D1480575

LEGISLATIVE ASSEMBLIES

Da Capo Press Reprints in

AMERICAN CONSTITUTIONAL AND LEGAL HISTORY

GENERAL EDITOR: LEONARD W. LEVY

Claremont Graduate School

LEGISLATIVE ASSEMBLIES

THEIR FRAMEWORK, MAKE-UP, CHARACTER, CHARACTERISTICS, HABITS, AND MANNERS

By Robert Luce

DA CAPO PRESS • NEW YORK • 1974

Library of Congress Cataloging in Publication Data

Luce, Robert, 1862-1946.
  Legislative assemblies.

  (Da Capo Press reprints in American constitutional
and legal history)
  Reprint of the ed. published by Houghton Mifflin,
Boston, issued as no. 2 of the author's series: The
science of legislation.
    1. Legislative bodies—United States.
  2. Legislative bodies. I. Title.
  JK2488.L8 1974   328.73   73-5617
  ISBN 0-306-70583-4

This Da Capo Press edition of *Legislative Assemblies* is
an unabridged republication of the first edition published
in Boston in 1924. It is reprinted by permission of The
President and Fellows of Harvard College

Published by Da Capo Press, Inc.
A Subsidiary of Plenum Publishing Corporation
227 West 17th Street, New York, N.Y. 10011

LEGISLATIVE ASSEMBLIES

THE SCIENCE OF LEGISLATION

LEGISLATIVE ASSEMBLIES

THEIR FRAMEWORK, MAKE–UP, CHARACTER, CHARACTERISTICS, HABITS, AND MANNERS

BY

ROBERT LUCE, A.M., LL.D.

A Member of the General Court of Massachusetts for nine years; of the Governor's Council, as Lieutenant-Governor; of a Constitutional Convention; and of the Congress of the United States

BOSTON AND NEW YORK

HOUGHTON MIFFLIN COMPANY

The Riverside Press Cambridge

1924

The Riverside Press
CAMBRIDGE · MASSACHUSETTS
PRINTED IN THE U.S.A.

CONTENTS

LEGISLATIVE ASSEMBLIES

LEGISLATIVE ASSEMBLIES

∙ ∙

CHAPTER I

THE FRAMEWORK

ACCIDENT made a legislative body of two Houses or Chambers — hence known as bi-cameral — the prevailing type in the modern world. For what is held to have been the first real Parliament, that of 1295, King Edward summoned nobles and prelates; directed the prelates to bring with them certain of the lower clergy; and ordered the election of knights of the shire, citizens, and burgesses. Here were six groups that might have treated with the King quite independently, but there was no powerful reason for independent action, and motives of convenience made some degree of fusion desirable. So when at the opening of Parliament the King with his Council had personally or by his commissioner received all who came, and the various Estates withdrew for deliberation upon the requests of the Crown, it was natural that the nobles and prelates, accustomed to act together in the Great Council, should deliberate together; and after a time for the knights of the shire, the citizens, and the burgesses to coalesce. The clergy had long been wont to vote their money grants in their purely clerical assemblies, the Convocations of Canterbury and York; they were reluctant to abandon their independence, and refused to take part in secular legislation, either because they thought it inconsistent with their calling or because they shrank from the burden; their attendance, irregular from the outset, presently stopped altogether; and so they failed in England to become a political Estate. Thus the six groupings that might easily have developed were reduced to two.

In mediæval Spain and France there were three Estates in three Houses. Sweden did not abolish the representation of four Estates until 1866, when a legislature of two branches was

3

substituted. On the other hand, in Scotland there was no distinction between the Estates, nor any division into two Houses; the different Estates always sat and voted together. Everywhere development was at the start a matter of chance, not premeditation. The significant thing is that the two-chamber idea was the one to survive. From this the fair conclusion is that it better met the need than any of the other combinations. It was the survival of the fittest. Nowadays, however, its merit is questioned. Proposals to substitute a single chamber are heard in many quarters. To weigh their merit calls for further help from history — the record of experience.

The Negative Voice

The development of the two-chamber idea in America shows no trace of conscious imitation of the English system. It grew out of the conditions of the times. Let it be recalled that our colonies began as trading companies, with what we should now call stockholders and boards of directors. The story of what happened in Massachusetts is the most illuminating. Its Directors were called Assistants, sometimes Magistrates. The charter of 1629 directed that there should be eighteen of them chosen from the body of the freemen, but up to 1680 the largest number actually serving was twelve, and it was usual to choose eight or nine. At first they were the important part of the Government, much as the directors are the important factor in conducting the affairs of a modern corporation. They exercised the legislative, the executive, and the judicial functions. Yet they were not allowed to get beyond the control of the stockholders. For instance the General Court, May 14, 1634, agreed, "that there shalbe x £ [ten pounds?] ffine sett upon ye Court of Assistants, & Mr. Mayhewe, for breach of an order of Court against imployeing Indeans to shoote with peeces, the one halfe to be payde by Mr. Pinchon & Mr. Mayhewe, offending therein, the other halfe by the Court of Assistants then in being, whoe gave leave thereunto." (A marginal note says: "This ffyne of x £ was remitted by the Court.")

The Assistants met as frequently as there was need, but stockholders' meetings — General Courts — were not held even the four times a year that the charter stipulated; in fact they came together but five times in the first five years. Furthermore, the power of the Assistants was enhanced through escaping the necessity of going out of office at stated times. By the order of October 18, 1630, the freemen were to choose Assistants "when there are to be chosen." The order of May 18, 1631, provided for Assistants "whom they shall desire to be chosen," and went on to say, "the like course to be holden when they, the said commons, shall see cause for any defect of misbehaviour to remove any one or more of the Assistants." This compelled judgment on men in office whose terms were not definitely ended, the inevitable result being that those once chosen were likely to keep their hold on the dignities, emoluments, and power of the position, thus becoming in effect an aristocracy with indefinite tenure.

The advantages thought to lie in this direction came near being perpetuated by precise recognition, for April 7, 1636, Winthrop's Journal tells us: "At a general court it was ordered, that a certain number of the magistrates should be chosen for life; (the reason was, for that it was showed from the word of God, etc., that the principal magistrates ought to be for life.) Accordingly, the 25th of the 3rd mo., John Winthrop, and Thomas Dudley were chosen to this place, and Henry Vane, by his place of governor, was president of this council for his year." This council for life lasted only three years, it being found to excite popular jealousy against the Magistrates. It seems to have been constituted in the hope of tempting over from England some of the peers, or gentry likely to become peers, since the members of such a council would be assured a place of dignity.

Winthrop evidently believed that the best interests of the colony called for control by the Magistrates. When in 1634 the principle of representation was applied, the freemen of the several settlements being empowered to choose two or three of their number to attend the General Court and "to have the full power and voices of all the said freemen derived to them for the making and establishing laws," he laid down the rule that they should not make any new laws, but prefer their grievances to the Court of Assistants; that is, the Magistrates. He thus reserved to the Magistrates the power to originate laws and to have the final word upon the proposals coming from the Deputies. Some years later, when the position of the Magistrates was under discussion, "one of the elders," Winthrop says, "wrote a small treatise, wherein scholastically and religiously he handled the question." He made a strong argument for the advantages of a form of government "mixt of Aristocracy and Democracy." In his notion the Magistrates were the "Aristocraticall branch." It is interesting to observe how he met the contention that as the number of Deputies exceeded those of the Magistrates, there was no reason why the votes of unequal numbers should be equal. To this he gave five replies:

"1: Not the number but the reason of them which are numbred is to be weighed.

"2: Tis not an Arithmeticall equality but a Geometricall that is to be attended to; that is, not equality of number, but of vertue.

"3: There is more disproportion betweene the wisedome and number and object of Electors sc: the major part of the country that choose the magistrate and the major part of the towne that choose the Deputy, then there is betweene the number of the elected sc. Magistrates and Deputies.

"4: Though among the Deputies there may be found those which doe excell compared with some of the magistrates yet generally the one being experienced the other lesse experienced wee may judge accordingly.

"5: If yet there remaine ought herin to be satisfyd it may be tempered by increasing the number of the one or diminishing the numbers of the other, or by qualifying the major part of the magistracy according to the proportion or two-thirds as 6 the major part of 9, 7 or 8 of eleven and as in some weighty motions of the venetian state policy tempers one part to the other, but doth not causelessly destroy either."[1]

The publication of this treatise was an episode in a controversy that vexed the colony during many years, a famous controversy, and one destined to prove of great consequence, for out of it came the American type of legislature — two elected bodies sitting in separate Houses, with agreement necessary for joint action.

The controversy began in 1634 when the inhabitants of Newtowne (now Cambridge), finding themselves crowded, asked of the General Court leave to remove to Connecticut. "This matter was debated divers days," says Winthrop in his Journal,

[1] *Mass. Hist. Soc. Proceedings*, 46, 283.

"and many reasons alleged pro and con." When at last the question was put to vote, "of the deputies fifteen were for their departure, and ten against it. The governor and two assistants were for it, and the deputy and all the rest of the assistants were against it, (except the secretary, who gave no vote;) whereupon no record was entered, because there were not six assistants in the vote, as the patent requires. Upon this grew a great difference between the governor and assistants, and the deputies. They would not yield the assistants a negative voice, and the others (considering how dangerous it might be to the commonwealth, if they should not keep that strength to balance the great number of the deputies) thought it safe to stand upon it. So, when they could proceed no farther, the whole court agreed to keep a day of humiliation to seek the Lord, which accordingly was done, in all the congregations, the 18th day of this month; and the 24th the court met again. Before they began, Mr. Cotton preached, (being desired by all the court, upon Mr. Hooker's instant excuse of his unfitness for that occasion). He took his text out of Hag. ii, 4, etc., out of which he laid down the nature or strength (as he termed it) of the magistracy, ministry, and people, viz., — the strength of the magistracy to be their authority; of the people, their liberty; and of the ministry, their purity; and showed how all of these had a negative voice, etc., and that yet the ultimate resolution, etc., ought to be in the whole body of the people, etc., with answer to all objections, and a declaration of the people's duty and right to maintain their true liberties against any unjust violence, etc., which gave great satisfaction to the company. And it pleased the Lord so to assist him, and to bless his own ordinance, that the affairs of the court went on cheerfully; and although all were not satisfied about the negative voice to be left to the magistrates, yet no man moved aught about it, and the congregation came and accepted of such enlargement as had formerly been offered them by Boston and Watertown; and so the fear of their removal to Connecticut was removed."

The issue was far from dead. At the General Court in March, 1635, "one of the deputies was questioned for denying the magistracy among us, affirming that the power of the government was but ministerial, etc. He had also much opposed the magistrates, and slighted them, and used many weak arguments against the negative voice, as himself acknowledged upon record. He was adjudged by all the court to be disabled for three years from bearing any public office." This Deputy, so democratic in his ideas, was Israel Stoughton, who, later returning to England, rose to be a Lieutenant-Colonel among the Ironsides; it was his son whose gift to Harvard led to the perpetuation of his name by Stoughton Hall. At the General Court in May "a petition was preferred by many of Dorchester, etc., for releasing the sentence against Mr. Stoughton the last General Court; but it was rejected, and the sentence affirmed by the country to be just." Of the same court Winthrop writes: "Divers jealousies, that had been between the magistrates and deputies, were now cleared, with full satisfaction to all parties."

It was an ingenious arrangement that they devised, an amplification of what now we call a conference committee. The record of March 3, 1635/6, reads: "No law, order, or sentence shall pass as an Act of the Court, without the consent of the greater part of the magistrates on the one part, and the greater number of the deputies on the other part; and for want of such accord, the cause or order shall be suspended, and if either party think it so material, there shall be forthwith a committee chosen, the one-half by the magistrates, and the other half by the deputies, and the committee so chosen to elect an umpire, who together shall have power to hear and determine the cause in question."[1]

Several years passed before the question of the negative voice came to the front again. Winthrop tells the important story at length, beginning with his Journal entry of June 22, 1642. "At the same General Court," he says, "there fell out a great business upon a very small occasion. Anno 1636, there was a stray sow in Boston, which was brought to Captain Keayne."

It should be understood that Keayne was a leading merchant of the town. He had already figured in the Journal, under date of November 9, 1639, as being "notorious above others observed and complained of" for oppression in the sale of foreign commodities; "and, being convented, he was charged with many particulars; in some, for taking above six-pence in the shilling profit; in some above eight-pence; and, in some small things, above two for one; and being hereof convict, (as

[1] *Records of the Colony of the Mass. Bay in N.E.*, I, 170.

appears by the record,) he was fined £200." The curious particulars of the discussion about the propriety of his charges and the extenuating circumstances will interest any student of the history of economics. After the Court censured him, the Church took him in hand, "where (as before he had done in court) he did, with tears, acknowledge and bewail his covetous and corrupt heart." His excuses led to a sermon by Mr. Cotton in which the preacher learnedly discussed the rules for trading. Keayne came near being excommunicated, but escaped with an admonition. Other episodes in his career put him in a better light. He was one of the promoters and was the first commander of the Ancient and Honorable Artillery Company, at times a delegate to the General Court, and evidently an influential citizen. He took a singular revenge on his critical fellow-citizens by leaving to the town three hundred pounds toward their first town-house, in a will of nearly two hundred pages, a large part of which was devoted to vindicating his mercantile honor.

These particulars about Keayne are of consequence here as throwing some light on the sow controversy, for evidently he had the sympathy of many of the well-to-do and was in disfavor with the plainer folk, who thought him an extortioner and very likely were jealous of his prosperity. To go on with the story of the sow brought to Keayne: "He had it cried divers times, and divers came to see it, but none made claim to it for near a year. He kept it in his yard with a sow of his own. Afterwards one Sherman's wife, having lost such a sow, laid claim to it, but came not to see it, till Captain Keayne had killed his own sow. After being showed the stray sow, and finding it to have other marks than she had claimed her sow by, she gave out that he had killed her sow. The noise hereof being spread about the town, the matter was brought before the elders of the church as a case of offence; many witnesses were examined and Captain Keayne was cleared."

Not satisfied with this, Mrs. Sherman went to law, and there followed a long course of litigation, with the suit on appeal finally reaching the General Court, then a trial court as well as a legislative body. It gave the best part of seven days to the case, without decision, "for there being nine magistrates and thirty deputies, no sentence could by law pass without the greater number of both, which neither plaintiff nor defendant had, for there were for the plaintiff two magistrates and fifteen deputies, and for the defendant seven magistrates and eight deputies, the other seven deputies stood doubtful. . . . The defendant being of ill report in the country for a hard dealer in his course of trading, and having been formerly censured in the court and in the church also, by admonition for such offences, carried many weak minds strongly against him. And the truth is, he was very worthy of blame in that kind, as divers others in the country were also in those times, though they were not detected as he was; yet to give every man his due, he was very useful to the country both by his hospitality and otherwise. But one dead fly spoils much good ointment."

Winthrop goes on to tell how there was great expectation in the country that the cause would pass against the Captain, "but falling out otherwise, gave occasion to many to speak unreverently of the court, especially of the magistrates, and the report went, that their negative voice had hindered the course of justice, and that these magistrates must be put out, that the power of the negative voice might be taken away."

Observe that had joint ballot prevailed, Mrs. Sherman would have won by 17 to 15, but that if the action of Magistrates and Deputies was to be taken separately, there was a deadlock — a victory for the Captain.

Before the Court broke up, the Governor tried to allay the feeling. He "tendered a declaration in nature of a pacification, whereby it might have appeared, that, howsoever the members of the court dissented in judgment, yet they were the same in affection, and had a charitable opinion of each other; but this was opposed by some of the plaintiff's part, so it was laid by." Thus Winthrop's customary rôle of peacemaker failed, which may indicate the intensity of the public feeling in the matter. He made it worse by forgetting that the man who gives an opinion would best not accompany it with his reasons. He proceeded to publish a declaration of the necessity of upholding the Magistrates. This took the form of a "Breaviate of the Case betwene Richard Sheareman plt. by petition & Capt. Robert Keaine defentt. about the title to A Straye Sow." It was an ingenious quibble to show that the vote of the Magistrates was not final, for the cause might have been argued again, or else committees might have been chosen, "to order the Cause according to Lawe." Passages of it gave so much offense that

Winthrop felt it necessary to explain and apologize in his speech to the General Court the next June. Although he refused to retract, he went on to say: "Howsoever that which I wrote was upon great provocation by some of the adverse party, and upon invitation from others to vindicate ourselves from that aspersion which was cast upon us, yet that was no sufficient warrant for me to break out into any distemper. I confess I was too prodigal of my brethren's reputation." Other language of like tenor he concluded with a sentence that would hardly be spoken by a Chief Executive of the present day: "These are all the Lord hath brought me to consider of, wherein I acknowledge my failings, and humbly intreat you will pardon and pass them by; if you please to accept my request, your silence shall be a sufficient testimony thereof unto me, and I hope I shall be more wise and watchful hereafter."

The "sow business," as Winthrop calls it, had become the great political issue of the hour. "That which made the people so unsatisfied, and unwilling the cause should rest as it stood, was the 20 pounds which the defendant had recovered against the plaintiff in an action of slander for saying he had stolen the sow, etc., and many of them could not distinguish this from the principal cause, as if she had been adjudged to pay 20 pounds for demanding her sow, and yet the defendant never took of this more than 3 pounds, for his charges of witnesses, etc., and offered to remit the whole, if she would have acknowledged the wrong she had done him. But he being accounted a rich man, and she a poor woman, this so wrought with the people, as being blinded with unreasonable compassion, they could not see, or not allow justice her reasonable course."

The constitutional bearing of the momentous controversy was upon the procedure of the General Court. Should there be in effect two branches, each with a negative on the other, each with power to prevent affirmative action, each with a "negative voice"?

To be sure, the reference then was wholly to the "negative voice" of the Magistrates (the Assistants, virtually the upper House, if such it was to be). Clearly, though, if the Magistrates could block the Deputies, the Deputies could block the Magistrates, and so the whole bi-cameral, two-chamber question was really at issue.

Winthrop's story concludes with this about the Court of

March, 1644: "Upon the motion of the deputies, it was ordered that the court should be divided in their consultations, the magistrates by themselves, and the deputies by themselves, what the one agreed upon they should send to the other, and if both agreed, then to pass, etc. This order determined the great contention about the negative voice." And had he the gift of prophecy, he might have added, "and in the end gave two chambers to every Legislature in the United States, as well as to the Federal Congress itself."

The separate Records of the "House of Deputies" begin with the 29th of May, 1644. The Charter made no provision for such a House, and its legality has therefore been questioned. Forty years later this gave occasion for one of the complaints believed to have led to vacating the Charter. However, the system had become an institution prized by the people, and it was destined to survive.

Winthrop was wrong in thinking that the controversy over the negative voice was in reality ended by the order of March, 1644. In November of that very year a new plan for choosing the General Court included a proposition that "the magistrates & deputies thus chosen shall sit togeather as a full & sufficient Generall Court, to act in all things by the major vote of the whole Court." It was ordered that by the last of the next month every town should vote on the plan, but no record of the result appears and it must have been in the negative. The "whereas" of the order had this clause: ". . . it being thought a matter worthy the triall, dureing the standing of this order, to have the use of the negative vote forborne," etc. We may infer that this took place, for immediately afterward appears an entry for a complainant in the case of his petition for his father against "the towne of Watertowne," with the further entry: "The deputies of Watertown, after the order was entered, tooke exception against it, alleadging that the major part of the magistrates did not vote for the complainant. It was hereupon put to the vote of the Court, whether the said order should not be judged to be good & effectuall, notwithstanding the allegation; and the vote was, that it should stand good." [1]

In the following May a joint committee of the two Houses was appointed "to consider of some way whereby ye negative vote may be tempered, that justice may have free passage." [2]

[1] *Records of the Colony of the Mass. Bay in N.E.*, II, 88–90.   [2] *Ibid.*, III, 11.

A year later, in the House of Deputies, May 6, 1646, "Itt was resolved, uppon the question, & that by vote, notwithstanding all the reasons alledged, that the Howse of Deputies should continew in their setting aparte & acting a parte from the Magistrates, according to the former order, as the most suitable to their condicions."[1] The next reference is that of October 18, 1648, when it was specifically declared that upon comparison at the end of the session of the "bills, lawes, petitions, &c." that had passed the Magistrates and Deputies, they were to be transcribed by the secretary of the Magistrates and the clerk of the Deputies; and those that had not passed both branches were to be put on file, "or otherwise disposed of, as the whole Courte shall appoint."[2]

From this time on it appears to have been generally conceded that the two bodies should act separately in matters of legislation, but there was still difference of opinion about matters of judicature. The Deputies, October 19, 1649, voted that cases brought before the General Court for review, or by order of the General Court, as in the case of disagreement of judges and juries, should be determined by the major vote of the Court met together; and all cases brought by way of complaint of unjust or unequal proceedings, should be determined by the major vote of the Deputies only.[3]

In the next year trouble came with an attempt to settle a question that still puzzles. It was ordered, October 18, 1650, that the interpretation of the law concerning the greater part of the Magistrates and the greater part of the Deputies, was to be understood as meaning the greater number of those present and voting.[4] This was repealed May 26, 1652, because it left "all or most of the cases formerly issued in the General Court doubtful and uncertain," and took away "the negative voice, both of Magistrates and Deputies, in making laws, as well as in cases of judicature, which was not intended, much less consented to." It was thereupon definitely declared that in the future, any case of judicature, either civil or criminal, should be determined by the major part of the whole Court.[5]

The marginal note in the Secretary's Journal reads, "Negative vote in use againe." That this was confined to legislation is

[1] *Records of the Colony of the Mass. Bay in N.E.*, III, 62.
[2] *Ibid.*, 260.   [3] *Ibid.*, 180.   [4] *Ibid.*, IV, pt. 1, 35.   [5] *Ibid.*, 62.

indicated by the provision in the codification of the laws made in 1660: "Forasmuch as after long experience, diverse inconveniences are found in the manner of proceeding in this Court, by Magistrates & deputies sitting together: It is therefore ordered by this Court & Authority thereof. That henceforth the Magistrates sitt apart, & act all business belonging to this Court by themselves, by drawing up bills, & orders, as they shall see good in their wisdom, which haveing agreed upon, they may present to the Deputies to be considered, & accordingly, to give their consent or dissent: The Deputies in like manner sitting by themselves, & consulting about such orders & Lawes, as they in their discretion and experience, shall find meet for the common good, which agreed on by them, they may present to the Magistrates, who haveing considered, thereof, may manifest their consent or dissent, thereto: And no law, order or sentence shall passe, or be accounted, an act of this Court, without Consent of the greater part of the Magistrates on the one partie, & the greater number of deputies, on the other partie, but all orders & conclusions, that have passed by approbation of Magistrates & Deputies as aforesayd, shall be accounted acts of this Court and accordingly be ingrossed, which on the last day of every session, shall be deliberately read over before the whole Court, Provided that if the Magistrates & Deputies, shall happen to differ in any case of Judicature, either civil or criminal, such case shall be determined by the Major Vote of the whole Court met together."

Nevertheless the dispute went on. It gained especial vigor in 1672 and 1673, when numerous messages on the subject passed between the two branches. Whitmore in his introduction to the Colonial Laws of Massachusetts quotes from one of these (to be found in the Archives, vol. 48, no. 114), showing the straits to which the Magistrates had been reduced. They were arguing plaintively that the consent of at least some of their number was necessary to make valid any act. The Records show (IV, pt. 2, p. 559) that May 7, 1673, a committee of ten was appointed to consider whether by the Charter there was a negative in any part of the General Court. Of the members three appear to have been Magistrates, two clergymen, and five Deputies, including their clerk. The report, dated September 1, 1673, is in the Archives, vol. 48, no. 125. It seems that eight members were present and three did not vote. According to Whitmore, the report, signed by the other five, was against there being such a negative power in either branch. My reading of it is just the reverse, — to the effect that there was a negative. Whitmore may have made a slip of the pen. The report makes no restriction of view to matters of judicature.

In the following October the Deputies voted : "For preventinge all future differences that may Arise in the Generall Court, it is Ordered by this Court & the Authority thereof that the Election of Officers, Admission of ffreemen, also matters of Councill & Judicature, togeather with any question or questions referring thereto, shall henceforth be heard debated & concluded by the Major Parte of the whole Court sittinge and votinge togeather any Law Usage or Custome to the Contrary notwithstandinge." The corresponding record for the other branch is : "The magistrates Consent hereto Provided it be such a major parte as our Patent requires to make a valid act." The dispute had come to center about this point, the same that had been at issue in 1650 and 1652. The Magistrates persistently refused to concede that less than half their whole number, regardless of the attendance, could pass laws or determine causes when in accord with the Deputies. So tenaciously did they hold to their contention that the attempt in 1685 to print a revision of the laws containing the obnoxious change, had to be abandoned.

In the Other Colonies

In the Plymouth Colony there was no such two-chamber development as in that of Massachusetts Bay. The division took a different course. By 1646 the attendance of the Deputies at three General Courts a year had been found burdensome, and so it was voted (October 20, 1646) that laws, orders, and ordinances should be made or repealed only at the Election Court in June, and that only the Magistrates should attend the other courts, which were to be restricted to matters of judicature. It was doubtless the controversy over the negative voice in the Bay Colony that led to some agitation for change in Plymouth, but June 6, 1650, it was voted to keep on as they had been doing, and that for the making and repealing of laws "the Magistrates and Committees or Deputies be considered as one body." [1]

[1] *Plymouth Colony Records*, xi, 54, 55, 56.

Apparently the Fundamental Orders of Connecticut (1638/9) did not contemplate that the Magistrates should sit apart from the Deputies, for the Court was to consist of the Governor, at least four Magistrates, and the greater part of the Deputies, this being what we should call a quorum; and the Governor, or Moderator, was to preside over them.   During six years the Deputies could outvote the Magistrates.   Then it may be that the echoes of the Massachusetts controversy reached the little colony on the banks of the Connecticut.   Whatever the cause, in February, 1644/5, an act was passed giving each body "a negative voice" upon the vote of the other.   Perhaps the example of the New Haven colony had something to do with it, for although the Fundamental Order for the government of New Haven (October 27, 1643) had provided that the Governor, Deputy Governor, Magistrates, and Deputies should all sit together, it also said, "Nothing shall pass an act of the Generall Court butt by the consent of the major part of the magistrates, and the greater part of Deputyes."

When in 1662 John Winthrop's son John got for Connecticut pretty much the charter he wanted, the provision about the Legislature was made to read as follows: "The Assistants, and Freemen of the said Company, or such of them (not exceeding Two Persons from each Place, Town, or City) who shall be from Time to Time thereunto elected or deputed by the major Part of the Freemen of the respective Towns, Cities, and Places for which they shall be elected or deputed, shall have a General Meeting, or Assembly, then and there to consult and advise in and about the Affairs and Business of the said Company; and the Governor . . . and such of the Assistants and Freemen of the said Company as shall be so elected or deputed . . . shall be called the General Assembly," etc.

In spite of the troubles in Massachusetts over the negative voice, there was in this Connecticut provision no clear facing of the problem.   Apparently no difficulties at once followed. All sat together for nearly twoscore years.   Gradually, however, the General Court began to assert authority over the doings of the Governor and Council, and in time was evolved the theory that its consent was necessary for all matters of consequence, out of which developed the order of October, 1698, dividing the General Assembly into two Houses, one consisting of the Governor and Council, the other of the Deputies.   Judge

Baldwin is of the opinion that this was accomplished by a forced construction of the Charter, if not a departure therefrom. "The constitutionality of this step," he says, "was long a subject of dispute, and the division was not stated in the published statute-books until after the Declaration of Independence, probably, in part, from the fear that, if stated, it might attract the notice of the British government, and serve as an occasion for revocation or forfeiture of the charter; and, in part, from an unwillingness on the part of the lower House to define exactly what privileges they had surrendered by consenting to sit apart. In elections of Colony officers to fill vacancies, which, by the charter, were to be made by the General Court, the lower House often contended that the vote must be taken in a joint convention, and on several occasions a failure to elect was only prevented by a temporizing policy on the part of the Council." [1]

In Rhode Island under the first patent the President and Assistants were executive officers and had no share in legislation *ex officio*. By the Charter of Charles II in 1663, legislative power was granted to the ten Assistants. They began sitting with the Deputies, but this brought controversy at once. The next year it was recorded that there had "been a long agetation about the motion whether the magistrates" should "sitt by themselves and the deputyes by themselves." In 1666 Warwick and Portsmouth successfully petitioned for separate sitting, but the law was quickly repealed. The "agetation" went on for a generation. Little by little the representatives of the people secured recognition of independent powers, and in 1696 separation took place.

Maryland began with one House, the members of the Council being also members of the Assembly. As early as 1642 the Burgesses expressed a desire to sit by themselves, but the Lieutenant-Governor denied the request. In 1650 came division into two Houses. In the course of the brief period when Puritan domination in England extended its influence to the colonies, there was return to a single House, but the reunion was only temporary and thereafter two Houses sat.

Notice that in Maryland the wish for each change came from the Burgesses. When the representative of the proprietor con-

[1] "Early History of the Ballot of Connecticut," *Papers of the Am. Hist. Assn.*, IV, 416 (1890).

trolled, he could issue writs summoning enough gentlemen to outvote the Burgesses in joint session. Under the brief Puritan régime, this was not feared, and by joint session the Burgesses could more easily have their way. Wherever the Charter prevented packing the upper House, the lower House was likely to prefer joint session. So it was in New Jersey. There the first Assembly, that of 1668, was bi-cameral. Friction followed. At last the Deputies sent a message to the Council: "We, finding so many and great Inconveniences by our not setting together, and your apprehensions so different to ours, and your Expectations that things must go according to your opinions, though we see no Reason for, much less Warrant from the Concessions, wherefore we think it vain to spend much Time of returning Answers by writings that are so exceeding dilatory, if not fruitless and endless, and therefore we think our way rather to break up our meeting, seeing the Order of the Concessions cannot be attended to." In other words, it was declared unconstitutional for the upper branch to thwart the lower branch, and so the lower branch went home. Seven years passed before there was another legal Assembly. Thereafter it was always bi-cameral.

In Virginia "before the year 1680," said Beverley, writing in 1705, "the Council sat in the same house with the Burgesses of Assembly, much resembling the model of the Scotch Parliament; and the Lord Colepepper, taking advantage of some disputes among·them, procured the Council to sit apart from the Assembly; and so they became two distinct Houses, in imitation of the two Houses of Parliament in England, the Lords and Commons; and so is the constitution at this day." This is to be disputed in two particulars. First, there was no imitation of Parliament, for a colonial Council occupied a place altogether different from that of the House of Lords. Secondly, the Burgesses had sat by themselves before 1680, at any rate at times, if John Fiske drew the right conclusion from an episode of 1676, after Bacon's Rebellion. It was then moved by one of the Governor's partisans in the House of Burgesses "to entreat the Governor would please to assign two of his Council to sit with and assist us in our debates, as had been usual." At this the friends of Bacon scowled, and somebody suggested such aid might not be necessary, whereat there was an uproar. The Berkeleyans urged that "it had been customary and ought not to be omitted," but a shrewd old Assemblyman named Presley replied, " 'Tis true it has been customary, but if we have any bad customs amongst us, we are come here to mend 'em." This happy retort was greeted with laughter, but the Cavalier feeling of loyalty to the King's representative was still strong, and Berkeley's friends had their way, apparently in a tumultuous fashion.[1]

Thomas Jefferson, writing his "Notes on Virginia" something more than a century later, complained bitterly of the division into two Houses. He quoted the essential rights secured by a solemn convention in 1651, when the colony, which still maintained its opposition to Cromwell and the Parliament, was induced to lay down arms — among them: "Secondly, that the Grand assembly as formerly shall convene and transact the affairs of Virginia." He went on to say: "Yet in every one of these points was this convention violated by subsequent Kings and Parliaments, and other infractions of their constitution, equally dangerous, committed. Their General Assembly, which was composed of the Council of State and Burgesses, sitting together and deciding by plurality of voices, was split into two Houses, by which the Council obtained a separate negative on their laws."[2]

The colonists in what is now New Hampshire were from 1641 to 1680 under the jurisdiction of Massachusetts. By a commission dated September 18, 1679, New Hampshire was set off, and from January 1, 1679/80, led an independent existence, with a separate President and Council. The members of the Council were not chosen by the people, as was the case in the neighboring colonies, but were appointed by the Crown, and could be dismissed by the President. Three years later the Council began sitting apart, as an upper House.

New York's first legislative assembly, convened by Governor Dongan in 1683, was bi-cameral, and the system was provided for in the "Charter of Libertys" sent by that body to the Duke of York, approved by him, and then vetoed. When Henry Slaughter was made Governor, in 1689, by his commission the representative assembly was revived, and from the first Legislature thereunder in 1691 the two Houses sat separately.

Pennsylvania was the only colony that began with two

[1] *Old Virginia and Her Neighbours*, II, 61.
[2] *Writings of Thomas Jefferson* (P. L. Ford ed.), III, 216 *et sqq.*

Houses and changed to one. From the time of Penn's first Frame of Government, 1682, until the revision made by the Charter of Privileges in 1701, save for the two years when control was in the Governor of New York, there were Council and Assembly. The new Charter made the Assembly the legislating body, and its only reference to a Council was incidental. When the Council was appointed, the commission of the members gave them only administrative powers. They were, however, to advise the Governor, and as he had a veto over the acts of the Assembly, the result was that the Councilors usurped indirectly a share in lawmaking. In time they arrived at proposing amendments, and instances are recorded of agreement by the Assembly when amendments had been so proposed. Yet it is also known that the Assembly at times held this interference by the Council a violation of rights. In fact the situation cannot be stretched to meet the theory that Pennsylvania as a province had any second chamber after the opening of the eighteenth century.

Delaware, an adjunct of Pennsylvania, followed her up to the Revolution in having only one legislative chamber.

The Declaration and Proposals of the Lord Proprietor of Carolina, in 1663, provided that the laws should be made by Deputies, "with the advise and consent of the Governor and Council." The Concessions of 1665, however, said that the Deputies were to join with the Governor and Council for the making of laws. The Fundamental Constitutions of 1669, fancifully framed by John Locke, had this article: "Seventy-one. There shall be a parliament, consisting of the proprietors or their deputies, the landgraves, and caziques, and one freeholder out of every precinct, to be chosen by the freeholders of the said precinct, respectively. They shall sit all together in one room, and have every member one vote." Nothing was to be proposed in this Parliament until it had first passed the Grand Council, so that here was to be in reality a two-chambered legislature. Locke's complexities proving quite unworkable, simpler machinery was substituted in practice. The Council kept the right of proposing all measures until 1693, when it was given also to the Assembly. The terms "General Assembly" and "Commons House of Assembly" thereafter used show that the two-chamber form had won acceptance.

The Charter of Georgia, in 1732, was granted to a Board

of Trustees, fifteen of whom were to be the "Common Council" and conduct the affairs of the colony. This body, sitting in London, governed for a score of years. In 1750 they voted for an Assembly. As they could not give it lawmaking power, they directed it should propose, debate, and represent. Two years later the Charter was abandoned and Georgia became a royal province. The usual form of government was thereupon provided on advice of the Lords Commissioners for Trade and Plantations — a Council appointed by the Crown, and an elected Assembly. One was styled the "Upper House of Assembly" and the other the "Commons House of Assembly." They sat separately.

New Hampshire, the first State to frame a Constitution, provided in the brief draft of January, 1776, for a Council, "to be a distinct and separate branch of the Legislature." It was to consist of twelve members, allotted to the five counties, to be chosen out of their own number by the "House of Representatives or Assembly." South Carolina, acting next, created an upper branch to be known as the "Legislative Council," to consist of thirteen members chosen by the "General Assembly" out of their own number, with no restriction as to allotment.

Then came Virginia with the first Senate so named and chosen as such at the polls. Thomas Jefferson is supposed to have suggested the name. His labors in the Continental Congress did not preclude him from sending to President Pendleton of the Virginia Convention a draft of a form of government. It followed New Hampshire and South Carolina in proposing an upper branch to be elected by the lower. It reached the Convention when there had already been substantial agreement on a plan based upon a draft by George Mason, which used no more specific designation than "upper branch." Jefferson's preamble and some other things were engrafted on the Mason plan, and inasmuch as the document adopted used the name "Senate," which Jefferson had used, it is fair to presume that the credit is his. The method of selection, however, was not his, for it was provided that there should be twenty-four members, for whose election the counties should be divided into twenty-four districts.

New Jersey copied from South Carolina the name "Legislative Council" and clung to it until 1844. This was the first State

to apportion one member to each county. Delaware called
its upper branch "the Council," substituting "Senate" in 1792.
It followed New Jersey in apportionment by counties, with
three to each. Maryland came along in November of 1776 with
a brand-new way of choosing Senators. Two electors were to
be chosen by each county, and one each by Annapolis and
Baltimore, who were to assemble and proceed to elect at large
fifteen Senators, nine of whom were to be residents on the
western and six on the eastern shore. This unique system
prevailed until 1837, when direct election was substituted, with
one Senator for each county and one for Baltimore. North
Carolina had a "Senate" from the start, and began with county
apportionment. New York also adopted "Senate"; South
Carolina changed to it in 1778; Massachusetts took it in 1780;
New Hampshire came to it in 1784. Rhode Island in 1795
changed the name "Upper House" to "House of Magistrates,"
but that never came into use; the term "Senator" supplanted
the term "Assistant," in May, 1799. Now all our upper
branches are Senates. "Legislative Council" is the almost
universal name for the upper House of British colonial bodies.

Speaking of names, it may as well be set forth here as anywhere that the colonial "General Court" survives only in the
Constitutions of Massachusetts and New Hampshire, and even
in them "Legislature" is also used. For some uncertain reason
the Connecticut Charter of 1662 and the Rhode Island Charter
of 1663 spoke of the "general meeting, or Assembly," and
"Assembly" proved more suited than "Court" to the colonial
fancy. The Massachusetts Bay Charters of 1629 and 1691
both spoke of "Court or Assembly," with variations making it
impossible to say just what designation was proper. Governor
Hutchinson in his "History" generally uses "Assembly" to
indicate the lower House, and "General Assembly" to designate
the lawmaking body as a whole. In one place (III, 245) he
speaks of "the three branches of the Legislature," which would
indicate that he included the Governor. From his phraseology
one would infer that "General Court" had gone out of use in
the period just before the Revolution, though it may be that
he had some prejudice against the name or thought it colloquial.
Virginia had begun with a "House of Burgesses," the towns
or "boroughs" predominating in that colony at the start, and
it kept the name until the Constitution of 1776 changed it to

"House of Delegates." Maryland followed Virginia in this. When the Carolina Legislature was permanently divided into two Houses, toward the end of the seventeenth century, the term "General Assembly" came into use. The North Carolina Constitution of 1776 named the lower branch the "House of Commons," and so it was called until the Constitution of 1868 substituted "House of Representatives." South Carolina first called its lower branch the "General Assembly," but made it "House of Representatives" in 1778. New Jersey also said "General Assembly." Delaware and Georgia preferred "House of Assembly." New York was content with unadorned "Assembly."

New Hampshire was the first to use "House of Representatives," but coupled with it, "or Assembly." Pennsylvania took it without alternative, as did Massachusetts, and now it is the usual name for the lower branch. "Legislature" appears in all the State Constitutions.

CHAPTER II

TWO CHAMBERS OR ONE

It has been said that more than half the American colonies began with uni-cameral Legislatures. If the statement is accurate, which is doubtful, it is but a half-truth. The one sitting of a powerless assembly in Georgia ought not to count; the Carolinas should really be put in the bi-cameral column; New Hampshire and Rhode Island had but the briefest acquaintance with the single chamber, before they got fairly under way. The fact is that the greater part of the colonies had no appreciable experience with the one-chamber system. Massachusetts, Connecticut, Maryland, and Virginia may be said to have given it a thorough trial before arriving at two chambers. Pennsylvania alone took the opposite course by changing in colonial times from two chambers to one.

When the Revolutionary crisis forced Americans to decide how to govern themselves, only those living in Pennsylvania and Delaware knew from personal experience anything about single-chambered Legislatures. Pennsylvania and her imitator, Vermont, alone saw fit to frame a State Constitution intrusting the making of laws to a single body uncontrolled. Frequently it is said that Georgia had only one chamber, but study of the Constitution of 1777 will disclose the fact that her Legislature was no more than technically uni-cameral. A Council there had an important part in lawmaking. This body was chosen by the Representatives from among their own number, two for each of the sizable counties. After the second reading of every bill, it had to be sent to the Council, "for their perusal and advice." To be sure, this gave the Councilors no power of direct veto, but the moral effect of their advice must have been considerable. Their right to propose amendments was recognized, for the Constitution said that when a committee from the Council came to the House with proposed amendments, its members should, while sitting and covered, deliver their reasons, the whole House at that time, except the Speaker, uncovered. A Senate was definitely created by the Constitution of 1789.

The Georgia plan of 1777 was not a long step from that of South Carolina, devised early in the year before. The "Congress" framing the South Carolina Constitution turned itself into a lower branch, the General Assembly, which was to elect out of its own number an upper branch, the Legislative Council.

Natural as it was that the newborn States should for the most part continue accustomed methods of lawmaking, this was not done without earnest discussion and much difference of opinion. Appointed upper Houses had everywhere brought friction. In Massachusetts the episode of the Mandamus Councilors bred bitterness. The temper of the people may be judged by the action of the town of Ashfield, which voted, October 4, 1774, "That the Assembly of this State consist of one Elective body, the members of which body shall be Annually elected." Massachusetts lived for nearly five years after Lexington and Concord with but one lawmaking body. Yet her leaders felt it was not wise for a permanent policy. John Adams, whose views on constitutional questions dominated in the end, set down those pertaining to this particular matter in 1776, in his "Thoughts on Government." [1] As a comprehensive statement of the arguments that decided our fathers, they are worth quoting, "I think," he said, "a people cannot be long free, nor ever happy, whose government is in one assembly. My reasons for this opinion are as follows:

"1. A single assembly is liable to all the vices, follies, and frailties of an individual; subject to fits of humor, starts of passion, flights of enthusiasm, partialities, or prejudice, and consequently productive of hasty results and absurd judgments. And all these errors ought to be corrected and defects supplied by some controlling power.

"2. A single assembly is apt to be avaricious, and in time will not scruple to exempt itself from burdens, which it will lay, without compunction, upon its constituents.

"3. A single assembly is apt to grow ambitious, and after a time will not hesitate to vote itself perpetual. This was one fault of the Long Parliament; but more remarkably of Holland, whose assembly first voted themselves from annual to septennial, and after a course of years, that all vacancies happening by death or otherwise, should be filled by themselves, without any application to constituents at all."

[1] *Works,* iv, 195.

Theophilus Parsons rewrote and strengthened this in the pamphlet known as "The Essex Result," which contained a report of the reasons for the rejection of the Constitution of 1778 by a convention of a dozen Essex County towns. He added: "The result of a single assembly will be hasty and indigested, and their judgments frequently absurd and inconsistent. There must be a second body to revise with coolness and wisdom and to control with firmness, independent upon the first, either for their creation, or existence. Yet the first must retain a right to a similar revision and controul over the second."

Over against the ideas of John Adams are to be set those of Benjamin Franklin. Adams wrote to Francis Dana, August 16, 1776:[1] "The Convention of Pennsylvania has voted for a single Assembly. Such is the force of habit; and what surprises me not a little is, that the American philosopher should have so far accommodated himself to the customs of his countrymen as to be a zealous advocate for it. No country ever will be long happy, or ever entirely safe and free, which is thus governed. The curse of a *jus vagum* will be their portion." None of Franklin's arguments in the debate on the question at that time have been preserved, unless we credit the common understanding that he then likened a legislative body having two branches to a cart with a pair of cattle hitched to each end, pulling in opposite directions. Of course it is possible that Adams erred in deducing Franklin's views from the action of the Convention, on the supposition that it was strongly influenced by "the American philosopher." Indeed, Burton Alva Konkle, in his elaborate book on "George Bryan and the Constitution of Pennsylvania," gives no part to Franklin in the saving of the single chamber, but credits it all to Bryan, a great champion of popular freedom, which the single chamber was supposed to encourage. Furthermore, Edward Channing, in his "History of the United States" (III, 439), seems to accept without question the opinion of Benjamin Rush [2] that Franklin was opposed to the single chamber. Rush said there was a pamphlet of the Doctor's printed in 1763 in which he supposed three branches preferable to two. Ford's bibliography of Franklin fails to note any such publication, there is no reference to it in any of the editions of his works, and search fails to pro-

[1] *Works*, IX, 429.   [2] *Pa. Mag. of History*, XXIX, 29.

duce any evidence corroborating Rush's statement. On the other hand, there is at any rate not the slightest question of Franklin's views thirteen years later when somebody published in the "Federal Gazette" (November 3, 1789), "Hints for the Members" of a Pennsylvania Convention. The giver of hints had argued: "A plural legislature is as necessary to good government as a single executive. It is not enough that your legislature should be numerous; it should also be divided. Numbers alone are not a sufficient barrier against the impulses of passion, the combination of interest, the intrigues of faction, the haste of folly, or the spirit of encroachment. One division should watch over and control the other, supply its wants, correct its blunders, and cross its designs, should they be criminal or erroneous. Wisdom is the specific quality of the legislature, grows out of the number of the body, and is made up of the portions of sense and knowledge which each member brings to it."

Franklin replied: "On this it may be asked: May not the wisdom brought to the legislature by each member be as effectual a barrier against the impulses of passion, etc., when the members are united in one body, as when they are divided? If one part of the legislature may control the operations of the other, may not the impulses of passion, the combinations of interest, the intrigues of faction, the haste of folly, or the spirit of encroachment in one of those bodies obstruct the good proposed by the other, and frustrate its advantages to the public? Have we not experienced in this State, when a province under the government of the proprietaries, the mischiefs of a second branch existing in the proprietary family, countenanced and aided by an aristocratic council? How many delays and what great expenses were occasioned in carrying on the public business; and what a train of mischiefs, even to the preventing of the defence of the province during several years, when distressed by an Indian war, by the iniquitous demand that the proprietary property should be exempt from taxation? The wisdom of a few members in one single legislative body, may it not frequently stifle bad motions in their infancy, and so prevent their being adopted? whereas, if those wise men, in case of a double legislature, should happen to be in that branch wherein the motion did not arise, may it not, after being adopted by the other, occasion long disputes and contentions between the two bodies, expensive to the public, obstructing the public business, and promoting factions among the people, many tempers naturally adhering obstinately to measures they have once publicly adopted? Have we not seen, in one of our neighboring States, a bad measure, adopted by one branch of the legislature, for want of the assistance of some more intelligent members who had been packed into the other, occasion many debates, conducted with much asperity, which could not be settled but by an expensive general appeal to the public? And have we not seen, in another neighboring State, a similar difference between the two branches, occasioning long debates and contentions, whereby the State was prevented for many months enjoying the advantage of having Senators in the Congress of the United States? And has our present legislature in one Assembly committed any errors of importance, which they have not remedied or may not easily remedy; more easily, probably, than if divided into two branches? And if the wisdom brought by the members to the Assembly is divided into two branches, may it not be too weak in each to support a good measure, or obstruct a bad one? The division of the legislature into two or three branches in England, was it the product of wisdom, or the effect of necessity, arising from the pre-existing prevalence of an odious feudal system? which government, notwithstanding this division, is now become, in fact, an absolute monarchy, since the . . . by bribing the representatives with the people's money, carries, by his ministers, all the measures that please him; which is equivalent to governing without a parliament, and renders the machine of government much more complex and expensive, and, from its being more complex, more easily put out of order. Has not the famous political fable of the snake, with two heads and one body, some useful instruction contained in it? She was going to a brook to drink, and in her way was to pass through a hedge, a twig of which opposed her direct course; one head chose to go on the right side of the twig, and the other on the left; so that time was spent in the contest, and, before the decision was completed, the poor snake died with thirst." [1]

Franklin argued in vain. The following year saw Pennsylvania fall into line with a Senate. So ended one of the battles royal in the long political fight between the conservatives of

[1] *Works of Benjamin Franklin* (John Bigelow ed.), x, 185–88.

the State, led by James Wilson, and those who under the leadership of George Bryan stood for democratic extremes. The defenders of popular liberty mourned the loss of a precious bulwark that when embodied in the Constitution had been gloried in and boasted of as a settled, established fact, for three quarters of a century,[1] and that seemed to them since then to have continued in justifying itself.

James Wilson more wisely interpreted the lessons of experience and saw things more clearly when he told the Pennsylvania Convention for ratifying the Federal Constitution, December 1, 1787 : "Though two bodies may not possess more wisdom or patriotism than what may be found in a single body, yet they will necessarily introduce a greater degree of precision. An indigested and inaccurate code of laws is one of the most dangerous things that can be introduced into any government. The force of this observation is well known by every gentleman who has attended to the laws of this State. This, sir, is a very important advantage that will arise from this division of the legislative authority." [2]

Another powerful thinker, James Iredell, had said to the North Carolina Convention, July 25, 1788 : " It will often happen that, in a single body, a bare majority will carry exceptionable and pernicious measures. The violent faction of a party may often form such a majority in a single body, and by that means the particular views or interests of a part of the community may be consulted, and those of the rest neglected or injured. Is there a single gentleman in this Convention, who has been a member of the Legislature, who has not found the minority in the most important questions to be often right? Is there a man here, who has been in either House, who has not at some times found the most solid advantages from the coöperation or opposition of the other? If a measure be right, which has been approved by one branch, the other will probably confirm it ; if it be wrong, it is fortunate that there is another branch to oppose or amend it." [3]

Notice that Iredell too was appealing to experience, the most convincing of teachers. Let it not be thought that the men who framed our Constitutions built them on the basis of *a priori* reasoning. They knew what had happened and they learned

[1] B. A. Konkle, *George Bryan and the Const. of Pa.*, 118.
[2] *Elliot's Debates*, II, 146.   [3] *Ibid.*, IV, 39.

from what they had observed.   Take another illustration, that
of the opening speech of Charles Pinckney in the South Carolina
Convention.   "In Maryland," he said, "one branch of their
legislature is a Senate, chosen, for five years, by electors chosen
by the people.   The knowledge and firmness which this body
have, upon all occasions, displayed, not only in the exercise of
their legislative duties, but in withstanding and defeating such
of the projects of the other House as appeared to them founded
in personal and local motives, have long since convinced me
that the Senate of Maryland is the best model of a Senate that
has yet been offered to the Union." [1]

The authors of "The Federalist," in their all-inclusive defense of the proposed Constitution, of course justified the
creation of a Senate.   In Nos. 62 and 63 they reviewed what
they described as the inconveniences which a republic must
suffer from the want of such an institution as the Senate.   "It
doubles the security to the people, by requiring the concurrence
of two distinct bodies in schemes of usurpation or perfidy, where
the ambition or corruption of one would otherwise be sufficient.
The necessity of a Senate is not less indicated by the propensity
of all single and numerous assemblies to yield to the impulse
of sudden and violent passions, and to be seduced by factious
leaders into intemperate and pernicious resolutions.   Another
defect to be supplied by a Senate lies in a want of due acquaintance with the objects and principles of legislation.   The mu-
tability in the public councils arising from a rapid succession
of new members, however qualified they may be, points out, in
the strongest manner, the necessity of some stable institution
in the government."

It is to be remembered that at this time there had been a
dozen years of experience with the weakness and inefficiency of
a Confederation governed by a single-chamber Congress.   When
the Articles of Confederation were drawn, the Committee had
rejected the suggestion of an annual Parliament of two Houses.
As Bancroft says, misled partly by the rooted distrust for which
the motive had ceased, and partly by erudition which studied
Hellenic councils and leagues as well as later confederacies, it
took for its pattern the constitution of the United Provinces,
with one House and no central power of final decision. [2]

One of the dangers feared by the framers of the new Constitu-

----

[1] *Elliot's Debates*, iv, 324.   [2] *Formation of the Constitution*, 11.

tion was that, however unfortunate this feature of the Confederation might seem to thoughtful men, it was so much approved by the masses that they might refuse a change. Indeed, one of the grievances of the insurgents who instigated Shays's Rebellion in Massachusetts was the existence of the State Senate. Elbridge Gerry observed in the Federal Convention, June 5, 1787, that in the Eastern States the people "have at this time the wildest ideas of government in the world. They were for abolishing the Senate in Massachusetts, and giving all the other powers of government to the other branch of the Legislature." [1]

This brief revelation of Gerry's temper in the matter is the more significant by reason of the fact that Gerry was by nature what we should now call a Democrat. He refused to sign the new Constitution because the rights of the citizen were not rendered secure.

In spite of the mass of evidence and argument, some American radicals persisted in doubts. For instance, William Maclay, the virulent and ever-suspicious Senator from Pennsylvania, wrote in his Journal May 25, 1789: "When I came home in the evening I told Mr. Wynkoop [a Representative from the same State] the business of the day. He said things of this kind made him think whether our style of government in Pennsylvania was not the best. Certain it is that a government with so many branches affords a larger field for caballing; first in the Lower House, and the moment a party finds a measure lost or likely to be lost, all engines are set to work in the Upper House. If they are likely to fail here, the last attempt is made with the President, and, as most pains are always taken by bad men and to support bad measures, the calculation seems in favor of the exertions and endeavors that are used, more than in the justness of the measure. On the other hand, a fuller field is open for investigation, but, unfortunately, intrigue and cabal take place of a fair inquiry."

The Journal of the Convention that framed the Constitution of Tennessee in 1796 shows that Andrew Jackson seconded a motion leading to a vote whereby the Convention at first decided in favor of one House. It changed its mind, however, and fell in with the tendency of the times. Of our three States that began with a single chamber, Georgia had reached two Houses in 1789, Pennsylvania in 1790. In the third, Vermont, which

[1] *Elliot's Debates*, v, 158.

had taken her Constitution chiefly from Pennsylvania, the Council of Censors recommended a Senate in 1793 and again in 1813. The proposal in 1813 was rejected in the House by a vote of 5 to 195. A like proposal in 1827 was defeated by 47 to 182. Gain for it continued until 1836, when it prevailed.

EXPERIENCE ABROAD

EUROPEAN experience with single chambers has not encouraged the spread of that system abroad. The Italian Republics of the Middle Ages notably taught the danger. John Adams showed that no part of the political history of mankind is more full of instructive lessons on the subject, or contains more striking proofs of the factious instability and turbulent misery of States under the domain of a single unchecked legislature, than the story of those Republics. (Adams in his remarkable "Defense of the American Constitution" — not the Federal Constitution, for it had not been drawn, but the State systems of government — was answering the criticisms of Turgot and de Mably on the two-chamber idea that the American States had put into their Constitutions.)

In February of 1649 the House of Commons resolved by 44 to 29 that "the House of Peers is useless and dangerous, and ought to be abolished." For four years the House of Commons ruled without check or veto. It was impulsive, arbitrary, tyrannical. Cromwell passed stern judgment on it. "As for Members of Parliament," he declared, "their pride and ambition and self-seeking, ingrossing all places of honor and profit to themselves and their friends, and their daily breaking forth into new and violent parties and factions; their delay of business and design to perpetuate themselves, and to continue the power in their own hands; their meddling in private matters between party and party, contrary to the institution of Parliament, and their injustice and partiality in those matters, and the scandalous lives of some of the chief of them; these things, my lord, do give much ground for the people to open their mouths against them and to dislike them, nor can they be kept within the bounds of justice and law or reason, they themselves being the supreme power of the nation, liable to no account, nor to be controlled or regulated by any other power; there being none superior or coördinate with them." So at last he put an end to what he called their prating.

In spite of that episode and of Italian experience, the French embodied the single chamber in the Constitution of 1791 by an almost unanimous vote of the National Assembly, and it was continued in the Constitution of 1793. To its inadequacy has been ascribed much of the folly of the time. The proceedings of the single chamber were marked by violence, instability, and excesses of the worst kind. Perhaps it is in some measure because of this that the older legislative bodies of the Continent to-day for the most part have two chambers.

The newer Constitutions show diversity of judgment. Before the World War the single chamber was to be found in a number of the smaller States of Germany, in those Swiss Cantons where the laws are made by representative bodies, in Greece, Bulgaria, and Serbia. There was, however, serious question as to its survival in Greece, and the Serbian experience had been such that, although perpetuated in the Constitution of Jugoslavia, it was by a majority of but a few votes. Finland and Esthonia took up with it, but it was rejected for Poland, though by only a narrow margin. The Russian Central Executive Committee, which at any rate ostensibly is the main lawmaking assembly, is made up of two bodies, the Union Council and the Council of Nationalities. Austria, using likewise the federated system, after the fashion of the United States has an upper branch representing the States and a lower representing the people. Rumania and Egypt preferred two Houses.

Especially significant was the adoption of the bi-cameral plan for the Irish Free State despite the dissatisfaction with the upper chamber in England and the fact that but one chamber was used in seven of the nine provinces of Canada (all save Quebec and Nova Scotia), that it had been preferred for South Africa, and that in the same year (1922) Queensland was doing away with the upper branch, the Legislative Council. Perhaps more weight was given to the knowledge that although the disputes between the two chambers in the Australasian colonies had been neither infrequent nor insignificant, yet in the long discussions preceding the formation of the Federal Commonwealth no proposal for a legislature of one chamber had any serious or influential support.

The single chamber appears in most of the Central American States — Guatemala, Honduras, Costa Rica, Salvador, Panama; and in most of the States of Argentina.

Arguments and Tendencies

In the course of the nineteenth century there was much more agitation of this subject in Europe than in America. John Stuart Mill, writing on "Representative Government" in 1861, said: "Of all topics relating to the theory of representative government, none has been the subject of more discussion, especially on the Continent, than what is known as the question of the Two Chambers. It has occupied a greater amount of the attention of thinkers than many questions of ten times its importance, and has been regarded as a sort of touchstone which distinguishes the partisans of limited from those of uncontrolled democracy." If he could have foreseen the controversy over the House of Lords, perhaps he would have ranked the importance of the question higher.

With us it has recently come to the front by reason of the sharp scrutiny brought to bear on all our governmental methods as a result of many influences uniting to demand reform and progress. Constitutional amendments for a single chamber were put before the people of Oregon in 1912 and 1914, of Oklahoma in 1914, and of Arizona in 1916. They did not prevail, but they at least showed serious desire. Governor Hodges of Kansas, the most aggressive champion of the change, proposed it to his Legislature in 1913 and made it the subject of earnest discussion in the West. Two years later two other Governors recommended it in their inaugural messages. Governor George W. Hunt of Arizona said: "It is becoming generally recognized, not only in Arizona, but in many other States, that the legislative body consisting of two separate Houses is unwieldy and results not infrequently in such an evasion of responsibility as defeats the ends of government. A single legislative body comprising not less than seven nor more than fifteen qualified representatives, selected by the people, compensated with an annual salary, and subject, like other officers, to recall, would, in my opinion, prove an economical innovation, resulting in efficient service and the definite fixing of responsibility for new legislation." The argument, however, did not win the approval of the people, for they rejected the proposed amendment by 11,631 to 22,286.

Governor Ernest Lister of Washington said: "I do not believe that a form of State government should be adopted that would place in the hands of the same officials legislative and administrative powers. I do believe, however, that better results would be obtained if we had one legislative body in the State consisting of say not to exceed twenty-five members, five elected from each Congressional district, which could be fixed as legislative districts, and by fixing the time of each regular session of the Legislature at ninety instead of sixty days." In his inaugural message of January, 1917, he repeated this belief.

In 1914 a proposal for a single legislative body with forty members passed each House in California, but could not be submitted to the people because it lacked five votes of a majority of the entire Legislature. In 1915 a committee of the Bar Association of Tennessee reported that the bi-cameral Legislature "belongs to that period when an aristocracy sought by means of the second House to perpetuate its privilege, and, therefore, has no place in a democracy like ours." The report proposed a Legislature consisting of a single house of thirty-three members. The Farmers Coöperative and Educational Union, with a membership of 35,000 in Nebraska, at its State Convention in January, 1918, unanimously approved the abolition of the State Senate. The Arkansas Constitutional Convention of 1918 at first voted for a uni-cameral Legislature with thirty-five members, but later reversed its action. In the Nebraska Constitutional Convention of 1920 a proposal for a one-House Legislature was lost by a tie vote. In 1921 the National Municipal League adopted a "Model State Constitution," carefully prepared and much studied, which would give but one lawmaking chamber, the Legislative Council attached thereto being merely advisory.

Evidently the question has vitality enough to call for analysis of the arguments.

The best argument for a thing is usually to be found in the circumstances of its origin, since that usually came about through a natural response to an evident need. Variety in legislative chambers began through the need of representing different Estates, different orders of men. So long as two chambers gave representation to the two predominant social groupings that may as well be called the classes and the masses as anything else — or if you prefer, the aristocrats and the democrats — advantages were evident. With the triumph of democracy, in our country at least, the walls protecting the upper House have crumbled. Property qualifications have disappeared. The constituencies of Senators and Representatives differ only in size. That in this respect they differ unevenly is nowadays made ground for complaint rather than praise. It is pointed out that this encourages unfair apportionments, regardless of numbers, as where each county gets one Senator, or, as in the case of Connecticut, with allotment of Representatives by towns. Because this usually gives an interest — the rural, farming interest — influence beyond its numerical ratio, it is now declared unfair where once the supposed benefit would have left no room for blame. Any representation of classes, indeed, is declared to be undemocratic. The only sort of representation of interests that still wins general approval is the representation of States in federations, and even this is challenged by those who fret because Delaware or Arizona carries as much weight as New York or Pennsylvania in the Federal Senate.

The old justifications have gone. Have new justifications come?

Yes; and they are neither few nor unimportant.

First I should place the lesson of experience that two chambers conduce to deliberate action. Long ago Paine saw that "the objection against a single House is, that it is always in a condition of committing itself too soon." [1] A story used to be told of George Washington. It may or may not have been true, but it is none the less illuminating. He was said to have been asked at a friend's table why we had aped the feudal institutions of Great Britain to the extent of having a select as well as a popular House in our Congress. His hostess had just helped him to a cup of tea, so hot that it was sending forth a cloud of steam. He poured a part of the tea into his saucer, and let it stand long enough to cool before drinking. "This cup," said he, "is the House of Representatives. Its contents have come directly from the people, who may be in a state of great excitement. This saucer is the Senate, in which I can hold the scalding liquid till its heat has subsided enough to make it safe to drink."

Nobody who has served in a large legislative body can fail to remember times when it was swept off its feet by some burst of eloquence, by a passionate appeal to sympathy, by some

[1] *The Rights of Man*, pt. II, p. 34.

highly colored story of injustice, when all rules would have been suspended and an unwise measure hurried to enactment had not the other House stood in the way of impulsive action.   To make haste slowly is nowhere more useful than in legislation. The danger is evident.   Yet the advocates of the single chamber have an answer not bad.   They say the Governor's veto and the referendum are safeguards enough.   They point to city governments.   During the greater part of the nineteenth century most American cities had Councils of two chambers.   Now these have been widely replaced by single chambers.   No harm has come.   In rebuttal, however, it is to be said that a City Council is not a lawmaking body.   Its acts have not the importance or standing of laws.   So the courts have held.   In Whitcomb's Case, 120 Mass. 123 (1876), Chief Justice Gray said: "The city council is not a Legislature.   It has no power to make laws, but merely to pass ordinances upon such local matters as the Legislature may commit to its charge, and subject to the paramount control of the Legislature."   The mistakes of a city council are seldom both serious and irretrievable.   Quite otherwise might it be with an Act of a State Legislature or Congress.

John Stuart Mill thought another line of reasoning more important.   "I attach little weight," he said, "to the argument oftenest heard for having two chambers — to prevent precipitancy, and compel a second deliberation; for it must be a very ill-constituted representative assembly in which the established forms of business do not require many more than two deliberations.   The consideration which tells most, in my judgment, in favor of two Chambers (and this I do regard of some moment) is the evil produced upon the mind of any holder of power, whether an individual or an assembly, by the consciousness of having only themselves to consult.   It is important that no set of persons should, in great affairs, be able, even temporarily, to make their *sic volo* prevail without asking any one else for his consent.   A majority in a single assembly, when it has assumed a permanent character — when composed of the same persons habitually acting together, and always assured of victory in their own House — easily becomes despotic and overweening, if released from the necessity of considering whether its acts will be concurred in by another constituted authority."[1]

Lecky saw the same evil.   "Of all the forms of government

[1] *Representative Government*, chap. XIII.

that are possible among mankind I do not know any which is likely to be worse than the government of a single omnipotent democratic chamber. It is at least as susceptible as an individual despot of the temptations that grow out of the possession of an uncontrolled power, and it is likely to act with much less sense of responsibility and much less real deliberation." [1]

Contrast this with the shallow epigram of Sieyès at the time of the French Revolution : "If a Second Chamber dissents from the First, it is mischievous; if it agrees, it is superfluous." Neither is true. Dissent proves, at least in theory, that the change proposed does not commend itself enough to give reasonable guarantee of its wisdom. Furthermore, dissent is at least as likely to block a bad measure as a good measure. In case of agreement, there is advantage in the double assurance of approval.

More serious and sincere are present-day rejoinders to such an argument as that of Mill for the advantages of consultation. It is replied that consultation may bring more harm than good. It conduces to bargaining, to an improper, harmful give-and-take. Worse than that, because much more common, it damages or even destroys the sense of responsibility. When two men join to do a foolish or a wrong thing, each can throw the blame on the other. The assertion is that were there but one House, it would feel a responsibility now lacking. It would be more honest and more courageous. This argument on the score of divided responsibility was among the considerations brought to the notice of the New York Convention of 1915 by the Bureau of Municipal Research in its report on "The Constitution and Government of the State of New York." It cited with apparent approval the averment that the two-chamber legislature "is destined to disappear from the State governments just so soon as the problem of constitution-making has been approached by the people with enough seriousness of purpose to demand that the representative branch be used as a means of establishing and enforcing responsibility instead of confusing it and compelling the people to look to an irresponsible 'boss' for protection." This is not quite clear to one outside the New York environment. The people of Massachusetts do not look to a "boss" for protection. The Legislature of that State is not and in our time never has been "bossed" either from within

[1] *Democracy and Liberty*, i, 299.

or from without.   Nothing there would hurt the chances of a bill more than the suspicion that a "boss" wanted it.   There is no adequate proof that in a majority of the States the people look to a "boss" for protection.   The innuendo is an illustration of the harm brought to the reputation of all American Legislatures by hasty generalizing from observation of one.

Furthermore, there is nothing to show that a "boss" can control two branches easier than he could one.   The intimation looks absurd on the face.   It is, indeed, true that two branches may make it easier for a "boss" or anybody else to thwart legislation, but they make it distinctly harder to get legislation. Is not the suspicion warranted that the charge comes from those who accept a proposal for change as *prima facie* commendable simply because it looks to change — those who by temperament think something else, anything else, must be better?

There can be control of both Houses only when the same political party has a majority in each (which is usually the case) and when party organization is so strong that it can make the majorities work in unison (which sometimes happens, though not so often as is supposed).   Party leaders usually concern themselves with but a small part of legislation.   There is always more or less of rivalry, jealousy, hostility in the relations between two branches.   The man is rare with hand steady enough and whip stout enough to drive the two at the same time.   In practice, the plausible theory that party organization destroys the checks and balances of the two-chamber system seldom works.

In this matter of checks and balances we find criticisms looking both ways.   Some, by averring that their disappearance has taken away from the two-chamber system its advantages, seem to admit that there were advantages.   Others, by blaming the system for its deadlocks, seem to imply that checks and balances are harmful.   A deadlock is a situation where each of two groups of men, ordinarily honest, is so sure it is right that it will not yield.   If each persists, the outcome is inaction. This means delay, and where each chamber has the strength and depth of feeling a deadlock shows, is it not on the whole advantageous to have delay until opinion enough can gather to compel action?

No argument is necessary to prove that the study of a measure by two Houses rather than one ought to bring to it more of criticism and ought to result in better legislation. The retort is that the possibility of a second examination tempts the body first scrutinizing to be hasty, careless, and slipshod in its work. Of course this can do no harm unless the second body assumes that the first scrutiny has been adequate and dispenses with any on its own part. That is possible, but my own observation does not lead me to think it frequent. Usually each House takes a malicious pleasure in detecting some bit of carelessness on the part of the other.

It is also averred that sometimes the second House resents being forced to take the responsibility of rejecting a measure already passed by the first House, and lets the measure go through.[1] This is also possible, but has not come within the range of my own observation.

Far more serious is the charge that bad bills are passed by one House in the confident expectation that they will be killed by the other. That takes place. Not a word is to be said in its excuse. Yet it may be pointed out that, if the second branch does its duty, no great harm has resulted. If it fails to do its duty, there is nothing to show that it would not likewise have failed had it been a single chamber. The fact is that while Legislatures like men are sometimes impelled by petty motives, yet good impulses predominate. Two Houses may now and then show themselves guilty of mean or sordid impulses, but such foolish exhibitions are so rare as to warrant ignoring them when set against the much more frequent instances of healthy, earnest rivalry in search for the public welfare.

It is urged both for and against two Houses that they hamper the influence of the individual member. On the one hand, it is argued that there is danger in the persuasive oratory of a brilliant man who can carry his point by appeal to passion or prejudice, and that it is useful to have a calmer consideration of his project by a body not subject to his eloquence. On the other hand, it is averred to be a misfortune that a master of a subject, one capable of convincing if he can get a hearing, may present his arguments to only one of the two bodies. In the other he must find some champion. It is almost certain he can find there nobody so well informed as himself on this particular matter, nobody willing to give all the time he has given to its

[1] Walker D. Hines, "Our Irresponsible State Governments," *Atlantic Monthly*, May, 1915.

mastery, nobody who will match his enthusiasm and zeal. Of course this condition militates against hasty changes in the statutes. Also it can be urged with force that no measure ought to become a law unless it can find at least two ardent supporters, one in each branch. Yet when you consider how many of the great reforms have been due to the energy of solitary men, inspired by individual conviction, it would appear that the bi-cameral method is not without its drawbacks.

This phase of the subject brings out another consideration. The psychologists are summoned to support the theory that the individual will is usually merged in the mass will of a legislating body. The result is the development of the mob spirit, where impulse gets the better of reason. Anybody who has served in a Legislature has seen this work. With two chambers it is not likely that each will be affected by a wave of prejudice or impatience or suspicion. Yet it is equally true that with two chambers the chance that a good measure will be thus defeated is twice as large as it is with one.

It is said that it is harder to corrupt each of two chambers than to corrupt a single chamber. Yet everybody knows that with two chambers the briber has two chances to accomplish defeat.

Two chambers divide some of the work, for a measure rejected by one, need not take the time of the other. Against this is put the time taken by a second consideration of measures that one body has approved. As to the time cost James D. Barnett, of the University of Oregon, writing in the "American Political Science Review" of August, 1915, on "The Bi-cameral System in State Legislation," made this statement: "Under the present conditions in our Legislatures the elimination of one House would reduce the mass of business submitted, approximately in proportion to the number of the members of the House eliminated, and thus by that much remove the difficulties in the way of deliberate action." Had he ever served in a Legislature, or if having served he had used his pencil, he would have found that but a small part of legislation originates in the brain of a member. Most of it is brought to members and that part would not be reduced in quantity by a single measure were there one House in place of two.

The money expense of a second chamber is a make-weight often thrown into the discussion. Stated without qualification, it is an unfair argument. If a second chamber is to be abolished simply because it adds to expense, then both chambers ought to be abolished, for the saving would be twice as great. Of course the real question is whether the extra cost of a second chamber is repaid by public benefit. The Bureau of Municipal Research was a little extravagant when it said the second chamber "adds enormously to the cost of government." [1] The cost of a Senate to each inhabitant of a State is trivial. It does not greatly increase what may be called the legislative overhead charges. If it is in fact a real safeguard, its cost is unimportant.

It has been urged that Constitutional Conventions have always been one-chambered bodies. True, but save in the earliest State period, when various Constitutions were put in force without submission to the people, the people have as a matter of fact almost invariably constituted a second chamber. We have come to the practically universal opinion that it is not safe to let a single body, unchecked, alter the fundamental law.

If in balancing the arguments I have thrown the scale in favor of the bi-cameral system, it is partly because long personal experience in the Massachusetts Legislature led me to believe its merits outweighed its defects. As to whether this is the case in other State Legislatures under present conditions, I can give no testimony based on personal observation, but no ground presents itself for thinking that in most of them the same considerations would not hold. /What will occur when our lawmaking methods are reorganized to meet modern needs is another story. Some day it is going to be recognized that government has come in our time to have two distinct functions — one it has always had, the function of justice; the other, the new function of business. When these come to be handled separately, the function of business may very well call for unicameral treatment, as in the case of all business corporations. Justice, however, the rights and wrongs of men, will always call for those methods that secure adequate caution, deliberation, reflection, assurance.

[1] *The Const. and Govt. of the State of N.Y.*, 63 (May, 1915).

CHAPTER III

SENATES

SENATES are among the oldest of human institutions. Their name reveals their history. The Latin *senatus* comes from *senex* — old man. First the aged head of the family ruled, then the aged members of the tribe. When leadership passed over to individuals, they naturally consulted the venerable. Doubtless there had been innumerable councils of such before "the Lord said unto Moses, Gather unto me seventy men of the elders of Israel," and before "Moses went out, and told the people the words of the Lord, and gathered the seventy men of the elders of the people, and set them round about the tabernacle." [1] From that day to this, the "elders" have played a conspicuous part in church history. They have even given to a great sect its name, for "Presbyterian" comes from a Latin word for "elder." In secular affairs another name tells the same tale, for "Aldermen" were once "Ealdor (elder) men."

It is among the Greeks that we can first trace the development of the Council of Elders into something approaching a modern Senate. [2] The Homeric poems show us a Council of chiefs or old men, and occasional meetings of a listening Agora — the assembly of the people. The next step was the defining of this Council under the Constitution Lycurgus is supposed to have given to Sparta not later than 825 B.C. The number of the Council was then fixed at thirty — the two Kings and twenty-eight ancient men, not appointed until sixty years old and holding office for life. These limitations appear to have given historians warrant for speaking henceforward of a "Senate." Plutarch ranks its establishment as the most important change Lycurgus made. Having a power equal to that of the Kings in matters of great consequence, and, as Plato expresses it, allaying and qualifying the fiery genius of the royal office, the Spartan Senate gave safety and steadiness to the commonwealth. The twenty-eight always adhered to the Kings so far

---

[1] *Numbers*, XI, 17, 24. [2] George Grote, *History of Greece, passim.*

as to resist democracy, and on the other hand supported the people against the establishment of absolute monarchy. It came to pass that the assembly of the people merely accepted or rejected what had been previously determined in the Senate. This they did without open discussion or power of amendment, and, if they decided crookedly, the Senate with the Kings could reverse their decision.

Solon modified and improved the Spartan idea for Athens. He enlarged the powers of its ancient Council, known as the Senate of the Areopagus from the place where it sat. He gave it an ample supervision over the execution of the laws, and imposed on it the censorial duty of inspecting the lives and occupations of the citizens, as well as of punishing men of idle and dissolute habits. Its judicial powers are most mentioned. The nine Archons passed into it and sat for life. Down to the time of Pericles it was the most important body in the State.

The novelty Solon devised was a second Senate, the proboleutic or preconsidering Senate, with intimate and especial reference to the public assembly — to prepare matters for its discussion, to convoke and superintend its meetings, and to insure the execution of its decrees. As first constituted by Solon, this Senate had four hundred members, taken in equal proportions from the four tribes. They were not chosen by lot as in the more advanced stage of the democracy, but were elected by the people. Members of the fourth or poorest class, though sharing in the election, were not themselves eligible.

Grote finds in the era of Solon (594 B.C.) "the first known example of a genuine and disinterested constitutional reform, and the first foundation stone of that great fabric which afterwards became the type of democracy in Greece." Solon is said to have contemplated that, by means of the two Senates, the State would be held fast, as if it were with a double anchor, against all shocks and storms. While Solon was yet alive, though very old, Peisistratus usurped the power in Athens and much of Solon's work seemed for the time to be undone. The forms of government persisted, however, after a fashion, and revived after the fall of the Peisistratid dynasty in 510 B.C., fifty years after the first usurpation of its founder. Cleisthenes was the new leader of constitutional government. The annually changed Senate, instead of being composed of four hundred members taken in equal proportion from each of the old four tribes, was enlarged to five hundred, taken equally from each of the new ten tribes. It comes before us, under the name of "Senate of Five Hundred," as an active and indispensable body throughout the whole Athenian democracy; and the practice now seems to have begun of selecting the Senators by lot.

From the time of Cleisthenes, the Senate of Five Hundred steps far beyond its original duty of preparing matters for the discussion of the ecclesia; it embraces, besides, a large circle of administrative and general superintendence, that hardly admits of any definition. Its sittings become constant, with the exception of special holidays, and the year is distributed into ten portions called Prytanies, the fifty Senators of each tribe taking by turns the duty of constant attendance during one prytany. The remaining Senators, not belonging to the prytan-izing tribe, may of course attend if they choose; but the at-tendance of nine among them, one from each of the remaining nine tribes, is imperatively necessary to constitute a valid meeting, and to insure a constant representation of the collec-tive people.

In Rome likewise the ancient Council of Elders grew into a Senate. Tradition has it that originally the Council was made up of the heads of families or clans. After the clan-elders ceased to exist, the King selected, but probably was bound by custom to see that each clan was represented. When a member died, the King would name another from the same clan. Out of this grew the life tenure of the Senators, subject to termination by the Censors. About 351 b.c. the filling of vacancies was transferred from the Consuls (who had succeeded the Kings) to the Censors. Certain classes of magistrates on completing their terms of office became Senators, and the Censors chose others enough to fill up the ranks. From three hundred in number they grew to six hundred under the Em-perors.

Originally when the King had a proposal to submit to the people, he first took the advice of the Council of Elders. After the Council had been transformed into the Senate, that body kept and never lost its formal character of being a council of advisers. Nominally it had no legislative authority. Really it ruled, until well into the last century of the Republic. Up to that time it controlled by the force of custom, which pre-scribed that no magistrate should submit any important matter

to the people without the advice of the Senate, and that no
magistrate should decline to submit such a matter if the Senate
requested. The veto was to be exercised by a magistrate only
if the Senate so advised, and was to be withheld when it so
counseled. If any magistrate balked, the Senate had for a
weapon of last resort the veto of some more friendly or sub-
missive magistrate. At first it also had the duty of what was
virtually the passing upon the constitutionality of measures after
the people had acted, but this was withdrawn about 339 B.C.
Another curtailment of power came in 286 B.C., with the Lex
Hortensia, providing that the resolutions of the Assembly of
the Plebs might receive the sanction of law even without ratification by the Senate. When Sulla seized power, he took from
the Assembly the right to discuss laws without authorization
from the Senate, but in the general undoing of Sulla's work a
few years later Pompey gave back to the tribunes the power to
initiate legislation. With the turmoils that changed Rome from
republic to empire, the Senate lost such of its authority as had
survived the usurpations of the demagogues, and under the
Emperors it was little more than a sham.

The House of Lords is another Senate that traces its origin
to a council. It succeeded the Great Council of Norman
times, and that in turn had succeeded the Anglo-Saxon Witenagemot, a comparatively small body of councilors, made up for
the most part of Bishops, Abbots, Ealdormen or Earls, and
King's Thegns. When Parliaments came, peers and prelates
are known to have deliberated on at least some occasions apart
from the King's Council, but presently they came to control
and then to be the Great Council, combining in themselves the
work of advising the Crown and of sharing in legislation. They
were not, however, known as the House of Lords until the time
of Henry VIII.

Up to the period of the Reformation, the spiritual Lords
generally made a majority of the upper House. Then their
number fell to twenty-six. The two archbishops and twenty-
four bishops now have seats; a junior bishop has to wait until
he holds the see of Durham, Winchester, or London. Judges
have been among the members and the upper House has exercised judicial functions from the time Parliament began. At
present there are four salaried lords-of-appeal in ordinary. On
retirement they hold their peerages during life. The four,

presided over by the Lord Chancellor, compose the supreme tribunal of the kingdom. Technically speaking, all the other members have a right to join with them, and some of those with legal training occasionally so do, but in most instances they work alone.

The House of Lords has grown something more than fourfold in six centuries. To the model Parliament of 1295 were summoned less that one hundred forty. By the time of Henry VII the number had fallen to eighty or less. To the first Parliament of Charles II were summoned almost precisely the same number as in 1295. With the eighteenth century began the lavish creation of peers. More than half the peerages of to-day have been created within the last half-century, and only a few of the rest can be called ancient. The total membership has now gone beyond seven hundred.

Colonial Councils

American colonial upper chambers were commonly spoken of as "Councils," but neither in origin nor in character were they like the councils from which sprang the Senates of ancient times or the English House of Lords. The earliest of them were substantially boards of directors of trading companies. In the older New England colonies the fact that they were not appointed by the Crown, but were elected, till just before the outbreak of the Revolutionary War, clearly distinguishes them from what has been more generally meant by "Council."

Furthermore, some of the fundamental characteristics of the English parliamentary framework were never embodied in any colonial organization actually put into effect. "Estates" were not recognized as such; the clergy had no seats; judges did not sit as such. There were no inherited memberships in the upper House. Life memberships were exceptional and temporary. Only in Massachusetts was carried out an attempt to transplant these features of aristocracy from England. Lord Say and Sele, Lord Brooke, and other peers with Puritan sympathies sought changes that would encourage them to come to America, and with other things an acknowledgment of hereditary right to a seat in the upper House. The colonists began to make appointments for life; but, as for the establishment of hereditary dignity, they answered by the hand of Cotton: "Where

God blesseth any branch of any noble or any generous family
with a spirit and gifts fit for government, it would be a taking of
God's name in vain to put such a talent under a bushel, and a
sin against the honor of magistracy to neglect such in our popular
elections. But, if God should not delight to furnish some of
their posterity with gifts fit for magistracy, we should expose
them rather to reproach and prejudice, and the commonwealth
with them, if we should call them forth, when God doth not, to
public authority."

The people, moreover, were uneasy at any permanent concession of office. Saltonstall, "that much-honored and upright-
hearted servant of Christ," loudly reproved "the sinful innovation," and advocated its reform; nor would the freemen be
quieted till, in 1639, it was made a law that those who were
appointed Magistrates for life should yet not be Magistrates
except in those years in which they should be regularly chosen
at the annual election.[1]

If, nevertheless, it should still be thought that our forefathers
copied the English House of Lords, let further proof to the contrary be brought from the writings of the time. These do not,
indeed, disprove that the smaller branch was meant to be what
they called an aristocratical body, and this of course savors of a
House of Lords, but clearly no such relation as that between the
Lords and the Commons was contemplated. What the aristocrats of the Massachusetts Bay Colony really had in mind is
best learned from the words of John Winthrop, their ablest
spokesman. Winthrop was trained as a lawyer and had
practiced his profession up to the time he came to America.
For his day he was far advanced in the mysteries of political
science. He had a clear idea of what he was about. Control
by the learned few was really his aim. You may find it set
forth in a formal discourse on government that he published
in 1644 by reason of the demand that the Deputies should share
in the exercise of judicial power. Its title was: "Arbitrary
Government Described: and the Government of the Massachusetts Vindicated from that Aspersion." The vindication,
however, was not founded on any allegation that the people
ruled, but on his conclusion from the terms of the Charter that
the freemen had "the power of Liberty." This he gave to them
in contrast with "the power of Authority," which he ascribed

[1] George Bancroft, *Hist. of the U.S.*, I, 258.

to the Governor, Deputy Governor, and Assistants. The plain people made short work of such metaphysical distinctions. Hair-splitting was not to their taste. A committee of the House of Deputies, passing on the treatise, bluntly said: "Concerninge the distinction therein made of the bodye Politick, & the members thereof, in attributing Authoritye to the one, & onely Libertye to the other: we finde not any suche distinction in the Patent." [1]

Winthrop had argued of the Deputies: "They have libertye of Counsell in all the generall Assemblyes, so as without their counsell & consent, no Lawes, decrees, or orders, of any publike nature or concernment, nor any Taxes, impositions, impresses, or other burdens of what kinde soever, can be imposed upon them, their familyes or estates, by any Authoritye in the Government." To this the committee of the Deputies replied: "Concerninge the Clause recited therein (respecting the generall Court) which gives only Libertye to the ffreemen, to advise & Counsell, instead of power & Authoritye (which the Patent allowes) we conceive it a takinge aweye of the power & priviledges of the ffreemen."

The House appears to have approved by vote the findings of its committee. Thereupon Winthrop retorted that his distinction was "warranted by the Patent (as in other places so) particularly in that clause, which sayeth that the Governour, etc., shall call the ffreemen to consult & advise etc. which is an acte of Libertye & not of Authoritye & for the other parte of their power, which is matter of Election, the late Bodye of Libertyes sayth it is their constant Libertye, not Authoritye."

In the last of the tracts that Winthrop wrote on the negative voice controversy, he set forth distinctly his conception of the place and power of the Deputies, as follows:

"1: They have the same place & power which the ffreemen assembled in a Generall Court ought to have: according to the Order of 34.

"2: These, joyned with the magistrates in any generall Court have (together with them) all the power legislative, & the chiefe power juditiall, of this bodye Politick.

"3: Neither the Magistrates alone, nor the Deputyes alone, without the consent eache of other, in any generall court, have any power at all.

[1] *Life and Letters of John Winthrop*, II, 441, 456.

"4 : The Deputyes are no magistrates nor (considered alone) have any judiciary power." [1]

Be it noted that he drew a clear distinction between the House of Lords in England and the Magistrates in the Colony: "Thos Nobles represent onely their owne familyes, but our magistrates doe represent the Authoritye of all the people." Clearly it was not Winthrop's idea that the upper branch represented the interests of one Estate, one class or rank or condition of the people. For two centuries that view, the English view, was to fight for a place in our system of government, to be at last defeated. If Winthrop was right, the idea of class representation was a usurper, an invader, anomalous, foreign to our first principles. Yet if not in theory, at any rate in practice, it won the acceptance of the colony from the start. Although the people chose the Governor and Assistants, for a generation their choice was confined to what Hutchinson describes as "the principal gentlemen of family, estate, understanding, and integrity."

It was the easier to do this because, ignoring the injunction of the Charter that eighteen should be elected, they confined themselves to eight or ten. At first the purpose was to leave room for persons of quality expected from England. Then it came to be realized that filling the quota would give a better chance to aspiring men not in favor with those already in power. The Deputies, too, may have been glad to keep down the number of Assistants, for officers were elected by majority vote of the whole Court, and the fewer the Magistrates, the less their influence on elections. At last the home government took umbrage at this violation of the Charter and flatly demanded that the full number of Assistants be chosen. Hutchinson quotes "one who lived at that time" as saying, that "when King Charles commanded them to fill up their numbers in government, which they had neglected, the new persons empowered were *Dii minorum gentium;* and one of their divines told them in public, they were in danger of being undone by creeping statesmen." [2] It was at the General Court in May, 1680, that the full number was first chosen.

The construction at the outset put on the Charter of 1691, which Hutchinson says was favored by the practice under the

---

[1] *Life and Letters of John Winthrop,* II, 430.
[2] Gov. Thomas Hutchinson, *History of Massachusetts Bay* (3d ed.), II, 11.

former Charter, made the Lieutenant-Governor and Secretary members of the Council in addition to its twenty-eight elected members, but the second year both were elected, with only twenty-six others, as Assistants. When the quarrels of pre-revolutionary times brought the matter in issue, Governor Bernard "was fully persuaded that both Lieutenant-Governor and Secretary were designed by the charter to be of the Council, and that Mr. Mather, the Agent, who was consulted in framing the charter, had fixed upon the number twenty-eight, in imitation of Lycurgus' senators, who were of a like number, and being added to the two Kings, who only retained a voice with the other Senators, made up thirty." [1]

Under the old Charter the freemen had elected the Assistants. Now it was directed that they should be chosen by the General Court. At the first election it was made a question whether by the General Court or Assembly was intended the House of Representatives only, or the whole three branches. Hutchinson tells us it had been handed down, by tradition, that, "after some time spent in messages and replies, the Council of the former year gave up the point, and sent Major Walley, one of their number, to acquaint the House with it; but when he came to the door he heard the Speaker putting the question to the House, and finding they had conceded to the Council, he returned without delivering his message; and a committee coming soon after from the House to bring up the vote, the Council by this accident retained a privilege which they have been in the exercise of ever since; and, no doubt, it is in a great measure owing to this, that any great change in the House has rarely been effected, even when there have been very warm altercations between the two Houses the preceding year." [2]

Hutchinson's personal experience with the General Court led him to write of its history with more than usual understanding. For instance, note how he treats an episode of 1719, when in the course of one of the quarrels with the Governor, a resolve sent up by the lower branch bore this indorsement: "Sent *to the upper house* for their concurrence." Hutchinson comments: "The *upper house* was a new name for the Council, and designed as a fleer, and to intimate that they might consider

[1] Gov. Thomas Hutchinson, *History of Massachusetts Bay* (3d ed.), III, 176.
[2] *Ibid.*, II, 15.

themselves in another capacity than as a privy council. Perhaps if Cromwell's epithet for the House of Lords had come into their minds, it would have been *the other House*. Taunts and language which tend to irritate can upon no occasion be justifiable from one branch of the Legislature to the other. Upon an agreement and harmony the interest of the people depends. Upon different apprehensions of this interest, if it be the real object, the several branches, by the persuasive voice of reason, will strive to convince each other, and be willing to be convinced, as truth shall appear. The Council thought themselves unkindly treated, and by a message desired the House to alter their vote; but they refused to do it and gave their reasons for the new form," averring that in several particulars they had received new and unusual treatment. "The House having in this manner expressed their resentment returned to their old style." [1]　In passing, attention may be called to the fact that at any rate by the time Hutchinson wrote, "the House" had come to be the common designation of the lower branch.

In 1766, when the rupture between Governor Bernard and the General Court of Massachusetts Bay was getting serious, the House failed to elect to the Council the Lieutenant-Governor, the Secretary, one of the judges of the Superior Court, and the Attorney-General, whereupon the Governor refused his consent to six of the men elected, "who appeared to him to be most unfit for the office." There was nothing illegal about this on either side, but Hutchinson says that while the House had kept up its right by constant use, though with one exception never before making so great a change at once, Governors had from disuse almost lost their right of negativing the Council. He seems to have had in mind the preceding twenty-five years, for in 1741 Governor Belcher had negatived thirteen of the men elected. On that occasion the House would choose none in the stead of those rejected, and Hutchinson says it had for many years neglected to comply with the Charter in this regard. Bernard now tried to get it to fill the places of the six rejected, but that would not have been a prudent move on the part of the men opposing him, so they skillfully replied that they were "under no apprehension of any bad effects, especially when they reflect on the ability and integrity of the Councilors he had approved of, and they beg to be

[1] Gov. Thomas Hutchinson, *History of Massachusetts Bay* (3d ed.), II, 205.

excused from any unnecessary search after palliatives or expedients." [1]

Hutchinson's general comment on the upper branch is worth quoting as the contemporary judgment of an able and learned man, perhaps prejudiced, but now believed to have been sincere. "It is very difficult," he wrote, "to form a second branch of legislature, analogous to the second branch in the English constitution. The colonies are not ripe for hereditary honours, otherwise there seems no more room for exception to them there, than in Ireland. In the charter governments of Connecticut and Rhode Island, this branch is more dependent upon the people in general than the House of Representatives; the first being elected by the freemen in general, the last by the freemen of their several towns; and there having been instances, in those colonies, where the Representatives have had virtue enough to withstand popular prejudices when the Council have not. In the royal governments, as they are called, the Council can scarcely be considered as a distinct branch; frequently they receive their appointment from the recommendation of the Governor; they are always liable to be suspended by him, and if it be without sufficient cause, the remoteness of the colonies from the place where redress is to be obtained, and the expense of soliciting it, are, very often, sufficient to discourage from applying for it. In Massachusetts, this branch is dependent both upon the Governor and people; and we have seen, at different times, the influence of the one or the other over this branch, according to the degree of spirit and resolution which has respectively prevailed. We have seen instances also of counsellors, who have had fortitude enough to resist an undue influence from either, and who from year to year have had violent opposition to their election. We have seen so many good men members, that I may not give the epithet [rotten?] to this branch which is sometimes used for the small boroughs in England. But we have often seen, that the most likely way to secure a seat for many years is to be of no importance, and therefore it must be pronounced defective. Neither in Massachusetts, nor in the royal governments, do we meet with that glorious independence, which makes the House of Lords the bulwark of the English constitution, and which has sometimes saved the liberties of the people from threatened

[1] Gov. Thomas Hutchinson, *History of Massachusetts Bay* (3d ed.), III, 148-52.

encroachments, and at other times put a stop to advances making upon the royal prerogative." [1]

One result of Hutchinson's long and embittered quarrel with the General Court, together with the other episodes that hurried Massachusetts toward the final break with the mother country, was that when Parliament passed the Act "for the better regulating the government of the province of the Massachusetts Bay," the number of Councilors was increased to thirty-six. The right of choosing them was taken away from the Representatives, and the power of selection vested in the Crown, after August 1, 1774. This power was exercised by the issue of writs of mandamus, and the Councilors named were execrated as the "Mandamus Councilors." The people assembled in large numbers and compelled many to resign. Fourteen resisted popular sentiment, whereupon the First Provincial Congress, voting October 21, 1774, resolved that those of them who did not within ten days acknowledge their misconduct and renounce their commissions, "ought to be considered as infamous betrayers of their country; and that a committee of Congress be ordered to cause their names to be published repeatedly, that the inhabitants of their province, by having them entered on the records of each town, as rebels against the State, may send them down to posterity with the infamy they deserve."

Meantime, at the annual meeting of the General Court, May 25, 1774, twenty-eight Councilors had been chosen in accordance with the provisions of the Charter of William and Mary. General Gage, exercising the charter prerogative of veto, rejected thirteen of these. The others were invited by the Provincial Congress, October 28, 1774, to sit with it, barring the Honorable Samuel Danforth, who had also been made a Mandamus Councilor and had been sworn as such, although he publicly declared his determination not to act under his commission. A month later a committee was appointed "to wait on such gentlemen of his majesty's constitutional Council of this province who are now in town at the request of this Congress, and acquaint them that this Congress respectfully acknowledge their cheerful attendance, but will not be ready to offer any matters for their advice, until a quorum of that

[1] Gov. Thomas Hutchinson, *History of Massachusetts Bay* (3d ed.), II, 15 (1760–67).

honorable board shall appear, and which is soon expected; and that in the mean time a seat is provided for them in this house, if they shall see cause to be present." [1] No further mention of them is to be found in the index of the Journals of the First, Second, and Third Congresses. Apparently they never exercised the function of a second chamber.

In Rhode Island, after some hesitation over the meaning of the Charter of 1663, it was decided that the Assistants (who composed the upper branch) were to be chosen by popular vote. In Connecticut they were at first chosen by the General Assembly, but later the Charter was construed as permitting their choice in the town meetings. A singular method was devised. In September each freeman voted for twenty men to be candidates at the election in the following April, when twelve out of the highest twenty were chosen.

In Pennsylvania the upper branch was elected by the people at the start, but the process did not long survive. By the original Frame, the Council, as it was called, had seventy-two members, an absurdly large number for a little colony and quickly found topheavy. The Governor presided and had three votes, but no veto. This Council had the exclusive right of initiating legislation as well as of summoning and dissolving the General Assembly. Penn had a clear idea of what was intended. "The people," he said, "have their representatives in the Provincial Councell to prepare, and the Assembly as it is called has only the power of aye or no, yea or nay. If they turn debators, or Judges, or complainers, you overthrow the Charter quite in the very root of the constitution of it, for that is to usurp the Provincial councel's part in the Charter and to forfeit the charter itself; here would be two assemblys and two representatives, whereas they are but one, to two works, one prepares and proposes, the other assents or denys — the negative voice is by that in them and that is not a debateing, mending, altering, but an accepting power." [2]

Such concentration of power proved intolerable. The Assembly at once petitioned for the right of initiation. Conferences followed, resulting in a revision of the Frame of Government, whereby the Council was reduced to three members from each county, the Assembly was to have six from each county, the triple vote of the Governor was abolished, and bills proposed by the Council were to be published twenty days before the meeting of the General Assembly. During the brief suspension of Penn's powers, when Governor Fletcher of New York had charge, the Council was appointed, but when in 1694 Penn's powers were restored, it became again elective and it was so continued by the Frame of Government of 1696 that took its name from Deputy Governor Markham. The new instrument, however, gave the lower branch as well as the Council the right to initiate measures. The situation was not yet satisfactory. An elected Council was not working well. So when Penn came over again, in 1700, discussion was renewed, with the result that in 1701 the Council became appointive and at the same time lost all direct share in legislation, apparently a compromise with important concession from both sides. Thereafter the Legislature of Pennsylvania consisted of the Governor and one House, for almost a century.

In North Carolina for seven years the Council was appointed by the Governor. For a score of years after 1670 there were ten members, half elected by the lower House, and the other half named to represent the proprietors. It was found that the Council had little to do except the proposing of laws, and that even this was obnoxious to the people. So in 1691 the Proprietors abolished the Grand Council and substituted a Council made up of Deputies alone. That in turn went by the board, in 1724, being replaced by an appointed Council to have a membership of twelve or less.

In New York, Councils were appointed under both Dutch and English rule. The number of members varied. Director Kieft found one Councilor enough, perhaps too much. Governor Bellomont enjoyed the advice of thirteen.

In Virginia there were usually a dozen, appointed by the Crown, almost always upon the recommendation of the Governor, and serving for life or during good behavior. The Governor could suspend, but very rarely exercised that power. In practice appointment was limited to men of means, for the Councilors filled the most important offices in the province, and if they were poor and defaulted, the Government would lose the funds misappropriated. The Governor usually sat with the Virginia Council until 1725.

It is not necessary to particularize further. Suffice it to say that in general the colonial type of government came to be that of a popular assembly, accompanied by a Council, which, except in Pennsylvania, served as an upper branch for purposes of legislation. Everywhere this upper branch also had certain administrative powers or powers of an advisory nature that made it also part of the executive branch of government. To illustrate, in 1678 the General Court of Connecticut ordered that the Governor, Lieutenant-Governor, and Assistants should be a Council to act for the Commonwealth during the recesses of the Court. Or, again for illustration, the Assistants in Massachusetts were from the first also known as the Magistrates and had the duties suggested by that name. Appointed by Proprietors or Governors in all but three of the colonies, with tenure of office at the control of the appointing power, the Councils were not responsible to the people and represented neither the people as a whole nor any specific interest in the community.

UPPER BRANCHES IN THE STATES

WHEN the Revolution transformed the provinces into commonwealths, upper branches saw more radical changes than almost any other of the familiar political institutions. Stripped of most of their executive and judicial powers, they became in point of fundamental functions little more than counterparts of the lower branches. Resemblances between the provincial Council and the British House of Lords suggesting relationship, virtually disappeared. As a matter of fact that relationship never existed. Yet, ignoring the individuality of American Senates, many writers have assumed that they were nothing but daughters of the House of Lords. For example, Stevens says: "The Senate of the United States is, in reality, a development from the House of Lords and the Privy Council, jointly; and as both these bodies came originally from the older legislative council of England, it is evolved, through them, from that ancient Great Council and the Witenagemot." [1]

Still farther afield was Freeman, the eminent English historian. "The historical connexion between the written Constitution of the United States and the unwritten Constitution of England," he declared, "is a truth on which I have often tried to insist, and not least when I was lecturing on such matters in the United States themselves. I will not here go

[1] *Sources of the Constitution*, 77.

into the subject at length; it may be enough to speak of the most remarkable case of closeness with which the daughter has, wherever it has been possible, reproduced the parent. This is the prevalence of legislative bodies composed of two Houses, a system which may be studied alike in the Union, in the States, and in many at least of the cities. We are so familiar with the system of two Houses, from its reproduction in countless later constitutions, that we are apt to forget that, when the Federal Constitution of the United States was drawn up, that system was by no means the rule, and that its adoption in the Constitution of the United States was a remarkable instance of cleaving to the institutions of the mother-country. Though the United States Senate, the representative of the separate being and political equality of the States, has some functions quite different from those of the House of Lords, yet it could have hardly come into the heads of constitution-makers who were not familiar with the House of Lords." [1]

This was quite wrong. When our Federal Constitution was adopted, two-chamber legislation had been familiar here for a century and a half. There were no less than eleven almost independent States that had continued it when framing their Constitutions, and all the delegates in the Convention of 1787, except those from Pennsylvania and Delaware, were by personal experience familiar with its working. There is no indication even that the House of Lords was studied to see if its example might so much as modify the colonial institution. In the eighty-five numbers of "The Federalist" I note but three references to the House of Lords by name, and these are of a purely incidental and casual nature. Once it is referred to as the British Senate, and then by way of showing its contrast to what the authors of our Constitution had devised. "Unfortunately, however, for the anti-federal argument," said Hamilton or Madison in No. 63, "the British history informs us that this hereditary assembly has not been able to defend itself against the continual encroachments of the House of Representatives and that it no sooner lost the support of the monarch, than it was actually crushed by the weight of the popular branch."

In almost every essential detail the Senate of the United States differs from the House of Lords. The American Senate has no hereditary memberships. Its members serve for a

[1] *Some Impressions of the United States* (1883), 116.

fixed term of years instead of for life. They represent, not classes nor estates, but geographical divisions, and each Senator must live in the division he represents. The number of Senators cannot be increased save upon the admission of new States. Their presiding officer is elected, under a system that makes him virtually the choice of the people. They receive salaries. They have no titles. They are not aristocrats. They have no judicial duties save in the rare instances of impeachment. They share in the executive power to the extent of ratifying various appointments and they have a hand in the making of treaties. It is true that in the actual processes of lawmaking there are resemblances between Congress and Parliament, but these processes were familiar to lawmakers for generations before our Congress was formed.

To sum it up, we find the differences many and essential, the resemblances few and inevitable. Bishop Stubbs had it right when he observed: "A strong current of similar events will produce coincidences in the history of nations whose whole institutions are distinct; much more will like circumstances force similarly constituted nations into like expedients; nay, great legislators will think together even if the events that suggest the thought be of the most dissimilar character. No amount of analogy between two systems can by itself prove the actual derivation of the one from the other." [1]

Our State Senates are not so sharply differentiated from the lower Houses as to call for much of separate attention. They do not get it from the people. Fault-finding is usually directed at "the Legislature," not at either branch. Nowadays the qualifications for electors and elected are much the same in respect to each. Some difference springs from the variance in the length of term. The only universal difference having important result is in the matter of size. As the larger branch averages to have about three times as many members as the smaller, it is argued that the vote of a Senator counts for three times as much as that of a Representative. This has combined with the effect of tradition to make service in the upper branch esteemed as somewhat more of an honor than service in the lower branch. The use of the words "upper" and "lower" has no doubt helped this notion. Custom nowadays calls for "Hon." to be prefixed to the name of a Senator, but not to that

[1] *Constitutional History of England*, i, 207.

of a Representative. In general the result has been election first to the lower branch and then promotion to the upper. Consequently the age of Senators averages to be somewhat greater than that of Representatives. This would tend to make a Senate somewhat more decorous and dignified in its proceedings, even if that were not assured by its smaller size.

Another characteristic of State Senates is their comparative freedom from attempts at oratory. Time was when half a hundred men were enough to invite the eloquence of a Webster or a Clay. To-day the same number within the walls of a State Senate chamber will listen with patience to nothing but the conversational style, and the less even of that, the better. Senators carry their points in the lobbies or the lounging rooms, by discussion in small groups. Most matters are decided before they are reached in the calendar. Argument on the floor rarely changes the result.

It is far from clear that this is fortunate. The benefits of publicity are lost. Minority criticism fails of its advantages. Secret influences are unchecked. As a result the work of Senates arouses suspicions too often well founded. That frequently leads Representatives who have legitimate ambition for political advancement and who are jealous of their reputations, to avoid election to the Senate. If gifted with powers of persuasion or born with a liking for parliamentary conflict, they find a congenial forum in the House, which they will not exchange for what they come to think the dull and dreary conditions of the Senate. This may account for the fact that Senates have comparatively few members of whom the newspapers ever speak as "brilliant." It also explains why so few Congressmen have served in State Senates. Ordinarily a seat in the upper branch of a State Legislature is the honorable rounding out of a political career, beyond which ambition either does not go or is not likely to be gratified.

Recent activities in the search for improvement in governmental processes have not failed to overlook State Senates. Some think the best way to reform them is to abolish them. Others think the wise course would be to reshape their functions. It has been suggested that it might be well to return to the colonial idea of an upper branch combining executive with legislative duties, at the same time a Privy Council and a Senate. One proposal is to make it a small body, with long terms, sitting continuously, paid well enough to let the members give all their time to the service of the State and assured of pensions if not reëlected after two or three terms. This should secure a body of legislative and administrative experts. If the development of what is known as the commission form of government continues, something of this sort may presently be reached.

ARRANGEMENTS FOR CONTINUITY

ONE way of discriminating the upper from the lower branch was found by our fathers in an arrangement securing continuity for the Senate.

By William Penn's Charter of Liberties to Pennsylvania in 1682, the members of the Provincial Council were to be replaced one third each year. The plan was incorporated in the Frame of Government promulgated in the following year, but does not appear in the Frame of Government of 1696. It was not forgotten. When Virginia came to the making of her first Constitution, she embodied the idea therein. One quarter of the Senators (who were elected for a four years' term) were to retire each year. With biennial elections in 1850 it was necessary to change this so that half the Senators retired each two years. The Constitution framed in 1864 by delegates from such parts of the State as were then within the Union lines omitted the alternating proviso, but it was renewed in 1870, to be again omitted in 1902.

Delaware followed Virginia, replacing one third of her Senators each year from 1776 to 1831.

The Constitution drafted for New York by John Jay in 1777 provided a four-year term for Senators, of whom one quarter should be replaced each year. When in 1846 a two-year term was substituted, alternation was dropped. The Constitutional Commission of 1872–73 recommended a return to the four-year term, with one Senator from each of eight districts going out each year, but the Legislature did not approve the proposal nor submit it to the people.

The examples of Virginia, Delaware, and New York led the Federal Convention of 1787 to adopt the idea for the Senate of the United States, the choice settling on alternation by thirds, with change every two years. That in turn made adoption of the system common, though not universal, in the

State Constitutions framed thereafter. When in 1790 Pennsylvania created a Senate, one quarter of its members were to be replaced each year. In 1838 this was changed to one third each year, a system lasting until 1874, when it was provided that one half should go out each two years. One quarter of Kentucky's Senators were replaced each year from the time of her second Constitution (1799) till that of 1850, when with biennials the change was made to replacing half each two years. Up to the time of the adoption of biennial elections by Ohio (1851), her Senators went out one half each year. Louisiana retired half her Senators every two years until 1879. Indiana replaced one third of her Senators each year until biennials came with the Constitution of 1851; then the Senate was divided into classes, one half going out each two years. Mississippi began (1817) with dividing her Senators into three classes; made it two in 1868; and abandoned the system in 1890.

Illinois has always had half of her Senators go out every two years. From 1819 to 1846, when biennials were adopted, Alabama Senators went out one third each year. Then it was changed to one half every two years; and with quadrennial elections provided in 1901, alternation disappeared. Missouri has from the start (1820) replaced half her Senators each two years. So long as Michigan retained annual elections (1835 to 1850) Senators were chosen for two-year terms and one half went out each year. Arkansas has always had half her Senators go out each two years. In the Republic of Texas (1836) Senators had three-year terms and went out one third each year; in the State, at first (1845) with four-year terms, one half each two years; in 1868, with six-year terms, one third each two years; returning in 1876 to four-year terms, half out each two years.

Maryland, by amendment to her Constitution in 1837, adopted the alternating system for the Senators, one third to be chosen every two years. In 1851 this was changed so that half should be elected every two years. While annual elections prevailed in Florida (1838–47), half the Senators went out each year; since, half have retired each two years. New Jersey adopted the alternating system for Senators in 1844, one third being replaced each year. Half the Iowa Senate has always gone out each two years. While Wisconsin had annual election, half the Senate went out each year; with biennials, this was changed to half each two years. California's course has been likewise. Half the Senators of Minnesota, Oregon, Colorado, North Dakota, Montana, Washington, Wyoming, Utah, Oklahoma, go out each two years. Half the West Virginia Senate went out each year until biennials came, and since then it has been half each two years. Nevada began by having half her Senators go out each two years, but dropped the plan.

At least three times Vermont has refused to make her Senate continuous, part of the Senators to go out at a time, the proposal being rejected twice by Conventions after recommendation by the Council of Censors, and once by the Legislature.

Under the programme recommended by the Bryce Conference for England, the members of the second chamber would be elected for terms of twelve years, one third to retire every four years. The twelve-year term appealed to those who drafted the Constitution for the Irish Free State, but they excepted the university members, who are to be chosen for six years, and they preferred that one half of the university members and one quarter of the others should retire every three years. This means that, assuming no dissolutions, there will be election of Deputies and Senators at the same time only once in twelve years. As but a quarter or so of the Senators will then be exposed to the passing gale, reasonable stability seems to be assured. In Chile and the Commonwealth of Australia one half of the Senators retire every three years; in France; the Netherlands, Argentina, and Brazil, one third. The Egyptian Senate will respond even less slowly to changes in public opinion, for one half of its members are to retire only every five years.

Continuity in the upper branch has generally been viewed as a desirable check on hasty, ill-considered reversal of governmental policy. Calm observers of our public life would undoubtedly agree that on the whole this has been found advantageous, but it must be admitted that there is another side to the question. It is charged that occasionally upper Houses get too far out of harmony with the popular will. Sweden has a remedy. There the King may dissolve the upper House, thus compelling new choice of the entire membership at one time. The Crown made one of the rare uses of this prerogative in the summer of 1919, because of the opposition of the upper

House to the eight-hour day. The result was a reduction of the number of Conservatives from 86 to 39, an increase of the Social-Democrats from 19 to 48, and changes in other group representation which made the Chamber far more liberal. No elections were held for the lower House, where a coalition of Liberals and Social-Democrats already controlled. Thus the two branches were brought into the accord necessary for the complete support of a Ministry.

CHAPTER IV

CHOOSING SENATORS

DETERMINING the membership of the upper House is a matter on which both opinion and practice widely differ, and there is likely to be much more of experiment before the wise course is clear. Hereditary membership, after the test of centuries in the English House of Lords, has run afoul of democratic tendencies that bid fair to work its undoing. When our fathers came to the making of Constitutions, they would have none of it. Three of the New England colonies had been wont to elect their upper Houses, and the practice was so in accord with the spirit of the times that naturally it was put into the various Constitutions. Judgments varied only as to the manner of election. As a rule direct vote by the people won preference, but there were exceptions. New Hampshire, South Carolina, and Maryland of the original States preferred indirect election at the start, and Kentucky imitated Maryland for seven years.

Direct election of Senators came to be universal in the States long before it won enough support to secure substitution in the Federal Constitution for the system of choice by Legislatures that had commended itself to the Convention of 1787. De Tocqueville thought the superiority of the Federal Senate due to the manner of its selection. "Men who are chosen in this manner," he wrote, "accurately represent the majority of the nation which governs them; but they represent the elevated thoughts which are current in the community, the general propensities which prompt its nobler actions, rather than the petty passions which disturb, or the vices which disgrace it."

Note the singular failure of prophecy in what he went on to say: "The time may be already anticipated at which the American republics will be obliged to introduce the plan of election by an elected body more frequently into their system of representation, or they will incur no small risk of perishing miserably among the shoals of democracy." On the contrary, we have dispensed with that plan and there are no signs of our perishing miserably. The fight was long and at times bitter. Public sentiment, of course, first found its expression in the House of Representatives rather than in the body assailed. Six times between 1893 and 1911 the lower branch passed the necessary resolution by overwhelming majorities, but until 1911 it was never allowed to come to a vote in the Senate. Then it was at first defeated, but four months later (June 12) it was approved, 64 to 24. So strong was the tide of public sentiment that inside of two years the necessary three quarters of the State Legislatures had ratified the amendment, and in May of 1913 it took effect.

The Senators of France are chosen indirectly. They number three hundred. Three quarters of them are chosen for terms of nine years by electoral colleges in the Departments, each consisting of the deputies, councilors-general, and district councilors (members of the councils for local government), and representatives from the municipal council of every commune, the last-named class forming a large majority. The other quarter were under the organic law of 1875 to be elected for life, at first by the National Assembly, and then vacancies to be filled by elections for life by the Senate itself. In 1884 more democratic ideas prevailed and provision was made for the gradual disappearance of the life class. The last of its number died in 1918.

Austria, copying in general outline the federal plan of the United States when framing its Constitution in 1920, preferred our old system of indirect election of members of the upper branch by the legislative bodies of the various States. Ireland decided to try something new — a combination of the direct and indirect principles. Although the people, voting at large, are to elect, it is to be from a panel of three times as many as are to be chosen, two thirds nominated by the lower branch of Parliament and one third by the upper, together with retiring and former Senators wishing to be candidates. Direct election was preferred by Poland and Czecho-Slovakia. All three make the unusual provision that youth shall have no part in the choice of Senators, Ireland and Poland restricting the electorate therefor to citizens thirty years old or more, and Czecho-Slovakia to those at least twenty-six years of age.

Methods of choosing the members of the second chamber in England were thoroughly considered by the Conference, appointed by the Prime Minister in 1917, to study reform of the House of Lords. This Conference, headed by Viscount Bryce and comprising thirty of the most thoughtful and experienced public men of the country, after nearly fifty sittings and six months of discussion, made in April of 1918 a report of great interest and significance. Direct election was rejected because, if a second chamber had a "mandate" from the people equal to that of the House of Commons, the second chamber would be likely to claim equal financial powers, and tend to fall into conflict with that principle of the Constitution which assigns to the Commons the function of making and unmaking Administrations. Ministers would have two masters to serve and to fear. The second chamber would be little more than a duplicate of the House of Commons, and might either, as being the less attractive body, come to be composed mainly of the surplus material of the latter, or (alternatively) by the longer tenure of its members become ultimately the more attractive, possibly the more influential legislative body. With the large constituencies necessary for a comparatively small chamber, the expense of election would be heavier, and thus an advantage would be given to wealthy candidates.

Also election by local authorities failed to win approval. It was argued that if the county and borough councils, grouped in local areas of suitable size, were to choose, party politics would certainly be brought into the selection of those councils hitherto elected on non-partisan lines, and the party spirit would be intensified where in mild form it already existed, which would prove a misfortune.

Another plan was that of placing the selection in the hands of some weighty, impartial, and independent authority, such as a joint standing committee drawn in equal or nearly equal numbers from both Houses of Parliament. This proposal found considerable support in the Conference, but the majority thought it essential to provide a broader basis for the second chamber, so that it should be as far as possible a representative body. This basis they found in election by the Parliament itself. So they recommended that the House of Commons should be divided into groups territorially, twelve for England and Wales, one for Scotland, the matter of Irish allotment being postponed. By the single transferable vote method of proportional representation each group should elect a number of members of the second chamber proportionate to the population of the areas represented. However, this was to provide for but 246 members of the second chamber. In addition 81 members should be chosen from among the Peers, by a joint standing committee of the two Houses, the number gradually to be reduced to 30, and the remaining 51 seats to be thrown open to persons not Peers. This was for the sake of preserving the historical continuity of the reconstructed second chamber with the ancient House of Lords, that the respect of the nation for the second chamber might be greater, and also to make probable the retention of the services of certain Peers noteworthy for distinguished ability and long experience in legislation.

Eight of the members of the Conference dissented from the recommendation of election by the House of Commons. They feared partisanship, an excess of control by party organizations, bargains of the most undesirable kind, and an irresistible temptation to choose on grounds other than those of eminence or fitness. To this the majority replied that the groups would be anxious to return persons of high political standing, and also to study local sentiment. Thus they would not be subservient to the control of party managers.

APPOINTMENT

THE Bryce Conference rejected the method of naming by the Crown through its Ministers. It was thought such a plan would be unlikely to find favor with the country, because it did not provide any guarantees for the fitness of the persons who might be nominated, and because it would be liable to be frequently employed as a reward for political party services. A provision requiring that the persons to be nominated should be taken from certain prescribed categories would not furnish an answer to these objections.

The Conference had at command plenty of experience to which it might have pointed in support of its conclusion. In Italy, for example, where the King appoints the men recommended by the Premier at the head of the party controlling the lower House, it has been found that appointment is unsuited to the system of party government, especially when the tenure is for life. When party control of the lower House changes, it is only by accident that the new Premier will find the upper House in sympathy with him. If the two Houses are of opposite political beliefs, the upper House must either fight or submit. If it fights, then the Premier may advise the King to create peers enough to change the majority. A notable instance of this was in 1890 when as many as seventy-five Senators were added. The result has been to weaken the prestige of the Senate and so to lessen its power that it is little more than a revising body, sometimes managing to get important amendments in detail, but rarely opposing the lower House in any matter of consequence. Senators must have filled high office; or have acquired fame in literature, science, or some other pursuit leading to the benefit of the nation; or be taken from some other specified classes.

In Canada the appointment of Senators has proved even less satisfactory. When Lord Elgin was Governor-General, he found the lack of harmony between the two Houses so embarrassing that he persuaded the home Government to make the upper House in the Union elective, but this failed to achieve its purpose, and when the Dominion was constituted, the Senate was made an appointed body. It was thought that this might open the door of opportunity to able men fitted by character and ability for high public service, yet without those qualities that are too often necessary for success in a popular election. It was hoped that the result would be a dignified body commanding respect by reason of the individual worth of its members, and furnishing a conservative element that would prevent hasty, ill-conceived, undigested legislation. It is averred, however, that the Senate has in every respect disappointed the hopes of its sponsors. "The typical Senator conforms to one of three types: he is either a generous subscriber to party funds — a type not unknown even in hereditary chambers; or a successful business man who has been or may be useful to some powerful interest favored by the dominant political party; or a mere party hack, rewarded — perhaps not illegitimately — for political services or political complaisance by the dignity of a Senatorship." [1]

Proposals for a change have not been infrequent, but there is no approach to agreement as to what should be done. Some want Senators elected by constituencies larger than those of the House of Commons. Others want election by the provincial Parliaments. Views vary as to the desirable length of term. The success of those provinces, all but two, that get along with

[1] J. A. R. Marriott, *Second Chambers*, 147.

a single chamber leads some to argue that there is no need for a Dominion Senate at all. Professor Leacock, of McGill University, Montreal, familiar, of course, with the situation, says that, whatever may be the nominal constitutional power of such a Senate, it is in reality unable to act as a counterbalancing force to the House elected by the people. The parliamentary life and parliamentary power are centered in the House of Commons.[1] He further says: "In the case of a conflict between the two, public opinion is generally in favor of the House which more immediately stands for the vote of the people, and circumscribes to a large extent the resistance that can be offered by the upper House to the more popular body. This is the explanation of the relatively feeble power of the Senates of France, Italy, and Canada." [2]

It is probably true that public opinion has more often sided with the course of lower Houses, not alone in the countries he mentions, but also everywhere else. It is not clear, however, that this is the chief reason why the powers of upper Houses have diminished. In fact that had not occurred in the case of the United States Senate when it was elected indirectly and therefore was more remote from popular sympathy than the lower House. On the contrary, the Senate had gained in power to such an extent that the hope of curbing it was one of the reasons for making its election direct. Our State Senates, too, mostly have longer terms than those of the lower House, and by reason of larger constituencies are less responsive to public opinion. Yet their power does not wane. With us, however, cabinet government introduces no complications. Very likely we should observe the same effects if we had ministries that must prevail or perish. It is this difference that leads English and Canadian writers to see in the lack of harmony between two branches nothing but defects where we find in it certain definite advantages. We want one House to check the other.

Observe that when the Australians came to set up their Commonwealth and decided to have a Senate, four of their States had been accustomed to elect Senators; two were familiar with Senators appointed for life; and near by was New Zealand, with Senators appointed for a term of years. Election was the method of choice selected.

[1] *Elements of Political Science*, 166.   [2] *Ibid.*, 171.

From the Lower House

THE method of choosing the upper branch that prevails in Norway is worth noting. There the Parliament, known as the Storthing, upon assembling as one body, selects a quarter of its members to serve as an upper House, the Lagthing; the remaining three quarters serve as the lower House. T. S. Tyng embodied that form of choice in the Draft of a Frame of Government he published in the "Political Science Quarterly" for June, 1912. He did not wish to have the choice restricted to the membership of the electing body, but he thought that body would naturally elect chiefly from its own members and would be best able to judge of their legislative knowledge and skill.

Somewhat the same idea appealed to Thomas Paine and to Thomas Jefferson. Paine comes down to us with a reputation for erratic genius that discourages serious consideration of his views. Yet it is to be remembered that his "Common Sense" was a potent instrument in securing the Declaration of Independence, and "The Crisis" was of great encouragement in a dark hour — patriotic aids that secured from Congress in 1785 its public approbation, with what it called a "liberal gratification" (although the amount was but three thousand dollars); from Pennsylvania five hundred pounds in currency; and from New York a fine estate of three hundred acres. To a constant interest and activity in public affairs as a citizen, he added the experience of Secretary to the Committee of Foreign Affairs in Congress for nearly two years; of clerk of the Pennsylvania Legislature; and of a member of the National Convention of France for many months during the most exciting period of the French Revolution. In the "Rights of Man" (1791–92) he said (pt. 2, chap. IV) it had been proposed to have but one representation, and to divide that representation by lot into two or three parts, bills to be debated in each, and then the whole to come together for general debate and determination by vote. The wording indicates that Paine may not have conceived the idea, but who suggested it does not appear.

Paine found occasion to set forth the notion in more detail when writing, in 1805, "To the Citizens of Pennsylvania, On the Proposals for Calling a Convention." Said he: "The Pennsylvania Convention of 1776 copied nothing from the English Government. It formed a Constitution on the basis of honesty. The defect of that Constitution was the precipitancy to which the Legislatures might be subject in enacting laws. All the members of that Legislature, established by that Constitution, sat in one chamber, and debated in one body, and thus subjected them to precipitancy. But this precipitancy was provided against, but not effectually. The Constitution ordered that the laws, before being finally enacted, should be published for public consideration. But as no given time was fixed for that consideration, nor any means for collecting its effects, nor were there any public newspapers in the State but what were printed in Philadelphia, the provision did not reach the intention of it, and thus a good and wise intention sunk into mere form, which is generally the case when the means are not adequate to the end. . . .

"Had the number of representatives in the Legislature, established by that Constitution, been increased, and instead of their sitting together in one chamber, and debating and voting all at one time, to have divided them by lot into two equal parts, and to have sat in separate chambers, the advantage would have been, that one half by not being entangled in the first debate, nor having committed itself by voting, would be silently possessed of the arguments, for and against, of the former part, and be in a calm condition to review the whole. And instead of one chamber, or one House, or by whatever name they may be called, negativing the vote of the other, which is now the case, and which admits of inconsistencies, even to absurdities, to have added the votes of both chambers together, and the majority of the whole to be the final decision. There would be reason in this, but there is none in the present mode. The instance that occurred in the Pennsylvania Senate, in the year 1800, on the bill for choosing electors, where a small majority in that House controlled and negatived a large majority in the other House, shows the absurdity of such a division of legislative power.

"To know if any theory be true or rational, in the practice, the method is, to carry it to its greatest extent; if it be not true upon the whole, or be absurd, it is so in all its parts, however small. For instance,

"If one House consists of two hundred members and the other fifty, which is about the proportion they are in some of the States, and if a proposed law be carried on the affirmative in

the larger House with only one dissenting voice, and be negatived in the smaller House by a majority of one, the event will
be, that twenty-seven control and govern two hundred and
twenty-three, which is too absurd even for argument, and totally inconsistent with the principles of representative government, which know no difference in the value and importance
of its members but what arises from their virtues and talents
and not at all from the name of the House or chamber where
they sit in."

Meantime the idea had won the favor of Jefferson, who put
it into "Notes for a Constitution" that have survived. They
are in the rough and without date, but the paper is water-
marked 1794. One of them begins: "The Legislature shall
form one House only for the verification of their credentials, or
for what relates to their privileges. For all other purposes
they shall be separated by lot into two chambers." [1] This was
to be repeated on the first day of each week of the session.

Note that the approval came from a man who had been a
member of legislative bodies or in the closest touch with them
for thirty years — in the Virginia House of Burgesses, in Congress, as minister plenipotentiary, and as Secretary of State.

A modification of the idea has recently come very near being
put to the test in an American State. Oklahoma in 1914 cast
94,986 votes for and 71,742 against an amendment reducing the
Legislature to a House of Representatives of eighty members, from which a subordinate body of fifteen Commissioners
was to be chosen. The proposition failed by reason of not getting a majority of the votes cast at the election.

REPRESENTATION OF PROPERTY

JEFFERSON must have modified his views in this matter somewhat, for in his "Notes on Virginia" (1782) he had written:
"The Senate is by its constitution, too homogeneous with the
House of Delegates. Being chosen by the same electors, at
the same time, and out of the same subjects, the choice falls of
course on men of the same description. The purpose of establishing different houses of legislation is to introduce the influence of different interests or different principles." And: "In
some of the American States, the Delegates and Senators are

[1] *Writings of Thomas Jefferson* (P. L. Ford ed.), VI, 520.

so chosen as that the first represent the persons, and the second the property of the State. But with us, wealth and wisdom have equal chance for admission into both Houses. We do not therefore derive from the separation by our Legislature into two Houses, those benefits which a proper complication of principles is capable of producing, and those which alone can compensate the evils which may be produced by their dissensions."

The statesmen who drew up the Federal Constitution were strong believers in the theory that the two branches should be a check on each other as a result of representing different interests. Repeatedly you may find this argued by the authors of "The Federalist." For instance, Hamilton wrote in No. 34: "It is well known that in the Roman republic the legislative authority, in the last resort, resided for ages in two different political bodies — not as branches of the same legislature, but as distinct and independent legislatures, in each of which an opposite interest prevailed: in one the patrician; in the other, the plebeian. Many arguments might have been adduced to prove the fitness of two such seemingly contradictory authorities, each having power to *annul* or *repeal* the acts of the other. But a man would have been regarded as frantic who should have attempted at Rome to disprove their existence. It will be readily understood that I allude to the *comitia centuriata* and the *comitia tributa*. The former, in which the people voted by centuries, was so arranged as to give a superiority to the patrician interest; in the latter, in which numbers prevailed, the plebeian interest had an entire predominancy. And yet these two legislatures coexisted for ages, and the Roman republic attained to the utmost height of human greatness."

It was Hamilton or Madison who wrote in No. 62: "As the improbability of sinister combinations will be in proportion to the dissimilarity in the genius of the two bodies, it must be politic to distinguish them from each other by every circumstance which will consist with a due harmony in all proper measures, and with the genuine principles of republican government."

And in No. 63, after citing the Senates of Sparta, Rome, and Carthage, it was said: "These examples, though as unfit for the imitation, as they are repugnant to the genius, of America, are, notwithstanding, when compared with the fugitive and turbulent existence of other ancient republics, very instructive proofs of the necessity of some institution that will blend stability with liberty."

A foremost authority of our own time, Woodrow Wilson, thought along the same lines. The Senate, he observed, is valuable in our democracy in proportion as it is undemocratic. "I think that a philosophical analysis of any successful and beneficent system of self-government will disclose the fact that its only effectual checks consist in a mixture of elements, in a combination of seemingly contradictory political principles; that the British Government is perfect in proportion as it is unmonarchical, and ours safe in proportion as it is undemocratic; that the Senate saves us often from headlong popular tyranny." [1]

To many of the constitution-makers of the Revolutionary period, the possession of property presented itself as the most appropriate test for giving a distinctive character to the upper House. It meant a particular representation for the landed interest. It assured a conservative element in the government. In the Federal Convention, although Gerry of Massachusetts opposed property as a basis of representation, [2] the example of his State in apportioning Senators according to wealth appealed to other members. Abraham Baldwin of Georgia thought the second branch ought to be the representation of property, and therefore that in forming it some reference ought to be had to the relative wealth of the constituents. He cited Massachusetts. [3]

Pierce Butler of South Carolina urged the same thing, [4] and contended strenuously that property was the only just measure of representation. Yates quotes Butler as saying: "Money is strength; and every State ought to have its weight in the national council in proportion to the quantity it possesses." Dickinson moved to add the words, "according to the taxes and contributions of each State, actually collected and paid into the national treasury." [5]

Yates says Wilson read Franklin's written remarks to the effect "that representation ought to be in proportion to the importance of numbers and wealth in each State." It is not easy to reconcile this with what Franklin replied two years

[1] *Congressional Government*, 226.
[2] *Elliot's Debates*, I, 406. [3] *Ibid.*, v, 260. [4] *Ibid.*, v, 275, 281. [5] *Ibid.*, I, 405.

later to the proposal that there should be an upper branch in the Pennsylvania Legislature, based on property. "Private property," he said, "is a creature of society, and is subject to the calls of that society, whenever its necessities shall require it, even to its last farthing; its contributions to the public exigencies are not to be considered as conferring a benefit on the public, entitling the contributors to the distinctions of honor and power, but as the return of an obligation previously received, or the payment of a just debt. The combinations are not like those of a set of merchants, who club their property in different proportions for building and freighting a ship, and may therefore have some right to vote in the disposition of the voyage in a greater or less degree according to their respective contributions; but the important ends of civil society, and the personal securities of life and liberty there, remain the same in every member of the society; and the poorest continues to have an equal claim to them with the most opulent, whatever difference time, chance, or industry may occasion in their circumstances." [1]

The matter received particularly thorough discussion in the Massachusetts Convention of 1820. The original Constitution of that State provided there should be forty Senators, elected by districts not less than thirteen in number, with not more than six Senators from any one district; and that "the General Court, in assigning the numbers to be elected by the respective districts, shall govern themselves by the proportion of public taxes paid by the said districts." This last provision led to about one tenth of the debate in the Convention of 1820. The ablest members of that able body shared therein.

General H. A. S. Dearborn opened in behalf of basing senatorial representation on population alone. He did not know whence the principle of the taxation basis had been derived. It was not to be found in the organization of any of the republics, ancient or modern. It did not exist in Greece, Rome, Venice, or Genoa. The only reason he had ever heard to justify it was that the taxes are paid in proportion to property, and that the principle of proportionment was designed for the protection of property. But this protection was not necessary. He appealed to the magnanimity of the rich to yield to the poor their equal proportion of rights. The people would constantly pro-

[1] *Works of Benjamin Franklin* (John Bigelow ed.), x, 189.

test, and at some time or other it would be necessary to yield to their importunity.

Judge Isaac Parker, President of the Convention and later Chief Justice, took the opposite view. There was, he said, no State in the Union, except Connecticut, Rhode Island, and Maine, that had not established a check by a different mode of representation of the people in the two branches. It might now be considered the unanimous voice of the civilized world that a system of checks and balances in the different departments of government, and between the branches of the Legislature, was essential to the preservation of liberty.

Levi Lincoln of Worcester, who became Governor five years later, held our government to be one of the people, not of property. Representation is founded on the interests of the people. It is because they have rights that they have assumed the power of self-government. Property is incompetent to sustain a free government. In a government of freemen property is valuable only as the people are intelligent. Were it not for a government of the people, the people would be without property. If it was a sound principle that property should confer the right of representation, it ought not to be restricted. Imposing the restriction was admitting that the principle was false and unjust.

The Honorable Richard Sullivan of Brookline pointed out that in a well-balanced republic the personal rights of the citizen are well secured, and rarely in danger; while nine in ten of all the laws relate in some measure to property. As the security of property, next after personal security, is the great end and object of government, its use as the basis of representation in the Senate was the most reasonable and proper.

Judge Samuel S. Wilde declared it was a principle admitted in all private corporations that all persons who have a larger share should have a larger vote. So in the community. That portion which contributes most to the public burdens should have the greatest weight in the government.

James T. Austin held that a representation founded on taxation was a representation of the whole people, and our Senators were elected on popular principles. Rich men alone might be elected if rich men alone had the privilege of voting; but that was not the case.

George Blake objected to the change proposed because, in his judgment, "it would have the effect to transform the most beautiful feature of the Constitution into a mass of deformity — to introduce confusion in place of order — injustice in place of justice." He said that he had used the other day a very improper figure, when he called the Senate the rich man's citadel. It was no more the citadel of the rich than of the poor man. It was the only branch of government which was particularly designed for the protection of property; and this protection was as important for those who have little as for those who have much.

Leverett Saltonstall of Salem believed property should be represented because it is the greatest object of civil society; it is not mere inert matter, but a living principle, which keeps the great machine of society in motion. It is the universal stimulus.

Joseph Locke of Billerica reached like conclusions, but by a different argument. He said he observed that some went on the principle that the Senate was founded on the basis of property. This was not true. The basis was taxation. The wealthy districts were allowed a greater proportion of representation in the Senate, not with a view to the protection of property, but because they were made to contribute so much to the support of the public burdens.

John Adams, the venerable ex-President, said he rose with fear and trembling to say a few words on the question. "It is now forty years since I have intermingled in debate in any public assembly. My memory and strength of utterance fail me, so that it is utterly impossible for me to discuss the subject on the broad ground on which gentlemen who have spoken before me, have considered it. No man pretends that all are born with equal property, but with equal rights to acquire property. The great object is to render property secure. Without the security of property, neither arts, nor manufactures, nor commerce, nor literature, nor science can exist. It is the foundation upon which civilization rests. There would be no security for life and liberty even, if property were not secure. Aristides ruined the Constitution of Solon, by destroying the balance between property and numbers, and, in consequence, a torrent of popular commotion broke in and desolated the republic. Let us come to Rome; property was infinitely more regarded than here, and it was only while the balance was maintained that the liberties of the people were preserved. In France, at the time of the Revolution, those who were without property were in the proportion of fifty to one. It was by destroying the balance that the Revolution was produced. All writers agree that there are twenty persons in Great Britain who have no property, to one that has. If the radicals should succeed in obtaining universal suffrage, they will overturn the whole kingdom, and turn those who have property out of their houses. The people in England, in favor of universal suffrage, are ruining themselves. Our ancestors have made a pecuniary qualification necessary for office, and necessary for electors, and all the wise men in the world have agreed in the same thing."

Judge William Prescott asked who could predict the consequences of changing the basis on which one of the departments of the government was founded — a system of representation founded on equal justice, on equal rights, and on that spirit of compromise on which alone government can be founded, and by which alone defects can be amended. It is not for the benefit of a few rich men that this provision is made, but for the men of moderate property and all men who have property. The very rich, when their property becomes insecure, may leave the country and carry their property with them. It is not so with men of moderate property. They must stay by their country and protect its rights.

Joseph Story, Justice of the Supreme Court of the United States, he who was to write the authoritative book on the National Constitution, paid one of the most eloquent tributes to property that can be found. "When I look around and consider the blessings which property bestows, I cannot persuade myself that gentlemen are serious in their views, that it does not deserve our utmost protection. I do not speak here of your opulent and munificent citizens, whose wealth has spread itself into a thousand channels of charity and public benevolence. I speak not of these, not because they are not worthy of all praise; but because I would dwell rather on those general blessings, which prosperity diffuses through the whole mass of the community. Who is there that has not a friend or relative in distress, looking up to him for assistance? Who is there that is not called upon to administer to the sick and the suffering, to those who are in the depth of poverty and distress, to those of his own household, to the stranger beside the gate?

The circle of kindness commences with the humblest, and extends wider and wider as we rise to the highest in society, each person administering in his own way to the wants of those around him.   It is thus that property becomes the source of comforts of every kind, and dispenses its blessings in every form.   In this way it conduces to the public good by promoting private happiness; and every man from the humblest, possessing property, to the highest in the State, contributes his proportion to the general mass of comfort.   It is in this view that I consider property as the source of all the comforts and advantages we enjoy, and every man, from him who possesses but a single dollar up to him who possesses the greatest fortune, is equally interested in its security and preservation.   Gentlemen have argued as if personal rights were the only proper objects of government.   But what, I would ask, is life worth, if a man cannot eat in security the bread earned by his own industry? It is a mistaken theory that government is founded for one object only.   It is organized for the protection of life, liberty, and property, and all the comforts of society — to enable us to indulge in our domestic affections, and quietly to enjoy our homes and our firesides."

Nevertheless, the friends of the rights of man persisted. Henry H. Childs of Pittsfield admitted he had no expectation of distinguishing himself as a public speaker, but he felt it his duty to his constituents and himself not to give a silent vote. He could see nothing in wealth to entitle it to a representation, and its natural influence showed it did not need a representation.

Levi Lincoln took the floor again.   The basis of wealth, he averred, is transient.   If property is mine to-day, it may be another's to-morrow.   A representation of the people, predicated on this phantom, would seem idle.   Wealth consists not in money, but in the productive labor of the country, in the soil and its produce.   Found the representation on this substantial property, which cannot be affected by accident, and it will have some permanent basis.

And then came the giant of the debate, to close it — Daniel Webster — with an oration worthy the fame he had already won.   Yet, as men now for the most part view the question, he was on the wrong side.   His powerful argument was based on what would to-day be deemed false premises.   The struggle for the abolition of slavery, the Civil War, the spread of democratic ideas, the growth of the country in prosperity and happiness under a constantly widening conception of political equality, have combined to make the mass of Americans believe the logic of the greatest American of his time was in this matter unsound. Yet it is worth while seeing how he reasoned.

The Senate, he said, is not to be a check on the people, but on the House of Representatives. It is the case of an authority given to one agent to check or control the acts of another. And if it be wise to give one agent the power of controlling or checking another, it is equally wise, most manifestly, that there should be some difference of character, sentiment, feeling, or origin in that agent who is to possess this control. Otherwise, it is not at all probable that the control will ever be exercised. To require the consent of two agents to the validity of an act, and yet to appoint agents so similar, in all respects, as to create a moral certainty that what one does the other will do also, would be inconsistent and nugatory. There can be no effectual control without some difference of origin, or character, or interest, or feeling, or sentiment. And the great question; in this country, has been where to find or how to create this difference, in governments entirely elective and popular.

In support of the Massachusetts answer to this question, Webster went on to justify its principle. He took this principle to be well established by writers of the greatest authority. In the first place, those who have treated of natural law have maintained, as a principle of law, that, as far as the object of society is the protection of something in which the members possess unequal shares, it is just that the weight of each person in the common councils should bear a relation and proportion to his interest. Such is the sentiment of Grotius, and he referred, in support of it, to several institutions among the ancient states. Those authors who have written more particularly on the subject of political institutions have, many of them, maintained similar sentiments. Not, indeed, that every man's power should be in exact proportion to his property, but that, in a general sense, and in a general form, property, as such, should have its weight and influence in political arrangement. Montesquieu speaks, with approbation, of the early Roman regulation, made by Servius Tullius, by which the people were distributed into classes according to their property, and the public burdens apportioned in each individual, according to the degree of power which he possessed in the government. One of the most ingenious of political writers is Mr. Harrington, an author not now read so much as he deserves. It is his leading object in his "Oceana" to prove that power naturally and necessarily follows property. He maintains that a government founded on property is legitimately founded; and that a government founded on the disregard of property is founded in injustice, and can only be maintained by military force. "It is strange," says Mr. Pope in one of his recorded conversations, "that Harrington should be the first man to find out so evident and demonstrable a truth, as that of property being the true base and *measure* of power." In truth he was not the first; the idea is as old as political science itself. It may be found in Aristotle, Lord Bacon, Sir Walter Raleigh, and other writers.

The true principle of a free and popular government, continued the speaker, would seem to be so to construct it as to give to all, or at least to a very great majority, an interest in its preservation; to found it, as other things are founded, on men's interest. The stability of government requires that those who desire its continuance should be more powerful than those who desire its dissolution. The freest government, if it could exist, would not be long acceptable, if the tendency of the laws were to create a rapid accumulation of property in a few hands, and to render the great mass of the population dependent and penniless. In such a case the popular power must break in upon the rights of property, or else the influence of property must limit and control the exercise of popular power. Universal suffrage, for example, could not long exist in a community where there was great inequality of property. In the nature of things those who have not property, and see their neighbors possess much more than they think them to need, cannot be favorable to laws made for the protection of property. When this class becomes numerous, it becomes clamorous. It looks on property as its prey and plunder, and is naturally ready, at all times, for violence and revolution. It would seem, then, to be the part of political wisdom to ground government on property; and to establish such distribution of property, by the laws which require its transmission and alienation, as to interest the great majority of society in the protection of the government. Life and personal liberty are, no doubt, to be protected by law; property is also to be protected by law, and is the fund out of which the means for protecting life and liberty are usually furnished. We have no experience that teaches us that any other rights are safe, where property is not safe. Confiscation and plunder are generally, in revolutionary commotions, not far from banishment, imprisonment, and death. It would be monstrous to give even the name government to any association in which the rights of property should not be competently secured. The disastrous revolutions which the world has witnessed; those political thunderstorms and earthquakes which have overthrown the pillars of society from their very deepest foundations, have been revolutions *against property*.

To this terrific onslaught by the champions of property, the untrained spokesmen of the people could make no adequate defense. The Convention had previously voted, 236 to 145, to change the basis of senatorial representation. General Dearborn had consented to reconsideration. After the battle was over, he found himself defeated by close to an exact reversal of the vote, for it now stood 164 to 247. Massachusetts was to wait twenty years longer before her Senators should be chosen by population and with no regard to property.

One of the great contests in the New York Convention of the following year (1821) was on the proposal to make the qualifications of electors for Senators and Governor the same as for electors of Assemblymen. The landed interests fought stoutly to save their preponderating influence in the upper branch, Chancellor Kent and Judge Spencer being their champions, while Erastus Root, Martin Van Buren, and others espoused the cause of equal rights, and won. In the course of his argument Chancellor Kent said: "By the report before us, we propose to annihilate, at one stroke, all those property distinctions, and to bow before the idol of universal suffrage. That extreme democratic principle, when applied to the legislative and executive departments of government, has been regarded with terror by the wise men of every age, because in every European republic, ancient and modern, in which it has been tried, it has terminated disastrously, and been productive of corruption, injustice, violence, and tyranny. And dare we flatter ourselves that we are a peculiar people, who can run the career of history, exempted from the passions which have disturbed and corrupted the rest of mankind? If we are like other races of men, with similar follies and vices, then I greatly fear that our posterity will have reason to deplore, in sackcloth and ashes, the delusion of the day. . . . I shall feel grateful if we may be permitted to retain the stability and security of a Senate, bottomed on the freehold property of the State. Such a body, so constituted, may prove a sheet anchor amidst the future factions and storms of the Republic."

Without it, he said, the agricultural interest is committed to the winds. "It should be the representative of the landed interest and its security against the caprice of the motley assemblage of paupers, emigrants, journeymen, manufacturers, and those undefinable classes of inhabitants which a State and city like ours is calculated to invite."

Martin Van Buren saw the other side of the shield. "When the people of this State shall have so far degenerated, when the principles of good order and good government which now happily characterize our people and afford security to our institutions shall have so far given way to anarchy and violence as to lead to an attack on private property, either by an agrarian law or by an attempt to throw all public burdens on any particular class of men, then all constitutional provisions will be idle and unavailing, because they will have lost all their force and influence."

From 1777 the New York apportionment for Senators had been made by four great districts, according to the number of freeholders of a hundred pounds or more, with a census and reapportionment every seven years. Now this was changed to eight districts based on population, with four Senators to each. In 1846 came the single district system.

New Hampshire since 1784 has allotted Senators to counties in proportion to taxes. North Carolina, beginning with one Senator for each county, changed in 1835 to the property basis, apportionment being "in proportion to the public taxes," and this was the system until 1868. Elsewhere apportionment has generally been by counties, with no direct recognition of property, although in a few cases where allotments were specifically set forth in the Constitution, comparative wealth may have been taken into account. To-day, except in New Hampshire, property as a basis for senatorial apportionment has disappeared.

The Bryce Conference rejected the proposal that a reconstituted House of Lords should be elected on the basis of a property qualification possessed by a privileged class of voters, and also the proposal of a property qualification for persons to be elected, both being deemed unsuitable to modern conditions.

In Cuba one half of the electorate for Senators "shall consist of citizens paying the greatest amount of taxes."

The argument that an upper House shall represent property as property arrogates to it a privilege denied to any other focus or field of human activity, such as religion, science, literature, art. That a man should be able to enjoy the fruits of his labors with security may or may not be the most important thing in life, but it is certainly not the only important thing. Furthermore, the theory that property should be represented as such is incapable of logical application in government. Corporations meet the main difficulty by giving each stockholder as many votes as he has shares, but this would be out of the question in government, save in the roughest sort of way.

CHAPTER V

THE QUESTION OF SIZE

AMERICAN lawmaking bodies were instituted and have developed without any approach to uniformity in the matter of size. No theory, no principle, no rule, can be deduced from the figures. Haphazard at the start, they have since shown nothing more than tendencies.

It would be useless to rehearse in detail the accidents of colonial assemblies. Suffice it to say that in New England, where the town was the social and political unit, the practice of giving representation to each town led to proportionate growth of the lower Houses as the number of towns increased. Elsewhere the county or parish was the more familiar unit, and once a colony had become fairly well settled, the number of counties and parishes remained without much change, and as a rule their representation was not much enlarged.

South Carolina was the only State outside New England to begin with a large House; it had 202 members, out of whom 13 were taken for the upper House. Georgia began with a House large for its population, having 90 members, but a dozen years afterward reduced the number and at the end of the century it had only 62. North Carolina gave two members to each county; Virginia likewise, with some extra; Maryland, four to a county; Pennsylvania six (with Philadelphia treated as a county); and Delaware seven, but as it had only three counties the result was the smallest House in the land, as befitted the smallest State. New Jersey made it three to a county. New York said "at least 70," in all, setting a definite figure of 100 in 1801, enlarged to 128 in 1821. Pennsylvania in 1790 devised a new kind of constitutional provision, a maximum and a minimum figure, respectively 100 and 60. As new States came in, they copied this. Kentucky (1792) said the lower House should have not less than 40 nor more than 100 members. Tennessee made the limits 22 and 26 until there should be 40,000 taxable inhabitants, after which the maximum was to be 40. Ohio, Indiana, and Illinois all took up with the idea,

Ohio starting with a range of 24 to 36, Indiana 25 to 36, Illinois 27 to 36, and provision for enlargement with growth of population beyond a specified point. Louisiana made the range 25 to 50.

Pennsylvania, too, was the first to provide for some sort of ratio between the upper and lower Houses. When in 1790 it created a Senate, it directed that the number of Senators should not be more than one third nor less than one quarter of the number of Representatives. Tennessee, Ohio, Indiana, and Illinois copied the plan, but made the limits one half and one third. Connecticut's first Constitution, that of 1818, made the Senate small, only 12, but ten years later the maximum and minimum method was substituted with the limits 24 and 18, changed in 1901 to 36 and 24. Maryland had but 15 members of the upper House at the start; Louisiana, 14; South Carolina, 13, which in 1790 had grown to 37; Virginia, 24, increased to 32 in 1830.

Maine, in 1819, devised a singular scheme. The House was to be of not less than 100 members, nor, at the start, more than 150. As population grew, it might be enlarged to a maximum of 200, and after that, every ten years, the people were to give in their votes as to whether the number should be increased or diminished. This intricate device survived until 1841, when by amendment the number was set at 151. The Senate was to start with 20 members, and to grow not to exceed 31, a provision it has not been found necessary to change. Missouri began (1820) by permitting the Senate to have anywhere from 14 to 33 members, but in 1865 fixed the number at 34. The House at first was to have not exceeding 100; in 1849 the number was fixed at 140; and this was raised to 200 in 1865. Michigan (1835) said the members of the House should not be less than 48 nor more than 100; and changed the 48 in 1850 to 64. At the start the Senate was to be as nearly equal as might be, to one third of the House. In 1850 its number was fixed at 32.

It would serve little good to detail the variations in the newer States. They tell much the same story, without important novelties. The outcome of it all is that our Legislatures average to have 37 Senators and 117 Representatives. Omitting New England, the average membership of the lower House is 100. In 1919 there were 1760 members of upper Houses, 5643 of lower Houses. In New England alone there were 1399 Representatives. The largest Senate is that of Minnesota, 67; the smallest, Delaware, 17. The smallest lower Houses are those of Delaware and Arizona, each 35.

The largest lower House, that of New Hampshire, calls for more than the bald statement that in 1919 it had 404 members, inasmuch as the experience of that State in all these many years has not been such as yet to convince the two thirds of the people who must consent to change, that large Houses are hurtful. However, four times within twenty years proposals to reduce the size have had much more than a majority, the vote in 1902 being 20,295 for to 13,069 against, in 1912 21,399 to 10,952, in 1920 48,598 to 28,121, in 1921 30,275 to 23,271. In each case change would have left a House much larger than the normal. The amendment submitted in 1920 would have reduced it only to between 300 and 325.

What has been printed about the New Hampshire situation probably does not reveal accurately the reasons that have prevented reduction, but taken at its face value, indicates that the educating influence of a large body has at least been a powerful consideration. For instance, in the Convention of 1902 Gilman Marston, for many years prominent in the public life of the State, was quoted as believing the amount of money spent in maintaining so large a House was more than offset by its educational value, giving opportunity for many to learn by experience how to conduct public business. A Concord correspondent, evidently a thoughtful observer, writing to the "Boston Herald" April 16, 1915, elaborated the same view. He gave it as his opinion that in some ways the big New Hampshire Legislature is one of the finest institutions in the country. "While its size may sometimes militate against rapid transaction of business, though this could not be successfully asserted of the present Legislature, this very size redounds to the advantage of the State in an educational way and in keeping the populace informed upon and interested in public matters to an unusual degree. The big Legislature gives a large body of men a training in public affairs, teaches them parliamentary practice, gives them discrimination in weighing public questions, national as well as State, as they arise. These benefits do not accrue solely to the Representative himself. He becomes a center of instruction in his community, if he is a man worth electing. The big Legislature is a university extension course that reaches thousands, has the effect of a correspondence school giving instruction in public problems." Ex-Senator William E. Chandler told the Convention of 1902 that he was not in favor of small Legislatures, though he would reduce the New Hampshire House to about three hundred.

New Hampshire goes to extremes. With a House one of the largest legislative bodies in the world, it has a Senate of 24 members that is one of the smallest. The Convention of 1850 recommended that the Senate be enlarged to 30 members, to be elected by 15 districts, but the amendment was rejected. The Convention of 1912 proposed increasing the Senate to 36 members, and dividing the State into senatorial districts on the basis of population, but this too was rejected, the vote being 19,433 for and 13,931 against, not the required two thirds.

Massachusetts had a long experience with a large House. It varied in size according as the towns cared or not to bear the expense of representation, in exciting times running up to six or seven hundred members, but often getting down to between two and three hundred, occasionally even below two hundred. Judge Story was its Speaker at a period when it was most numerous and, as he told the Convention of 1820, when it was under the most powerful excitements. "I am sorry to say it, but such is my opinion," he declared, "that in no proper sense could it be called a deliberative assembly. From the excess of numbers deliberation became almost impossible; and but for the good sense and discretion of those who usually led in the debates, it would have been impracticable to have transacted business with anything like accuracy or safety. I wish most deeply and earnestly to preserve to my native State a *deliberative* Legislature, where the sound judgment, and discretion, and sagacity of its best citizens may be felt and heard and understood at all times and under all circumstances. I should feel the liberties of the State secure, if this point were once fairly gained." [1]

Even Judge Story, with all his experience and ability, could not then persuade the State to change, and appeals equally earnest in the Convention of 1853 were equally vain at the moment, but the arguments of that Convention were not to be long delayed in fruition. The Committee on Retrenchment and Reform told the Senate, April 21, 1857, it was persuaded that no intelli-

[1] *Mass. Conv. of 1820*, 293.

gent man could be familiar with the course of proceedings in the House without being fully convinced that it was altogether too large to secure accuracy and dispatch in the prosecution of business. The people had come to be of the same opinion and in 1857 ratified an amendment reducing the size of the House to 240.

George S. Boutwell had been a member and had become Governor before this. He had wide experience with legislative bodies in the course of his long life. Toward its close I asked him whether he thought large or small Houses preferable. He answered: "Large Houses." He thought they better reflected the public will and were less open to undesirable influences.

The matter came up in the Pennsylvania Convention of 1873, and Wayne MacVeagh said: "As you increase power, as you increase responsibility, so you increase the character of the men you summon to the post. And therefore I am firmly convinced that fifteen Senators and forty-five Representatives would furnish you a far better bulwark against the rising tides of political corruption than three hundred Senators and one thousand Representatives." [1]

Governor Julius Converse of Vermont, writing in February, 1873, to a delegate in that same Convention, said the main ground for the failure of frequent attempts to reduce the number of Representatives in Vermont had been the security against corruption given by the larger number. He heartily concurred in the opinion that it prevented fraud and corruption. Governor Jewell of Connecticut said: "In my opinion a large number of Representatives is a certain guard against corruption." [2]

Opinion still differs. For illustration of its contradictions, take the views of two Governors as given to the Governors' Conference of 1913. Governor Colquitt of Texas said: "I went to the State Senate where I served for four years, with the belief that the number of legislators should be reduced. Our State Senate, under the Constitution, is limited to thirty-one members. I found that the vote of a single member would control sometimes, to the extent of defeating a meritorious measure, or the passage of one that was not meritorious, and therefore I became convinced that the number of members in the State

---

[1] *Debates of the Penn. Convention of 1873*, I, 329. [2] *Ibid.*, II, 281.

Senate of Texas should be increased. I believe in large legislative bodies, because they proceed slowly." [1]

On the other hand, Governor Hodges of Kansas told how in
his message of the previous March he had proposed a one-House
Legislature of not to exceed sixteen members, and he said his
most violent critic had proposed a one-House Legislature of
thirty. More recently Emmet O'Neal, former Governor of
Alabama, expressed the opinion that the most important and
necessary reform for his State would be a radical decrease in
the membership of the Legislature. He thought the House
should not have more than thirty members, two from each Congressional district and ten from the State at large; the Senate
fifteen, one from each Congressional district and five at large. [2]

William D. Jelks, Governor of Alabama, is another who thinks
Legislatures too large. A model body, in his opinion, would
be, say, ten members, sitting a large part of the time. [3] Senator
George W. Norris of Nebraska advocates a one-House Legis-
lature with a membership not to exceed twenty or thirty for a
State like his own. [4]

Ohio in 1913 by a vote of 240,066 to 417,528 defeated an
amendment that would have reduced the number of Senators to
twenty-two and the number of Representatives to fifty.

Congress during the Revolutionary War and afterward under
the Confederation was an elastic body. Each State was to
send not less than two nor more than seven Delegates, and
as each State had to bear the expense of its Delegates, there
was a strong motive for keeping down the number. At times,
indeed, some States were not represented at all. In the Federal Convention the outcome of much discussion was an agreement that the new Congress should have one member for not
less than 30,000 inhabitants, except that each State was to
have at least one. No proposal of the Convention aroused
more criticism. The authors of "The Federalist" recognized
"the weight of character and the apparent force of argument
with which it has been assailed." They said (in No. 55)
that "the charges exhibited against it are, first, that so small
a number of representatives will be an unsafe depositary of the
public interests; secondly that they will not possess a proper

---

[1] *Proceedings*, 306.   [2] *Address to the Ala. State Bar Assn.*, July 13, 1917.
[3] Letter to Mass. Com. on Information and Data for Const. Conv. of 1917.
[4] *New York Times*, January 28, 1923.

knowledge of the local circumstances of their numerous constituents; thirdly, that they will be taken from that class of
citizens which will sympathize least with the feelings of the
mass of the people, and be most likely to aim at a permanent
elevation of the few on the depression of the many; fourthly,
that defective as the number will be in the first instance, it will
be more and more disproportionate, by the increase of the
people, and the obstacles which will prevent a correspondent
increase of the representatives."

The reply was worthy of those able men who made of "The
Federalist" an invaluable treasury of political science. It was
Hamilton or Madison who wrote: "Nothing can be more falla-
cious than to found our political calculations on arithmetical
principles. Sixty or seventy men may be more properly trusted
with a given degree of power than six or seven. But it does not
follow that six or seven hundred would be proportionately a
better depositary. And if we carry on the supposition to six
or seven thousand, the whole reasoning ought to be reversed.
The truth is, that in all cases a certain number at least seems to
be necessary to secure the benefits of free consultation and discussion, and to guard against too easy a combination for improper purposes; as, on the other hand, the number ought at
most to be kept within a certain limit, in order to avoid the confusion and intemperance of a multitude. In all very numerous
assemblies, of whatever character composed, passion never
fails to wrest the scepter from reason. Had every Athenian
citizen been a Socrates, every Athenian assembly would still
have been a mob."

It is equally timely to-day to read what was said in No. 58,
the authorship again being that of either Hamilton or Madison:
"In all legislative assemblies the greater the number composing
them may be, the fewer will be the men who will in fact direct
their proceedings. In the first place, the more numerous an
assembly may be, of whatever characters composed, the greater
is known to be the ascendancy of passion over reason. In the
next place, the larger the number, the greater will be the proportion of members of limited information and of weak capacities. Now, it is precisely on characters of this description that
the eloquence and address of the few are known to act with all
their force. In the ancient republics, where the whole body of
the people assembled in person, a single orator, or an artful

statesman, was generally seen to rule with as complete a sway as if a scepter had been placed in his single hand. On the same principle, the more multitudinous a representative assembly may be rendered, the more it will partake of the infirmities incident to collective meetings of the people. Ignorance will be the dupe of cunning, and passion the slave of sophistry and declamation. The people can never err more than in supposing that by multiplying their representatives beyond a certain limit, they strengthen the barrier against the government of a few. Experience will forever admonish them that, on the contrary, after securing a sufficient number for the purposes of safety, of local information, and of diffusive sympathy with the whole society, they will counteract their own views by every addition to their representatives."

Nevertheless, these arguments did not appease the critics. They returned to the attack in every State Convention for passing on the Federal Constitution, and the topic has been a favorite theme for discussion from that day to this.

Beginning with 65 members, the apportionment after the census of 1790 raised the number of the lower House of Congress to 106; after 1800 to 142; after 1810 to 186. This was alarming. Ezekiel Whitman in the Maine Convention of 1819 called it a very inconvenient size. "It is with difficulty," he declared, "that the House can transact the public business. Hence it is that we have seen a simple proposition debated in that body for weeks in succession. The case of John Anderson and the questions relative to the Seminole War, and to internal improvements, consumed a fortnight each." Nevertheless, after 1820 the number jumped to 213, and after 1830 to 242. Then a determined stand was made and the total was kept close to that figure until after the Civil War. With the census of 1870, however, pressure became too strong and the apportionment added a fifth to the number, bringing it to 293.

It was in this decade that Senator George F. Hoar, writing in the "North American Review" for February, 1879, on "The Conduct of Business in Congress," said that "the great point, the restoration to the House of its function as a deliberative assembly, can only be fully accomplished by a reduction of its members." After the census of the following year, the number was increased to 332, then after 1890 to 357, and after 1900 to 385, increased to 391 upon the admission of Oklahoma. While it was at that figure, a competent observer, one of the keenest of Washington correspondents, Robert Lincoln O'Brien, discussed in the "Outlook" (December 2, 1905) "The Troubles of the New Congressman." "Why cannot the work in the House be important?" he asked. "What is the matter? A fundamental source of trouble lies in the present size of that body. . . . New legislation, aside from the routine appropriations, should be added to the statute-books only after great deliberation, and a small group can do this better than a mass-meeting. The size of the House is the reason always assigned for the code of rules which concentrates power in the hands of the old members. And why is the House so large? Because the absurd practice has grown up of making the apportionment after each census in such a way that no State will lose representation. . . . Until some Congressional leader arises with the nerve to say that two hundred members would make a good working body, adjusting the ratio of representation accordingly, the disillusionment which Washington brings to the new Congressman will go on."

Then after 1910 the number was increased to 435!

The House of Commons is much larger. Its membership, 670 before the Representation of the People Act enlarged it to 707 in 1918, has become 615 as a result of the establishment of the Irish Free State. Criticism of the size is not wanting. For instance, Lord George Hamilton, speaking with the weight of long personal experience, declares: "The House of Commons is numerically far too large for the purposes of debate or legislation." [1] He points out that "the chamber of the House itself, including the accommodation of the galleries, from which members cannot speak, will barely contain half its number." However, only on rare occasions of political importance are the benches filled. The chamber of our House of Representatives is more commodious and I have never seen the seating capacity taxed by the House itself.

The House of Lords is nominally even larger than the House of Commons. When the Lords debated the subject through nearly all of the sitting of March 22, 1923, Marquess Curzon said there were 741 on the Roll, but deducting some names duplicated, with minors not effective members, and the Royal Princes, who do not take part in debates, he made about 700

---

[1] *Parliamentary Reminiscences*, 210.

the total of those who could, if they chose, take part in the proceedings. The motion of Lord Newton, "That it is desirable that the members of this House should be reduced," was agreed to, but no attempt was made to fix upon an exact number. In 1921 (July 18), resolutions outlining the reform scheme of the Government, moved by Viscount Peel, contemplated a House of about 350. As the purpose of the motion was to get the opinions of the Peers, action was postponed. A bill of Lord Lansdowne in 1911 following prolonged investigation had proposed 350; and the Bryce Conference of 1918 had suggested 342.

Do not infer from the figures of the present membership of the House of Lords that in action it is an unwieldy body. Lord Newton, speaking in 1923, had found that in the previous three sessions an average of 208 of the Peers had not attended at all, and 207 did not appear as much as ten times in a session. However, the situation is viewed as dangerous because of the possibility ever present that the habitual absentees may be induced to attend at a time of crisis, the fear being that, ignorant of parliamentary processes and not having heard debate, they may turn the scale unwisely. One of the purposes contemplated in the various schemes for reconstituting the House is the securing of better attendance from a varied membership, even with its total of but one half that of to-day.

With the perplexities of the English problem in the foreground, the men who drafted the Constitution for the Irish Free State created a Senate of fifty-six members, in addition to those from the Universities. Still smaller will be the upper branch of what seems to be meant for the chief lawmaking body in Russia. In the "Council of Nationalities" each of the four "united and autonomous socialist soviet republics" is to be represented by five members, each of the autonomous provinces by one member, and two other republics each by one member. Supposing that the number of autonomous provinces, which is not specified, will not in any case be large, the total bids fair to seem remarkably small for so huge a country.

The lower branch in Russia, the "Union Council," is to have 371 members. The French Chamber has 626 members; the Italian, 508. The new German Constitution said nothing about size. There is to be one member of the Reichstag for every 60,000 votes cast for a list under the system of proportional representation adopted, so that the size is determined by the extent of the voting, and likewise the number of members from each district. The lower branch in Czecho-Slovakia is to have 300 members; the upper, 150. The Canadian House as a result of the latest census will have 245 members.

The mass of argument in this matter may be summed up as follows:

Large Houses are likely to secure representation of a greater variety of social interests, by having in their membership men of all the professions and many pursuits. A much more extensive knowledge of local conditions and local opinion is available. Venal influences cannot turn a large body from the path of duty. Bribery and corruption have less chance, log-rolling is harder, all secret influences are hampered. In speeches and votes personal friendships are less likely to embarrass or swerve. Many more citizens can profit by a share in the educating effect of legislative service, and in turn the schooling in public affairs is much more widely diffused by them throughout the community. More voters know their Representatives and therefore take personal interest in the work of the Legislature. State-wide acquaintance is fostered. Large bodies move more slowly and therefore with less danger from hasty change. There are more men among whom to divide the work of committees.

On the other hand, as Cardinal de Retz said, every assembly of more than a hundred is a mob. In other words, large bodies are subject to the mob spirit, which replaces reason with impulse. Prejudice and passion sway large bodies. They tempt to partisan debate, which has been called the foe of reasonableness; to oratory, likewise called the foe of logic. Deliberation is declared impossible. Compromise and concession are hindered. It is harder to recede or accept correction before hundreds than before tens. A smaller proportion of the membership takes part in the business. Time is wasted; sessions are protracted.

Small Houses show less disposition to talk and to abuse freedom of debate. Their members are less inclined to pose. Yet each feels himself of more consequence, adding to his sense of responsibility. What every member does, is known. He can be watched and be strictly held accountable. The members get more thoroughly educated in public affairs. Party spirit is mitigated by friendly relations. Fewer bills are introduced, and sessions are correspondingly shortened. Money for salaries is saved.

On the other hand, in a small House the single member has dangerous power. His one vote has the greater chance to defeat a good bill or pass a bad bill. This makes the absence of a few members a more serious matter.

Such a contradiction of arguments so numerous makes it gross presumption for any one man to speak dogmatically. Appreciating the need of modesty where so many thoughtful men have failed to reach anything like agreement, I venture a conclusion of my own with no other hope than that as an opinion it may count for one. It is to the effect that for the purpose of embodying the common will in statutes of general purport concerned with principles and policies, the larger the House the better; and that for the purpose of transacting the business of government, the administrative business now so unwisely imposed on representative bodies elected by popular vote, the smaller the House the better. When the time comes that these two distinct functions are separated, with the legislature restricted to principles and policies, and with the making of rules and regulations transferred to some sort of administrative agency, then the type of House found in New Hampshire and Massachusetts or at Washington will prove the safer and wiser.

CHAPTER VI

LENGTH OF TERMS

PARLIAMENT in the thirty-five years after 1295 (when it reached the form we now understand by that name) was summoned forty-four times. So there was nothing of novelty in the statute 4 Edw. III, c. 14, saying, "It is accorded that Parliament shall be holden every year once, [and] [or] more often if need be." Of the next thirty years there were but three without a Parliament. Even these omissions, however, were so irksome that in 26 Edw. III, c. 10, it was granted, "for redress of divers mischiefs and grievances which daily happen, a Parliament shall be holden or be the Parliament holden *every year*, as another time was ordained by statute." Yet the practice by no means suited everybody. Each session involved a fresh election, and the wages of the members, met by the localities, proved no slight burden. Every session meant more money or some favor for the King. Thus frequent sessions came to signify frequent taxation, so that there was no unanimity of complaint if the King now and then disregarded the law on the subject. He found an excuse in the wording of the statute by averring that the words "if need be" modified the whole of the rest of the sentence, instead of only "more often." In the next century omissions became more frequent, and intervals longer. In the sixteenth century there were but twenty-four Parliaments and in the first half of the seventeenth only ten. No Parliament sat between 1604 and 1614, or between 1628 and 1640 — a fact worth remembering for its probable influence on the colonists who were then laying the foundations of American institutions.

Up to the time of Henry VIII Parliaments lived, as a rule, through but one session, being dissolved as soon as the single important piece of business for which they met had been finished. Then the work came to be more diversified and sessions were prolonged. The Reformation Parliament of Henry VIII lasted seven years. It was, however, not yet established that Parliament was an essential part of the government machine. In the forty-five years of the reign of Elizabeth, the thirteen sessions

98

of ten Parliaments covered less than three years all told, with an average of little more than three weeks a year. Sir J. R. Seeley thinks that in describing the government of Elizabeth's reign, it would not have been natural to mention Parliament at all. "Not exactly that Parliament was subservient, but that in general, Parliament was not there." [1]

Under James I Parliament began to assert itself, and, of course, it is commonplace to say that the story of the reign of Charles I is the story of the struggle between Parliament and the Crown. When the Long Parliament met, in 1640, after there had been no summons for eleven years, one of its earliest measures was aimed at such an abuse, and early in 1641 was passed, almost unanimously, the first of the Triennial Acts. At the end of three years any Parliament should be automatically dissolved, and then within three years the Chancellor or Keeper of the Seal was to issue writs for a new Parliament, under pain of disability to hold his office and of further punishment. The King gave unwilling consent to the act, but the nation welcomed it with bonfires and joyous acclaim. Yet the very Parliament that passed it sat for thirteen years before it was dissolved by Cromwell.

When the throne was restored to the Stuarts, the second Charles was restless under the three-year provision, and in 1664 he openly revolted. He said he loved Parliaments, but "would never suffer a Parliament to come together by the means prescribed by that bill." Thereupon the compliant Houses promptly repealed the statute as "in derogation of His Majesty's just rights and prerogative," yet with a clause in the repealing act saying that Parliaments should not in future be intermitted above three years at the most. This left it possible for any one Parliament to sit as long as the King chose, and he saw fit to keep the sitting Parliament in existence until January of 1679, its life of nearly eighteen years being the longest in English annals.

In 1677 Shaftesbury moved an address for dissolution. On the strength of the statute of Edward III he urged that by reason of the recent prorogation of a year and a half the Parliament had ceased legally to exist. His rival Danby represented the address as a contempt of the House, and the Lords at his bidding threw Shaftesbury and some of his supporters into the Tower.

[1] *Introduction to Political Science*, 256.

The episode won strength for the principle, and when a dozen years later William of Orange was sent for, that principle found a place in the Bill of Rights. The thirteenth clause of the memorable declaration reads: "For redress of all grievances, and for the amending, strengthening, and preserving of the laws, Parliaments ought to be held frequently."

In 1693 Shrewsbury revived the triennial idea, presenting to the Lords a bill providing that the Parliament then sitting should expire in 1694, and that no future Parliament should last longer than three years. The Lords passed it almost unanimously, in spite of the opposition of William, to whom the notion was almost as obnoxious as it had been to both the first and second Charles. In the House of Commons there was a sharp contest. Macaulay tells [1] us that old Titus, who had been a politician in the days of the Commonwealth, entertained the House with a speech after the pattern fashionable in Puritan days. Parliaments, Titus said, resembled the manna which God bestowed on the chosen people. They were excellent while they were fresh; but if kept too long they became noisome; and foul words were engendered by the corruption of that which had been sweeter than honey. Most of the Whigs supported the bill; the Tories opposed. The House yielded to the pressure of public opinion, but not without a pang and a struggle.

Following the Jacobite Rebellion of 1715 came a further change of the term. It was alleged that there seemed great probability of a renewal of the contest over the throne, or at any rate of very serious riots at the election due to be held in 1717. So the ministers proposed that the existing Parliament should have its term extended to seven years. Steele (he of "The Tatler") in the House of Commons warmly advocated the change. He declared that ever since the enactment of the Triennial Act the nation had been in a series of contentions. "The first year of a Triennial Parliament has been spent in vindictive decisions and animosities about the late elections. The second session has entered into business, but rather with a spirit of contradiction to what the prevailing set of men in former Parliaments had brought to pass than for a disinterested zeal for the common good. The third session has languished in the pursuit of what little was intended to be done in the sec-

---

[1] *History of England*, chap. xix.

ond; and the approach of an ensuing election has terrified the members into a servile management, according as their respective principals were disposed toward the question before them in the House. Thus the state of England has been like that of a vessel in distress at sea; the pilot and mariners have been wholly employed in keeping the ship from sinking; the art of navigation was useless, and they never pretended to make sail." Lord Somers, who died on the day the Septennial Bill was passed, was reported to have said of it, in his last moments, "I think it will be the greatest support possible to the liberty of the country."

The preamble of the bill alleged that the Triennial Act had been found "very grievous and burdensome, by occasioning much greater and more continued expenses in order to elections of members to serve in Parliament, and more violent and lasting heats and animosities among the subjects of this realm, than were ever known before." This matter of expense is believed to have been the real motive behind the bill, the Jacobite excitements being only the pretext. With the increased importance of the House of Commons and the greater desire for seats, the cost of elections had grown rapidly. As but three years of tenure were possible, members confronted by the early prospect of another contest naturally wanted a higher subsidy than would be the case with a seven-year tenure.

Many attempts were made to repeal the Septennial Act. Hallam doubted whether, if any of them had succeeded, with a return to triennial Parliaments, there would have been much perceptible difference in the course of government. Said he: "It will be found, I believe, on a retrospect of the last hundred years, that the House of Commons would have acted, in the main, on the same principles had the elections been more frequent; and certainly the effects of a dissolution, when it has occurred in the regular order, have seldom been very important."

One of the five points of the "People's Charter" of 1848 was restriction of the duration of Parliaments to one year. With the other radical demands of the programme, it failed of acceptance. No change came until 1911, when a subsidiary feature of the Parliament Act that emasculated the House of Lords was a provision for a five-year term of the Commons. By reason of the World War the operation of this provision was suspended. For the Irish Free State, which may be presumed to have prof-

ited somewhat by English example, the term of the Chamber
of Deputies was made (1922) four years.

France has experimented much in the matter. In 1791 the
term of the Chamber was made two years; in 1795, three years;
in 1799, five. The Constitutional Charter granted by Louis
XVIII in 1814 provided that one fifth of the Chamber should
be renewed each year, but this lasted only a decade, for the
success of the reactionaries in 1824 was followed by a law extending the life of the Chamber to seven years, with entire
change at the end of that period. In 1848 the term was made
three years; in 1852, six; in 1875, four. Yet end of discussion
was not reached. Once at least, in 1902, the Deputies passed a
resolution changing the term to six years, but the Senate did
not concur. The Briand Ministry in 1910 proposed the six-
year term, with one third of the members to retire every two
years.

In Germany the Reichstag, at first not to live more than three
years, had its term extended in 1888 to five. The Constitution
framed for the German Commonwealth in 1919 said the National Assembly should be elected for four years. In Italy the
Chamber of Deputies is to be dissolved at the end of five years,
but earlier dissolutions seem to be practically inevitable. In
Belgium the term is four years, in Norway three; in Sweden
and Switzerland, three for members of the lower House. The
Canadian House of Commons sits for five years unless sooner
dissolved; the terms of some of the Provincial Legislatures are
five years; of others, four. The duration of the Parliaments
of the Australian Commonwealth, its six States, and New
Zealand is limited to three years; of the Parliament of the
Union of South Africa, to five years. The lower branches in
Brazil and Chile are to be elected for three years; in the
Netherlands for four; in Egypt for five. Argentina alone, as
far as I have observed, secures continuous existence by having
both branches renewed by portions, the Senators one third
every three years and the Deputies one half every two years.
Constitutions following the World War prescribed in Poland a
five-year term, for both branches; in Jugoslavia, Austria, and
Rumania, four years; in Esthonia, three years, and that term,
established in the Organic Law of Finland in 1906, was not
changed by its Constitution of 1919. Deputies in Czecho-
Slovakia are to be chosen for six years. Austria has the unusual

provision that the term, to be computed from the day of the first meeting, shall continue to the day on which a new Nationalrat meets, but the arrangement is such that this extension of life cannot exceed thirty days.

PERIODS

THE election of members of a legislative body for a fixed period appears to have been a distinctively American device. In England, the Crown has always had the power to end the life of a Parliament at pleasure. In the United States every Congress and Legislature exists during a predetermined period, prescribed by a written Constitution. This has given us a more definite and significant use of the word "term" than it has in England. With us, "term" corresponds to the prescribed life-period. For the sake of clarity it may better be used than the word "session" when referring to such a life-period. "Session" confuses by its varied applications. Accuracy will be furthered by restricting it here to that period of fairly continuous legislative labor which nowadays ordinarily covers a few months and never more than a year. Thus each Congress, lasting for two years, has two regular sessions, one usually of from six to eight months, the other of three. To discriminate, "sitting" may be used for the day's work.

Time was when several sessions in a year were not uncommon. The Charter of Massachusetts Bay provided for four General Courts each year, and although at first the exigencies of the new colony reduced this with common consent to one a year, known as the Spring Court of Elections, presently demand for observance of the Charter sprang up, and in 1634 it was ordered that henceforth there should be four General Courts yearly. When provision was made for representation, at first the Deputies were chosen for each Court. Such frequent elections and so many sessions were quickly found burdensome, and in March of 1635/6, it was ordered that only two Courts should be held annually, one in May for elections and other affairs, and one in October for making laws and for other public occasions. It would seem that the colonists were apprehensive lest this might be followed by a change to elections for much longer terms and perhaps the substitution of the English system. Otherwise it is not easy to account for Paragraph 68 of the Body of Liberties

(1641), in which it was said: "Because we cannot forsee what
varietie and weight of occasions may fall into future consideration, and what counsells we may stand in neede of, we decree.
That the Deputies (to attend the Generall Court in behalf of the
Countrie) shall not at any time be stated or inacted, but from
Court to Court, or at the most for but one yeare, that the Countrie may have an Annuall libertie to do in that case what is most
behoofefull for the best welfaire thereof." Massachusetts did
not abandon the principle here enunciated until well into the
twentieth century. In 1642 it began electing its Legislature
once a year and continued so to do until 1920, the necessary
constitutional amendment being adopted in 1918.

Virginia was less successful in shaking off English precedents.
Before the end of the period from 1652 to 1660, when its people
were governing themselves, they enacted that their legislators
should be elected every two years, but in 1662, when the laws
were revised, with a declaration that those omitted were repealed, this was among the laws omitted. As elections were
held up to 1666, it has been questioned whether this particular
omission was intentional, but clearly the English attitude toward
the matter won favor in Virginia, for an Assembly lasted from
1666 to 1676, after the fashion of continuity that Charles had
adopted. Inevitably the members got quite out of harmony
with their constituents. Grievances were ignored and the
ground was prepared for Bacon's Rebellion. That promised
for a time the revival of old privileges, but the hope proved
vain, for it did not survive Bacon's death. Instructions
were sent over to Berkeley in 1677 that Assemblies should
be called but once in two years and should sit not more than
fourteen days, save for special reasons. By 1700 the custom of
proroguing Assemblies from session to session had become very
common. The records show from one to seven sessions held
by one Assembly without renewal by election. However,
Beverley (1705) says that the time of meeting of the Assembly
had been either once a year or once in every two years; "and
seldom two entire years passed without an Assembly." In
1762 the Burgesses declared frequent new Assemblies more
satisfactory to the people, and petitioned the King to allow
them one new Assembly every three years at least. In the
course of the same session, however, it was enacted that no
Assembly should continue longer than seven years, and that the

Assembly then in existence, unless sooner dissolved by the Governor, should legally expire May 26, 1768, five and a half years after the passage of the act. In reality none ever existed seven years.[1] From 1619 to 1776 there were about one hundred and twenty sessions of the Virginia Assembly.

The Fundamental Constitutions drawn for Carolina in 1669 provided: "A new Parliament shall be assembled the first Monday of the month of November every second year." The temporary Constitution of 1670, however, simply directed the Governor to call an Assembly "as soon as conveniently you can after the receipt of these instructions," with nothing further about their sessions. It is known that the Assemblies in North Carolina were almost regularly biennial for a long time. Burrington, the first royal Governor of that Province, was told to follow its laws and usages on the subject, and it is supposed he found the practice of biennial elections established. Interference with it shortly before the Revolution led Mr. Maclaine to say, in the Convention of 1788, for considering the proposed Federal Constitution: "I believe you remember — and perhaps every member here remembers — that this country was very happy under biennial elections. In North Carolina, the Representatives were formerly chosen by ballot biennially. It was changed under the royal government, and the mode pointed out by the King." [2]

In South Carolina under the Proprietors a statute was passed limiting the life of an Assembly to two years. In 1721 this was changed to three years. A law of 1745 provided for annual elections and another of 1748 for biennial elections, but both were rejected by the King and the old Triennial Act remained in force.

The Concession and Agreement of the Lords Proprietors of the Province of New Cesarea, or New Jersey (1664), provided for a General Assembly of twelve Deputies or Representatives, which was to have power to appoint the time of meeting and "to adjourn their sessions from time to time to such times and places as they shall think convenient." In 1672 this was modified so that to the Governor and Council was given the power of summons and adjournment. The Fundamentals of the Province of West New Jersey (1681) called for an annual meeting

[1] E. I. Miller, *The Legislature of the Province of Virginia*, 49.
[2] *Elliot's Debates*, IV, 29.

of a General Free Assembly, at a day certain, though the Governor with the consent of the Council might convene it earlier if need be. By the Fundamental Constitutions of East New Jersey (1683) the Great Council was to meet each April. This was the lower branch, and it furnishes the only instance that has come to my notice where continuity of membership has been sought in a lower House of this country. The provision was that one third of its members should be elected each year. After the Proprietors of East and West New Jersey surrendered their rights to the Crown, sessions came wholly within the control of the Governor. They were frequent until the Assembly that met in 1721, but of the six years before the next one was summoned, two went without a meeting, and then another was not chosen for six years. The people complained and the Assembly of 1733 passed a Triennial Bill, which was assented to by the Governor and Council, but was rejected by the King. Other measures of like nature were brought forward in the course of the next decade, one a bill for septennial elections that passed the House in 1740, but none prevailed. After 1744 there seems to have been no further complaint of consequence.

Penn's Charter of Liberties (1682) provided annual elections for Pennsylvania and that colony rejoiced in its good fortune. When Andrew Hamilton, Speaker of the Assembly, in 1739 took leave of the House on account of his age and infirmities, he said: "It is our great happiness that instead of triennial Assemblies, a privilege which several other colonies have long endeavored to obtain, ours are annual; and for that reason as well as others, less liable to be practiced upon or corrupted, either with money or presents." [1]

In New York Representatives were at first not chosen for any fixed time. An Assembly that met in June, 1716, was dissolved August 10, 1726. Dissolution was at the pleasure of the Governor and Council. A dissolution resulted from a transfer of the Crown, and sometimes, but not always, the death of a Governor was deemed to have the same effect. Also it often happened that a new Governor began his official career by calling a new Assembly. The refusal of an Assembly to give the Governor the appropriations he wanted was reason enough for dissolving it. Thus, in 1729, Governor Burnett sent one home because it had not "granted His Majesty's revenue in so ample

---

[1] Robert Proud, *Hist. of Penn.*, ii, 217.

and honorable manner as they had done formerly." In 1736 Clarke found an Assembly defiant of the King's instructions. One he dissolved. The new one told him they would raise no money for more than one year at a time; "nor do we think it convenient to do even that, until such laws are passed as we conceive to be necessary for the safety of the inhabitants of this colony, who have reposed in us a trust for that only purpose, and, by the grace of God, we will endeavor not to deceive them." Clarke submitted, and, bartering law against law, consented to a bill assuring frequent elections. Its preamble declared that "the frequent Electing of the Members that Constitute the General Assembly of this Colony and meeting of the same in General Assembly not only tends very much to preserve the liberty and safety of the inhabitants of this Colony, but also tends to create a good and lasting harmony and agreement, necessary for the honor and Interest of his Majesty and the Safety and well-being of his Subjects here, to subsist betwixt the governors for the time being and the inhabitants of this colony; and, to establish and preserve the same upon the most solid, firm, and lasting foundation." The act required an annual meeting of the Assembly in the city of New York; and, if an Assembly were dissolved, that writs of election for a new Assembly should be issued within six months after the dissolution. The term of members was fixed at three years. An elaborate argument was made in favor of the act, laying stress upon the practice of annual election in New England and Pennsylvania, but the Board of Trade recommended disallowance and an order in council was issued accordingly.[1] Then in 1743, by an act which, in the preamble, recited that the parliamentary term in England had been fixed at seven years, and that the colonial Legislature "conceive it their duty, as it is their inclination, to copy after so wise an example," the term of the existing Assembly, and of all subsequent Assemblies, was limited to seven years; and this term continued during the remainder of the colonial period.[2]

In New Hampshire, on the death of George I, the Assembly, which had existed five years, was of course dissolved; and writs for the election of another were issued in the name of

---

[1] E. B. Greene, *Provincial America*, 176, citing *Doc. Hist. of New York*, IV, 243 *et seq.*
[2] C. Z. Lincoln, *Const. Hist. of New York*, III, 146, 147.

George II. The long continuance of this Assembly was principally owing to the absence of Governor Shute, in whose administration it began; and to the uncertainty of his return or the appointment of a successor. It had been deemed a grievance, and an attempt had been made in 1724 to limit the duration of Assemblies to three years, in conformity with the custom of England. At the meeting of the new Assembly, the first business it took up was a motion for a Triennial Act. The Lieutenant-Governor was disposed to gratify it, and the Houses agreed in framing an act for a triennial Assembly.

The royal Governors did not as a rule like such limitations on their prerogatives. It was an interesting complaint that Governor Sharpe of Maryland sent to Lord Baltimore, June 6, 1754: "I will beg leave to submit to your Lordship's Consideration whether it will be impracticable or improper to fall on any method to put a Stop to such Perverseness as might generally be perceived in the proceedings of our Lower Houses of Assembly which is in great measure owing to the short Duration of our Sessions which terminate at the end of 3 years; few Gentlemen will submit to the inconveniences that such as canvass for Seats in that House must necessarily subject themselves to; by which means there are too many Instances of the lowest Persons at least men of small fortunes no Soul & very mean Capacities appearing as Representatives of their respective Counties; As there would be no want I apprehend of Gentlemen to appear as Candidates if the Drudgery of Electioneering was to return less frequently. I submit to your Lordship's Wisdom whether there may be any impropriety (if a more agreeable Choice of Members should be made) in continuing the next Assembly for more years than has been lately usual or customary." [1]

Argument of this sort at last led the home Government, in 1767, to declare itself definitely on the whole subject of limitations of a Governor's power in this particular, by a general instruction directing the Governors not to assent to any act fixing the duration of an Assembly.[2]

---

[1] *Maryland Archives*, 1; *Correspondence Gov. Sharpe*, 68 (as quoted by C. F. Bishop, *History of Elections in the American Colonies*, 34).
[2] E. B. Greene, *The Provincial Governor*, 156.

FREQUENCY OF ELECTIONS

ALTHOUGH colonial grievance related chiefly to the length of intervals between sessions, it included infrequency of elections. There was, indeed, just ground for complaint when a Governor refused to dissolve a compliant Assembly. Yet nothing before the Revolution has come to my notice indicating that the frequency of elections had received discussion of much consequence on its own account, apart from controversies with the Executive. Then philosophizing statesmen began to treat it independently. In 1776 John Adams wrote to John Penn:[1] "That the representatives may often mix with their constituents, and frequently render them an account of their stewardship, elections ought to be frequent:

"Like bubbles on the sea of matter borne,
They rise, they break, and to that sea return."

Some of the States put the idea into their Bills of Rights. Virginia said: "That the legislative and executive powers of the State should be separate and distinct from the judiciary; and that the members of the two first may be restrained from oppression, by feeling and participating the burdens of the people, they should, at fixed periods, be reduced to a private station, return into that body from which they were originally taken, and the vacancies be supplied by frequent, certain, and regular elections, in which all, or any part of the former members, to be again eligible, or ineligible, as the laws shall direct." Pennsylvania said much the same thing (1776) in fewer words: "That those who are employed in the legislative and executive business of the State, may be restrained from oppression, the people have a right at such periods as they may think proper, to reduce their public officers to a private station, and supply the vacancies by certain and regular elections." Maryland said in November: "The right in the people to participate in the Legislature is the best security of liberty, and the foundation of all free government; for this purpose, elections ought to be free and frequent."

North Carolina in December declared itself still more concisely, saying, "for redress of grievances, and for amending and strengthening the laws, elections ought to be often held."

[1] *Works*, IV, 205.

Vermont the next year copied the Pennsylvania wording. Of course John Adams put the idea into the Constitution he wrote for Massachusetts, his form being: "In order to prevent those who are invested with authority from becoming oppressors, the people have a right, at such periods and in such manner as they shall establish by their frame of government, to cause their public officers to return to private life; and to fill up vacant places by certain and regular elections and appointments."

In these declarations of a general principle, it was not necessary to define frequency, but in the working parts of the Constitutions that was essential. Experience with the royal Governors had made the people totally unwilling to give any control of the matter to executives. If it was left to the Legislatures, there was no knowing how far they might prolong their own existence. Election at fixed intervals was familiar, and in some of the States the custom of election at a definite time each year had been long established. So it was almost inevitable that what has now come to be the universal custom in the United States should be preferred rather than the English system of dissolutions and general elections as chance may bring them.

The period between elections that had prevailed in the greater part of New England for more than a century commended itself to all the original States except South Carolina. In the letter to John Penn from which quotation has been made, Adams further said: "These elections may be septennial or triennial; but, for my own part, I think they ought to be annual; for there is not in all science a maxim more infallible than this, where annual elections end, there slavery begins." The phraseology indicates that the saying was not new, but its source has not come to my knowledge. It caught the public fancy in the early days of constitution-making, was long repeated whenever controversy arose, and has had a powerful influence on our institutions. Yet it is a purely arbitrary delimitation, with no basis of reason in itself.

That the Eastern and Middle States should accept the annual period with little discussion was not unnatural. Its acceptance by most of the South is more surprising. Perhaps the explanation is that given by Sikes in regard to what happened in North Carolina. He says both parties favored annual elections. "The conservative party had little confidence in any of the Constitutions that had been formed by the different colonies, but thought that annual elections would be some check on the oppressive tyranny of an oppressive Legislature. The ultra-democratic party believed that where annual elections ended, there tyranny began." [1]

A dozen years later Maclaine, in the Convention considering the Federal Constitution, showed himself unconvinced. "Notwithstanding the contest for annual elections," he said, "perhaps biennial elections would still be better for this country. Our laws would certainly be less fluctuating." [2] Yet even Georgia did not go with South Carolina in clinging to the biennial period, nor did Kentucky in 1792, but Tennessee (1796) chose biennial elections.

The Articles of Confederation provided that delegates to Congress should be annually appointed by the States. Doubtless the unsatisfactory experience with the Congresses under the Confederation led the Convention of 1787 to hope for better results from two-year terms for Representatives. "The Federalist" devoted two numbers (52 and 53) to proving that biennial elections for the House were neither too frequent nor too rare. The argument was based chiefly on the greater scope of information necessary for Federal legislation. "The question then may be put into this simple form: does the period of two years bear no greater proportion to the knowledge requisite for Federal legislation than one year does to the knowledge requisite for State legislation? The very statement of the question, in this form, suggests the answer that ought to be given to it."

In the Massachusetts Convention for ratifying the Constitution, the provision for biennial election of Congressmen received more attention than any other, being particularly obnoxious to the critics. General Samuel Thompson, from Topsham, in what is now Maine, fought hard against it. The reporter of the debates, ordinarily non-committal, was moved by the General's eloquence to say: "Here the General broke out in the following pathetic apostrophe: 'O my country! never give up your annual elections; young men, never give up your jewel!'" "He apologized for his zeal," says the reporter, but the apostrophe so satisfied him that he seems to have repeated it with frequency.

[1] *The Transition of North Carolina from Colony to Commonwealth*, 74.
[2] *Elliot's Debates*, IV, 29.

Dr. John Taylor said that annual election had "been considered as the safeguard of the liberties of the people; and the annihilation of it, the avenue through which tyranny will enter." In view of the fact that the right of electing Representatives in Congress would be a new privilege acquired by the people, Thomas Dawes thought it would be in favor of the people if their Representatives should be elected even for forty years instead of two. On the other hand, the Honorable Abraham White would rather they should be chosen for six months. Fisher Ames, with the craft of the skilled debater, disarmed his opponents at the start by confessing and declaring that his zeal for frequent elections was not inferior to theirs. "I consider it," he said, "as one of the first securities for popular liberty, in which its very essence may be supposed to reside." Then he went on to lay down a reasonable proposition: "The term of election must be so long, that the Representative may understand the interests of the people, and yet so limited, that his fidelity may be secured by a dependence upon their approbation." It did not follow because annual elections are safe, that biennial elections are dangerous. He thought biennial elections ought to be preferred "from the extent of the country to be governed, the objects of their legislation, and the more perfect security of our liberty." Faction and enthusiasm, he said, are the instruments by which popular government are destroyed. A democracy is a volcano, which conceals the fiery materials of its own destruction. These will produce an eruption, and carry desolation in their way. The people always mean right, and if time is allowed for reflection and information, they will do right. "I would not have the first wish, the momentary impulse of the public mind, become law. For it is not always the sense of the people, with whom I admit that all power resides. On great questions, we first hear the loud clamors of passion, artifice, and faction. I consider biennial elections as a security that the sober second thought of the people shall be law."

General John Brooks of Medford (afterward Governor) combated the notion that the liberties of the people depended on the duration of Parliament — "with much ability," says the reporter. Next General Thompson was called to order, on the ground that he reflected on the last administration of the State when he said if it had continued one year longer "our liberties would have been lost and the country involved in blood; not so much, Sir, from their bad conduct, but from the suspicions of the people of them." Christopher Gore (also afterward Governor) and Rufus King ransacked history to show that biennial elections would not be dangerous. Judge Dana thanked God he was one of the people, and expressed his satisfaction with the biennial idea.

Tennessee came into the Union in 1796 with a Constitution providing for biennial elections, doubtless through the influence of South Carolina's example. Ohio followed with annual elections, then Louisiana with biennial, next Indiana and Mississippi with annual, and the same year (1818) Illinois preferred biennial. The next year Maine made them annual and then Missouri made them biennial.

In the decade beginning with 1831 the pendulum began to swing toward biennials. Delaware that year, Mississippi the next, changed from annual to biennial, and in 1835 North Carolina followed. Although Michigan and Florida came in with annuals, Arkansas chose biennials, and then in 1840 Georgia shifted to biennials.

It was about this time that State Legislatures began to fall into disrepute. The reckless appropriations that helped bring the financial panic of 1837, the loans of public credit to canals and railroads, the introduction of corporation influences — these and other causes began to convince the people that Legislatures were an evil to be mitigated by curtailment. The next eleven years saw the biennial doctrine make rapid headway. In that time Maryland, Alabama, Florida, Virginia, Kentucky, Ohio, and Indiana all changed to biennials. Iowa was admitted with them. Wisconsin, however, entered in 1848 with annual elections and California likewise in 1849.

Of the eighteen States admitted since 1850, only West Virginia started with annual elections, and she changed to biennials in 1872. Of the older States, Michigan changed to biennials in 1868, Vermont in 1870, Pennsylvania in 1873, New Hampshire in 1877, Maine in 1880, Wisconsin in 1881, Connecticut in 1884, Rhode Island in 1911, Massachusetts in 1918. New York and New Jersey are the only States still electing the members of the lower House every year.

Four States have gone to the extreme of elections every four years — Louisiana in 1879, Mississippi in 1890, Alabama in

1901, and Maryland in 1922, the full four-year programme to begin with the election of 1926. E. F. Noel, Governor of Mississippi from 1908 to 1912, after having served two terms of four years each in the Senate, and in the House before the change of 1890, an experience surely giving weight to his conclusions, thinks no harm whatever has resulted in his State from four-year terms for all State and county officers, including Senators and Representatives. He says he has never heard a complaint since the change was made. Like so many others, he sees in annual elections constant turmoil, loss of popular interest, and the injury that comes from keeping officials constantly canvassing, thus distracting attention from official duties.[1]

An amendment that would have provided quadrennial elections for Senators and Representatives was rejected in South Dakota in 1914 by a vote of 29,746 to 45,061. The new Constitution proposed for Arkansas in 1918 would have established quadrennial elections, but of course it cannot be known whether it was this that caused the rejection of the whole instrument. The model State Constitution drafted for submission to the National Municipal League in November of 1920 would give Representatives a four-year term.

For and Against Biennials

Surely biennial elections have had a test long enough and broad enough to warrant the expectation of satisfactory judgment. Yet the candid man must admit that the balance of considerations is far from clear. Forced to a vote, a thoughtful observer must recognize that his decision will depend on the weight he himself attaches to groups of considerations that have little relation to each other. It is like choosing between an apple and an orange, not between two apples nor between two oranges.

The starting-point of judgment should be the demonstrated fact that frequent elections conduce to reëlection. Reversing it, the longer the term, the less the probability of reëlection. For instance, in Vermont in 1868, the last year under the annual system, eleven Senators and ninety-six Representatives were reëlected. Of the thirty members of the Senate of 1919, one had been in the Senate and nine in the House of 1917; of the

[1] Letter to Mass. Com. to Compile Information and Data for Conv. of 1917.

246 members in the House of 1919, fifteen had been in the House of 1917.

This sort of thing has been a frequent result of adopting biennials, but such contrasts are not to be found everywhere, for in many States the rotation system had already, before annual elections were superseded, reduced to a negligible minimum the amount of reëlection. In Connecticut, for example, it had fallen to about one tenth. Charles R. Buckalew urged biennials on the Pennsylvania Convention of 1873 in the hope that they might check this evil. Their adoption worked no such reform as Mr. Buckalew sought. In the House of 1916 there were but fifty-six members who served in that of 1914 — less than thirty per cent. Possibly, however, the situation is improving, for of the members of the House of 1918 ninety-five — nearly one half — were reëlected to that of 1920. No figures have come to my notice showing that in a single instance the lengthening of the term has resulted in longer average service. Always a bad situation has not been bettered, or rather a bad situation has been made distinctly worse.

The arithmetic of the problem is complicated by the consideration that while frequent elections encourage reëlection and so conduce to long periods of public service, yet patently the man who is not going to be reëlected, anyhow, will be useful (or the reverse) proportionately in some degree to the length of his term. That is one reason why argument has of late been heard for extending the terms of Representatives in Congress. The two-year term proved to be generally acceptable until after the Civil War, but since then numerous resolutions have been introduced looking to its extension. Most of the proposals for change have looked to a three-year term, but some have been for a four-year term, or even six years. Bourke Cockran told the House (June 2, 1906) that the gravest cause of its incapacity is in the term of its members. "The Congress does not convene till the month of December preceding the choice of its successor," he said. "From the very moment he takes his oath of office before this desk, each member is plunged into the throes of a struggle for reëlection. How can he perform his duties impartially and fearlessly while three fourths of his attention must be distracted by the exigencies of his own position? You may say that the honest and efficient member will neglect his personal interests and devote himself exclusively to his representative duties. Well, Mr. Speaker, what duty can be higher than seeing that his district is well represented? (Laughter.) And he must think himself the very best representative his district could find or else he could not justify himself in coming here. The House is reduced to this position: In the first — the longer and more important — session, every member is striving for renomination and reëlection from the very hour he is sworn in until the adjournment, and in the second session he has either been beaten, in which case his interest in the session is sensibly reduced, if not wholly extinguished, or else he has been reëlected, in which case his sense of security is apt to be too great for efficiency. (Applause and laughter.) His whole service, except under very exceptional conditions, is confined to two sessions. In the first everything tends to make him incapable. In the second, he may be indifferent. (Laughter.) We declare at every stage that the House is declining in influence. Yet we lose no chance to push it farther along on the downward slope. To me the wonder is not that the House has declined in consequence, but that any of its consequence survives."[1]

To emphasize this aspect of the case is wholly natural in a member of a legislative body, who inevitably looks at things in their relation to himself and his fortunes. Detachment is hard for him. He cannot get quite the right perspective. So over against Cockran's argument may usefully be set the conclusions of a Massachusetts newspaper man, R. L. Bridgman, who for a generation has watched and studied Legislatures, building up a deserved reputation for intelligence in observation and soundness of judgment. It was not in a hastily written newspaper article, but in a well-considered book on "Biennial Elections" that he said (p. 14):

"Will the State be safer with Representatives holding terms so long that they will not yield unwisely to popular excitement, or will it be safer with Representatives holding terms so short that they will not defy the wishes of their constituents? Only one candid answer is possible with those who have watched for a long time the course of legislation. The short term is unquestionably the safer. The occasions of danger from popular excitement are comparatively rare. The occasions from temptation to the legislator are almost constant. The member who feels that he will never come again, that, under the system of

[1] *Cong. Record*, XL, pt. 9, 8832.

courtesy and rotation which prevails some other man is sure
to take his place the next year, is much more likely to disregard
the wishes of his constituents than the member who feels that
his reëlection depends upon his fidelity to them. If two-year
terms were introduced, the members, to a larger extent than now,
would be absolutely certain that they would not be reëlected.
They would be less sensitive to the wishes of their constituents.
They would be more susceptible to corrupt influences. They
would be more watchful to make as much personal gain as possible out of their political careers. Self, not the public, would
be more likely to be the chief consideration."

Two other arguments have played a large part in the decisions
on this question — that on the score of expense, and that on the
score of disturbance. It is true elections cost only half as much
if held only half as often. It is also true that elections disturb
the placid repose of society, or at any rate divert men from customary occupations. Neither of these arguments ought to be
deemed relatively of importance. If government is our most
serious concern, then money and thought and time and energy
can be expended on nothing of more consequence. It is amusing, and it is sad, to see the complaint of too much politics go
hand in hand with the complaint of misgovernment. What
illogical creatures we are! We scold our legislators because
they don't come up to our expectations, and then we scold
because we are asked to do anything about it. We want
automatic righteousness. Sorry will be the day when we rely
on that and that alone for the preservation of our liberties.
Then there will be no elections. One man or a group of men
will save us all that expense and trouble.

There is a way out of the dilemma. It has not the slightest
chance of meeting common approval yet, but it will always be
open and some time may get serious consideration. It is not
a new idea. Marshall's biography of Washington, in a note
to page 353 of vol. 5, adds: "It has been published by the enemies of Mr. Hamilton, that he was in favour of a President and
Senate who should hold their office during good behaviour."
J. T. Austin, in his "Life of Elbridge Gerry" (ii, 21, note), says
that whether by enemy or friend the publication was substantially true, unless indeed some equivocation may be played upon
the words "in favour," and that it may be conceived he was
in fact *not in favour* of his own proposition. "Col. H. him-

self, in a letter to Col. Pickering in 1803, when the extreme unpopularity of such a proposition was most manifest, and after the overthrow of the political party of which those gentlemen were the chiefs, owing, as it unquestionably was, to their high toned notions of government, availed himself of some such ingenious distinction. He avows making the proposition, which it was well-known to him was on record, and would one day be published. 'The highest toned propositions which I made in the convention were for a President, Senate and judges, during good behaviour'; but he leaves the reader to infer that his mind had not settled down definitely in approbation of his own proposals."

In our time Albert Stickney has written a book, "The Political Problem," in developing the theory that gain would come from having all those who may be elected to office, legislators as well as officials, serve during good behavior. As he puts it (p. 113), "that means the abolition of tenure by election for the members of the popular assembly, as well as for the chief executive, and the substituting in its place tenure at the will of the people; in other words, each member of the popular assembly, though originally chosen by the citizens of his electoral district, would be responsible, after he was chosen, not to his single district or to its citizens, but only to the whole people, that is, to the popular assembly itself." Stating it more concretely, a Representative would hold his place until ousted from it by his fellow Representatives. Mr. Stickney thinks that under such a system first-class men would be chosen, safe men, of good repute, with experience in affairs. Ordinarily they would be men somewhat advanced in years, who had led laborious lives; successful men, and therefore generally men of some means. "Membership in these popular assemblies, if men did their work faithfully, would be very laborious. Members who were honest would get small remuneration in money; and all that they could gain in reputation, they would get in a comparatively short time. Many of them, after a reasonable term of service, would ask to retire." If there were no resignations or removals, death would make a practically complete change once in about fifteen years. This change, though steady, would be gradual. "The machinery would not be deranged. Work would not be interrupted. The membership would have stability and mobility combined. New blood and brain would be continually coming in, and at the same time the body would at all times have a large proportion of members of experience."

Nothing so revolutionary as this would to-day be considered with patience by the people. They would reject it instantly as "undemocratic." Some of its purposes, however, serious and respectable purposes at that, can be achieved by a step that would not be revolutionary nor even unfamiliar. The arrangements for continuity found in most of our Senates could be extended to the rest and also to the lower branches. This has of late been under discussion in Vermont, where the evils produced by the biennial system and by the demand for rotation in office have been especially conspicuous and detrimental. The suggestion is that members of both branches be elected for four-year terms, one half retiring with each two years. This would insure some degree of experience in at least half of the membership.

SENATORIAL SERVICE

THE election of members of the upper House for terms longer than those of the lower House appears at least once in colonial times. Penn's Charter of Liberties (1682) provided that members of the Provincial Council should be chosen for three-year terms, one third going out each year. This was embodied in the Frame of Government of that year, but Markham's Frame of Government of 1796 dropped the provision.

In some of the early State Constitutions the idea was revived. Virginia took the lead with a four-year term for Senators and has continued the policy without change. Delaware made it three years, changing to four in 1831. Maryland made it five years, changed to six in 1837, and then to four in 1851. New York began with four years. In the Convention of 1846 the proposal to continue that term had only 17 votes; 42 voted for three years; and by 80 to 23 it was in the end put at two years. The Commission of 1872–73 proposed a return to the four-year term, but the Legislature did not approve and so it was not submitted to the people. In 1894 the term was changed to three years.

The provision of six years as the senatorial term made by the Federal Constitution gave the idea of a longer term for the upper branch such approval that it has been embodied in much the greater part of the State Constitutions since adopted.

In but one of the newer States, however, has the duration been made six years. Texas went to that figure in 1868, but returned to four in 1876. Four was the figure Pennsylvania chose when in 1790 she created her first Senate; in 1838 it was changed to three, but in 1873 the State went back to four. In 1790, also, South Carolina made it four years. Georgia has tried four methods. Her first Senators, provided for in 1789, were to be elected every third year. Annual election was substituted in 1795; this was changed to biennial in 1840 with the adoption of the biennial system; in 1868 the four-year term was substituted; and in 1877 return was made to the two-year term. Most of the newer States started with four years. Indiana, Alabama, Mississippi, however, all began with three years and later changed to four. New Jersey, beginning with the annual election of Senators, changed it to triennial in 1844. Nevada is one of the few States that have ever shortened the term; it began with four years and changed to two. At present thirty-one States have four-year terms; one State makes it three years; and sixteen prefer two years.

In seventeen States the terms of Senators and Representatives are of the same length; in thirty-one the terms of Senators are longer — twice as long in all save New Jersey, where they are three times as long.

Of countries with terms of members of the upper branch longer than those of the United States Senate, in Ireland the term is twelve years; Egypt, ten; France, the Netherlands, Sweden, Argentina, and Brazil, nine; Czecho-Slovakia, eight. It is not without significance that Belgium, which up to 1921 had an eight-year term for Senators, changed it to four when in that year revising the Constitution.

One argument in behalf of long terms for Senators was well put by Governor Hoffman of New York, in his message of 1872, recommending a Constitutional Commission: "The chief object of a Senate should be to review the action of the other House, to check and restrain improvident, hasty, or unwise legislation; and, for the best discharge of this duty, it should be composed of men well versed in public affairs. Its name imports that it is to be a council of men of long experience. Every inducement should be held out to attract the right men to service in this body. The public cannot expect, any more than a private person, to command valuable services unless it offers an adequate reward. This reward need not be wholly pecuniary; the dignity of an office is often a more powerful inducement to the class of men we need in the public service. A long term and a large constituency would greatly enhance the dignity of the office of Senator, and make it attractive to our most distinguished citizens. If the senatorial term were made four or five years and the State were divided into a small number of senatorial districts, so as to throw the choice of Senator upon a large constituency, and the compensation made a fair one, I do not doubt that the ablest and most experienced of our public men would be found ready to apply themselves in the Senate to the important duty of securing good laws for the people."

Much of this was sound, but the Governor drew the long bow when he said this programme would attract the most distinguished citizens of a State. All that can reasonably be hoped is that it would attract better men than would otherwise listen.

Opinions differ as to whether there is gain from long senatorial terms through their effect in delaying response to change in public opinion. Conservatives say it is well to prevent quick answer to every veering gust. Radicals say the popular will ought to prevail, forthwith. Experience has shown that party control of the National Senate follows much more speedily the shifts in the attitude of the voters than would be expected in view of the six-year term. Yet it lags far enough behind to give reasonable protection against whim and impulse.

CHAPTER VII

FREQUENCY AND LENGTH OF SESSIONS

FREQUENCY of election and frequency of session are in theory quite distinct problems, but in practice they are often confounded. Common usage, converting an adjective into a noun, has applied the word "biennials" indiscriminately to elections and sessions. Much clearer thinking would result if the two things could be kept separate. Really all that relates them is the fact that the interval between the first day of one session and the first day of the next session cannot be longer than the interval between elections. These two intervals may be of the same length, or that between the first days of sessions may be as much shorter than that between elections as judgment dictates, even to the point of having no interval at all, as in the case of continuous session. The determination is wholly arbitrary.

Regularity of sessions developed as a matter of convenience. At first the King summoned a Parliament when he wanted the nation to give him money. Inasmuch as a Parliament meant a contribution, complaint of frequent assembling was natural. On one occasion the grant to the King was made upon condition that "no other Parliament should be holden from the Calends of March till Michaelmas." In the course of time, when evils of an opposite nature developed, the nation decided not to appropriate money for more than a year. Hence an annual session became a necessity. It is to-day the rule for all the English Dominions that their Parliaments shall sit annually and that in the event of dissolution twelve months shall not intervene between the last session of one Parliament and the first of another. In 1867 Bismarck wanted triennial sessions for Germany, and in 1888, when the term of the Reichstag was changed to five years, he wanted the sessions held only every other year, but it kept on meeting annually. The Constitution adopted in 1919 stipulated a meeting each year. Such is the requirement in Belgium, France, Portugal, and indeed most of the other countries of the world.

The American colonies, begun on a corporate basis, naturally carried out the corporation practice of having meetings of members and of their Councils, or Boards, or Directors, at stated intervals. The stockholders of the Massachusetts Bay Colony were to meet four times a year, the directors (the Assistants) oftener. It proved inconvenient for the stockholders to gather so frequently and for a while an annual meeting sufficed. Between this practice and the charter requirement, compromise was made on two General Courts a year — a system that lasted for nearly two centuries. The Governor could, "upon urgent occasion," call a General Court at any other time. In Connecticut many extra sessions were held. In 1645 the Court met seven times; in 1658 it met five times, twice in a single month. The two regular sessions a year were replaced by one when the State Constitution was framed, in 1818. Rhode Island continued the practice of two sessions a year, one at Newport and the other at Providence, even after framing her Constitution in 1842. A dozen years later an annual session was substituted, to meet at Newport and adjourn to Providence.

Under the royal Governors the irregularity of sessions was a bitter grievance with the colonists. They conceived it to be a serious infringement of their liberties, and when in their Declaration of Independence they arraigned the King, assuming him to be responsible for everything his Governors had done, they charged: "He has refused for a long time, after such dissolutions, to cause others to be elected; whereby the Legislative Powers, incapable of annihilation, have returned to the People at large for their exercise; the State remaining in the meantime exposed to all the danger of invasion from without, and convulsions within."

So when Maryland came to draft a Bill of Rights for its first Constitution, in August of 1776, it said: "For redress of grievances, and for amending, strengthening and preserving the laws the Legislature ought to be frequently convened." Massachusetts amplified this into: "The Legislature ought frequently to assemble for the redress of grievances, for correcting, strengthening, and confirming the laws, and for making new laws, as the common good may require." New Hampshire in 1784 copied Massachusetts word for word.

When the Federal Constitution was framed, it was thought that the new national government would relieve the States of much of their work. Hamilton called attention to this in No. 84 of "The Federalist." "The business of the United States," he said, "has hitherto occupied the State Legislatures, as well as Congress. The latter has made requisitions which the former have had to provide for. Hence it has happened that the sessions of the State Legislatures have been protracted greatly beyond what was necessary for the execution of the mere local business of the States. More than half their time has been frequently employed in matters which related to the United States." Perhaps Tennessee, drawing up a Constitution in 1796, had this in mind when it provided for biennial sessions of the Legislature, therein departing from the example of South Carolina, which in 1776 had made sessions annual although making elections biennial. Since Tennessee's decision all the States starting with biennial elections have made sessions biennial, and most of those changing from annual to biennial elections have at the same time changed to biennial sessions. Georgia, adopting both biennial elections and biennial sessions in 1840, changed sessions back to annual in 1865, made them biennial again in 1877, and came back to annual once more in 1891, with a fifty-day limit on each session, unfinished business going over from the first session of a term to the second. Florida, adopting biennial elections and sessions in 1847, made sessions annual in 1865, returning them to biennial ten years later. Texas, which as a Republic (1836) had annual elections, came in as a State (1845) with both elections and sessions biennial, made sessions annual in 1868, and changed them to biennial in 1876.

Maryland furnished a unique episode, due to politics. She had annual sessions until 1846. The substitution then of biennial sessions was not quietly accepted and the contest was renewed in the Convention of 1851, the result being a compromise by which sessions were to be annual for three years and thereafter biennial.

Two States, Mississippi in 1890 and Alabama in 1901, reached the extreme of making sessions quadrennial. In Mississippi, however, a special session was provided, midway the quadrennial regular sessions. This was limited to thirty days unless extended by the Governor, and restricted to considering appropriations and matters designated by the Governor in the call. Since then the State has changed back to biennial sessions.

Louisiana (1879) and Maryland (1922) adopting quadrennial elections continued biennial sessions (with one three-year interval in Maryland to synchronize the programme). The proposed Constitution rejected by Arkansas in 1918 would have made regular sessions quadrennial, with a midway session limited to thirty days and restricted to consideration of general appropriation bills and to investigation of the accounts of State officers and the management and condition of State institutions. Governor Nestos of North Dakota in his message to the Legislature of 1923 proposed quadrennial sessions.

The result of the four-year system in Alabama has been intelligently and instructively set forth by Governor Emmet O'Neal of that State.[1] Speaking with personal knowledge and a judgment evidently well-ripened by experience, he discussed the matter with skill, vigor, and cogency that ought to win for his views the respectful attention of any who may have thought the lessening of legislative sessions a cure-all. His conclusion was that the quadrennial only intensifies the evils of the biennial system.

Governor O'Neal did not find that lessening the number of sessions lessens the volume of legislation. Of this he said: "From the date of its admission as a State till the adoption of the Constitution in 1875, the Legislature of Alabama met annually. The most notable change which was effected by that Constitution was the establishment of biennial sessions limited to sixty legislative days. Notwithstanding the restrictions upon legislative competency and legislative activity provided by the Constitution of 1875, it was found, when the Constitutional Convention of 1901 assembled, that the biennial session, limited to sixty days, had not checked or lessened, but rather increased, the volume of legislative enactments. Hence the Constitutional Convention of 1901, in a spirit of impatience, disappointed by the results of the biennial session, boldly embarked the State upon a new and untried experiment — that of quadrennial sessions of the Legislature limited to fifty days. If intermissions of two years in the meeting of the lawmaking body could not put a stop to excessive legislative activity, it was vainly believed that by increasing the interval from two to four years we could find the panacea for all of our legislative ills. . . . No one will deny that in all the States of the Union,

[1] " Distrust of State Legislatures," *North American Review*, May, 1914.

with their increasing population, industrial and economic development, and wealth, legislation on various subjects is absolutely necessary, and that many laws require revision and modification; but the evil feared, and which it was proposed to eliminate, was the passage and repeal of too many laws, by means of greater deliberation and consideration of all matters of legislation. Yet, paradoxical as it may seem, the remedy has proven to be the chief cause of the evil we have sought to avoid. . . . Biennial sessions only increase legislative pressure."

It is but fair to say, however, that opinion in Alabama is divided. To William D. Jelks, Governor of that State from 1901 to 1907, it does not appear that the provision for quadrennial sessions "has worked to the detriment of the State in any respect." He thinks it is not true, or, if true, only true in a measure, that quadrennial sessions have resulted in ill-digested legislation, for he sees no special occasion for ill-digested legislation growing out of the fact that the Legislature is presumably in session only for one period in four years. Governor Charles Henderson also approves the quadrennial plan. He thinks the evils gotten rid of by it overbalance the advantages of biennial sessions.[1] The State voted in 1916 against returning to the biennial plan, by 42,946 to 51,284.

Whether the actual volume of law is reduced by holding sessions less frequently, is a disputed point. Von Holst declared "the legislative statistics of the States which have tried both plans show that with annual sessions just as many laws are passed each year as with biennial sessions are passed every second year."[2] On the other hand, C. L. Jones, writing more recently, says: "One of the favorite ways to reduce the evil of 'over-legislation' has been to cut down the number of sessions and even to limit the time the Legislature may remain in session. No better example can be found of our patchwork methods of treating the problems of lawmaking. The result of attempts to cram legislation into short periods has not been to lessen the number of 'bad laws,' nor to lessen the number of laws passed."[3]

In the matter of number, Professor Jones may have had in mind only the effect of limiting the length of sessions. It would

[1] Letters to Mass. Com. to Compile Information and Data for Conv. of 1917.
[2] *Constitutional Law of the U.S.*, 270.   [3] *Statute Law Making* (1912), 13.

be hard to get satisfactory statistical proof on this point. Observation, however, is quite enough without figures to warrant contesting a collateral dictum of Von Holst. Said he: "The experience of the States which have annual legislative sessions has shown that the Legislatures, when they do not find enough to do, always know how to make something to do. Once assembled, they seem to feel in duty bound to sit for a certain time and to pass a certain number of laws." If any Legislature in the land ever fails to find enough to do, it has never come to my knowledge. The trouble is just the opposite — there is everywhere too much to do. The one Legislature with which I am thoroughly acquainted, sitting annually, feels in duty bound neither to sit for a certain time nor to pass a certain number of laws; it wants to get through as soon as it can with a clear conscience, and it passes laws only to the degree compelled by public pressure, the bulk of the criticism on it concerning not what it does but what it leaves undone. Were it to enact in a biennial session only as many bills as it now enacts in an annual session, the volume of that criticism would be greatly increased.

The indisputable thing is that if the demands of the citizens are to be met as much in biennial sessions as they are in annual sessions, just as many laws must result from one system as the other. One exception has to be made to this. With annual sessions laws are more quickly repealed and changes are more speedily made. This may be unfortunate; it may be fortunate. Governor O'Neal concluded that lengthening the interval between sessions was distinctly harmful in this respect. "The vice of the system," he said, "was that it denied the people for four years the right to repeal or revise vicious or unwise legislation. The right of the people to self-government was suspended for four years, and during that period they were forced to endure without remedy the evil effects of any bad laws that might exist upon the statute-books."

Thomas Paine, writing "Of Constitutions, Government, and Charters," in 1805, said: "Legislatures are elected annually, not only for the purpose of giving the people, in their elective character, the opportunity of showing their approbation of those who have acted right, by reëlecting them, and rejecting those who have acted wrong; but also for the purpose of correcting the wrong (where any wrong has been done) of a former Legislature." With men who are so constituted as to

think all change obnoxious *per se*, this observation will carry
little weight. They would rather bear those ills they have
than fly to others that they know not of. They sympathize
with that love of status which Sir Henry Maine found to be the
characteristic of uncivilized communities. Nevertheless there
cannot be improvement without change, and laws must be
changed if society is to advance. The carper delights to speak
of the process as "tinkering." If he would himself but once
try to write a law of any but the simplest nature, he might
learn that no more difficult task perplexes human ingenuity.
Rarely can the most expert of legislators anticipate all possibilities. The occasion for amendment is virtually inevitable.
As a rule the sooner the amendment can be made, the better.

This does not condone foolish changes nor those that are
trivial. It assumes that laws are enacted for reasonable purposes, in response to genuine demand, which is of course a
broad assumption, open to many exceptions, yet the right starting point for the man who has faith in the virtue of the form
of government under which he lives. Such a man will prefer
annual sessions if their net result is to better the statute-book.

It is, however, denied that frequent sessions get better legislation. On the contrary, it has been frequently urged that the
result of fewer sessions would be improvement in the laws.
For instance, Von Holst said "it is evident that many laws which
were at least unnecessary have been enacted" by Legislatures
sitting annually; "and unnecessary laws, simply because they
are unnecessary, always do harm. The stability of relations
so essential to the welfare of the State and of society is thus quite
uselessly destroyed and a highly dangerous craving for excitement fostered. That there is much truth in this argument,
cannot be disputed by any one who examines the facts without
prejudice." Risking the suspicion of prejudice, I venture to
question the accuracy of the premise on which this conclusion
was based. There are no unnecessary laws, that is, laws thought
unnecessary by everybody. Need is a matter of opinion and a
matter of degree. Furthermore, there is no proof that the
average importance of enactments in biennial is greater than
of those in annual sessions. The opposite is to be expected.
Self-interest being the most powerful motive with most men, if
there must be selection between measures, those that serve the
selfish purpose of somebody will have the right of way if in-

genuity can prevail.   The measures really of most consequence to the general welfare are those more likely to be slighted.

Governor O'Neal summed up the actual experience of his own State with the declaration, "Instead of preventing, the quadrennial system has proven to be the most prolific source yet devised for hasty and ill-considered legislation." Simon Sterne pursued this phase of the matter with logic in an address to the American Bar Association, Aug. 24, 1884. "To cut in half the time of the session of our Legislature, as a cure for bad legislation," he said, "is not only to prove ourselves ignorant of the cure for our evils, but to ignore the causes of the evils. Insufficient time for investigation, inadequate machinery for investigation, as preliminary to legislation, absence of notice to parties to be affected by proposed legislation, hurry, want of method and of publicity, absence of deliberation, are among the main causes of bad legislation.   Now, how will this be cured by biennial Legislatures, with the consequent doubling, at the least, of the pressure upon the Legislature when it does meet? Reducing the time for deliberation increases the hurry, and necessarily dispenses with the little method that is still observable."   And further: "This proposed remedy is contrary to the tendencies of modern civilization; it is the abdication of a function, not its specialization and development; it is the merest refuge of imbecility, a confession that on this subject we are bankrupted in thought; that instead of being able to turn out better laws by selecting better legislators and improving their methods, our invention offers no other cure than to close the gates of our legislative mills every other year, in the vain hope that in the alternative year they may produce better wares."

Up to this point it has been a question of comparison — legislation better or worse.   It is also to be observed that relief from legislation positively bad, legislation vicious or venal, has been sought by making sessions less frequent.   For instance, T. R. White tells us in his "Commentaries on the Constitution of Pennsylvania" (187) that in the Convention of 1873 the real reason for the proposed change was a feeling on the part of the majority of the Convention that less evil was likely to be done by a Legislature meeting once in two years than by one meeting every year.   The proposal was frankly stated by its advocates to be a companion provision to the clause forbidding local and special legislation, both clauses being meant to reduce to a minimum the opportunities for evil legislation. Governor O'Neal thought the whole argument in favor of biennial sessions is evidently based on the assumption that because our Legislatures have passed bad laws, have often proven corrupt, have many times flagrantly betrayed the interests of their constituents, and have allowed public-service and favor-seeking corporations and other great industrial enterprises to secure franchises, privileges, and exemptions detrimental to the public welfare, and have converted our lawmaking bodies into agencies of class advantage and personal profit, representative government has proven a failure, and that all efforts to reform or improve conditions are hopeless. I quite agree with what he proceeded to say: "This is the language of despair, and the conclusion is not as correct as it may seem obvious. The corruption and incompetence of many of our Legislatures may be admitted; but it does not necessarily follow that the people can never trust their representatives to serve them honestly and efficiently."

It would be impossible to show that a change from annual to biennial sessions has lessened venality or has diminished the aggregate amount of dishonest legislation.

It would be equally impossible to show that such a change has improved the quality of legislators. The hope was that less frequent elections and sessions would result in bringing to the Legislature greater public attention, and thus make it a more desirable field of activity for men of ability. There is no proof that this result has followed.

It was also hoped that increasing the interval between sessions would increase the sense of responsibility on the part of legislators. It was thought that when a new law could be revised or repealed twelve months later, men were more careless or indifferent than they would be if the correction of mistakes must be delayed two years. On the face of it, this looks reasonable, but in the course of my own experience in annual sessions I cannot recall ever having had ground to think that any fellow-member was careless or indifferent because his work could be speedily undone. Yet in candor it should be recorded that the Massachusetts Recess Committee of 1915 said that with biennial sessions "matters would receive more careful consideration."

There remains the argument on the score of expense, perhaps

the argument most commonly urged. One answer to it is that a single bad law may cost the State more than the whole expense of a legislative session, and if it were due to the inexperience of legislators or other characteristics of infrequent sessions, the saving they might bring would be a case of penny wise and pound foolish.

Turning to some of the definite objections to infrequent sessions, we find one of grave consequence in the embarrassment they cause to the conduct of the business of a Commonwealth. It is hard enough to forecast conditions for a year. Little beyond this is ever attempted in private business. Occasionally big corporations commit themselves to programmes, maybe of an engineering nature, that will take several years to complete, but the well-nigh universal rule is to have annual meetings, from which it is fair to conclude that the shrewdness of the business world is in accord on the proposition that twelve months is the interval between decisions and revisions that best suits the conditions of life.

Governor Cornell of New York in 1882 was of the opinion that "provision for the support of all departments of the State government, can be made two years in advance, quite as well as for a single year," and so many other able statesmen have been of the same belief, that it would be rash indeed to dogmatize the other way. Yet my own impression, confirmed by experience in the legislative position most concerned with appropriations, the chairmanship of the House Committee known in Massachusetts as that on Ways and Means, is that it would be better to have more rather than less frequent contact between the Legislature and the administrative departments. The budget cannot well be made up for less than a twelvemonth, but there should be more elasticity than the present system permits. In corporation affairs administrative officials can get relief in the event of emergencies or changed conditions or unforeseen opportunities, by recourse to the President or the Board of Directors. The same chance is open to municipal departments, for all city councils are in session that is virtually continuous. Only in our State and Federal affairs do we tie ourselves down to infrequent chances for readjustment. E. E. Agger, writing on "The Budget in American Commonwealths," [1] held it to be an ameliorating circumstance that "the activities

[1] *Columbia Univ. Studies*, xxv, no. 2, p. 63 (1907).

of the average American State are relatively few and unchange-able." This was the case when most of our States adopted biennial sessions, but it is not the case to-day. Recent admin-istrative reorganization in Massachusetts found a hundred or more Bureaus, Departments, and Commissions to be grouped. Other populous States have likewise developed their activities. Everywhere the functions of government are broadening their scope. Sooner or later they will compel application of the same principles that have proved efficacious and economical in the world of commerce and industry.

One of the weaknesses of the biennial session system neces-sarily comes from the fact that under it the employment of a permanent legislative staff is out of the question. This tends to perpetuate the bane of so many Legislatures — the office-seeking that distracts and encumbers the members. Governor Thomas Ford, of Illinois, in his "History" of that State, where he well knew the Legislature from its beginning in 1818 down to 1847, gives a lively picture of what was then the common experience, and still may be seen in many States. "The mem-bers of the Legislature," says he (p. 285), "after having been elected, feeling victorious and triumphant over their adversaries at home, come up to the seat of government in a happy state of exultation of mind and self-complacency, which make the compliments with which they are received most soothing and agreeable. The whole world of aspirants for office comes with them. A Speaker of the lower House, and officers of the two Houses, are to be elected, the first thing. For these offices there are many candidates. I have known more than one hundred candidates for door-keepers of the two Houses. Be-sides these, there are numerous candidates for secretaryships and clerkships. The members exhibit themselves in public places, where they can be approached, flattered, supplicated, and teased, by the several aspirants for office, who fly round from one member to another, with great glee and activity, making themselves agreeable, until after the election."

Annual election of members of the lower branch and annual sessions are now found only in New York and New Jersey. Four States — Massachusetts, Rhode Island, South Carolina, and Georgia — prefer the combination of biennial elections with annual sessions, after the manner of Congress. Governor J. Q. A. Brackett urged such a combination on Massachusetts in his inaugural address of 1890. He argued that a Legislature elected for two years and meeting annually would at its second session be composed wholly of experienced members. He believed "the members would be disposed to postpone to the second session propositions of questionable expediency coming before them at the first, in order that they might have ample time for their consideration. On the other hand, they would not be inclined, except in special exigencies, to enter again upon the consideration of questions which had been finally disposed of at the first. This would save much of the time now taken up each year in hearings and discussions upon the same subject by successive Legislatures. It would lessen the tendency to the enactment of laws by one Legislature and their repeal by the next, and thereby tend to remove the objection often expressed as to the uncertainty of the law occasioned by frequent changes therein."

R. L. Bridgman pointed out that the reverse of Governor Brackett's proposition is also true — "that at its first session the Legislature would be practically composed wholly of inexperienced members. More than this, the experience which it would have in its second session would be only that learned by observation of the errors of its own inexperience; whereas, by the present system of annual elections, the experience gained is by observation of the traditions and customs handed down, with more or less improvement, from year to year, and which are the result of the accumulated trials and wisdom of a century." Each was assuming that biennial elections would diminish the number of reëlections. To weigh the gains and the losses would be no easy matter. Massachusetts decided in 1918 to put it to the test.

Experience has not shown that biennial or quadrennial sessions cure the evils at which they were aimed. They have not been accompanied by legislative improvement. On the other hand, Governor O'Neal may have been right in saying that "there is less alarm or apprehension in those States which have annual sessions of the Legislature, at the convening of the lawmaking body than in those where the biennial or quadrennial system prevails." The steadily growing pressure of work is compelling a revision of judgments. Charles McCarthy, the Wisconsin legislative expert, expressed the belief that "it will not be long until some kind of annual session will be necessary if hasty legislation is to be avoided." He is not alone in that opinion. The half dozen States that preserve the annual session seem to me wise.

A correspondent of the "Nation" suggested, February 1, 1912, that regular sessions be abolished, and that each year at city and town elections the question be put on the ballot, "Shall the Legislature meet this year?" Nothing more pregnant with disaster could be urged. The result would be, to use a time-honored metaphor, the bursting of the dam that has piled up water until it drives everything before it and works havoc throughout the valley. The innate conservatism of the majority, the wish of most men to be let alone, the powerful influences of invested capital, these and other forces would unite to get an annual majority against the sitting of Legislatures until at last the spirit of revolution broke bonds. It is well to remember the wisdom of Montesquieu: "The motion of the people is always either too remiss or too violent. Sometimes with a hundred thousand arms they overturn all before them; and sometimes with a hundred thousand feet they creep like insects."

If we were to throw away all that Englishmen gained by triennial and septennial acts, to throw away what our fathers won on the battle-fields of the Revolution, if we were to return to the mediæval system of having lawmaking bodies meet at somebody's pleasure — whether that of monarch or majority is all the same in essence — practical difficulties of the most serious nature would arise. Regularly repeated and systematic appropriations are indispensable to good government. It is unthinkable that republics in our time will entrust to any man, Board, or Commission, the power of the purse, the right to tax, the unrestricted authority to spend. Then, too, the redress of grievances is one of the prime functions of legislatures — the justice higher and broader than any that can be dispensed in courts of law. Shall the aggrieved await the whim of the majority before being heard? Not even in the matter of routine administrative detail that now is allowed unwisely to take up so much of the time of lawmakers and to encumber the statute-books so needlessly, would irregular sessions at intervals meet the rational needs of the community. Laws are enacted because the world moves, because Science and Invention never sleep, because even Custom always marches. Our ills come

not because laws are in the van, but because they are so far in
the rear.   The Legislature always lags.

Special Sessions

There are signs that the reaction has begun.   Almost unconsciously the States are resorting to methods of evading constitutional obstacles that stand in the way of getting the work
done.   Whenever a Constitution blocks the natural paths of
community action, others will be sought, if the occasion is urgent.   The significant thing in this instance is not that there is
evasion, but that it would not take place if the common instinct
did not demand and justify.

The resort is to adjourned and special sessions.   In Ohio
the annual session came back as a regular practice under the
guise of adjournment.   When the matter was under consideration in the Pennsylvania Convention of 1873, a letter was read
from General Thomas L. Young, a prominent member of the
Ohio Senate, in which he said that since the biennial session
provision went into effect, in 1852, the Legislature had met
every winter but one.   "In a State as large as Ohio," he said,
"we have found it necessary to meet annually.   The people
and their varied wants and interests demand it, and if your
Convention should adopt our plan, you would make a grave
mistake."   In spite of this advice, Pennsylvania not only
changed to biennial elections but directed that after 1878 the
General Assembly should hold no adjourned session.   It might,
however, meet when convened by the Governor.   In 1883 an
extra session lasted six months.   In 1891 the Senate sat a month.
In 1906 an important programme was put through in a
month.

In many other States the extra session has been more or less
frequently employed to meet exigencies more or less genuine.
The chance of such evasions was not unrecognized by the constitution-makers who were set on curtailing legislative activity.
Tennessee appears to have been the first State to see harm in
letting special sessions transact any business they please.   From
the start in 1796, regular sessions had there been biennial, and
doubtless the spirit of that system had been violated by miscellaneous business in special sessions.   Anyhow, the Constitution
of 1834 declared: "They shall enter on no legislative business

except that for which they were especially called together."
Illinois, which also began with biennials (1818), copied thirty
years later the Tennessee provision. Its inelasticity led to a
singular episode in 1911. While a special session was still
sitting, other matters than those specified in the call seemed to
require action, and the Governor called another special session
to convene at once, so that two special sessions were going on
simultaneously.

Nevada, in 1864, had anticipated such an embarrassment by
adding to the Tennessee provision power to consider "such other
legislative business as the Governor may call to the attention of
the Legislature while in session." Missouri in 1865 followed
substantially the Tennessee provision, ten years later adding that
of Nevada. Florida in 1868 forbade action at a special session
on anything other than the business set forth by the Governor
in his proclamation or later called to attention by him, save with
unanimous consent of both Houses; evidently this was found
too severe, for in 1885 permission to act on other business was
permitted upon a two-thirds vote. West Virginia in 1872 restricted special sessions to business stated in the proclamation,
and thereafter other States rapidly fell in line so that at this
writing there are thirty with restriction. The Governor con-
trols in all save Alabama, Arkansas, and Florida, where business other than that which he recommends can be taken up by
a two-thirds vote, and in Mississippi, where impeachments and
examination into the accounts of State officers are permissible
at "extraordinary sessions," and appropriation and revenue
bills at the "special sessions" that come regularly between the
quadrennial regular sessions. In the California case of People
v. Blanding, 63 Cal. 333, it was held that the Senate might ratify
appointments, though not mentioned in the Governor's recommendations. The court believed the prohibition extended
only to legislation and that this was not legislation.

In New York, where the Constitution says that at extraordinary sessions no subject shall be acted upon except such as
the Governor may recommend for consideration, the Legislature
chanced to be in extraordinary session when occasion appeared
for the impeachment of Governor Sulzer. Of course the Governor had not recommended his own trial. Might he be brought
to the bar? The argument was that inasmuch as the Assembly
had the right to impeach, it was inconceivable that the right

might not be exercised at any time. This view prevailed, the impeachment proceeded, and the Governor was convicted.

President Grant in his message at the opening of Congress in December, 1873, proposed a constitutional amendment providing that an extra session of Congress should consider nothing but what the Executive might submit. There is no record that Congress gave the proposal any attention. With the pressure of work that prevails to-day, such limitation would be most unfortunate.

In the States where the Constitutions do not define the nature of the extraordinary occasions upon which a Governor is to call a special session, the decision as to the need rests entirely with him. No external power can successfully question his motives. The courts have no jurisdiction.

In England the King may at any time by proclamation appoint Parliament to meet at the expiration of fourteen days from the date of the proclamation; and this without regard to the period to which Parliament may stand prorogued or adjourned. The President of the United States "may, on extraordinary occasions, convene both Houses, or either of them." There have been twenty or more of special sessions of Congress, and in addition about two-score brief special sessions of the Senate held usually for the confirmation of appointments at the beginning of a presidential term. Calling a special session of both Houses has so often brought bad luck to the President, particularly at the beginning of an administration, that it has come to be looked on with an almost superstitious aversion. The misfortunes of John Adams and of Madison made so deep an impression of this sort on political leaders that after Madison's two extra sessions, no other was called for a quarter of a century. Blaine recalled that in September, 1837, Van Buren began the ill-fortune of his administration by assembling Congress three months in advance of its regular session. John Tyler in turn never recovered from the dissensions and disasters of the extra session of May, 1841, — though it was precipitated upon him by a call issued by President Harrison. All these extra sessions except the one in Van Buren's administration had been held in May. No wonder, therefore, that ill luck came to be associated with that month. When the necessity of assembling Congress was forced upon Lincoln by the firing on Sumter, Seward warned him that in any event he must not have the session begin in May.[1] This reminded Mr. Bryce of the superstition against May marriages mentioned by John Knox apropos of the marriage of Mary Queen of Scots and Darnley.

LIMITING THE LIFE

WHEN railroad and other mercenary influences had begun to undermine public confidence in the Legislatures, New Jersey found a new application for the ingenious idea that the way to handle an evil is to lessen its opportunity. The shorter the session, the less harm it can do. In 1683 the Fundamental Constitutions of East New Jersey had directed that the Great Council should meet each April 20 and sit until the 20th of July unless the Governor and Council thought fit to continue the session longer. It was not this method of specific limitation that the New Jersey of 1844 chose, but another method to accomplish the same result, that of limiting the number of days for which the lawmakers could get full pay. So her new Constitution directed that for forty days they should get three dollars a day and after that a dollar and a. half. The device caught the fancy of New York, which two years later carried it farther by prescribing that at the end of a hundred days the wage of three dollars a day should stop altogether. Iowa in the same year copied the New Jersey plan more nearly, making the pay two dollars a day for fifty days, and after that one dollar. It is significant that these three States, the first to try the experiment from the salary side, all abandoned it, Iowa in 1857, New York in 1874, and New Jersey in 1875.

The more straightforward plan, that of imposing a definite time limit, was first resorted to by Louisiana, in 1845, the period being fixed at sixty days, and that is still the Louisiana practice. In 1850 Virginia and Kentucky followed the example. Virginia began with a ninety-day limit, which could be extended not more than thirty days on concurrence of three fifths of the members elected to each House. In 1864 the ninety days were changed to sixty, in 1870 back to ninety, in 1902 again to sixty, the privilege of extension continuing, but in 1902 it was provided that there should be no pay beyond the first sixty days. Kentucky made the limit sixty days, unless extended by a two-thirds vote of all the members elected to each House, an exception

[1] James G. Blaine, *Twenty Years in Congress*, II, 55.

that was dropped in 1890, when the length of the session was limited definitely to "sixty legislative days," exclusive of Sundays and legal holidays, with the declaration that "a legislative day shall be construed to mean a calendar day." In the following year Maryland and Indiana took up with the plan. Maryland said that after the next two sessions, the Legislature should sit only from the first Wednesday in January to the 10th of March, about 100 days. The Constitution of 1864, as if to emphasize disapproval of this, said: "The General Assembly shall continue its session so long as in its judgment the public interest may require." However, three years later a limitation of ninety days was imposed. Indiana made it sixty-one days — good measure for two months.

Since that time (1851) sixteen States have put a time limit on sessions and sixteen have put a time limit on salaries, all save three continuing the practice up to this writing. California after paying legislators for not more than sixty days of the sessions between 1879 and 1908, then by popular vote substituted a salary of $1000 with no limit on the total length of sessions. Colorado, beginning with a time limit of forty days, changed it in 1884 to ninety days, and then in 1910 abolished the limit, at the same time substituting a salary of $1000 for the biennial session in place of the seven dollars a day previously paid. Governor Ammons of that State said at the Governors' Conference of 1913: "We found that in actual practice a limitation was the most convenient way of jobbing legislation or defeating it." [1] Nebraska in 1920 substituted a salary without time limit for the provision that pay by the day should not be given for more than sixty days at any one session or one hundred days in the term.

On the other hand, in 1914 the voters of Wyoming by 16,966 for to 8,479 against, not a majority of the electors, rejected an amendment extending the length of the session to sixty days, and providing that no bill should be introduced after the first forty. In 1915 the voters of Texas decisively defeated an amendment that would have given their legislators a fixed salary and would have permitted regular sessions to continue until they had disposed of their business.

As it stands now there are twenty-one States with time limits, ranging from forty days in Wyoming to about five months in

[1] *Proceedings*, 277.

Connecticut (1912), sixty days being the favorite number, adopted by a dozen States. There are fourteen States with wage restrictions, from forty days in South Carolina and Oregon, to seventy-five days in Tennessee, ten preferring sixty days. Of these fourteen States, Missouri drops from five dollars to a dollar a day after the first seventy days; Oklahoma from six and Texas from five dollars a day to two dollars after sixty days. All told (Virginia having been counted in both the time limit and wage restriction groups) there are thirty-four States with and fourteen without some sort of provision directly or indirectly limiting the length of regular legislative sessions.

The most ridiculous of all limits has been that imposed by the Legislature of Ohio in 1896 when it passed a resolution for a Constitutional Convention and provided it should not sit more than ninety days.

Other countries have not all avoided the evils of limited sessions. The Swedish Riksdag may stay in session four months unless earlier dissolved by the King. Although the Norwegian Storthing is to stay in session as long as it thinks proper, that is not to be for more than two months without the permission of the King. In Japan the limit is three months, but the time may be extended by imperial order; in Chile four months, which the President may extend for fifty days. Argentina specifies the time, five months, and the President may extend. In Brazil, although the Constitution says the Congress is to continue in session four months, it may be prorogued or adjourned, and there is the further stipulation that the Congress alone shall have the right to decide respecting the extension or adjournment of its sessions.

Our Congress once escaped some degree of limitation only by a veto of the President. In 1836 it undertook to secure that the first session should always end on the second Monday of May unless the two Houses should otherwise provide. President Jackson held that according to the provisions of the Constitution the day of adjournment is not subject to legislative enactment, but is a matter to be decided by each Congress for itself. Though his view was attacked in the Senate by such authorities on the Constitution as Webster, Clay, Calhoun and Leigh, not enough votes could be mustered to overcome the veto.

Massachusetts had an equally narrow escape. The Convention of 1853 proposed giving the General Court power to fix the compensation of its own members, with the proviso that they should not be paid for more than a hundred days, but this fell with the rest of the revision when submitted to the people. To the Legislature of 1857 were presented petitions from about forty towns, signed by more than three thousand voters, asking an amendment to limit sessions to a hundred days. The Committee on Retrenchment and Reform thereupon advised an amendment like the Virginia provision, limiting the session to ninety days unless by vote of three fifths of the members elected to each House, it be extended not to exceed thirty days. This passed the Legislature of 1857. In the following year it passed the House, 138 to 26, but was defeated in the Senate, 15 to 19. As in the Senate only a majority was required, a change of three votes would have sent the measure to the people and very likely have inflicted on the State what most of her citizens who are experienced in public affairs would now call a misfortune.

It is an instructive commentary on human nature that the practical effect of limiting pay was to limit sessions, precisely as expected. Public spirit does not impel legislators to work after their wages stop. There may have been a few exceptions, but the only one coming to my notice — and that not in the case of a Legislature, but of a kindred body — was to the credit of the New York Constitutional Convention of 1894, which sat beyond the time for which the Legislature had provided compensation. This was the reverse of the spirit that about forty years earlier showed itself in discovery of a way to evade the constitutional purpose in the matter of the legislative provision then in force. At the end of the hundred days for which the members of the Legislature were paid, they adjourned, and the Governor called a special session to attend to important canal matters, whereupon the per diem came to life. Here was a loop-hole that needed plugging. New York did not stop it up, preferring in 1874 to get rid of the whole thing, but other States were more pertinacious and sought remedies in putting restrictions on special sessions. Nine of the States that have a time limit on regular sessions have one also on special sessions, five of them making it thirty days. Five that restrict pay at regular sessions also restrict it at special sessions. New Hampshire and Nebraska, with no time limit, restrict pay at special sessions, one to fifteen and the other to ten days, and Wisconsin forbids payment for special sessions. Idaho, discouraging long regular sessions by restricting pay to sixty days, and Texas by lessening it after sixty days, handle special sessions by a time limit. The intermediate sessions that Mississippi calls special, although they come regularly, are limited to thirty days unless the Governor extends them by proclamation, which must be for a specific length of time.

The Alabama Constitution of 1901 when providing for quadrennial sessions, said that after the first one, which might last sixty days, the Legislature should not "remain in session longer than fifty days." Nevertheless, regular sessions have in reality lasted more than one hundred days. The Constitution is ingeniously evaded by giving over to committee work the days in excess of fifty. Inasmuch as the framers of the Constitution did not think to specify that the pay of members (four dollars a day) should be only for the days of actual session, they pay themselves for the committee workdays, thus nullifying the intent of the provision.

It seems incredible that men should have expected from the curtailment of sessions any result other than that which has actually followed. Everywhere it has produced bad work, slovenly, slipshod, hurtful. Whatever theory one who has had no experience in a Legislature may evolve, as a practical matter it proves impossible for such a body in a brief time to organize, appoint committees, accustom its large proportion of new members to the routine of procedure, hold hearings and executive sessions of committees, report on one or two thousand propositions, give approved measures all their readings, reconcile the views of two branches — in brief, operate the necessarily ponderous machinery of legislation, and do it right in forty, fifty, sixty, or even a hundred days. Proofs by the score, testimony by the page, could be amassed, but it will here suffice to present only what may be necessary for illustration.

In 1912 the people of Arkansas, aggrieved by the length and expense of sessions and the character of the output, voted three to one for an initiated amendment limiting sessions to sixty days. On the face of it, the record of the 1913 Legislature seemed to show that the results desired had been accomplished. The cost of that Legislature was about $76,000 against $200,000 in 1911. In 140 days of 1911 were passed 502 acts, resolutions, and memorials, covering 1958 pages; in 60 days of 1913 were passed 368 such measures, covering 1560 pages. That, however, is not the whole story. As typical of what happened, we are told that two acts were passed relating to the erection of power dams and two to prevent the introduction of insect pests, in the latter case two different Boards being created to carry them out. After the Legislature adjourned, it was discovered that the general appropriation bill had not been passed by both Houses in the same form.[1] Extolling the limitation of sessions, Governor Warren T. McCray of Indiana, in the "Illinois Journal of Commerce" for August, 1923, ignored the implications of his own statement that of the ninety or more bills of a general nature passed by the latest Indiana Legislature, "fully three fourths were designed to correct existing laws which had proved defective in their operation in some minor particular."

Kansas pays its lawmakers for fifty days. In 1913 they sat forty-nine days or parts of days. Governor Hodges told the Governors' Conference later in the year that the Session Laws made a book of 594 pages, and contained 376 laws and resolutions. Excluding appropriation bills, thirty-six important new laws were enacted, the rest being local acts, amendments, or matters trivial in nature. Something like seven laws passed both Houses for each day. "It is hardly possible," said the Governor, "for a member to read seven enactments a day, and it is an impossibility for him to comprehend and understand them." After a quarter of a century of experience in New York with limiting sessions by paying members for only a hundred days, Governor Hoffman in his message of 1872 urging a Constitutional Convention, said: "The provision has had no good practical effect. It has not lessened the amount of legislation, it has simply caused the members to act with more haste." The clerk of the Arizona House of Representatives was quoted by the Massachusetts Joint Special Committee on Legislative Procedure, 1915, as saying: "In an experience with Legislatures in Colorado, Oklahoma, and Arizona, I have seen more vicious legislation passed during the rush of the closing day of a limited Legislature than during all the rest of the session." That Committee after a statistical analysis of the work of Legislatures with and without limited sessions, concluded it would be unwise

[1] D. Y. Thomas (Univ. of Ark.), "Direct Legislation in Arkansas," *Pol. Sc. Qy.*, March, 1914.

for Massachusetts to adopt any such change as would hamper "the calm deliberation and careful consideration so necessary to well-drafted legislation."

With equal sagacity the Committee further said: "Paradoxical as it may seem, most States have tried to cure the defect of poorly considered legislation by giving their Legislatures less time to consider matters." It might have pointed out other weaknesses of the device. It might have recalled what George B. Upton told the Massachusetts Convention of 1853, after he had served in the Legislature for seven years. He declared that if the Convention limited sessions to ninety or a hundred days, it would, in his judgment, give to the minority a greater power than was ever given to any body of men. "Under such circumstances, place me in the Legislature, with a strong minority, and I will defeat any project which is demanded by a majority of the people of this State. To avoid this, you must give to the majority an arbitrary power to stop all discussion and put it down, in order to bring your session to a close, and to pass the measures which ought to be passed." May it not be that Mr. Upton put his finger on what came to be a powerful help to the development of boss control in many American Legislatures? If there is time to do only part of the work, somebody must select what shall get the preference. A premium is put on dictation. The strong man thereby adds to his power because of artificial and abnormal conditions.

Another danger is that as the end of a brief session approaches, with much business remaining on which there is sure to be contest, the Legislature will send the inconspicuous bills to the Governor without due consideration, shirking its own responsibilities.

One of the few Western States not limiting sessions directly or indirectly is Wisconsin. The head of its Legislative Reference Department, Charles McCarthy, an acute observer of the processes of lawmaking, voiced his thankfulness: "In spite of cheap clamor concerning the time spent by the Legislature in session, this has been a great blessing to the State. With hundreds of laws to be provided, any one of which may be tested before the courts for years, it would indeed be foolish to fail to give reasonable time or intelligent care to these bills. It is a good investment in the end."[1] Yet Wisconsin is restless.

[1] *The Wisconsin Idea*, 206.

Attorney General W. C. Owen had occasion in 1915 to give an opinion to the effect that it is not competent for a Legislature to limit its legislative powers by a rule limiting the number of bills that may be introduced.

If Constitutions are to limit sessions, they ought also to forbid more business to come before the Legislature than can be well performed. Citizens ought to be fined for having grievances to be redressed. If they persist in asking justice, the best remedy would be to stop Legislatures from sitting at all.

Putting on a time limit is perhaps the most preposterous device men ever conceived for the remedy of political ills. No railroad, banking, or manufacturing corporation would be so silly as to try to improve an inefficient directorate by a vote compelling directors' meetings to adjourn after two hours or restricting such meetings to two months in the year. If the administration of justice became conspicuously defective, nobody would risk his reputation for sanity by advising that the courts should sit only from New Year's Day to Easter. A Legislature is in part a Board of Directors, conducting what has become a gigantic enterprise, involving the annual expenditure of many millions of dollars. It is in part what it always has been, a court for the redress of grievances, for protecting the weak against the strong, for dealing out the higher justice. If it is inefficient in matter of business, if it is inadequate in point of justice, is the wise remedy to be the curtailment of opportunity? No, every dictate of reason and common sense declares that precisely the opposite course should be pursued. In the ordinary affairs of life when we find work is not being thoroughly done, we demand that more time and thought and energy shall be put into the work. That is precisely what we should demand of men who undertake to legislate for us.

France has the right idea. There the National Assembly must remain in session at least five months out of twelve. The new Constitution of Egypt possibly goes too far in making it six. At the other extreme is the provision in the Netherlands that the regular annual session shall last at least twenty days, a provision of slight apparent value except in the way of preventing dissolution solely by reason of discontent with the result of an election. Wiser is the Belgian Constitution with its requirement that the Chambers must meet every year for at least forty days. As a matter of fact they usually sit on three times as many days, but that does not affect the theory of a fixed minimum instead of a fixed maximum. The fixed minimum recognizes the demands of justice and progress. Are they not the more important considerations?

The cry for short sessions is nothing new. At the opening of the Parliament in 1601, the Speaker reported an intimation from the Queen through the Lord Keeper that the Parliament should be short. "And therefore she willed that the members of this House should not spend the time in frivolous, vain, and unnecessary motions and arguments, but only should bend all their best endeavours and travails wholly to the devising and making of the most necessary and wholesome laws for the good and benefit of the commonwealth and the realm."

Governor William Gaston, of Massachusetts, said in his inaugural message, January 7, 1875: "I find upon examination of the messages of my predecessors, that short sessions have long been the subjects of Executive commendation. Upon examination of the length of sessions, I find that their advice has not produced flattering results. Although somewhat discouraged by this circumstance, I shall venture to follow in the line of their example and give similar advice." It has become the well-nigh universal custom for Governors, presiding officers of Senate and House, and particularly the newspapers, to give like counsel. Apparently nobody ever stops to wonder if it be sound. In that selfsame message Governor Gaston said, "The legislation of the State is becoming too voluminous and complex." A thousand others have made the same comment, in every corner of the land, seemingly without a moment's thought of its true significance. Legislation is voluminous and complex, not because legislators want it so, but because of community demands. Society itself has become vastly more complex, and its interests have become vastly more voluminous, than was the case a century ago. The industrial revolution that began with the application of steam to the operation of machinery and locomotives, and received fresh impetus from the varied applications of electricity, has been accompanied by a social revolution, one phase of which is an unprecedented extension of the functions of government. It is this that has put the great strain on our methods of lawmaking, or rather of governing, for a great part of the new work imposed on Legislatures is not genuine lawmaking at all, but the making of rules and regulations for the administration of coöperative undertakings.

Before the nature of the new troubles and difficulties was apparent, such a remedy as the shortening of sessions did not appear so absurd as it appears to-day. It was not at first understood that the increase in the number of enactments was no sporadic result of a diseased public mind, but was the natural response to new social conditions. It ought to be now clear to everybody that the growth of the work of the State is the manifestation of a common purpose, earnest, deliberate, and likely to have a material degree of continuity and permanence. The outlook indicates still greater growth of this work. The State bids fair to take over more and yet more of the tasks hitherto left to individuals, and to enter upon more and more tasks hitherto not attempted at all.

This means more and more work for Legislatures or for some other like instrumentalities of government. Evidently a new need must somehow be met.

CHAPTER VIII

SOME POSSIBLE RELIEFS

To meet modern conditions, if the customary allotment of time cannot be more effectively used, there should be increase of time or lessening of work or both.

As a matter of fact various improvements in methods and processes that have been discussed in "Legislative Procedure" would let more work be done in the same time. Here may be added some consideration of benefits of the same sort that would come from rearrangement.

The time schedule of the Federal Government ought to be reconstructed. The Fourth of March as Inauguration Day should be abandoned, but if not, a new Congress should meet on that day. With each Congress first convened March 4, the two-year term could have three regular sessions that would in my judgment conduce to more and better work, with much less hardship to members. As things go now, there are two regular sessions, one known as "the long session," which before the World War had been averaging seven months in length, and the other known as "the short session," of three months. Partly by reason of the growth of work, partly from unusual causes, special sessions have of late been the rule. Of the seven Congresses beginning with 1909, only one was without a special session, but it is to be hoped that the exceptional needs will not continue.

If the normal amount of business should now call for a month more of work in each term than the average for the period 1889–1909, then Congress would meet the situation by working twelve months out of every twenty-four. This it could most conveniently arrange by using for work the first six months of each calendar year. Several factors combine to make such a programme desirable. By reason of the campaign and election, autumn sittings are open to objection every other year. In the intervening years the session might begin November 1 (as was contemplated in part by the bill that President Jackson vetoed in 1836 because it also fixed a date for adjournment), and this would have the decided advantage of permitting adjournment earlier in the following summer — an advantage particularly desirable every four years in view of the custom of holding the national conventions in June. Perhaps, though, the programme would balance better if the winter session began each year on the same date. With no meeting in November, it would not be wise to try to meet in December. The inevitable recess from before Christmas to after New Year's has shown December convening hardly worth while. If the session should open in January, the member who had settled his family in apartment or residence would find it much more convenient to have their abiding place continuous each year until summer than to alternate between long and short tarryings. By reason of the climatic conditions of Washington in mid-summer, adjournment ought to come not later than July 1.

The ideal schedule, then, if March 4 must continue as Inauguration Day, would be to have the first regular session of a term run from March 4 to July 1 or earlier; the second from January 1 to July 1 or earlier; the third from January 1 to March 3; and so on.

The Legislatures, without increasing the total of their days of sitting, could probably accomplish more and do their work better by resort to a practice familiar in Massachusetts years ago, a practice abandoned just before railroads came to remove the chief objections it had developed, those connected with travel. There were two sessions of the General Court each year, one in May seldom exceeding a fortnight, ending with adjournment to the following winter. In the Convention of 1820 much debate arose over the proposal to change to an annual session, beginning with the first Wednesday in January, and in the end an amendment to that effect was submitted by the Convention. It was not at the time adopted, but a like amendment prevailed eleven years later.

By the debate in 1820 it appears that a great part of the business of the May session was of a private nature. "It is now almost invariably the practice," said Leverett Saltonstall of Salem, "it is indeed an established rule, to pass an order of notice in all these cases; with a very few exceptions they are made returnable at the next session of the General Court. No act would pass unless an order of notice had been issued, nor except in especial cases, unless the order is returnable at a subsequent session." He would appeal to gentlemen of experience in the Legislature, to the members of the standing committees, if many of these projects do not expire between the sessions. Nothing more is heard of them. The passions have had time to cool. "What will be the effect of the proposed alteration in business of this kind? If there is but one session a year, orders will be returnable at the same session at which they are presented. The interest of the parties will be kept alive. The passions will continue excited, their ardor will have no time to abate. As to public laws the same reason will apply and with at least equal force. Now most important subjects are referred from one session to the next. It is seldom that an important public law passes at the same session in which it is proposed. It is postponed to the close of the session, and then, almost of course, it is referred to the next. In the meantime it is published, and at the next session public opinion is found against it, or the plan is abandoned by its author. But if this alteration takes place what will be the course? Will the new projects for improvement be referred? Who that is acquainted with the benevolent ardor of our reformers can believe that? Great attempts will be made to carry them through at the single session, and laws will thus often pass, which otherwise would not." [1]

Procedure, meant to accomplish somewhat the same benefit that Mr. Saltonstall found in the old Massachusetts practice, has recently been adopted in California. The Legislature meets every second year on the first Monday after the first day of January, and continues in session for a period not exceeding thirty days. A recess is then taken for not less than thirty days. In the first part of the session any member of either House may introduce as many bills as he pleases. On reassembling after the recess, however, no member can introduce more than two bills, and to introduce any he must have the consent of three fourths of the members. When Lieutenant-Governor Wallace was asked in the Governors' Conference of 1913 what had been the result, he replied that as the plan had been tried but once, he could not give much helpful information. "Most of our members would say that it is a failure, that it is a waste of time and quite ineffective. And there are those who would say it is very valuable, because it has aroused the interest

[1] *Mass. Convention of 1820*, 87 *et seq*

of the people and because it has given them an opportunity, after the introduction of a bill, to consider that bill. My impression is, it is like a great many other things — it has its very good side, and not quite as good as the father of the measure expected it would have when he had it introduced. . . . It has this weakness, that at the end of the first section of the session, when it comes to the last day or two, members will introduce bills that have no particular meaning, that have to be amended and remodeled at the next session. . . . I think it is a good thing, but a long ways from perfect." [1]

In March of 1917 Arthur P. Will, Chief of the Legislative Counsel Bureau of California, wrote to me: "Of late considerable doubt has developed regarding the advantage of the plan and there are proposals to return to the old style." From another source I am informed that one objection arises from geographical conditions peculiar to California. The members from the Southern part of the State, it is said, now the more numerous, go home for the recess, consult in regard to the more important measures proposed, reach agreements, and on their return present a united front, dominating the situation.

In spite of such uncertain testimony, the conditions in Massachusetts seemed in 1918 to warrant putting the split session within the power of its General Court. The Constitution forbade adjournment for more than two days at a time. The gradual advancement of the time limit on the introduction of business had reached a point where if the Houses had the power and saw fit, it could be arranged to have nothing but the routine of organization and the reference of bills in the first week or two, and then a recess during which the committees might work. At the end of the recess enough reports would be ready for steady occupation in the two chambers. Men on the minor committees would have most of the recess free for their own concerns; the major committees could work steadily, without the waste of time produced by the uncertainty as to the length of a daily sitting of the House. It proved possible to persuade the Convention itself to test the principle. After sitting on ten days in June, it adjourned on the 26th until July 10th and then adjourned for another week, committees sitting in the intervals. After this there proved to be enough work ready for the usual course of consideration. The success of the

[1] *Proceedings of the Governors' Conference of 1913*, 307, 308.

experiment led the Convention to advise an amendment of the Constitution authorizing the General Court within the first sixty days of a session to take a recess or recesses amounting to not more than thirty days. This was adopted by the people. As yet the General Court has not taken advantage of the new power, for that body is most reluctant to change its habits, but doubtless the need of time-saving processes will presently compel it to rearrange its accustomed schedule.

It is interesting and significant to find the Constitution of Czecho-Slovakia calling for two regular sessions each year, spring and fall; and that of Russia requiring the Central Executive Committee, which seems to be the chief lawmaking body, to meet three times a year.

LONGER SESSIONS

RATHER than reform their processes, the chief legislative assemblies of the world have followed the line of least resistance by lengthening their sessions. The first ten Congresses averaged to be in session 283 days (including Sundays and holidays); the second ten, 313; the third, 329; the fourth (excluding long recesses), 339; the fifth, 344; the sixth (to March 3, 1909), 331. The next seven Congresses averaged 570 days — nine and a half months of each year (for a Congress covers two years).

Parliament has kept pace with Congress. Before the World War it was the English practice for the Houses to come together early in February, and usually sit until some time in August, occasionally into September. In the nine years 1902–10 the House of Commons averaged to sit on 141 days (Sundays omitted), but as it averaged to work eight hours and a half a day, where the lower branch of Congress averaged only about five and a half, the two bodies were not very far apart in the actual time of sitting. In this period the frequency of autumn sessions began to make the strain serious. In the nine years before the outbreak of the War, there were only two without autumn sessions. Mr. Balfour strongly deplored this when testifying in the spring of 1914 before the Select Committee on House of Commons Procedure. That the House had been compelled to sit such a large proportion of each year in so many recent years, he thought really a very serious blot on the Parliamentary system. He was convinced that Mr. Gladstone was right in saying that the utility of the House was greatly impaired if it was compelled to sit during too many months. "I do not believe," Mr. Balfour declared, "the Departments can do their business if the House is going to sit ten months in the year. I do not believe the Ministers can give the necessary time for thinking out great schemes of social reform, whatever they are, and I do not believe the members can give that [desirable?] interest or zest in debates which are continued for an undue period." Lord George Hamilton, publishing his "Parliamentary Reminiscences and Reflections" two years later, concluded the last chapter with a list of the indispensable reforms in his judgment "necessary for the preservation and continuance of our national life and of our Empire." At the very head he placed: "First, we must reform the existing procedure of the House of Commons and curtail the duration of the session. At present men of character and ability and accustomed to a busy life decline to waste ten months of the calendar year in an atmosphere of self-advertising talk and lobby intrigue."

Before the War the French Assembly was going beyond both Parliament and Congress in amount of work, averaging to sit two hundred days.

There are those who think that the enormous increase in the scope of our Federal activities will prevent Congress from ever returning to the average of sittings customary before the War. They say it will have to recognize that in order to come nearer doing its work properly, it must sit continuously, except for reasonable and regular vacations. This will not be a novelty. During the Revolutionary War it was both customary and necessary for Congress to sit all the time, and after the war until the formation of the Union the practice continued, except for short intervals when the government was left in the hands of committees of the States. To be sure, reasons then prevailed that do not now exist. Congress was the executive as well as the legislative. From motives of economy the States generally kept their representation down to the minimum, and the indifference about attending, together with the provision that nine States must approve action, made delay constant and the work could not be finished promptly. At times the representation was so scanty that one eighth of the members present could block the most important measures. Of course the situation is now quite otherwise, but it may be worth remembering that continuous session of our chief lawmaking body would not be unprecedented.

It would, however, in some respects be unfortunate. Congressmen ought to have personal touch with their constituencies as often as practicable, both to inform and to be informed. Furthermore, the conscientious member finds that the work at Washington makes no small drain upon his vitality. Time and opportunity for recreation are limited. Not a few of the members find it necessary to live in cramped quarters devoid of accustomed home comforts. The summer season is trying. Most of the men are no longer young, and to carry the load of responsibility through nearly all the year over-taxes their strength. Their work would be the better and their lives the longer if their noses were not kept on the grindstone more than half the year.

For the State Legislatures the conditions are different. With the range of their duties, the variety of their problems, the volume of their work, far more extensive than in the case of Congress, is it wholly preposterous that they should sit continuously? We are quite accustomed to see the legislative branches of our city governments sit at regular intervals through the year. Only accidental considerations kept our State legislative bodies from developing the same practice. In colonial times and indeed up to the development of our railroad systems, the slowness of travel made any but periodical gatherings out of the question. The obstacle has disappeared in our more populous States. If it were thought desirable, it would be perfectly feasible now in many of the States to have Legislatures meet with the regularity and frequency of a City Council. Augustus decreed that the Roman Senate should assemble twice every month for the dispatch of business, and required that at least four hundred members should be present at every sitting. In the sultry and pestilential months of September and October he released them from this fatiguing service, except only a smaller number chosen by lot, who were constrained still to meet on the stated days.[1] Much the same system was urged on the New York Constitutional Convention of 1915 by Merton E. Lewis, First Deputy Attorney General. He wanted the Legislature to meet in the first week of every month in the year except July and August. He argued that more men would

---

[1] Charles Merivale, *History of the Romans under the Empire*, iii, 394.

find it possible to give up a definite week in every month than can be found to give time for a continuous service of four or five or more months, broken only by hasty and unsatisfactory visits home at week-ends. There would be no closing days of the session with its congestion, as the unfinished business of one month would go over to the next month. There would be no thirty-day period during which the Governor would have to pass upon from five hundred to a thousand bills. There would be greater deliberation if provision were made that no bill could be acted upon in the month of its introduction except in an emergency pointed out by message from the Governor. That would give the members three weeks to consider the calendar of the next month.

Dudley S. A. Cosby, writing in the "Westminster Review" for October, 1905, of the situation in England, declared it might be said without exaggeration that it was an absolute impossibility for any Government to carry out a quarter of the legislation necessary, in the time at the disposal of the House. He urged sessions throughout the year, with Saturdays to Mondays free, and suitably distributed holidays.

PRESSURE IN THE CLOSING DAYS

To get rid of the congestion in the closing days of the session would be a most important gain. To the pernicious effect of that congestion, perhaps more than to any other one cause, is due the inferior quality of our legislation. After reading the story of what takes place as our Legislatures draw to an end, the marvel is that the statutory product is not far worse. The tale was told by four Governors at the Conference of 1913. Governor Hodges described the Kansas session of that year. "In the closing days, as in all Legislatures," he said, "there was lawmaking in hot haste, bills were rushed through under omnibus roll-calls, and the result was a lot of more or less crude and ill-digested laws, some of which are puzzles for even learned jurists to interpret with anything like satisfaction to themselves or to the public." He went on to say that notwithstanding the fact that his executive clerk and the Attorney General did their best to scrutinize all bills, two chapters duplicated two others; one chapter of old law was repealed three times; a new chapter was immediately amended by the succeeding chapter; an old chapter repealed by a new one was amended and repealed by another. A bill came to him containing a negative reversing its purpose. Two bills were exact duplicates. A number of bills passed both Houses without any enacting clauses — absolutely necessary to their validity as laws. All told he had to return fifteen bills for correction, and in the Sessions Laws will be found a large number of resolutions authorizing corrections in acts.

Governor Stewart of Montana, where sessions are limited to sixty days, said the worst thing they had to contend with in his State was "the tendency of the two Houses to dilly-dally along during the early part of the session." On the last day of the preceding session 125 bills came to him, and he had something like 175 or 200 when the Legislature adjourned.

Ex-Governor Gilchrist of Florida, spoke to like effect: "I dare say it has been the experience of every gentleman on the floor who has served in a Legislature where the Legislature sat for sixty days, that for the first forty days of the session there is very little work done. They pass about thirty or forty per cent of the bills, and they dump them all in during the last ten or twelve days of the session. In Florida, two or three hundred bills go to the Governor during the last four days of a sixty-day session." [1]

That the evil is not confined to States with limited sessions, was shown by the testimony of Governor Dunne of Illinois. "Three fourths of all the legislation that was passed at this last session by the Illinois Legislature," he said, "was passed within the last ten days of the Legislature, and I will state to you gentlemen, upon my word, that when the bills were engrossed and handed to the Governor, after they had been submitted to the Attorney General to pass upon their constitutionality, I was compelled to pass upon nearly two hundred bills of vital importance to the State of Illinois, within five days." [2] Since then conditions have become worse yet. Of the 361 bills passing both Houses in 1921, final passage was given to 315 in the last seventy-two hours.

In the first eight weeks of the eleven through which the New Jersey Legislature of 1923 sat, 36 bills were presented to the Governor; in the next three, 217. An examination of the work of the General Assembly of Iowa shows it has been customary

[1] *Proceedings*, 267.   [2] *Ibid.*, 271.

in that State to pass in the last ten days of the session more than two thirds of all the bills enacted.   Indiana is even more blameworthy, if the record of the session of 1917 was not exceptional.   According to John A. Lapp[1] one hundred and fifty laws were dumped on the desk of the Governor in the last two days, less than fifty having been previously sent to him. Says Mr. Lapp: "The last night of the session members could be found enrolling their own bills in any part of the capitol in order to get them signed by the presiding officer before adjournment.   What a splendid chance to slip jokers into bills!   What a splendid opportunity for the clever gentlemen who knew exactly what they wanted!   In this confusion many good laws came through in such shape as to render them invalid."   Mr. Lapp's judgment is that it is utterly impossible to do the work in sixty-one days.

A report drawn by Simon Sterne, for the special committee of the New York Board of Trade and Transportation on Constitutional Amendments, dated May 31, 1894, castigated deservedly what was going on in New York.   "Toward the end of the session bills then introduced are frequently not printed; they are acted upon by committees, if at all, under great pressure to finish their work before the end of the session.   They are frequently not placed in the hands of any standing committee, but are read from the clerk's desk 'by title,' and at once put upon their passage, and when the vote is taken it is generally taken in ignorance of the scope and purport of the measure. In these last days of the session votes are generally bargained away for counter votes from fellow-members by what is known as log-rolling.   We can make clear to our minds the monstrous character of this proceeding if we would suppose a court of justice, on finding its calendar encumbered with causes which cannot be tried before the summer vacation, dispensing with the taking of the testimony of witnesses and argument of counsel, and deciding such cases upon the pleadings alone.   The miscarriage and travesty of justice which would result from such a course partakes of the same nature, if we would but see it, of the mischief which is annually enacted at Albany, and at most, if not at all, other capitals of the country, in the corrupt and slipshod method of grinding out laws toward the end of a legislative session."

[1] Quoted by Ogg and Ray, *Int. to Am. Govt.*, 599.

It is true that this preposterous state of things is general, but it is not universal. The Massachusetts Legislature, at any rate, is not guilty of such enormities. No matter what the desire of its members to get through and go home, the ordinary forms of committee reference, hearing, and report are observed to the end. If there is suspension of the rule calling for reading on separate days, it is done with due regard to the rights of minorities and with all the care for thorough work that could reasonably be expected. In brief, cause for serious complaint does not in fact exist. There can be no question, however, that reform is sadly needed in most of the States, and in some respects there is chance for gain even in the best of our Legislatures.

Governor Ammons of Colorado writes me that his only suggestion for remedy is to compel the disposition of all bills before the fixing of the final date of adjournment. He says the limit on the length of sessions was removed in his State because of the fact that the Legislature did very little work at the beginning of the session, and left a great deal undone or passed legislation in bad shape during the rush at the close of the session. The final days were also used to defeat legislation or, as was often the case, to change laws to an undesirable form. "The constitutional amendment said nothing about finishing business before the day of adjournment was fixed, and so each General Assembly has fixed a day with a good deal the same result as that which attended the old system."

But why fix a day for adjournment? In the Legislature with which I am familiar, that of Massachusetts, it is not deemed necessary. The only approach to it is the custom under which the presiding officers of the two branches, when they find the work drawing to a close, see that a rule is passed making the morning and the afternoon each a legislative day, letting bills get two readings within twenty-four hours. So little remains to be done, that this exposes members to no danger of surprise. It would not be accurate to say there is no hurry whatever in the closing hours, but up to the last moment nothing is done to stifle debate.

The trouble many other Legislatures seem to invite, is in Massachusetts now almost wholly avoided by a precaution put into effect before the session is half through. Committees are by rule required to report before a specified date on all matters that have been referred to them, and as no new business can be introduced after the first few days of the session except with an approval from the Committee on Rules that is not easily secured, or by a four-fifths vote rejecting an adverse decision of that Committee, very little new work is added. Figures from the Massachusetts Blue Books give a striking example of what can be done in the way of reform, without blare of trumpets, without exaggerated abuse, solely by the development of a healthy public spirit manifesting itself in a system of rules gradually perfected by thoughtful legislators working modestly, almost silently, for the common welfare. Here are the totals of the measures acted upon by the Governor on the last day of the session (none being thereafter signed in Massachusetts):

YEAR	ACTS	RESOLVES	TOTAL
1855	71*	9	80
1875	28	16	44
1895	39	9	48
1915	7	1	8

* Including one veto

Of course the maintenance of such a system as has produced this result is largely a matter of custom. If a Legislature is not pervaded by a spirit of respect for its own rules, its case is hopeless. All to be said is that if a Legislature really wants to lessen the crush of work at the end of a session, by spreading discussion on the floor over the later weeks, it can be done, just as in at least one State it actually is done, and has been done for years.

Some of the States have tried to meet the situation by constitutional provisions. Thus Indiana said in 1851: "No bill shall be presented to the Governor within two days next previous to the final adjournment of the General Assembly." In practice, however, bills are passed up to the last day, though only such as the Governor is willing to consider; the provision has, therefore, simply the effect of giving him an absolute veto on all bills passed in the last two days of the session.[1] Minnesota's Constitution reads: "No bill shall be passed by either House of the Legislature upon the day prescribed for the adjournment of the two Houses. But this section shall not be so construed as to preclude the enrollment of a bill, or the signa-

[1] Paul S. Reinsch, *American Legislatures*, 140.

ture and passage from one House to the other, or the reports thereon from a committee, or its transmission to the executive for his signature." The only effect is to shorten the session by one day for legislative purposes; the last day is devoted to corrections of the Journal, and to the passage of resolutions and memorials. Texas in 1876 said: "No bill shall be passed which has not been presented and referred to and reported from a committee at least three days before the final adjournment of the Legislature." Louisiana in 1879 said no appropriation of money should be made in the last five days of the session. Mississippi in 1890 added revenue bills to a like prohibition. Alabama in 1901 confined the injunction to revenue bills, and so did Oklahoma in 1907.

In so far as such provisions are meant to lessen the crush at the end of the session, they are more or less futile. Their only practical advantage lies in giving the Governor a little more time for considering whether to sign or veto. The topic is not one that ought to be handled by organic law. The evils can be and ought to be met by legislative rules. Looking in this direction is the joint rule of the Pennsylvania Legislature which forbids the passage of any bill, resolution, or order to which the Governor's signature is required, on the day of adjournment. That, however, is not the right way to get at the trouble. The real solution lies in rules such as those of Massachusetts securing the early introduction of business and prompt reports from committees. If a Legislature will live up to the spirit of such a programme, as the Massachusetts Legislature does, and if the preposterous idea of limiting the length of sessions is abandoned, what is now one of the greatest obstacles to good lawmaking by the States, will become insignificant.

Congress has always shown the need of protection. It would be possible to bring proofs from the story of the closing hours of every term. Let one description suffice, that of the last day of the very first Congress of the United States, which may not only portray the evil, but also convince that it is not the product of a degenerate age. Senator Maclay with his usual vivacity and acerbity tells us what took place on the 3d of March, 1791. "As well might I write the rambles of Harlequin Ranger or the vagaries of a pantomime," his Journal reads, "as to attempt to minute the business of this morning. What with the exits and the entrances of our Otis [the Secretary of the Senate], the announcings, the advancings, speechings, drawings, and with-drawings of Buckley [Beckley (?) Clerk of the House] and Lear [Secretary of the President], and the comings and goings of our committee of enrollment, etc., and the consequent running of door-keepers, opening and slamming of doors, the House seemed in a continual hurricane. Speaking would have been idle, for nobody would or could hear. Had all the business been pre-viously digested, matter or form would have been of little consequence. This, however, was not the case. It was patch-ing, piecing, altering, and amending, and even originating new business. It was, however, only for Ellsworth, King, or some of Hamilton's people to rise, and the thing was generally done."

This was one of Maclay's slurs on the "court" faction. Hav-ing therewith again voiced his dislike of the President's friends, he went on: "But they had overshot themselves; for, owing to little unforeseen impediments, there was no possibility of working all through, and there was to be a great dinner which must be absolutely attended to. Terrible, indeed, but no alter-native — the House must meet at six o'clock.

"In the evening by candle-light. When I saw the merry mood in which the Senate assembled, I was ready to laugh. When I considered the occasion, I was almost disposed to give way to a very different emotion. I did, however, neither the one nor the other; and, feeling myself as little importance as I had ever done in my life, I took pen and paper and determined, if possible, to keep pace with the hurry of business as it passed."

Then he notes some of the measures. On one he would have been glad to speak, but — "To speak in the present up-roar was like letting off a pop-gun in a thunderstorm." After a time he gave up his notations, for "there was now such con-fusion with Otis, Beckley, Lear, our committee of enrollment, etc., that I confess I lost their arrangement. Indeed, I am apt to believe if they had any they lost it themselves. They all agreed at last that the business was done. The President left the chair, and the members scampered down stairs."

In the 4th Congress there was a proposal in the Senate for a rule forbidding the origination of a law of general importance within the last ten days of the session, and declaring that the Senate would act on none received from the House within that time, but the proposal was not adopted.[1] The 17th Congress

[1] *Annals of Congress*, 2d Sess., 4th Cong., 576, 1577.

added to the joint rules: "No bill that shall have passed one House shall be sent for concurrence to the other on either of the three last days of the session"; and, "No bill or resolution that shall have passed the House of Representatives and the Senate shall be presented to the President of the United States, for his approbation, on the last day of the session." At almost every session thereafter, while the joint rules were in force, one or both of these rules would be suspended in favor of certain or all of the bills of the session. Thus, of 142 bills passed in 1832–33, 90 were signed under suspension of the rules. At first it was held that these rules could be suspended whenever a majority wished, without a day's notice; but in 1836 it was held that it required unanimous consent to consider a resolution from the House suspending the rules, on the same day that it was received. In 1852 the rules were amended so as to provide that such a motion should "always be in order, be immediately considered and decided without debate." In the 44th Congress the Senate held that there were no joint rules, the House not having adopted the resolution sent to it by the Senate readopting those of the previous session. "Thus, since 1876, there has not been even the restraint of the 16th and 17th joint rules on the pushing of important business to the end of the session." [1]

The difficulty is not one peculiar to the United States, nor is it modern. As far back as 1668 the House of Lords had occasion to make a standing order that in the case of bills coming up near the time of adjournment, no argument (such as shortness of time) should thereafter be used to precipitate their passing, but that due consideration should be had, according to the course of Parliament. It has been found necessary to limit the reception of bills from the Commons to a period of the session when there is time enough to consider them.[2]

UNFINISHED BUSINESS

MUCH of the trouble is due to the effect of the session's end upon pending bills.

Bacon, in his Abridgment (title "Court of Parliament" F.), says, "the diversity between a prorogation and an adjournment or continuance of the Parliament is, that by the prorogation

---

[1] Clara H. Kerr, *Origin and Development of the U.S. Senate*, 51, 52.
[2] H. Cox, *Institutions of the English Government*, 168.

in open court there is a session, and then such bills as passed in either House, or by both Houses, and had no royal assent to them, must, at the next assembly, begin again . . . but if it be only adjourned or continued, all things continue in the same state they were in before the adjournment or continuance." An English government having business it cannot finish in the course of the regular session, and does not want to abandon, will sometimes resort to an adjournment instead of a prorogation. The need of such an awkward device is unfortunate. Some simpler way ought to be found to prevent the waste of time and energy that takes place under the present system. Every year the end of the session comes without action on measures to which Ministers and House have given much effort, and the work has to begin over again and be largely repeated at the next session. Numerous attempts have been made to remedy the evil. When in 1890 a majority report advised the House to carry unfinished business from one session to the next, Mr. Gladstone, then leading the Opposition, showed that like proposals had been under consideration by the House for forty years, and in every instance, in every shape, had been universally condemned. Gladstone's formidable opposition prevailed, no attempt being made to frame a Standing Order.

The matter was discussed before the Select Committee on House of Commons Procedure that reported in 1914. Asquith said he had always been in favor of carrying things over, but recognized it was an opinion shared by hardly any of the great Parliamentarians of his time. He recalled that not only Gladstone but also Sir William Harcourt strongly opposed the idea. J. Ramsay MacDonald said he would be quite willing to let a bill be carried over at the end of the Committee stage, but not before. Sir Courtenay Ilbert attached no great importance to the proposal, because often in the course of discussion of a bill it is found that it ought to be very much re-cast, and its friends would be much hampered if they should be tied down in the succeeding session to the bill introduced in the session before. So he thought no great amount of time would be saved by carrying over. The Draft Report recommended by the Chairman and supported by three members of the Select Committee would have provided for a day toward the end of a session when the House should decide what if any bills that had passed through Committee or reached a later stage, should be carried over to the next session. Upon motion therein put without debate, a bill as carried over should maintain its position.

Michael MacDonagh says in "The Pageant of Parliament" (II, 225) that the proposal to carry over uncompleted bills has always been consistently rejected by the House of Commons on the ground principally that the power of the Government would be greatly strengthened by any system that would facilitate the rapid progress of business, which is regarded as a thing not at all to be desired.

Some relief has been applied in the matter of private bills, such as those relating to railway construction or municipal utilities. They are treated by a semi-judicial process highly expensive to both sides, and it would be absurdly wasteful to require a repetition of this because the work had not been finished by the end of a session. So, usually in the few cases when the business is not completed, a special order provides that the parliamentary steps already taken shall be taken again formally at the opening of the next session, letting the affair proceed from the point it had reached.

The French Senate remains indefinitely in possession of all matters not completed, the theory being that as it is renewed by thirds, it is continuous. In the lower branch a measure is not dropped at the end of a session, but survives during the continuance of the Chamber. Only upon complete renewal of the Chamber is the slate wiped clean.

In this country constitution-makers have not always discriminated with precision in the use of the words "adjourn" and "prorogue." Jefferson gave it correctly in his Manual, following the English definition, and the courts have held "adjournment" equivalent to "postponement," but the implications of "adjournment" are not always meant when the word is used in provisions about legislative sessions. However, the principle is observed, and in nearly all our lawmaking bodies everything dies with the end of the session. Soon after the Federal Constitution was put into effect, Congress decided on that rule, but the inconveniences of its application to the two sessions of a single Congress led in 1818 to provision that business should go over from one session of the House to the next, though not beyond the life of the Congress. Uncertainty whether this applied to House bills that had not been acted on in the Senate brought in 1848 a joint rule meeting the case. It remained to provide for committee work, and in 1860 the rule was amended so that all business before committees should be resumed at the next session of the same Congress.

The seriousness of the situation may be gathered from the fact that of 900 bills reported to the House in the 65th Congress, 435 were still pending at adjournment. Though the work was cleaned up somewhat better in the 66th, yet of 1095 bills reported to the House, 316 failed to get action before the end of the term.

The 67th House was widely criticized by the uninformed on the score of general inefficiency, yet at any rate mathematically it excelled its predecessors with 1450 committee reports, and adjourned with only 280 reported bills pending, but to accomplish this result required four sessions, covering 624 calendar days out of 730, and even at that one fifth of the work, measured by number of bills, was unfinished.

Georgia, with biennial elections and annual sessions, like Congress continues unfinished business from the first session of a term to the second, giving it there the same place in the calendar that it held at the end of the first session.[1]

Indiana with biennial sessions provides by statute that the unfinished business of any session goes into the calendar of the next in the same order in which it stood at the termination of the previous session; and may be taken up and disposed of in the same manner in which it might have been disposed of at the previous session, subject to such change in rules of procedure as either House may make.[2] The latest "Rules" at hand show no reference to the subject.

There may be other States having like provision, but it is not common. Yet with the steady growth in the pressure of business, more attention is likely to be paid to the practice. Clearly there is now great waste of effort in going over the same ground session after session. To be sure, there are advantages in the way of preventing bad legislation, but whoever does not assume that all laws anybody else wants are inevitably unwise, must admit that some desirable laws get unnecessary labor to a deplorable degree before at last they have run the long gantlet. Would any great harm follow if the approval of House or Senate stood through following sessions unless reversed in the same

[1] *Park's Annotated Code (1914)*, sec. 349.
[2] *Burns' Annotated Indiana Statutes*, sec. 755-7.

branch by positive action? Or why not let a favorable committee report survive unless a subsequent House should see fit to recommit the matter? This would not be permitted to lessen the time spent on controverted questions of importance, but it might get out of the way more quickly some of the minor matters that now waste much time in the mere moving of the machinery.

Congress is looking toward more continuity of action. Hope that some day it may achieve real reform came with the preparation of a tariff bill by the Ways and Means Committee of the 54th Congress, and its presentation on the first day of the 55th, and also the introduction of the General Deficiency Bill, which had failed in the 54th because of a Senate amendment. Another straw was thought to be the law enacted by the 53rd Congress, providing that the Speaker of one Congress should appoint a Committee on Accounts from the members elected to the next Congress, to serve during the interval before the meeting of the new House. Yet few if any important steps toward the desirable end have since been taken. The reform drags.

Technical difficulties make it awkward to correct the situation. The courts are disposed to limit strictly the powers of a legislative body to the duration of its life. For example, in Cliff v. Parsons, 90 Iowa 665 (1894), when the Secretary of a Senate was displaced and he contended that under Sec. 13 of the Code his term was to continue during the session at which he had been elected, the Court, holding that the statute abridged the constitutional powers of the Senate to choose its own officers in such manner and for such time as it might please, pointed out that no General Assembly has any power to control the right of either House of any subsequent General Assembly in this respect. It has long been familiar law that, as was held in Brighton v. Kirner, 22 Wis. 54 (1867), one Legislature cannot bind another as to the mode in which it shall exercise its constitutional power of repeal or enactment. However, if the will to meet the situation should presently develop, there is little doubt that custom would soon give the weight of law to such practices as might be adopted, so that successive Legislatures would accept continuity as a procedure not to be questioned.

Two of the new European Republics have begun an interesting

experiment that may much lessen the volume of unfinished business. In Poland if the Senate does not within thirty days raise any objection to a bill that has come from the lower branch, the President is to direct its publication as a statute. In Czecho-Slovakia the Senate must within a month act on budget and army bills coming from the Chamber, and within six weeks on other bills; the Chamber must within three months act on bills from the Senate. Otherwise assent is to be presumed. In the case of expiration of term, prorogation, or dissolution in the course of the period thus prescribed, a like period is to be allowed from the first day of the next session. Herein Czecho-Slovakia abandons the rule that bills die with the end of a session. The two branches may by agreement alter the periods prescribed, but, though the language is not clear, it would seem that this cannot be done in the case of budget and army bills. Other countries have devised ways for the lower branch to coerce the upper, but as far as I have observed this is the only case where the upper can compel the lower to act or else acquiesce.

In such a practice those who want more of result from our legislative bodies can see marked advantage. Those who want legislation hindered and lessened will see in it little but harm. Anyhow, it should save much waste of effort.

Lessening the Work

To meet the ever-growing pressure by lessening the volume of work to be done within the limits of sessions, is a tendency that appears in many directions. Resort to recess committees and other expedients for preliminary preparation has been discussed in "Legislative Procedure" (pp. 175, 577). A subsidiary advantage of the budget reform as generally applied looks in the same direction. How this can be carried farther is illustrated by provisions to be found in the Mexican Constitution. If that document had been more respected, it would have more weight as an authority, but although no conclusions as to efficiency can be drawn, yet as matter of interest we may note a programme that might have happier results elsewhere. The revision of 1917 continued an institution that had been known for many years — a standing committee to sit during recesses. It is composed of fourteen Senators and fifteen Representatives, and one of its duties is to report on all pending measures so that they may be considered at the next session.

The German Constitution directs the Reichstag to appoint a standing committee "for the protection of the rights of the representative body over against the National Ministry, for the period between sessions and after the end of the legislative term." Just what it may do, is left indefinite. Provision is also made for a standing committee on foreign affairs to act when the Reichstag is not sitting, but the functions of this one too are not set forth. Czecho-Slovakia is more explicit, with a programme going beyond that of any other republic organized on familiar lines. A committee of twenty-four, eight from the upper branch and sixteen from the lower (with a like number of alternates), between sessions "shall act on all matters of immediate urgency, even if in ordinary circumstances they should require the enactment of legislation, and shall exercise control of all government and executive powers." Measures legislative in their nature must be recommended by the Government with the approval of the President, and lose their validity if not approved by both chambers within two months after the beginning of the following session. In Russia the "Præsidium" of the chief lawmaking body represents in the period between its sessions "the highest legislative, executive, and regulating organ of the Union." This Præsidium, with twenty-one members, is to include the members of the Præsidiums of both branches, which appear to correspond to our Committee on Rules. The Constitution specifically empowers it to issue "decrees, regulations, and orders."

In a more important particular the legislative framework of Russia suggests the direction in which republics may yet move for relief from the pressure on their present lawmaking bodies. The rest of the world is still in a mood to think that nothing good can come out of Russia, but when time has softened somewhat the memories of the suffering and tragedy wrought by the Bolsheviks, when their follies and futilities have become history, perhaps at any rate students will find that the episode has not been wholly without useful contribution to political science. Then there may be serious consideration of the creation by the Bolsheviks of what might be called a super-legislature. The Congress of Soviets, which originally was to be convened at least twice a year and as the Constitution now stands is to assemble once a year, is a one-chamber body that seems likely to concern itself with the larger questions of government and to lay down general principles. Below this comes what is called the "Central Executive Committee." As we use the term this is not a committee at all, but is virtually a self-contained legislature of the bi-cameral type, large and representative. To be sure, the 371 members of the lower branch are named by the Congress of Soviets, but it is to be from the republics in proportion to population, and though the members of the upper branch are to be confirmed by the Congress of Soviets, they are to be representatives of the republics. This body seems to be designed to attend to what may be termed the secondary grade of legislation, less in importance, but according to our experience far the greater in bulk.

It will be seen that this is the division of labor toward which many of our American States are tending in their use of constitutional conventions for enactment of the most important laws.

Everywhere the bulk of the minor legislation is largely administrative in its nature. When it comes to be recognized that the work now done by our legislative bodies is of two sorts which can and ought to be dealt with independently, when the line is drawn between the making of laws and the administering of public affairs, if the details of administration are not turned over to administrators after the English fashion, it may be that we also shall resort to two legislatures. One of these may be large and may sit infrequently, for considering broad questions of public policy, for agreeing on programmes, for passing on budgets. The other may be a small body sitting continuously or at regular intervals not far apart, after the fashion of a Board of Directors, with control of all matters of administrative detail. Then the larger body will have time to do its work right.

CHAPTER IX

PLACE AND TIME

AMERICAN judgment has differed widely as to whether law-making is done better in centers of population or at a distance from the influences of big cities. In thirteen of the States the largest city is the capital, in eight others one of the larger cities. Speaking broadly, more than half the States prefer the smaller place for their capital, or at any rate do not yield to demands that the seat of government shall be moved to a larger place. However, inertia, expense, and property interests are powerful obstacles in the way of change, and it is not safe to predict what would be the common attitude were the question to be faced afresh.

There was a large element of accident in the original location of our capitals. Naturally the first colonial assemblies were held where the chief settlements began. Rhode Island, formed by a union of towns, made the Legislature peripatetic. Successive sessions of the General Assembly in the years 1789–90 were held in September, at Newport; in October, at East Greenwich; in October-November, at South Kingstown; and in January at Providence. In the following September, the session was held at Bristol.[1] Not until 1900 were sessions confined to Providence. Connecticut, likewise an amalgamation, divided the perquisites of the capital between Hartford and New Haven until 1873. When East and West New Jersey came into one province, each brought its capital and insisted on a share in the honors — a constant source of friction between Assembly and Governor, as well as of annoyance to everybody, yet prejudice could not be overcome.

Perhaps Massachusetts was the first to weigh deliberately the relative advantages of large and small capitals. In a message to the House of Representatives, June 7, 1770, Lieutenant-Governor Hutchinson recalled the discussion. "In 1747 or 1748," he said, "when the Court House, in Boston, had been consumed by fire, the major part of the then House of Repre-

[1] *R. I. Col. Records*, x, *passim*.

sentatives was averse to rebuilding it, and disposed to build a house for the General Court in some town in the country. Being then one of the Representatives of Boston, I used my influence, in every way I could, with propriety, in favor of rebuilding the Court House in Boston, but finally could prevail thus far, and no farther. The House, upon the question whether a grant should be made, for rebuilding the Court House, was equally divided; and I, being the Speaker of the House, gave my casting vote in favor of the town." [1] By so narrow a margin did Boston escape the loss of what she would now hold her crowning honor.

In 1754 a committee of the House was appointed to consider a proper place for a Court House at a distance from Boston, but nothing came of it. Ten years later, fire again threw lurid light on the problem, if only a side-light. By reason of small-pox in Boston, the General Court was sitting in Cambridge, the Governor and Council using the library on the upper floor of Harvard Hall, the Representatives below. On a very tempestuous night in January, the beams caught from the large fire left burning in the Library and the building was destroyed. The benevolent Thomas Hollis, who had been one of the most munificent contributors to the lost library, wrote when helping to repair the loss: "I am preparing and going on with my mite to Harvard College, and lament the loss it has suffered exceedingly; but hope a public library will no more be turned into a council room." On this occasion there was great mourning. The Governor sent a message of condolence to the Representatives; the newspapers bewailed it as "a ruinous loss"; and the mother-country and the colonies were stirred up to repair the mischief.[2]

The disputes that led up to the Revolution gave the Governors chance to assert their right to assemble Legislatures where they pleased. One of the complaints made of the King in the Declaration of Independence was: "He has called together legislative bodies at places unusual, uncomfortable, and distant from the depository of their public records, for the sole purpose of fatiguing them into compliance with his measures." Massachusetts had more reason than any other colony to make the complaint. At this distance of time it is hard to take the

[1] *Mass. State Papers*, 216.
[2] Harriet Martineau, *Retrospect of Western Travel*, II, 98.

matter as gravely as it was taken then, and it now looks more like a pretext than a reason for revolution, but doubtless it was serious enough to our forefathers. That the royal Governors did not view it quite so solemnly, may be inferred from one bit of grim humor. In 1770 the General Court, sitting against its will in the chapel of Harvard College, sent an address of remonstrance to the Governor, pointing out, among other things, the inconvenience of sitting in Cambridge, whereupon the Governor replied: "If you think the benefit which the students receive by attending your debates is not equal to what they may gain in their studies, they may easily be restrained, and then your sitting in the College will be little or no inconvenience." [1]

After North Carolina framed its Constitution in 1776, there was no established seat of government. The Legislature went from town to town. Different towns were anxious for it, and this begat jealousies. It was not till 1788 that a permanent seat of government was selected, Raleigh. Vermont had a like experience. Before 1808 its Legislature had held sessions in fifteen different towns, one of which, Charlestown, was outside the present limits of the State, though then in its Eastern Union. In that year, as if partly fulfilling the threat of Ethan Allen, it gathered among the fastnesses of the mountains, and established a permanent residence at Montpelier, which town was chosen as the capital because it was near the geographical center of the State. "A large wooden structure, three stories in height and of quaint fashion, was erected for a State House. The seats of the Representatives' Hall were of unpainted white plank, which so invited the jackknives of the true-born Yankee legislators that in a quarter of a century they were literally whittled into uselessness." [2]

Nearly every State might furnish some interesting tale about the location of its capital, and the story of establishing the seat of the national government on the Potomac would be a chapter by itself. Here, however, there is occasion only to call attention to the effect of locations on legislative work. William Schouler indicated it in the Massachusetts Convention of 1853. Said he: "I think the true reason why we have had so long sessions of the Legislature during the last few years, is on ac-

---

[1] L. A. Frothingham, *A Brief History of the Constitution and Government of Massachusetts*, 16.
[2] R. E. Robinson, *Vermont*, 264.

count of the great facilities afforded gentlemen for reaching
their homes by means of the railroads. If you will look at
the Rules and Orders of the last House, you will find that more
than one third of the members boarded at home, within the
range of sixty miles. It is impossible to get evening sessions,
as we used to have during the last part of the session. I recollect before we had these facilities for traveling, we used to
have sessions at nine o'clock in the morning and continue the
session until six in the evening, and then the legislative sessions
did not exceed ninety days. But during the last three or four
years, since the construction of so many railroads, affording
such facilities for members to reach home, they will go home
every day, and there are enough of them, with the Boston members, to vote to adjourn when they ought not to adjourn, in
order that they may reach the cars in time. I do not think that
the Legislature does more business than formerly. You cannot get committees together in the morning, or evening, because
members have gone home." [1]

Since then the effect of rapid transit has become even more
important. More than three quarters of the members of the
Massachusetts Legislature now live at home through the session, for the most part carrying on their private affairs much as
usual. Inevitably sessions are much longer than in States
where the capital is less accessible. In most of the States,
indeed, the greater part of the members have nothing but
legislative work to take their attention during five days of each
week, and they can attend to it with little distraction. For
this reason not a little is to be said in favor of having the State
House in a small place, not too easily reached. On the other
hand, there is undoubtedly force in what President Lowell
of Harvard University said to a committee of the New York
Constitutional Convention, June 10, 1915. "Massachusetts,"
he declared, "has one advantage over New York, which is not
an inconsiderable one, and that is, as the Legislature sits in
Boston, it gets a great deal better chance to hear public opinion,
and to get men coming there constantly, before the committees.
There are a great many more appearances of citizens at committee hearings than in any other Legislature that I know of
in the United States, and that is an advantage." [2] This seems

[1] *Debates in Mass. Conv. of 1853*, I, 782.
[2] *N.Y. Conv. Doc. No. 14*, 129.

to me a more serious consideration than that which caught the attention of Mr. Bryce. He thought that since a small town is neither attractive socially. nor convenient for business men or lawyers, the placing of a capital in such a town has an unfavorable effect on the quality of legislators. It may be that the ablest men of a State, living for the most part in or near its largest city, will be less willing to make the sacrifice of legislative service if its work must be done in some place distant from their homes, but it is not conspicuous that in States where the capital is in the largest city the members from that city are markedly superior to those coming from the smaller places.

The Beginning

No great importance seems at first to have been attached to the time of convening the Legislatures. Four of the original States did not at the start take the trouble to cover the matter in their Constitutions, but now provision is made everywhere. Three of the States specify that the date shall be as determined by law, and nine naming a date, permit another to be substituted by law. The rest name a date without alternative. In Iowa and Nevada the Governor may convene before the prescribed time.

Congress is to assemble on the first Monday in December, "unless they shall by law appoint a different day." This clause did not appear in the draft of the Constitution recommended to the Federal Convention by the Committee on Detail, but was inserted on motion of Mr. Randolph, seconded by Mr. Madison, by a vote of eight States to two. It seems to have been a compromise between those who would leave the matter entirely to Congress, and those who feared that in such case disputes would arise. The report of the debate does not indicate that anybody thought of having the President take any part in the matter, other of course than might result from his power of vetoing a bill setting or changing the date. It seems to have been taken for granted that it was prudent to authorize the President to convene Congress "on extraordinary occasions," although the right to convene the Senate by itself did not go without question. The expression of his power to call what has come to be known as a special session, may or may not be held to exclude Congress from exercising such a power by itself.

The question came near having more than academic importance while President Wilson was abroad, negotiating the Peace Treaty in 1919. Upon the ending of the 65th Congress, it was feared in some quarters that the President might not at once summon the 66th, and as important appropriation bills that had failed of passage ought to be taken up again at once, the dilemma would be serious if the President failed to act. Senator La Follette urged a change in the Constitution to meet such exigencies, so that Congress could convene itself. Others believed there was no need for such an amendment, thinking the power already in existence. The President, however, deprived the contention of immediate consequence by calling a special session.

The Legislatures of three of the States may have a free hand in the matter through the chance that tied it up with the New England custom of having two sessions a year. The original Massachusetts Constitution (1780), specifying that the legislative body should meet every year on the last Wednesday in May, added — "and at such other times as they shall judge necessary." This clause survived when the meeting time was changed from May to January and regular sessions became annual. No change in this respect was made when biennial elections were adopted, in 1918. New Hampshire copied the provision in 1784, and Connecticut in 1818. Yet in 1920 when the matter bade fair to be of importance in Connecticut by reason of the desire to secure ratification of the Federal amendment granting suffrage to women in time for them to take part in the presidential campaign, former Governor Baldwin, a jurist of high standing, was quoted as holding that the Legislature could not convene itself.

The issue was raised in Oklahoma in September of 1923 when a majority of the members of the Legislature, which was not then in session, gathered in the State House to determine whether Governor Walton should be impeached. Refused admission to the legislative chambers, they tried to proceed in the corridors, but under warrant of the state of martial law that had been proclaimed, the commanding officer of the military district ordered and compelled the assemblage to disperse. Although the members contended that their meeting was legal and declared their intention of taking the question to the courts, judicial determination was prevented by decision to put on the ballot, at a special election about to be held, the question of authorizing a special session. The people voted such authority, and the Governor was thereafter in due course impeached and removed.

If the question ever reaches the courts, it does not seem to me probable that they will hold it within the power of a Legislature to convene itself in the lack of constitutional direction as to procedure. Possibly, though, the signature of a majority appended to a call would be held sufficient if ample notice had been given and the rights of a minority protected in all other respects. The Louisiana Constitution of 1921 wisely took thought of the contingency by providing that if the Governor should ignore a petition for a special session signed by two thirds of the members, the Lieutenant-Governor or the Speaker of the House or both of them should issue the call.

At any time the question may become serious in those States where the Legislatures regularly assemble only once in two years, and of course the chance of trouble is greater with quadrennial sessions. Naturally its importance attracted the attention of Governor O'Neal of Alabama, which has the quadrennial system. He told the Alabama State Bar Association in 1917 that "the right of the people through their trusted representatives to make, revise, or repeal laws, should not be dependent upon the pleasure or caprice even of the Governor." Such a view seems incontestable. Nothing in our Constitutional history suggests that the framers of our Constitutions, State or Federal, ever contemplated that the legislative branch should be under the control of the executive branch in this particular. On the other hand, the universal distrust of the executive branch that prevailed when our early Constitutions were framed, leaves little doubt that if their authors had thought it necessary to particularize, they would have declared the legislative branch to have at least equal power with the executive in the matter of assemblage.

The President of France must, in the course of a recess, convene the Houses on the request of an absolute majority of each. The German Constitution adopted in 1919 provided that in case of adjournment, the Reichstag is to determine the day of reassembling, but its President must call it together at an earlier date on demand of the President of the Commonwealth or of one third of the Deputies. The National Ministry is to convene the upper branch on demand of one third of its members. Likewise, in the Irish Free State the Chamber is to fix the date of reassembling, but no provision appears for earlier convocation on demand of members. The Constitution of Czecho-Slovakia provides that on the application of half the members of either Chamber, made to the Prime Minister, the President must summon an extraordinary session, and furthermore that if four months have elapsed since the last ordinary session, two fifths of either branch may compel summons within a fortnight. The President of Poland may convoke the Sejm at any time and is bound to do it within two weeks on request of one third of the Deputies. In Austria the President of either House must call it together immediately on demand of a quarter of the members or of the Federal Ministry. Although the chief lawmaking body in Russia, the Central Executive Committee, is to meet anyhow three times a year in regular session, it seems to have been thought prudent to provide that extraordinary sessions shall be held on the decision of the governing committee (the Præsidium) of either branch, or on demand of the Central Executive Committee of one of the Republics. What might be called the Super-legislature, the Congress of the Soviets, which is to meet once a year, may be convened in extraordinary session by the Central Executive Committee on its own decision, or on demand of either of its branches or of any two Republics. The State Assembly of Esthonia likewise has a Præsidium, which may summon an extraordinary session, and it must so do on demand of a quarter of the members or of the Government. In Egypt the King must convene the Parliament on petition signed by an absolute majority of either House.

In Italy, where annual assemblage is not prescribed, Premier Giolitti announced in the summer of 1920 what was described as a concession to the Chamber of Deputies, in the shape of power to convoke itself instead of having to wait for a royal summons. The initiative was put in the hands of the nine standing committees, which by majority action might require the Government to issue a call, the Government, however, having the right to name the dates at which the session should begin and end. This was looked upon as an important increase of parliamentary power.

American Legislatures are for the most part convened about two months after their election. A different practice in the case of Congress has long been the object of serious criticism. Accident imposed on the nation a schedule that has worked much mischief and threatens more, even at times to the point of serious crisis. The framers of the Federal Constitution set no date for its going into effect, by reason of the uncertainty as to when ratification might be completed. It was the Continental Congress that named the first Wednesday of March, 1789 (which fell on the 4th), as the day for beginning under the new Constitution, and although a quorum of both Houses did not appear till a month later, it was assumed that the terms of Senators and Representatives had begun on the 4th of March. Perhaps the first Congress was justified in enacting that the terms of the President and Vice-President should also date from March 4, when in fact Washington and Adams did not take office until April 30, their actual service thus being shortened by nearly two months, but there is to-day little probability that the Supreme Court would approve any shortening or lengthening of terms by statute, and so March 4 will be the determining day until the Constitution is amended. The power of Congress to fix a date for the regular assembling earlier than December has never been exercised, with the result that save when a special session is called, the members of the House do not come together for thirteen months after they have been elected.

Various harms follow. Chief of them is the failure to give reasonably prompt effect to the will of the people as shown in an election. If the voters have decided upon a change in party control, confusion and uncertainty prevail until it has been accomplished. At present the old Congress pursues one of its regular sessions after it may have been rebuked and disowned. The conditions are all against good work in that session. Defeated members have lost their interest and zeal; they may be sulky and obstinate. Sometimes they are even bluntly told they have no moral right to speak and vote on the issues that have prevailed in the campaign, to persist when the popular will has been definitely shown. As a whole the House loses the sense of responsibility. It shirks. It postpones what it can.

Furthermore, whenever a Representative does not begin his work until thirteen months after he has been elected, there remain but five or six months, possibly less, before he may have to begin his campaign for renomination. He will have had almost no chance to show his mettle, to earn either praise or blame, for he will hardly have mastered even the elements of Congressional procedure, much less have achieved any prominence. Surely the work of a full term should be known to his constituents before they pass judgment.

Of course there are arguments the other way. The ultra-conservatives dread to have the popular will speedily carried out, for they fear whim and prejudice and passion. They think it well that the country should have time to cool off after the excitements of a campaign, and that those to whom power has been newly entrusted will use it the more wisely if many months have elapsed. To this it may fairly be rejoined that our institutions are based on the principle of majority rule. The presumption always is that the popular will should prevail. Frequent elections were provided for the very purpose of permitting it to prevail. And anyhow the conditions are such that precipitate, ill-considered action would be well-nigh impossible, for the mills of Congress grind very, very slowly at the best. Committees deliberate and are deliberate. Each of two Houses will take its time. The power to delay, especially in the Senate, is great. Congress is the last place in which to worry about hurry.

When as cautious and conservative a body as the American Bar Association concluded the situation ought to be changed, we may conclude that the need was both clear and important. So it was not surprising that the Senate of the 67th Congress gave serious consideration to the arguments presented by a committee of the Association, and by a vote of 63 to 6 approved, February 13, 1923, a constitutional amendment providing that the terms of Senators and Representatives shall begin on the first Monday of the January following their election, and that of the President and Vice-President two weeks later, with assemblage of Congress on the first Monday in January of each year. The House did not find time to act on the matter before adjournment, but it seemed not at all improbable that the change will not much longer be deferred.

No such serious change in governmental habits can wholly escape embarrassments, and in Washington will appear one already familiar in those State capitols where the budget system has been put in force. There Executives are being asked to lay before the legislative branch, usually but eight weeks or so after election day, an exhaustive, complete financial programme for which they are supposed to assume personal responsibility in every detail. Perhaps this is no unreasonable demand in the case of a Governor reëlected, but probably half the time the Executive is a novice, often without even the benefit of legislative experience. Under such circumstances he must rely largely on the judgment of administrative officials, and if there has been a change in party control, this may prove awkward.

An incoming President could be saved from such a situation if the fiscal year of the Government should be changed to correspond with the calendar year, instead of beginning July 1, as is now the case. Then it would be safe to let a new President delay presenting his budget for a month or two. There are in fact strong arguments for making the change, anyway. Much of the public work is seasonal and ought not to be dislocated by appropriations beginning or ending in midsummer. The schedule now in force leads to much waste of time and money.

There must also be remembered the need for recommendation other than financial in the inaugural message. With this in mind Governor Emmet O'Neal of Alabama expressed the belief that the Legislature should be assembled only after the incoming Governor has had some months of experience in office, some opportunity to give careful study to the wants of the State, and enough time to prepare such legislation as he may ascertain is required for a wise, economical, and efficient administration.[1] In his message of 1923 Governor McCray of Indiana suggested that the Legislature be convened at the beginning of the second and fourth years of the Governor's term. There is much force in the argument for such a change in schedule. Against it will be urged the importance of giving effect as early as possible to the will of the people as expressed at the polls. The conflict of needs gives one more occasion for the hope that presently by separating the treatment of policies and practices, of laws and regulations, of principles and details, we may reach more orderly and efficient methods of government.

[1] Address to Alabama State Bar Assn., July 13, 1917.

The Ending

"Adjournment" of legislative bodies means properly the temporary cessation of business, which is to be resumed on the next legislative day or at a time certain. Invariably, at any rate in practice, it is in this country nowadays a function of the body itself.

"Prorogation" signifies a final cessation of the business of the session. It does not preclude another session if the time of prorogation is not coincident with the end of the term. In the United States it is a function of the legislative body, though sometimes coupled with what is in practice, with very rare exceptions, a purely formal share on the part of the Executive. Where the cabinet form of government prevails, the share of the Executive is greater, sometimes reaching the point of predominance.

"Dissolution" involves the death of the assembly. It is now the recourse under the cabinet form of government when before the natural term of an assembly has been finished, the Executive determines that another shall be elected.

In England, up to Puritan times, it was the theory as well as the practice that the life of a Parliament was at the pleasure of the King. The attack on this principle was among the noteworthy constitutional episodes of the Puritan Revolution. One of the first acts of the Parliament that assembled in November of 1640 was the passage of a Triennial Bill, which not only provided that the interval between Parliaments should never be more than three years, but also provided that no future Parliament should be dissolved or adjourned, without its own consent, within less than fifty days from the opening of its session. This did not protect the Parliament that passed the bill from the danger that its audacities might bring it to a speedy end, and so in May of 1641 it passed another against its own dissolution without its own consent. Under this bulwark it became the famous Long Parliament, and its career led Blackstone to say a century and more afterward (i, 188): "If nothing had a right to prorogue or dissolve a Parliament but itself, it might happen to become perpetual. And this would be extremely dangerous, if at any time it should attempt to encroach upon the executive power: as was fatally experienced by the unfortunate King Charles the First; who having unadvisedly passed an act to continue the Parliament then in being till such time as it should please to dissolve itself, at last fell a sacrifice to that inordinate power, which he himself had consented to give them."

This very Parliament, however, was destined to perish in spite of itself, at the hands of the *de facto* executive it had helped to put in power, namely, Oliver Cromwell. One morning in April, 1653, he learned that the House was hurriedly passing a bill that in the new Parliament to be elected would have kept their seats to the fifty or sixty men who had been left by Pride's Purge, and were derisively called the Rump. Cromwell hastened to the House, listened to the impassioned eloquence of Sir Harry Vane for a while, and then strode into the middle of the chamber, exclaiming, "I will put an end to your prating." Calling in his soldiers, he ordered them to clear the House. As the members crowded to the door, he reviled them with bitter words. Sir Harry Vane refused to cringe and told him his act was "against all right and all honor." Cromwell retorted in kind, ending with, "The Lord deliver me from Sir Harry Vane!" The Speaker refused to leave his seat till Harrison offered to lend him a hand to come down. Cromwell himself lifted the mace from the table. "What shall we do with this bauble?" he said. "Take it away." And so ended the doctrine that a Parliament might sit as long as it pleased.

When lawmaking bodies began in America, the notion that they could have anything to say about their own existence had not yet become familiar. The records of the first of them, that which met at James City, Virginia, July 30, 1619, read, for August 4: "This daye (by reason of extreame heat, both paste and likely to ensue, and by that meanes of the alteration of the healthes of diverse of the general Assembly) the Governour, who himselfe also was not well, resolved should be the last of this first session." When in 1642 the London Company sought to secure a return of its charter for Virginia, the Assembly approved a long remonstrance to be sent to the King, and voted that, "taking into serious consideration the many and weighty business begun in this present grand assembly, and which yet do remain unfinished," the Assembly should be adjourned to the 2d day of June. This was the first continuance of a session by adjournment, and the members were so anxious to forestall criticism after dissolution, that they issued to the people "A

Remonstrance of the Grand Assembly," telling the important things they had accomplished by the protracted session, and justifying themselves.

The first charter of the Massachusetts Bay Colony was silent on the subject, and so, there being nothing to prevent, the colonists grasped the chance to keep the control in their own hands. The entry of the proceedings of the General Court, May 14, 1634, reads: "It is likewise ordered, that there shalbe foure Generall Courts held yearely, to be summoned by the Governor, for the tyme being, & not to be dissolved without the consent of the major parte of the Court." The Charter of 1691 gave the powers of adjournment, prorogation, and dissolution to the Governor, but in terms uncertain enough to permit a controversy that Hutchinson describes. In 1721, he tells us, no grants had been made, and no officers for the ensuing year had been constituted; the House, notwithstanding, sent a message to the Governor to desire the Court might rise. He refused to gratify them. "Thursday the 13th of July had been appointed for a public fast. The members desired to be at home with their families, and on Wednesday, by a vote, they adjourned themselves to Tuesday in the next week. The House of Commons adjourn for as long time, without any immediate act of royal authority, but, I presume, never contrary to a signification of the mind of the King; and the adjournments over holidays are as much established, by ancient usage, as the ordinary adjournments from day to day, and, being conformed to by both Houses of Parliament, no inconvenience can arise. But the charter was urged by the Governor to be the rule in this assembly, not the analogy between a Massachusetts House of Representatives and the Commons of Great Britain. The Governor, by the charter, has the sole power of adjourning, proroguing, and dissolving the General Court. Taken strictly, it would be extremely inconvenient; for the act of the Governor would be necessary every day. Upon a reasonable construction, therefore, the House had always adjourned from day to day, but never for so great a number of days. The Council, who were obliged to spend near a week without business, unanimously voted, upon hearing the House had adjourned, that such adjournment, without his excellency's knowledge and consent, was irregular and not agreeable to the charter. The Governor (Dudley) afterwards made this adjournment one of the principal articles of complaint against the House," which presently acknowledged his authority in the matter and said he ought to have been informed before they adjourned, "and that it was so designed and casually omitted." But they carefully distinguished between the power of adjourning the General Court and adjourning the House of Representatives, whereupon the Governor called them before him, scolded them, and dissolved the Court.[1]

Partly in view of the uncertainty as to the time for which the House might adjourn, an explanatory charter was thought necessary, and such a charter accordingly passed the seals. It read: "Whereas no power is granted by the said recited letters Patents to the said House of Representatives to adjourn themselves for any time whatsoever, by means whereof divers Doubts and Controversies have arisen within our said Province to the Interruption of the Publick Business thereof and the obstruccion of Our Service," the Representatives might adjourn themselves for two days or less, but not longer without the consent of the Governor.

The Concession and Agreement of the Lords Proprietors of the Province of New Cesarea, or New Jersey, 1664, provided for a General Assembly of twelve Deputies or Representatives which was to have power to appoint its own time of meeting and "to adjourn their sessions from time to time to such times and places as they shall think convenient." In 1672 this was modified so that to the Governor and Council was given the power of summons and adjournment. The Fundamental Constitutions of East New Jersey, 1683, called for the Great Council to meet each April 20 and "sit upon their own adjournments, if they see meet," till the 20th of July, "unless the Governor and Common Council think fit to continue them longer."

By Penn's Charter of Liberties to Pennsylvania in 1682, the Provincial Council was "to continue and sit upon its own adjournments." The General Assembly was to sit until the Governor and Council informed it they had nothing further to propose. In 1696 Governor Markham's Frame of Government, giving the Assembly the right to originate measures, provided that the Assembly likewise should "sit upon their own adjournments." The same phrase, used in Penn's Charter of Privileges in 1701, brought to an issue the differences between

---

[1] Gov. Thomas Hutchinson, *History of Massachusetts*, 3d ed., II, 232–35.

the parties that had developed. The Council, representing those who stood for privilege, held that the right was limited to short periods, but the popular party, controlling the Assembly, took the opposite view and decided the matter by adjourning. Thereupon to make a show of power the Council went through the form of prorogation to the day the lawmakers had set for reassembling. However, the battle was looked upon as won by the popular body, led by David Lloyd.[1] When Andrew Hamilton, Speaker of the Assembly, took leave of the House, on account of his age and infirmities, in 1729, he said: "We sit upon our own adjournments, when we please, and as long as we think necessary; and we are not to be sent a packing in the middle of a debate, and disabled from representing our just grievances to our gracious sovereign, if there should be occasion; which has often been the fate of Assemblies in other places."[2] The privilege was always a matter of pride to Pennsylvanians.

North Carolina furnishes another illustration of colonial quarrels over this matter. Governor Everard in 1725, the first year of his administration, fearing to encounter the popular party, prorogued the Assembly before it had met. The lower House refused to recognize the validity of such a prorogation, and assembling on the day originally set, proceeded to organize. All they could do brought no recognition from the Governor, whose action they stigmatized as illegal. They declared that at their next meeting they would transact no business until their privileges had been confirmed by the Governor and Council, voted an address to the Proprietors, and then adjourned till the day for which they had already been prorogued. On reassembling, they declared that they did so according to adjournment, recognized the officers elected at the previous meeting, and in various other ways tried to establish the legality of their previous assembling.[3]

When in 1754 seven of the colonies sent delegates to a Congress at Albany, Benjamin Franklin drew a Plan of Union which interests us here because of its novel suggestion for a course halfway between the extreme views in this matter of adjournment. Its provision was "that the Grand Council shall neither

[1] Isaac Sharpless, *Two Centuries of Pennsylvania History*, 98.
[2] Robert Proud, *History of Pennsylvania*, II, 217.
[3] J. S. Bassett, *The Constitutional Beginnings of North Carolina*, 62.

be dissolved, prorogued, nor continued sitting longer than six weeks at a time, without their own consent or the special command of the Crown." The fear was that the President-General might abuse power in this regard should it be entrusted to him.

The royal Governors found fresh occasion to use the power of dissolving Assemblies, in the controversies that ripened into Revolution. Two characteristic instances may be cited. One was that of the attempt by Governor Gage in Massachusetts to get rid of the bothersome General Court sitting in Salem in June of 1774. On the 17th, according to the Journal, the Governor directed the Secretary to acquaint the two Houses, it was his pleasure the General Assembly should be dissolved; and to declare the same dissolved accordingly. "The Secretary went to the Court House, and finding the door of the Representative's Chamber locked, directed the Messenger to go in, and acquaint the Speaker, that the Secretary had a message from his Excellency to the honorable House, and desired he might be admitted, to deliver it. The Messenger soon returned, and said he had acquainted the Speaker, who mentioned it to the House; and their orders were, to keep the door fast. Whereupon, the following proclamation was published on the stairs leading to the Representative's Chamber, in presence of a number of Members of the House, and divers other persons; and immediately after in Council." [1]

The purpose of the Massachusetts General Court in this proceeding was the same as that which produced a like episode in South Carolina, namely, the desire to appoint Deputies to the General Congress at Philadelphia and provide for their expenses. Lieutenant-Governor Bull was Acting Governor. By a secret understanding the members of the Commons' House were on hand at eight o'clock in the morning of that day instead of waiting till ten or eleven as usual. They at once organized and sent a committee to tell the Governor they had met. He was still in bed. Old custom required that he should send communications to the Commons' House by the Master in Chancery. Before the Governor could put on his clothes, have the attendance of the Master to carry his message, and secure the presence of two of his Council to represent the upper House, the Commons' House had confirmed the appointment

[1] *Mass. State Papers*, 416.

of the Deputies and had provided for a sum not to exceed
£1500 sterling, to defray their expenses.   Too late the Governor
prorogued the Assembly.[1]

Friction of this sort over questions of adjournment gave
Thomas Jefferson warrant for putting among the injuries and
usurpations of the King that were set forth in the Declaration
of Independence when submitting facts to a candid world:
"He has dissolved representative houses repeatedly, for opposing with manly firmness his invasions on the rights of the
people."   In view of such belief, it is not strange that as each
colony came to draw up a Constitution, it took particular care
to anticipate trouble on this score.   New Hampshire led
(January 5, 1776) with a Constitution not providing for a chief
executive, and so its precaution in this regard was to keep either
House from coercing the other.   To this end it provided that
neither branch without the consent of the other should adjourn for a longer time than from Saturday to Monday.   South
Carolina, coming next, in March, created a President, and
specifically denied him the power to adjourn, prorogue, or
dissolve the legislative body, and gave either branch the power
to adjourn itself independently.   Virginia made like provision
in June.   New Jersey, in July, put the control in the hands of
the lower branch, with the familiar phrase — "sit upon their
own adjournments"; the upper branch was to be convened at
all times when the Assembly was sitting.   Pennsylvania, with
its single House, used the New Jersey phrase, Vermont as usual
copying Pennsylvania.   Delaware allowed its two branches to
adjourn independently, but stipulated that the two should
always sit at the same time and place.

Maryland was the first to anticipate possible differences between the branches; it provided that if they adjourned to different times, the Governor should select one of the dates, or a
day between.   North Carolina let each branch "sit upon their
own adjournments," but added, "from day to day"; for
longer adjournments they were to proceed "jointly, by ballot."
In Georgia the House of Assembly was to have "power of adjournment to any time or times within the year."

In New York neither branch could adjourn itself for more
than two days without the consent of the other.   There a new
idea appeared, or rather an old idea, for it was the provincial

[1] Edward McCrady, *Hist. of So. Carolina*, II, 745–47.

practice continued. Apparently New Yorkers had not felt keenly the injuries suffered by other colonies at the hands of royal Governors, which had led the framers of previous Constitutions either specifically to deny the Governor the right of prorogation or else, while silent on that point, to give the power of adjournment to the Legislature. The New York Convention thought it protection enough, while giving the Governor the right of prorogation, to provide that the prorogations should not exceed sixty days in the course of any one year. George Clinton, the first Governor of New York under the Constitution, prorogued the first Legislature twice before it actually met, and Governor Tompkins exercised the power once, in 1812. It was not perpetuated in the second Constitution.

In Massachusetts either branch was to be able to adjourn itself for not more than two days at a time, and the Governor was to adjourn or prorogue to any time the two Houses should desire; he was to prorogue for not more than ninety days in any one recess, a provision that disappeared when in 1831 annual sessions were substituted for semi-annual; in case of disagreement between the two Houses, the Governor, with advice of the Council, could "adjourn or prorogue" for not exceeding ninety days. New Hampshire in 1784 copied the Massachusetts provisions. When Vermont in 1836 created a senate, it provided that if they disagreed about adjournment the Governor might adjourn them to such time as he should think proper. In about half the States the Governor now has like authority, with, as a rule, the restriction that he must not adjourn beyond the first day of the next regular session, but in Delaware he may not adjourn more than three months, in Kentucky and Pennsylvania more than four months, and in Georgia there is the unique provision that he may adjourn either or both Houses. In South Carolina if either House remains without a quorum five days, the Governor may adjourn to a time not beyond the date of the next annual session.

Thirty-six of the States now forbid either House to adjourn for more than three days without the consent of the other; seven say for more than two days. Apparently Massachusetts and New Hampshire are the only States where the Houses acting jointly may not adjourn themselves as they see fit. The amendment adopted by Massachusetts in 1918 permits recesses by concurrent vote, not exceeding thirty days in the aggregate and all within the first sixty days of the session, but for the rest of the session the two-day limit prevails. The restriction is often an awkward obstacle to reasonable adjournments, compelling evasion by sittings at which with common consent no business is transacted nor attempt made to get a quorum; yet it has at least the merit of saving quarrels between the branches. Missouri is singular in a provision dating from 1865 to the effect that an adjournment or recess of the General Assembly for more than three days shall have the effect of and be an adjournment *sine die;* and that an adjournment for three days or less shall be construed as not interrupting the session, "but as continuing the session for all the purposes mentioned in section sixteen of this article" — the section about the *per diem* of members.

When the Constitution of the United States was framed, State precedents were followed in this provision: "Neither house, during the session of Congress, shall, without the consent of the other, adjourn for more than three days, nor to any other place than that in which the two houses shall be sitting." In case of disagreement between the Houses with respect to the time of adjournment, the President may adjourn them to such time as he shall think proper. Occasion arose for an appeal to President Wilson to use this power, and there may have been previous instances of the same sort, but no President has ever used it. Andrew Jackson, however, reminded Congress of its existence and nature. In 1836, when he refused to sign the bill that would have set the second Monday in May for the adjournment of the first regular session of each subsequent Congress, he cited the constitutional provision about his power in case of disagreement between the Houses, as one with which the bill was not in accord. His opponents, among the ablest and strongest men in the Senate, could muster only 16 Yeas to 23 Nays, and so the bill was rejected. Thereupon the House virtually admitted the force of Jackson's contention by passing a bill providing for assemblage November 1, with reference to adjournment omitted, the measure, however, failing to become law.

As matter of curiosity rather than because of any real significance, it may be interesting to note that at least two States see fit to determine with precision the hour for ending a session. Michigan put into her Constitution of 1850: "The Legislature, on the day of final adjournment, shall adjourn at twelve o'clock noon." New Mexico copied this in 1910. Arkansas had the same provision in her Constitution of 1868, but dropped it in 1874. The rejected New York Constitution of 1867 contained it. When Cass was a United States Senator and Benton in the House, they urged that Congress expired at 12 midnight of the 3d of March, that no formal adjournment was necessary, and that it was the duty of the presiding officer to leave the chair. Speaker Carlisle, in April, 1888, said it had since then been the invariable practice of the House, and he thought it was so before, to remain in session on the legislative day of March 3 until 12 M. of March 4. The practice continues.

In nearly all the rest of the world where representative institutions are found, the power of dissolution is an important adjunct of the system of ministerial responsibility, being the means of an appeal to the electorate, to find out whether the balance of parties has shifted. Germany was an exception while an empire. There the lower branch could be dissolved at any time by the upper branch, with the consent of the Emperor. The result was to develop the power of dissolution into a means for breaking down resistance in the lower branch, and it was so used on several noteworthy occasions. Under the new Constitution the National Assembly is to determine the close of sessions, but the President of the Commonwealth may dissolve it, though he may not take this step twice for the same cause. In Prussia the Diet may be dissolved by itself; or by a majority of the Prime Minister, the President of the Diet, and the President of the Council of State; or by a referendum invoked by popular initiative or the Council of State. In Czecho-Slovakia the President has the right to dissolve, though not in the last six months of his term. Poland provides for dissolution by a two-thirds vote of the Sejm, or by the President with the consent of three fifths of all the Senators, in each case the Senate being automatically dissolved, but the session handling the budget cannot be closed before the budget has been voted. In Jugoslavia the King may dissolve if the State budget has been fixed and if the decree is signed by all the Ministers. In Austria the Nationalrat may dissolve itself. A French President cannot dissolve the Chamber without the consent of the Senate, and the failure of that body to exercise this power of control is held to be in part responsible for the frequent changes of Cabinets.

Protection against coercing or stifling the legislative branch by prolonged or repeated adjournments is in France found in the provision that though the President may adjourn the Houses, it must not be for more than a month nor can it take place more than twice in the same session. The restriction on the President of Poland and the King of Egypt is likewise, except that neither can adjourn the same ordinary session more than once. The President of Czecho-Slovakia may prorogue Parliament for not longer than a month, but not more frequently than once a year.

The Irish Free State leaves adjournments in the control of Parliament, the lower branch being empowered to end sessions, save that the sessions of the Senate may not be concluded without its consent. The Constitution follows the British policy of putting the power of dissolution in the hands of the Executive, stipulating that the Representative of the Crown, who is entrusted with the function as a matter of form, shall never exercise it save on the advice of the Executive Council. Nevertheless this policy, one of the most venerable of British institutions, is nowadays by no means universally approved in England itself. On the contrary, there are those who see in it the most serious menace of parliamentary government. Herbert Sidebotham points out [1] that each dissolution fines each member a thousand pounds in election costs, a fine that tells heavily against the free and independent Parliament the country wants. The vote that brings about a General Election may prejudice half a dozen other reforms of moment. The suggested remedy is a Parliament chosen for three, four, or five years, to sit for its natural term unless it agrees by a vote that it cannot carry on. If one Ministry fails, let another be tried.

[1] *Political Profiles*, 253–56.

CHAPTER X

ELECTION AND QUALIFICATION

The first requirement for admission to an elected lawmaking body is that the applicant shall have been duly elected.

For nearly three hundred years after the shaping of Parliament as we now know it, seats in the House of Commons were not prized enough to make of much importance the question of who should decide election contests, and the matter appears to have been left to the King in Council. Under the Tudors the situation changed, and we find the Commons coming to think it their right to determine their membership themselves. In Mary's time they appointed a committee to inquire whether Mr. Alexander Nowell, prebendary of Westminster, might be a member, and the next day it was declared that as he had a voice in Convocation, he could not also sit in the House.

Under Elizabeth their right to determine contested elections was definitely established. It was in 1586 that she ordered the Speaker to signify to the House her displeasure that it had been "troubled with a thing impertinent for them to deal with, and only belonging to the charge and office of the Lord Chancellor, whom she had appointed to confer with the judges about the returns for the county of Norfolk, and to act therein according to justice and right." Nevertheless, the House appointed a Committee to examine into the returns, and this committee reported that "they had not thought it proper to inquire of the Chancellor what he had done, because they thought it prejudicial to the privilege of the House to have the same determined by others than such as were members thereof. And though they thought very reverently of the said Lord Chancellor and judges, and knew them to be competent judges in their places; yet in this case they took them not for judges in Parliament in this House." This was agreed to by the whole House.

James the First had no intention of submitting to such an inroad on his prerogatives if he could help it. So when he issued the proclamation calling together his first Parliament, he directed that the returns should be filed in chancery, which thus was to pass on the sufficiency of elections. For Parliament to accept this would be the undoing of what had been achieved in the preceding reign. So it took the first chance to assert its privileges by seating, for the county of Buckingham, an outlaw, Sir Francis Goodwin, elected in the face of the King's command that no outlaws should be chosen. The Lords interfered by asking a conference in the matter, saying the King so desired. Thereupon the Commons sent the Speaker and a numerous deputation to discuss the matter with the King, who insisted that the House ought not to meddle with the returns. Conferences and disputes followed. At last His Majesty sent for the Speaker and told him that as an absolute King he desired and commanded that there should be a conference between the House and the judges. Upon this unexpected message, says the Journal, there grew some amazement and silence. But at last one stood up and said: "The prince's command is like a thunderbolt: his command upon our allegiance like the roaring of a lion. To his command there is no contradiction; but how or in what manner we should now proceed to perform obedience, that will be the question." It was resolved to confer with the judges in the presence of the King and Council, whereupon the King worked out a compromise by setting the election aside and ordering a new writ. Although the Commons did not get what they set out to get, they are credited with having won. By 1624 they had come to look on it as their "antient and natural undoubted privilege and power" to examine the validity of elections and returns.

In 1703 one Ashby, a burgess of Aylesbury, brought suit against the returning officer for refusing his vote. Three judges of the Queen's Bench quashed the proceedings, on the ground that the House of Commons alone had jurisdiction in all cases relating to elections. Lord Chief Justice Holt took the opposite view, and so did the House of Lords, to which appeal was carried. A bitter quarrel followed between the two Houses. Suspended by prorogation, it was renewed at the next session, when the Commons committed the parties to Newgate. Then a new phase developed, over the question of habeas corpus, the majority of the court holding they were not warranted in setting the men at liberty against the commitment of the House. The Lords took up the cudgels with fresh zeal, and at last the question reached the Queen, who cleverly evaded it by putting an immediate end to the session.

It was in this controversy that the Commons, highly irritated over the course of Chief Justice Holt, sent a serjeant-at-arms to bring Holt before them. That doughty defender of judicial independence bade the messenger begone. Thereupon the House sent the Speaker, who came with many members. To him the Chief Justice replied: "Go back to your chair, Mr. Speaker, you may depend upon it, or within five minutes I will send you to Newgate; you speak of your authority, but I tell you I sit here as an interpreter of the laws, and a distributer of justice, and, were the whole House of Commons in your belly, I will not stir one foot." The Speaker was prudent enough to return and the House with equal prudence let the matter drop.

The determination by vote in the House of Commons of what the English call election petitions and what we call contested elections, became unsatisfactory as the development of political parties brought in its train the motive for rank injustice. A scandalous evil developed. In 1770 Mr. Grenville attacked this with a proposal to transfer decision from the House itself to a committee. His plan was to have thirteen members elected by the sitting members and petitioners from a list of forty-nine who had been chosen by ballot, to whom each party should add a nominee. This tribunal was to decide without appeal. The Grenville Act was continued from time to time; and in 1774 Sir Edward Sandys brought in a bill to make it perpetual. This encountered strong opposition, especially from Fox, who dreaded the surrender of the privileges of the House; but the successful operation of the Act, in the five cases that had already been tried under its provisions, was so generally acknowledged, that the bill was passed by a large majority. "This happy event," wrote Lord Chatham, "is a dawn of better times: it is the last prop of Parliament: should it be lost in its passage, the legislature will fall into incurable contempt, and detestation of the nation. . . . The Act does honor to the statute-book, and will endear forever the memory of the framer."

For a time, says May,[1] this measure undoubtedly introduced marked improvement in the judicature of the House of Commons. But too soon it became evident that corruption and party spirit had not been overcome. Right was generally

[1] *Const. Hist. of England*, i, 291–94.

discovered to be on the side of that candidate who professed the same political opinions as a majority of the committee.   In 1839, by Sir Robert Peel's Act, committees were reduced to six members, and nominated by an impartial body, the general committee of elections.   The principle was adhered to in later Acts, with additional securities for impartiality; and the committee was reduced to five members.   The evil was thus greatly diminished.

Yet the sinister influence of party was not wholly overcome. In the nominated election committees, one party or the other necessarily had a majority of one; and though these tribunals became more able and judicial, their constitution and proceedings often exposed them to imputations of political bias.   In 1868 the Chancellor of the Exchequer was forced to say that the "tribunal had not proved satisfactory"; expenditures had grown; corrupt practices had not declined; the decisions had been uncertain and contradictory.   From all this the Chancellor inferred, and the House proved to be of the opinion, that there was in the principle something essentially vicious.   It was then decided to place the matter in the hands of judges, one from each of the great divisions of the Law Courts (Queen's Bench, Common Pleas, and Exchequer), others to be added to the list if the number of cases required it.   Bryce, writing in 1904, said that under this plan the decisions of the judges had not always been consistent, and sometimes had been generally thought to be mistaken; sometimes the judges were too technical in annulling an election for some small breach of the law, sometimes they failed to annul it where there had been extensive corruption, the specific instances of which it is hard to prove.   Yet on the whole, he thought, the act had worked well; there was at any rate no demand for return to the old system.   Criticism arises because of the delay in the proceedings and protraction of the trial; inevitable expense to parties irrespective of results; inadequacy of existing arrangements to secure for the successful party the costs actually awarded.   In 1897 a select committee investigated.   Its report recommended some changes, but made no suggestion of any fundamental alteration.

In Massachusetts Bay it would seem that there was early occasion for deciding what should be done in such matters, for we find that at a General Court March 4, 1634/5, it was ordered " that when the deputyes of severall townes are mett togeather before any Generall Court, it shalbe lawfull for them, or the major parte of them, to heare & determine any difference that may arise about the election of any of their members, & to order things amongst themselves that may concerne the well ordering of their body." [1]

When four years later Connecticut borrowed its basic principles from the charter and laws of the parent colony, it developed the Massachusetts notion on this point into an elaborate provision of the Fundamental Orders:

"9. It is ordered and decreed, that the deputyes thus chosen shall have power and liberty to appoynt a tyme and place of meeting togather before any Generall Courte to advise and consult of all such things as may concerne the good of the publicke, as also to examine their owne Elections, whether according to the order, and if they or the gretest prte of them find any election to be illegall they may seclud such for present fro their meeting, and returne the same and their resons to the Courte; and if yt proue true, the Courte may fyne the prty or prtyes so intruding and the Towne, if they see cause, and giue out a warrant to goe to a newe election in a legall way, either *in whole or in prte*."

The first contested election case in Massachusetts, as far as observed, is recorded under date of May 30, 1644, in the Journal of the House of Deputies. After one Steevens had been legally chosen a deputy by the town of Gloucester (then called Gloster), "uppon some private differences falleinge out betweene ye church & him in ye intrime," the freemen of that town chose one Bruin in his stead. The Court ordered that Bruin "bee sent home agayne, & that ye towne of Gloster is desired to send ye said Mr. Steevens, first chosen." The town or any one or more of them, might complain against Steevens; "& if it shall appeare that such their alegacions shall render him unfitt for ye service of this Courte, than this howse shall acco. it theire dutie to deale with him as an offending member thereof." [2]

After the Province Charter went into effect, the General Court, in 1692, framed an enactment with a phrase that has come down to this day and is now the accustomed formula. It read: "The representatives assembled in any great and general court shall be the sole judges of the elections and qualifications of their own members, and may from time to time settle,

---

[1] *Records of the Colony of the Mass. Bay in N.E.*, i, 142.   [2] *Ibid.*, iii, 3.

order and purge their house, and make such necessary orders for the due regulation thereof, as they shall see occasion." In the same year the Virginia Burgesses declared that the House was the sole judge of the capacity or incapacity of its members. Sheriffs who tried to determine such questions were declared guilty of a breach of privilege, and two of them were ordered under arrest.[1]

The principle was by that time undoubtedly established. To be sure, at the meeting of His Majesty's Privy Council in 1684, when the New York Charter of Liberties was under discussion, the clause of that instrument which gave to the Assembly with the consent of the Governor power to judge of undue elections and of the qualifications of members, was objected to on the ground that "it may be inconvenient and is not practised in some other Plantations." Notwithstanding the opinion of the Privy Council, C. F. Bishop, who has made a thorough study of the general subject, believes that he has found evidence enough to justify him in stating that as a general rule contested elections in the American colonies were everywhere decided by the body to whose membership the candidates aspired.[2]

One of the rare instances in this country where a legislative body has been denied that right, resulted from the quarrel in 1707 between Lord Cornbury, Governor of New Jersey, and his Assembly. In order that a majority of the Assembly might be his friends, two of the Council alleged that three members-elect of the lower branch did not have the necessary property qualification. Thereupon the Governor refused to swear these three members. Thus, as reads the complaint sent to the Lords Commissioners for Trade and Plantations, "the undertakers obtained a majority by one in the House of Representatives, who adjourned the hearings of this case, until they had reaped the fruits of their iniquity." Cornbury persisted that he had a right to pass on qualifications, but the Board of Trade wrote to him that he "would do well to leave the Determination about Elections of Representatives to that House, and not to intermeddle therein." His removal in 1708 put an end to the dispute. The next year the Assembly embodied in an act regulating the qualifications of Representatives, the provision that the House "are and shall be judges of the qualifications of their own members."

[1] E. B. Green, *Provincial America*, 73.
[2] *History of Elections in the American Colonies*, 187.

In 1735 Governor Belcher of New Hampshire tried to assert a right to pass on the qualifications of members, but the House resisted stoutly and had its way.[1]

In North Carolina by the revision of the laws in 1715, each marshal or his deputy who had been in charge of an election, was required to attend the Assembly during the first three days of the session, in order to be at hand to give evidence in contested election cases.

New Jersey was the first State to specify that the Assembly should be "judges of the qualifications and elections of their own members." Pennsylvania and Delaware copied the specification, and now in one form or another it is to be found in the Constitution of every State, save that Minnesota uses the word "eligibility" instead of "qualifications." Maryland, however, added in 1851 the restrictive clause, "subject to the laws of the State," changed in 1867 to, "as prescribed by the Constitution and Laws of the State," thus permitting one Legislature to hamper succeeding Legislatures, which is unique. Very likely the purpose was to make it possible by statute to bring in the help of the courts. Various States had sought protection against the dangers of leaving decision to uncontrolled or unaided Houses. Pennsylvania had been incited by the Grenville Act to provide in 1790: "Contested elections shall be determined by a committee, to be selected, formed and regulated in such manner as shall be directed by law." This followed the sentence: "Each House shall judge of the qualifications of its members." The words "elections and" that preceded "qualifications" in the Constitution of 1776 were now omitted, showing clearly it was meant to give final authority to the committee, as in England under the Grenville Act. Kentucky copied this two years later, but in 1799 changed it to read: "Each House of the General Assembly shall judge of the qualifications, elections, and returns of its members; but a contested election shall be determined in such manner as shall be directed by law." Louisiana copied this in 1812, and so did Iowa in 1846. Minnesota, in 1857, was loath to go that far, and said instead: "The Legislature shall prescribe by law the manner in which evidence in cases of contested seats in either House shall be taken." West Virginia followed Kentucky in substance, and so did Texas in 1866.

[1] *New Hampshire Provincial Papers*, IV, 680–84.

The subject aroused earnest discussion in the Pennsylvania Convention of 1873. Harry White said: "Contested elections in our Legislature have, to a certain extent, been a mockery upon its legislative and upon its judicial tribunals. The Legislature of 1839, in following the Constitutional Convention of 1790, thought they were wise in following the precedent which George Granville adopted in the English Parliament in 1770, and thought, when this matter of lot was agreed upon and secured for trying these cases, a panacea for all excitements resulting from political contests had been secured. But the experience of the past few years in Pennsylvania, where this system only obtains, has been to contravene this conclusion."[1] Theodore Cuyler declared: "This decision of contested election cases has done more to shake the confidence of the people of Pennsylvania in the purity and integrity of their courts than any other class of questions that has come before them."[2] John M. Broomall testified: "I have witnessed some twenty contested elections and taken part in them, and I am obliged to confess, although it is humiliating, that in almost every instance the votes that were cast were cast according to party predilections. I believe that has been the case in every instance, with an occasional exception, where the members of the majority, perceiving that their votes were not needed to secure their friend his seat, came forward and appeased their conscience by casting their votes for the opposite party. This is simply humiliating."[3]

The outcome of the discussion was a change to: "The trial and determination of contested elections of electors of President and Vice President, members of the General Assembly, and of all public officers, whether State, judicial, municipal or local, shall be by the courts of law, or by one or more of the law judges thereof"; the General Assembly to regulate details by general law. Accordingly in 1874 it was provided by statute that contested elections of Senators and Representatives should be tried and determined by the Court of Common Pleas of the county of residence of the person returned.

To one not a lawyer the constitutional provision in Pennsylvania would probably seem incapable of more than one meaning, but the Supreme Court of that State found another. In the case of *In re* Contested Election of McNeill, 111 Pa. 235 (1885),

[1] *Debates*, II, 336. [2] *Ibid.*, II, 399. [3] *Ibid.*, II, 567.

the court said, by Chief Justice Mercur: "A careful reading of this section 17 shows that its purpose is not to take from each House the power to judge of the election and qualification of its members, given by section 9, cited. Its purpose is merely to provide a method of procuring and presenting to the respective House the evidence and information necessary for an intelligent decision, and to secure early action." Presumably a like conclusion would be reached in other States that have constitutional provisions for the determination of contested elections by courts. In three State Constitutions the insertion of a single word has put the matter beyond doubt. Connecticut said in 1818: "Each House shall be the *final* judge of the election returns, and qualifications of its own members." Arkansas in 1874 and Missouri in 1875 said each House should be the "sole" judge.

At least two New York Governors have tried to get the transfer of jurisdiction of contested election cases to the courts. In 1890 Governor David B. Hill sent a special message to the Legislature, urging an amendment. He thought the power vested in each House had been frequently abused. "Worthy of maintenance as this ancient privilege was regarded in the times when the Crown assumed prerogatives which rightly belonged to the representatives of the people, there is no longer any excuse for its retention in legislative bodies, when a State or a nation has an elective, stable, and independent judiciary." He also suggested action by the Legislature that would bring the subject to the attention of Congress, with a view to a similar amendment to the Federal Constitution. In 1891 he renewed his recommendation, and said concerning the proposed amendment of the Federal Constitution, that "the distinguished Speaker of the House of Representatives [Thomas B. Reed] had given the plan his strong endorsement." The Legislature passed such an amendment. In 1892 Governor Roswell P. Flower urged it, remarking that "since the last annual election, by the mutual consent of both parties to the contest, the highest court practically exercised that jurisdiction in several cases, and with excellent results"; and that "jurisdiction over the determination of such cases properly belongs to the courts." The Legislature passed the amendment the second time, but it was rejected at the polls by 5352 votes.[1]

[1] C. Z. Lincoln, *Const. Hist. of New York*, II, 581, 582.

Constitutional amendment is necessary to accomplish the reforms because our courts would probably refuse final jurisdiction. Such is the inference to be drawn from a recent position taken by the Supreme Court of Massachusetts. A statute had been passed giving three judges of the Superior Court power to declare void an election in which they might find corrupt practices. When it came before the full bench in the case of Dinan v. Swig, 223 Mass. 516 (1916), the court held that the constitutional provision making the House of Representatives the judge of the returns, elections, and qualifications of its members, vested the power exclusively. "No other department of the government has any authority under the Constitution to adjudicate upon that subject. . . . It is a prerogative belonging to each House, which each alone can exercise. It is not susceptible of being deputed. . . . No legislative body can be the sole judge of the election and qualifications of its members when it is obliged to accept as final a decision touching the purity of the election of one of its members made by another department of the government in an inquiry to which that legislative body is not a member and which it has not caused to be instituted."

Reform is even more needed in Congress than in the State Legislatures, because the waste of time in Congress is more costly and because there as a rule the evil effects of partisanship are more prevalent. The waste of time has been enormous. Some idea of its aggregate may be had from knowing that more than eleven hundred pages of Hinds' monumental volumes of "Precedents of the House of Representatives" are filled with matter on the subject.

At the outset the House undertook to examine the evidence and vouchers as reported to it by the committee. When in 1791 the seat of General Anthony Wayne, member-elect from Georgia, was contested by James Jackson, counsel were admitted within the bar, exhibits and proofs were presented, and the petitioner and the sitting member were fully heard. Wayne lost his seat by a unanimous vote and then it was refused to Jackson on a tie vote, the Speaker voting against him. At once it was recognized that this procedure would never do. The sifting of evidence would have to be left to the committee. That accomplished, there remained the bothersome problem of how the testimony should be taken. This was met in haphazard fashion until 1851, when a statute was enacted bringing about some degree of uniformity in procedure, but it is still unsatisfactory.

In the debate of 1851 one member said: "This thing of contesting the right to a seat upon this floor has become the greatest of all humbugs in this age of humbugs." The lack of orderly method had helped fasten the worst faults of partisanship on the process. These had begun to be conspicuous in the days of Andrew Jackson, when party spirit ran high. In the debate on the case of Letcher v. Moore, in 1834, it was charged that party considerations were influencing the decision, and the charge was repeated in the North Carolina case of Newland v. Graham in 1836. Unquestionably such considerations played a big part in the famous "Broad Seal" case of 1839 and 1840, when the control of the House depended on whether five Whigs or five Democrats had been elected in New Jersey. That was the time when on the fourth day of the bitter struggle over organization, John Quincy Adams cut the Gordian knot by offering a resolution the Clerk had refused to put, and by announcing his intention to put it himself, whereupon he was appointed chairman and in the end straightened out the perplexing situation. On this occasion the minority of the Elections Committee deliberately charged the majority with acting on partisan considerations.

Matters went from bad to worse. Henry L. Dawes, who was for eight years at the head of the Elections Committee, wrote in 1870: "All traces of a judicial character in these proceedings are fast fading away, and the precedents are losing all sanction." Just after that, however, there was a revival of virtue. George Frisbie Hoar tells about it in his "Autobiography" (I, 268). "I served my second term [1871–73] on the Committee on Elections," he says, "under the chairmanship of George W. McCrary. Election cases in the House up to that time were, as they always were in the English House of Commons and as they have been too often in the Senate, determined entirely by party feeling. Whenever there was a plausible reason for making a contest, the dominant party in the House almost always awarded the seat to the man of its own side. There is a well-authenticated story of Thaddeus Stevens, that going into the room of the Committee on Elections, of which he was a member, he found a hearing going on. He asked one of his Republican colleagues what was the point in the case. 'There is not much point to it,' was the answer. 'They are both damned scoundrels.' 'Well,' said Stevens, 'which is the Republican damned scoundrel? I want to go for the Republican damned scoundrel.'

"We had a good many contests. But the Committee determined to settle all the questions before it as they would if they were judges in a court of justice. The powerful influence of Mr. McCrary, the Chairman, aided largely to bring about that result. The Democratic minority soon discovered that we were sincere and in earnest. They met us in a like spirit. I believe the Committee on Elections during that Congress reported on every case with absolute impartiality, and the House followed their lead."

Such a high level of political morality could not be maintained. The witty George D. Robinson, who went to Congress from Massachusetts in 1877, was asked what were party questions. "I know of none," said he, "except election cases." With this may be matched the epigram of Speaker Reed on the same subject: "The House never divides on strictly partisan lines except when it is acting judicially." Writing in the "North American Review" for July, 1890, Mr. Reed said more seriously: "The decision of election cases invariably increases the majority of the party which organizes the House, and which therefore appoints the Committee on Elections. Probably there is not a single instance on record where the minority was increased by the decision of contested cases." The record may not have been quite so shameful as that, but in essence the charge was true.

Conditions improved a little in the dozen years following. Computation showed that from 1865 up to and including 1903, although the majority deprived the minority of seats eighty-two times, yet it deprived itself of seats nine times. Nevertheless Samuel W. McCall was undoubtedly justified in writing in 1904: "I think it is very rare that a close election case is decided upon judicial grounds." Of late the situation has much bettered. In recent Congresses most of the committee reports have been distinctly fair and usually made by a unanimous vote. The House itself, however, sometimes inclines to be more partisan than its committees. With a revival of intense partisanship throughout the country, the Representatives would probably at once revert to the old system of putting expediency ahead of justice.

The danger of this is far from the only reason why the conditions should be at once reformed, by turning over to the courts as much of the work as possible.   Representative Frederick W. Dallinger of Massachusetts was confirmed in this conclusion by eight years of service on one of the Committees on Elections, and in 1923 the committee of which he was Chairman reported his bill to have the Circuit Court of Appeals pass upon the question of the right of a member to his seat, in case of contest, with final decision still to lie in the House, by reason of the constitutional provision.   In the excellent report accompanying the bill Mr. Dallinger pointed out that in addition to the danger of partisan decisions by the House itself, partisanship may at any time work serious mischief at an earlier stage, when State officials determine who is prima facie entitled to a seat.   As the organization of the House is effected by those presenting proper credentials, the results may be far-reaching in case there is a close contest for the Speakership, which has happened more than once.   Under Mr. Dallinger's plan, the court would issue the credentials, thus lessening the danger of unfairness.

Furthermore, proceedings would be much expedited.   As things go now, few cases can be brought to decision within a year after the term begins, and not infrequently the decisive vote will not be reached in the House till the last week of the last session.   In the 67th Congress three cases were disposed of at two o'clock in the morning of the last day.   In this instance it chanced that no seats were vacated, but sometimes it happens that a member will be ousted close to the very end of his term, in which case he draws his salary up to the day of the vote, and the man who gets the seat draws pay for the full term, causing sad waste of public funds.

Another gain would be the avoidance of many frivolous contests.   Often defeated candidates, counting on partisan support to bolster up doubtful charges, will put committees and the House itself to much trouble, when they would not have presumed to lay their contentions before a court.

Mr. Dallinger's bill could not be brought up in the House, by reason of the pressure of other business at the end of the session, but there is ground for hope that it may have better fortune speedily.   Not a single reason of weight militates against it, and it ought to prevail.

With the constant elaboration of election laws and the growth of a public opinion that frowns on the more flagrant abuses, it is probable that the number of contests, in both Federal and State elections, will diminish.   Already the gain has been marked.   In the first fifty years of Congress, 71 seats were contested ; in the next fifty years, 278.   Then in a single decade there were 88 cases, but the total for the next two decades was only 72.   The five Houses from 1913 to 1923 averaged but about six cases each.   By 1879 the work confronting the Elections Committee had become so great that Roger Q. Mills suggested its division. The suggestion bore fruit in 1895 with the creation of three Election Committees, of nine members each.   They survive, but two could now usually do all the work without hardship.

By the volumes of Massachusetts Election Cases it appears that from 1780 to 1852 there were 297 cases, an average of four a year.   From 1853 to 1885 there were 124, giving an average slightly smaller.   From 1886 to 1902, only 34 were reported, an average of but little more than two a year.   Since then there have been so few cases that appointment to the Committee on Elections is now viewed as an empty honor.   Doubtless in time the same gains will be made throughout the country, for sooner or later the suffrage will everywhere get the adequate protection of the law.

Inferring from the German Constitution of 1919, we may conclude that occasion for systematic treatment of election cases has not been confined to England and the United States.   In Germany disputed elections are to be decided by an Electoral Commission, made up of members of the National Assembly and members of the National Administrative Court, the latter to be appointed by the President of the Commonwealth on the nomination of the President of the Court.   Proceedings apart from the hearings before the Commission will be conducted by a National Commissioner appointed by the President.   Prussia has made like provision.   Austria and Poland put the matter in the hands of the Supreme Court, and Czecho-Slovakia provides for an "electoral court," but Jugoslavia says the National Skupshtina shall scrutinize the credentials of its own members and shall decide about them.

Canada, which in 1851 had created "the general committee of elections," with six members appointed by the Speaker, its decisions to be final and conclusive, now by the statute of 1886 as amended in 1915 designates various courts that are to have jurisdiction, two judges to be "trial" judges and their decision to be final. If they differ, they are to certify their difference and make no report. Appeals lie to the Supreme Court, the decision of which is to be final.

Egypt furnishes a novelty in the provision that a mandate can be declared invalid (which presumably means that credentials can be rejected and perhaps that a member can be unseated), only by a two-thirds vote. Although each House is to judge as to the validity of elections, the power of validation may be conferred on some other authority.

COMPETENCY

AMERICAN Charters and Constitutions when directing who may and who may not be chosen to write laws, have more often laid the emphasis on disqualification than on qualification. In other words, it has been more common to exclude the presumably incompetent than to invite the probably competent. In the early days there were a few well-meant, high-sounding, platitudinous, quite ineffective designations of the kind of men to be elected. Thus William Penn set forth in his Frame of Government of 1682 that "seventy-two persons of most note for their wisdom, virtue and ability" should be chosen. When Pennsylvania came to make her Constitution of 1776, this was shortened into "persons most noted for wisdom and virtue," from which it may or may not be inferred that there was despair of getting persons of ability. Even the hope of wisdom and virtue is not found in the Constitution of 1790.

New Hampshire began with the demand that her Assembly should be composed of "reputable" freeholders and inhabitants, but abandoned the demand in 1784. Maryland was more persistent. The injunction of 1776 that Delegates should be elected "of the most wise, sensible, and discreet of the people," was not dropped until 1851. Vermont has clung to the dream of Penn, as transmitted to her through the Pennsylvania Constitution she copied in great part. It appears to be still the case that the Representatives of the Freemen of the Green Mountain State are to be "persons most noted for wisdom and virtue"; but no such requirement was imposed when a Senate was created.

The Irish Free State seeks the ideal by prescribing that Senators shall be citizens who have done honor to the nation by reason of useful public service or who, because of special qualifications or attainments, represent important aspects of the national life.

Turning to the negative phase of the matter, observe that the scope of the word "qualifications" has not escaped dispute. Does it mean those that are set forth in the fundamental law, or may the adjudicating body use its own judgment in respect of particulars not therein covered? Much is to be said for the contention of the strict constructionist that legislative bodies have no powers not expressly delegated, but my own belief is that in this matter the weight of common sense is with those who argue for plenary powers. Is it not absurd to suppose that an assembly may not exclude an idiot or a leper? And if it be granted that an assembly may in any case whatever go beyond the written word, how escape the conclusion that the matter is one of judgment?

AGE, SEX, EDUCATION

OF specific disqualifications, the most natural and clearly the most proper is that on the score of age. By the common law of England a man was of full age at twenty-one. How that period came to be accepted, is lost in the mists of antiquity. It was not the civil law, for in Rome full age was not till twenty-five years. Our English ancestors decided that at the age of twelve a male might take the oath of allegiance, at fourteen might choose his guardian, at seventeen might be an executor, and at twenty-one, with complete power to alienate his lands, goods, and chattels, to dispose of his property and himself, was of "full age." This inevitably became a test of his fitness to serve in Parliament. Apparently, however, no occasion for its use came until the time of James the First. A speech by Recorder Martin in the tenth year of that monarch is mentioned with commendation by Dr. Welwood in his "Memoirs." The membership of forty youths not above twenty years of age, and some not exceeding sixteen, caused the grave old lawyer to say, that "it was the ancient custom for old men to make laws for young men ; but that now he saw the case altered, and that there were children elected into the great council of the nation, which came to invade and invert nature, and to enact laws to govern their fathers."

Evidently the evil was becoming serious, for in 1621 it was proposed to insert in a bill relating to the election of members, a provision that they should be at least twenty-one years old. In the debate Mr. Weston said: "It is not fit that they should make laws for the kingdom, who are not liable to the law." Two years later Sir Edward Coke declared: "Many under the age of twenty-one sit here by connivance, but, if questioned, would be put out." That the offenders were the scions of great families, made their presence doubly distasteful to the Puritan elders, who, if we may believe Prynne's Tract, muttered that Parliament was not a place in which to enter whelps. Under the Commonwealth the prejudice against youth went so far that in 1658 some opposed the admission of Lord Falkland, barely of legal age, on the ground that he had not sown his wild oats. The impudent youngster retorted: "If I have not, I may sow them in this House, where there are plenty of geese to pick them up."

In spite of growing discontent, the practice of winking at the presence of lads clearly under age, long continued. Hatsell tells us (II, 5) that in 1690 on the hearing of a controverted election, the petitioner, Trenchard, was admitted by his counsel to be a minor, but notwithstanding, upon a question and division, was declared to be duly elected. Soon afterward an act was passed (7th William III) making null and void the election of anybody not of full age. Even this did not cure the evil. As late as 1787 two youths who were to rank among the greatest leaders of the House of Commons — Shaftesbury and Fox — took their seats before they had reached twenty-one years.

Lord Oranmore and Browne, debating the question of the size of the House of Lords, March 22, 1923, suggested that no Peer should be allowed to take his seat until he had attained the age of thirty; and also that no Peer should be allowed to exercise his full functions in the House, as to debate and voting, until for three years he had passed through a probationary period, which should include attendance at one Private Bill Committee at least. Very likely English experience had something to do with the decision of the Irish Free State to require age of at least thirty-five years in the case of its Senators. The members of its lower branch need be but twenty-one.

No trace of trouble over the matter in colonial times comes to my notice, and it appears to have received little attention when the original States drew their Constitutions. None of them at first deviated from the common law principle in prescribing qualifications for the lower branch. As to Senators Virginia, Maryland, and South Carolina alone entertained the notion that they should be what the word implies — older men. Even these States did not seek gray hairs, for Virginia and Maryland set the limit at but twenty-five years, South Carolina at thirty. The Revolution was the work of young men, and those who achieved it were not eager to deprive themselves of its fruits in the way of opportunity for important public service.

As they themselves grew in years, some of them came to attach more importance to maturity. New Hampshire in her second Constitution (1784) inserted a thirty-year requirement for Senators, and the advisability of this won enough recognition to secure its insertion in the Federal Constitution by unanimous vote. Discussion was aroused only by the question of a requirement for members of the lower House. Colonel Mason moved to make twenty-five years a qualification. He thought it absurd that a man to-day should not be permitted by law to make a bargain for himself, and to-morrow should be permitted to manage the affairs of a great nation. It was the more extraordinary, as every man carried with him, in his own experience, a scale for measuring the deficiencies of young politicians; since he would, if interrogated, be obliged to declare that his political opinions at the age of twenty-one were too crude and erroneous to merit an influence on public measures. It had been said, that Congress had proved a good school for our young men. It might be so, for anything he knew; but if it were, he chose that they should bear the expense of their own education.

James Wilson thought the motion tended to damp the efforts of genius and of laudable ambition. There was no more reason for incapacitating youth than age, where the requisite qualifications were found. Many instances might be mentioned of signal services to the public, rendered in high stations, before the age of twenty-five. The present Mr. Pitt and Lord Bolingbroke were striking instances.

The outcome of the debate was that seven States voted for and three against the amendment.

Doubtless it was this example that moved Delaware in 1792 to raise the limit for the lower House, twenty-four years being for some odd reason the figure chosen. When Kentucky and

Missouri were admitted, they chose the same figure, and all three keep it to this day. Ohio, in 1802, took the Federal limit, twenty-five years, and stood by it until 1851. Mississippi also experimented, starting with a requirement of twenty-two years, but dropped to twenty-one in 1832. Virginia made the requirement twenty-five years from 1830 to 1850. Arkansas began as a State and Texas as a Republic, in 1836, with the twenty-five year figure, but Texas made it twenty-one as a State and Arkansas came to that in 1868. Illinois raised the figure to twenty-five in 1848, returning to twenty-one in 1870. South Carolina tried a twenty-two year limit from 1868 to 1895. Some of the newer States have been surprisingly cautious in the matter, Colorado, South Dakota, Utah, and Arizona all making the figure twenty-five years. They are the only States with that qualification to-day.

Regarding tendencies it is just as hard to draw any inferences from changes in requirements for Senators as it is from those for Representatives. Five States have raised the figure, five States have lowered it. Five have had three different limits so far, and one, Virginia, has had four requirements, starting with twenty-five years, making it thirty in 1830, twenty-five in 1850, and in 1870 opening the office "to any person qualified to vote for members of the General Assembly." At present six States make the figure thirty years; one each twenty-seven and twenty-six years; twenty-two, twenty-five years; one, twenty-four years; and the rest, twenty-one years, although Oregon is the only State naming that figure, the others applying it by reference or implication.

Age limitations, like other constitutional provisions, carried less weight in the early days of Constitutions than they carry now. My studies lead me to believe, pessimists to the contrary notwithstanding, that we are a more law-abiding people than were our forefathers. Perhaps, though, in this particular a stronger reason is to be found in the fact that the increase in the number of years which must be given to training for the professions brings men into prominence much later in life than was the case in the Revolutionary period and long afterward. Furthermore, when there were frontiers, pioneers, and raw communities, youth had chances and advantages not to be found in a matured society. It is told of John Breckenridge that when he was only nineteen years old and about to set out from home for his third year in college, he was elected to represent his county in the Virginia House of Delegates. When he reached Williamsburg, the House set the election aside, but his frontier constituents promptly reëlected him, whereupon he was once more refused a seat. A third time he was chosen. Then the House yielded and the young student left the study of books for the study of measures and men.

Nearly a score of years later the youthful appearance of another Virginian, John Randolph of Roanoke, led the Clerk of the House of Representatives at Washington to ask his age. "Ask my constituents," was the only answer Randolph deigned to make. As a matter of fact he was a year above the limit, but had he been a year below, it probably would have made no difference. In the previous Congress William C. C. Claiborne of Tennessee had taken his seat without question, though if the date given for his birth is correct, he was but twenty-two years old. Henry Clay was four months less than thirty years of age when he took the oath as a Senator of the United States, December 29, 1806.

Such instances, not uncommon in our legislative bodies in their early years, became rarer as conditions changed. It is significant that when John Young Brown of Kentucky was elected to the 36th Congress, he refrained from taking his seat at the first session, but coming of age three days after it adjourned, he took the oath at the second. The chances would be strongly against the admission to-day either to Congress or any State Legislature, of any man known to be under the specified age limit.

By the way, if our legislative bodies deserve the abuse heaped upon them (which is very far from being established), it is not because of their immaturity. The average age of the Senators in a recent Massachusetts Legislature was forty-five years, and of the Representatives, forty-four. Less than one tenth of the members were under thirty; about one tenth were more than sixty. The members of the United States Senate average about fifty-nine years; of the House, fifty-four.

In other countries age standards have varied arbitrarily. In Athens although a youth attained voting privileges at nineteen, he was not permitted to speak in the public assemblies for some years afterward, and could not hold office before he was thirty. In Sparta no man received personal or political independence until he was thirty. Rome gave limited political functions at seventeen, full capacity at twenty-five. Where the civil law inherited from the Romans prevails to-day, there is a tendency to apply to legislators its rule that a man becomes of age at twenty-five, but the practice is far from uniform. For instance, an Italian Deputy must be thirty years old, an Italian, Belgian, or French Senator forty. The same age was required of French Deputies as of Senators from 1814 to 1830, the limit then being reduced to thirty years. That was a unique provision of the Constitution drafted for France in 1795, which stipulated that to be a member of the Council of Ancients (the upper House) a man had to be not only forty years old, but also married or a widower. Possibly it is to be regretted that there has been no survival of demanding the beneficial influence of matrimony.

In Switzerland a lad of fourteen could take part in the Landsgemeinde, but toward the middle of the fifteenth century the age of political majority was fixed at sixteen in some of the cantons.

In Austria members of the lower branch must be more than twenty-four years of age; as to the upper branch the Constitution lives up to the federal theory by leaving the matter to the States, requiring only the same conditions of eligibility as those for membership in their Landtags. In Czecho-Slovakia Senators are to be at least forty-five years old, Deputies thirty. Poland has a figure five years lower for each branch. In the single chamber of Jugoslavia members are to be at least thirty years old. Egyptian Senators must be forty years old, Deputies thirty. Prussia has set twenty-five years as the limit in each branch. The Constitution of the German Commonwealth, on the other hand, makes no specific reference to age or sex qualifications for office, but by declaring all citizens to be eligible for public office and giving the suffrage to all men and women more than twenty years of age, indirectly makes that the limit.

Among the delegates to the Convention framing this Constitution were thirty-seven women. In removing all discrimination on the score of sex, Germany has but responded to the tendency of the time. With woman suffrage it was inevitable that the eligibility of women for office would not be long contested. Already this has been recognized elsewhere. Twenty-four women were returned to the Finnish Parliament in 1916. For some time women had been chosen to American Legislatures here and there in Western States; two were chosen in 1917 to the Legislature of the Canadian Province of Alberta. The first woman member of the Congress of the United States was elected in 1916; no woman was elected to the next Congress; one to that following, with two others later to fill vacancies.

In England the attendance of a woman at Westminster has been a revival. In early times peeresses in their own rights and abbesses at the head of religious orders were summoned to attend Parliament. Presently they fell into the habit of sending men proxies, and by the times of the Stuarts the practice of issuing summonses to them had disappeared. When the Representation of the People Act gave women the suffrage in 1918, it was held by the law officers of the Crown not to confer on them the right to sit in Parliament, whereupon correcting legislation was promptly enacted. Lady Astor was the first woman to take her seat, late in 1919. The correcting act provided that no person should be disqualified by sex or marriage from the exercise of any public function. What this might mean, came in issue in 1922 when Lady Rhondda, a peeress in her own right, petitioned that she might sit in the House of Lords. At first the Committee on Privileges reported favorably, but the Lords sent the matter back, whereupon the Attorney General argued strongly that the holding of the dignity of a peerage could not be construed as a public function and the committee voted against the petition, 20 to 4. Its granting would have opened the doors to a score or more of other peeresses — a prospect not viewed with equanimity by a majority of the Lords. Yet undoubtedly wherever the suffrage is granted to women, many of them will presently be found in all types of legislative bodies.

Arizona is the only State of the Union to impose any specific educational test. With a view, no doubt, to its Spanish-speaking inhabitants, it requires the ability to read, write, speak, and understand the English language well enough to perform the duties of a member without the aid of an interpreter. As in general our States require directly or indirectly that Senators and Representatives shall have the qualifications of an elector, it may be broadly stated that illiterates are barred where there are educational qualifications for the suffrage.

The desirability of giving at least some small degree of formal recognition to the advantages of the higher education has been in effect met in England and now in Ireland by university representation in the House of Commons. Indirectly the same result is after a fashion accomplished in Belgium, Italy, Spain, and Egypt by the provisions about the choice of Senators from certain specified classes, to most of which it is inconceivable that a man of little or no education could attain.

CHAPTER XI

OTHER REQUIREMENTS

CITIZENSHIP as a qualification for office was a matter of negligible consequence in colonial days. The common requirement of property for the exercise of the suffrage or any share in public affairs, was enough to secure the desired attachment to local interests. It was the change worked by the Revolution that led men to begin to think they should take precaution against putting their affairs in the hands of outsiders and newcomers.

The plan of a Constitution laid before the Federal Convention by Charles Pinckney contemplated four years of citizenship for Senators and left blank the requirement for Representatives. The report of the Committee on Detail filled the blank with three years. Colonel Mason thought that was not enough to ensure the local knowledge a Representative ought to have. "It might also happen that a rich foreign nation, for example, Great Britain, might send over her tools, who might bribe their way into the legislature for insidious purposes." He wanted it seven years, but after hearing argument, thought seven years too long, though he "would never agree to part with the principle." Rutledge and Gouverneur Morris stood for seven years. On the other hand, Ellsworth thought one year enough. Later, Morris moved to make the qualification for Senators fourteen instead of four years of citizenship, Pinckney seconding him. Ellsworth opposed the motion, as discouraging meritorious aliens from emigrating to this country. Mason would have restrained eligibility to natives, had it not been for the fact that many not natives had acquired great credit in the Revolution. Madison thought any restriction in the Constitution unnecessary and improper. Butler was decidedly opposed to the admission of foreigners without long residence. Doctor Franklin would be sorry to see anything like illiberality, though not against a reasonable time. Randolph would go as far as seven years, but no farther. Wilson rose with peculiar feelings. He was not a native and foresaw he might be excluded from participating under a Constitution he had shared in making. Morris spoke strongly for his motion but in vain, as only four States voted for it, with seven against. Next he moved for thirteen years, and lost; Pinckney for ten years, and lost. Then nine years secured the support of six States, a majority. The debate returning to Representatives, Wilson and Randolph wanted the requirements for them four years. Gerry preferred to confine eligibility to natives. Williamson preferred nine years of residence. Hamilton and Madison wanted to leave it to the Legislatures. All motions for a figure other than that of seven years, failed of a majority.

The most noteworthy instance where the question of citizenship has resulted in exclusion from an American legislative body, was that of Albert Gallatin, who came to be a famous Secretary of the Treasury and played an otherwise important part in public life. Gallatin took his seat as a member of the United States Senate from Pennsylvania December 2, 1793. He had landed in Massachusetts in 1780, had formed the intention of becoming a citizen in the summer of 1783, and had taken the oath of citizenship and allegiance to Virginia in 1785, so that he had not actually been a citizen for the nine years prescribed by the Constitution. When he took the Virginia oath, however, the government was that of the Confederation, under the Constitution of which the free inhabitants of each of the States, paupers, vagabonds, and fugitives from justice excepted, were to "be entitled to all privileges and immunities of free citizens in the several States." Gallatin himself thought it a nice and difficult point, likely to be decided by a party vote, for parties were already forming. His election was declared void by a vote of 14 to 12. His biographer doubts if a majority would have been secured against him had he not seriously annoyed the Federal leaders by introducing a resolution calling for an elaborate statement of the debt, which they found most embarrassing.

Excluded from the Senate in February, 1794, Gallatin came back as a member of the House in December of the following year and proceeded to make himself more obnoxious than ever to the Federalists. They tried to get at him when they passed the fatal Alien and Naturalization Bills of 1798. These did not reach Gallatin, but they helped kill the Federalist party. The new Naturalization Act prolonged the period of residence before a man could become a citizen, from five to fourteen years.

Harper in the House debate urged that nothing but birth should entitle a man to citizenship. Otis offered a resolution that no man alien-born unless already a citizen, should thereafter hold office here. Massachusetts and Connecticut Legislatures recommended to Congress that no person thereafter naturalized should be eligible to either House. The only result was to help defeat John Adams and make Thomas Jefferson President. In the year after Jefferson took his seat, Albert Gallatin became his Secretary of the Treasury, and the period required before naturalization was put back to five years.

The obstinate remnant of the Federalist party that in 1814 held the famous Hartford Convention, which might have led New England to secession but for the ending of the war, persisted in trying to revive the alien issue. "The easy admission of naturalized foreigners, to places of trust, honor, or profit," the delegates resolved, "operating as an inducement to the malcontent subjects of the old world to come to these States, in quest of executive patronage, and to repay it by an abject devotion to executive measures," was part of the policy that had brought the country into "this vicissitude." Therefore they proposed a constitutional amendment excluding from office foreigners thereafter arriving in the United States.[1]

From that day to this at intervals of a score of years more or less, agitations against the foreign-born, and particularly against those of the Roman Catholic faith, have disturbed the public tranquillity. The most serious was that which reached its height about 1855, called the Know-Nothing movement. It has been the only outbreak of prejudice that has come dangerously near to lessening the opportunities of new-comers. The Legislature of Massachusetts, overwhelmingly controlled in that year by the apostles of Native Americanism, gave the first passage to a constitutional amendment confining political, judicial, or military office to the native-born (or children of American parents born without the jurisdiction of the United States). The next year this passed the Senate by 17 to 6, but failed of the necessary two thirds in the House, the vote being 166 to 128.

Maine is the only State requiring a period of citizenship in the United States to have passed before a man can take his seat in Senate or House, the requirement being five years. Seven-

[1] Theodore Dwight, *History of the Hartford Convention*, 369, 373.

teen other States, however, have deemed it necessary to specify citizenship in the United States as a qualification. Thirty require a man to have been a citizen, inhabitant, or resident of the State for periods varying from one to seven years, New Hampshire being at the extreme with a seven-year requirement, and Kentucky next with a six-year requirement, each for Senators. The Constitution proposed for Arkansas and rejected in 1918 would have added to the qualifications for Senators and Representatives the requirement of citizenship of ten years in the United States.

RESIDENCE

ORIGINALLY it was expected that men summoned to Parliament should be residents of the county or borough sending them. The words *"de comitatu tuo"* in the writ to the sheriff are supposed to have implied this. Early in the fifteenth century any doubt that may have existed was removed by the statute 1 Henry V, which expressly commanded residence as a qualification. With the political jealousies of Tudor times, with the growth of commercial interests, and with the wider scope of social relations, strangers began to covet the borough memberships and to canvass for them. A way to evade the statute was found in admitting non-residents to the free burghership, and presently the statute itself came to be looked on as inoperative.

In Elizabeth's reign an attempt was made to secure its repeal. Norton argued (1571) that the repealing bill would take away all pretense for sending unfit men, as was too often seen, and remove any objection that might be started to the sufficiency of the present Parliament, wherein, for the most part, against positive law strangers to their several boroughs had been chosen; that persons able and fit for so great an employment ought to be preferred without regard to their inhabitancy, since a man could not be presumed to be the wiser for being a resident burgess; and that the whole body of the realm, and the service of the same, was rather to be respected than any private regard of place or person. Hallam says ("Const. Hist." i. 265): "This is a remarkable, and perhaps the earliest assertion, of an important constitutional principle, that each member of the House of Commons is deputed to serve, not only for his constituents, but for the whole kingdom; a principle which marks the distinction between a modern English Parliament and such deputations of the Estates as were assembled in several continental kingdoms; a principle to which the House of Commons is indebted for its weight and dignity, as well as its beneficial efficiency, and which none but the servile worshippers of the populace are ever found to gainsay."

Evasion of the law increased. By the opening of the seventeenth century, at any rate, counties as well as boroughs were disregarding it. In an election of 1601 Sir Edward Hobbie said in reply to one of the arguments of Sergeant Harris: "If you stand on that, I think, there are few Knights in the House lawfully chosen; for the words of the Writ and Statute are that he must be commorant [an inhabitant] within the county, which but few are." To this, says Sir Simonds D'Ewes in his Journal, "not one word was answered, and that clause was hushed up." At last, in the case of Onslow v. Repley, 1681, Lord Chief-Justice Pemberton for the Court of King's Bench ruled that "little regard was to be had to that ancient statute 1 Henry V, forasmuch as common practice hath ever since been to the contrary." This is believed to have been almost the only instance in which desuetude has avowedly nullified a statute. The law was formally repealed by 14 Geo. III, c. 50.

On the Continent the general practice does not require Deputies to be residents of their districts. In Canada, and probably in the other English Dominions, residence is not required.

In this matter as in so many other particulars, the records of the American colonies show there was no general imitation of English procedure, but that each colony worked out a practice to suit its own needs. Thus in Plymouth, compact, with but a few towns, there was no occasion whatever for electing non-resident representatives, but on the contrary every reason for having each town represented by men of its own. So when representatives were created, March 5, 1638, the vote provided "they choose them onely of the ffreemen of the said Towne whereof they are." [1] On the other hand in the Massachusetts Bay Colony distances quickly became a serious factor in communication and Boston began gathering to herself more than numerically her fair share of the abler men. So as early as 1641 we find it declared, in No. 68 of the "Body of Liberties": "It is the libertie of the freemen to choose such

[1] *Plymouth Colony Records*, x, 31.

deputies for the Generall Court out of themselves, either in their own Townes or elsewhere as they judge fitest."

Possibly there was question of this, for when in November, 1644, a new plan for choosing the General Court was proposed, its author took care to specify, "further, to the end the ablest gifted men may be made use of in so weighty a worke, it shalbe at the liberty of the freemen to choose them, in their own sheires, or elsewhere, as they shall see best." [1] No record appears of action on the plan, but the practice of electing non-resident Deputies became common without further statutory recognition. For example, Captain John Hull, the famous mintmaster, who was from first to last a citizen of Boston, represented Westfield in 1674, Concord in 1676, and Salisbury in 1680.

The first Governor under the new Charter given to Massachusetts Bay in 1691, Sir William Phips, speedily found himself opposed by a strong faction, known as the court or prerogative party, friends of the old charter, the conservatives of their day, who wanted Phips removed. Late in 1693 a motion for an address to the King against this action, that is, in favor of Phips, was carried in the lower branch of the General Court by only a bare majority, the vote standing 26 to 24. It happened that various representatives of country towns who were residents of Boston, were friends of Phips. Thereupon his enemies conceived the ingenious idea that they could advance their cause by getting rid of these men through changing the law so that Representatives would have to live in the towns they represented. Evidently the argument for the change won over enough of the friends of Phips to give success to the stratagem, for an entry in Judge Sewall's Diary for November 25 reads: "Representatives vote that none be chosen Representatives but persons resident in the Towns for which they are chosen, and having Free-Hold there, &c."

Perhaps some who were friendly to the Governor had the wool pulled over their eyes. Perhaps there were those not unwilling to stab him in the back. Anyhow the amended bill went to the upper branch and Sewall's entry for the 28th tells what there fell out: "The Bill for regulating the choice of Representatives was brought in with the clause relating to Residency of the Persons to be chosen for. The Dissent also of 21 Deputies was

[1] *Records of the Colony of the Mass. Bay in N. E.*, II, 88.

brought in with it, alledging the vote was contrary to Charter, Custom of England, of the Province, hindred men of the fairest estates from Representing a Town where their Estates lay, except also resident; might prove destructive to the Province." After giving the names of the dissenters, he says: "The clause was read, and the Dissent 2 or 3 times by the Secretary, and then put to the Vote, Governour not being there." Nine are recorded "Content" and eight "Not content." Sewall takes the pains to add: "Governour came in presently after had done voting." An imaginative historian, fond of reconstructing an episode on a phrase as a foundation, might enjoy himself in drawing from this the inference that, if something had not delayed the Governor, his presence might have shamed the opposition enough to change at least one vote, in which case the injury of the residence requirement might never have been inflicted on Massachusetts.

When Governor Hutchinson came to describe this happening, he observed [1] that though the provision was generally looked upon as a privilege and a point gained by the people, "it certainly was occasioned by what is commonly called the prerogative party in government, and, however salutary, was designed as an abridgment of liberty." Whatever the effects may have been up to Hutchinson's time, since then they have been of a nature to make it doubtful whether even his rhetorical concession, "however salutary," was justifiable. Many thoughtful men would now look on the incident as a striking illustration of the unfortunate origin of destiny-shaping institutions in episodes trivial of themselves and having no manner of relation other than sequential, to the results they produced.

From the legal point of view, a strict construction of the Charter would seem to justify the twenty-one Deputies who declared the change to be contrary to its provisions, for the Charter contains nothing that can be fairly construed into a restriction upon the choice of the electors, save that it should be from freeholders. Herein it differed from some of the other Charters. For instance, that of Connecticut in 1662 speaks of "Two Persons from each Place, Town, or city," to be elected or deputed. Penn's first Frame of Government contains no suggestion of a residence restriction, but that of the next year

[1] *History*, II, 79.

(1683) said the Provincial Council was to consist of eighteen persons, "three out of each county," and the Assembly of thirty-six, "being six out of each county," so that the phrase "out of" might be presumed to imply residence. The same phrase appears in the Fundamental Constitutions for the Province of East New Jersey, 1683.

It is not probable that the practice of restriction to residents prevailed in provincial New York, for nothing to that effect was put into her State Constitution. Apparently it was thought at the time of the Convention of 1846 that there was restriction, for when the single district system was under consideration and it was proposed that a district might name any resident of the county, though outside the district, Mr. Nicholas gave as a reason to the contrary: "If the Constitution sanctions the election of candidates out of the district where they are to be voted for, it must defeat the principal objects of the single district system, which are to prevent political combinations in large counties, and to bring the candidate and his constituents nearer together, so that candidates may be generally known within their district." Yet when in 1858 a seat was contested on the ground of non-residence, Lyman Tremain, Attorney General, reported to the Assembly that, in his opinion, "there is nothing in the Constitution or laws of this State which prohibits the people in any Assembly district from electing a member to represent them in the Assembly of this State, who resides in another district."

In 1709 the General Assembly of New Jersey enacted that no one should be elected thereto who was "not inhabiting and usually resident himself, and likewise with his family (if any he hath) the day of the date of the writ of summons," but this was aimed to exclude those residing in neighboring provinces.

Colonial Virginia followed the English rule that candidates might offer themselves regardless of residence. We find Patrick Henry chosen from Louisa County in 1765, though not then living within its borders. The Constitution of 1776, however, declared that the Representatives should be chosen "of such men as actually reside in and are freeholders of the same counties, or duly qualified according to law." It is said that at the election in Fauquier, in the spring of 1784, the old friends and constituents of John Marshall in that county again elected him a member of the General Assembly, although he was

no longer an actual resident in the county. Perhaps his retention of a freehold there was held to make him "duly qualified
according to law."

From 1778 to 1865 citizens of South Carolina might be chosen
to the Legislature from districts in which they did not reside,
with the restriction that a Senator must have an estate and
freehold of his own right in the district electing him, to the value
of 7000 pounds, and a Representative, of 3500 pounds.

New York is now the only State that does not require a State
Senator or Representative to be an elector, inhabitant, or resident of the district he represents. Fifteen States specify even
that removal of a member from the district shall vacate the
office.

Two thirds of the States prescribe the time for which a
Senator or Representative must have lived in the district.
Three require two years; most of the others, one year. Massachusetts oddly omits a time specification for Senators while
requiring a year for Representatives. Many of the States by
stipulating that the Senator or Representative shall be an
elector of the district, impose in effect a time requirement.

Upon the adoption of the Federal Constitution, James
Madison was defeated for election to the United States Senate,
through the influence of Patrick Henry in the Virginia Legislature. Thereupon Madison's friends sought to elect him to the
House. Trying to prevent this, Henry contrived, it is charged,
an unfair apportionment that threw Madison into a district
supposed to be hostile — a device suggesting that the "Gerry-
mander" ought to have been called the "Henrymander."
At the same time an act was passed restricting candidacies to
residents. Nevertheless Madison won.

Restriction to residents was destined to be held unconstitutional by Congress. The first case to come up was that of
William Pinkney of Maryland. That State in 1790 enacted a
law requiring residence in the district at the time of election
and for twelve months before. Pinkney was an able lawyer,
destined to become recognized as the head of the American
bar. It is said he made a powerful argument in support of his
claim to be returned, and he was by the Executive Council
declared duly elected, but the issue was avoided by his declining
the honor on account of his professional pursuits and the state
of his private affairs. The restriction was brought to the de-

cisive test in November of 1807 when there was exhaustive debate on whether William McCreery was entitled to his seat. The committee reported the law unconstitutional and in the end the House voted not to oust McCreery.

Nevertheless it was enacted in Massachusetts that a Congressman should be an inhabitant of his district. Governor John A. Andrew did not approve of this and in his second inaugural message (1862) recommended that the provision be dropped, declaring it unconstitutional. Yet a redistricting bill was passed repeating the provision. Andrew vetoed it, saying in the course of his message: "I cannot think that Daniel Webster was more familiar with the Plymouth district and its people, merely for the fact of his legal domicile in Marshfield, where he spent a few weeks of the year, than he was with the people and interests of the Boston district, where he had resided for years, and where were the seat and center of his political, social, and business life. Nor can I think that the transference of the town of Quincy from one district to another, rendered John Quincy Adams any more or less fitted to represent either the one or the other of them." The act was passed over the veto, but the provision was in several instances practically disregarded, and when in 1882 Governor Long called attention to Governor Andrew's arguments, with approval, the provision was dropped.

Whether or not supported by statute, it has become the unwritten law in most of the States that the member must be a resident of his district. There are occasional exceptions. Downtown constituencies in New York City are often represented by men living in uptown districts. Massachusetts has occasionally seen the election of a man not residing in the district. In at least one notable instance, the nomination was given by a minority party with little expectation of success, but by one of the unexpected turns of the political wheel, it proved to be fortunate. Had such a result been expected, it is improbable that the politicians of the district in question would have let the nomination go beyond their borders.

In many instances compliance with the letter of the law has been all that public sentiment has asked. Summer residents, with domicile secured by presence on the day when the assessors make their rounds, often meet the requirements of constituencies. And once established in Congress, many members have secured reëlection for term after term, although having meantime become virtually residents of Washington or some large city. A reasonable inference would be that non-residence has not been so objectionable to constituencies at large, as to the politicians controlling nominating conventions, who have naturally sought to keep honors in hand. With the spread of direct nomination, it would not be surprising to see more non-residents chosen.

The custom of confining choice to residents, whether in the case of Representatives in Congress or of those in Legislatures, is perhaps the most harmful that has afflicted American politics. The only thing to be said for it is that in theory it should conduce to benefit by securing knowledge of local conditions and local opinion. Even this turns out in practice to be more of harm than a gain, for it encourages legislation from the local point of view rather than that of the State or Nation as a whole. It incites sectionalism. It fosters log-rolling. It makes legislation selfish. It offers reward to every legislator who thinks his first duty the getting of special favors for his constituency. It endangers the political future of every legislator who opposes "porkbarrel" bills and who will not admit that his prime function is to despoil the public treasury for the benefit of his own district.

Another injury lies in its effect on the quality of our legislative bodies. It assumes an even distribution of experience and ability. Such a distribution was more nearly the case a century ago than it is now. The growth of cities has enormously increased their attractiveness for strong men, because of the opportunities they offer for wealth and power and fame. To-day the larger cities contain the offices and counting-rooms of by far the larger number of leaders in nearly every line of endeavor. At the same time within the cities themselves the influences toward social segregation have crowded the exceptional men into a few of the wards. The result is that in some city neighborhoods there are ten, twenty, a hundred times as many men fitted for lawmaking as in rural districts of the same population, or in other parts of the city itself.

If it is the fact that the work of government ought not to be a specialized occupation, that citizens should engage in it but temporarily, that the best results are to be secured by a system not much removed from the method of filling juries, by lot, then the argument falls to the ground. Few thoughtful men, however, will be able to see why government does not deserve expert work as much as any other task. No sane man now thinks that the interpreter of law, the Judge, ought to be chosen at random without regard to his qualifications for the work. It is not yet so generally agreed that the administrator of law should be a trained expert, but the conviction of that fact is making rapid progress and we may both confidently and thankfully look forward to its common acceptance before many decades have passed. There remains unregenerate only that department of government concerned with the framing of law.

As far as my observation goes, ours is the only country in the world that thereby deliberately discourages men from entering on a public career. We say to the youth that in the practice of law or medicine, in the ministry, in every kind of engineering, in business, in every other occupation save that of public service, faithful endeavor shall secure that opportunity for continuous labor which alone promises fame and fortune, and of greater importance, promises that satisfaction of the wish to make life useful, which is the source of the noblest effort and the cause of the highest achievement. In politics alone is a youth confronted with not merely the possibility but with the strong probability that his career will be cut short by some one of a hundred kinds of accident. The first change in the party control of his district will throw him off the ladder, and once off he is likely never to get back. In this way the Progressive uprising of 1912 ended the opportunities of scores upon scores of men who had learned something of official duties. Most of them, compelled to turn their thoughts and ambitions into other channels, have never made even the attempt to renew their interest in public affairs. Should they aspire again to be chosen to office, they will be seriously handicapped by the record of defeat, for the public refuses to recall the reason of defeat, and the politician always inclines to back the candidate with the prestige of never having been beaten.

The ambitious youth cannot even make a start in public life unless he lives in a district where a majority of the voters are of his political way of thinking. The man with the making of a statesman in him may live a long life in a district not of his political faith and never be entrusted with so much as a single term in the Legislature. This automatically excludes from the public service nearly half of the capable men in the greater part of the States of the Union. Only in the South, where by reason of the negro problem one party overwhelmingly predominates, is the pernicious effect insignificant.

It is a condition that emphasizes the worst phases of the party system. Every legislator knows that the least deviation from party subservience will endanger his whole political future. If by a single vote he alienates the good-will of the party leaders of his district, he cannot as in other countries turn to some constituency not out of sympathy with this particular position. If he is defeated in a district where organized labor is in control, he cannot appeal to a district of farmers. In short, his usefulness may end when he happens to get out of touch with the controlling faction of the group among whom he happens to dwell.

The system takes no account of where a man's interests may lie or where his activities may be applied. The arbitrary assumption is that their locality is where he happens to sleep on a specified night in the year. Once that may have been a reasonable test. To-day it is inconsistent with the fact that hundreds of thousands of men pass most of their waking hours at distances more or less remote from their abodes, working in cities and sleeping in suburbs. More of the intellectual and business leaders of Boston sleep outside its artificial bounds than sleep within. Large numbers of the strong men with offices on Manhattan Island have their homes beyond the Harlem or East River, or live in another State, New Jersey. Much the same thing is true of Chicago and most of the other great cities.

Furthermore, with the spread of prosperity and the more rational attitude toward annual periods of rest and recreation, large numbers of men now have two homes, one for winter and one for summer, usually many miles apart and often in different States. This gives them property interests in two localities and acquaintance with the conditions and needs of each.

City growth has made representation by wards absurd. Men are rarely known by more than a few of their neighbors in cities, and the selection between candidates gets none of the benefit of personal acquaintance that used to be found. Then, too, there is no important reason why a ward of a crowded city should have independent representation in the Legislature even if only locality interest is to be considered. Likewise in the country, conditions no longer justify old methods. When each town had separate representation, there was warrant for the belief that personal knowledge of candidates helped toward wise choice, and something was to be said for having local interests voiced at the State House. Nowadays, except in some of the New England States, one Representative is sent by a group of towns, occasionally a numerous group, and the old justifications have disappeared.

It would be vain to hope that these things will be speedily recognized by the mass of the electorate. Abolition of the residence requirement would be very hard to achieve ; the people would cling tenaciously to the idea of locality representation. A palliative, however, if not a remedy, ought not to be out of the question. Such a palliative might be found in the choice of a part of the State Representatives and Senators "at large," either by Congressional districts or on a State ticket, and some of the Congressmen "at large," as occasionally practiced in some States. The honor that would inevitably be attached to election at large, however artificial in itself, would incite the candidacies of capable men. They would go to Legislature or Congress without the embarrassment of petty local obligation. They would take a broader view of public questions.

WEALTH

THE ancients were not agreed as to whether public officers should be men of means. Solon provided for the election of the magistrates of Athens from the first three only of the four classes into which he divided the people, these three consisting of persons of easy fortunes. Aristotle, however, in "The Politics" (bk. VI) urged that no property qualification should be required for offices, or only a very small one. When Augustus reformed the Roman Senate, he raised the qualification to twelve hundred thousand sesterces, equivalent to about fifty thousand dollars of our money. In his censorial capacity he ejected the impoverished.

In England custom began in the seventeenth century to make it hard for the poor man to serve in Parliament. Constituencies stopped paying wages when men began to be eager for election. Competition between the newly rich increased electioneering expenses amazingly. Next the very evil that handicapped the man without money, that of wholesale bribery, became the cause of legislation seeming to deprive him of what little chance he had, for in 1710 it was enacted that no man should be elected for a county unless he had an income of £600 a year, or for a borough unless he had an income of £300 a year. In each case this income was to be from land. Swift, in "The Examiner," described the measure as "the greatest security that was ever contrived for preserving the Constitution, which otherwise might in a little time be wholly at the mercy of the monied interest."

From the first the law was evaded. It did not require that a member should continue to have such an income. So a colorable transfer of property was made to the impecunious member-elect, which was canceled or reversed as soon as he had taken his seat. The practice became recognized and in effect legitimate. Burke, Pitt, Fox, and Sheridan were among the famous men who were always notoriously disqualified and met the letter of the law only by fictitious methods. There is abundant evidence that hundreds of members swore to the ownership of property they never possessed. Yet in one conspicuous case conscience (let us hope it was) prevailed. In 1826 the poet Southey, who had been elected a member for Downton while he was absent on the Continent, addressed a letter to the Speaker in which he stated that he did not possess the estate required by law, and the House thereupon, after waiting the proper time, issued a writ for a new election.

In 1838 the nominal monopoly of the land-owners was surrendered and personal property was added as a qualification, but this did not content the masses, who made the abolition of all property qualifications one of the five articles of the People's Charter. Although their agitation was not at once successful, its purpose in this particular was ostensibly accomplished in 1858 by repeal of the obnoxious, invidious, unjust law.

As a matter of fact, however, it continued to be next to useless for men without money resources to entertain ambitions for a seat in Parliament. The cost of election stood in the way. In the reign of Anne a start was made toward establishing the pernicious principle that the personal interest of a candidate justified requiring him to bear some part of the official expenses of conducting elections, and by the middle of the century this had become accepted doctrine. Up to the time of the reforms of 1832 there was no legal requirement that the candidate should bear all the costs of the returning officers, but the result was effected by custom. After the Reform Bill of 1832 it was made possible to collect these official costs by law. If there was no contest, the candidate on nomination paid $125. If the seat was contested, in boroughs the official costs ran from $500 to $3500, and in counties from $750 to $5000, according to the number of electors on the register, and were apportioned equally between the candidates. Not until 1918 were the official costs put upon the taxpayers.

Unofficial expenditures, though now much limited, still handicap the poor man. Furthermore, under a system whereby candidates are customarily selected by a central political committee, the party managers want men who can contribute handsomely to the local political clubs. "The electors at large," says Sidney Low, "have a natural affection for the lavish public-spirited person, who is always ready to respond to local solicitations with a sufficient cheque. Church guilds, musical societies, charitable committees, football and cricket clubs, flourish under the fertilising stream, and tap its sources with unblushing rapacity. The wealthy M.P. or candidate groans but pays. Sometimes if he is 'nursing' the place assiduously, the constituency, in its corporate capacity, may receive a *douceur* in the shape of a public library, or an open space, or a swimming bath. A considerable proportion of the English members of Parliament would be satisfied if their annual outlay upon their division [district] came to no more than £500. Many spend less, some a great deal more. There are large county divisions, and certain small and greedy urban communities, in which the annual expenditure could be reckoned in thousands of pounds rather than hundreds." [1]

The result of all this is that no poor man is elected to Parliament unless with the help of contributions from friends or partisans.

In a few of the other countries of the world the possession of wealth by a legislator is either required or formally recognized as desirable. The rich are among the classes from which Senators must be or may be chosen in Belgium, Italy, Spain, and Egypt. In the Netherlands members of the upper House must be among the highest taxpayers, limited in each Province to one for every fifteen hundred persons, or else hold or have held

[1] *The Governance of England*, 180.

one or more of the important public offices designated by law. Sweden has property qualifications for both branches. In Argentina the Senators must enjoy a specified annual income or its equivalent in capital; in Chile both Senators and Deputies must have a specified income, the minimum for a Senator being four times as large as that for a Deputy.

In the colonies that became the United States, property qualifications for membership in the Assemblies went for the most part hand in hand with those for the suffrage. Only three made a marked distinction. South Carolina and New Jersey required £1000 and New Hampshire £300 for members. A freehold was usually required. Pennsylvania, Delaware, and Virginia specified the number of acres of land; in other cases the value of the freehold in money was determined. In South Carolina land and slaves or an equivalent in personal property was demanded. The location of the property was usually specified. The earlier statutes provided merely that the property should be in the colony. Later on, however, there was a tendency to require that Deputies to the Assembly should possess a freehold in the district represented. In New Jersey the Deputy was to own property in the division — East or West Jersey — from which he was elected. In Connecticut the Deputy was to be a freeman; the freemen were to elect Deputies from their own number and the freemen were required to own a certain amount of property in the town. Hence, although it was not directly so provided by statute, ownership of property in the town represented was required. Most of the colonies required it by statute. New Hampshire, on the other hand, provided that the property might be anywhere in the colony.[1]

The delegates to the only Assembly that sat in Georgia as a colony were selected under a singular restriction, due to the desire to encourage the silk industry. From June, 1751, to June, 1753, no person could be a Deputy unless he had "a hundred mulberry trees planted and properly fenced upon every fifty acres he possessed." After 1753, a Deputy was to have been a person who had strictly conformed to the limitation of the number of negro slaves in proportion to his white servants, who had at least one female in his family instructed in the art

[1] F. H. Miller, "Legal Qualifications for Office in America," *Am. Hist. Assn. Ann. Report for 1899*, I, 96, 97.

of reeling silk, and who yearly produced fifteen pounds of silk upon fifty acres of land, and the like quantity upon every fifty acres he possessed. "But as the Trustees are desirous of seeing some immediate good effects from this Assembly, and are sensible that at present there are not many in the province who may have the necessary qualifications," the members of the first Assembly were wisely exempted from the operation of these rules.[1]

Accustomed as they were to property qualifications for office holding, it was not surprising that seven of the original States framed their Constitutions with specifications as to the amount a Representative or Senator should possess. Virginia, Delaware, and New York did not specify amounts but required that the choice should be confined to freeholders. Pennsylvania was the most liberal, naming no property qualifications, but the election was confined to taxpayers and the Declaration of Rights implied restriction when it said: "All free men having a sufficient common interest with, and attachment to the community, have a right to elect officers, or to be elected into office." Vermont, framing a Constitution independently in 1777, long before she was admitted as a State, was the first to reach the position that since then has won well-nigh universal acceptance. Her Bill of Rights copied the Pennsylvania phraseology, but the Frame of Government imposed not even the taxpaying quali-fication for election to the General Assembly.

In the Federal Convention there was difference of opinion over this as over nearly every other matter. Colonel Mason wanted a property qualification for Senators. Gouverneur Morris wanted Senators unpaid, which would confine the second branch to rich men; "of such the second branch ought to consist." He appears, however, to have opposed specific qualifications, for later on when Colonel Mason cited with approval those of Queen Anne's law for members of Parliament, Morris said they had been disregarded in practice, "and were but a scheme of the landed against the monied interest." Dickinson was against qualifications. He doubted the policy of interweaving into a republican Constitution a veneration for wealth. He had always understood that a veneration for poverty and virtue were the objects of republican encouragement. To this Gerry retorted, "if property be one object of government,

---

[1] C. F. Bishop, *The History of Elections in the American Colonies*, 44.

provisions to secure it cannot be improper" — a surprising rejoinder from one of a democratic spirit that was a generation later to make him Vice-President, after leading the fight against the aristocrats of his own State.

Pinckney thought it "essential that the members of the Legislature, the Executive, and the Judges, should be possessed of competent property to make them independent and respectable." Rutledge, in seconding Pinckney's motion, said the committee could not agree on the qualifications, "being embarrassed by the danger, on the one side of displeasing the people, by making them high, and on the other, of rendering them nugatory, by making them low." Doctor Franklin expressed his dislike to everything that tended to debase the spirit of the common people. If honesty was often the companion of wealth, and if poverty was exposed to peculiar temptation, it was not less true that the possession of property increased the desire of more property. Some of the greatest rogues he was ever acquainted with were the richest rogues. Pinckney's motion was rejected, Madison's Journal tells us, by so general a "No" that the States were not called.

When the draft came before the State Conventions for ratification, this matter did not escape attention. In Massachusetts Rufus King met the criticism that a property qualification had been omitted. He did not think it necessary; he never knew that property was an index to abilities. "We often see men," said he, "who, though being destitute of property, are superior in knowledge and rectitude. The men who have most injured the country, have most commonly been rich men. Such a qualification was proposed in the Convention, but by the delegates of Massachusetts it was contested that it should not obtain." He observed that no such qualification was required by the Confederation.[1]

Either Madison at Philadelphia gained the wrong impression of Gerry's idea or else King had forgotten. It must have been a little awkward for him to push the argument while the Constitution of Massachusetts itself was recognizing the claim of property to representation and requiring its possession by lawmakers.

A year after Vermont had come into the Union without any property qualifications for legislators, Kentucky, the second

[1] *Debates of Mass. Convention of 1788*, 133.

State to be admitted (1792), made no reference to the matter in her Bill of Rights, but followed Vermont's example in practice.

It has been frequently supposed that the advanced principles of Vermont and Kentucky won speedy support and that with the triumph of Jeffersonian democracy a wave of revolt against property qualifications swept through the land. Such was not the case. It was Jacksonian democracy that opened the door of opportunity to the impecunious. To be sure, Maryland abolished all property qualifications for office in 1810, and Alabama and Maine left them out of their Constitutions in 1819, but it was with Jackson that the reform gained impetus. Before his second term had expired, Mississippi, Tennessee, and Georgia had abolished property qualifications for office, Michigan and Arkansas had come in without them. Thenceforward the progress was rapid. Florida framed a Constitution without them in 1838; Massachusetts dropped them in 1840, New Jersey in 1844, Connecticut, New York, and Louisiana in 1845; the newer States would have none of them; the older States remaining unreformed, got rid of them soon after the war, except Rhode Island, which clung to them until 1888, and Missouri, which requires her Senators and Representatives to have paid a State and county tax within the year before election.

Nothing leads me to suppose that property qualifications were ever more effective here than in England. The case of John Turner, elected to the Massachusetts General Court in 1786, throws light on the attitude of that time. Sundry of his neighbors alleged want of qualification, whereupon only 25 out of 113 members of the House would vote that he was obliged to prove himself a qualified member. Of course with the burden of proof put on the petitioners, their case was hopeless. The next day the House voted the evidence they had produced was insufficient.[1]

In the Louisiana Convention of 1844–45, reference to a property qualification caused a delegate to cite a case in the House of Representatives of that State, when he was a member, as proof that the qualification was not only odious to the people of the State, but was disregarded by them. The seat of a member had been contested on the ground that he did not possess landed estate to the value of $500 as required by the Constitution of 1812, but the committee on elections, though

---

[1] *Mass. Election Cases*, i, 22.

knowing the facts, would not take notice of them, neither would the House.[1]

The disappearance of the property qualification in America would make discussion of the subject purely academic were it not that the possession of wealth continues to be a factor in the choice of our public servants. To-day, however, more frequently the possession of wealth brings opposition than favor. Among the masses there is, as there always has been and doubtless always will be, widespread suspicion of the well-to-do. It is one of the phases of the eternal conflict between aristocracy and democracy. Let me quote the temperate statement of some considerations bearing on the question, made by Henry Sidgwick in his thoughtful book, "The Elements of Politics" (378–80). "On the one hand," he says, "it is fairly urged that legislation is an art that can hardly be fairly undertaken except by persons of high intellectual culture: and that only those whose income is above the average are likely to have had the time and means necessary for the acquisition of such culture. On the other hand it may be replied that legislation is an art that is yet in a very rudimentary condition, in respect of the application of science and systematic method: that the knowledge and intellectual training, really useful for purposes of practical politics, which an ordinary legislator from the ranks of cultivated society has obtained from schools and colleges and books, is not very important in extent; nor beyond what an intellect of exceptional vigor can acquire in any class of society, in spite of the disadvantages of a short education and a life spent in manual labor. It may be urged further that the limitation of eligibility to a minority of comparatively wealthy persons is incompatible with an adequate realization of the general aims of representative government; since, in order to obtain the varied empirical knowledge and the sympathetic insight into the needs of all sections of society, which we saw to be the characteristic merit of this form of government, it is necessary that every class of electors should be free to choose its own members. Moreover, the limitation must have a tendency to diminish the interest taken by the poorer classes in the election of legislators, and to weaken their confidence in the members elected. These arguments seem to me very strong against any formal and rigid limitation of eligibility."

[1] F. N. Thorpe, *Const. Hist. of the Am. People*, i, 412.

Yet he swings the balance toward wealth. "I do not mean," he says, "that it would ever be possible — or desirable — to compose a legislature entirely of persons whose mere wealth renders them unlikely subjects for corruption: but in a body whose members are to a great extent drawn from this class it will generally be easier to keep up a severe tone of public opinion in reference to the pecuniary temptations to which a legislator is exposed. If, finally, it be said that an assembly in which comparatively rich men preponderate will tend, in framing legislative measures, to have special regard to the class-interest of the rich, I should consider it a valuable security for just legislation in a country where the suffrage is widely extended; in view of the great danger that the apparent interests of the poor, who form the numerical majority, will be preferred to the real ultimate interests of the whole community."

My own preference would be to urge other considerations, more suited to American modes of thought. On this side of the water men are more concerned with what a man does than with what he is. We are perhaps too indifferent to culture and too fond of achievement. Whether wisely or not, we are most interested in the fruits of a man's labors because they attest the labors, because they are an index of capacity. That is why many Americans would not agree with the confidence of Francis C. Lowell when he said: "It is obvious that men should be chosen for public office, not because they are rich or poor, not because they live in one place or in another, not because they deserve distinction, not because they are respectable or even virtuous, but simply and solely because they will serve the public better than any one else."[1] The wisdom of the concluding reason is incontestable. Is it not, however, fair to urge that the preceding reasons are corollaries rather than contrasts? Ordinarily the possession of a competency acquired by the effort of the owner indicates energy, diligence, persistence, patience, temperance, good judgment, and other qualities desirable in legislators. It will be a sorry day for democracy when it holds the proof of such qualities to be a reason for refusing to make use of them.

[1] "Legislative Shortcomings," *Atlantic Monthly*, March, 1897.

Religious Tests

PARTICULAR statement of religious qualifications for office was not as a rule deemed necessary in the American colonies, specifications for citizenship sufficing. Massachusetts Bay furnished one exception, its General Court enacting October 18, 1654: "Forasmuch as, according to the present form of government of this jurisdiction, the safety of the Commonwealth, the right administration of justice, the preservation of the peace, and purity of the churches of Christ therein, under God, doth much depend upon the piety, wisdom, and soundness of the General Court, not only Magistrates, but Deputies, it is therefore ordered by this Court, and the authority thereof, that no man, although a freeman, shall be accepted as a deputy in the General Court, that is unsound in judgment concerning the main points of the Christian Religion as they have been held forth and acknowledged by the generality of the Protestant Orthodox writers, or that is scandalous in his conversation, or that is unfaithful to the government; and it is further ordered, that it shall not be lawful for any freeman to make choice of any such person as aforesaid that is known to himself to be under such offence or offences before specified, upon pain or penalty of five pounds, and that the cases of such persons to be tried by the whole General Court." [1]

That the spirit of this was not neglected, is shown by an episode Hutchinson records, writing of the year 1721: "An odd affair happened in the House, this sitting of the Court. One of the members sat down in prayer time. The Speaker, after prayers, asked him the reason of it. He said he could not join with them in calling God '*our* Father.' The House immediately resolved, 'that Philip Taber be expelled this House as not worthy to continue a member thereof.'" [2]

In 1663 the High Sheriff of Lower Norfolk represented to the Virginia House of Burgesses that Mr. John Porter, one of the Burgesses of that county, was "loving to the Quakers and stood well affected towards them, and had been at their meetings, and was so far an Anabaptist as to be against the baptising of children," whereupon Porter was "dismissed this House," after he had confessed that he was well affected to the Quakers.[3]

---

[1] *Records of the Colony of the Mass. Bay in N.E.*, IV, pt. 1, 206.

[2] *Hist. of Massachusetts*, 3d ed., II, 227, note.

[3] Hening, *Virginia Statutes at Large*, II, 198.

In 1704 the Assembly of South Carolina, by a margin of but one vote, made the Church of England the established church of that colony and enacted that the sacrament should be taken according to its practices by every Assemblyman who had not taken it within twelve months. He was to take it in open Assembly or else deliver a proper certificate, signed by a minister, or prove the fact by two witnesses on oath. It is said that more than two thirds of the people of the province were dissenters, and of course they balked at such a rigid requirement. So they sent representatives to London to protest, whereupon the proprietors consented that the law should be repealed, which was done in 1706. Meanwhile, in November, 1705, the new Deputy Governor of North Carolina, Thomas Carey, had caused an act to be passed imposing a fine on any person who should enter into an office before taking an oath of qualification, and another declaring void the election of any person who should promote his own candidacy. Not only did these provisions bar the Quakers, but also by resort to the second one the election of any Presbyterian or other dissenter who was objectionable might be declared void on the slight pretext that he had promoted his own election.[1] Here too the objecting colonists sent protest to England, where John Porter, who bore it, secured an instrument in writing, or commission, for the settling of the government, by which the laws imposing oaths were suspended.

By the election law enacted in Pennsylvania in 1705 a man could not take his seat in the Assembly before he had made and subscribed to long declarations and profession of his Christian belief. He had to renounce transubstantiation; to declare the worship of the Virgin Mary or other Saints superstitious; to profess faith in the Trinity; and to acknowledge the Scriptures given by divine inspiration.

Whether or not elsewhere there were definite enactments thus excluding Catholics from office, in practical effect they were kept out in probably all the colonies except New York and Maryland. Jews were under the ban in New York, a contested election case there deciding (1737) that they could not hold office.[2]

Intolerance, however, did not extend in every direction.

---

[1] S. A'C. Ashe, *Hist. of North Carolina*, I, 160.
[2] *Colonial Docs. of N.Y.*, VI, 56, note.

Although by the Fundamental Constitutions of East New Jersey (1683), no man was to be admitted as a member of the Great or Common Council, or to any other place of public trust, who did not profess faith in Jesus Christ, yet no man was to be admitted who would not solemnly declare that he did not seek the turning out of any in the government, or their ruin or prejudice in person or estate, because they were in his opinion heretics, or differed in judgment from him. In West New Jersey (1681) none of the free people were to be "rendered uncapable of office in respect of their faith and worship." After the union of the two colonies, the Quakers were much oppressed, but in 1713 they secured equal standing with men of other beliefs through the passage of a bill permitting them to affirm instead of taking oath, and qualifying them to serve as jurors or "execute any office or place of trust or profit."

In view of this early history, it was singular that New Jersey should be the first as a State to make religious discrimination in the matter of office holding. Although in appearance hearty in declarations for freedom of conscience and against religious establishment, yet when that State said no "inhabitant of this Colony shall be denied the enjoyment of any civil right, merely on account of his religious principles," it put the word "Protestant" before "inhabitant"; and it declared as capable of being elected to office, "all persons, professing a belief in the faith of any Protestant sect, who shall demean themselves peaceably under the government."

The delegates chosen to form a State Constitution for Pennsylvania were required to believe in the Holy Trinity and the divine inspiration of the Scriptures.[1] The Constitution they drew, required every member of the General Assembly to make and subscribe this declaration: "I do believe in one God, the creator and governor of the universe, the rewarder of the good and the punisher of the wicked. And I do acknowledge the Scriptures of the Old and New Testament to be given by Divine inspiration." This was not repeated in the Constitution of 1790, but in its place appeared: "No person, who acknowledges the being of a God and a future state of rewards and punishments, shall, on account of his religious sentiments, be disqualified to hold any office or place of trust or profit under this commonwealth." This provision continues.

[1] *Works of Benjamin Franklin*, John Bigelow ed., IX, 431, note.

Delaware, acting at the same time with Pennsylvania, required members of each House to profess faith in the Trinity, and acknowledge the Scriptures to be given by divine inspiration.

In Maryland, although as one might expect from the history of that province, the first Constitution (1776) was for the times unusually liberal in the matter of freedom of conscience, yet "a declaration of a belief in the Christian religion" was to be required. This was repeated in the Constitution of 1851, but with the exception — "if the party shall profess to be a Jew, the declaration shall be of his belief in a future state of rewards and punishments." In 1864 the requirements were consolidated into "a declaration of belief in the Christian religion, or in the existence of a God, and in a future state of rewards and punishments." In 1868 this was shortened into "a declaration of belief in the existence of God."

North Carolina originally declared that "no person who shall deny the Being of God, or the truth of the Protestant religion, or the divine authority of either the Old or New Testament, or shall hold religious principles incompatible with the freedom and safety of the State, shall be capable of holding any office or place of trust within the State." This was the handiwork of an excellent and cultivated patriot, Rev. Dr. David Caldwell of Guilford, who thought it improper for men of his cloth to be mixed up in politics. Samuel Johnston, writing to Mrs. Hannah Iredell, December 13, 1776, said of the proposal: "This was carried after a very warm debate, and has blown up such a flame that everything is in danger of being thrown into confusion."[1] The prohibition was held not to exclude from the Legislature, but from civil offices, yet may be here mentioned because the experience with it illustrates the temper of the years that followed. In spite of it Thomas Burke, who "publicly professed and openly avowed the Catholic faith," after being a member of the Continental Congress, was elected Governor. In the Convention of 1835 it was said that Catholics had filled all offices, from Governor down to constable. The most distinguished of them, William Gaston, who without protest on the score of religion had been a member of the State Senate, Speaker of the House of Commons, and member of Congress, was in 1833 chosen a Justice of the Supreme Court. He ex-

[1] J. W. Moore, *Hist. of North Carolina*, 229.

plained in a letter how he could hold office in spite of the clause
in question. He held the Constitution to be based on the
general principles of civil and religious liberty; therefore all
citizens not clearly disqualified were competent to hold office.
What is the Protestant religion? We have no establishment
to determine that religion and pronounce on schism and heresy.
The Constitution has not defined the Protestant religion, has
not excluded Catholics or any other denomination *eo nomine.*
Is a belief in the Catholic a denial of the truth of the Protestant
religion? For these and other reasons Judge Gaston concluded
he was not disqualified and that he had "no right by any over-
nice scruples to be instrumental in practically interpolating
into that instrument an odious provision which it does not
contain." [1] The Convention of 1836 replaced the word "Protestant" with "Christian." In 1868 the restriction was limited
to "all persons who shall deny the being of Almighty God,"
and this was repeated in 1876.

Georgia and Vermont began (1777) by confining Representatives to believers in the Protestant religion, and in the following
year South Carolina, revising her Constitution, put in a like
provision. One of the same sort was in the rejected Massachusetts Constitution of 1778, and that which was adopted in 1780
required any person chosen Governor, Lieutenant-Governor,
Councilor, Senator, or Representative to declare that he believed the Christian religion and had a firm persuasion of its
truth. Also any person elected or appointed to State office
had to take oath or affirm that no foreign prelate had or ought
to have any jurisdiction, superiority, preëminence, authority,
dispensing or other power in any matter ecclesiastical or spiritual — which was an awkward declaration for a true Catholic
to make.

The Federal Constitution said "no religious test shall ever
be required as a qualification to any office or public trust under
the United States." Charles Pinckney of South Carolina was
the broad-minded statesman who proposed this. Apparently
his motion to amend by its insertion went through almost without opposition. We know only that Roger Sherman "thought
it unnecessary, the prevailing liberality being a sufficient security against such tests," but after Gouverneur Morris and
General Pinckney had spoken for the motion, it was agreed

[1] S. B. Weeks, *Church and State in North Carolina*, 61–64.

to, *nem. con.* It was not, however, to go unnoticed in the State Conventions. In Massachusetts three clergymen came to its defense. There were seventeen clergymen in the Convention, only eight of whom seem to have addressed it on any subject whatever, and of these eight only three touched upon the religious test. It is instructive indeed that not one of the three opposed the Constitution on this ground. On the contrary, their observations about freedom of conscience were of a liberality astonishing for that day, and may even now be republished with admiration and profit.

The Reverend Daniel Shute of Hingham said: "To object to the latter part of the paragraph under consideration, which excludes a religious test, is, I am sensible, very popular; for the most of men, somehow, are rigidly tenacious of their own sentiments in religion, and disposed to impose them upon others as the standard of truth. If, in my sentiments upon the point in view, I should differ from some in this honorable body, I only wish from them the exercise of that candor with which true religion is adapted to inspire the honest and well-disposed mind. To establish a religious test as a qualification for offices in the proposed Federal Constitution, appears to me, Sir, would be attended with injurious consequences to some individuals, and with no advantage to the whole. . . . Unprincipled and dishonest men will not hesitate to subscribe to anything that may open the way for their advancement, and put them into a situation the better to execute their base and iniquitous designs. Honest men, alone, therefore, however well qualified to serve the public, would be excluded by it, and their country be deprived of the benefit of their abilities. . . . Far from limiting my charity and confidence to men of my own denomination in religion, I suppose, and I believe, Sir, that there are worthy characters among men of every denomination — among the Quakers, the Baptists, the Church of England, the Papists, and even among those who have no other guide in the way to virtue and heaven, than the dictates of natural religion. . . . The presumption is that the eyes of the people will be upon the faithful in the land, and, from a regard to their own safety, they will choose for their rulers men of known abilities — of known probity — of good moral character. The apostle Peter tells us that God is no respecter of persons, but in every nation he that feareth him and worketh righteousness, is acceptable to him. And I know of no reason, why men of such a character, in a community, of whatever denomination in religion, *cæteris paribus*, with other suitable qualifications, should not be acceptable to the people, and why they may not be employed by them with safety and advantage in the important offices of government. The exclusion of a religious test in the proposed Constitution, therefore, clearly appears to me, Sir, to be, in favor of its adoption." [1]

The Reverend Phillips Payson of Chelsea said: "Such were the abilities and integrity of the gentlemen who constructed the Constitution, as not to admit of the presumption that they would have betrayed so much vanity as to attempt to erect bulwarks and barriers to the throne of God. . . . The great object of religion being God supreme, and the seat of religion in man being heart or conscience, *i.e.*, the reason God has given us, employed on our moral actions, in their most important consequences, as related to the tribunal of God, hence I infer, that God alone is the God of the conscience, and consequently, attempts to erect human tribunals for the consciences of men, are impious encroachments upon the prerogatives of God. Upon these principles, had there been a religious test, as a qualification for office, it would, in my opinion, have been a great blemish to the instrument." [2]

The Reverend Isaac Backus of Middleborough said: "Nothing is more evident, both in reason and in the holy Scriptures, than that religion is ever a matter between God and individuals; and therefore no man or men can impose a religious test without invading the essential prerogatives of our Lord Jesus Christ. Ministers first assumed this power under the Christian name; and then Constantine approved of the practice, when he adopted the professions of Christianity, as an engine of state policy. And let the history of all nations be searched, from that day to this, and it will appear that the imposing of religious tests hath been the greatest engine of tyranny in the world. And I rejoice to see so many gentlemen who are now giving in the rights of conscience, in this great and important matter. Some serious minds discover a concern lest, if all religious tests should be excluded, the Congress would hereafter establish Popery or some other tyrannical way of worship. But it is most certain that no such way of worship can be established without any religious test." [3]

[1] *Debates in Mass. Convention of 1788*, p. 220.   [2] *Ibid.*, 222.   [3] *Ibid.*, 251.

New Hampshire, which had not referred to the matter in the skeleton Constitution of 1776, required in 1784 that legislators should be of the Protestant religion. The Convention of 1850 advised taking out the religious test, but the people could not be persuaded to abandon the relic of prejudice until 1877. Ex-Senator Chandler told the Convention of 1902 that it was never enforced, and was obsolete for years before it was abolished.

It will be seen that of the twelve States (including Vermont) with Constitutions when the Federal Union was formed, all but Virginia and New York had imposed the test. Sentiment was changing, however, and few of the new States were to show intolerance. Of these Tennessee said in 1796: "No person who denies the being of God, or a future state of rewards and punishments, shall hold any office in the civil department of this State." Mississippi copied this in 1816. Arkansas copied part of it in 1836, but opened the door a little by omitting reference to a future state of rewards and punishments. On the other hand, States that had inserted the test were one by one dropping it. Christian charity won the first victory in Georgia, which reversed her position on this matter in the year when the Union was formed. South Carolina followed the good example in the next year. In 1792 Delaware made amends by going farther in her Bill of Rights than Pennsylvania had gone two years before, saying: "No religious test shall be required as a qualification to any office, or public trust, under this State."

In that same year Kentucky framed a Constitution declaring: "The civil rights, privileges, or capacities of any citizen shall in no ways be diminished or enlarged on account of his religion." Vermont dropped her requirement in 1793. Ohio began (1802) with substantially the Delaware declaration, as did Indiana (1816), Illinois (1818), Alabama (1819), and Maine (1820).

The subject was discussed at length in the Massachusetts Convention of 1820. Daniel Webster, opening the debate, argued that no man has a right to an office and that those who confer office may annex any such conditions to it as they think proper. If they prefer one man to another, they may act on that preference. "Between two candidates, otherwise equally qualified," he said, "the people at an election may decide in favor of one because he is a Christian, and against the other because he is not. They may repeat this preference at the next election, on the same ground, and may continue it, from year to year. Now, if the people may, without injustice, act upon this preference and from a sole regard to this qualification, and refuse in any instance to depart from it, they have an equally clear right to *prescribe* this qualification beforehand." Finding the declaration in the Constitution, and hearing of no practical harm from it, he would have been willing to retain it, but he did not consider its retention essential, for another part of the Constitution recognized in the fullest manner the benefits which civil society derives from those Christian institutions which cherish piety, morality, and religion.

On the other hand, James T. Austin held that every one who contributes to the expenses of government and bears his share of the public burthens, has a right to be a candidate for popular favor. This was the general rule. He admitted there were exceptions. We have the right to demand the qualifications of age, property, and residence, because they are necessary to insure the proper performance of the duties of the office. But this qualification related to opinions which do not bear upon the duties of government and are not connected with the public safety. This was the distinction — if we pass this line there is no place to stop.

There were twenty-one clergymen in the Convention and they were far from unanimous. The Reverend Joseph Tuckerman and the Reverend Edmund Foster wanted the test retained, on the usual grounds. But the Reverend Thomas Baldwin believed sufficient the solemn oath required of legislators; the Reverend Paul Dean thought that while it was important that men who rule over a Christian country should be Christians, it ought to be effected by other means than by the Constitution; and the Reverend N. W. Williams had yet to learn the propriety of requiring as a qualification for office such a profession as is required for admission to the church of God. In the end a motion to retain the old declaration was lost, 176 to 242; the people ratified the change, 13,782 to 12,480; and Massachusetts took her stand on the side of liberality.

New Jersey saw the light in 1844; Arkansas in 1868.

About two thirds of the States now specify in one way or another that religious belief shall not be a bar to holding civil office. In Arkansas, Maryland, Mississippi, North and South Carolina,

Pennsylvania, Tennessee, and Texas, atheists are still nominally excluded; in Pennsylvania and Tennessee, those also who do not believe in a future state of rewards and punishments. In the other States the absence of specification implies that there are no restrictions in this particular, for it is inconceivable that anybody to-day would raise a question of the common law, no matter what once it may have been.

To trace the growth of religious liberty in its relation to the lawmaking bodies of other lands, would be of itself a gigantic task and need not here be undertaken. It may, however, be useful merely to mention some of the decisive episodes in English parliamentary history of the last hundred years.

In the matter of the admission of Catholics the Duke of Wellington had to yield in 1829, and bring in a bill like that designed by Pitt. When in 1832 a Quaker (Mr. Pease) was returned as a member, the difficulty about the oath was quickly settled by letting him affirm, but another was less easily handled. It was a rule that the hat might be kept on while sitting, but must be taken off when moving about in the House. Some friend of Mr. Pease, to obviate this, instructed the doorkeeper to remove the hat gently and retain it till he quitted the House. In the course of a year or two he put it on and off for himself. Controversy over the admission of Jews lasted from 1849, when Baron Lionel de Rothschild was returned as one of the members for the City of London, till 1860, when the question acquired a permanent settlement, though the Jew still held his title by a standing order of the Commons and not under the law. In 1880 began the prolonged contest in the case of Charles Bradlaugh, a free-thinker of extreme type, who declared the oath was not binding on his conscience and asked to be allowed instead to affirm. When this was refused he desired to swear, but against this it was urged that a man without religious belief could not take an oath. After exciting controversy the House by 275 to 230 resolved that Bradlaugh should neither affirm nor swear. The story is one of devices and expedients and motions, odious scenes of physical violence, hard-fought actions in law-courts, conflicts between the House of Commons and the constituency, — in short, an intolerable scandal. In 1883 a serious attempt was made to change the law, but the Affirmation Bill was cast out by a majority of three, in spite of Mr. Gladstone's noble speech. In the course of that Parliament

Bradlaugh was never allowed to discharge his duty as a member, but after the election of 1885, when being once more chosen by Northampton, he went to the table to take the oath, the Speaker would suffer no intervention against him. In 1888 Bradlaugh himself secured the passage of an affirmation law, and in 1891 the House formally struck from its records the resolution of ten years earlier.[1]

[1] John Morley, *Life of W. E. Gladstone*, iii, 11–21.

CHAPTER XII

VARIOUS EXCLUSIONS

The eligibility of clergymen to be members of Parliament came to the front dramatically by reason of the election of Horne Tooke in 1801. Tooke, a radical agitator, had been a thorn in the flesh of the government from the outbreak of the American Revolution. In the debate on the attempt to exclude him, the Bishop of Rochester saw but one objection to the election of persons in holy orders — the unbecoming nature of the electioneering system, "the means by which candidates were obliged to seek admittance into the lower House, such as opening houses of entertainment, and truckling to every voter," which would form more or less of a difficulty to all scrupulous men. Lord Thurlow characterized the bill as one of disfranchisement. Lord Eldon supported it. Horne Tooke said "deacons and priests had sat in Parliament for more than a century, but at last one got in who opposed the Minister of the day, and then Parliament determined that there should no more be any deacons and priests admitted amongst them." The precedents collected by the committee were obscure and inconclusive. Occasionally clergymen sat in the House in its early years, but their right was at least doubtful from the time when it was recognized that by being represented in Convocation they should be taxed in Convocation. The House refused to exclude Tooke, but promptly passed an act (41 Geo. III, c. 63) by which it was declared that "no person having been ordained to the office of priest or deacon, or being a minister of the Church of Scotland" should be capable of being elected, and if any such person should sit or vote, he was to be liable to a fine of £500 for each day, to any one who might sue for it. Tooke, having been chosen before the passage of the act, was excepted from its operation. The Roman Catholic clergy were excluded by 10 Geo. IV, c. 7, s. 9.

Italy forbids the presence of priests in its lower House and so does Brazil. In Victoria and South Australia clergymen are excluded from Parliament. The Japanese electoral law of 1889 disqualified for membership in the House of Representatives all Shinto or Buddhist priests, Christian clergymen, or other teachers of religion.

Objection to clergymen as lawmakers rarely reached the point of exclusion by law in the American colonies until Revolutionary times. In Maryland, indeed, from the start, no priest, clergyman, or preacher of the gospel sat in the Assembly,[1] but this was exceptional, as was the act of Virginia, passed in the troublous days of the Commonwealth, declaring "it is unpresidential [unprecedented], and may produce bad consequences" [2] — in spite of which fear the ban seems later to have been there removed.

When the Revolution came, many of the clergy of the Church of England were naturally Royalists, and in those States where their influence had been strong, the framers of Constitutions took revenge by excluding them from Assemblies. Virginia led, in 1776, but not wishing to discriminate, declared "all ministers of the gospel, of every denomination, incapable of being elected members of either House of Assembly, or the Privy Council." Maryland, North Carolina, and Georgia copied this in substance. New York saw fit to explain and justify. "Whereas," it said, "the ministers of the gospel are, by their profession, dedicated to the service of God and the care of souls, and ought not to be diverted from the great duties of their function; therefore, no minister of the gospel, or priest of any denomination whatsoever, shall, at any time hereafter, under any pretence or description whatever, be eligible to, or capable of holding, any civil or military office or place within this State." This so pleased South Carolina that it was put into her second Constitution (1778), with the substitution of "public preacher of any religious persuasion" in place of "priest of any denomination," and with a limitation to two years after ending the exercise of the pastoral function.

All the Southern States coming afterward into the Union, save only Alabama and Arkansas, put the exclusion into their Constitutions. No Northern State imitated New York. In Massachusetts, however, I find that when the election of the Reverend Samuel Perley, returned a member from Gray in 1788, was controverted, the petitioners gave among their reasons — "Because we suppose, that those, who impose

[1] W. H. Browne, *Maryland*, 57.   [2] Hening, *Virginia Statutes at Large*, I, 378.

taxes upon us, ought to be those only who pay a proportion of those taxes, which the said Perley, being a minister of the gospel, is not obliged by law to do." The petitioners got leave to withdraw.

Repentance and reaction began with Georgia, which, framing a new Constitution in 1798, dropped the exclusion. Two years later Thomas Jefferson, who wanted to be remembered for the bill he wrote establishing religious freedom in Virginia, awoke to his inconsistency in approving the denial of rights to clergymen. When in 1783 there was a general idea that a Convention would be called to revise the Constitution of his State, he prepared a scheme that he meant to propose. Writing to Jeremiah Moor, August 14, 1800, he said of it: "I observe an abridgment of the right of being elected, which after seventeen years more of experience and reflection, I do not approve. It is the incapacitation of a clergyman from being elected. The clergy, by getting themselves established by law, and ingrafted into the machine of government, have been a very formidable engine against the civil and religious rights of man. They are still so in many countries and even in some of these United States. Even in 1783, we doubted the stability of our recent measures for reducing them to the footing of other useful callings. It now appears that our means were effectual. The clergy here seem to have relinquished all pretension to privilege and to stand on a footing with lawyers, physicians, &c. They ought therefore to possess the same rights." [1]

Nevertheless no other State than Georgia dropped the exclusion until Mississippi revised her Constitution in 1832. Louisiana (1852) was the only other Southern State to drop it before the Civil War, and she put it back from 1864 to 1868. The probability is that when the rest of the States made revisions before the War, they retained the exclusion not through fear of the political influence of clergymen, but because they thought the arena of politics unsuited to the cloth. In the Maryland Convention of 1851 Mr. Chandler, of Baltimore County, sought to strike out the obnoxious clause, but was defeated two to one. New York saw the light in 1846, an attempt to retain the provision being defeated in the Convention of that year by 77 to 33. In 1872 an attempt to restore it was unsuccessful.

---

[1] *Writings of Jefferson*, P. L. Ford, ed., VII, 454.

Half a dozen of the Southern States removed the disability from clergymen in the Constitutions drawn after the War. Kentucky came to removal in 1891. Now only Maryland and Tennessee persist in narrowness.

Nobody would contend that clergymen as a class should play the part in public life that naturally falls to lawyers. As a rule they do well to refrain from prominence in party strife. On the other hand, it is desirable that many points of view shall be represented in the lawmaking bodies of a republic. Under normal conditions the chances of the suffrage will send one or two clergymen into each Legislature. Exceptionally they may be numerous. For instance, in the Know-Nothing Legislature of Massachusetts that sat in 1855 there were twenty-four clergymen, four times as many as the year before, but nothing like it has been known since. The record of that particular Legislature was not such as to encourage a wish for its repetition. The presence of so many clergymen was not by itself the cause, but probably it helped. There can be too much of a good thing.

Lawyers, now conspicuous if not dominant in all lawmaking bodies, have not always been welcome members. Hostility toward them goes back to the middle of the fourteenth century, when a Parliament called "Learned" because it contained so many members learned in the law, won the ill will of the royal favorites whose exactions were thereby thwarted. So it was petitioned that "Nul home de ley soient retournez ni acceptez chevaliers des Countees." As a result it was enacted in 1373 that no lawyer practicing in the King's court should be returned knight of the shire. It was alleged that the lawyers used their places merely to advance the interests of their private clients. Soon after Henry IV came to the throne, his urgent need of money and his fear that his demands would be refused by a Parliament too intelligent, led him to put into the summons, "Nolumus quod aliquis homo ad legem aliqualiter sit electus." By this he kept out lawyers from the boroughs as well as the counties. Coke says this "made the Parliament fruitless, and never a good law passed thereat, and called the 'lack-learning Parliament.'"

The law against lawyers, obsolete for centuries, was not formally repealed until 1871.

The Massachusetts General Court in 1663 ordered "That no person who is a usuall & common atturney in any inferiour

Court shall be admitted to sitt as a deputy in this Court."[1] Such a provision, however, does not necessarily indicate a mistrust of lawyers. Undoubtedly they were disliked, but the stronger reason for their exclusion was that the General Court was virtually the Court of Appeal. The separation of legislative and judicial functions had but begun. Many years were to pass before it would be prudent to let a lawyer sit in a body that might have to adjudge his cause. Hutchinson said he did not recollect that Boston ever chose a lawyer to represent it until 1738, when John Read was elected, but he was left out the next year. In 1758 and 1759 Benjamin Pratt was a member. According to Hutchinson, who was himself an able lawyer, "these were men of the first character in their profession." And he goes on to say: "Lawyers have ever since taken the lead, and been much employed in the publick measures of this, and of the other colonies, and of the Continental Congress."[2] Save for the record, it would be needless to say that practicing attorneys, as such, are no longer excluded from any of our lawmaking bodies.

When Pennsylvania's first Constitution (1776) forbade members of the House of Representatives to hold any other office, it excepted only office in the militia. The revision of 1790, extending the prohibition to members of Congress, added to the militia exception that of "attorney at law," and so it still stands. The presumption is that somebody told the Convention that attorneys were or might be held to be officers under the Commonwealth or the United States. Two years later Delaware also took the precaution to put the standing of attorneys beyond dispute, and the example has since been followed by Colorado and North Dakota.

About a third of the States have thought it necessary in their Constitutions to exempt from the offices that legislators may not hold, those of Justice of the Peace or Notary Public or both. On the other hand, New Jersey specifically forbids Justices of the Peace to sit in the Legislature. Such variations are accounted for by the difference in the functions of these officials in various States.

Of course a quite different phase of the matter is presented by lawyer legislators who have clients interested in legislation.

[1] *Records of the Colony of the Mass. Bay in N.E.*, iv, pt. 2, 87.
[2] *History of Massachusetts*, iii, 104.

This was discussed at length in the Pennsylvania Convention of 1872. The tenor of the arguments is worth noting for illustration of the change in political standards that has come about in the course of half a century.[1] Thomas Howard stated the situation: "If there is an evil to which the people of this Commonwealth have had their attention steadily directed for the last twenty-five years, it is the scandal, the public, the notorious scandal, that the lawyers of private corporations are at Harrisburg upon the floor working for the passage of laws for their regular employers." As to an attorney or employee of a corporation, Samuel C. T. Dodd asked: "If the people see fit to elect a man in such employment to the Legislature, by what right shall we interfere with their choice? The responsibility is with them, and upon them falls the consequence." C. A. Black agreed that the people had the right to elect an attorney of a corporation if they chose so to do. Andrew Reed could not see any reason why an agent or attorney of any corporation, or any other person, after he gets on the floor of the Legislature and discloses that he is such an agent or that he has such an interest, should be prevented from speaking on a bill. He thought such a man the proper one to speak on it, as he is the most capable of explaining what the bill means. Theodore Cuyler held it to be false doctrine that the great corporations should not have their interests represented. "Elsewhere, in other countries, great corporations are especially represented, and it is thought to be a wise thing in legislation that it should be so." He cited the British Universities and the City of London.

Opposite views were forcibly presented, but the instructive fact is that the idea of the presence of corporation counsel in the Legislature did not then seem repugnant to men apparently conscientious.

In the few instances where State Constitutions have excluded men of certain occupations, it has been because of peculiar conditions attaching thereto. Thus, no president, professor, or instructor of Harvard College was eligible to be a member of the Massachusetts General Court from 1780 to 1877, because Harvard was a quasi-public institution, the State having a share in its management. Florida, framing its Constitution when the abuse of State banks had helped bring on a great

[1] *Debates*, III, 7 *et seq.*

crisis, said no officer of a bank should be Representative, Senator, or Governor, and the provision stood until 1865. Virginia emulated Florida in 1850, but confined the disqualification to members of the Assembly; this lasted for twenty years. In 1872, when railroad influences were demoralizing many legislative bodies, Congress included, West Virginia said, as she still says, that no salaried officer of any railroad company shall be a member of the Legislature.

Hungary excluded members of financial societies having relations with the State, and administrators of subsidized railroads.

Government contractors are disqualified from serving in Parliament. Contracts for the public service gave to English statesmen of the eighteenth century a method of corrupting members of Parliament that has never been extensively used on this side of the water. Favors were generously dispensed by the ministry of the hour to members who saw no wrong in accepting from the public treasury an exorbitant price for rum or beef for the navy, or some other kind of supplies. In the course of the War of the American Revolution, the abuse became more scandalous than ever, or else the stolid conscience of the Englishmen of that day began to quicken. In 1779 Sir Phillips Jennings Clerke got leave to bring in a bill disqualifying contractors from sitting in Parliament except where the contracts were obtained at a public bidding. The first year he lost in the Commons, the next in the Lords, and the third in the Commons again, but his idea was gaining strength. In 1782 Fox supported modification of the proposal by omitting the exceptions in favor of contracts obtained at a public bidding and by extending the measure to cover existing as well as future contracts. The reform was favored and put through by the Rockingham ministry, which came into office immediately afterward. The Act 22 Geo. III, c. 45, declares that any person who shall, directly or indirectly, or by any one in trust for him, undertake any contract with a government department, shall be incapable of being elected, or of sitting or voting during the time he shall hold such contract, or any share thereof, or any benefit or emolument arising from the same; but the Act does not affect stockholders in incorporated trading companies, contracting in their corporate capacity. The penalties for violations of the Act are peculiarly severe: a contractor sitting or voting is liable to forfeit 500 pounds for every day on which he shall sit or vote, to any person who may sue for the same; and every person against whom this penalty shall be recovered, is incapable of holding any contract.

Something of the evil must have been known here also in the time of the Revolutionary War, for we find the men who drew the Constitution for Maryland in 1776 putting into it a provision that no person receiving the profits or any part of the profits arising on any agency for the supply of clothing or provisions for the army or navy, should have a seat in the General Assembly or Council; and every Senator, Delegate to Assembly or Congress, member of the Council, and Governor was required before taking office to make oath that he would not receive such profits. The next month North Carolina made the same sort of provision, though omitting the oath. South Carolina, when revising its Constitution in 1790, forbade any contractor or agent of a contractor of the army or navy of the State or the United States, to sit in the Legislature, and Delaware did likewise in 1792. All these States except Delaware have now dropped the prohibition, but meanwhile others have adopted the idea, though not restricting it to army and navy contracts. Illinois in 1848 and Michigan in 1850 forbade any member of the General Assembly to be interested either directly or indirectly in any contract with the State or any county thereof, which might be authorized by law passed in the course of his term or for a year afterward. West Virginia copied this in 1872. Three years later Nebraska took it with the addition of city contracts, also providing that no person with an unadjusted claim against the State should sit in the Legislature. Five other States have since then followed the example of Illinois and Michigan.

That less than a quarter of the States now have this sort of prohibition in their Constitutions, indicates that the evil aimed at is no longer of importance in the Legislatures. Somebody, in 1806, thought it was of consequence enough in Congress to warrant introducing a constitutional amendment for the exclusion of government contractors from the House. Two years later a like resolution was offered including the Senate as well as the House. This may have been suggested by the connection of Senator Smith of Maryland with a Baltimore firm that had large contracts with the Government. The proposal for an amendment failed, but an Act of Congress approved April 21, 1808, forbade a member of Congress being interested in a government contract. In 1867 there was occasion for the passage of a joint resolution canceling a contract for the transportation of mails, made by a man subsequently elected to Congress. Of late years no complaint has attracted attention.

The difficulties of the problem may be illustrated by what took place in Canada in 1887 as a result of the law forbidding a seat in the House of Commons to any person interested in a government contract. A large number of members were involved in the controversy that arose. Mr. Currier, a member of a firm that had supplied lumber to the Department of Public Works, and Mr. Norris, one of the owners of a line of steamers that had carried rails for the government, believing they had infringed the law, though unwittingly, resigned their seats. Mr. Anglin, the Speaker, was the proprietor of a newspaper that had received public money for printing and stationery furnished to the Post Office Department. A committee came to the conclusion that his election was void, and this led to the resignation of Mr. Anglin and of others who had entered into such contracts.[1]

Governmental activities have now so broadened that hardship and injustice must follow attempt to keep lawmakers entirely free from business dealings direct or indirect with any of the agencies of government. Extreme application of the principle would shut out of the public service nearly all transporters, manufacturers, and traders, for it is a rare man in commerce or industry who never has occasion to enter upon his books a charge against some public department, or who does not at least indirectly profit by some public undertaking. The problem is further complicated by the extent of the corporation method of concentrating capital. It would hardly be maintained that a stockholder in a railroad should not sit in Congress, solely on the ground that the railroad transports government supplies. Evidently it is a situation where the law cannot wisely attempt to draw the line between propriety and impropriety. Each case must be settled on its own merits, as may seem equitable to the persons involved and to public opinion.

[1] Sir J. G. Bourinot, *Parliamentary Procedure and Practice in the Dominion of Canada*, 143.

At one time monopolists were excluded from Parliament. Under Elizabeth the grants of exclusive privileges in manufacture and trade had become a great popular grievance. After four days of hot debate in the House the Queen saved herself the mortification of defeat by saying she would revoke all grants found injurious by fair trial at law. The evil was not ended, and in the early days of the reign of James I, Sir Edward Coke complained bitterly of it, but much relief came with the statute 21 Jac. I, c. 3, which declared monopolies to be contrary to law and void, except patents to authors of new inventions, and also patents concerning printing, saltpeter, gunpowder, great ordnance, and shot.

The hostility to monopolists continued and one of the first activities of the Long Parliament was directed against them, Pym and Colepepper making the principal speeches. It was resolved — "That all projectors and monopolists whatsoever; or that have any share or have had any share, in any monopolies; or that do receive, or lately have received, any benefit from any monopoly or project; or that have procured any warrant or command for the restraint or molesting of any that have refused to conform themselves to any such proclamations or projects; are disabled by order of this House to sit here in this House; and if any man here knows any monopolist, that he shall nominate him; that any member of this House that is a monopolist or projector shall repair to Mr. Speaker that a new warrant may issue forth; or otherwise, that he shall be dealt with as with a stranger, that hath no power to sit here." [1] Several members resigned or were expelled in pursuance of this resolution. Possibly it was this agitation that inspired the colony of Massachusetts Bay to declare in the Body of Liberties adopted in 1641: "No monopolies shall be granted or allowed amongst us, but of such new Inventions that are profitable to the Countrie, and that for a short time." It does not come to my notice, however, that on this side of the water monopolists were ever excluded from Legislatures.

James I on entering England called a Parliament and commanded the people not to send any outlaws or bankrupts. The somewhat famous controversy that followed, over the right of the King to dictate in the matter of qualifications, resulted from the election of Sir Francis Goodwin, an outlaw. Two

[1] *Parl. Hist.*, II, 651.

centuries later Parliament itself saw fit to exclude bankrupts, by the 52 George III, c. 144. To-day a bankrupt may be elected to Parliament, but he is not permitted to take his seat until the adjudication is annulled, or until he obtains his discharge from the Court with a certificate that his financial difficulties were due to no misconduct on his part; and if he fails to obtain a certificate of discharge within six months, the seat is declared vacant. Nothing of the sort in American legislative history has come to my notice.

A third of our States stipulate that tax collectors or other officials who may be in debt to the government, shall not be eligible until their accounts have been settled.

In Sweden persons whose taxes are in arrears are disqualified for election. When it was discovered that a Liberal candidate for the Riksdag, M. O. Larsson, had seven years before omitted to pay his taxes, thirteen shillings in amount, it was. decided by the returning officer, and confirmed on appeal, that 6700 voting papers containing his name were null and void, and on a fresh count the Protectionist was found to have gained the election by a majority of more than 2900.[1]

Poland is unique in saying that a Deputy may not be the responsible editor of a periodical publication.

CRIME AS A BAR

THE State Constitutions contain a great variety of provisions meant to keep out of the Legislature or out of all public office men found guilty of crimes of moral turpitude. Generally the exclusions are positive, sometimes they are to be secured through laws the Legislatures are directed to enact. Generally they are to be perpetual, sometimes they can be terminated. It would be needlessly tedious to try to detail or classify thoroughly all these provisions. It may be said, however, that embezzlement of public funds ends a man's officeholding in half a dozen States, and so with felony. Infamous crime in general is a bar in eight; forgery is specified in at least three; Georgia in 1877 included larceny, going farther than Florida, which in 1868 had directed legislation to exclude on this ground. Idaho forbids the holding of any civil office to a person confined in prison on conviction of a criminal offense, and Louisiana in

---

[1] R. Dickinson, *Foreign Parliaments*, 151.

1898 put into her Constitution a clause excluding from holding any office or appointment of honor, trust, or profit, "those actually confined in any public prison," as well as "all interdicted persons." Exclusion is indirectly accomplished in a score of States by refusing the suffrage because of this crime or that, and then restricting candidacy for office to voters.

About half the States specify bribery as a disqualification, a dozen or so restricting it to bribery in elections, half a dozen or more referring to bribery of legislators, sometimes of office-holders. At least one (South Dakota) disqualifies perpetually a member or officer of a Legislature convicted of having sworn falsely or of violating his oath. In Pennsylvania any candidate guilty of bribery, fraud, or willful violation of any election law, shall be forever disqualified from holding any office of trust or profit. Like penalty threatens any Maryland man, not only for bribery but also for giving or causing to be given an illegal vote. This corresponds to the law in England, where a man found guilty of corrupt practices at elections is forever incapable of sitting for the constituency in which the offense was committed, nor can he be chosen for any other place until seven years after the offense.

Constitutional provisions aimed at one of the crimes most dangerous to the body politic, that of dueling, have particular interest not only in their relation to parliamentary history, but also as a notable instance of how a democratic community sometimes resorts to the most solemn expression of its will in order to suppress customs that have become obnoxious. The duel was devised in the early Middle Ages for the purpose of getting truthful statements in the matter of inheritances. From what was prescribed by Emperors as part of a judicial proceeding, grew a matter of chivalry. Long after it had ceased to have any justification, men clung to it as they cling to it yet in a few parts of the world, through a perverted conception of honor. Of late years it has blotted few pages of legislative annals, but time was when any man prominent in public life was in danger from its menace. In England such statesmen as Fox, Pitt, Castlereagh, Canning, Sheridan, Grattan, Curran, O'Connell, Peel, and Disraeli, challenged or fought on points of honor. The most celebrated of English duels of the last hundred years was that between the Duke of Wellington and Lord Winchelsea, arising from reflections made by Winchelsea on the Duke's conduct in connection with the Catholic Emancipation Bill. The Duke missed; the Lord fired in the air and then apologized. Now the practice has become almost extinct in England.

In this country duels were rare up to the time of the Revolution, but from then till the Civil War they were frequent, especially in the South. Even so eminent a man as George Washington found no sharp words of reprobation for the practice when Lafayette consulted him about a challenge to Lord Carlisle. The French officers had taken offense at words derogatory to France, in an address signed by the British Commissioners, Carlisle's name leading, and as Lafayette was the highest in rank of the French, the duty of resenting fell to him. Washington refused his approbation and mildly remonstrated: "The generous spirit of chivalry, exploded by the rest of the world, finds a refuge, my dear friend, in the sensibility of your nation only. But it is in vain to cherish it, unless you can find antagonists to support it; and however well adapted it might have been to the times in which it existed, in our days it is to be feared, that your opponent, sheltering himself behind modern opinions, and under his present public character of commissioner, would turn a virtue of such ancient date into ridicule." Nevertheless, Lafayette persisted, but Lord Carlisle declined the challenge in a good-humored and civil reply, to the effect that he was responsible only to his country and King for his public conduct and language.[1]

The Revolutionary Congress punished a man who sent a challenge to a member of that body, but for many years afterward objection to the code was not seriously pressed. When in 1796 Senator James Gunn, of Georgia, sent a challenge to Abraham Baldwin, a Representative from the same State, all the House did was to declare it a breach of its privileges. The death of that great statesman, Alexander Hamilton, at the hands of Aaron Burr, Vice-President of the United States, in 1804, shocked the country more because an eminent man had died, than because he had been put to death by another. Senator Benton's graphic account of the Clay-Randolph duel in 1826 mildly reprobates the practice. He himself killed a Mr. Lucas and engaged in other "affairs."

Opinion was changing, however, and in 1838 there was wide-

[1] *Washington's Writings*, VI, 78.

spread indignation and horror at the tragic fate of Representative Jonathan Cilley. After serving as Speaker of the House in Maine, he had been in Congress but a few months, when, at the age of thirty-six, he met death in the shape of a rifle bullet fired by a fellow-member, William J. Graves, of Kentucky, in a duel fought at Bladensburg, near Washington, with weapons of Cilley's choice. The matter was made all the worse by the officiousness of Representative Wise, of Virginia, whose words in debate had been questioned by Cilley, and who acted as a second for Graves. After two shots Wise broke off a truce between the combatants, and many believed the two Southerners had conspired to assassinate a fellow-member from the North who was obnoxious to them. A Committee of the House recommended the expulsion of Graves, and the censure of Wise, and of Representative Jones, of Tennessee, who also had acted as a second, but after long debate and a parliamentary struggle of intensity, the whole subject was laid on the table. Both Graves and Wise denied all vindictive feeling, and their constituencies sustained them, but in New England they were viewed as murderers.

The conscience of the nation was not so stirred again by dueling for twenty years. Then, in 1859, Senator Broderick, of California, a man respected by his associates of all parties for the purity of his life and his scrupulous honesty, was killed in combat with Judge Terry, for words spoken in a political campaign. Terry won the toss and chose pistols — weapons with which he was at home, for he was a Texan, a dead shot, and accustomed to affairs of honor. The duel was at ten paces. As Broderick raised his weapon, it went off prematurely, owing to the delicacy of the trigger. A second later, Terry, taking deliberate aim, shot him through the breast. Such cold-blooded murder outraged the country. Since then no memorable duels have been fought by men in public office. When a few months afterward a hot personal debate took place in the House between Branch, of North Carolina, and Grow, of Pennsylvania, with the result that Branch sent Grow what was virtually a challenge, the dignified refusal of Grow cost him no respect worth having.

The moral sense of the people had been slowly waking. To abhorrence of the barbarous practice was added recognition of the loss suffered by the community when a promising career was so uselessly ended. Furthermore, there was an indirect injury of no small consequence through the effect on the freedom and candor of discussion in the public councils. At any moment the frank and outspoken champion of a cause exciting strong personal feeling ran the danger of having to stake his life on the chance of a duel, or else be held up to scorn as a coward.

Connecticut was the first State to recognize the evil by a constitutional provision. When her first Constitution was framed, in 1818, dueling was classed by it with other offenses for which infamous punishment is inflicted, with forfeiture of the privileges of an elector as an additional penalty. In the following year Alabama declared the General Assembly should have power to pass penal laws "to suppress the evil practice of dueling, extending to disqualification from office or the tenure thereof." Virginia came next, in 1830, authorizing the Legislature to provide perpetual exclusion from office for anybody who should send, accept, or knowingly carry a challenge, or fight a duel, act as a second, or in any way aid or assist. Two years later Mississippi prescribed that every legislator should take an oath that he had not been engaged in a duel since January 1, 1833, nor would be so engaged during his continuance in office.

Tennessee in 1834 explicitly disqualified duelists, and so did Florida in 1838, putting in the restriction, however, that the penalty should extend to the sending or accepting of a challenge only when the probable issue might be the death of the challenger or challenged. One of the amendments adopted by Pennsylvania in 1838, disqualified duelists, and Judge Woodward told the Convention of 1873 that the strong feeling in favor of this amendment may have carried the others at the polls. He wished it retained, and though various members thought the habits of society had so changed that a duel had become morally impossible in Pennsylvania, not only did the Convention vote for retaining the main part of the article, but also it struck out the permission to the Executive to remit the offense, so that now there is in that State no escape from perpetual deprivation of the right to hold any office of honor or profit.

With the action of Louisiana in 1845 began a more rapid succession of constitutional disqualifications on this score, fourteen States acting before the Civil War. Iowa in 1846 went to the length of putting her disqualification into the Bill of Rights. The debate in the Kentucky Convention of 1849 was typical. Objection was made to putting criminal law in the constitution. Dueling was the fairest mode of fighting known. It was a restraint on the bully in high life. The people never respected a coward, and in Kentucky no man could succeed in public or private life if he suffered himself to be insulted. In Louisville there had been but two deaths from duels in seventy years. On the other hand it was urged that the killing of a man in a duel was murder of the most deliberate and malicious description. Kentucky was the only country in which no man had ever been punished for giving, accepting, or carrying a challenge, or for killing his antagonist in a duel. By 58 to 34 was passed the section requiring the members of the General Assembly, all public officers, and members of the bar, before entering upon their duties, to swear or affirm that since the adoption of the Constitution they had not fought a duel with deadly weapons with a citizen of the State, within or without its borders, nor had assisted in a duel in any way.[1] Also disqualification was provided, but with the proviso that the Governor might pardon after five years.

Conventions in the course of and immediately after the War in some cases dropped provisions aimed at duelists, in other cases modified them, because they had been found too drastic, or general disqualifications by reason of infamous crime were thought enough, or the practice had so waned as to remove the need for exceptional penalty. Louisiana dropped the provision in 1864. Arkansas, in 1864, first providing perpetual disqualification from office, added the suffrage in 1868, and in 1874 took out the suffrage and restricted the office disqualification to ten years. Florida in 1865 put in the proviso that the legal disability should not accrue until after trial and conviction according to due form of law. Maryland in 1867 authorized removal of the disability by act of Legislature. Georgia, first inserting the disqualification in 1868, tempered it in 1877 by adding the power of pardon. On the other hand, Virginia, which in 1830 had left the matter to the Legislature, in 1870 made the exclusion explicit by constitutional provision. Illinois took a contrary course that same year by dropping the provision entirely. Colorado, in 1876, was the last State framing

[1] F. N. Thorpe, *Const. Hist. of the Am. People*, II, 126 *et seq.*

a first Constitution, to deem specific reference to the evil necessary.

Florida in her Constitution of 1868 said, and still says, that the Legislature is to enact the necessary laws to exclude from every office of honor, power, trust, or profit, civil or military, within the State, and from the right of suffrage, all persons who shall make, or become directly or indirectly interested in, any bet or wager, the result of which shall depend upon any election. Do not suppose, however, that such a provision is primarily a matter of morals. The basis for it is the possibility of vitiating the expression of the public will by giving voters a pecuniary interest in the result, sometimes accomplished by forming large pools, in which shares are sold. In that light the provision has much more justification than one put into the Constitution of South Carolina in 1895, which says: "It shall be unlawful for any person holding an office of honor, trust, or profit to engage in gambling or betting on games of chance; and any such officer, upon conviction thereof, shall become thereby disqualified from the further exercise of the functions of the office, and the office of said person shall become vacant, as in the case of resignation or death."

South Carolina has another unique provision, aimed at lynching. It excludes from office (save in the event of pardon by the Governor), any State, county, or municipal officer through whose negligence, permission, or connivance a prisoner has been taken by a mob, and has suffered bodily violence or death. Three of the States exclude, or direct laws to exclude, on conviction of any malfeasance in office. Ever since 1786 Vermont has disqualified from all office any person taking greater fees than the law allows. A singular precaution against a particular kind of malfeasance is the Minnesota provision that if the presiding officer of either branch of the Legislature refuses to sign a bill that has passed both Houses, he shall become incapable of holding a seat in either branch of the Legislature or any other office of honor or profit.

That a man has been declared a criminal by State law, does not of itself prevent him from being elected to Congress. When James A. Peterson, nominated in Minnesota as a candidate for the United States Senate, was convicted of a felony and sentenced to imprisonment, the court refused to order his name to be kept off the ballot, holding that the provisions of the State

Constitution imposing restrictions on the right to hold public office could have no application to the office of United States Senator.[1]

DUAL OFFICE-HOLDING

IN the earliest days of representative government it was seen that a man dependent on the bounty of the King for his livelihood was not a fit man to share in bargaining with the King through the process known as Parliament. Also it was soon recognized that the perquisites of office are a bait that may tempt lawmakers away from the exercise of independent judgment. So we find as early as 1348, in the 22d Edward III, the Commons praying the King, "That no person summoned to Parliament should be either a Taxer, Collector, or Receiver of the Fifteenth then granted." And again, in the 25th of Edward III, the Knights, Citizens, and Burgesses were virtuous enough to pray, "That none of them be made Collectors of the aid then granted."

It will be observed that two dangers were here anticipated, one threatened by the election of an office-holder to Parliament, the other by the appointment of a member of Parliament to office. These two aspects of dual office-holding are rarely discriminated, probably because the steps taken against the evils involved have usually been taken with both aspects in mind at the same time. For our purpose, however, it seems best to give in connection with "Qualifications" the facts relating to the election of office-holders to lawmaking bodies, and later on those concerning the appointment of members of such bodies to office, although the two subjects so overlap that precise separation is impossible.

In colonial times there was no general attempt to deliminate sharply the three branches of government, but here and there may be noted something like instinctive recognition of its desirability. For example, in Virginia tobacco inspectors were not only excluded from the House but also were not allowed to take any part in the election of members, or even be present at the polls. Finally, in 1742 and 1748 a tobacco inspector could not become a Burgess until two years after vacating the office. Sheriffs or others holding places of profit in the government were not eligible, and Burgesses were exempt from being

[1] State v. Schmall, 167 N. W., 481 (1918).

compelled to serve as sheriff. By the act of 1762 Burgesses were prohibited from holding any other office of profit, and the acts regarding sheriffs and tobacco inspectors were reaffirmed.[1] Maryland disqualified sheriffs, and also ordinary-keepers, who had to be licensed. The New York Assembly in 1770 disqualified judicial officers, but the act was disallowed.

The presumption is that in the case of sheriffs the objection was the same as in England. Hatsell found that when in 1614 Sir George Selby, sheriff for Durham, had been elected Knight of the Shire for Northumberland, his election was declared void; and said he supposed the reason was the necessity sheriffs are under of residing in their counties during the greater part of the time.[2] A notable application of the rule was in the case of the great lawyer, Sir Edward Coke. The activity with which he opposed the arbitrary measures of James the First, and the amazing fund of knowledge with which he supported the privileges of the House of Commons, furnished reason enough for Charles to try, by appointing him sheriff, to exclude him from a seat in the House. Hatsell says this measure so far succeeded that, though the House would not come to any decision on the question, Coke certainly never sat in the second Parliament summoned by Charles.

S. G. Fisher finds in the Georgia charter of 1732 a conscious attempt to keep the powers more distinctly separated. The charter provided that no person holding an office of profit under the corporation should be a member of the corporation. Mr. Fisher reasons that "the corporation, or members of the company, made the laws and appointed the council which carried on the company's executive business; so that the corporation was, in effect, the legislative department; and the provision for more distinct separateness meant that no member of the legislative department should hold any office in the executive department, or, presumably, in the judicial department, if there was one."[3]

There may have been such a conscious purpose, but is it not more likely to have been some development of corporation practice in England? Montesquieu had not then published the epoch-making book that spread throughout the colonies faith in the separation of powers.

[1] E. I. Miller, *The Legislature of the Province of Virginia*, 56.
[2] *Precedents*, II, 22, 24.   [3] S. G. Fisher, *Evolution of the Const. of the U.S.*, iii.

The Montesquieu doctrine, gaining well-nigh universal acceptance when the first American States were in the making, led Virginia to say that no person should exercise the powers of more than one of the three departments of government at the same time, except that justices of the county courts might be eligible to either House of Assembly. New Jersey excluded from the Assembly the judges, sheriffs, and all other persons "possessed of any post of profit under the government," save only justices of the peace. Pennsylvania said no member while continuing such should hold any other office except in the militia. Maryland excluded any person holding a place of profit or receiving any part of the profits thereof. North Carolina specified certain officials who should not sit in the General Assembly. Other States have found an astonishing number of ways to say in general that a legislator shall not hold any office — or "any other office," if it be that a member of a Legislature is himself an officer.

The most considerable exception has been of officers of the militia, specified by about half the States. The recent change in the status of the militia, brought under Federal control, may raise some interesting problems in this particular. It has not been American practice to encourage the election of regular army or navy officers as lawmakers, but there is no objection to their presence in Parliament or, so far as I am aware, in most of the legislative bodies on the Continent. Indeed Germany goes to the point of saying that members of the military forces need no leave in order to exercise their functions as either national or State legislators, and, if they become candidates for election, the necessary leave to carry on their campaigns shall be granted. Poland deemed it desirable to specify that members of the army in active service shall not be excluded. France, however, in the Organic Law of November 30, 1875, declared that no soldier or sailor in active service on land or sea, whatever his rank or position, might be elected a member of the Chamber of Deputies.

Four of our States let any postmasters sit, and seven admit those with small incomes. Whether county or municipal officers are "officers under the State," might furnish occupation to the hair-splitters. Three States have seen fit specifically to exclude county officers and four keep out prosecuting attorneys. New York, by amendment approved at the polls in

1873, excluded "any officer under any city government" who was such at the time of election or for a hundred days previously, and it vacated the seat of any legislator who accepted such office. Kentucky went farther in 1890, making ineligible "an officer of any county, city, town, or other municipality, or an employe thereof." Nebraska and Ohio have thought it prudent to clear up the situation by specifically exempting township officers, and Nebraska adds precinct officers. When J. H. Murphy was at the same time Mayor of Davenport, Iowa, and a State Senator, it was held that his salary of $100 as Mayor was not lucrative and he was allowed to keep his seat in the General Assembly.

The exclusion of municipal officers from the central lawmaking body, is no novelty. On the 25th of June, 1604, it was resolved by the House of Commons, "That no Mayor should be elected, returned, or allowed to serve as a Member of this House"; and this was to continue as an Act or Order of the House forever.[1]

Three members of the First General Assembly in Iowa were alleged to be disqualified by having accepted lucrative offices, but it was held that ineligibility does not become a disqualification after election to the Assembly.

The creation of a central government in America gave rise to the perplexing problem of whether an officer of that government ought to be allowed to sit in a State Legislature. In 1789 this was long and warmly agitated in the Massachusetts General Court. The judge of a district court, the attorney, and the marshal of the district were members. The Senate voted 13 to 11 against vacating the seat of the marshal, and the House voted the other way, 137 to 24, on the question of substituting a general declaration for the report of the committee.

Early in 1813 Amos Kendall, then studying law in Groton, on a visit to Boston listened with great interest to a debate in the Senate upon a question whether officers in the army of the United States could rightfully hold seats in that body. Two of the Democratic Senators, Tuttle and Ripley, had been appointed colonels in the regular army. One of them had taken his seat in the Senate. There was at the time nothing in the Constitution of Massachusetts or of the United States which rendered a seat in the State Senate and an appointment in

---

[1] Hatsell, *Precedents*, ii, 21.

the United States army incompatible, and the argument rested
entirely on the incongruity of the two relations. The lobby of
the Senate was crowded. "The speech of Harrison Gray Otis
was a superb display of eloquence, but full of bitterness and
sarcasm." By the entire Federal vote and a part of the Republican vote, led by Mr. Lincoln, the seats of Colonels Tuttle
and Ripley were declared vacated.[1] The Reverend Solomon
Aiken of Dracut was deprived of his seat in the General Court of
1815–16 because he had accepted an appointment as chaplain in
the United States Army. Upon reëlection the next year he
was again excluded, by a vote of 264 to 12. One of the amendments adopted as a result of the Convention of 1820 ended the
question as far as Massachusetts was concerned, by providing
that no Federal officer, except a postmaster, should be eligible
as a member of the Legislature.

In New York the two Houses by resolution in 1790 declared
the thing improper. Governor Clinton had occasion to remind
the Legislature of this in January of 1821, apropos of the fact
that Mr. Skinner was a member of the Senate and Council of
Appointment, while holding the office of a judge of the District
Court of the United States. The joint committee on the
message repudiated the resolution of 1790 in no unmeasured
terms, severely censuring the Governor for his position. Yet
the Convention of the fall of that same year put into the Constitution the provision that no member of Congress, nor any
person holding an office, either civil or military, under the
government of the United States, should be eligible to a seat
in either branch of the Legislature.

Reverse the proposition and the question of constitutionality
arises. The States have no power to add to the qualifications required for a United States Senator or Representative; and all
provisions in their statutes or Constitutions that forbid a
member of the Legislature or other State officer from being
chosen Senator have been rejected by the United States Senate
as void. The Constitution of Illinois tried to prevent the
election to any office under the United States of a judge of the
Supreme or Circuit Court. Nevertheless Judge Lyman Trumbull of the Supreme Court and Judge Samuel S. Marshall of the
Circuit Court were elected to the Congress that met in December
of 1855. Their seats were contested, but only five members of

[1] Wm. Stickney, *Autobiography of Amos Kendall*, 76.

the House appear by the vote to have doubted the unconstitutionality of the State provision. Trumbull had not taken his seat, having been elected to the Senate. There the matter was debated, and by 35 to 8 he was declared entitled to his place. In 1884 the same question arose over a like provision in the Constitution of Kansas, and the position was reaffirmed.[1] Although doubts would seem to have been clarified long ago, the problem vexed at least one court as late as 1918. In the State of Washington it was held that provisions in State Constitutions making judges ineligible to offices or employments other than judicial during their terms, could not prevent the nomination of a judge for Congress.[2]

In France the exercise of public duties paid for out of the treasury of the State is declared to be incompatible with the office of Deputy, save in the case of a few specified exceptions. On the other hand, the Constitutions of Germany, Prussia, and Austria distinctly recognize the right of public officials to serve in a representative capacity, encouraging them indeed by prescribing that they shall have leave of absence to conduct their campaigns. In Poland public employees (other than Ministers, Under-Secretaries of State, and professors in academic schools) automatically get leave of absence when elected Deputies, and the years during which they serve as such are considered "years of service," presumably for retirement, pension, and similar purposes. However, administrative, revenue, and judicial officials of the State, other than those employed in the central departments, may not be elected in the districts in which they are performing their judicial duties. Jugoslavia has a unique provision to the effect that political, financial, and forest officials, as well as officials of the agrarian reform, whatever that is, cannot be candidates unless they have given up office a year before the announcement of the election.

[1] Hinds, *Precedents*, I, 384–89.   [2] State *v.* Howell, 175 Pac. Rep., 569.

CHAPTER XIII

MEMBERSHIP MATTERS

No Englishman duly qualified and lawfully elected, may refuse to take his seat in Parliament, even though he were elected against his will. No Englishman once seated may resign. The theory is that the office is a trust not for private but for public benefit. "The country and the commonwealth," it was said long ago, "have such an interest in every man that when by lawful election he is appointed to the public service, he cannot by an unwillingness or refusal of his own, make himself incapable; for that were to prefer the will or contentment of a private man before the desire and satisfaction of the whole country, and a ready way to put by the sufficient men, who are commonly those who least endeavor to obtain the place." [1]

In the early days of this country, when every man's help was sorely needed, men were not allowed to evade the duties of public office. The Plymouth Colony Revision of 1636 contained these paragraphs:

"That if at any time any shall be elected to the office of Governor & will not hold according to the election that then he be amerced in 20 pownds starling ffine.

"That if any elected to the office of Assistant refuse to hold according to eleccion that then he be amerced in ten pownds starling ffine.

"That in case one & the same person should be elected Governor a second yeare having held the place the foregoing yeare it should be lawfull for him to refuse without any amercement unles they can prevaile with him by entreaty." [2]

As increase of numbers made available more men for the responsibilities of leadership, such provisions became less important, and we find the third of the foregoing repealed in 1639, the others in 1645.

Thomas Dudley, rather obstinate and somewhat opinionated, brought the matter to the front in Massachusetts. Winthrop's Journal has these entries:

[1] John Glanville, *Reports of Certain Cases, etc.*, 101.
[2] *Plymouth Colony Records*, xi, 10.

April 3, 1632. "At a court at Boston, the deputy, Mr. Dudley, went away before the court was ended, and then the secretary delivered the Governor a letter from him, directed to the Governor and Assistants, wherein he declared a resignation of his deputyship and place of Assistant; but it was not allowed."

May 1. "The Governor and Assistants met at Boston to consider of the deputy his deserting his place. The points discussed were two. The 1st, upon what grounds he did it; 2d, whether it were good or void. For the 1st, his main reason was for the public peace; because he must needs discharge his conscience in speaking freely; and he saw that bred disturbance, etc. For the 2d, it was maintained by all, that he could not leave his place, except by the same power which put him in; yet he would not be put from his contrary opinion, nor would be persuaded to continue till the General Court, which was to be the 9th of this month."

May 8. "A General Court at Boston. The Deputy Governor, Thomas Dudley, Esq., having submitted the validity of his resignation to the vote of the Court, it was adjudged a nullity, and he accepted of his place again, and the Governor and he being reconciled the day before, all things were carried very lovingly amongst all, etc., and the people carried themselves with much silence and modesty."

Dudley, however, cherished his views. Ten years later we find the proof of his pertinacity, by the entry of May 18, 1642: "The Court of Elections was. Mr. Winthrop was again chosen Governor, and Mr. Endecott Deputy Governor. This being done, Mr. Dudley went away, and though he were chosen an Assistant, yet he would not accept it. Some of the elders went to his house to deal with him. His answer was that he had sufficient reasons to excuse and warrant his refusal, which he did not think fit to publish, but would impart to any one or two of them whom they should appoint, which he did accordingly. The elders acquainted the Court with what they had done, but not with the reasons of his refusal, only that they thought them not sufficient. The Court sent a magistrate and two Deputies to desire him to come to the Court, for as a Counsellor he was to assist in the General Court. The next day he came, and after some excuse he consented to accept the place, so that the Court would declare that if at any time he should depart out of the jurisdiction (which he protested he did not intend), no oath, either of officer, Counsellor, or Assistant should hold him in any bond where he stood. This he desired, not for his own·satisfaction, but that it might be a satisfaction to others who might scruple his liberty herein. After much debate the Court made a general order which gave him satisfaction."

In the early days of Maryland one Weston pleaded that he was not a freeman because he had no land or certain dwelling, but the Assembly voted he was a freeman and compelled him to serve.[1] Need for such compulsion disappeared long ago and probably nowhere in the world would its exercise to-day be attempted. At last accounts the Constitution of Norway still said that every one who is elected a Representative is bound to accept, unless he. has been a Minister or Councilor of State and is chosen by a district in which he is not a voter, or is prevented by reasons the Storthing considers lawful; but having served in the three regular sessions following an election, he is not bound to serve again. The chances are the provision is a dead letter.

Apparently it was once thought that a line could be drawn between refusal to begin and refusal to continue service, or else that eminent parliamentary authority, L. S. Cushing, editing the first volume of "Massachusetts Election Cases," would not have said (in a note on page 30) : "It is probably true that every person elected a member of a legislative assembly may decline the office, but if he accepts, and takes his seat, it may be doubted whether he can resign without the consent of the body of which he is a member." In his authoritative work on the "Law and Practice of Legislative Assemblies" he reiterated the doubt, but added that the consent of the assembly is always implied unless there is some expression to the contrary. Presumably his doubt sprang from the English rule, which always has been that no Englishman once seated in Parliament may resign. In practice the rule has little or no effect. By statute the member who accepts a civil office vacates his seat. There are certain nominal offices with no duties attached to them that are kept alive for use when a member wishes to withdraw from the House. That most commonly used and best known is the stewardship of the Chiltern Hundreds. A member may not get one of these appointments of right, but it is seldom or never refused. Upon appointment, resignation of course immediately follows.

The Virginian Assembly once went to the extreme of holding

[1] *Maryland Archives*, i, 176.

it could not relieve a Burgess of the duties of membership even when his constituents had formally requested that the privilege of absence from the sittings be granted to him. The House was of the belief that once a seat had been taken, it could not be vacated by the action of the House unless the occupant had been found guilty of some heinous offense.[1] Gradually, however, the opposite view gained support. It seems to have won acceptance by the time when Pennsylvania furnished the most interesting resignation story in American annals. There the Quakers controlled the Assembly from the start up to 1756. Then the outbreak of the French and Indian War brought a serious dilemma, for the Quakers could not consistently vote money for military purposes. The only recourse seemed to be the taking away of their power and to that end a bill was introduced in Parliament to exclude from the Pennsylvania Assembly all who would not take the Oath of Allegiance, which no Quaker would take. Powerful Friends intervened, securing delay until two of their number could go to the colony and try persuasion. Before their arrival several of the Quaker members refused to be candidates for reëlection and afterward others consented to resign, in number enough to give the majority to adherents of other faiths. Once Quaker control had been ended, it was never resumed.

Nowadays it is not probable that a protest against resignation would get serious attention anywhere.

In Congress, from the beginning, it has been the practice to hold that a member ceases to be such from the moment his resignation is handed in at the Clerk's desk. The practice was questioned in 1870, when B. F. Whittemore, of South Carolina, handed in his resignation while the House was considering the advice of its Committee on Military Affairs that he be expelled for having sold appointments to the Military and Naval Academies. N. P. Banks and H. L. Dawes urged that a member of a parliamentary body could not resign without the consent of that body, since the contrary doctrine would menace its very existence. It was, however, decided that the resignation was valid. The motion for expulsion was laid on the table, and resolutions condemning Whittemore's conduct were passed.

One of the disqualifications urged against Senator James Davis in the first General Assembly of Iowa was that he had

---

[1] P. A. Bruce, *Institutional Hist. of Va.*, II, 466.

resigned his office, but it was held that inasmuch as the resignation had not been accepted, it had not taken effect.

Failure to attend will be treated as a resignation. In 1870 David S. Draper, of Great Barrington, elected to the Massachusetts House, did not present himself for qualification as a member. On the 20th of January the House directed its Committee on Elections to ascertain whether he intended to qualify. He made an indefinite answer, whereupon the House declared the seat vacant and ordered a new election.

EXPULSION

FROM time immemorial it has been deemed the right of legislative bodies to expel members thought unfit. Some of the notable instances will show the grounds that have been held to warrant exercise of the power. The first case recorded in Parliament was that of one Terrill, who was sent to the Tower for telling Henry VII of the measures then under discussion in the House. Both he and his posterity were disabled from ever serving as members. In 1580 Arthur Hall, Burgess for Grantham, was charged with having caused to be published a book "not only reproaching some particular good members of the House, but also very much slanderous and derogatory to its general authority, power, and state, and prejudicial to the validity of its proceedings in making and establishing of laws." He had previously incurred the displeasure of the Commons, in 1572, when he was ordered to appear at the bar to answer for "sundry lewd speeches," used as well in the House as elsewhere. Regarding him now as incorrigible, the House exhausted its wrath in punishments. In spite of his humble submission, they unanimously expelled him, imposed a fine of five hundred marks, and sent him to the Tower until he should make a satisfactory retraction. Four years later the famous Doctor Parry suffered because he spoke warmly in denouncing as cruel and bloody a bill inflicting the penalty of death on Jesuits and seminary priests. Charged with opposing a bill approved by a committee, he was ordered into the custody of the sergeant, the Speaker was directed to reprimand him upon his knees, and on his failing to make an acceptable apology, he was voted out of the House.

In the reign of James I, De Lolme recalls,[1] Sir Giles Montpesson, having been guilty of monopolies, and other acts of great oppression on the people, was not only expelled from the House of Commons, but was impeached, was prosecuted with the greatest warmth by the House, and finally was condemned by the Lords to be publicly degraded from his rank of a knight, to be held forever an infamous person, and to be imprisoned during life. In the same reign, Sir John Benet, having been found guilty of corrupt practices, such as taking exorbitant fees, and the like, in his capacity of judge of the Prerogative Court of Canterbury, was expelled the House, and prosecuted. In 1641, Henry Benson, having been detected in selling protections, experienced likewise the indignation of the House and was expelled. "In fine," says De Lolme, "in order, as it were, to make it completely notorious, that neither the condition of representative of the people, nor even any degree of influence in their House, could excuse any one of them from strictly observing the rules of justice, the Commons did, on one occasion, pass the most severe censure they had the power to inflict, upon their Speaker himself, for having, in a single instance attempted to convert the discharge of his duty, as Speaker, into the means of private emolument, — Sir John Trevor, Speaker of the House of Commons, having, in the sixth year of the reign of King William, received a thousand guineas from the city of London, 'as a gratuity for the trouble he had taken with regard to the passing of the *Orphan Bill*,' was voted guilty of a high crime and misdemeanour, and expelled the House. Even the inconsiderable sum of twenty guineas, which Mr. Hungerford, another member, had been weak enough to accept on the same score, was looked upon as deserving the notice of the House, and he was likewise expelled."

In 1796, Colonel Cawthorne, by a court-martial found guilty of embezzlement, cashiered, and rendered unfit to serve the King in any military capacity whatever, was expelled as an unfit person to hold a seat in Parliament. In 1812, Benjamin Walsh, a stock-broker, having been convicted at the Old Bailey of a fraud upon Sir Thomas Plomer, met with the same fate; the plea in mitigation, that he had paid four thousand guineas for his seat for Wooton Bassett, did not avail to save him, notwithstanding the wishes and recorded opinions of Sir Samuel

[1] *The Constitution of England*, bk. II, ch. 16.

Romilly. "I thought it extremely dangerous," Romilly says in his diary, "that the House should assume to itself a power of expelling any of its members merely on the ground of their having been guilty of gross immorality. Such a censorial power cannot be intrusted to a popular assembly, acting, as it often necessarily must act, under the influence of a political prejudice, without being liable to the greatest abuse."

The history of exclusion and expulsion in this country begins with its very first legislative body, for when the Virginia House of Burgesses met in 1619, there was occasion to question the admission of the Burgesses from Martin's Hundred. Martin's patent exempted him from obedience to the laws and authority of the colony except in matters of defense. Moreover, his people had made trouble by dealing unfairly with the Indians. It was a dangerous situation and the leaders felt his Burgesses ought not to be admitted unless he would surrender part of his patent. This he refused to do and so his men were excluded. In later years there were various cases of expulsion and disqualification.[1] For instance, in 1652, John Hammod, from the lower parish of Isle of Wight county, was expelled because he was "notoriously knowne a scandalous person and a frequent disturber of the peace of the country, by libell and other illegall practices." At the same session James Pyland, from the upper parish of the same county, was expelled as "an abetter of Mr. Thomas Woodward in his mutinous and rebellious declaration, and concerning his the said Mr. Pyland blasphemous chatechisme." [2]

The Assembly of 1655 endorsed the principle involved in these cases by enacting that Burgesses should be "such and no other than such as are persons of knowne integrity and of good conversation." This was reaffirmed in 1658. The same year it was enacted that persons guilty of "the odious sinnes of drunkennesse, blasphemous swearing and cursing, scandalous living in adultery and ffornication," besides being fined were to be held incapable of being witnesses or of holding any public office. Bribers were disqualified, even if the bribe were only promised and not delivered. In the session of 1742, one Henry Downs was charged with having helped to steal sheep; it was said that he had once confessed this offense in open court, and

[1] E. I. Miller, *The Legislature of the Province of Virginia*, 51, 52, 94.
[2] Hening, *Va. Statutes at Large*, i, 374.

had been punished by fifteen lashes on the bare back, by being put into the stocks, and then by being sold into servitude for one year and nine months, to pay fees. The House declared he was guilty, expelled him, and disqualified him to sit in that Assembly. The same penalty was applied to William Andrews, whom the committee declared guilty of "many male and scandalous Practices, in the Office of Inspector." That he, had been dismissed from the offices of inspector and justice was evidence of his guilt.

The South Carolina Statutes of 1685 were passed by only seven members of the Parliament, the other thirteen having been expelled by the Governor for refusing to acknowledge the validity of the Fundamental Constitutions that John Locke had provided for the colony.

In that same year at the first meeting of the Pennsylvania Assembly after William Penn had gone back home, Nicholas More, one of the leading men in the province, who had been Chairman of the first Assembly and Speaker of the second, and was now Chief Justice and also a member of the Assembly, was accused of acting illegally and arbitrarily. Thereupon the Assembly expelled him, voting him "a public enemy to the Province and Territories, and a violator of the privileges of the freemen." [1]

In the course of a long and sharp letter to the New Jersey Assembly of 1707, the Governor, Lord Cornbury, complained: "You have taken upon you, to administer an oath to one of your members, and have expelled him the House for refusing to take an oath, which you could not legally administer to him. This is most certainly robbing that member of his property, and a most notorious assuming to yourselves a negative voice to the freeholders election of their representatives; for which there can be no precedent found." In reply the Assembly quibbled by saying: "We never did administer an oath (tho' we think we have power so to do), what oaths were administered were administered by justices of the peace before us. We expell'd that member for several contempts for which we are not accountable to your excellency, nor no body else in this province: We might lawfully expel him, and if we had so thought fit, might have rendered him incapable of ever sitting in this House; and of this many precedents may be produced."

[1] Edward Channing, *Hist. of the U.S.*, ii, 122.

About this time Major William Sandford signed an address to the Queen which the House three years later voted to be "a false and scandalous representation of the representative body of this province," and because of it they expelled him in spite of his plea that he signed as a member of the Council.

Expulsion was getting to be a habit in New Jersey. When in May of 1714 Governor Hunter summoned the Assembly to meet again and only nine members appeared, warrants were sent to several others, bringing four, whereupon the thirteen voted expulsion of all the rest of the members, including the Speaker, "for contempt of authority and neglect of the service of their country." Also it was voted that those expelled might not sit if upon a new election they should be returned. Nevertheless, several of them were reëlected. They were refused their seats and the electors were obliged to vote over again.

When the Plymouth Colony revised its laws in 1658, the last clause of the law of 1638 concerning deputies was changed to read: "That all such Courts as Majestrates and Deputies are to acte in makeing of lawes and being assembled the Court in the first place take notice of theire members and if they find any unfitt for such a trust that they and the reason therof bee returned to the towne from whence they were sent that they may make choise of more fitt and able persons to send in their stead as the time will permitt." [1] On the 4th of July, 1673, it was enacted by the Court that "those that are or shalbe sent from the severall Townes for to serve as deputies shall have a voate with the Majestrates in the purging of the Court untill by the above-said disaccepted." [2]

The provision that the places of members sent home should be filled by the election of others, is to be noted in contrast to the contemporaneous practice of Rhode Island. At the fourth General Court of her two colonies, in May of 1650, it was ordered that in case any member upon complaint and trial, should prove to be unfit to hold his seat, the Assembly might suspend him and choose another in his place. Long afterward the Supreme Court of Massachusetts had occasion to address itself to this point. It was in 1826 that in an Opinion given to the House the Justices said (5 Pick. 517) that death, resignation, or removal out of the State were contingencies of which towns may be supposed to take the risk, when they make their

[1] *Plymouth Colony Records*, XI, 92.   [2] *Ibid.*, 235.

election, but in the case of a seat vacated by the interference of
the constituted authorities, they thought the place might be
supplied by the town represented, because the inhabitants of
the town would otherwise be deprived of their voice in the legislative department, without their consent, and this would be
contrary to one of the fundamental principles of a free representative government. To be sure, the Justices were asked
about a case where the authorities, that is, the General Court,
had "called the Representative to another sphere of public
duty," and it might be held that if a district send a bad man to
the Legislature, the district might be taking the same risk as in
the case of death, resignation, or removal, but the general practice probably is to have the vacancy caused by expulsion filled
by another election when time permits.

The troubles of the Revolutionary period gave the Legislatures of the new States plenty of occasion to pass judgment on
members. For instance, in Massachusetts James Perry, of
Easton, was charged with having sold a quantity of rye for the
troops of the State (then on service in Rhode Island), at an extravagant price, namely, eighteen shillings a bushel in the new
money, the Continental currency, though it appeared he had
agreed to return the money to the Colonel buying, any time
within two months at the rate of eight shillings hard for eighteen
of the new. The committee, however, reported that he had no
intention of depreciating the currency or injuring the State,
and the report was approved.

The membership of Tories was not uncontested. In 1781
Abiel Lovejoy, returned a member from Vassalborough, was
accused as "not friendly to the cause of America." On his
agreeing not to attempt to sit in the House, no further proceedings then took place, but when the next year he was elected
again, he was ordered to withdraw from the House until the
evidence should be produced, and then the matter seems to
have been dropped. In 1783 Jerathmiel Bowers of Swansey was
excluded because by a resolve of 1777 he had been disqualified
from holding any position of honor or profit in the commonwealth. In the same year the House ordered Abiel Wood, of
Pownalborough, to appear in his place and expelled him because he did not obey; a former General Court had put him
under bond not to correspond in any way with the enemy.

In 1784 opinion had begun to change, for when Joshua Hubbard of Kittery was charged with having been an enemy to the country through the most difficult periods of the war, refusing to aid in raising money to carry it on, saying he hoped Great Britain would conquer, suffering himself to be carried to gaol rather than take arms or help raise money, trying to join the Quakers in order to avoid taking part in the contest, and subsequently relinquishing his pretensions to Quakerism when the affairs of the country wore a more promising aspect — yet the committee said if all this were proved it would not disqualify him and he was allowed to remain. The next year John Williams of Deerfield, who in 1783 had been indicted for the part he had taken in the war, in favor of Great Britain, pleaded the benefit of the sixth article in the treaty and was allowed to keep his seat. This put an end to further questioning of Representatives-elect in this particular.

Shays's Rebellion in 1786 cost Moses Harvey of Montague his place, the ground being that he had been convicted of sedition and sentenced to an ignominious punishment. Two cases are recorded where sentence led to suspension rather than expulsion. In 1784–85 Jeremiah Learned of Oxford, under indictment for "seditiously and riotously opposing the collection of public taxes," was suspended until he should be tried. In 1807–08 the Governor sent a communication to the House, stating that John Waite of Falmouth had been convicted of forgery, and on the motion of Joseph Story of Salem, who was to become the foremost commentator on constitutional law, Learned was suspended until he should be tried.

In those days there was no hesitation to recall old offenses. Elisha Fuller of Ludlow was convicted in 1791 of forging a certificate, purporting to be signed by two Selectmen, whereby they recommended him as "a person of sober life and conversation, and well qualified for the business of a retailer of spirituous liquors." He had been sentenced to pay a fine, did not get a pardon or a reversal of the judgment, and ten years later was excluded from a seat in the General Court. James Morrell of Falmouth was more fortunate in 1816–17. He had been indicted in 1814 for stealing a town order to the amount of $15.12. The verdict had been set aside and a new trial ordered. The indictment, however, was quashed and the legislative committee vindicated him by refusing to recommend action.

Massachusetts has always acted in this matter under what

may be called the common parliamentary law. In other words no specific constitutional authorization has been thought necessary. Her Supreme Court set forth the principle in Hiss *v.* Bartlett, 3 Gray 468 (1855). "The power of expulsion," said Chief Justice Lemuel Shaw, "is a necessary and incidental power, to enable the House to perform its high functions, and is necessary to the safety of the State. It is a power of protection. A member may be physically, mentally, or morally, wholly unfit; he may be afflicted with a contagious disease, or insane, or noisy, violent and disorderly, or in the habit of using profane, obscene, or abusive language. It is necessary to put extreme cases, to test a principle. If the power exists, the House must necessarily be the sole judge of the exigency which may justify and require its exercise."

New Hampshire, New York, North Carolina, Kansas, and South Dakota have also refrained from explicitly referring to the power in their Constitutions. In Kansas the Supreme Court has found the power in the right of each House to be the judge of the qualifications of its members. The question rose in connection with a statute giving the court trying the cause, authority to remove any State, district, county, or township officer found intoxicated in any public place. When, in 1878, this threatened to bring about the removal of a member of the Legislature, it was held [1] that the power to judge of qualifications was continuous, running through the entire term.

Some States have found occasion to mention the power of expulsion in their Constitutions, through the wish to limit it in one way or another. For instance, South Carolina said at the start: "The General Assembly and Legislative Council, respectively, shall enjoy all other privileges which have at any time been claimed or exercised by the Commons House of Assembly, but the Legislative Council shall have no power of expelling their own members." The inference is that expulsion had been a privilege claimed or exercised. Why it was denied to the Legislative Council is matter of surmise; perhaps it was because that body had only thirteen members. The prohibition was dropped in 1778, leaving the matter to be presumed from the clause about "other privileges."

Pennsylvania and Delaware, holding their Conventions at about the same time and in many particulars continuing

[1] State ex rel. *v.* Gilmore, 20 Kas. 551 (1878).

brotherly relations, each specified that a member might be expelled, but not a second time for, in Pennsylvania, "the same cause," in Delaware, "the same offense," which was restricted to "misbehavior." Maryland was more cautious, making the ground for expulsion "a great misdemeanor." Vermont copied Pennsylvania, but in 1786 changed the restriction, "not a second time for the same cause," into, "not for causes known to their constituents antecedent to their election," which continues to this day.

The idea that a vote larger than a majority ought to be required, appears to have been conceived in the Pennsylvania Convention that adjourned in February of 1790; and was at once copied by the South Carolina Convention that completed its labors in the following June. It quickly won support, being adopted by Delaware and Kentucky in 1792, Tennessee in 1796, and by other States until now a two-thirds vote is the rule in every State referring to the matter except Vermont. Fifteen of the States carry the precaution to the point of requiring that such a vote shall be of all the members, and not merely of those present.

Nineteen States direct that a member shall not be expelled twice for the same "cause"; eight make it the same "offense." Just why there is this difference in words is not clear, for if the necessary number wanted to get rid of a fellow-member, they would accomplish it under either word. Yet in at least four instances when Constitutions have been revised, the word "cause" has been changed to "offense" and it is to be presumed some definite motive was in mind. Four States (Delaware, Virginia, Florida, Louisiana) have had such a restriction for a time and then dropped it. Texas dropped it for eight years and then (1876) put it back. It was in the rejected New York Constitution of 1867. Illinois from 1848 to 1870 said: "The reason for such expulsion shall be entered upon the Journal, with the names of the members voting upon the question." Michigan from 1835 to 1908 said, after the fashion of Vermont, a member should not be expelled "for any cause known to his constituents antecedent to his election," and Arkansas said substantially the same thing from 1868 to 1874. Idaho says expulsion is to be "for good cause shown."

Ohio, which from the start permitted expulsion by a two-thirds vote, though not a second time for the same cause, added a separate provision in 1912: "Laws shall be passed providing for the prompt removal from office, upon complaint and hearing, of all officers, including State officers, judges and members of the General Assembly, for any misconduct involving moral turpitude or for any other cause provided by law; and this method of removal shall be in addition to impeachment or other method of removal authorized by the Constitution."

In Kansas a law of that kind came before the Supreme Court, in the case above cited of State *v.* Gilmore. Was there no provision for the removal of Gilmore from office by impeachment? It is claimed, said Justice Brewer, "that by the decision in the Blount case, it was long ago held by the United States Senate, that the members of that Senate were not subject to impeachment, and that by the common understanding and consent of all, this decision has been considered as applicable to members of all State Legislatures. So far as the Federal Legislature is concerned, the decision in the Blount case, though rendered by a closely divided Senate (14 to 11) has ever since been accepted as a correct exposition of the law, and that question is doubtless forever at rest." The Judge went on, however, to quote with approval the opinion of the Judge who decided the case in the District Court, drawing a distinction between the language of the Federal and State Constitutions. The Kansas phraseology was: "The Governor, and all other officers under the Constitution, shall be subject to impeachment." The lower court thought it not open to doubt that a member of the Legislature was an officer under the Constitution. The upper court, although quoting this with approval, did not find its enunciation necessary to the determination of the matter in issue, but sustained the judgment dismissing the petition, on the ground that the Legislature could not delegate its power to judge the qualifications of its own members.

The clause of the Federal Constitution relating to expulsion reads: "Each House may determine the rules of its proceedings, punish members for disorderly behavior, and, with the concurrence of two thirds, expel a member."

Does this mean that expulsion is a form of punishment for disorderly behavior, to be applied with the concurrence of two thirds? Does it cover only disorderly behavior in the House? Does it further mean that expulsion is to be applied for no other cause?

These questions present the most interesting problem that has arisen in Congress relating to the subject.

In 1797 President Adams transmitted to the Senate a letter purporting to have been written by William Blount, a Senator of Tennessee, for the purpose of inciting certain Indians of the South to act with British agents in an enterprise opposed to the interests of the United States and Spain. Blount, with only one vote to the contrary, was expelled as having been guilty of a high misdemeanor, entirely inconsistent with his public duty and trust as a Senator.

Ten years later Senator John Smith of Ohio, alleged to be implicated in the conspiracy of Aaron Burr, escaped expulsion by one vote. John Quincy Adams, making the report, argued eloquently that the power of expelling was without limitation. "When a man, whom his fellow-citizens have honored with their confidence, on the pledge of a spotless reputation, has degraded himself by the commission of infamous crimes, which become suddenly and unexpectedly revealed to the world, defective indeed would be that institution which should be impotent to discard from its bosom the contagion of such a member; which should have no remedy of amputation to apply until the poison had reached the heart."

At the time of the duel between Jonathan Cilley and William J. Graves, in which Cilley lost his life, and the House would not expel nor even censure Graves or his seconds, a protracted debate over technicalities ended in laying the matter on the table. The sectional quarrel had already blinded the eyes of men to justice and right. The prevalence of dueling up to that time was some excuse for the action of the House, but there was no valid excuse whatever for its refusal in 1856 to expel Preston S. Brooks after his brutal and cowardly assault on Senator Charles Sumner. To be sure, the assault was not on a member of the House and did not take place in the House, but the sober judgment of men would now say that if ever dishonorable, criminal conduct gave reason for expelling a member, it gave reason for expelling Brooks, unless passion and partisanship are to palliate offenses against decency and law.

Two years later the House refused to expel O. B. Matteson, who had resigned from the previous House to escape expulsion on the charge of inciting the use of a large sum of money for corruptly securing the passage of a certain resolution, and of defaming the House by declaring that a large number of members had pledged each other not to vote for any resolution granting money or lands unless they were paid for it. Three members of the committee, a majority, took the ground that the proceedings in the previous Congress constituted no disqualification and that the legislative power to punish members could not be used in regard to matters having no legal recognition.

On the other hand, in 1870 the House refused to let B. F. Whittemore, of South Carolina, take the oath and occupy his seat, when he had been reëlected after expulsion on the charge of selling appointments to the Military and Naval Academies, an offense treated as bribery. General Logan, for the committee, distinguished this from the Matteson case by saying Matteson had been elected to a Congress succeeding the one in which he had been censured, and which had no jurisdiction of the offense committed against its predecessor. This was an instance of exclusion, not expulsion, though apparently argued without drawing the distinction. In 1872 the House in the Crédit Mobilier affair preferred to censure rather than expel Oakes Ames and James Brooks, declining, however, to express doubt as to its power to expel.

The practice of polygamy next brought up the issue. In 1873 attempt was made to exclude George Q. Cannon, a Mormon delegate from Utah. The question was complicated by the fact that Cannon was a delegate from a territory and not a member from a State. Also there was doubt as to whether once sworn he should be excluded or expelled. No action was then taken, but in 1882 he was excluded. Polygamy again brought dispute in 1900, in the case of Brigham H. Roberts, when the subject received the most exhaustive discussion. Utah had now become a State, so that the delegate issue no longer perplexed, but the doubt as to whether procedure should be by exclusion or expulsion still troubled. Speaking of expulsion, the majority of the committee averred that the ablest lawyers, from the beginning of the Republic, had held that the House has no power to expel except for some cause relating to the context. They said that these propositions were established: "1. Neither House of Congress has ever expelled a Member for acts unrelated to him as a Member or inconsistent with his public trust and duty as such. 2. Both Houses have many times refused to expel where the guilt of the Member was apparent; where the refusal to expel was put upon the ground that the House or Senate, as the case might be, had no right to expel for an act unrelated to the member as such, or because it was committed prior to his election."

The minority of the committee quoted Story's comment on the Blount case, Story concluding: "It seems, therefore, to be settled by the Senate, upon full deliberation, that expulsion may be for any misdemeanor which, though not punishable by any statute, is inconsistent with the trust and duty of a Senator." Half a dozen of the leading constitutional authorities were cited in support of the view that the power to expel is unlimited. The long and hard-fought contest ended with the passage of a resolution, by 268 to 50, to the effect that Roberts, who had not been sworn in as a member, "ought not to have or hold a seat." The minority of the committee proposed a substitute to the effect that the status of Roberts as a polygamist, unlawfully cohabiting with several wives, afforded constitutional grounds for expulsion, but not for exclusion. This was rejected by a vote of 81 to 244. The importance of the point lies in the fact that a man may be excluded by a majority vote, but for expulsion a two-thirds vote is necessary.

In 1906 a majority of a Senate committee deemed Reed Smoot's membership in a religious hierarchy that countenanced and encouraged polygamy, a reason for removing him from the Senate. The Senate itself, however, refused either to exclude or expel.

Congress has been more lenient than many State Legislatures in the matter of expulsion. Even in the case of most disorderly behavior within its own walls, where its rights have not been open to question, it has been reluctant to act. Very early it gave notable proof of its charity. In the exciting days of John Adams' administration, when the quarrel with France was preparing the way for the Alien and Sedition Laws, Roger Griswold of Connecticut one morning taunted fiery Matthew Lyon of Vermont about his army record, whereupon Lyon spat in Griswold's face. By 52 to 44, not two thirds, the House failed to expel Lyon, who based his defense on the fact that the House was apparently not in session, the Speaker having left the chair while ballots were being counted. Three days after this vote, Griswold assaulted Lyon with a stout cane while Lyon was seated, writing. Lyon got the tongs from the fireplace and there was a lively affray, stopped with difficulty. This time the Speaker was in his chair, but the attempt to expel both of the pugnacious members failed and the House would not even censure them.

Grievous though the offense may have been then and on other occasions, much as the dignity of the House may seem to have suffered through forbearance to punish, yet on the whole it is perhaps fortunate that discipline has been no more severe. The power is full of danger. To be sure, it is a power that, as Doctor Johnson said, "necessity made just and precedents have made legal," even where not set forth in Constitution or statute. Yet it may easily be perverted by partisan abuse. For momentary ends the rights of constituencies may be destroyed, reputations may be blasted. The danger is all the greater because there is no chance of appeal. The courts deem themselves powerless. In French v. Senate, 146 Cal. 604 (1905), when four Senators had been expelled for taking bribes, it was held that under our form of government the judicial department has no power to revise even the most arbitrary and unfair action of the legislative department, or of either House thereof, taken in pursuance of the power committed exclusively to that department by the Constitution. "There is no provision authorizing courts to control, direct, supervise, or forbid, the exercise by either House of the power to expel a member."

Curiously enough, through some strange obliquity of human nature, expulsion often accomplishes a result precisely the opposite of its purpose. John Wilkes, profligate demagogue, became the most popular man in England largely because the House of Commons tried to get rid of him. A mean and sordid offense like that of Whittemore who sold cadet appointments was rewarded by immediate reëlection. In Canada, something more than a century ago, C. B. Bouc, convicted of a share in conspiracy to defraud, was expelled and reëlected several times, and finally had to be disqualified by statute. Not so blameworthy, perhaps, was the constituency that a generation later kept on reëlecting Mr. Christie, member from Gaspé, as fast as he was expelled, for one of the chief charges was that as an extreme partisan of the Government, he had badly advised the Governor, which suggests partisanship. Probably that was the chief factor in the expulsion two years later of William Lyon Mackenzie from the Legislative Assembly of Upper

Canada, because he was found "guilty of gross, scandalous, and malicious libels, intended and calculated to bring this House and the government of this province into contempt." Reëlected, he was declared incapable of holding a seat in that session, and when he again presented himself he was forcibly expelled by the Sergeant-at-Arms. Later all proceedings in the case were expunged from the Journals.

Episodes of this sort have strengthened the incredulity of the many persons who ascribe to "politics" all charges made against men seeking or holding public office. Such persons persist in discrediting or ignoring even irrefutable evidence. Blind and unreasoning sympathy for the under dog sways the prejudice of the multitude. Democracies love martyrs. Therefore it is the part of wisdom to accept the situation and very rarely to disturb a man who has been fairly elected a member of a lawmaking body.

For this reason it was probably fortunate that the Senate did not push the charges against Senator La Follette based on certain utterances in the course of the Great War. Whether the House might not wisely have ignored the conduct of Victor L. Berger, may or may not be later shown worth discussing, but apart from the political phase of the matter, the technical phase calls here for a word of explanation. Berger, the recognized leader of the Socialist Party, had been found guilty under the Espionage Act and sentenced to twenty years of imprisonment. His appeal was pending when the 66th Congress, to which he had been elected, came together. Upon the allegation that he was ineligible to a seat, he was not permitted to be sworn in as a member. This method of procedure would have been of importance if there had proved to be a marked difference of opinion in the House, for expulsion requires a two-thirds vote, whereas exclusion may be determined by a majority. Opinion, however, was almost unanimously against Berger, only one negative vote being recorded upon the resolution later accompanying the committee report to the effect that he was not entitled to his seat. The committee saw fit not to rely upon the sentence by the Court, but from its own investigation concluded that Berger had "given aid or comfort to the enemies" of the United States, which by the Fourteenth Amendment to the Constitution made him ineligible until Congress by a two-thirds vote should remove the disability. Upon reëlection to the same Congress he was again refused admission, but when elected to the 68th Congress no question about his admittance was raised.

Somewhat different were the circumstances in the case of the expulsion of five Socialist members of the New York Assembly in 1920. The New York Constitution does not specifically give the Legislature power of expulsion, so that the procedure took place under the provision that each House shall be the judge of the qualifications of its own members. The New York practice of having members-elect subscribe to the oath individually before organization did not give the opportunity found in Congress and probably most other legislative bodies, to challenge at the swearing-in time, and so recourse was had to the expedient of suspension during inquiry. At the opening of the investigation by committee that followed, the propriety of this suspension was denied by a special committee of the Association of the Bar of the City of New York, headed by Charles E. Hughes. The statement submitted by Mr. Hughes represented that the five Socialists had been permitted to take the oath; they had participated in the election of Speaker, and otherwise acted as members; no charge had been made against them prior to suspension; no charge was pending that they were not duly elected, did not possess the qualifications prescribed by the Constitution, were not of sound mind, had been convicted of any crime, were guilty of any violation of law, or were guilty of any misconduct while members. This was all true enough and justified the contention that "questions as to the existence of disqualification in the case of a member-elect are properly presented before he is admitted to membership in the Assembly." Such ought to be the practice, even though inconsistent with the custom of admitting a man alleged to be disqualified because not duly elected, and determining the fact later. Yet it may be questioned whether the Bar Committee was right in holding it to follow that a man once admitted "cannot be suspended or denied these privileges [of membership] pending inquiry, but only upon being expelled in case proper charges have been sustained after hearing." Parliamentary law gives the power to require an unruly member to withdraw, at least temporarily. Members have often been suspended pending inquiry as to alleged offenses. It would be impracticable to set any limit to the power of a legislative assembly in this particular. That is one of the things which must be left to the sense of decency and fitness.

The Bar Committee reached safer ground when it argued that a man may not be denied the privilege of taking the oath' of office, and that the oath once taken may not be denied adequacy, merely because of any alleged opinion, state of mind, or intent, claimed to be inconsistent with the oath; and that inasmuch as the Constitution of New York ordains that no other oath, declaration, or test save that set forth in the Constitution shall be required as a qualification for office of public trust, the Assembly has no authority to establish any test of loyalty or political principle as a qualification of membership. Technically this was sound and in a court of law might have prevailed, but State Legislatures are not courts of law, bound by forms and precedents. In such matters as this the Constitutions wisely leave their powers vague and general. Here the question is not one of individual rights, but of the authority necessary for the functioning of government. Every limitation prescribed would sooner or later interfere with the common welfare. Even though occasional harm may come from the abuse of authority or the unwise exercise of judgment, it is better to leave the lawmaking body untrammeled in determining upon the qualifications of men either to become or to remain members.

In this New York instance the most important thing was not procedure. The vital question was whether members of the Socialist party were so disloyal and traitorous that their oaths to support the Constitution could not be treated otherwise than as patently sham and a mere cloak for treachery.

After long controversy the five Socialists were expelled, whereupon in new elections they were returned by increased majorities. Again their right to seats was attacked, but on somewhat different grounds. In the first inquiry three of them had been held responsible for their own utterances and acts, and all five for their pledges to support a society or group known as the Socialist Party of America, which was charged with designing to change our form of government by other than constitutional methods. In the mean time a convention of the party had changed its Constitution to meet the fundamental objections of the Assembly. So it was decided now to unseat only the three who were believed to be open to charges on personal grounds. The same issue confronted the Assembly of 1921,

but the passions and prejudices fanned to a flame by the war
had begun to subside and it proved possible to avoid meeting
the question again.

The episode was altogether unfortunate. It established a
dangerous precedent in parliamentary procedure. It helped
radical agitation. It swelled the political revolt it was meant
to stifle. It threatened one of our liberties we have thought
vital, for freedom of speech seemed to be at stake. Unpatri-
otic, incendiary, revolutionary though the views of the five
Socialists may have been, very many thoughtful observers
deemed it impolitic and dangerous to deprive districts of representation because of the expression of political beliefs. The
Constitution of New York says: "Every citizen may freely
speak, write and publish his sentiments on all subjects, being
responsible for the abuse of that right." The spirit of our institutions demands the clearest evidence of such abuse.

Treason in time of war can hardly be questioned as a valid
ground for expulsion, but with this exception moral turpitude
is about the only occasion to which there may be prudent resort. Nowadays nothing short of expulsion would be deemed
fitting upon the discovery of moral turpitude. Surely in this
respect there has been advance since 1689 when the case of
Captain Churchill vexed Parliament. He had refused to take
some merchant ships under the protection of his man-of-war
unless he received a present of £200. As a member of Parliament, how should he be treated? It was made a party question. Admiral Russell and Mr. Smith urged that he was
zealous and hearty for the Government, and hoped that an
ounce of misdemeanor could not weigh down a pound of merit.
Sir Edward Seymour on the contrary advocated extreme rigor:
"It is said he is a gentleman of merit, but no man of the fleet
can come before you, but as much may be said for him. But
who would not for £200 have a reprimand here, and go do the
same thing again! Send him to the Tower, and declare him
not capable to serve at sea again." The doctrine of loose morality prevailed and Captain Churchill suffered no more than a
short term of imprisonment. He ingenuously confessed that he
would rather fight three battles with the French than one with
the House of Commons.[1]

[1] W. C. Townsend, *Hist. of the House of Commons*, II, 95.

VACANCIES

IN England, the House of Commons has always regarded the right of determining upon the existence of vacancies, and of taking measures to fill them, as essential to its free and independent existence; and consequently has asserted and maintained it as a most important and undoubted privilege, resting upon the same foundation with the right of determining upon the elections and returns of its members.[1] One of Queen Elizabeth's Parliaments did not sit for five years, and in that time many members died, others left the country, others fell sick. The Lord Chancellor directed new writs for choosing men in their places. This resulted in certain members consenting to be reported as dead, or incurably sick, that other persons with whom they might bargain or agree, could be chosen.[2] The opportunity for the influence of the Crown strengthened the conviction that the House should keep the matter in its own hands. Such an abuse would be impossible now, but control is still of importance in England, more so than with us, because a change of governments may come about there through the results of by-elections.

It is probable that the English practice made it the common law that legislative bodies shall control the filling of vacancies where there is no constitutional direction to the contrary. Anyhow, several of the American colonies appear to have proceeded on that assumption when they framed their first State Constitutions. Virginia, however, saw fit to specify that each House should direct writs of election "for the supplying intermediate vacancies." Pennsylvania said the President (as the Governor was first styled) should "supply every vacancy in any office," but it is doubtful if this extended to members of the House of Representatives. The matter was made clear by the Constitution of 1790, which directed that the Speaker of each House should issue the necessary writs of election. In North Carolina the two Houses were to "direct writs of election"; in Georgia the single House was to do the same. In South Carolina the presiding officers were to issue writs for filling vacancies occurring between sessions.

---

[1] L. S. Cushing, *Law and Practice of Legislative Assemblies*, 186.
[2] Preface to John Glanville, *Reports of Certain Cases*, xxvi.

Massachusetts devised a peculiar way for filling vacancies in the Senate, giving the power to the Senate and House sitting jointly. New Hampshire in 1784 and Maine in 1819 copied this, but all three have now abandoned it, Massachusetts in 1860, New Hampshire in 1889, and Maine in 1899.

The prejudice against giving the Governor a share in the matter began to wear away soon after the Revolution. Georgia turned the issuing of writs of election over to him in 1789. Tennessee so provided in her first Constitution, that of 1796. Most of the newer States have taken the same course. Kentucky, however, began (1792) by directing that the Senate should fill its own vacancies by vote of the remaining members, and that for the House the Speaker should issue writs of election. In 1792 it was provided that the whole matter should be regulated by law. This was copied by Louisiana in 1812, and remained the practice there until 1879, when the authority was given to the Governor. North Carolina in 1835 empowered the Governor to proceed in the case of vacancies occurring before the meeting of the General Assembly, and in 1868 extended it to him in all cases, under such regulations as might be prescribed by law. As it stands now, under something more than half the Constitutions the Governor is to issue writs at all times, and in four cases he is to do it in the recess, under restrictions. In the other States the matter is left in the control of the Legislature.

The well-considered draft of a Model State Constitution adopted by the National Municipal League would save time and expense by having a vacancy filled by a majority vote of the remaining members from the district in which the vacancy occurs. The feasibility of this, however, is contingent on the use of proportional representation, with some such provision as that in the draft in question, calling for not less than five members from a district.

In the case of vacancies in Congress, the Federal Constitution provides that the executive authority of the State shall issue writs of election. How soon a Governor shall act in the case of a vacancy in Congress, is left to his sense of duty, as it generally is in the case of vacancies in Legislatures where he has the power to proceed.

An interesting instance of declaring a seat vacant was that concerned with Thaddeus Stevens, who was to become one of the best known and most powerful of Congressmen. In the winter of 1838–39 there was an exciting struggle over the organization of the Pennsylvania Senate. On the issue depended the question as to which of two rival Houses would be recognized. When decision in the Senate was disputed, a mob took possession. President Penrose of the Senate, various Senators, and along with them Stevens, who was there as a spectator, fled by jumping from the windows. After the riot the State militia was called out and President Van Buren was much exercised over the possibility of having to intervene with United States troops. The story is that Stevens ran off to Gettysburg and stayed there for about a month before returning to claim his seat in the House. Thereupon the House solemnly resolved that the seat was vacant, though it was said that others who had been out nearly as long were admitted without question.

If the candidate receiving the largest number of votes is ineligible, does a vacancy follow or should the candidate getting the next largest number be declared elected? England gives the seat to the second man, providing those who voted for the ineligible candidate knew of his ineligibility. The theory is that when an elector is apprised of the fact of disqualification, and notwithstanding gives his vote for the candidate ineligible, he takes upon himself the risk of losing his vote, if his construction of the law turns out to be wrong. Cushing thought this did not seem unreasonable.[1] It was, however, shown in the thorough debate on the subject in the contested case of Smith v. Brown, in Congress, in 1868, that Cushing's view was based on English and not on American precedents. The view of the committee in this case was opposed to that of Cushing, and was sustained in the House by a vote of 102 to 30. The question was again discussed in the case of Joseph C. Abbott, in 1872, this time in the Senate, where the same conclusion was reached, the vote being 42 to 10.[2] On numerous other occasions Congress has taken the same position.

The matter came near being of grave consequence at the time of the controversy over whether Hayes or Tilden had been elected President. The issue rose over the action of the Governor of Oregon in throwing out the vote for a candidate for presidential elector who was averred to be a Postmaster, thus

[1] *Law and Practice of Legislative Assemblies*, par. 179.
[2] Hinds, *Precedents*, I, 448, 478.

giving the certificate to one of the Democratic candidates. All the precedents were exhaustively discussed before the Electoral Commission. Its decision was to the effect that the majority candidate had in fact resigned his position as Postmaster, so that nothing was added to the precedents, but the arguments made a valuable contribution to the literature of the subject. They may be found in the volume on the "Electoral Count of 1877."

It was here brought out that the earliest American decision on the point was that of Chief Justice Chase of Maryland who in Hutcheson v. Tilden and Bordley (4 Harris and McHenry, 279) held that all votes given for an ineligible candidate are to be thrown away and rejected as having no force or operation of law, and decided that the next man in the poll had been properly declared elected. It was shown that since then this view has been applied in several cases by the legislative department of Maryland.

Our courts have followed the English line of reasoning in a few other instances, and notably in Indiana. There in Gulick v. New (14 Ind. 93) the court said: "While it is true that the votes of the majority should rule, the tenable ground appears to be that if the majority should vote for one wholly incapable of taking the office, having notice of such incapacity, or should perversely refuse or negligently fail to exercise their choice, those, although in a minority, who should legitimately choose one eligible to the position, should be heeded." In 1831 the Supreme Court of Maine gave an Opinion (7 Me. 497) in answer to questions of the House of Representatives, one of which was: "Can ballots having the names of persons on them, who do not possess the constitutional qualifications of a Representative, be counted as votes under the 5th section of the 4th article, part 1st of the Constitution, so as to prevent a majority of the votes given for eligible persons constituting a choice?" The Court replied: "To the fourth question proposed, without a particular statement of reasons, we merely answer in the negative." By thus disregarding certain scattering votes cast for an ineligible person, an election that would otherwise have been defeated through the requirement of an absolute majority, was effected.

In a recent Wisconsin case where the majority of the Court followed the English reasoning, stress was laid on the effect of knowledge by the voters. Frank T. Tucker, candidate for Attorney-General in the primary, died under tragic circumstances that might fairly be argued to have become generally known. In spite of Tucker's death, leaders of the party advised voting for him nevertheless. Said the majority of the Court: "The great weight of authority, English and American, is to the effect that votes knowingly cast for a candidate who cannot possibly exercise the functions of the office if elected, are thrown away, and it seems to us that this should be so." The three dissenting Justices also evoked "the great weight of authority," and found that in this country it is in harmony with the rule that ineligibility does not void ballots nor give the election to the next man, and they said this rule had been laid down in several Wisconsin cases.[1] In 1917 Woll v. Jensen, 36 No. Dak. 250, followed the minority opinion in the Wisconsin case.

Singular provision against vacancies is made by some of the Central American republics. They elect substitutes, somewhat after our practice of electing alternates for delegates to conventions. In Costa Rica there is to be one substitute Deputy and one substitute Senator for every three and remainder from each Province. If less than three Senators or Deputies are sent by a Province, nevertheless there is to be a substitute. Honduras elects one Deputy and one substitute for every ten thousand inhabitants; it has no Senate. Nicaragua elects one Deputy and one substitute for every fifteen thousand inhabitants, one sitting and one substitute Senator for every two Deputies. In Panama "there shall be substitutes to take the place of the regular incumbents in case they fail to appear absolutely or temporarily." The device also appears in the new Constitution of Austria, with one alternate to be elected for each member of the Bundesrat, the upper branch. Perhaps the restriction thereto had something to do with the evident intention to constitute that body in conformity with the federal principle of the representation of States, although as they are to be represented therein in proportion to the number of their citizens, it is not quite clear why the same system of alternates should not have been used for the lower branch too.

[1] State ex rel. Bancroft v. Frear, 144 Wis. 79 (1910).

CHAPTER XIV

QUALITY PAST AND PRESENT

"STUDENTS of our government all agree," said Governor Emmet O'Neal, of Alabama, in 1914, "that there has been a steady decline in the average standard of ability, independence, and intelligence of the membership of our State Legislatures."[1] In the same year Ogden L. Mills told the New York Academy of Political Science that "it is becoming increasingly hard to get our ablest men to become Senators and Assemblymen and that those positions are no longer looked upon with the same degree of honor as they were in the early days of the Republic." E. L. Godkin, trenchant critic, had recognized the incipient stages of this decadence seventeen years before, finding it in scope far wider than the narrow limit of American State Legislatures. "There is not a country in the world, living under parliamentary government," he declared, "which has not begun to complain of the decline in the quality of its legislators. More and more, it is said, the work of governments is falling into the hands of men to whom even small pay is important, and who are suspected of adding to their income by corruption. The withdrawal of the more intelligent class from legislative duties is more and more lamented, and the complaint is somewhat justified by the mass of crude, hasty, incoherent, and unnecessary laws which are poured on the world at every session. It is increasingly difficult to-day to get a man of serious knowledge of any subject to go to Congress, if he have other pursuits and other sources of income. To get him to go to the State Legislature, in any of the populous and busy States, is well-nigh impossible."[2]

Let us travel back to that halcyon time when the best men went to the Legislature. It was not in 1875, for then Henry Reed doubtless spoke precise truth when he said: "It is true that most State Legislatures are composed of men of low tone, ignorant, selfish, and easily debauched; it is also true that

---

[1] "Distrust of State Legislatures," *No. Am. Review*, May, 1914.
[2] "The Decline of Legislatures," *Atlantic Monthly*, July, 1897.

transportation corporations are often recklessly managed, and are apt to be in the hands of unscrupulous men, and the relation between them and the State government is sooner or later one of bargain and sale." [1]

Congress was no better, for Gideon Welles wrote, in his diary December 12, 1866: "It is pitiable to see how little sense of right, real independence, and what limited comprehension are possessed by our legislators. They are the tame victims and participators of villainous conspirators." And on the 24th: "There is less statesmanship, less principle, less honest legislation than usual. There is fanaticism, demagogism, recklessness. The radicals, who constitute more than three fourths, are managed and controlled by leaders who have no more regard for the Constitution than for an old almanac, and the remaining fourth are mostly party men, not patriots. . . . Four fifths of the members are small party men, creatures of corner groceries, without any knowledge of the science of government or of our Constitutions. With them all, the great, overpowering purpose and aim are office and patronage."

It must have been that the Civil War brought depravity in its train, for even while it was in progress, in 1862, we find Sidney G. Fisher declaring: "The Government is below the mental and moral level, even of the masses. Go among them. Talk to the farmer in his field, the blacksmith at his anvil, the carpenter at his bench — even the American laboring man who works for hire, in the Northern States — and compare their conversation, so full of good sense and sound feeling, with the ignorance, vulgarity, personality, and narrow partisan spirit of an ordinary Congressional debate, and with disclosures made by investigating committees. Evidently the mind and moral sentiment of the community are not represented." [2]

The lawmaking bodies of the States were no better off, if we may trust the judgment of Anthony Trollope, who came to this country in 1861. Nothing, said he after his visit, had struck him so much in America as the fact that the State Legislatures were puny powers. He found that the two professions of lawmaking and of governing had become unfashionable, low in estimation, and of no repute in the States. "Whether or no the best citizens of a State will ever be induced to serve in the

---

[1] "Some Late Efforts at Constitutional Reform," *No. Am. Review*, July, 1875.
[2] *The Trial of the Constitution*, 347.

State Legislature by a nobler consideration than that of pay, or by a higher tone of political morals than that now existing, I cannot say." And later on: "The theory has been that public affairs should be in the hands of little men."[1]

That being the wretched case threescore years and more ago, what must be our plight to-day when we have fallen so much below our fathers! But they, too, had fathers vastly their superior in virtue and intelligence. Read the glowing tribute paid to the merits of Congressmen in 1841 by another English observer, Charles Dickens, after visiting the Capitol at Washington:

"Did I recognize in this assembly, a body of men, who, applying themselves in a new world to correct some of the falsehoods and vices of the old, purified the avenues to Public Life, paved the dirty ways to Place and Power, debated and made laws for the Common Good, and had no party but their Country?

"I saw in them, the wheels that move the meanest perversion of virtuous Political Machinery that the worst tools ever wrought. Despicable trickery at elections; underhanded tamperings with public officers; cowardly attacks upon opponents, with scurrilous newspapers for shields, and hired pens for daggers; shameful trucklings to mercenary knaves, whose claim to be considered, is, that every day and week they sow new crops of ruin with their venal types, which are the dragon's teeth of yore, in everything but sharpness; aidings and abettings of every bad inclination in the popular mind, and artful suppressions of all its good influences: such things as these, and in a word, Dishonest Faction in its most depraved and unblushing form, stared out from every corner of the crowded hall.

"Did I see among them, the intelligence and refinement: The true, honest, patriotic heart of America? Here and there, were drops of its blood and life, but they scarcely colored the stream of desperate adventurers which sets that way for profit and for pay. It is the game of these men, and of their profligate organs, to make the strife of politics so fierce and brutal, and so destructive of all self-respect in worthy men, that sensitive and delicately-minded persons shall be kept aloof, and they, and such as they, be left to battle out their selfish views unchecked. And thus the lowest of all scrambling fights goes on, and they who in other countries would, from their intel-

[1] *North America*, 216, 509.

ligence and station, most aspire to make the laws, do here recoil the farthest from that degradation." [1]

A panegyric not quite so emphatic, but yet earnest, was that of still another visitor, De Tocqueville, who wrote his "Democracy in America" half a dozen years earlier. "On entering the House of Representatives at Washington," he said, "one is struck by the vulgar demeanor of that great assembly. The eye frequently does not discover a man of celebrity within its walls. Its members are almost all obscure individuals, whose names present no associations to the mind: they are mostly village lawyers, men in trade, or even persons belonging to the lower classes of society. In a country in which education is very general, it is said that the representatives of the people do not always know how to write correctly."

Yet another visitor of that period was Harriet Martineau, who passed two years here in thorough travel, meeting the leading statesmen of the time, and, on the whole, making just and accurate observations. From her we learn that in this retrospect we have not yet reached the time when the best men were elected, for she said: "It has become the established method of seeking office, not only to declare a coincidence of opinion with the supposed majority, on the great topics on which the candidate will have to speak and act while in office, but to deny, or conceal, or assert anything else which it is supposed will please the same majority. The consequence is, that the best men are not in office. The morally inferior who succeed, use their power for selfish purposes, to a sufficient extent to corrupt their constituents, in their turn. . . . I often mentioned this to men in office, or seeking to be so; and they received it with a smile or laugh which wrung my heart. Of all heart-withering things, political scepticism in a republic is one of the most painful. I told Mr. Clay my observations in both kinds. 'Let them laugh,' cried he, with an honorable warmth; 'and do you go on requiring honesty; and you will find it.' " [2]

Miss Martineau, De Tocqueville, Dickens, all observed our public life in the period when the influences of Jacksonian Democracy are supposed to have lowered its tone. For more satisfactory proofs of the decorum, dignity, chivalry, that marked our predecessors in so much greater degree than ourselves, let us go farther back, to the first decade of the century, and read

[1] *American Notes*, ed. of 1910, 143.   [2] *Society in America*, I, 85.

a story, little known, that appeared in the "New York Evening Post" of December 13, 1805:

"Oppugnation — The United States Gazette hints at a street affray, between two gentlemen in Philadelphia, and the particulars have since been verbally communicated; but the personal respect we bear one of them, prevents our making it a newspaper story. Not so with that of which we shall now give our readers the particulars, something the true english style.

"On Friday last the well known Leib, one of the representatives of Pennsylvania, and the leader of the Duane party, and Joseph H. Nicholson, one of the representatives of Maryland, met in the Congress Lobby about 1 o'clock; when Leib immediately called Nicholson a liar, and thereupon commenced one of the best fought battles recorded in the annals of Congressional pugilism.

"The Fight"

[It will suffice to quote the description of three of the rounds, typical of the whole.]

"1st round. Nicholson hit Leib in the mouth and knocked him down.

"7. Nicholson knocked down his man without ceremony — 20 to 2 on Nicholson.

"44. Nicholson gave his opponent another favourite hit on the throat, and Leib fell exhausted.

"The fight continued until the 64th round, but a detail of the rounds could be no gratification to our readers. Leib had received such blows as deterred him from again facing his man. He protracted the fight, falling after making a feeble hit. In the round which ended the fight, those who backed him advised him to resign, which he did, after a combat of one hour and seventeen minutes.

"The combatants were alike very much beaten; but although Nicholson could scarcely see out of either eye, he appeared quite fresh. Leib was everything that has been said of him. Against any other man but Nicholson, he must gain a conquest off hand. He fights without fear, and his blows are such as leave evident marks behind. He, however, uses his left hand but seldom, for if he could perform with it equal to his opponent, he might with safety bid him defiance. Vivat Respublica."

The particularity of this account lends it the color of truth, and the likelihood of ground for it is increased by the fact that both men resigned in the following year. Yet it is hard to reconcile the story with the record of the men, for Nicholson was afterward Chief Justice of the sixth judicial district, and judge of the Court of Appeals, and Leib was a United States Senator from 1809 to 1814. As Mark Twain said of the report of his death, it may have been greatly exaggerated.

Perhaps more trustworthy and inspiring knowledge is to be had of the lawmakers in "the early days of the Republic." Surely we may expect to find unalloyed patriotism, the recognition of merit, the victory of virtue, among the demigods who created the nation. Let us see how nobly they bore themselves in the first Congress. Fisher Ames may speak for the House of Representatives. On the 23d of March, 1790, he wrote to his friend George Richards Minot of "the violence, personality, low wit, violation of order, and rambling from the point, which have lowered the House extremely in the debate on the Quaker memorial. The Quakers have been abused, the eastern States inveighed against, the chairman rudely charged with partiality. Language low, indecent, and profane has been used; wit equally stale and wretched has been attempted; in short, we have sunk below the General Court in the disorderly moment of the bawling nomination of a committee, or even of country (rather Boston) town-meeting." [1]

These, however, were the words of a spokesman for the aristocrats of Massachusetts, the well-born, as John Adams called them, and perhaps Ames was uncharitable to those of the baser sort. So turn to one more democratic in his instincts, a true champion of equality, William Maclay of Pennsylvania, member of the first American Senate. In his Journal, charmingly frank and continuously tart, he wrote under date of August 29, 1789: "With the Senate I certainly am disgusted. I came here expecting every man to act the part of a god; that the most delicate honor, the most exalted wisdom, the most refined generosity, was to govern every act and be seen in every deed. What must my feelings be on finding rough and rude manners, glaring folly, and the basest selfishness in almost every public transaction! They are not always successful, it is true; but is it not dreadful to find them in such a place?" Also read the last words in his Journal, March 3, 1791: "As I left the

[1] *Works*, I, 75.

Hall, I gave it a look with that kind of satisfaction which a man feels on leaving a place where he has been ill at ease, being fully satisfied that many a culprit has served two years at the wheelbarrow without feeling half the pain and mortification that I experienced in my honorable station." He saw dishonor in the acts of most of his colleagues, grossly shown, he believed, in the bill for assumption of State debts and in other money transactions.

Now we are getting back to "the fathers." Perhaps, though, they fell from grace when they had created a Federal Congress, or it may be that as usual after wars there had been corruption of morals and manners. Let us look, then, to the state of the Congress of the Confederation in the darkest hours of the Revolution, surely a time when patriotism ought to have secured that self-sacrifice which leads the noblest to accept the burdens of public office. Yet Alexander Hamilton wrote to George Clinton, February 13, 1778: "There is a matter, which often obtrudes itself upon my mind, and which requires the attention of every person of sense and influence among us; I mean a degeneracy of representation in the great council of America. It is a melancholy truth, sir, the effects of which we daily see and feel, that there is not so much wisdom in a certain body as there ought to be, and as the success of our affairs absolutely demands. Many members of it are no doubt men, in every respect, fit for the trust; but this cannot be said of it as a body. Folly, caprice, a want of foresight, comprehension, and dignity, characterize the general tenor of their actions." [1]

Hamilton ascribed this chiefly to the fact that the ablest men, outside those who had gone into the army, had been retained for the service of the respective States in civil capacities, so let us go back to the year before the outbreak of war, when no army had been officered and the very best citizens of the thirteen colonies had been sent to Philadelphia, where they were to brew Independence. John Adams shall be our authority as to their qualifications and conduct. After two or three months of dilly-dallying, he became impatient. "The deliberations of Congress," he declared, "are spun out to an immeasurable length. There is so much wit, sense, learning, acuteness, subtlety, eloquence, etc., among fifty gentlemen, . . . that an immensity of time is spent unnecessarily. . . . This assembly

[1] *Writings of George Washington*, v, 508.

is like no other that ever existed. Every man in it is a great man, an orator, a critic, a statesman; and therefore every man upon every question must show his oratory, his criticism, and his political abilities. The consequence of this is, that business is drawn and spun out to an immeasurable length. I believe, if it was moved and seconded that we should come to a resolution that three and two make five, we should be entertained with logic and rhetoric, law, history, politics, and mathematics; and then — we should pass the resolution, unanimously, in the affirmative. . . . These great wits, these subtle critics, these refined geniuses, these learned lawyers, are so fond of showing their parts and powers, as to make their consultations very tedious. Young Ned Rutledge is a perfect bob-o-lincoln — a swallow, a sparrow, a peacock; excessively vain, excessively weak, and excessively variable and unsteady; jejune, inane, and puerile."

Turn from Congresses to Assemblies, and let us gather proofs of the decadence of State Legislatures. Prepare to expect a striking contrast between the merits of the fathers and the shortcomings of our own generation, for do we not read in that perspicacious journal, "The Nation," how much more honorable were those who have gone before? "In the old days," it says, "the New England Legislatures were 'General Courts,' not merely in formal title, but in common parlance. Somewhat of the dignity of the judge went along with them. The pay was almost nothing; the illicit profits quite so; but the personal honor of the position was very considerable. The farm communities, therefore, almost invariably sent up to the State capitals their best men, and sent them up over and over again. Usually it was the country squire, but, if a farmer, it was the farmer who was the leader in town meeting, apt to be the best lettered man of his class, and usually the owner of many well-ordered acres. He took his election, moreover, not only as a matter of grave personal responsibility, but as a civic badge of the highest dignity and as a sort of decoration. In actual legislation he may have been an opinionated, cramped partisan, but his integrity was flawless, and pride of place as well as his conscience checked the slightest tendency to a dishonorable act." [1]

Now for some contemporary judgment, for instance, that of

[1] *The Nation*, June 23, 1892.

Elbridge Gerry, signer of the Declaration of Independence and afterward Governor of his State. In the Federal Convention of 1787 he said: "In Massachusetts, the worst men get into the legislature. Several members of that body had lately been convicted of infamous crimes. Men of indigence, ignorance, and baseness, spare no pains, however dirty, to carry their point against men who are superior to the artifices practised." [1]

That epoch, so far better than ours, yet was itself evidently one of degeneracy. We are told that in colonial Virginia, for example, it had been considered an honor to hold office, and office-holding tended even to become the badge of a class. A member of the parish vestry was nearly always chosen to represent the county in the House of Burgesses. If not a vestryman, the member of the House was sure to be a representative of the same ruling class, and jealous of its privileges. Bishop Meade makes the statement that there were not three members of the Virginia Convention of 1776 who were not vestrymen of the Established Church. [2] What a change we find in a few years, if we are to accept the opinion of James Madison, voiced in the Convention of 1787, according to the report of one of his speeches as given in his own Journal. He appealed to his colleague, Colonel Mason, "to vouch another fact not less notorious in Virginia [than the partiality of its Legislature to its own members in appointments to office,] that the backwardness of the best citizens to engage in legislative service gave but too great success to unfit characters."

Many another citation could be made from the debates of the same Convention showing the low opinion in which its members held the State Legislatures. Since, however, it is the tendency of members of one lawmaking body to think unkindly of those of another, let us for more genial language look to an outsider, say General James M. Varnum, who wrote a letter to George Washington, telling why Rhode Island was not represented in the Federal Convention: "Permit me, Sir, to observe, that the measures of our present Legislature do not exhibit the real character of the State. They are equally reprobated and abhorred by gentlemen of the learned professions, by the whole mercantile body, and by most of the respectable farmers

---

[1] *Elliot's Debates*, v, 160.
[2] H. R. McIlwaine, *The Struggle of Protestant Dissenters for Religious Toleration in Virginia*, 13.

and mechanics. The majority of the administration is composed of a licentious number of men, destitute of education, and many of them void of principle. From anarchy and confusion they derive their temporary consequence; and this they endeavor to prolong by debauching the merits of the common people, whose attention is wholly devoted to the abolition of debts, public and private." [1]

Or take the judgment of A. Maclaine, of North Carolina, who in the year before the Convention assembled, in writing to James Iredell spoke of the many wicked and scandalous acts of the preceding session of the Legislature; attributed these to want of principle and want of knowledge; and said he was sick of legislating. "There is no dealing with fools and knaves," he observed, just as if he were speaking to-day — "unless they are powerfully opposed. There will be no living in the country without a reform, and in truth it will be a disgrace to live in it." [2] Three years earlier James Hogg, who, we are told, was a North Carolina gentleman distinguished at the bar for ability, and in social life for refinement and elegance, also writing to Iredell had said : "A set of unprincipled men, who sacrifice everything to their popularity and private views, seem to have acquired too much influence in all our Assemblies." [3] This was no relapse, if we are to set any store by the judgment of Samuel Johnston, one of the foremost of the North Carolina radicals, who wrote to Iredell while the Revolutionary War was stirring all hearts to patriotism, in December of 1776, that every member of the Constitutional Convention of his State who had "the least pretensions to be a gentleman" was suspected by the others, whom he describes as "a set of men without reading, experience, or principle to govern them." [4] His colleagues in the first Legislature were many of them "fools and knaves, who by their low Arts have worked themselves into the good graces of the populace."

This might suggest that the turmoil of the Revolution threw the scum to the top. Doubtless we shall find power in the hands of wiser, purer men if we but look to the years before war had wrenched society from its moorings. Yet Governor Martin of North Carolina in 1773 declared the House consisted, for the

<hr>

[1] *Elliot's Debates*, v, 577.
[2] *Life and Correspondence of James Iredell*, ii, 138.
[3] *Ibid.*, ii, 46.   [4] *Ibid.*, i, 338.

most part, "of men in the lowest state of ignorance, that are gulled into absurdities by a few artful and designing men, influenced by selfish and interested motives."[1]

Of course he was a prejudiced critic, for he wrote when revolt against Governors was in the air and in every colony "the poor misguided herd," as Martin called them, were making things most uncomfortable. So jump back two generations, into calmer surroundings, when presumably none but the best were chosen to make laws. Surely that ought to have been the case in Virginia, most prosperous, wealthy, and aristocratic of the colonies, where the landed gentry had in the course of a hundred years brought into full bloom a chivalrous society, refined, proud, masterful. Governor Spotswood described the men these patricians chose to make their laws. How astonishing to find that two hundred years ago the best citizens failed to get elected to office! In 1711 Spotswood repined because the Assembly was composed "of men of narrow fortunes and mean understandings." In the Assembly of 1713–14 the Burgesses were "persons of the meanest capacities and most indifferent circumstances, and whose chief recommendation to the Post is their declared resolution to raise no taxes upon the People for any occasion whatever." Again, in 1723, he noticed a tendency toward "excluding the gentlemen from being Burgesses, and choosing only persons of mean figure and character." He said the same mean spirit was shown by the Burgesses expelling two members "for having the generosity to serve without pay," on the plea that they were bribers.[2]

Here we are, two centuries back, when men were brave and disinterested and regardless of their own political fortunes, and the Governor could declare of the members that "some of them have so little shame, as publicly to declare that if, in Assembly, anything should be proposed which they judged might be disagreeable to their constituents, they would oppose it, though they knew in their conscience, it would be for the good of the country."

But why take the time farther to trace the degeneracy of public men generation by generation, or even century by century? Let us rather at one leap go back two thousand five hundred years and see how human nature has fallen. "How

---

[1] *N. Ca. Colonial Records*, ix, 698.
[2] E. I. Miller, *The Legislature of the Province of Virginia*, 53, 54.

can a man serve the prince? When out of office, his sole object is to attain it; and when he has attained it, his only anxiety is to keep it. In his unprincipled dread of losing his place he will readily go all lengths." The sentiment has a familiar ring. It might have been taken from any periodical or newspaper of to-day, if "public" were substituted for "prince." Yet these were the words of no modern cynic, no embittered pessimist, no canting fault-finder. They were spoken by Confucius, the greatest sage of his time, one of the greatest sages of all time. He knew human nature. It was the same then as it is to-day. Whether in Orient or Occident, whether yesterday, or when history began, always the proof may be found that some men, usually many men, have in public service failed to convince their fellows of their unselfishness, their valor, their virtue.

DIFFICULTIES OF COMPARISON

ERROR in the comparisons of legislative bodies at different periods, comes from contrasting selected groups of members. One important factor is overlooked, one all-important factor — the base-line from which measurements are to be taken. Mount Katahdin, rising from a plain, is imposing in its grandeur. Yet the city of Denver is higher above the sea than the summit of Katahdin, and were Katahdin in Colorado it would be but a minor peak of the Rockies. The statesmen of one epoch may so tower above the average of intelligence and ability as to seem demigods. Men of like capacity might at another period hardly rise above the crowd.

Furthermore, if one of the periods compared is in the present, double is the difficulty. We judge a man of the past at any given moment of his life, not alone by what he then was and had been, but also with the knowledge of what he afterward became. When Benedict Arnold returned from that terrible march to Quebec, he was a hero to his contemporaries, but we of to-day can never conceive him a hero. On the other hand, who in 1850 would have named Abraham Lincoln as one of the great men in the Congress where he served?

Yet again, the times confuse the issue. The same men debating the Kansas-Nebraska question might seem giants; debating a silver coinage or ship-purchase bill they might seem pigmies.

The greater part of our men of national repute sat earlier in
some State Legislature. Wiseacres shake their heads and say,
"We have no Legislatures now like those in which were Lincoln
or Hoar, Henry or Marshall." Yet in every Legislature to-day
are men who ten or twenty years from now will be famous in
their turn. The Massachusetts House of Representatives in
1895 and 1896 was not conspicuously better than at any other
period in a generation. The surviving members of those two
years held a reunion in 1916. It was found that one of them
had become Governor; five had been sent to the Governor's
Council, and five to Congress; one had been made a Federal
Judge and eleven had become Judges of State courts; six had
been chosen Mayors, four District Attorneys, one Attorney
General, and one State Treasurer; forty had served in the
State Senate, one as its President; ten had become bank presi-
dents; many of the others had achieved responsible positions
in professional or business life. The record was not exceptional. It would be duplicated by the twenty-year story of
every Massachusetts Legislature within the memory of man,
and by that of the Legislature in many another State. It
may even be true of New York, in spite of the averment of
Ogden L. Mills to the New York Academy of Political Science
that the Legislature "no longer furnishes a real stepping stone
to the larger and more responsible positions in public life."
Mr. Mills has been contradicted by his own experience, for the
New York Senate, where his service was noteworthy, furnished
him a stepping stone to the national House. Strong men are
likely to be promoted everywhere.

Deterioration is alleged in the case of Congress with the
same carelessness as in the case of the State Legislatures. In
reply take the testimony of S. J. Barrows, who was steno-
graphic secretary to Seward and in the Department of State from
1867 to 1871; later a Unitarian clergyman and editor of the
"Christian Register"; and then a member of the 55th Congress,
from Massachusetts. In 1903 he wrote: "As a newspaper
correspondent at Washington more than thirty years ago, I had
a good opportunity to study public men at a period when a great
crisis in our history had brought many of the strongest men to
the front. If there were giants in those days there are giants
in ours. There has been no diminution in the intellectual
stature of this battalion of our public men. As to particular

districts in the House, and certain States in the Senate, a comparison of past and present might be unfortunate; but, taking both bodies as a whole, there has been no abatement in intelligence, knowledge, practical sagacity, statesmanlike grasp of public questions, or brilliancy in oratory. After going through the list of States and districts past and present, I find not the slightest reason to believe that the Congress of 1871 was any stronger than the Congress of 1900." [1]

Just comparisons between different legislative bodies of the same period ought to be easier than those perverted by the illusions of time, but here, too, there is inevitable error. Distant hills are always greenest. Arcadia is beyond the sea. Therefore, Congress is thought by most Americans to be inferior at any rate to Parliament, and probably to many other national councils. Here again let Mr. Barrows be quoted, to the contrary. Three times he represented this country in the International Parliamentary Union, when it held sessions in Paris, Brussels, and Christiania, and he was thus brought in contact with 350 or more of picked representatives of European parliaments. "In point of linguistic facility," he said, "the representatives of polyglot countries, like Switzerland, Austria, or Belgium, are far ahead of our own; but in everything else which goes to make up the qualifications of a good representative, I have failed to mark any important difference, except those differences of method and tradition, which mark the difference between Europe and America."

Naturally Bryce made comparisons. "As respects ability," he concluded, "the Senate cannot be profitably compared with the English House of Lords, because that assembly consists of some twenty eminent and as many ordinary men attending regularly, with a multitude of undistinguished persons who though members, are only occasional visitors, and take no real share in the deliberations. Setting the Senate beside the House of Commons, one may say that the average natural capacity of its seventy-six members is not above that of the seventy-six best men in the English House." This is fairer than it seems. The House of Commons for the greater part bounds the ambitions of English statesmen. From it there is no promotion, for it is well understood that when a member is made a peer, save

[1] "Is Our National Congress Representative?" *No. Am. Review*, November, 1903.

in rare instances, it is the courteous way of bowing him out of public life. Most of British political ability is in the Commons. There political careers are begun and ended. With us, the lower branch is the avenue to the higher. Some very able men, indeed, prefer to stay in the House, but more seek the Senate at the first opportunity. Then, too, men who have risen to be Governors of States often step directly into the Senate from the executive chamber. For these reasons, it is significant that Mr. Bryce at least did not rank our ablest group of legislators below the ablest English group of the same number.

Another English observer, acquainted with both bodies, Sydney Brooks, writing more recently than Bryce,[1] differentiates the House of Commons from the French and American legislatures by saying: "First, it is a body with a far higher social standing; secondly, it is better educated; thirdly, it is much wealthier. Nothing amazes Englishmen who visit Washington so much as to find that in the polished, agreeable, and distinctive society that graces and is graced by the national capital, Congressmen have no part — even less part than a French Deputy in the Parisian world. In England an M.P., unless he be an Irishman, is at once a man of social position not only in the provinces, but also in London. He has, at any rate, the entrée, and it depends entirely on himself whether or no he converts it into a permanent foothold. Then, again, a very large percentage of members are 'varsity men. They have received, or most of them have received, the best education that England can offer, and they carry its stamp through life. And finally an immense majority of them are rich men. It has been said that there is nowhere where a poor man feels so out of place as in the House of Commons."

Here, it will be noticed, is no question of native intellectual ability, but only of certain particulars that in fact do not for the most part greatly appeal to sober-thinking Americans. We are wholly indifferent to the social standing of our statesmen, or else, indeed, view with some suspicion those who frequent tea-tables and drawing-rooms. The mass of our people do not look on the higher education as assuring capacity for public service. Some of them magnify the merits of wealth, but for its own sake wealth does not command political support. In short, we are quite willing to grant that the House of Commons may surpass

[1] "The House of Commons," *Harper's Weekly*, March 5, 1904.

the House of Representatives in these three particulars, and yet not be willing to concede superiority in the things we deem essential for statesmanship.

FAULT-FINDING AND ABUSE

IT is to be feared that not only visitors from abroad, but also many of our own countrymen, have been over-willing to see in Washington what they expected to see. Democracies delight in finding fault with their servants. The habit has grown on us until we are possessed by it. Newspapers, prospering the mor⌐ as they succeed in printing what the public wants to read, encourage the habit by catering to it. "So much criticism has been levelled by the press at the *personnel* of the House of Representatives, and so many insinuations are constantly indulged in against the habits and integrity of its members," wrote Hilary A. Herbert, "that every newly elected representative on coming into that body within recent years must have confessed to himself a feeling of profound surprise at what he has seen. He has heard much of corruption, but he sees no evidences of its existence. Possibly among so many, there may be some who are corrupt, but the body, as a whole, may challenge comparison for integrity and fidelity with any in the world; he has heard of dissipation, but he finds that, with very few exceptions, the members are remarkable for sobriety and steady habits; and what surprises him most of all is the average ability and range of information possessed by those around him." [1]

A more discriminating judgment is that of Professor Henry C. Emery, who as Chairman of the Tariff Board had good chance to watch Congressmen at short range. Said he to the students of the Sheffield Scientific School of Yale in 1912: "The representatives of the people in either branch of Congress are probably much more honest and decidedly less intelligent than you young men think them to be. There is a certain glamour about positions of this kind and I have no doubt that you exaggerate in your minds the capacity of the average Congressman and what you consider the great genius of the few leaders who have made themselves conspicuous. On the other hand, just as you make them in your minds more than plain human

---

[1] "The House of Representatives and the House of Commons," *No. Am. Review*, March, 1894.

beings in the matter of intelligence, you make them rather less than plain human beings in the way of plotting, scheming, and planning. This is partly due to the fact that they are distant from you; partly due also, I suppose, to a certain tendency of youth to exaggerate all qualities whether good or bad. I have heard my father [Chief Justice Emery of Maine] remark, after a long life of varied experience with all classes of men, that the longer he lived the more he came to trust in the honesty of men and the less he came to trust in their intelligence." [1]

In the matter of the Legislatures as in that of Congress, fair appraisal is a rarity. So nearly universal has been the misconception and the misrepresentation that even as keen an observer as Bryce was deceived. He concluded that "the real blemishes in the system of State government are all found in the composition or conduct of the Legislatures"; and he put first in the list of blemishes — "Inferiority in point of knowledge, of skill, and sometimes of conscience, of the bulk of the men who fill these bodies." Describing the institutions of a land not his own and necessarily relying on the opinion of others, Bryce was excusable, but it is not so easy to forgive an American who says: "Very often the legislative body is below the average citizenship of the community." [2]

To rebut such charges, first let me quote two Massachusetts men of character and standing that ought to secure credence for their testimony. After service in the Legislature, one was to become a leading Senator of the United States, the other a Federal Judge. Henry Cabot Lodge said: "A very common illusion is that in this country legislative bodies are more or less bad and stupid, and that every man who can be called a politician, is from the name alone a person of inferior character and ability. This pernicious nonsense is fostered by the manner in which many newspapers, especially those which from love of paradox call themselves independent, habitually speak either thoughtlessly or intentionally of all men in public life. If a young member of the Legislature happens to suffer from any such illusion as to Legislatures and politicians, he will soon be cured of it. If he plunges with rash confidence into debate, he will find himself most probably overmatched in argument, and contending with men who are vastly his superiors in practical

---

[1] *Politician, Party and People*, 90.
[2] J. R. Commons, *Proportional Representation*, 164.

knowledge of public affairs. He will soon find also, that his associates are a body of honest, right-thinking, and rightly-intentioned men, of more than average ability and character. Legislatures vary; and in any Legislature there can be found persons who are stupid and selfish, and sometimes corrupt. The same statement, however, is true of any business, trade or profession. But our Legislatures on the average, and as a rule, will compare favorably with an equal number of persons taken from any portion of the community, and the members are usually men of reputation in their own neighborhood for force and capacity." [1]

Likewise speaking from personal experience F. C. Lowell said : "If the average man be asked why a session of the Legislature is dreaded by many intelligent persons, he will answer that the quality of the individual legislators is poor, and that few of them are men of good standing in their individual communities. This statement he will hold to be obviously true beyond the possibility of doubt. He supposes them to be, for the most part, machine politicians of small capacity and doubtful honesty, actuated mainly by party spirit and personal ambition — men who are but little trusted by their neighbors in the other affairs of life. To prove positively the unsoundness of this common opinion is impossible, of course, for respectability, reputation, and good standing in the community are largely matters of opinion. I can only say that I believe the members of the Massachusetts House, as individuals apart from their office, to be much better men than their critics suppose. A House of 240 members must always contain some men who are not honest, reputable, or intelligent ; but the better the members are known as individuals, the more plainly does it appear that the great majority of them are altogether respectable and well intentioned, and that many of them are men who in their respective communities are actually chosen, and chosen naturally and properly, to fill important positions of private and corporate trust. Considering human nature, it is rather remarkable that universal suffrage is so discriminating." [2]

Precisely such would be my own conclusions, reached likewise after service in the Massachusetts Legislature. It will, however, be instantly retorted that the Massachusetts Legis-

[1] "A First Term in the Legislature," *Youth's Companion*, January 10, 1889.
[2] "Legislative Shortcomings," *Atlantic Monthly*, March, 1897.

lature is exceptional, the best in the land.   That is not for a
Massachusetts man to deny.   Yet there are other States where
defenders of the lawmakers are not wholly wanting.   For
instance Charles McCarthy, who knew more about them than
most people, answered the question — "What sort of men compose the Wisconsin legislature?"   Said he: "It has long been
the custom to laugh at legislators and to belittle the politicians
who are our lawmakers.   To the average citizen the legislator
in general appears as a very ordinary individual who is a politician for what he can make out of it.   I confess that I was
agreeably surprised to find that, however the case may be elsewhere, the Wisconsin Legislature is composed of men far above
the average in every respect.   The average wealth is very high
and the average intelligence is still higher.   Among them are
sharp, shrewd merchants, bright young lawyers, sober, progressive farmers, retired engineers and business men.   The
average legislator in Wisconsin is, further, a church-going man."

Mr. McCarthy also observed: "It is evident that the Wisconsin Legislature is, on the whole, improving from year to
year.   There are not as many brilliant leaders as formerly, but
neither are there as many stupid or corrupt men.   The primary
seems to elect a middle class average man of independence and
intelligence.   The old system tended to elect either brilliant,
well-known men or those who were merely pawns in the game.
Under the primary, individuals announce their intention of
becoming candidates and fearlessly run for office.   Legislators
have often admitted to the writer that they would not attempt
to run for office under the old system.   No one has to ask for
that privilege now." [1]

Surely weight will not be denied to the judgment of Herbert
S. Hadley, whose distinguished service as Governor of Missouri
gave him a nation-wide reputation, and who later became Professor of Law in Colorado University.   Says he: "I have had
occasion to know somewhat intimately a number of State Legislatures, and while I realize that this particular branch of the
public service is the favorite editorial and rhetorical chopping
block of critics and reformers, my opinion is that we get surprisingly good results in actual legislation when we consider
the necessary haste and unscientific methods under which their
work is usually performed.   Further, I never knew a State

[1] *The Wisconsin Idea*, 90 (1912).

Legislature that was not fully representative. By that I mean that with a few exceptions the legislators represent more than the average of ability and integrity of their constituents, and understand fully and try to represent faithfully the interests and needs of their different districts." [1]

Governors are not usually expected to look at the legislative branch with generous eyes, yet another of them, J. F. Fort, who had been the Chief Executive of New Jersey, said to the Economic Club of Boston, November 29, 1915: "The members of the Legislature are generally conscientious, honest, honorable men, and a whole lot of the criticism that falls on them is unjust." That verdict is typical of what you may get from any fair man who can speak as a result of personal observation.

Professor Paul S. Reinsch, after a comprehensive study of the whole field of American legislative work, declared: "It has become almost fashionable to talk of State Legislatures as bodies in which men of ability and respectable character are in a disappearing minority, and yet even the most superficial acquaintance with actual Legislatures will immediately reveal the fact that they are very fairly representative of the American people, and that there is in them a great deal of honest effort to grapple with the difficult problems of legislation, misguided though this effort may be at times for lack of authentic information and thwarted by certain vicious arrangements in our political system. The State Legislatures by no means deserve to be treated as unimportant or cast aside as vitiated beyond hope. Such superficial views must give way to an intelligent study of the workings of these institutions, to a sane and impartial criticism; and before all, there ought to be a sustained effort to support the men who are with honest purpose struggling for equitable and effective legislation, by giving them countenance and by raising their achievements to that plane of public importance which they deserve." [2]

The denunciation of a whole Legislature, say of two hundred men, because a score of those men are weak or venal or vicious, is wholly unjust. That calls for a percentage of virtue which would not be expected from any group in the community, unless it be the clergy; and the Twelve Disciples had one Judas.

---

[1] "Power, Duty, and Responsibility of the Individual Citizen," *Am. Bar Ass'n Journal*, April, 1923.
[2] *American Legislatures and Legislative Methods*, 128.

Let any newspaper writer run over in his mind the characteristics of his associates and see if he is prepared to say that not one in ten of them would accept money for suppressing an item of news. Let him ask himself how many would suppress it at the request of a personal friend, in disregard of the interests of his employer. Would the words "quack" and "shyster" have come into general use if the medical and legal professions were immaculate? Surely their members are fortified with a higher degree of education than can be expected of a representative assembly. Or if you turn for comparison to the business world, does the record of failure indicate an average of capacity, does our common experience with business ethics suggest an average of integrity, higher than that of a State Legislature?

It is not easy to understand why democracies abuse their servants. If it were just, yet would it be folly. The psychologists have proved that praise is wiser than blame. The effects of the two influences on school children have been studied. It is found that scolding is distinctly less useful than approbation. Scolding makes men as well as children callous, indifferent, stubborn. Yet democracies persist in scolding their servants, thus inciting them to be cynics. The result is that the man in public life, living in an atmosphere of suspicion, constantly misrepresented, rarely commended, too often ends by losing his enthusiasm, his courage, even his self-respect. Sometimes he concludes he may as well be hung for an old sheep as a lamb. Sometimes in disgust he abandons what chance he may have of a career. When press and public by sneer and slur make public life obnoxious, why wonder that it is not attractive to more men of brains and ambition? The marvel is not that its level is lower than might be wished, but that this level succeeds in keeping where it really is.

CHAPTER XV

CAPACITY AND TRAINING

IF it were true that our representative bodies fall below their constituencies in honesty, capacity, intelligence, then would we all agree that there is something radically wrong in the system. If, however, the representative body equals its constituency in these respects, is it adequate? Bryce held that Europe and America answer this question differently. He thought he found a fundamental difference between the conception of the respective positions and duties of a representative body and of the nation at large entertained by Americans, and the conception that prevailed in Europe hitherto. "Europeans," he said, "have thought of a legislature as belonging to the governing class. In America there is no such class. Europeans think that the legislature ought to consist of the best men in the country, Americans that it ought to be a fair average sample of the country. Europeans think that it ought to lead the nation, Americans that it ought to follow the nation."

The generalization may be true of Europeans, though its validity to-day is not so clear as it was a generation ago. The rise to power of such men as Lloyd George and Mussolini, the increase in the number of labor representatives in Parliament and of Socialists in the Reichstag, the revolution in Russia — these are signs of the times. Leaders are no longer universally from the well-born. In England itself are men who believe representative government there has fallen to the same low level they delight to ascribe to America. One of the most caustic of recent English critics avers: "It is not treated as remarkable, it is treated as a matter of course, that neither in Congress nor the House of Commons is there any adequate representation of the real thought of the time, of its science, invention and enterprise, of its art and feeling, of its religion and purpose. When one speaks of Congressmen or Members of Parliament, one thinks, to be plain about it, of intellectual riffraff. When one hears of a preëminent man in the English-speaking community, even though that preëminence may be in political or social science, one is struck by a sense of incongruity if he happens to be also in the Legislature." [1]

The judgment is severe, and if deserved by Parliament, which I greatly doubt, it is not deserved by Congress. As far as American lawmaking bodies are concerned, such charges are based on the misconception illustrated by Bryce's assertion that we think they ought to be "a fair average sample of the country." His idea of "average" in this connection may be gathered from another passage in his great book, where he said: "The fact is, that the Americans have ignored in all their legislative, as in many of their administrative arrangements, the differences of capacity between man and man. They under-rate the difficulties of government and over-rate the capacities of the man of common sense. Great are the blessings of equality; but what follies are committed in its name!"

This reveals the defect in his scathing arraignment of American Legislatures. He assumed their members to be all equal, over-estimated the influence of vice, under-estimated the influence of virtue; gave too much weight to ignorance and stupidity, too little to the solid qualities of leaders. Doubtless therein he reflected the views of American informants who without personal acquaintance with Legislatures, condemned them *en masse* because of their shortcomings.

The fact is that American thought as embodied in American institutions does not contemplate a dead level of mediocrity in a representative body, nor anything in the nature of an average, but does contemplate the representation in a general way of all classes in the community, a great variety of occupations, different degrees of prosperity and education — a mirror, as it were, to reflect society. This conception, I know, is not that of all Americans. Professor Commons, for example, in his book on "Proportional Representation" (p. 164) asks the question: "Do we want only average men to govern us and make our laws?" Querying whether we want anybody to govern us, let us go on to see the argument he builds on the assumption that choice has some relation to averages. He says: "We do not select *average* physicians to save our lives, average ministers to interpret the gospel, nor average tailors, bakers, and carpenters to clothe, feed, and shelter us. We select men of exceptional native ability, who through training have become experts and

[1] H. G. Wells, *Social Forces in England and America*, 306 (1914).

professionals, men versed in their callings. So in this most important of our delegated services, this revising and framing our laws which regulate the very structure of society, and make our lives, our rights, our religion, and our enjoyments possible, in this supreme service, why should we not select men far above the average? Should they not be men who are grounded in jurisprudence, sociology, political economy, comparative legislation, besides possessing that infinite tact known as statesmanship?"

Does not fallacy run all through this? Surely some of us do select average physicians, ministers, tailors, bakers, and carpenters. Some of us select those below the average. Otherwise, none would make a living save men of "exceptional native ability," there would be none of the average class, and none below the line — which is mathematically absurd.

Doubtless Professor Commons meant that on every occasion when we need help, we intend to get the best we can, but judgments, wants, opportunities, purses, all vary so much that in any connection the truism is of small importance and particularly in the matters of public employment does it throw little light on the situation.

Another misleading figure is the half-truth so often used in blaming representative government, that the stream cannot rise higher than its source. It is as deceptive as the assertion that the Mississippi River runs uphill because its mouth is farther than its source from the center of the earth. The fact is that only in exceptional instances does a Representative fail to be better than the mean of his constituency. From the very nature of the case this is inevitable. Normally the representative is chosen because of some superiority. To be sure, it may be superiority in a particular that would not be admitted by all to be the wisest test. And no matter what the standard, there may be others, perhaps many others, who would excel him. Nevertheless, the underlying purpose of the electorate is not to choose a man because he is thought inferior, but is to choose a man believed to be superior. Otherwise election contradicts itself. Alexander Hamilton was right when he said in "The Federalist" (No. 35): "Where the qualifications of the electors are the same, whether they have to choose a small or a large number, their votes will fall upon those in whom they have most confidence; whether these happen to be men of large fortunes, or of moderate property, or of no property at all."

Lord Brougham worked out the idea in more detail. "The representatives are chosen; they are selected; they are set apart from the mass, because of some qualities that distinguish them from that mass; these qualities are such as to give a pledge of their greater fitness for the functions of government. In one man it is greater wisdom; in another, more ample wealth; in a third, higher birth; in a fourth, greater information. In almost every one integrity or respectable character is a ground of choice, and prudence or discretion, itself a virtue, the parent of some and the guardian of all the virtues, is hardly ever left out of the account in determining the choice of those persons who are to act for the community in the conduct of their most important affairs. Hence the influence of the ignorant, the heedless, the stupid, the profligate, is reduced to a small amount in the conduct of the government; for, generally speaking, the same persons who, being unfit to be themselves trusted with power, would ill-use it, are very capable of making a good choice enough of a representative." [1]

It would be exaggeration to ascribe so thoughtful and deliberate a manner of choice to an American electorate, even if it were a quite accurate description of a British constituency, which I doubt, but it is within bounds to present this as a reasonably faithful portrayal of the spirit of an election whether in England or the United States, even though the electors may be for the most part quite unconscious of their own motives or impulses. The result, as Sir J. R. Seeley puts it, is that the representative system is essentially aristocratic. "As there may be an elective monarchy, so there may be an elective aristocracy, and such is every representative Parliament. It is an elective aristocracy. It is a body of men who have been selected by the community as more fit than the average to attend to public affairs, to make and unmake the government. These men have stood out in some way above the rest; that is, they are an aristocracy." [2]

A corollary of this not commonly understood is that our lawmakers, evidently above the median point in some noticeable particulars, are likely to be above that point in other particulars not so conspicuous. Of late the psychologists have demonstrated that in human nature good traits go together. To him

[1] "The British Constitution," *Works*, XI, 60.
[2] *Introduction to Political Science*, 330.

that hath a superior intellect is given also on the average a superior character. The able persons in the world in the long run are the most clean, decent, just, and kind.[1]

Lord Brougham gave a striking illustration of how the political stream rises higher than its source. Commenting on the remarkable freedom of Parliament from corruption during the half century and more of his membership, he said: "I question if any one election had ever taken place during the same time in which many electors had not been influenced by some corrupt motive or other in the exercise of this sacred trust."[2] A thousand instances to the same effect could be gathered from the history of representation in America. Some of our greatest statesmen have entered public life through noisome channels. Many and many of our Representatives have in their public service risen far above the environment out of which they came. It is almost invariably the case that in point of integrity as well as capacity they are superior to the rank and file of their constituents.

Office and the Exceptional Man

The critics, however, are dissatisfied because exceptional men are not more numerous in the public life of America. Half a century ago John Stuart Mill declared it an admitted fact that in the American democracy, the highly cultivated members of the community, except such of them as were willing to sacrifice their own opinions and modes of judgment, and become the servile mouthpieces of their inferiors in knowledge, seldom even offered themselves for Congress or the State Legislatures, so little likelihood had they of being elected.[3] Equally censorious, Bryce said of our State Legislatures that "the men who combine high talent with character and energy are too much occupied in practicing their profession or pushing their business to undertake the dreary task of wrangling over gas and railroad bills in committees, or exerting themselves to win some advantage for the locality that returns them." Numerous American critics entertain kindred notions. One of them, Walker D. Hines,

---

[1] Edward L. Thorndike, "Intelligence and Its Uses," *Harper's Monthly*, January, 1920.
[2] "The British Constitution," *Works*, XI, 62.
[3] *Representative Government*, chap. VII.

went so far as to say it is generally agreed that comparatively few men of ability and force seek public office, and almost none stay in it.[1]

Exaggerated though such charges may be, yet candor demands recognition of the fact that they are not without an element of truth. An American who would have the public life of his country rise to higher levels, should seek the obstacles in order that he may do what he can to help remove them. Such was, of course, the purpose of Moorfield Storey when in his Presidential Address to the American Bar Association in 1894, he named "among many reasons which make so many able and honorable men prefer private life": The necessity of seeking office; the methods employed to secure nominations; large contributions to campaign expenses; the sacrifice of independence; hard work; small pay; abundant criticism; and slender appreciation of good service.

I should agree with Mr. Storey that the abundance of criticism and the slender appreciation of good service are genuine deterrents. Some of his other reasons seem to me less weighty. The work is no harder than in any other field of important endeavor. The pay would have no more influence on the nobler ambition than it has, for example, in the field of education. The sacrifice of independence is not a sacrifice to the man temperamentally adapted to collective action; furthermore, some of the most conspicuous successes have been made by self-willed statesmen. Large contributions to campaign expenses are not essential to political advancement in the case of anybody more than ordinarily qualified for such advancement. It is true that methods frequently employed to secure nominations are distasteful to high-minded men, but it is not impossible to get recognition without them, and for the most part they are no more undignified than the practices commonly used in the commercial world for getting trade. As for the necessity of seeking office, it is to be admitted that an artificial prejudice based upon a wrong conception of the relation of the citizen to the State, has in one corner of the world kept many a man from his duty by the credence it has won for the preposterous notion that the office should seek the man, and not the man the office. This notion was for some time common, and can hardly yet be said to be uncommon, in the northeastern corner of the United

[1] "Our Irresponsible State Governments," *Atlantic Monthly*, May, 1915.

States. If it exists anywhere else in the civilized world, it is, as far as I can learn, sporadic.

Ancient and mediæval history has not disclosed to me any epoch or any region where it was held dishonorable for a man to disclose a wish to serve his fellows. Where men qualified for public service, refrained from seeking it, the motive was selfish. Thus in the early years of Parliament, when election to it was viewed as a burden, the office had to seek the man because it meant expense and inconvenience. In the latter half of the fifteenth century the advantages of a seat in Parliament began to outweigh the disadvantages. From that day to this it has been a customary and a creditable thing for Englishmen openly, frankly, and earnestly to solicit the suffrages of electors. There is nothing to indicate that in our colonial era the wisdom of this custom was questioned. Apparently the notion that it was wrong, came into being as part of the general feeling produced by the Revolution, that everything English was out of place under a republican form of government. Large numbers of the people during and after the Revolutionary War thought that the reverse of the English way of doing things must be the democratic way of doing things. Andrew Jackson, ultra democrat, voiced this when in 1798 he was elected by the Legislature to a seat on the bench of the Supreme Court of Tennessee. It was, he said, a post he accepted in obedience to his favorite maxim, that the citizen of a free commonwealth should never seek and never decline public duty.[1]

For some inexplicable reason the doctrine gained its firmest foothold in New England. There for a century it was common belief that there was something unseemly in seeking public office. It was possible for George S. Boutwell to say in his "Sixty Years in Public Affairs" that he had never asked for personal support at the hands of anybody. In the Middle States there was less prejudice against ambition, yet Grover Cleveland wrote to a young friend February 4, 1885: "I never sought an office of any kind in my life."[2]

The opposite spirit dominated the South, or at any rate its aristocratic parts, where English traditions survived. P. A. Bruce, who has made careful study of colonial Virginia, finds it was the becoming step there for every young man of promise

[1] *Parton's Life of Andrew Jackson*, I, 227.
[2] *Writings and Speeches of Grover Cleveland*, 338.

and fortune, whether in possession or prospect, to enter the House almost as soon as he came of age, in order that he might, while still young, acquire some experience of public affairs. "Perhaps not a single heir to a well-known name, high social position, and large estate, who was also distinguished for marked capacity, failed to present himself almost immediately after he had passed his minority, to the voters of his county as a candidate for this honor." [1]

George Washington followed the general practice in asking the suffrages of his neighbors. It is amusing to read of the deprecating, beseeching, vociferating conduct of candidates on election days when John Marshall ran for office. Young Southerners went into politics as frankly as young Northerners went into trading, thinking it the normal thing to ask for what they wanted. As a result the open competition between the ablest men of the South gave it a representation in Congress much superior to that of the North, where it was thought improper for men conscious of political capacity, to try for the chance to exercise it. In the South, statesmen were trained. In the North, they were the product of accident. In the South, a political career was encouraged. In the North, it was discouraged. So it came about that in the twoscore years of Congressional contest leading up to the Civil War, the South with less population and less real power, won far more of the forensic victories.

It was the Southern view of political propriety that spread through the West. When Abraham Lincoln was twenty-two years old and a clerk in Denton Offutt's store in New Salem, Illinois, he offered himself to the voters of the vicinity as a candidate for the Legislature, with thirteen other citizens fired by like ambition. According to custom he issued a circular or handbill in which he modestly set forth his sentiments. He received less than a third of the votes, but in his own town got all save three. At the next election, in 1834, his name headed the list.

It continues to be the practice in the West for men to proclaim their aspirations with a frankness that would shock the East. In many places at election time you may read newspaper advertisements of candidates, written in the first person and signed, announcing their desire for votes. An Eastern candidate still

[1] *Institutional Hist. of Va.*, II, 423–24.

usually induces the editor to insert a news paragraph saying that, in response to the urgent solicitation of many friends, Mr. So-and-So has consented to be a candidate for such-and-such an office. The truth is that the multitude of counselors can usually be counted on the fingers of one hand. Yet the pretense persists. Of course there are exceptions. In boss-governed districts, the boss sometimes chooses his candidate without suggestion from anybody. There are places where groups of public-spirited citizens deliberately select men to be asked to run. Yet it is safe to say that far the greater number of candidacies are nowadays self-begun, as they ought to be. The man who does not within himself conceive a desire to serve his fellows in public office, is as little likely to be useful in such work as the man who without ambition or preference permits himself to be injected into the clinic, the bar, or the pulpit.

SCHOLARSHIP

OF course the fallacy that the office should seek the man, deters the man of fine susceptibilities more often than the man of coarser grain. The result is to lessen the proportion of refined and educated men who enter public life in regions where the doctrine carries weight. There are observers who would deny that this is an unmixed evil. For instance, S. J. Barrows said: "It would be absurd to characterize representative government as a failure because the ablest men, academically considered, are not always chosen by a community to represent it. Those who make such criticisms have rather in mind an aristocracy or an oligarchy, neither of which must be confounded with democracy. They overlook the fact, also, that the man who is academically the ablest may be politically and personally the weakest." [1]

I do not for a moment suppose Mr. Barrows meant to deplore the presence of the scholar in politics. He was one himself. What he meant to bring out, I take it, is that scholarship alone does not guarantee usefulness in public position. No man of sense denies that academic training is a help. Flippancy to the contrary notwithstanding, the fact is that education is more highly valued as an asset by those who are without it

[1] "Is Our National Congress Representative?" *No. Am. Review*, November, 1903.

than by those who have it. Thomas Wentworth Higginson wrote advisedly of this, in combating the impression that college-bred men are disliked in politics, and have to encounter prejudice and mistrust, simply by reason of education. "As a rule, it may be assumed," he said, "that any jeer at a 'scholar in politics' proceeds from some other scholar in politics. It was almost pathetic to me to see, while in the Massachusetts Legislature, the undue respect and expectation with which the more studious men in that body were habitually treated by other members, who perhaps knew far more than they about the matters of practical business with which Legislatures are mainly occupied. It was, if analyzed, a tribute to a supposed breadth of mind which did not always exist, or to a command of language which proved quite inadequate. Many a college graduate stammers and repeats himself, while a man from the anvil or the country store says what he has to say and sits down. . . . I have much oftener been saddened by the too great deference of men who were my superiors in everything but a diploma than I have been amazed by their jealousy or mistrust." [1]

This generous disclaimer from a man who was himself of exceptional culture, did his modesty credit, but may have been somewhat exaggerated. My own observation of the Massachusetts Legislature has been to the effect that the influence there exercised by college-bred men, an influence wholly out of proportion to their numbers, is justified by their capacity as legislators. Indeed their usefulness is such that it is safe to say no factor that would increase their numbers should be neglected.

It is, however, not the case that the educated classes in America are under-represented, numerically speaking. About two thirds of the members of Congress have received education of college or law-school. He who believes in schooling and fears it may not have been gaining ground, will be enlightened by knowing that of 354 men who sat in the Continental Congress from its first meeting in 1774 to its last in 1788, only one third, 118 in all, were college graduates. [2]

We may expect a smaller percentage of college education in State Assemblies, but here too there has been a decided advance,

---

[1] "On the Outskirts of Public Life," *Atlantic Monthly*, February, 1898.
[2] James A. Garfield, "A Century of Congress," *Atlantic Monthly*, July, 1877.

if we may judge from the statistics of four Massachusetts Conventions. In each of those of 1780, 1820, and 1853, a little less than one fifth of the delegates could boast a college education. In the Convention of 1917 the proportion had doubled, to two fifths. These were all bodies of three or four hundred men. Of the 280 members of the Massachusetts Legislature of 1920, 61 held college degrees and 53 others had gone beyond the high school or academy, making all told two fifths with more than ordinary schooling. This was a little higher ratio than Samuel P. Orth found in analyzing the membership of the Legislatures of Vermont, Ohio, Indiana, and Missouri, for their figures gave one fifth as having received college training, and enough more with academy or professional training to make the total one third. The proportion of college-bred men in some Western Legislatures is markedly increasing. In the Iowa Assembly, for example, it has risen to about half the membership.

Do not infer, however, that any considerable number of these men have that specialized training which would particularly fit them for grappling with the problems of political science. Rarely among the two or three hundred members of an American Legislature would you find one who had ever turned the pages of Hooker, Hobbes, Locke; rarely would you find one who had read Adam Smith from end to end, or with more than a most cursory knowledge of Ricardo, Bentham, or Spencer. The college men know something of history and many of them have worried through the rudiments of political economy, but very, very few are the men who come to the making of laws with that exhaustive preparation now demanded of experts in all the higher occupations.

Lawyers Making Law

The nearest approach to special qualification is found among the lawyers. Massachusetts Conventions present a striking phenomenon in this respect. Less than seven per cent of the delegates in 1780 had been trained for the bar; in 1820 the proportion was sixteen per cent; in 1853 it was eighteen per cent; and in 1917 it jumped to forty-seven per cent, a figure all the more suggestive because that radical proposal, the Initiative and Referendum, was the issue in the campaign, with a decided majority of the winners pledged to its support. Apropos of this it may be recalled that the French Revolution and the Reign of Terror were brought about by the country lawyers of France who controlled the National Assembly.

Nowadays three fifths or more of the members of Congress are lawyers. Particularly in the West and South the path of political preferment to high position lies through the office of Prosecuting Attorney or Judge. With the State Legislatures, for some reason not quite clear, it is different. A writer in the "New York Times" for March 20, 1910, examined the membership of the Legislatures of twenty States taken at random, well scattered, and found that in every one of the Western States except Colorado, farmers greatly outnumbered lawyers. In two of the Central States, Wisconsin and Missouri, the farmers outnumbered the lawyers, in Minnesota it was a tie, and in three others the lawyers exceeded. In only two of the seven Eastern States examined were the lawyers in the lead. In Pennsylvania he found manufacturers having the largest representation, and in Connecticut merchants. John A. Lapp, writing in the "Annals of the American Academy" for September, 1912, reported in the preceding Legislatures of Vermont, New York, Indiana, and Michigan about thirty-seven per cent farmers, twenty-four per cent in business or manufacturing, and only twenty per cent lawyers. A little less than one quarter of the 240 Massachusetts Representatives in 1920 had been admitted to the bar. In the South the lawyers have kept their hold on public office better than in any other part of the country. Everywhere they continue to exert more influence on legislation than would be expected merely from their numbers. The presiding officers and the chairmen of important committees are usually lawyers.

The preponderating influence of lawyers in the lawmaking bodies of English-speaking peoples has long been prolific of criticism. Prejudice against the members of the bar crops up repeatedly in the history of Parliament. For instance, James I wrote to Secretary Calvert, desiring the House "to go on cheerfully in their business, rejecting the curious wrangling of lawyers upon words and syllables." In his speech of 1623 "the wisest fool in Christendom" told his Parliament: "Let not any stir you up to law questions, debates, quirks, tricks, and jerks." At the time of the Revolution Lord Halifax cautioned the constituencies against choosing lawyers, who almost all had narrow minds, and by the whole scope of their studies found themselves pressed to adhere to the King and his prerogative. "For this general odium," says Townsend,[1] "the venality of some and tergiversation of other great lawyers, who trafficked with their powers of speech, may perhaps in some degree account. The exactions of Dudley, wresting the law to iniquity, suggesting in his guilty flight the impost of ship-money; the late repentance of Coke, becoming in his old age, but not till then, a tribune of the people, may in part explain this deep-rooted aversion. But a still stronger motive of dislike may be traced to the trivial jealousy which the weak entertain against the strong, depreciating those arts of oratory with which themselves may be unacquainted; undervaluing that research and laborious investigation for which they have neither leisure nor capacity; measuring by a money standard, those acquire-ments which though it may retain, gold cannot purchase. The gift of ready elocution, the self-possession, apt address, unfailing facility of speech, and those attendant evils, the habits of pro-lixity and repetition, an unsparing consumption of time, and minute subtlety, tend to weariness, and irritate and annoy the most impatient, the least merciful in criticism, of all audiences — a crowded House of Commons."

It might have been thought that with the spread of intelli-gence, a better understanding of the nature and purposes of law, and the broadening of the profession itself, lawyers might have won a higher place in British esteem, but the prejudice against them is as intolerant as ever, judging by the keen criticism of H. G. Wells, written no longer ago than 1912. "Steadily with the ascendancy of the House of Commons," he says, "the barristers have ousted other types of men from political power. The decline of the House of Lords has been the last triumph of the House of Lawyers, and we are governed now to a large extent not so much by the people for the people as by the barris-ters for the barristers. They set the tone of political life. And since they are the most specialised, the most specifically trained of all the professions, since their training is absolutely antag-onistic to the creative impulses of the constructive artist and the controlled experiments of the scientific man, since the business is with evidence and advantages and the skillful use of evidence and advantages, and not with understanding, they are the least statesmanlike of all educated men, and they give our

[1] *History of the House of Commons,* I, 333 *et sqq.*

public life a tone as hopelessly discordant with our very great and urgent social needs as one could well imagine. They do not want to deal at all with great and urgent social needs. They play a game, a long and interesting game, with parties as sides, a game that rewards the industrious player with prominence, place, power, and great rewards, and the less that game involves the passionate interests of other men, the less it draws them into participation and angry interference, the better for the steady development of the politician's career. A distinguished and active fruitlessness, leaving the world at last as he found it, is the political barrister's ideal career." [1]

At this writing the House of Commons contains ninety-eight lawyers, exactly the same number as the preceding House contained. Assuming that there has been no great change in ten years, if Mr. Wells finds such menace in less than one sixth of the membership, what would he say to the outlook for the United States, where more than three fifths of the Representatives in the national House are members of the bar?

The English attitude toward lawyers in the period when the American colonies were settled, is well illustrated by an article in the Fundamental Constitutions that John Locke prepared and the Earl of Shaftesbury amended for Carolina in 1669 : "Seventy. It shall be a base and vile thing to plead for money or reward ; nor shall any one (except he be a near kinsman, not farther off than cousin-german to the party concerned) be permitted to plead another man's cause, till, before the judge in open court, he hath taken oath that he does not plead for money or reward, nor hath nor will receive, nor directly nor indirectly bargained with the party whose cause he is going to plead, for money or any other reward for pleading his cause."

In that same year the Delegates to the Maryland Assembly presented to the upper House a paper of seven grievances, one of them to the effect that attorneys were a grand grievance. The upper House replied that as to attorneys, they were a useful class of citizens, indispensable, indeed, to those who could not attend to their law business in person, and if they were guilty of any misfeasance, there was the law to punish them. [2]

As champions of the people in the grievances against the mother country, such men as Otis and John Adams in Massa-

[1] *Social Forces in England and America*, 59.
[2] W. H. Browne, *Maryland*, 121, 122.

chusetts, Patrick Henry in Virginia, made themselves famous, broke down prejudice, and won respect for the usefulness of lawyers in public concerns. Their share in the framing of Constitutions and the other work of establishing new governments completed the winning of public confidence. Ever since then they have been foremost in American public life.

After the Revolution the lawyers completed the task of ousting the parsons from their position of dominance in the community. The liberalizing tendencies of the times weakened the influence of the church. The oratory of the bar came to interest more than that of the pulpit. Read the incredible stories of the effect of such eloquence as that of Patrick Henry. In the next generation wonder how the ponderous periods of Daniel Webster could have enthralled his hearers. Study that glorious epoch when the compelling advocate was the idol of the people, and the baneful influence of corporations had not yet quenched popular esteem. Then you will understand how the great lawyers of America got the chance to be her great statesmen.

Now power is changing hands again. The lawyers, after eclipsing the clergy, are passing into the shadow of the editors. Whatever may be the case in England, the bar no longer dominates the public opinion of the United States. In many of our legislative bodies, regardless of membership statistics, the lawyer as such has lost his mastery. That this is altogether a gain, should not go without question. There are considerations both ways. For this reason with me the strictures of Mr. Wells carry less weight than the calm, temperate judgment of Henry Sidgwick, who sets forth the situation with fairness, thoroughness, and acumen. "We may lay down without hesitation," he says,[1] "that men who have that thorough knowledge of law which we can, generally speaking, only expect to find in able and experienced members of the legal profession, should have a large and responsible share in lawmaking. Proposed laws should be drawn up by lawyers, and any changes made in the draft should be carefully revised by lawyers. But, for several reasons, it does not seem desirable to entrust the substantial work of legislation entirely — or even mainly — to them alone.

"Firstly, the deductive operation of applying complicated general rules accurately and faithfully to particular cases is

[1] *The Elements of Politics*, 355–57.

very different from the inductive operation of collecting, comparing, estimating the good and bad consequences of actual laws, and considering the consequences of proposed or possible measures. In either case, a knowledge of law, as it is, is required: but the use made of the knowledge, the habit of mind that it generates, the special points needful to be observed, the special difficulties that have to be faced and overcome, are obviously different in the two cases. Persons, therefore, may be highly skilled by nature and practice for the *application* of law, which is the habitual intellectual work of the judge, without being qualified for the *modification* of law which is the proper work of the legislator. Again, in the judicial administration of law, it is most needful that the judge should have a scrupulous respect for the law that has actually been laid down: that he should resist not only the coarser temptation of warping it under the influence of bribery, intimidation, party feeling, or personal affection, but also the subtler temptation, to twist it in the direction of equity and utility; since, as each judge would be likely to twist it somewhat differently, the certainty of law, which is more important than any increase of equity that could be obtained in this way, would be lost: moreover, if this well-meant warping of rules were allowed, it would be indefinitely more difficult to resist than the influence of sinister interests. But this scrupulous reverence for existing law, though a needful habit of mind, is likely to prevent the heads of the legal profession from being unbiassed judges of proposed improvements in law; especially as such improvements are likely to render a certain amount of their painfully gained knowledge and elaborately contrived methods useless, and to impose on them the necessity of learning new rules and new methods. We need not suppose this last consideration consciously to operate as a motive, it is sufficient if it gives an unconscious bias.

"Hence, however desirable it may be to give leading lawyers a large and responsible share in the work of constructing laws, they are commonly more qualified to be *builders* than *architects* in this work."

The delicate way in which this last is put, commends itself. A less discriminating writer, though, might have said with more explicitness that lawyers are liable to be poor lawmakers because their mental habit is backward looking. Their whole training has taught them ever to rely on precedents. They worship the past. This has its advantages, but among them is not a facility for meeting present needs and anticipating tomorrow.

Nevertheless, in spite of the limitations developed by the training of the lawyer, that training brings at the same time certain capacities which will promise him the chance for leadership. Furthermore, as Professor Reinsch has pointed out, lawyers, though not to the same degree as formerly, still constitute the most representative profession in the community. In their practice they come in contact with all classes and conditions in our social and economic life, and they have unequaled opportunities of observing the workings of law. "So," he well says, "while a government entirely carried on by lawyers would be extremely undesirable, a republic resting upon a written Constitution and free from a dominating caste, can hardly be conceived of without considerable prominence being accorded in public affairs to the profession of law." [1]

Everywhere in the United States the judiciary committee is the most important of all the committees and generally its members are all lawyers. Indeed in the California Senate, and possibly elsewhere, it is customary to put on that committee every member who is an attorney-at-law. This raises an interesting query. Is it wise to have a judiciary committee in the hands of lawyers? The custom is so prevalent that at first blush the question strikes one as superfluous. Yet at least one Congressman of long experience has given serious reasons for answering it in the negative. "For two Congresses the Judiciary Committee of the House never did agree and a majority never signed any proposition that they reported to the House," said ex-Speaker Grow, as he recalled the failures of the committee he had appointed thirty-seven years before, in the War Congress of 1861. "It was new legislation. We were making new laws, and, as I have said a number of times, with my experience, if I had to make up a judiciary committee for legislation, there should not be more than three lawyers on it, just enough to give construction to adjudicated phrases by the courts, and the rest should be composed of good common-sense members. Now, that Congress — the first session of the 37th Congress — disposed of more legislation in twenty-seven

[1] *American Legislatures*, 288.

days than was ever disposed of in any session of Congress since the Republic began. But the Judiciary Committee selected from the most able lawyers of the House, from their reputation and by the positions they held at home, were not able to agree much of the time. The questions were new ones, like the confiscation of rebel property. It was to carry on internecine war which we then had for the first time, and its lawyers, able judges, coming from the highest courts of their States, in many cases, like lawyers in all cases, must adhere to precedent. They said no such thing was ever heard of as such and such laws, and hence their disagreements. But they brought the business before the House, and the House disposed of it." [1]

FARMERS AND CITY FOLK

In "The Independent" for July 24, 1916, William B. Bailey commented on a chart he had prepared, showing the relation between the number of members of Congress and the population credited to various occupations, the chart having the title — "Our Misrepresentative Congress — With too many Lawyers and not enough Farmers and other Folks." Since that view is common, his comparisons may serve as a basis for criticism. He said there were about twenty-five million males twenty-one years of age or more gainfully employed in this country. Of these 120,000 were lawyers. Thus, about three fifths of the members of Congress were chosen from a group comprising less than one-half of 1 per cent of the gainfully employed males. On the other hand, only 3 per cent of the members were previously farmers, although 30 per cent of the gainfully employed males in this country were in this large group. The chance of a lawyer going to Congress was apparently twelve hundred times as great as that of a farmer.

Here we find once more the familiar assumption that unless representation is numerical, it is "misrepresentative." Is it, however, true that if three tenths of the men in this country are farmers, we would have better government if three tenths of our Congressmen were farmers? Note the recollection by George S. Boutwell of the Massachusetts Legislature of 1842 and thereabouts. "In those days the farmers constituted a majority of the House. They were generally men of intelli-

[1] *Congressional Record*, House, April 13, 1898.

gence, and they held about the same relation to the business of the House, that juries hold to the business of the Courts. They listened to the arguments, reasoned upon the case, and not infrequently the decision was made by them." [1]

Add to this what Nahum Baldwin, of Mercer, said in the Convention that framed the Constitution of Maine, in 1819 : "Now, sir, I have said it, and am bold to say it again, that one gentleman from Portland has more influence in this Convention, than the whole delegation from Somerset County, which is twenty-nine members. [He was from Somerset.] The reason is obvious. The members from country places are mostly farmers; and they will generally sit from one end of the session to the other without saying a word. Where there is an assemblage of the most brilliant talents and literary accomplishments from all parts of the State, the farmer is loath to expose his ignorance and weakness, and hazard being made the butt of ridicule for his blunders and every day language. And if now and then one dares venture out, and blunder on in his home made, every day, farmer dialect, his only security is confidence. If he has plenty of brass, and a good share of common sense, he may possibly jog on, and hold up his end tolerably well, in a ludicrous manner; but such instances are rare. For the most part (and I repeat it with confidence), one man who is master of all the alluring, persuasive, and insinuating charms of eloquence, will carry more sway in a legislative body, than thirty silent members from the country."

This had much of truth. Yet it was overdrawn. Sometimes the plain common sense of the farmer is weightier than the polished oratory. There is a speech by Jonathan Smith, of Lanesborough, in the Debates of the Massachusetts Convention of 1788 for ratifying the Federal Constitution (pp. 203 *et sqq.*) that will recall to any man who has served long in a State Legislature, the satisfaction he has felt when some honest, blunt yeoman has risen after many days of silence, to confound with a few pregnant, pithy, rude sentences the demagogues who have been wasting the time and patience of the assembly by specious pleas to prejudice and suspicion. "Mr. President," said Jonathan Smith, "I am a plain man and get my living by the plough. I am not used to speak in public, but I beg your leave to say a few words to my brother plough-joggers in this House.

[1] *Sixty Years in Public Affairs*, I, 104.

I have lived in a part of the country where I have known the worth of good government by the want of it. . . . When I saw this Constitution, I found that it was a cure for these disorders. It was just such a thing as we wanted. I got a copy of it and read it over and over. I had been a member of the Convention to form our own State Constitution, and had learnt something of the checks and balances of power, and I found them all here. I did not go to any lawyer, to ask his opinion; we have no lawyer in our town, and we do well enough without. I formed my own opinion, — and was pleased with this Constitution. My honorable old daddy over there" — (he pointed to Mr. Singletary, who had just told the Convention that "these lawyers, and men of learning, and moneyed men, that talk so finely, and gloss over matters so smoothly, to make us, poor, illiterate people, swallow down the pill, expect to get into Congress themselves; they expect to be managers of this Constitution, and get all the power and all the money into their own hands, and then they will swallow up all us little folks, like the great Leviathan, Mr. President; yes, just as the whale swallowed up Jonah") — "My honorable old daddy there, won't think that I expect to be a Congressman, and swallow up the liberties of the people. I never had any post, nor do I want one, and before I am done you will think that I don't deserve one. But I don't think any worse of the Constitution because lawyers, and men of learning, and moneyed men, are fond of it. I don't suspect that they want to get into Congress and abuse their power. I am not of such a jealous make. They that are honest men themselves are not apt to suspect other people. I don't know why our constituents have not as good a right to be jealous of us as we seem to be of the Congress, and I think these gentlemen who are so very suspicious that as soon as a man gets into power he turns rogue, had better look at home."

Long before this, George Alsop, in "A Character of the Province of Maryland" (1666), had found much the same traits in rustic lawmakers. "These men that determine on these matters for the Republique," he wrote, "are called Burgesses, and they commonly sit in Junto about six weeks, being for the most part good ordinary Householders of the several Counties, which do more by a plain and honest Conscience, than by artificial Syllogisms drest up in gilded Orations."

In our time the development of cities has led to sharp contrast between the representation of rural and urban districts. George W. Woodward observed in the Pennsylvania Convention of 1873: "I do not mean to say that populations in the rural districts are any better or purer than populations in urban districts; but such is the working of our system that our great cities send into the Legislature the men who give us the worst legislation of any class of representatives. They ought to send there the most intelligent and leading minds of the country, for they contain them. Intellect, like capital, centers in these great cities; but when have these great cities been duly represented in the Legislature of Pennsylvania? What gentleman will rise now in his place and say they are represented to-day as they ought to be? That the intellect, and culture, and enterprise of Philadelphia are represented to-day in the Legislature of Pennsylvania as they ought to be? No man will say it. When have they ever been so represented? Never in our day. When will they be so represented? Never in our day." [1]

That the best choice is made by the country districts, was the conclusion of F. C. Lowell, writing from experience in the Massachusetts Legislature.[2] He suggested as a reason that in the country districts the population is stable, and the average income is so small that the legislative salary makes a desirable addition. In the cities, and especially in the larger cities, men of the widest and most successful experience in business seldom find time for legislative service. Yet he was more charitable than Mr. Woodward to the Representatives from cities. He had found them usually men of some acquaintance with affairs, whose principal desire, when elected, is to do that which is right and for the public interest. These statements, he knew, might be strenuously controverted, but he could say that experience had converted him from the opposite belief.

My own observation has led me to much the same conclusion as that of Judge Lowell. To it I should add, however, that though the purpose of city Representatives is to do the right thing, they come mainly from environments where the common conception of what is the right thing differs greatly from that prevailing outside the densely populated areas. The fundamental characteristic of city politics is found in the prevalence of the belief that there is nothing dishonorable in deriving from

[1] *Debates*, II, 174.
[2] "Legislative Shortcomings," *Atlantic Monthly*, March, 1917.

public office pecuniary advantage beside that which comes from salaries. The normal thing is private gain from public office. The demoralizing effect of this on candidacies need but be suggested. It is an effect common in the manufacturing communities as well as in the great centers of population.

Furthermore the influence of rural regions, by reason of the rotation system and also because of the comparative scarcity of strong men, due to the drain by the cities, is less than it should be. The net result is that it is no great exaggeration to say Massachusetts is governed by the suburbs of Boston. They keep Representatives and Senators long in office. Useful men from them can attend at the near-by State House without great personal sacrifice, generally continuing business or professional activities during sessions. Standards of public duty are high. Pressure from office-seekers is small. Favors for constituents are seldom asked. Punishment is rarely meted out because of differences of opinion on isolated questions. Taking everything into consideration, the lot of a suburban member of a Massachusetts Legislature is about as agreeable as comes to any lawmaker in the land.

Of course these are generalizations. Many good men come from the heart of the big city, from the manufacturing town, from the village or the farm. The greater part of the leaders, however, are what in many parts of the land, though rarely in Boston, are called commuters.

It is an old cry in this country that there are in public life too few business men. In 1802 Thomas Jefferson, then President, wrote to Cæsar A. Rodney: "Congress is not yet engaged in business of any note. We want men of business among them. I really wish you were here." [1] From that day to this it has been a common complaint that we ought to send more men of affairs to Congress and Legislatures. Jefferson's argument is of course weighty, but the expediting of the public business is not the only purpose of government, although it is an important purpose.

As a matter of fact, business men, however successful in their natural fields of activity, often fall below professional men in the work of lawmaking. The life of the business man trains him to look on every transaction from the point of view of profit, and his own profit at that. His life is essentially selfish, not

---

[1] *Writings of Jefferson*, P. L. Ford ed., VIII, 187.

altruistic. Furthermore, it has little room for theory, but concentrates itself on fact. Lawmaking (other than administrative) is wholly a matter of theory — based on fact, to be sure, but theory nevertheless. Therefore it calls for broad vision, inclusive generalization, logical thought. These things may or may not be found in the man whose years have been spent in trade. Nothing in his experience makes it more probable that he will have them than anybody else. On the other hand, they ought to be found in any man who has been trained in one of the professions, for the law, the pulpit, medicine, engineering, and like pursuits have theory and logic for their very foundations, and their inspiration is altruistic.

Whether from business or professional life, a man is not likely to go far or stay long in politics if he has not some qualities that commend him exceptionally to his fellows. Often it is complained that the social qualities get too much consideration from constituencies. It is said with a sneer that this or that man has succeeded because he is "a good mixer." Of course geniality is by itself not enough, but it is nevertheless a commendable quality in any aspirant for votes. It betokens a warm heart, generosity, charity, sympathy. Best of all it promises good nature, the quality that more than any other makes life happy.

Singularly enough, a liking for sociability has brought suspicion on a large group of men in public life, through their membership in secret societies. For instance, George H. Haynes, writing of "Representation in State Legislatures," has said: "It certainly is no mere coincidence that in the Massachusetts Senate every other man is a Mason, while in the House more than one third of the members belong to the same order. Nearly the same proportions are found in the New Hampshire Legislature. Other secret orders have nearly as large a representation. While such figures give no evidence of class action within the Legislature, they certainly do make it clear that membership in one of the more influential secret orders constitutes a strong 'pull' in securing a nomination and election." [1] Post hoc, propter hoc! Of course the fact is that men who join societies are as a rule more companionable, sociable, friendly than those who do not. Their society associations give them chance to widen their circle of acquaintance. A man who aspires to serve his fellows is likely to be a man who seeks their companionship.

[1] *Annals of the American Academy*, March, 1900, 81.

It should, indeed, be thought matter for congratulation that so many of the Americans in representative positions are men of broad human sympathies, acquainted with life in many aspects, trained in the school of men. Again let me quote that acute philosopher, Henry Sidgwick. "The ideal legislator," he admirably says, "must have an insight into the actual relation of the laws to the social life of the community regulated; the manner in which they modify the conduct of the individuals whom they affect; the consequences, proximate and remote, that are likely to result from any change in them. To obtain this insight he ought to have such an acquaintance with particular facts as it is difficult to obtain otherwise than from actual experience, or at least intimate converse with men of experience; and he ought also to possess such knowledge as is obtainable of the general tendencies of social development and the effects of different social causes. Taking men as they are, we shall hardly expect to find many whose knowledge qualifies them for dealing in a statesmanlike manner with all the problems presented to a modern legislative body; if so, it becomes important in constructing our legislative organ to aim at including an adequate selection of persons who, with general ability, combine special experience in different departments of social life. This, then, is one argument for the representative system, as now applied in most countries that share West-European civilisation; that the periodical election of legislators by different divisions, sufficiently numerous, of the whole community, tends to give us, if not ideal statesmen, at any rate a body of men who possess in the aggregate the special empirical knowledge that is most indispensable."[1]

It will be observed that this lays no stress on the intellectual capacity, the education, the training, or the social standing of the individual representative. It emphasizes the aggregate. It explains why after all it makes no great difference which of two men is elected to office. Toward the end of his life George Grote, the eminent statesman-historian, said he had come to perceive that the choice between one man and another among the English people signified less than he used formerly to think it did. "The English mind is of one pattern, take whatsoever class you will. The same favorite prejudices, amiable and otherwise; the same antipathies, coupled with ill-regulated though

[1] *The Elements of Politics*, 357.

benevolent efforts to eradicate human evils, are well-nigh universal." That could be said of any American Commonwealth. Our differences are for the most part superficial. In the great essentials of habit and thought we are one. So our lawmaking bodies, ever changing in elements, change in spirit only as the community itself changes. Like a river they are never, yet always, the same. Like the surface of that ever-flowing river, they truthfully reflect the scene. If that scene be ugly or beautiful, so will be its reflection.

CHAPTER XVI

ROTATION IN OFFICE

OUR lawmaking bodies may be representative, their members may be as well qualified for the work as the conditions of a broad suffrage permit, and yet they may fall short in efficiency. If this be the case in the matter of American Legislatures, one reason is to be found in the practice whereunder utilizing the benefits of experience is discouraged. It is not a new practice nor American in its origin. Aristotle gave it as among the characteristics of democracy that all should rule each, and each in his turn over all; that no one should hold the same office twice, or not often except in the case of military offices; that the tenure of all offices, or of as many as possible, should be brief.[1] One of the French Constitutions of the period of the Revolution permitted Deputies, chosen for three-year terms, to serve not more than six years.

The principle has been applied, at least to some degree, in the purest of modern democracies, Switzerland. There the lawmaking body, known as the Federal Assembly, has two Houses, each of which chooses its own President and Vice-President, with the proviso that they shall not be eligible to these offices in the next regular session. The same insistence on rotation in office is found in the executive body, the Federal Council, chosen for three years, which elects one of its members President of the Confederation to serve for one year only, and not to be eligible for reëlection. Nevertheless, the Swiss habit is to reëlect the members of the federal legislative branch, and the same is true in the case of the cantons. Winchester found rejection of a sitting member to be a rare exception. Death or voluntary retirement accounted for nineteen out of twenty-one new members of the Assembly chosen at the preceding general election. Referring to this sure tenure of officials generally, the President of the Confederation said in a public address: "Facts and not persons are what interest us. If you were to take ten Swiss, every one of them would know

---

[1] *The Politics*, bk. VI.

344

whether the country was well governed or not; but I venture to say that nine of them would not be able to tell the name of the President, and the tenth, who might think he knew it, would be mistaken." [1] Bryce thinks the existence of the Referendum facilitates retention in office by the Swiss.

The New England colonies are commonly supposed to have more nearly approached pure democracy than any other governments from ancient times to their day. As a matter of fact, they were in one aspect theocracies, in another aristocracies, but democratic impulses now and then successfully revolted. Massachusetts Bay saw that happen once, by reason of this matter of rotation in office. Winthrop's Journal tells of it with humor all the more delicious because doubtless wholly unintentional. His entry for May 14, 1634, says: "At the general court Mr. Cotton preached, and delivered this doctrine, that a magistrate ought not to be turned into the condition of a private man without just cause, and to be publicly convict, no more than the magistrates may not turn a private man out of his freehold, etc. This falling in question in the court, and the opinion of the rest of the ministers being asked, it was referred to further consideration." The next paragraph reads: "The court chose a new governor, viz. Thomas Dudley, Esq., the former deputy." Winthrop did not deem it necessary to specify that the Governor who failed of reëlection was John Winthrop. Thus abruptly did the electors disown Cotton's doctrine.

Neither Winthrop nor Cotton was a democrat at heart. Later Winthrop wrote: "The best part of a community is always the least, and of that best part the wiser is always the lesser." Cotton wrote to Lord Say in 1636: "Democracy, I do not conceive that ever God did ordain as a fit government either for church or commonwealth. If the people be governor, who shall be governed?" He preached his opinions with more effective result five years later. Winthrop tells of it in his Journal, under date of November 12, 1641: "At this session Mr. Hathorn, one of the deputies, and usually one of their speakers, made a motion to some other of the deputies of leaving out two of their ancientest magistrates, because they were grown poor, and spake reproachfully of them under that motion. This coming to Mr. Cotton his knowledge, he took occasion

[1] *The Swiss Republic*, 80.

from his text, the next lecture day, to confute, and sharply (in his mild manner) to reprove such miscarriage, which he termed a slighting or dishonoring of parents, and told the country, that such as were decayed in their estates by attending the service of the country ought to be maintained by the country, and not set aside for their poverty, being otherwise so well gifted, and approved by long experience to be faithful. This public reproof gave such a check to the former motion that it was never revived after."

Information as to the colonial habit in the matter of representatives is meager, but lack of uniformity may be inferred from the fact that though in the first years of Maryland less than a quarter of the Delegates would be reëlected, in the half-century before the Revolution from fifty to seventy per cent would be sent back. In the early days of Rhode Island the Deputies were always changing more or less. The office was deemed a burden, which but few would assume for more than one or two sessions, as required by law.[1] Pennsylvania was the first colony to have the rotation idea put into its frame of government. William Penn's Charter of Liberties provided that (after seven years) when a member of the Provincial Council (the upper branch) ended his three years' term, he should be "uncapable of being Chosen again for one whole year following that so all may be fittest for the Government and have Experience of the Care and burthen of it." The provision disappeared in 1696, but it was not forgotten. When the Convention of 1776, over which Benjamin Franklin presided, and which he no doubt inspired, created but one legislative body, it said: "No person shall be capable of being elected a member to serve in the House of Representatives of the freemen of this Commonwealth more than four years in seven." It was also provided that a delegate of the State in Congress should serve no longer than two years successively and be incapable of·reëlection for three years afterward; that any person having served as a member of the Supreme Executive Council of the State for three successive years, should be incapable of holding that office for four years afterward; and that one third of the Council should be replaced each year. "By this mode of election and continual rotation," it was explained, "more men will be trained to public business, there

[1] S. G. Arnold, *Hist. of R.I.*, i, 368.

will in every subsequent year be found in the Council a number of persons acquainted with the proceedings of the foregoing years, whereby the business will be more consistently conducted, and moreover the danger of establishing an inconvenient aristocracy will be effectually prevented."

Franklin persisted to the end in his admiration of the idea. Madison reports him as saying in the Federal Convention: "It seems to have been imagined by some, that the returning to the mass of the people was degrading the magistrate. This, he thought, was contrary to republican principles. In free governments, the rulers are the servants, and the people their superiors and sovereigns. For the former, therefore, to return among the latter, was not to *degrade*, but to *promote*, them. And it would be imposing an unreasonable burden on them, to keep them always in a state of servitude, and not allow them to become again one of the masters." [1]

Not all Pennsylvanians were of the same opinion. "A Citizen of Philadelphia," namely, Pelatiah Webster, writing in 1783 the pamphlet that Hannis Taylor thinks furnished the scheme of our Federal Constitution — "A Dissertation on the Political Union and Constitution of the Thirteen United States of North America" — said: "This doctrine of rotation was first proposed by some sprightly geniuses of brilliant politics with this cogent reason: that by introducing a rotation in the public offices we should have a great number of men trained up to public service, but it appears to me that it will be more likely to produce many jacks at all trades, but good at none. I think that frequent elections are a sufficient security against the continuance of men in public office whose conduct is not approved, and there can be no reason for excluding those whose conduct is approved, and who are allowed to be better qualified than any men who can be found to supply their places." Such became the conviction of the people of the State, and in the very year when Franklin died, 1790, they adopted a new Constitution in which this favorite theory of his found no place.

Another of the great men of the time who believed in rotation was Thomas Jefferson. His State had put into the Bill of Rights of the Constitution of 1776: "The legislative and executive powers of the State should be separate and distinct from the judiciary; and that the members of the two first

[1] *Elliot's Debates*, v, 369.

may be restrained from oppression, by feeling and participating the burdens of the people, they should, at fixed periods, be reduced to a private station, return into that body from which they were originally taken, and the vacancies be supplied by frequent, certain, and regular elections, in which all, or any part of the former members, to be again eligible, or ineligible, as the laws shall direct." It was in the spirit of this that Jefferson prepared, probably not long after the framing of the Virginia Constitution, a resolution for the rotation of members of the Continental Congress. It was rejected, but is worth quoting for the light it sheds on one phase of the opinion of that day:

"To prevent every danger which might arise to American freedom by continuing too long in office the members of the Continental Congress, to preserve to that body the confidence of their friends, and to disarm the malignant imputation of their enemies: It is earnestly recommended to the several Provinces, Assemblies or conventions of the United colonies that in their future elections of delegates to the Continental Congress one half at least of the persons chosen be such as were not of the delegation next preceeding, and the residue be of such as shall not have served in that office longer than two years." [1]

When the Federal Constitution had been drawn, Jefferson wrote to Madison, December 20, 1787, that a feature of it he disliked, and strongly disliked, was the abandonment of the principle of rotation in office, "and most particularly in the case of the President." He was not the only man to reach that office who may have changed his views about the desirability of second terms.

Maryland followed Virginia in making an abstract statement of the principle, but confined it to the executive branch, saying: "That a long continuance, in the first executive departments of honor or trust, is dangerous to liberty; a rotation, therefore, in those departments, is one of the best securities of permanent freedom." No other State referred to it until John Adams came to write the Constitution of Massachusetts. In 1776 he had given the idea half-hearted approval. "A rotation of all offices," he had said, "as well of representatives as of counsellors, has many advocates, and is contended for

_____
[1] *Writings of Thomas Jefferson*, P. L. Ford ed., II, 61.

with many plausible arguments. It would be attended, no doubt, with many advantages; and if the society has a sufficient number of suitable characters to supply the great number of vacancies which would be made by such a rotation, I can see no objections to it. These persons may be allowed to serve for three years, and then be excluded three years, or for any longer or shorter term." [1] Four years later he put into the Bill of Rights of his State: "In order to prevent those who are vested with authority from becoming oppressors, the people have a right, at such periods and in such manner as they shall establish by their frame of government, to cause their public officers to return to private life; and to fill up vacant places by certain and regular elections and appointments."

The chances are that Pennsylvania was responsible for fastening the rotation system on the Confederation. A few weeks after the Pennsylvania Constitution provided that no man should sit in Congress more than two years successively, nor be capable of reëlection for three years afterward, Maryland improved thereon by stipulating "that there be a rotation, in such manner, that at least two of the number be annually changed; and no person shall be capable of being a Delegate to Congress for more than three years in any term of six years." North Carolina found another variation by providing, a month later, that no person should be elected to serve in Congress for more than three years successively. Virginia, by statute, copied this in 1777.[2] Richard Henry Lee said the act was aimed at him. Vermont followed the example of Pennsylvania in the same year. When in November the Congress itself acted by promulgating Articles of Confederation, it preferred that part of the Maryland declaration which said no person should be capable of being a Delegate for more than three years in any term of six years. New Hampshire in 1784 saw fit to put this in her Constitution, for just what purpose is not clear. Massachusetts had not thought it necessary in 1780. Perhaps New Hampshire wanted it for her own guidance in case the Articles should be changed.

When at the opening of the Federal Convention of 1787 Edmund Randolph presented a plan, he embodied in it the Confederation idea of ineligibility for reëlection. His reso-

---

[1] John Adams, "Thoughts on Government," *Works*, IV, 197.
[2] Hening, *Statutes at Large*, IX, 299.

lution to this purpose, however, was rejected without a single vote in its favor — indeed, as far as Madison's Journal shows, without a word of discussion. Two months later Elbridge Gerry presented a resolution of the Massachusetts Legislature instructing the deputies of that State not to depart from the rotation established under the Confederation, nor to agree to give members of Congress a capacity to hold offices under the government. He addressed himself, however, entirely to the second instruction, and the first was ignored. At the end of the Convention, he gave the reëligibility of Senators as one of the reasons impelling him to refuse to sign, but made no reference to it in relation to Representatives.

The friends of rotation were not to be thus easily suppressed. In the State Conventions that followed for ratification, they made themselves heard by protests emphatic. In New York Gilbert Livingston moved a resolution to the effect that no person should be eligible as a Senator for more than six years in any term of twelve years. Said he: "In such a situation, men are apt to forget their dependence, lose their sympathy, and contract selfish habits. Factions are apt to be formed, if the body becomes permanent. The Senators will associate only with men of their own class, and thus become strange to the condition of the common people. They should not only return, and be obliged to live with the people, but return to their former rank of citizenship, both to revive their sense of dependence, and to gain a knowledge of the country." [1]

Robert R. Livingston (the chancellor), taking the opposite view, exclaimed: "What singular policy to cut off the hand which has just qualified itself for action!" And farther on — "This rotation is an absurd species of ostracism — a mode of proscribing eminent merit, and banishing from stations of trust those who have filled them with the greatest faithfulness. Besides, it takes away the strongest stimulus to public virtue — the hope of honors and rewards. The acquisition of abilities is hardly worth the trouble, unless one is to enjoy the satisfaction of employing them for the good of one's country. We all know that experience is indispensably necessary to good government. Shall we, then, drive experience into obscurity?"

John Lansing came to the defense of the proposal: "The objects of this amendment are, first, to place the Senators in

[1] *Elliot's Debates*, II, 288 *et sqq.*

such a position of dependence on their several State Legislatures, as will induce them to pay a constant regard to the good of their constituents; secondly, to oblige them to return, at certain periods, to their fellow-citizens, that, by mingling with the people, they may recover that knowledge of their interests, and revive that sympathy with their feelings, which power and an exalted station are too apt to efface from the minds of rulers."

Melancton Smith was of the same mind: "As the clause now stands, there is no doubt that Senators will hold their offices perpetually. . . . I think a rotation in the government is a very important and truly republican institution. It is a circumstance strongly in favor of rotation, that it will have a tendency to diffuse a more general spirit of emulation, and to bring forward into office the genius and abilities of the continent: the ambition of gaining the qualifications necessary to govern will be in some proportion to the chance of success. If the office is to be perpetually confined to a few, other men, of equal talents and virtue, but not possessed of so extensive an influence, may be discouraged from aspiring to it. The more perfectly we are versed in the political science, the more firmly will the happy principles of republicanism be supported. The true policy of Constitutions will be to increase the information of the country, and disseminate the knowledge of government as universally as possible. If this be done, we shall have, in any dangerous emergency, a numerous body of enlightened citizens, ready for the call of their country." [1]

Alexander Hamilton replied to Smith: "When a man knows he must quit his station, let his merit be what it may, he will turn his attention chiefly to his own emolument; nay, he will feel temptations, which few other situations furnish, to perpetuate his power by unconstitutional usurpations. Men will pursue their interests. It is as easy to change human nature as to oppose the strong current of the human passions."

No separate vote appears to have been taken on the resolution.

In Massachusetts Charles Turner declared: "Knowing the numerous arts that designing men are prone to, to secure their election, and perpetuate themselves, it is my hearty wish that a rotation may be provided for."

[1] *Elliot's Debates*, II, 309, 310.

Theophilus Parsons, however, saw great and insuperable objections to a rotation. It is an abridgment of the rights of the people, and it may deprive them, at critical seasons, of the services of the most important characters in the nation. It deprives a man of honorable ambition, whose highest glory is the applause of his fellow-citizens, of an efficient motive to great and patriotic exertions. The people individually have no method of testifying their esteem, but by a reëlection; and shall they be deprived of the honest satisfaction of wreathing for their friend and patriot a crown of laurel more durable than monarchy can bestow?

In Virginia George Mason, one of her foremost statesmen, held nothing so essential to the preservation of a republican government as a periodical rotation. Nothing so strongly impels a man to regard the interest of his constituents as the certainty of returning to the general mass of the people, whence he was taken, where he must participate their burdens. It is a great defect in the Senate that they are not ineligible at the end of six years. The biennial exclusion of one third of them will have no effect, as they can be reëlected.

When a greater Virginian, George Washington, accepted the Presidency, to which he had been called by the unanimous voice of the people, it was not his intention to remain in office more than one term. Toward its end he wrote to Madison, asking his advice about the Farewell Address he contemplated, and in this letter, he suggested that one of the reasons to be given for retirement should be: "As the spirit of government may render a rotation in the elective offices of it more congenial with the ideas the people have of liberty and safety."[1]

SPREAD OF THE DOCTRINE

It will be seen that the statesmen of the Revolutionary period were divided on the question, with the rotation theory evidently gaining popularity. After democratic ideas won the ascendancy under Jefferson and his successors, that theory made rapid headway and by Jackson's time it had swept the country. Jackson himself in his very first message came out squarely for it. "There are, perhaps," he said, "few men who can for any great length of time enjoy office and power without being

[1] *Washington's Writings*, xii, 383.

more or less under the influence of feelings unfavorable to the faithful discharge of their public duties. Their integrity may be proof against improper considerations immediately addressed to themselves, but they are apt to acquire a habit of looking with indifference upon the public interests and of tolerating conduct from which an unpracticed man would revolt. Office is considered as a species of property, and government rather as a means of promoting individual interests than as an instrument created solely for the service of the people. Corruption in some and in others a perversion of correct feelings and principles divert government from its legitimate ends and make it an engine for the support of the few at the expense of the many. The duties of all public officers are, or at least admit of being made, so plain and simple that men of intelligence may readily qualify themselves for their performance; and I can not but believe that more is lost by the long continuance of men in office than is generally to be gained by their experience. I submit, therefore, to your consideration whether the efficiency of the Government would not be promoted and official industry and integrity better secured by a general extension of the law which limits appointments to four years."

The disastrous effects of such doctrine quickly showed themselves. Harriet Martineau, who traveled through the country a few years later, told of some of them after her return to England. "I was frequently reminded by friends," she wrote, "of what is undoubtedly very true, the great perils of office in the United States, as an excuse for the want of honesty in officials. It is perfectly true that it is ruin to a professional man without fortune, to enter public life for a time, and then be driven back into private life. I knew a Senator of the United States, who had served for nearly his twice six years, and who then had to begin life again, as regarded his profession. I knew a Representative of the United States, a wealthy man, with a large family, who is doubting still, as he has been for a few years past, whether he shall give up commerce or public life, or go on trying to hold them both; but at the very next election after he has relinquished his commercial affairs, he may be thrown out of politics." [1]

A few of our own thinkers saw the danger of the system. One of them was Thomas H. Benton, who knew by experience of

[1] *Society in America*, I, 107.

thirty years as a Senator, what influence and capacity come to the man who gets the chance to develop his powers. No stronger support for his argument could be found than his own growth. "Short terms of service," he said, "are good on account of their responsibility, and two years is a good legal term; but every contrivance is vicious, and also inconsistent with the reëligibility permitted by the Constitution, which prevents the people from continuing a member as long as they deem him useful to them. Statesmen are not improvised in any country; and in our own, as well as in Great Britain, great political reputations have only been acquired after long service." What superiority the Senate might have over the House, he ascribed in part to the caucus system of the House, and to rotation in office, "which brings in men unknown to the people and turns them out as they begin to be useful; to be succeeded by other new beginners, who are in turn turned out to make room for more new ones; all by virtue of arrangements which look to individual interests and not to the public good." [1]

In the State Legislatures the victory of the rotation idea was even more pronounced than in Congress. For instance, from the debates of the Michigan Constitutional Convention of 1850 it is to be learned that rotation had then become so customary as to make it exceedingly difficult to elect a member of the Legislature twice in succession.

West Virginia put rotation squarely into her first Constitution (1862), saying: "When two or more counties are formed into a delegate district, the Legislature shall provide by law that the delegates to be chosen by the voters of the district shall be in rotation, residents of each county, for a greater or less number of terms, proportioned as nearly as can be conveniently done to the white population of the several counties in the district." This disappeared in 1872.

In 1848 J. D. Hammond, in the "Life and Times of Silas Wright," wrote (p. 341): "The people of the State of New York, and particularly those of them who belong to the Democratic party, are partial to a rotation in office. They believe that no one citizen to the exclusion of others ought for any considerable time to enjoy the emoluments of office. Perhaps their notions in this respect are carried too far, and that in their zeal for an equal distribution of the honors and emoluments

[1] *Thirty Years' View*, i, 207.

of office, they do not sufficiently consider that the office is created for the benefit of the public, and not for that of the incumbent." Great indeed had been the change of public temper since the period of the first New York Constitution, when there were eighteen members who sat from ten to twenty years each, with an average of more than thirteen years.[1]

The most striking and saddening record is that of Connecticut. Roger Sherman had said in the Federal Convention: "In Connecticut we have existed one hundred and thirty-two years under an annual government; and as long as a man behaves himself well, he is never turned out of office." [2] In the early period William Hillhouse of New London served in the General Court for fifty-eight years. As elections to the lower House of that body were semi-annual, he was sent by his town to 116 successive sessions. Between 1783 and 1801, only one Assistant who did not decline a reëlection, failed to receive it, but this was no doubt largely because of the device by which the names were voted on one by one in the order of the list arranged by the Legislature. The exception was in the case of General James Wadsworth, who lost his seat because he opposed the ratification of the Federal Constitution. In 1802 William Williams had been an Assistant since George the Third was King; Oliver Ellsworth had been first elected in 1780; another had sat since 1784, another since 1785.[3]

What has happened since is concisely told by the table (on page 356) Clarence Deming toilfully prepared. The work it meant is suggested by his modest statement that there are probably a few immaterial errors, "as the table involved the comparison by the writer of nearly five thousand names of members of the General Assembly." [4]

When Mr. Deming performed this useful work, he said that in a large proportion of the smaller towns it had become a tradition that a Representative, once elected, had exhausted his claim to the office; and only at the peril of a local split in his party could he seek a reëlection.

In 1892 the percentage of reëlection rose to 9.2 per cent; in 1897, it fell to 2.8 per cent. Since then the showing has been

[1] Thurlow Weed, *Autobiography*, 200.
[2] Yates' Minutes, *Elliot's Debates*, I, 450.
[3] Simeon E. Baldwin, "The Three Constitutions of Conn.," *New Haven Hist. Soc. Papers*, v.
[4] *Political Science Quarterly*, IV, 426.

somewhat less ominous. Of the 258 members of the House in 1919, 57 had been in the House of 1917, and 30 others had previously served in Legislature or Constitutional Convention or both.

YEAR	WHOLE NUMBER OF REPRESENTATIVES	REËLECTED FROM PREVIOUS YEAR	PER CENT REËLECTED
1790............	171	109	63.7
1800............	189	102	54.0
1810............	199	83	41.7
1820............	204	53	26.0
1830............	208	47	22.6
1840............	212	27	12.7
1850............	222	27	12.2
1860............	236	30	12.7
1870............	239	24	10.0
1880............	246	23	9.3
1889............	249	13	5.2

Turning to the West we also find conditions frequently so deplorable as to make good legislation a matter of wonderment. According to the figures given by C. L. Jones in his book on "Statute Law Making," of 120 members of the Minnesota House of 1911, 75 were new; of 143 in Missouri, 102 were new; of 95 in the North Dakota House of 1909, 71 were new. In these three Western States, then, about seven Representatives out of every ten were without experience. It further appears by the Jones figures that one out of every ten had served two terms; one out of twenty-five, three terms. Samuel P. Orth averred in the "Atlantic Monthly" for December, 1904, that in Indiana about one quarter of the House had served before. Governor Hodges told the Governors' Conference of 1913 that the terms of the members of the Kansas House do not as a rule cover more than one session. "Generally, an overwhelming majority of the House of Representatives are first-termers, and without legislative experience. The same thing is often true of the Senate." [1] In the West Virginia Legislature of 1915 almost nine tenths of the members were novices; in the Nebraska Legislature of 1913, almost seven tenths.

[1] *Proceedings*, 251.

THE CONSIDERATIONS

CHARLES R. BUCKALEW, one of the able members of the Pennsylvania Convention of 1873, arguing for biennial elections in what proved a vain hope that changes of membership would be fewer if elections were less frequent, recalled that under the annual system then prevailing, at one session there were 76 new members out of 100, and very often the number of new, undisciplined men in the House was between 60 and 70. "The habit of our people," he said, "has been to reëlect members for but one term — for a second term. The consequence is, that the grade of ability in the House of Representatives has come to be very low. Intelligence and discipline, acquaintance with public business, and, along with these that legitimate influence which holds public men steady — I mean the expectation of reëlection or continuance in public service — all these are wanting, the inevitable result of which is the degradation of public life. Members in that House not trained to high ideas of honor and patriotism and public spirit, it is believed, have sometimes yielded to the influences about them. And why? Why, one reason has been that they have seen before them no prospect of continuance in public service. They have regarded themselves as men of the moment, to serve in a position in which they have been placed but for a few weeks or a few months and then to retire. They have known that no exhibition of capacity, no exhibition of high honor and public spirit could continue beyond the short service to which our Constitution and the habits of our people have brought us." [1]

No volumes of Convention debates show a more thorough discussion of legislative ills, and a more earnest effort to remedy them, than those of the body Mr. Buckalew addressed. Its recommendations and those of other States revising their Constitutions about the same time, with other evidence of varying character, warrant the conclusion that it was the period when our State Legislatures fell to their lowest level. A contemporary account of the situation lays stress on rotation as a cause. It says: "In the State Constitutions which have been adopted within the last five years, special efforts have been made by the reformers who drew them up to prevent fraudulent or tricky legislation. That this evil exists, every session of every

[1] *Debates of the Penn. Convention of 1873*, I, 359.

State Legislature gives renewed proof in the shape of bills passed in the absence of a quorum, bills containing clauses smuggled into them and not voted upon at all, bills passed so hastily as to prevent proper consideration, bills passed in the guise of amendments or joint resolutions. As a general rule, these fraudulent acts are to be traced to one or two interested persons, and do not by any means necessarily imply that a majority of the legislative body approves or countenances them. Like any public body, the Legislature *qua* Legislature is interested in having its proceedings orderly and honest; and no doubt if our Legislatures to-day, as formerly, had that feeling of permanency which comes from the reëlection, year after year, of a considerable number of veterans, they might be relied upon to protect themselves against fraud. But from causes which are so well known and understood that there is no need to recapitulate them, the modern Legislature is a body of the most fluctuating character, possessing so few men of legislative experience that these count for nothing, and sitting for so short a time that their proceedings attract small attention. There are few among them who know more than the rudiments of parliamentary law; while to the shrewder and more cunning the nice and complicated system elaborated in Cushing's and other manuals seems designed to confuse the unwary, and to offer opportunities of the richest kind to the wise. Parliamentary law, in fact, in modern times, affords just the weapon which the dishonest legislator needs to impose on the body of which he is a member." [1]

This appeared in a journal that has never tried to catch flies with honey. Its preference for vinegar is well known. Yet even though the severity of its judgments leads the reader to be on his guard against hyperbole, that they contain an element of justice is as rarely to be gainsaid as it is to be denied that they perform a valuable public service. The strictures on the rotation system were warranted in 1875. They are just as applicable to-day, except so far as the volume of the evil may have been reduced.

Unquestionably in this evil may be found one of the great causes for the weaknesses of our legislative bodies. They are so largely made up of inexperienced men that the wonder is their work is no worse. Men without experience do no great

[1] "A New Kind of Veto," *The Nation*, July 15, 1875.

harm if they are associated with others who are familiar with legislative methods and problems. The smaller the bulk of experience, the more the waste of time and the greater the danger of unwise legislation. Repeatedly it has been seen that when waves of popular indignation or excitement have swept into a Congress or Legislature a larger number of new men than usual, there has been a distinct drop in the quality of legislation. The proposition ought to need no argument. It stands to reason that novices cannot do such good work as experts.

Since the best legislation is a growth rather than an invention, it is particularly important that a considerable part of the legislators should know something of its history. Otherwise a Legislature cannot begin where its predecessor left off, but must take up the subject *de novo*, without the benefit of what study and discussion have previously been given to it. As far as reliance is to be placed on information and advice from the outside, the new legislator is hampered by the lack of that capacity for discrimination which usually nothing but experience can give. At first he will lend an equally ready ear to the expert and to the demagogue, to the man of balance and the man without balance, to the doer and to the dreamer. For most men wise action depends on the power to appraise the judgments of others. This power is rarely a gift, usually an acquisition. At any rate it is strengthened by experience.

The matter was approached from another angle by George W. Biddle in the Pennsylvania Convention of 1873. "While it is quite true," he said, "that a good representative would, by experience, become a better one, it is equally true and a great deal more dangerous to the community represented, that a bad representative becomes a great deal worse by long continuance in office. The balance of disadvantage, let me say, is vastly against continuing for a long term the bad representative. If there be danger to be apprehended from corruption, much more is to be apprehended from those who are familiar with the arts and tricks of legislation, and who, grown hardy by constant experiment, endeavor to pervert the whole machinery of legislation to their own advantage and to the detriment of their constituency." [1]

That kind of argument was much more common in the early

[1] *Debates of the Penn. Convention of 1873*, I, 367.

days of the Republic than it is now. Our fathers were filled with fears. Their bitter experience with the evils of misgovernment by arbitrary rulers led them to crowd their Constitutions with checks and balances and all sorts of devices for restraining bad men. Ours is a more optimistic, less suspicious age. The mass of the people instead of wanting less government, want more. At every turn they press for an extension of governmental activities. Wise or not, that is the fact, and one must reckon with facts. If, then, government has become far and away the most important of social activities, with the probability of a steadily widening range of functions, it becomes of greater consequence than ever that those who conduct government shall have all the help that training and experience can give.

However, it is possible to lay too much stress on some of the evils of rotation. For example, take an illustration of extreme criticism in "The Nation" of June 23, 1892: "How absolutely fatal to any theory of legislative responsibility such a state of affairs must be, is obvious. It simply tempts a man of easy-going principles to make the most of his 'good time' as a legislator; if corrupt, to sell his vote and influence as often as he can; and, even if both able and honest, it spurs him on with no hope of appreciation by his constituents and consequently of continued usefulness." My personal observation of fellow-members has given me no ground to think that in practice such harmful effects are serious. The prospect of a short term of office more often makes men courageous than indifferent. He gives too little credit to the inherent virtues of mankind who thinks men often become careless of duty because the rewards of its performance will not be surely and quickly attained.

Or again, note what was said by Francis C. Lowell (afterward Judge), writing an admirable article on "Legislative Shortcomings," in the "Atlantic Monthly" of March, 1897, as a result of his experience while a member of the Massachusetts House: "Rotation in office makes a legislative expert almost an impossibility. As no lawyer or physician would ever submit to a professional education if he were allowed to practice his profession but for a year or two in the course of his life, so no man will undertake serious legislative study if his knowledge, the result of his faithful and long-continued labor, can be made profitable but for a few months. Even if a man were found, ready to give years of study for so scanty a return of usefulness, he would be denied the opportunity of sufficient legislative practice, without which his study would probably be misleading. Try to imagine for a moment the effect upon the community of compelling all physicians, merchants, and manufacturers to retire from business after an experience of only a year or two."

The spirit of the criticism is just and the purpose laudable, but candor calls for the admission that to liken the work of the legislator to that of the lawyer, physician, merchant, or manufacturer is somewhat inaccurate. The suggestion of such relationship is not new. You may find Sir William Blackstone saying in his "Commentaries on the Laws of England" (i, 9), a century and a half ago: "It is perfectly amazing that there should be no other state of life, no other occupation, art, or science, in which some method of instruction is not looked upon as a requisite, except only the science of legislation, the noblest and most difficult of any. Apprenticeships are held necessary to almost every art, commercial or mechanical; a long course of reading and study must form the divine, the physician, and the practical professor of the laws: but every man of superior fortune thinks himself *born* a legislator. Yet Tully was of a different opinion. 'It is necessary,' says he, 'for a Senator to be thoroughly acquainted with the constitution; and this,' he declares, 'is a knowledge of the most extensive nature; a matter of science, of diligence, of reflection; without which no Senator can possibly be fit for his office.'"

In the matter of such eminent authority as that of Blackstone and Cicero, it is presumptuous to differ and superfluous to approve. Yet I venture to do both. I contest the implication that a specialized technical training is as important to the legislator as it is in the occupations commonly spoken of as the arts and sciences. Of course a knowledge of the rudiments of parliamentary law is indispensable for useful service, but enough of that for ordinary purposes is easily acquired. It is helpful to know something of the art of bill-drafting, but not indispensable, for expert help is at hand in every well-regulated legislative body. The study of the law undoubtedly helps a man to be a better lawmaker in some particulars. To be well grounded in political and constitutional history, has decided advantages. Yet none of these things bear the same relation

to the work of the legislator that, for example, the study of
anatomy bears to the work of the physician. In a legislative
body, the more important thing is a catholic knowledge of
men and matters. It is of more consequence that the lawmaker should know a little of many things, than a great deal of
a few things.

It does not follow that one man of common sense is as fitted
to make laws as another, even when the acquirement of knowledge has been the same. Qualities of temperament may fit
or unfit. The gift of speech may turn the balance. It may be
that any one of a dozen other considerations ought to have
compelling force. Therefore whatever interferes with their
operation, endangers wise choice. For this reason it was a
sound observation of Burke, in his "Reflections on the Revolution in France," that "no rotation; no appointment by lot;
no mode of election operating in the spirit of sortition or rotation,
can be generally good in a government conversant in extensive
objects. Because they have no tendency, direct or indirect,
to select the man with a view to the duty, or to accommodate
the one to the other."

Besides its baneful effect in opening the doors of the council
chamber to many inferior men, rotation hurts by depriving
every man its victim of the chance to profit by that education
which the service itself gives. A legislative body is a school
and there are few occupations where practice teaches more.

Shall we then keep on reëlecting everybody during good
behavior? By no means. That would be inconsistent with
the fundamental purpose of frequent elections, which is to
keep the legislative body in harmony with changing public
sentiment. For the administrative part of present-day legislative work, reëlection during good behavior would be admirable.
For the law-declaring part of it, gradual change is eminently
desirable. When the time comes that the administrative part
is put in trained hands, as sooner or later it will come, then
the administrative body will have long terms and common sense
will forbid replacing a man as long as he is efficient. In the
meantime, while we continue the anomalous and indefensible
policy of allowing the same body both to declare the general
law and to make the rules and regulations for the conduct
of public enterprises, we must combine as far as we may the
policy of permanence and the policy of rotation. That will

work itself out in fashion adequate though crude, if constituencies can be persuaded to follow the practice of giving the ordinary legislator one reëlection and of sending the well-fitted legislator as long as he will consent to serve. Every man who conducts himself decently in his first term ought to have reëlection for the sake of maintaining a custom that has enough merit to over-balance all other considerations, the custom of rewarding conscientious service, however commonplace it may be. Beyond the one reëlection, capacity should be the test.

Remedies and the Outlook

Massachusetts has furnished the shining example of how to get out of the quagmire. Perhaps it never suffered from rotation so much as some of the other States, but yet it suffered. One instance was that which followed the Know-Nothing eruption in 1854, exceptional, to be sure, but worth recalling for an anecdote Frank B. Sanborn tells. Governor Emory Washburn was denied a reëlection. When the new legislators came up to take the oath of office in 1855, most of them being new and unknown persons who had supplanted men of experience formerly coming to the General Court, Governor Washburn is said to have remarked, after the oaths had all been taken, "You are now qualified, gentlemen — so far as taking the oath of office can qualify you — to sit as members of the General Court." To which the Secretary of State added the usual chorus — "God save the Commonwealth of Massachusetts!" [1]

Governor Thomas Talbot said in his inaugural address of 1879: "The present method of classifying the towns for the choice of Representatives is not satisfactory. It deprives the State of the continued services of many valuable members, and returns to each successive House a large majority of new and inexperienced men. This retards the despatch of business, and tends to defective legislation." Where wards or towns were grouped in districts, it was the custom to assign in order one or two terms, rarely more, to each ward or town. Only an exceptionally courageous or fortunate Representative seeking a career of more than the allotted span, could overcome the unwritten agreements of local leaders who controlled conventions.

---

[1] *Reminiscences of Seventy Years*, 44.

In helping to break down the system of party nomination by conventions in Massachusetts, and replacing it with direct nomination, in 1902, one of the purposes I had in mind was to lessen the damage wrought by these rotation arrangements. One of my able colleagues, with capacity that made him afterward President of the Senate and then sent him to Congress, was refused more than one term in the House because the small town from which he came was said to be entitled to send a man only one year in ten. Many cases of a like nature had come to my notice. It was my belief that the mass of the people did not want this sort of thing. No motive leads the people to wish bad government. They have every motive to wish efficiency. Their daily observation in all the other affairs of life tells them that experience makes capacity more efficient. By reason of common sense it is instinctive with them to want to retain useful public servants. Left to themselves, they would put common sense into practice. They were kept from this by narrow-minded, self-interested, small politicians, who used the convention system to "pass the honors round" and thereby increase their own petty power. Whether or not direct nominations caused what followed the enactment for Representatives in 1902, of course no man can positively say, but here is the record of reëlections out of 240 members:

Year	Reëlected	Per cent
1895...............	99	41
1905...............	113	47
1915...............	134	56

If it is the fact that direct nomination increased reëlection by a third, that alone would go far to justify the reform.

These figures do not tell the whole story, for they cover only men reëlected to Legislatures immediately succeeding, and to the same branch. Of the 280 members of the Massachusetts Senate and House in 1916, 206 had previously served in the Legislature — almost three quarters. Every Senator had lawmaking experience. There were fifty-seven members who had been elected to one branch or the other four or more times. One had been elected eleven times. Since then the adoption of biennial elections has unfortunately had the usual result. To the Senate of 1923 only sixteen of the forty members who served in the sessions of 1921–22 were returned, and to the House only 117 of the 240 old members came back. Nevertheless the showing is not bad. Taking into account the professional and business obligations that prevent many legislators from consenting to serve more than a term or two, no great gain over the present situation is possible. It is in advance of that in most if not all of the other States in the Union.

In Congress, too, the situation is improving. In the 42d Congress, which met in 1871, 53 per cent of the members had served before; in the 50th, 63 per cent; in the 62d, 70 per cent; in the 64th, 74 per cent; in the 66th, 76 per cent. When a quarter of the members returned to private life March 4, 1919, they had averaged to serve a little more than seven and a half years each. Omitting about a dozen of exceptionally long service, the average of the others had been almost exactly three terms — six years.

When Edward A. Freeman wrote "Some Impressions of the United States," in 1883, after a visit to us, he said (p. 118) he had "to explain more than once that it was a rare thing in England for a member of Parliament to lose his seat, unless he had given some offense to his own party, or unless the other party had grown strong enough to bring in a man of its own." And when Mr. Bryce made his first observations of us, he found occasion to say that in England the proportion of members reëlected is much higher than here. "It was remarked as a novelty in the Parliament of 1885, elected after a sweeping measure for the redistribution of seats, that about one-third of the members had not sat in the Parliament of 1880. Any one can see how much influence this constant change in the composition of the American House must have upon its legislative efficiency."

Fortunately there no longer remains much warrant for comparisons of this sort to our discredit. Indeed, considering certain essential differences in the situation, it is possible that our showing is somewhat the better. Henry Jones Ford has suggested one difference, in explaining why in Canada members are not so keen about retaining their seats as in England.[1] He

[1] "American and Canadian Political Methods," *No. Am. Review*, November, 1911.

points out that attendance at a provincial capital is very different from living in London. Washington, to be sure, is not a provincial capital and life there has its attractions, of a kind, but they are not of the vital interest to most men that a sojourn in New York would present. By the way, Professor Ford says that in Canada enough members drop out from one cause or another after a five-year term to change about two thirds of the membership of the legislative assembly.

Apparently constituencies are coming to understand that long service brings their Congressmen influence and power, with reflected satisfaction to themselves. In 1922 the Speaker of the national House was serving his fifteenth two-year term, a former Speaker his twenty-third, the majority leader his thirteenth, and ten important committee chairmanships were held by men whose periods of service averaged more than twenty years.

It would not be candid to assert that such a state of affairs is without disadvantages. Like every other question of public policy, this has two sides. It is altogether probable that Congress is less responsive to opinion than is desirable, because its leaders are for the most part men who were started on their careers by issues now no longer uppermost in the public mind, and who, having passed the meridian of life, have reached the age when most men dislike to face fresh problems and to change their points of view. It is hard for them to keep up with the times. They are liable to get out of touch with progress in the arts and sciences, industry and commerce, all the ever-changing relations of society. Yet in my judgment long service on the whole brings to the country decidedly more gain than loss.

CHAPTER XVII

THE LOBBY

"LOBBY," a small hall, anteroom, or waiting-room, has by figure of speech come to be applied in the United States to the men who frequent the approaches to legislative chambers for the purpose of addressing individual argument to lawmakers or of otherwise influencing votes. Doubtless ever since representative assemblies began, citizens have visited them for purposes of persuasion. Certainly the practice was known in the colonial days of America. E. P. Tanner, in his exhaustive monograph on the Province of New Jersey,[1] says of its General Assembly that there seems to have been at times no little of what we now call lobbying. The nearly successful effort of George Willocks, an outsider, about 1720, to control the 7th Assembly against Burnet, presumably to further his own business interests, is a striking example.

When the colonies had come together, their Congress began at once to be the scene of individual pressure, and under the new Constitution Alexander Hamilton speedily developed the fine art of lobbying. No one can read the story of the assumption of the State debts and the location of the capital without wondering whether the legislative manipulators of our day have really gone much beyond our forefathers in point of questionable practices. Very likely, though, the origin of the professional lobby ought not to be set at a date much farther back than that of the war between Andrew Jackson and the United States Bank over the charter question. Thereafter, with the mushroom growth of corporations and their need of special legislation, lobbying as a business grew rapidly. A. R. Spofford, long Librarian of Congress and steeped in its history, tells of some of the episodes.[2]

In the course of the Kansas excitement in Buchanan's administration, two powerful lobbies struck hands to put two distasteful measures through Congress, the Lecompton Consti-

[1] Col. Univ. Studies, xxx, 342.
[2] "Lobby," *Lalor's Cycl. of Pol. Science*, ii, 780, 781.

tution bill (an administration measure), and the Chaffee india-
rubber extension patent, which kept a band of lobbyists in pay
at Washington for two years. Both measures failed, though
more than $100,000 was spent. The testimony before the
Covode committee of investigation did not show corruption in
a single member of Congress. In the case of President Johnson's trial by impeachment, in 1868, there was an extensive
lobby operating back and forth between Washington and New
York, and early knowledge of the unexpected acquittal was
traded upon by men outside of Congress, but the managers
found no evidence whatever that any Senator received money
for his vote. In the case of the Pacific mail steamship subsidy
lobby, in 1872, more than $800,000 was expended, of which
$300,000 went to an ex-Congressman, and remained entirely
unaccounted for, and the rest was divided among lobbyists,
journalists, and obscure employees for supposed influence in
House or Senate. The subsidy, which was passed, was for the
annual sum of $500,000, but the grant was repealed two years
later, and the Ways and Means committee reported, on investigation, that no money was found to have been paid to
any member of Congress. At times in our history there has
been a British lobby, with the most polished accompaniments,
devoted to watching legislation affecting the great importing
and shipping interests. We have even had a French lobby,
more than once, since M. Genet undertook to influence American
opinion against the neutrality policy of Washington in 1793.
There was what was called a Danish lobby in 1868, having as
an object Mr. Seward's treaty for the purchase of the Danish
West Indies, but no money was used, save for writing and
printing.

Something may be gathered about the rise of lobbying as an
occupation in the State Legislatures, from the delightful description by L. E. Chittenden, in his "Personal Reminiscences"
(p. 33 et seq.), of his membership in the "Third House" at the
capital of Vermont in 1850. There were few general laws;
railroads, banks, bridges, turnpikes, cemeteries, almost all
corporations were created by special charter. Banks, railroads,
and other corporations occupied three fourths of the time of the
Legislature. Much of the legislation was absurd, more of it
dangerous. Existing corporations found it necessary to be
represented by counsel at the State capital during the whole

session. There were thus brought together many lawyers who had little to do but to watch the daily Journal and the interests of their corporation clients. "We had come to be known as the 'Third House.' We met daily in the State Library, and lampooned everybody who deserved our attention, especially the members of the two *lower* Houses. More effective work for our clients was accomplished by the satirical items which we made for the newspapers than by our legitimate work before the committees." The rogues organized in burlesque, with a Speaker and ludicrous standing committees. They made a great success by publishing the " Third House Journal," the climax of which they capped with the "Magna Charta of the Moosalamoo Bank." Chittenden gives it in full and says it will become known to future generations, if historians do justice to the Third House, not only as the most comprehensive, but as positively the last special bank charter presented to the Vermont Legislature. "Republics are notoriously ungrateful, and instead of approving our patriotic labors, the members of the lower House denounced us as a set of pestiferous scamps who lay awake nights to invent new schemes for ridiculing our superiors." Apparently the evil of special bank charters was laughed out of Vermont. Herein may be found a useful hint for reformers.

Special legislation was the noisome fount from which at the same period sprang the same evil in Massachusetts. Henry Wilson told of it in the Convention of 1853. The previous Legislature had passed 158 acts increasing the capital stock of corporations, or creating new corporations. "Those of us who have been here during the past seven years," said Wilson, "know how the members have been bored by this lobby system, that has grown up under this system of granting special acts for manufacturing, banking, insurance, railway, and other business purposes. Sir, I want to see this lobby system, which corrupts and degrades legislation, broken up, and it can only be done by removing the cause which created it. The removal of that cause, the destruction of this lobby system, will not only shorten sessions at least one third, but it will tend to the purification of legislation. General laws for corporation purposes will save us from the disgraceful scenes which have been enacted here during the past few years, when the State House has been made an encampment of the agents of antagonistic corporation interests who have beleaguered the Legislature for days and weeks." [1]

Later in the Convention Mr. Wilson declared: "I do not believe there has been a Legislature during the last six years, aye, ten years, through which we could carry any proposition against the railway influence and power." Otis P. Lord, of Salem, agreed with him "that the railroad interest is now too strong even for the Legislature; and when it gets to be too strong for the Legislature, everything else is as a mere rope of sand." [2] James S. Whitney, of Conway, thought "the gentleman has well said that the railroad corporations in this State constitute a power greater than any other in the State." [3] In another debate Robert Rantoul, of Beverly, said: "The fair page of the history of Massachusetts has never yet been sullied by the record of any instance of corruption or wickedness; but I know, sir, from my own observation, and from the information I have derived elsewhere, that there has been a vast amount of outside influence exercised in regard to getting matters through the Legislature." [4]

In the course of the next quarter of a century the evil of lobbying grew until it became important enough to win recognition in the Constitutions. Alabama seems to have been the first State to dignify it with notice, saying in 1874: "The offense of corrupt solicitation of members of the General Assembly, or of public officers of this State, or of any municipal division thereof, and any occupation or practice of solicitation of such member or officers to influence their official action shall be defined by law, and shall be punished by fine and imprisonment." The statute in accordance therewith follows the wording of the provision in the Constitution, which, it will be seen, does not necessarily mean that the practice of solicitation shall have the element of corruption, in order to entail punishment. However, in the statutory definition of bribery the limiting "corruptly" is used, and presumably the court would imply it here.

Three years later the Georgia Constitution was made to say, succinctly and absurdly: "Lobbying is declared to be a crime, and the General Assembly shall enforce this provision by suitable penalties." That meant nothing, for it did not define.

[1] *Debates in Mass. Conv. of 1853*, i, 785.   [2] *Ibid.*, ii, 259, 260.
[3] *Ibid.*, 265.   [4] *Ibid.*, i, 847.

There was no more agreement then than there is now, as to what is lobbying. It would be impossible to put into words that would meet the needs of a criminal court, a definition likely to find general acceptance as covering the phases of the practice urged as reprehensible. California, the second State to make a constitutional declaration, tried to define and palpably failed. It said, in 1879: "Any person who seeks to influence the vote of a member of the Legislature by bribery, promise of reward, intimidation, or any other dishonest means, shall be guilty of lobbying, which is hereby declared a felony." Promise of reward is one kind of bribery. Intimidation should probably be classed as contempt, a breach of privilege. The catch-all, "any other dishonest means," leaves wide open the question of what is dishonest, and is quite useless unless the courts are to create crimes after the fashion of the old common law.

The propriety of treating such a subject in a Constitution is open to grave question. It is matter for statutes. There can be no question of the complete authority of a Legislature to regulate its own processes and to protect itself. Upon this authority many of the Legislatures have taken action. Massachusetts was the first to go into the matter thoroughly. In 1887 a legislative investigation showed that about $20,000 had been distributed among men supposed to be able to exercise influence in the matter of a town-division bill. The measure was vetoed by the Republican Governor on the ground that whatever its merits, the methods used were so reprehensible as to call for disapproval by withholding signature. Because the Republicans, controlling the Legislature, failed to take any steps to suppress the evil of which this was a symptom, the Democrats made it a party issue, and their ablest orator, William E. Russell, young and brilliant, presently helped arouse public opinion to the point of compelling legislation. In the House they had an efficient legislator in the person of Josiah Quincy, who wrote the report of a committee that investigated the passage of an elevated railroad bill on which about thirty-five counsel and lobbyists had been employed, at a total expense paid or specifically contracted of about $33,000, with much more yet to be paid. Accompanying the report was a bill that became law as Chapter 456 of the Acts of 1890 and has served as the model for numerous like laws elsewhere.

The reliance was to be on publicity. Men who for hire work to help or hinder legislation, whether as legislative counsel (those who appear at public hearings) or as legislative agents (lobbyists), must register their employment in advance, and at the end of the session their employers must report the amount paid.

Laws of such a type have in view only the moral effect, and bearing that in mind, it may be fairly said that the publicity laws have been salutary. It was neither the intention that they should, nor the expectation that they would, stop lobbying. Unfortunately some of their advocates gave the opposite impression in argument or prophecy, and the public has been correspondingly disappointed. All that was hoped, or could reasonably be hoped, was the restraint on improper practices that comes from publicity.

Could publicity have been completely secured, such evil as there is in lobbying would have become insignificant. It has been secured only in part. The record of payments to legislative counsel is fairly thorough, save that the attorneys employed by some corporations receive annual salaries and the part that might properly be charged up to legislative work is not known. This, however, does no mischief of consequence unless the salary is used to cover up on the corporation books certain classes of questionable outlay. The record of payments to legislative agents, the real lobbyists, is generally believed to be grossly incomplete. As in the case of the laws against corrupt practices at elections, only the honest man obeys, the very man you do not worry about. The man who will bribe, will lie about it.

If this were all the story, no credit would attach to the publicity laws, but there is another side to the matter, and one of real importance. These laws have played a useful part in the campaign for raising the standards of conduct by and toward legislators that has accomplished so much in the last two or three decades. They have given formal, official recognition to the fact that for attorneys to appear before legislative committees is a legitimate and honorable practice. They have declared it to be the creed of the community that paid argument addressed otherwise to legislators is honorable at least when it is aboveboard. To establish these things has been worth while.

Wisconsin has gone beyond publicity. Governor R. M. La Follette in his message to the Legislature of that State January 12, 1905, urged upon its consideration the enactment of a law that should make it "an offense, punishable by the heaviest money penalty and by imprisonment as well, for any lobby agent or lobby representative, employed and paid for his services by others, to attempt personally and directly to influence any member of the Legislature to vote for or against any measure affecting the interests represented by such lobbyist." In a special message, May 25, he repeated this, and in the course of discussion of the subject at length, said: "Every legitimate argument which any lobbyist has to offer, and which any legislator ought to hear, can be presented before committees, before the legislators as a body, through the press, from the public platform, and through printed briefs and arguments placed in the hands of all members and accessible to the public." He concluded his message by saying: "I commend to your considerate judgment the enactment of a statute making it a penal offense for a paid lobbyist to approach a legislator privately or personally upon any matter which is the subject of legislation."

The Legislature heeded the Governor's opinion and enacted that it should be unlawful for any legislative counsel or agent to influence any legislator personally and directly otherwise than by appearing before the regular committees, or by newspaper publications, or by public addresses, or by written or printed statements, arguments, or briefs delivered to each member, twenty-five copies to be first deposited with the Secretary of State.

This hits everybody employed to influence legislation, whether specifically, or in the course of duty as an officer of a corporation or of a society philanthropic, moral, or benevolent in its nature. Since agency does not necessarily involve remuneration, here in its broadest form is embodied the contention of those who think it unwise that any person representing another, whether paid or not, shall have private conference with a legislator concerning any matter of legislation. This view is widely entertained and deserves careful scrutiny.

ATTITUDE OF THE COURTS

IT is the view that has been taken for the most part by the courts. The first of a long line of American decisions expressing it was that in the Kentucky case of Wood *v.* McCann, 6 Dana 366 (1838), where the defendant had employed the plaintiff to aid him in getting a bill through the Legislature to legalize his divorce from a former wife and his marriage with another. Said Chief Justice Robertson: "It is certainly all-important to just and wise legislation, and therefore to the most essential interest of the public, that the Legislature should be perfectly free from any extraneous influence, which may either corrupt or deceive the members, or any one of them. . . . Certainly the law should not help to compel the payment of a fee to any man, whether of great or of little influence, for his personal solicitation in favor of the enactment of any law whatever. Nothing could be more suicidal or unwise than a contrary doctrine. A lawyer may be entitled to compensation for writing a petition, or even for making a public argument before the Legislature, or a committee thereof; but the law should not help him, or any other person, to recover a fee for exerting any personal influence, in any way, in any act of Legislature."

Here as in other of the cases the use of the phrase "personal influence" leaves something to be desired in the way of accuracy, and it is not always clear whether the judges have had in mind personal argument alone, or have been aiming at a variety of influences of a personal nature. The doubt came to the front in the case of Clippinger *v.* Hepbaugh, 5 Watts & Sargeant 315, decided in Pennsylvania five years later. The court held that a contract to use personal influence would be void, but note what Justice Rogers said in giving the opinion: "Already is there too much reason to believe that this indispensable branch of government [the legislative], without which our whole political fabric would crumble into ruins, has in some instances been contaminated by sinister and improper influences brought to bear on members." Whether or not the courts have meant to go beyond personal conference, that is at any rate included in their strictures.

"Personal influence to be exerted with the members of the Legislature" was held in Hunt *v.* Test, 8 Ala. 713 (1845), to be among the methods very clearly contrary to public policy.

Then came explicit censure of individual conversation, in the New York case of Harris v. Roof's Exrs., 10 Barb. 489 (1851). The Court held, by Justice Hand: "It is the duty of every legislative body, and every member of it, to give all proper and necessary attention to the business before it. And it certainly would imply a most unjustifiable dereliction of duty to hold that the employment of individuals to visit and importune the members, is necessary to obtain justice. Such practices would have a tendency to prevent free, honorable, and correct deliberation and action of this most important branch of sovereignty." So it was decided that no action would lie for services as a "lobby agent," they not having been performed before the House as a body, nor before its authorized committee.

Commenting on this case, Justice Selden, in Sedgwick v. Stanton, 4 Kernan 289 (1856), threw some light on the reasons for the judicial view: "The court did not mean to hold that one who has a claim against the State may not employ competent persons to aid him in properly presenting such claim to the Legislature, and in supporting it with the necessary proofs and arguments. Persons may no doubt be employed to conduct an application to the Legislature, as well as to conduct a suit at law; and may contract for and receive pay in preparing documents, collecting evidence, making statements of facts, or preparing and making oral or written arguments, provided all these are used or designed to be used before the Legislature or some committee thereof as a body; but they cannot with propriety be employed to exert their personal influence with individual members, or to labor in any form privately with such members out of the legislative halls. Whatever is laid before the Legislature in writing, or spoken openly or publicly in its presence or that of a committee, if false in fact, may be disproved, or if wrong in argument, may be refuted, but that which is whispered in the private ear of individual members is frequently beyond the reach of correction. The point of objection in this class of cases, then, is the personal and private nature of the services to be rendered."

In the same year the objection on the score of personal influence was maintained by the Wisconsin Court in Bryan v. Reynolds, 5 Wis. 200 (1856), and five years later a majority of the Vermont Court, in Powers v. Skinner, took the same ground, but Judge Barrett (with Judge Bennett approving) gave a dissenting opinion in which he declined to pronounce a contract void where there was no agreement to use improper means.

Then in 1863 the subject received thorough discussion in the Massachusetts case of Frost *v.* Belmont, 6 Allen 153. The town of Belmont had voted to raise money to reimburse the citizens' committee that had secured the incorporation of the town. A material amount had been reported by the committee as paid for lobby members — one item of $1180 paid at a "house of entertainment" — and sundry other questionable items. The Court forbade the town to pay, and Justice Chapman said, in part: "By the regular course of legislation, organs are provided through which any parties may fairly and openly approach the Legislature, and be heard with proofs and arguments respecting any legislative acts which they may be interested in, whether public or private. These organs are the various committees appointed to consider and report upon the matters to be acted upon by the whole body. When private interests are to be affected, notice is given of the hearings before these committees; and thus opportunity is given to adverse parties to meet face to face, and obtain a fair and open hearing. And though these committees properly dispense with many of the rules which regulate hearings before judicial tribunals, yet common fairness requires that neither party shall be permitted to have secret consultations and exercise secret influences, that are kept from the knowledge of the other party. The business of 'lobby members' is not to go fairly and openly before the committees, and present statements, proofs, and arguments that the other side has an opportunity to meet and refute, if they are wrong, but to go secretly to the members and ply them with statements and arguments that the other side cannot openly meet, however erroneous they may be; and to bring illegitimate influences to bear upon them. If the 'lobby member' is selected because of his political or personal influence, it aggravates the wrong. If his business is to unite various interests by means of projects that are called 'log-rolling,' it is still worse. The practice of procuring members of the Legislature to act under the influence of what they have eaten and drunk at houses of entertainment tends to render those of them who yield to such influences wholly unfit to act in such cases. They are disqualified from acting fairly towards interested parties, or towards the public. The tendency and object of these influences are to obtain by corruption what it is supposed cannot be obtained fairly."

In that same year an Indiana opinion held (Coquillard *v.* Bearse, 21 Ind. 479) that the agent could not do the work secretly. Justice Hunt, in Lyon *v.* Mitchell, 36 N.Y. 241 (1867), declared: "Personal solicitation of legislators or of judges is not a lawful subject of contract." Harris *v.* Simonson, 28 Hun. 318 (1882), discountenanced direct appeals to lawmakers and was quoted with approval in Cary *v.* Western Union Telegraph Co., 47 Hun. 610 (1888). Like views held by the Federal Justices were reviewed by Justice Morris in Owens *v.* Wilkinson, 20 App. D.C. 51 (1902), who summed them up by saying: "As we understand it, the rule to be deduced from the decisions of the Supreme Court of the United States which have been cited, is this — that agreements for professional services in the procurement of Congressional legislation, which involve personal solicitation of members of Congress, will not be enforced by the courts, whether improper means are used or not in such solicitation. . . . It may be remarked that in most cases it would be difficult, if not impossible, to prove the use of improper means to influence the action of those who are thus approached; and that for this reason also, as well as to remove the occasion of temptation, the courts refuse to lend their aid where there is any personal solicitation whatever, whether in itself legitimate or illegitimate."

The ultimate results of individual solicitation have loomed large in the judicial mind. Thus Mr. Justice Field, in delivering the opinion of the United States Supreme Court in Tool Co. *v.* Norris, 2 Wall. 45 (1864), pronounced: "All agreements for pecuniary considerations to control the business operations of the Government, or the regular administration of justice, or the appointment to public offices, or the ordinary course of legislation, are void as against public policy, without reference to the question whether improper means are contemplated or used in their execution. The law looks to the general tendency of such agreements; and it closes the door of temptation by refusing their recognition in any of the courts of the country." The same view was taken in Trist *v.* Child, 21 Wallace 441 (1874). Nicholas P. Trist, after waiting twenty years for Congress to pay a claim, employed an agent to get it through, with the result that Congress made an appropriation. The agent died, his son succeeded to the business and bargain, and Trist refused to keep the bargain, therein being upheld by the Court, which set its condemnation on the whole transaction. Although admitting there was no reason to believe that the services of the lawyers "involved anything corrupt or different from what is usually practised by all paid lobbyists in the prosecution of their business," the Court held, nevertheless, that all such contracts are contrary to public policy. "The theory of our Government," said Justice Swayne for the Court, "is that all public stations are trusts, and that those clothed with them are to be animated in the discharge of their duties solely by considerations of right, justice, and the public good. They are never to descend to a lower plane. But there is a correlative duty resting upon the citizen. In his intercourse with those in authority, whether executive or legislative, touching the performance of their functions, he is bound to respect truth, frankness, and integrity. Any departure from the line of rectitude in such cases is not only bad in morals, but involves a public wrong. . . . If the instances were numerous, open, and tolerated, they would be regarded as measuring the decay of the public morals and the degeneracy of the times. No prophetic spirit would be needed to foretell the consequences near at hand."

It is probable that in this case the offense was aggravated in the eyes of the court by the fact that the bargain was for payment of one fourth of the amount collected, to the agent. Contingent fees in matters of legislation have seemed particularly reprehensible to the courts. Apprehension on the same grounds has led at least one State, Kansas, to prohibit the employment of legislative counsel or agents on a contingent fee.

The early objections on the score of privacy have been broadened out in various State courts. Thus in Mills v. Mills, 40 N.Y. 543 (1869), it was held that a contract, the consideration of which was that one of the parties thereto would give all the aid in his power, spend such reasonable time as might be necessary, and generally use his utmost influence to procure the passage into law of a bill introduced into the Legislature, was void, as against public policy. Said Chief Justice Hunt: "It is a contract leading to secret, improper, and corrupt tampering with legislative action." Equally sweeping was the Oregon

Court in Sweeney *v.* McLeod, 15 Ore. 330 (1887) : "It is against public policy for any person to hire himself out to perform lobby service for another, and all contracts made or other acts done in furtherance of such purposes are illegal."

On the other hand there is a line of decisions intimating that the evil lies not so much in the privacy of the persuasion as in the concealment of the agency. Justice Grier expounded this in delivering the majority opinion of the United States Supreme Court in Marshall *v.* B. & O. R. R. Co., 16 How. 314 (1853). A. J. Marshall was to receive a sum of money from the Baltimore & Ohio Railroad Company if a certain private bill should become a law in Virginia. He was to use his means of persuasion to induce the Legislature to pass the law, but to appear as a stranger, and not as the agent of the corporation. Said Justice Grier : "Where persons act as counsel or agents, or in any representative capacity, it is due to those before whom they plead or solicit, that they should honestly appear in their true characters, so that their arguments and representations, openly and candidly made, may receive their just weight and consideration. A hired advocate or agent, assuming to act in a different character, is practising deceit on the Legislature. Advice or information flowing from the unbiased judgment of disinterested persons, will naturally be received with more confidence and less scrupulously examined than where the recommendations are known to be the result of pecuniary interest, or the arguments prompted and pressed by hope of a large contingent reward. . . . Influences secretly urged under false and covert pretenses must necessarily operate deleteriously on legislative action. . . . Bribes, in the shape of high contingent compensation, must necessarily lead to the use of improper means and the exercise of undue influence. Their necessary consequence is the demoralization of the agent who covenants for them ; he is soon brought to believe that any means which will produce so beneficial a result to himself are 'proper means'; and that a share of these profits may have the same effect in quickening the perceptions and warming the zeal of influential or 'careless' members in favor of his bill. The use of such means and such agents will have the effect to subject the State governments to the combined capital of wealthy corporations, and produce universal corruption, commencing with the representative and ending with the elector. Speculators in legislation, public and private, a compact corps of venal solicitors, vending their secret influence, will infest the capital of the Union and of every State, till corruption shall become the normal condition of the body politic, and it will be said of us as of Rome, — '*Omne Romae venale.*'"

In the following year the Maryland Court, in Wildey *v.* Collier, 7 Md. 273, took pains to avoid saying that a disclosed agency would be obnoxious: "We do not say that services of that kind may not be compensated when publicly rendered by advocates disclosing their true relation to the subject, but certainly not when the character in which they solicit is unknown." This foreshadowed the gradual shifting of the courts to other ground. In 1869 we find the California Court declaring, in Miles *v.* Thorne, 38 Cal. 335: "He had a legal right to urge its passage by all honorable means, provided he did not conceal, but openly acknowledged his interest in the measure." That view was reiterated in Foltz *v.* Cogswell, 86 Cal. 542 (1890): "While the evidence does show that the plaintiff endeavored to persuade some of the members individually to act favorably upon the bill she was seeking to have passed, it does not show that she used any dishonest, secret, or unfair means to accomplish her object. Besides, if she did not tell them that she was acting as an agent for pay, they must have known from the character of the bill that she was acting as the agent of Dr. Cogswell, which fact was sufficient, of itself, to disclose her motive."

It cannot be said that there is yet enough body of judicial opinion of this sort to warrant the assertion that the courts as a whole have reversed their position, but in effect their earlier views have been nullified by the course of the Legislatures, for statute after statute has now officially recognized and made legitimate the status and work of the legislative agent, whose chief function is well known to be that of individual communication with members. At first this result was reached negatively. Thus the Criminal Code of Oregon (Sec. 638) made it a misdemeanor for an agent to converse with and explain to, or in any manner attempt to influence any member of the Legislature without disclosing the interest of the person represented, the negative inference being that if the interest was disclosed, there was no misdemeanor. Then came the lobby law of Massachusetts, meant to secure disclosure of interest by registration, and such is fast becoming the general policy.

The various Legislatures that have proceeded in this direction seem to me to have taken more tenable ground than that of the courts in the bulk of their opinions or of Wisconsin in the statute induced by Governor La Follette. The contentions call for examination.

How to Present Argument

Starting with the accepted premise that legislators cannot rely on their own knowledge, but must look elsewhere for some part of the desirable information and opinion, how are they to be instructed? Governor La Follette said first that the arguments can be presented before committees. True, with limitations. Taking men as they are and not as they ought to be, recognize that a full attendance at a committee hearing is most exceptional. It would be impracticable to confine committee action to those members who have heard the arguments, and experience does not show that they will adequately inform those who were absent.

Next it is said that arguments can be presented before the legislators as a body, through printed briefs and arguments placed in the hands of all the members and accessible to the public. That also is true, with limitations, the most serious being that the legislator is flooded with printed matter on a multitude of topics, of which he has the time to digest not a tithe. Few members of State Legislatures are trained in the quick perusal and comprehension of printed argument — almost none outside the members of the professions, and they are in the minority. Theorists who urge this reliance, themselves accustomed to much reading and to persuasion through the eye rather than the ear, forget that to the mass of mankind print is not the normal avenue of intellectual approach. The controlling fact is that most legislators must be reached through the spoken word. The practical question is whether this word shall, as in the courtroom, be restricted to public utterance. Undoubtedly that would be best if competent spokesmen could be assured and if attention to them could be enforced. This, however, has in practice so far been found an impossibility. Adequate debate is the exception in our legislative bodies, for reasons set forth in "Legislative Procedure." Adequate attention can be secured by very few debaters. Anything like the systematic and sufficient presentation of arguments customary in courts of justice is in most cases out of the question.

Of La Follette's approved means of instruction, there remain to be considered the press and the platform. As to the platform it is to be said that but a small fraction of legislative problems ever get general discussion that is public and oral. Information secured in this way would be most fragmentary and insufficient. Editors are usually partisan rather than judicial. Readers usually look to only one journal for enlightenment.

However inadequate and imperfect these methods of informing, the critics would confine the legislator to them on the ground that the word spoken in familiar intercourse, which is our chief reliance in the ordinary relations of life, is too dangerous in matters legislative. This point of view is taken by even as judicious a man as President Lowell. "Clearly in those matters on which opinion cannot readily be formed by current public discussion," he says, "where a careful weighing of evidence is needed, it is important that the members should be placed in a judicial attitude and surrounded so far as possible by the safeguards that experience has proved essential in judicial proceedings. What confidence should we have in the verdict of a jury if the parties were allowed to interview the several jurors in private; and why should we put greater reliance on the decision of the legislators if this is almost their only source of information?" [1]

Is not the analogy imperfect? The prime function of a jury is to ascertain what has been done, often in order that a judge may determine what should be done. The Legislature is both jury and judge. Even in the one matter of the ascertainment of fact the conditions are quite different. A jury is properly presumed to have only the average training and development of the critical faculty. For its protection the courts have woven a stout net of rules about hearsay evidence, leading questions, and other perils. These rules are, to be sure, the result of centuries of experience with the wiles of attorneys, and they are not to be lightly dismissed. Yet even within the walls of a courtroom it sometimes seems as if justice would be advanced if jurymen were allowed to apply the processes of belief and disbelief to which they have always been accustomed in the routine affairs of life. Much more is it reasonable to

[1] A. L. Lowell, *Public Opinion*, 136.

think that legislators, men of more intellectual power and of more experience than the mass of mankind, may safely apply the processes familiar to them in their homes and in their occupations.

Ignorance of the facts is presumed on the part of the jury. More than that, ignorance is desired. In a capital case the talesman is likely to be rejected if he has any personal knowledge of the crime. On the contrary, it is the very theory of representative government that the legislator shall bring to its problems at least that amount of knowledge and opinion which the average citizen is presumed to possess, and he is usually chosen because he has more knowledge than others, with more definite opinion. Particularly in the matter of opinion it is expected also that he will fortify or modify his own by resorting to every accessible expression of the judgments of his constituents. This is precisely the reverse of the juryman's duty. The juryman may discuss the case only with his fellow jurymen, must not talk about it outside the jury room, must not read about it. If such a standard of conduct should be prescribed for a legislator, how could he honorably give ear to a constituent presenting grievances or submitting beliefs?

The fact is that we must rely on the legislator to decide what means he shall use to sift truth from falsehood. We must assume that he has the ordinary sense of honor and somewhat more than the ordinary degree of capacity. We must hope that he will be fair-minded, unprejudiced, reasonable. Nobody who has actually served in a Legislature will testify that contrary attributes are there the rule. The tendency to err is in precisely the opposite direction from that feared by the courts and other critics. Experience in public life inclines men to be skeptical rather than gullible. With every year of service the legislator becomes less credulous. Distrust is his danger.

It does not follow that no regulation of intercourse with legislators is wise or expedient. On the contrary, certain restrictions are desirable for the sake of decorum or convenience or some other palpable advantage. Thus it has come to be recognized that individual argument should not be addressed by citizens to members of a legislative body within its chamber while it is in session. American assemblies were long in reaching this conclusion. Senator Hoar, recalling that when he entered Congress in 1869, the corridors of the Capitol and the committee rooms were crowded with lobbyists, spoke of the custom of the two Houses permitting their members to introduce strangers on the floor. In Massachusetts the floor of the House was open to the public until 1890, when restrictions were imposed by rule. Before that time lobbyists came in freely and sat among the members. Since 1906 they have been excluded from the floor in Iowa by rules of the Houses. Elsewhere such rules are now not uncommon, but Legislatures may still be found where lobbyists can seat themselves beside members and ply their vocation undisturbed.

Surely no self-respecting Legislature will permit either the man who makes lobbying a business or any other citizen to go about the floor interviewing members. It would seem as if rules ought to suffice, and that Arizona was needlessly minute in putting into her Constitution: "The Legislature shall enact laws and adopt rules prohibiting the practice of lobbying on the floor of either House." Yet that rules do not always meet the need may be gathered from what Hichborn says about the California Legislature. He avers that one of the principal scandals of the Legislative session in 1907 was the openness with which machine lobbyists invaded Senate and Assembly chamber. They went so far as to move from member to member during roll-calls, giving Senator or Assemblyman, as the case might be, a proprietary tap on the shoulder, to direct his vote. In 1909 both Senate and Assembly adopted rules that no person engaged in presenting any business to the Legislature or its committees should be permitted to do business with a member while the House to which the member belonged was in session. Persons transgressing this rule were to be removed from the floor of the House in which the offense was committed, and kept out during the remainder of the session. The rule was employed in one instance only. Lobbying, in spite of the rule, continued on the floors of both Houses even during sessions. "When the Islais Creek Harbor bill was under consideration in the Assembly, for example, Carroll Cook, and others interested in the defeat of the measure as it had passed the Senate, appeared openly on the floor and in the lobby of the Assembly, even when the debate was going on, and worked for amendment of the measure to suit their aims. All this resulted in the greatest confusion. But Speaker Stanton seemed absolutely unable to cope with the situation. The lobbying and the confusion continued in spite of Stanton's efforts to enforce something of the appearance of order. Such scenes were often duplicated in the Senate." [1]

It is to be hoped that this picture was overdrawn, and that such episodes are not common throughout the land, but it is to be feared that there is far too much laxity in the matter. The Massachusetts rule, which excludes legislative counsel and agents from even the corridors and ante-rooms of the two Houses, is well enforced. At Washington I have never seen within the lobbies a man I knew to be a lobbyist, and rarely have I observed even in the corridors of the Capitol men who I had reason to suspect were being paid for buttonholing members. Save for attorneys who are sent to Washington on perfectly legitimate errands, not once a month does such a man cross the threshold of my room in the office building.

Systematized Influence

More difficult is the problem presented by that complex system of influence which is often meant when the term "lobbying" is used, rather than the simpler process of communicating specific argument from agent to member. The courts began to take notice of this when Justice Wright of New York delivered the opinion in Rose and Hawley v. Truax, 21 Barb. 361 (1855) : "It is against the genius and policy of our government that her legislative and executive officers shall be surrounded by swarms of hired retainers of the claimants upon public bounty or justice. The nuisance has become almost intolerable; and all that is required to make it quite so is for courts to tolerate contracts in respect to the services of these retainers, and, by action, enforce claims for their services."

Here was a novel proposition, that the courts may strike at an obnoxious system by refusing to support contracts that contribute to its maintenance. Whether such is a legitimate judicial function, may be left to the casuists who on the one side think that the bench should be the arbiter of public morals, and on the other hold that the Legislature should determine the scope of the police power. The defenders of the courts may in this particular field point further with pride to the vigorous language used in Kansas Pacific Railway Co. v. McCoy,

[1] Franklin Hichborn, *Story of Calif. Legislature of 1909*, chap. XXI.

8 Kan. 543 : "The use of money to influence legislation is not always wrong. It depends altogether on the manner of its use. If it be used to pay for the publication of circulars or pamphlets, or otherwise, for the collection or distribution of information openly and publicly among the members of the Legislature, there is nothing objectionable or improper. But if it be used directly in bribing, or indirectly in working up a personal influence upon individual members, conciliating them by suppers, presents, or any of that machinery so well known to lobbyists, which aims to secure a member's vote without reference to his judgment, then it is not only illegal, but one of the grossest infractions of social duty of which an individual can under the circumstances of the present day be guilty. It deserves not merely the condemnation of the courts, but the scorn and scourging of every honest citizen. For it is the way of death to republican institutions."

The reader may decide for himself whether or not that was improved upon a generation later in Le Tourneaux v. Gillies, 1 Cal. App. 546 (1905) : "It is not the policy of the law that the members of the Legislature should be subjected to the personal solicitation during the session of experienced and paid lobbyists. Men who are paid to influence legislation, and who become acquainted with and cultivate the friendship of members through dinners, wines, cigars, and personal attention, are certainly not assisting the State in providing good legislation. If such men escape public prosecution, it is no reason that the time of the courts should be taken up in aiding and assisting them in relation to their nefarious business. Courts will not permit themselves to be used for the purpose of aiding or enforcing such contracts. If such persons escape punishment through a public prosecution, they may consider themselves fortunate."

In Michigan the court was not so confident of the extent of its powers. Justice Grant said, in Randall v. News Association, 97 Mich. 136, that "however reprehensible it may be for a member of the Legislature to keep 'open house' for the entertainment of members, where they may partake of 'light refreshments, wine, beer, liquors, and cigars,' it falls short of establishing a case of bribery."

Whatever the boundaries of judicial power in this regard, it is quite clear that the existence and exercise of these powers

have had little or no effect on the evil. Its wane has been
due not to penalties, but to public opinion. The record is illuminating. For half a century the abuse flourished almost
unchecked. Nearly twoscore years after Henry Wilson denounced it in the Massachusetts Convention, Governor William
E. Russell found occasion for even stronger language when he
addressed the Legislature of 1891. Despite the passage of the
Lobby Law, the scandals of a few years later when the exploiters
quarreled over the gas spoils of Boston, surpassed anything
that had gone before, if we are to give any credence to Thomas
W. Lawson's revelations. More disheartening even were the
discoveries in the course of the New York insurance investigation, when it was reported to the New York Legislature that
the New York Life Insurance Company had paid out in ten
years $1,117,697 for "the supervision of matters of legislation."
This sum was paid, without adequate vouchers, to one man to
be used by him at his discretion. Said the committee: "Nothing disclosed by the investigation deserves more serious attention than the systematic efforts of the large insurance companies
to control a large part of the legislation of the State. They
have been organized into an offensive and defensive alliance to
procure or to prevent the passage of laws affecting not only
insurance, but a great variety of important interests to which,
through subsidiary companies or through the connection of
their officers, they have become related. Their operations
have extended beyond the State and the country has been
divided into districts so that each company might perform
conveniently its share of the work. Enormous sums have been
expended in a surreptitious manner. Irregular accounts have
been kept to conceal the payments for which proper vouchers
have not been required. This course of conduct has created a
widespread conviction that large portions of this money have
been dishonestly used." [1]

This awoke the conscience of the country. Lobbying of the
more obnoxious variety became distinctly "bad form." The
standards of legislative conduct have been distinctly raised.
Much more important, the standards of civilian conduct have
been raised still farther. Citizens of wealth and standing have
always been chiefly to blame. Therefore the appeal to their
sense of decency was of the more consequence. They thought

[1] *New York Assembly Doc. no. 41*, 1906.

themselves not without excuse. When acting independently they felt they had the right — when acting as trustees they felt it their duty — to organize against "strike" legislation, the bills introduced by venal legislators or at the behest of lobbyists, for "hold up" purposes. The more the men of wealth fed the lobby, the hungrier the lobby grew. Presently through the moneyed world spread the notion that all legislators were venal and all legislation must be bought. The lobbyist worked on the fear and folly of the capitalist. Sometimes the lobbyist bought, more often he only pretended to buy. A favorite trick was to learn by eavesdropping or otherwise how this or that member meant to vote, and then to sell the vote. My own vote was sold in this fashion at least once, and I have no doubt that to this day some Boston financier thinks me venal.

The system received a wound that in time may prove fatal, when right-minded men of public spirit faced the situation dispassionately, determined the cause of the disease, and applied themselves to the remedy. For instance, such a group of men in Boston, informally organized as a Public Franchise League, quietly arranged a conference with the financiers who really controlled the group of corporate interests most responsible for lobbying activities on Beacon Hill. It is no longer a secret that Louis D. Brandeis, now on the bench of the United States Supreme Court, was the spokesman of the Franchise League in making the agreement that followed. The bargain was that if the lobby in question should be abandoned, the League would undertake to protect the corporation concerned against strike legislation. The agreement has been faithfully executed. From that day to this all strike bills aimed at this corporation have been killed and no lobby has been necessary in order to get fair play.

Governor Folk of Missouri followed much the same line in 1905. Not waiting for the Legislature to protect itself or for private citizens to take the lead, he issued an order requiring lobbyists to register at the executive office upon coming to the capitol, and also on leaving; to state to the Governor and to the press the object of their visit; and to leave the city within a limit of thirty hours. Fear of inquiry into their methods led to compliance.[1] Furthermore, in return for a faithful ob-

[1] *Comp. Leg. Bull. no. 2*, Wis. Leg. Ref. Dept., 17.

servance of these rules the Governor promised the special interests that he would not allow any "hold up" measure to pass, an agreement which he kept by vetoing several bills that might fairly be suspected of that purpose.[1]

OLD EVILS THAT SURVIVE

Do not suppose that the evil of lobbying has been suppressed. There has been gain, thanks to an awakened public opinion and to some statutes and rules more or less useful, but part of the old abuses have not yet been reached and new ones are sure to develop as long as men can find money profit in influencing legislation. Of the old evils one that exists still in Massachusetts and doubtless in varying degree elsewhere, is to be found in the skill with which the lobbyist pollutes the very source of legislation by influencing the election of legislators. Contributions to the campaign funds of candidates were condemned by Governor Russell a generation ago, but they have continued. Moorfield Storey in his Presidential Address to the American Bar Association, August 22, 1894, well described the danger. "Many a man who would scorn to receive a bribe," he said, "will accept a contribution to his campaign expenses, apparently paid for the honorable purpose of advancing a political cause, but spent in helping him to gratify his cherished political ambition by defeating now his rivals in his own party convention and now his political opponent at the polls. He does not recognise the bribe, but he feels the obligation to the contributor, and that gratitude which is defined as a lively sense of favors to come makes him glad to repay the favor if he can before the next campaign makes necessary a fresh call for pecuniary help. A man must be singularly independent if he does not lend a kindly ear to the friend who has helped largely to elect him and upon whose aid he must again rely."

It is an evil that will never be completely cured until the public realizes the choice of its servants to be a public concern, not a private interest, and by assuming all election expenses removes the opportunity for temptation.

Another device employed for putting members under obligation, used particularly by public service corporations to help their lobbyists, is that of giving employment to voters upon

[1] Reinsch, *Am. Legislatures*, 255.

the request of their representatives. Once I was a candidate against a man who with another was said to have secured work thus for more than a thousand men in the preceding year, it happening that several unusual needs for laborers had coincided. It was no uncommon thing for members of the Legislature from Boston districts to pass a large part of their time in acting as free employment agencies. The abuse became so notorious and harmful that in 1902 the Legislature adopted this rule: "A member of either branch who directly or indirectly solicits for himself or others any position or office within the gift or control of a railroad corporation, street railway company, gas or electric light company, telegraph or telephone company, aqueduct or water company, or other public service corporation, shall be subject to suspension therefor, or to such other penalty as the branch of which he is a member may see fit to impose." In 1903 it was made by statute a penal offence for such corporations to appoint or discharge on the request of any legislator or virtually any public official, whether of State, county, city, or town.

Political in its nature is one brand of lobbying that rarely leads to the use of money and therefore is not so reprehensible as if it were essentially corrupt, but it is embarrassing and annoying in the extreme. That is the lobbying by office holders who seek increases of salary, oppose changes in the statutes relating to their work, ask special favors in the way of appropriations for their departments, or even mix in legislation not involving their personal interests. They will presume on their personal acquaintance and association with a legislator, making it awkward for him to say "No." Often active and influential members of the party organization, they may bring political pressure to bear, giving a member the impression that his political future is at stake, or indeed openly threatening defeat at the next election. Evidently they have even gone so far as to capitalize their opportunities extensively, taking pay for the exercise of their influence, if we may suppose that only such gross abuse would have led Alabama to say in her Constitution: "No State or county official shall, at any time during his term of office, accept either directly or indirectly any fee, money, office, appointment, employment, reward or thing of value, or of personal advantage, or the promise thereof, to lobby for or against any measure pending before the Legislature, or to give or withhold his influence to secure the passage or defeat of any such measure."

In my own State of Massachusetts the chief nuisance has been the solicitation on the score of salaries. Several speakers in the Convention of 1918 averred that even judges had haunted the lobbies of the General Court in their search for more pay. Also there is ground for complaint in the visits of county and city officials impelled by some phase of self-interest. The greater part of the occasion for this will be removed when the handling of administrative functions is separated from the real work of lawmaking, and some small body, semi-legislative, semi-executive, is entrusted with the business of government. Here as in so many other particulars the legislative branch is burdened and hindered by duties foreign to its proper field, which have been brought to it by the vast spread of the field of governmental activity, a growth with which the science of organization has been unable to keep pace.

Without waiting for such radical change, the Legislatures can and should free themselves from the irritations brought by the importunities of their own servants. The Iowa Senate by rule forbids any of its officers or employees to "solicit or endeavor to influence members of the Legislature in their official action," and declares that any person violating the rule shall be summarily dismissed. Like provisions are found in Colorado, Arizona, and some other States. If, however, a sense of propriety and decency does not curb the practice, it is to be doubted whether rules will accomplish much. Of course no self-respecting assembly would endure it in any serious degree.

Still another avenue of approach is through the press gallery. Reporters and correspondents have it within their power to exercise great influence on legislators. To the credit of the journalistic profession it is to be said that cases of abuse of this power for money considerations have been rare. There was an instance at Washington in 1860 when F. W. Walker was excluded for accepting money to further the interests of one Wendell before Congress, and we must assume that there was occasion for the passage of a resolution in 1875 depriving of the privilege of a seat in the gallery any reporter receiving any fee, bribe, or reward in connection with any legislation pending in either House. Here and there the annals of State Legislatures disclose unsavory instances of perverted newspaper con-

science, but in comparison with the opportunities they have
been remarkably few.

Importuning by office-seekers is one of the vexations of legislative life. Before the merit system of appointment made
progress through civil service reform, the nuisance had become
almost intolerable to right-minded men, and the marvel is that
when it was at its height any man with self-respect would endure the burden it brought to the legislator. How it affected
members of Congress half a century ago was told by James A.
Garfield: "One third of the working hours of Senators and
Representatives is hardly sufficient to meet the demands made
upon them in reference to appointments to office. The spirit
of that clause of the Constitution which shields them from arrest 'during their attendance at the session of their respective
houses, and in going to and returning from the same,' should
also shield them from being arrested from their legislative
work, morning, noon, and night, by office-seekers." [1]

Senator Hoar tells an amusing story of the ingenuity with
which one Congressman sought to salve his conscience while
avoiding the giving of offense.[2] It seems that Representative
James Buffington was very anxious about the matter of patronage and of getting offices for all his constituents. A great
many men applied for his support; frequently there were many
applications for the same office. He did not like to refuse
them. So he made it a rule to give all of them a letter of recommendation to the Departments. But he had an understanding with the appointing clerks that if he wrote his name Buffington with a "g" he desired that man should be appointed, but
if he wrote it Buffinton without the "g" he did not wish to be
taken seriously.

The spread of civil service reform has greatly lessened the
volume of annoyance, but there yet remains enough life in the
spoils system to make it a plague. And the astonishing thing
is that probably a majority of the legislators in this country
would restore it to its old-time virulence if they dared. Never
was a reform accepted with less grace by tnose to whom it
brought the most relief. As a rule men hate to lose even petty
power, and the loss of the chance to dispense favor and thereby
to advance political fortunes has been a bitter pill for the Ameri-

---

[1] "A Century of Congress," *Atlantic Monthly*, July, 1877.
[2] *Autobiography*, I, 227.

can politician. For this reason every attempt to complete the reform is doggedly fought, and we are yet far from that full acceptance of the merit system which alone will make it possible to undertake with safety and advantage the great extensions of public ownership and management, the great broadening of the field of public service, in these days so strenuously urged. Meanwhile the burden of the spoils system on lawmakers is as irksome as it is needless.

Legitimate Lobbying

In the general denunciation of lobbying, the sheep and the goats have suffered alike. It has too often been forgotten that high-minded men, animated by unselfish motives, legitimately resort to organization for giving effect to their views. No reason appears why they should not employ spokesmen, whether counsel or agents. The laborer is worthy of his hire; all of us must live; and the man who toils for righteousness must be fed and clothed and housed just as the man who works for iniquity. To be sure, righteousness and iniquity may depend on the point of view, but for the present purposes let us assume that they are to be discriminated by the degree of self-interest. If, then, reasonably unselfish purpose is to be encouraged, shall we restrain it by forbidding its achievement through paid argument? So little reason suggests itself for such restraint that it might be ignored were it not for the frequency with which we hear complaint of the presence of representatives of philanthropic, commercial, and industrial organizations at committee hearings and in the lobbies and corridors of capitols. Supersensitive legislators every now and then resent the pressure thus brought to bear.

The complaint is not reasonable. To be sure, unfair methods may be used by the men with virtuous purpose as well as by those who seek only private gain, and no word is to be spoken in defence of threats and persecution, but in practice it turns out that the methods of men with philanthropic motive are usually frank and honorable. Such men really benefit legislation. Even though we grant that the ideal of representative government would be secured by a body of statesmen who, unaided, unguided, self-sufficing, would out of their own consciousness evolve wisdom reflecting the public will, we know that no such body ever has existed or, while human nature is imperfect, ever will exist. If, then, legislators must to greater or less extent look elsewhere for information and judgment, where can they better turn than to the organizations of citizens who co-operate in behalf of principles?

There is one phase of the work of these organizations to which surely nobody can object. Besides giving information to legis-lators, they get information about legislation, and this is to the advantage both of Legislatures and of the public. No more useful opportunity is open to Chambers of Commerce and like bodies than that of watching and reporting what goes on in legislative halls. Their legislative agents may come near to being the often wished-for "people's lobbyists." Such agents should spread knowledge about the bills introduced, the times of com-mittee hearings, amendments adopted on the floor; behind them should be Committees on Legislation ready to act at a moment's notice if occasion arises to defeat a bad bill making headway or to help a good bill in danger.

It is also perfectly proper and not undesirable that public service and other business corporations shall have watchers in the capitols. Corporation directors are trustees for stock-holders whose numbers often run up into the thousands, and may well construe it to be part of their duty to see that at least there is knowledge of hostile legislation proposed. Likewise may be commended the growing practice of having the big municipal corporations represented in the lobbies. Boston has protected itself on many an occasion by the activities of the member of its law department entrusted with the work on Beacon Hill.

Along the same lines is the work of the legislative agents of the labor organizations. They give help to any legislator broad enough to be willing to consider the other man's point of view, and they carry back to their unions the broadening they them-selves unconsciously get through contact with the representa-tives of the other classes in the community. Of course the capitalist group can hardly be expected to look with equanimity on the efforts of the labor lobbyists, but the labor men return the distrust with good measure, and the conflicts of interest that follow help on the whole toward well-balanced, equitable legislation.

With attention called to all these varieties of lobbyists and

the useful purposes that many of them serve, will the reader
be surprised to learn that most legislators deem it useful, desirable, and in no way dishonorable, to give ear to such men?
No less notable and reputable a lawmaker than Thomas B. Reed
used to say when he was in the House that there were no terrors
for him in a call from a lobbyist, and that he was always willing
to go out and see one, unless he had reason to believe the man
a rascal. "If any person can tell me more about a pending
bill than I know already," he would ask, "why should it be my
duty to shun him?" All Mr. Reed insisted upon was that the
lobbyist should be clean-handed, stick to his legitimate business,
and hold his interviews with Congressmen outside the legislative chambers.

No lawmaker can know too much about the work before him.
Of much the greater part he can have no personal knowledge,
but must get it where he can. If he is a man intelligent enough
to make laws, he will be able to discount self-interest on the
part of his informant, to recognize truth and disregard falsehood,
to winnow the chaff from the grain. It is not a case of being
defiled by touching pitch, nor even of consorting with men of
doubtful quality. By far the greater part of the men whose
duty it is regularly or occasionally to communicate with lawmakers are men of high character and clean lives. A few are
knaves. In the public mind their brand of yeast spoils the
whole loaf. That belief is unwarranted and is unfair.

Exaggeration of the Evil

A review of the history of lobbying, the judicial opinions to
which it has given rise, the discussions that have led to the laws
on the subject, and all the rest of its literature, leads to astonish-
ment that so much is charged and so little is known. To be
sure, the mercenary phases of lobbying do not warrant the
hope of copious or exact information, for they are naturally
veiled in secrecy. A lobbyist is rarely called upon to give to
his principal a detailed report of his expenditures, and vouchers
are almost never required. Of course this creates the most
powerful temptation to exaggerate and falsify. The more the
lobbyist says he has used in bribes, the bigger his chance to
profit in so far as he pockets the money himself. Manifestly
the result is to add largely to the erroneous beliefs on the

subject. When such beliefs cannot be disproved by recorded facts, it is permissible to turn to the judgments of men in the best position to form them. In this instance they are the men who have had long experience in public life. If improper solicitation of legislators really goes on to anything like the degree charged by the muckrakers, surely those who are in the midst of it ought to know. Yet legislators of the highest standing, exceptional perspicacity, and years of opportunity for knowledge will be found almost unanimous in saying that the volume of the evil is most grossly exaggerated.

Should you say that they are the men never improperly approached, and that pride in their associations prompts too generous defence, let me call as a witness an observer, A. R. Spofford, who as Librarian of Congress had the advantage of intimate acquaintance without the handicap of being one of the men under fire. Said he: "While there is no reason to doubt that what is known as the lobby has existed in one or another form in the legislative history of all free governments, it is certain that the organization and power of this indefinite influence in political life has often been grossly exaggerated. In times of partisan excitement, when the advocates and opponents of any measure before the legislative body are full of zeal, wild stories are spread abroad through the press, connecting the names of public men with allegations of bribery and corruption. These stories are in the majority of cases utterly unfounded, and yet are as industriously circulated to meet a real or fancied public appetite for scandal, as if there were no law of libel in existence. Probably there is no public man of any notoriety in our political history who has not at some time been charged with acting or voting under the influence of the lobby."

And farther on: "The existence of a powerful and organized body has been assumed as successfully endeavoring to control our national legislation. Numerous as are the men whose casual employment may justify the application to them of the term lobbyist, the power and influence of the congressional lobby has been greatly over-rated. Congress is not a body of venal reprobates ready to be corrupted, but a body fairly representing the average intelligence and morality of the people. Bad legislation, of which we have more than enough, is the fruit of ignorance, not of corruption." [1]

[1] "Lobby," *Lalor's Cycl. of Pol. Science*, ii, 779–81.

Take a concrete example given by Mr. Spofford: "Enormous stories were told of a Russian lobby; how that only $5,000,000 out of the $7,200,000 paid for the purchase of Alaska ever reached Russia. The facts were that not a dollar was paid to a Congressman, but $27,000 was invested in skillful attorneys, and $3000 paid to one Washington newspaper, while the $2,170,000 was expended by the Russian minister, under instructions from his government, in munitions of war and machinery."

Is it surprising that some knowledge of what had been the facts in such cases led many of us to be skeptical when in May of 1913 President Wilson, provoked by the opposition to the tariff bill, attacked the lobby he averred to be working against it? May those of us with some actual experience in legislative surroundings, not be pardoned if we saw flaws in his argument? He described a lobby as "insidious" when "newspapers are filled with paid advertisements calculated to mislead the judgments of men." Since all advertisements imply payment and are commonly so understood by the public; since their purpose is to shape judgment and everybody so knows; and since whether they are "calculated to mislead" is a matter of opinion: that much of the President's charge was oratorical.

He went on to call a lobby insidious when "money without limit is being paid to sustain such a lobby." This was hyperbole, and hyperbole often has its legitimate use. The implication, however, that the use of money to shape opinion is *per se* objectionable, may not be instantly accepted. Were it true without qualifications, sorry would be the plight of a President elected as a result of opinion in part shaped through campaign expenditure of amounts running up into the millions.

Further he said that a lobby is insidious when "great bodies of astute men seek to create an artificial opinion and to overcome the interests of the public for their private profit." It may be suggested that any opinion which is created is artificial and that almost all opinion is created. However, that may be captious. Note rather the vital point, the implication that great bodies of astute men do in fact seek to overcome the interests of the public for their private profit. This I have no hesitation in absolutely denying. Of a dozen reasons, one might suffice, that it is utterly impossible to combine great bodies of men for any such purpose. It ought also to be said that no such thing is ever attempted.   Large bodies of men do in fact believe that the public interest will be advanced by enterprises that bring them individual profit.   For instance, a railroad benefits the inhabitants of the country it traverses, to a degree far greater than the aggregate of the benefits to its stockholders.   The bankruptcy of a railroad inconveniences or indeed positively injures the public more than the stockholders, in the total of the effects.   It is most unfortunate that men ignore the unity of interest between enterprise and public welfare.

Although the practice of lobbying continues in connection with every one of our lawmaking bodies, it is not true that through this channel any considerable amount of money reaches any considerable number of legislators.   Outside that which is spent in ways now held to be legitimate, most of the money is kept by the men supposed to be go-betweens, who pretend to accomplish bribes that are in reality never completed.   It is a gainful occupation equally easy and disgraceful.   If the member alleged to have been bribed, votes as the lobbyist has reported to his employer would be the case, the employer is quite content; if the member votes the other way, the employer dares not make any trouble.

Almost as simple and still more profitable is the resort to blackmail.   The lobbyist thinks up bills that would damage somebody having money.   These he presents on his own petition or that of a man of straw, or he gets some friendly member to introduce them, perhaps innocently, perhaps in collusion. The whole purpose is to get bought off.   Such bills are variously known as "strike bills," "hold-up bills," "regulators," "sandbaggers," or by some other familiar title, according to the whim of this or that Legislature.   In some States it is not uncommon for scores of these bills to appear at every session.   For the most part they are aimed at corporations.   At times they have been very profitable, not only to the lobbyists, but also to that small group of political degenerates in every Legislature who believe in making hay while the sun shines.   They will continue to be an easy way of extracting money from the purses of spineless men until public opinion makes it as disgraceful to corrupt as to be corrupted, and equally disgraceful whether the corruption is direct or indirect.

We have reached the point where it is generally agreed that

it is odious to pay a lawmaker for his vote. Unfortunately too many men otherwise honorable think still that it is not improper to pay somebody else to get a member's vote or influence legislative action, without overmuch scrutiny of the methods used. They are quite ready to pay the lobbyist without questioning his processes. They are nothing loath to retain lawyers or others supposed to be able to control certain members by influences political, social, or personal. They are unwilling to bribe but are willing to buy. Most of their money is wasted, but it does infinite harm, for it contributes in no small degree to that mistrust of legislative bodies which is the source of so much of the political unrest of our time.

CHAPTER XVIII

BRIBERY

THE story of bribery in connection with modern assemblies is not pleasant. To avoid its telling might be the wish of one who finds no satisfaction in dwelling on the weaknesses of human nature, and yet it cannot be escaped if we are to try to learn whether the ethical standards of mankind are rising, or whether present-day forms of government invite and develop the evil. There is a widespread belief that legislative corruption is novel or is more common than ever before. On this assumption blame is attached by some to democratic institutions; by others it is advanced as a proof of degeneracy. In various ways it contributes to that lack of confidence in representative government which is a conspicuous characteristic of our time. Therefore it is of no small importance to determine what are the facts, both as to the past and as to the present.

Bribery is an offense at common law. Originally in England it was confined to interference with the administration of justice, but presently it came to cover corrupt reward for the discharge of any public office. This appears to have been the conception of it in ancient times. At Athens the constant complaints of bribery were aimed chiefly at generals and others in administrative positions, as well as at demagogues who were bought to pursue this or that line of policy. "Of bribery in the popular courts of justice," says Freeman,[1] "we hear very little, and of bribery in the Assembly itself we hear absolutely nothing. That Assembly doubtless passed many foolish, hasty, and passionate votes, but we may be quite sure that it never passed a corrupt vote." On the other hand, the prevalence of venality among Athenian officials may be inferred from the injunction of Plato, in his ideal republic, that those who took presents for doing their duty should be punished in the severest manner. Let it not be supposed, however, that bribery was an evil peculiar to a form of government such as that of Athens.

[1] *Hist. of Federal Govt.*, I, 83 *et seq.*

As Freeman well said in another connection,[1] "it is absurd to infer that a democratic or a federal form of government has a necessary and special tendency to corruption, when it is certain that corruption has been and is rife under governments of other kinds." The fact is that in all ages and all climes men holding high public trusts have too often been guilty of betraying those trusts by the acceptance of bribes.

The historians agree that bribery of lawmakers first became a crying evil in the reign of Charles II. As Parliament gained in power, inevitably the Crown sought to achieve by secret means what it could no longer do openly. Its resort was to "influence" of every sort, that, as Seeley defines it,[2] being "a general name for all the different forms of persuasion which the Crown by its greatness, splendour, wealth, and patronage could exert upon individuals." Its worst phase is bribery.

The evil became notorious in the Pensioner Parliament, the body that under Charles II sat for seventeen years without dissolution. Many of its poorer members sold their votes for a very small gratuity.[3] Lord Clifford allowed £10,000 for buying them; Lord Denby increased the allowance. The practice became so obnoxious under William III that public opinion revolted. The Commons resolved February 17, 1694: "That the Lord Falkland, being a member of that House, by begging and receiving £2000 from His Majesty, contrary to the ordinary method of issuing and bestowing the King's money, was guilty of a high misdemeanour and breach of trust; and that he be committed to the Tower of London during the pleasure of the House." Accordingly he was sent to the Tower and kept there a few days, being released upon setting forth to the House that he was "highly sensible of their displeasure."

More famous is the case of the Speaker of the House, Sir John Trevor. Bishop Burnet says of him: "Being a Tory in principle, he undertook to manage that party, provided he was furnished with such sums of money as might purchase some votes; and by him began the practice of buying off men, in which hitherto the King [William III] had kept to stricter rules. I took the liberty once to complain to the King of this method.

[1] *Some Impressions of the U.S.*, 124 (1883).
[2] Sir J. R. Seeley, *Introduction to Political Science*, 261.
[3] John, Earl Russell, *An Essay on the Hist. of the English Govt. and Const.*, ed. of 1866, 201.

He said he hated it as much as any man could do; but he saw it was not possible, considering the corruption of the age, to avoid it, unless he would endanger the whole."

In 1695 a rumor spread that the funds of the City of London and the East India Company had been largely employed for corrupting great men, and the name of Sir John Trevor was among those mentioned. A committee was appointed to examine the books of the two corporations and it reported that in the preceding session the Speaker had received a thousand guineas for expediting a local bill. It was moved that he had been guilty of a high crime and misdemeanor, and he had to stand up and put the question. There was a loud cry of "Aye!" He called for the "Noes" and scarcely a voice was heard. He was forced to declare that the "Ayes" had it. As Macaulay says, a man of spirit would have given up the ghost with remorse and shame; and the unutterable ignominy of that moment left its mark even on the callous heart and brazen forehead of Trevor. Had he returned to the House on the following day, he would have had to put the question on a motion for his own expulsion. He therefore pleaded illness and shut himself up in his bedroom. Wharton soon brought down a royal message authorizing the Commons to elect another Speaker.

At that time it was resolved: "That the offer of any money, or other advantage, to any member of Parliament, for the promoting of any matter whatsoever, depending, or to be transacted, in Parliament, is a high crime and misdemeanor, and tends to the subversion of the English constitution." [1] Therein Parliament did not say what it thought, unless it was sincere in a momentary spasm of virtue. Surely the sop to conscience had been wholly forgotten when Robert Walpole became the real ruler of England. In the course of the score and more of years during which his dynasty lasted, he matured the art of bribery. Earl Russell, after showing the injustice of averring that Walpole was the first to govern England by corruption, goes on to say that he employed it with a coarseness which, by destroying the shame attendant upon it, overthrew the low barrier of virtue still subsisting, and extended the vice which thus openly displayed itself.[2] Lecky tells us there can be no doubt that a

[1] Sir Thomas Erskine May, *Law, Privileges, Proceedings, and Usages of Parliament*, 285.

[2] *An Essay on the Hist. of the English Govt. and Const.*, ed. 1866, 201.

large proportion of the immense expenditure of secret service money during Walpole's administration was devoted to the direct purchase of members of Parliament.[1] He governed by means of an assembly saturated with corruption, and he fully acquiesced in its conditions and resisted every attempt to improve it. He appears to have cordially accepted the maxim that government must be carried on by corruption or force, and he deliberately made corruption the basis of his rule.

It is instructive to note the frame of mind to which this brought so learned a philosopher as David Hume. His celebrated "Essays" were published in the year of Walpole's downfall, 1742, when two decades of vicious prosperity had benumbed the English conscience and perverted its powers of reasoning. In the sixth of those Essays you may read : "Political writers have established it as a maxim, that, in contriving any system of government, and fixing the several checks and controuls of the constitution, every man ought to be supposed a *knave*, and to have no other end, in all his actions, than private interest. By this interest we must govern him, and, by means of it, make him, notwithstanding his insatiable avarice and ambition, coöperate to public good. . . . It is, therefore, a just *political* maxim, *that every man must be supposed a knave :* Though at the same time, it appears somewhat strange, that a maxim should be true in *politics* which is false in *fact*. But to satisfy us on this head, we may consider, that men are generally more honest in their private than in their public capacity, and will go greater lengths to serve a party, than when their own private interest is alone concerned. Honour is a great check upon mankind; but where a considerable body of men act together, this check is, in a great measure, removed; since a man is sure to be approved of by his own party for what promotes the common interest; and he soon learns to despise the clamours of adversaries."

Henry Pelham took over the system of government by bribery and brought it to perfection. With the opening years of the reign of George III the climax was capped. Under Lord Bute, in 1762, the expenditure of secret service money rose to £82,168. Horace Walpole relates a startling tale of the purchase of votes by Fox in December, 1762, in support of Bute's preliminaries of peace. He avers that a shop was publicly opened at the Pay

[1] *England in the Eighteenth Century*, i, 395.

Office, whither the members flocked, and received the wages of their venality in bank-bills, even to so low a sum as £200, for their votes on the treaty; £25,000, as Martin, Secretary of Treasury, afterward owned, was issued in one morning; and in a single fortnight, a vast majority was purchased to approve the peace. The account is probably exaggerated, but doubtless there was basis for it, as it was in essence not unnatural for the times.

To Bute, says Lecky (I, 398), we owe the most gigantic and most wasteful of all forms of bribery, the custom of issuing loans on terms extravagantly advantageous to the lender, and distributing the shares among the supporters of the administration. Stock-jobbing became the fashion among the members, and was a scandal for a score of years. In 1781 Lord North contracted a loan of £12,000,000 to defray the cost of the disastrous American war. It was computed by Fox that a profit of £900,000 would be derived therefrom; and by others that half the loan was subscribed for by members of the House of Commons. Lord Rockingham said "the loan was made merely for the purpose of corrupting the Parliament to support a wicked, impolitic, and ruinous war."

Lotteries furnished another cloak for distributing the public funds where they would do the most good. In 1769 there were turned over to members twenty thousand lottery tickets that they could sell at a high premium.

Much money did its work without any subterfuge. The sums varied, Wraxall tells us,[1] from five hundred to eight hundred pounds a year, which sums were "conveyed" to gentlemen of the House of Commons "in a squeeze of the hand" as they passed the ministerial agent. It was the business of that agent in Lord Chatham's time to distribute "with *art* and *policy*" among the members who had no ostensible place, sums of money for their support during the session. It was no uncommon circumstance at the end of a session for a gentleman to receive five hundred or one thousand pounds "for his *service*." Such a gift seems to have been regarded as a customary compliment. It might be offered without offense, and if it was declined, an apology was felt to be due to the minister.[2]

The King was an accomplice in the system. From a letter

[1] Anecdotes and Speeches of Lord Chatham, I, 137.
[2] May, *Const. History of England*, I, 302.

he wrote in 1781 no other conclusion can be drawn than that he was in the habit of transmitting money to secure majorities for the Ministers fighting his battles. Before the end of his reign, however, more honorable notions prevailed. The system did not long survive the ministry of Lord North. Although in later years probably resorted to on rare and exceptional occasions, it virtually disappeared in the nineteenth century.

Observe that all this was bribery of members by the Government, reprehensible enough to be sure, but not quite so vicious as the bribery by which it was succeeded, that coming from outside. Bribery by private interests is to be debited to the invention of steam railroads. When they were young in England, one company was able to boast that it had command of one hundred suffrages in the House of Commons; and Francis, in his "History of the Railways," says that members were personally canvassed, solicitations were made to peers, influences of the most delicate nature were used, promises were given to vote for special lines before arguments were heard, advantages in all forms and phases were proposed, to suit the circumstances of some and the temper of others. Letters of allotment were tempting; human nature was frail; and the premium on five hundred shares irresistible.[1] We read of one bill that cost the Directors £82,000; of needy members "conciliated" by being paid £5000 for a strip of land worth £500; of members who systematically sold their parliamentary interest for money considerations.

This was but a passing phase, an episode of weakness under great temptation, disappearing with the motive. By 1860 so much of it had been forgotten that Lord Brougham seems to have felt justified in testifying: "I have sat in Parliament for about fifty years, and I never heard even a surmise against the purity of the members, except in some few cases of private bills promoted by joint stock companies. I had been considerably upwards of a quarter of a century in Parliament before I ever heard such a thing even whispered; and I am as certain as I am of my own existence, that during the whole of that period, not one act of a corrupt nature had ever been done by a member of either House." [2] This can be reconciled with the averments of the critics only by supposing that even when the

[1] Simon Sterne, "Legislation," *Lalor's Cycl. of Pol. Science*, II, 755.
[2] "The British Constitution," *Works*, XI, 62.

railroad outlay was at its worst, the volume of iniquity in Parliament was not so great as the pessimists alleged, that comparatively few members were implicated, and that honorable men like Lord Brougham had no personal knowledge of the scandal. Since that time only at rare intervals has there been ground for impeaching the integrity of members of Parliament. Taken as a whole its record in our day has been wonderfully clean. Contrasted with that of the seventeenth century, surely it gives warrant for the belief that the standards of English public life have been greatly elevated.

It is a most remarkable and significant thing that the debauching of Parliament which continued through the hundred years from Charles II to George III, found so little reflection in the public life of the Colonies. Only one noteworthy and considerable instance of what we now mean by corruption, before the Revolutionary War, has come to my notice. According to James Parton,[1] in the Virginia House of Burgesses of 1765 an attempt was made to bolster the falling fortunes of leading members by loans of public money. John Robinson, the Speaker of the House, who was also the Treasurer of the Province, had been in the habit for years of lending the public money to distressed members and others, himself becoming responsible to the government for the repayment. But these planters were doomed never to be again in a paying condition. Many of them borrowed, few repaid, until his deficit was £130,000. A ring was formed in the Assembly, for the double purpose of relieving the Speaker's estate from this menacing obligation, and of enabling him to accommodate others of the ring with further loans of public money. It was the intention of the ring to make the scheme work backward, and include the loans already effected. Patrick Henry killed the project with a sentence: "What, sir, is it proposed, then, to reclaim the spendthrift from his dissipation and extravagance by filling his pocket with money?" Robinson died the next year; the deficit could no longer be concealed; the real object of the scheme became apparent; and the Speaker's estate had to make good the loss.

This seems to have been an exceptional occurrence. For the most part the colonial assemblies approached independence with comparatively high standards and clean records. Just why the war should have conspicuously vitiated the temper of

[1] *Life of Thomas Jefferson*, 80.

public life, is a mystery. It might have been thought that the high ideals of patriotism glorified by the struggle, together with the pressing need for suppressing individual greed, would have made it a period of exceptional purity of conduct. Yet that the contrary was the effect, is the irresistible conclusion from the record of the time. Recall the lament of George Washington to James Warren, written March 31, 1779: "Speculation, peculation, engrossing, forestalling, with all their concomitants, afford too many melancholy proofs of the decay of public virtue, and too glaring instances of its being the interest and desire of too many, who would wish to be thought friends, to continue the war. Nothing, I am convinced, but the depreciation of our currency, proceeding in a great measure from the foregoing causes, aided by stock-jobbing and party dissensions, has fed the hopes of the enemy and kept the British arms in America to this day. They do not scruple to declare this themselves, and add, that we shall be our own conquerors."

Corruption seems to have been in the air. Else how can we account for such fears as those of Theophilus Parsons, afterward Chief Justice of Massachusetts, he who wrote in 1778 "The Essex Result," the pamphlet about the Convention at Ipswich that mainly led to the rejection of the first Constitution drafted for Massachusetts? "The legislative body will hold the purse strings," he predicted, "and men will struggle for a place in that body to acquire a share of the public wealth. It has always been the case. Bribery will be attempted, and the laws will not prevent it. All States have enacted severe laws against it, and they have been ineffectual." If this be thought to have been only the abstract reasoning of one who had found the most virtuous States to have become vicious, and the morals of all peoples, in all ages, to have been shockingly corrupted, note that he cited what he saw around him, as the ground for his fears. "Have we not," he asked, "already degenerated from the pure morals and disinterested patriotism of our ancestors? Are not our manners becoming soft and luxurious, and have not our vices began to shoot?"

Parsons was not the only Massachusetts statesman of the period to find in his surroundings occasion for alarm. Elbridge Gerry was another to discern in the public life of his day the promise of evil. Yates in his "Minutes of the Debates in the Federal Convention" quotes Gerry as saying he "supposed that in the national legislature there will be a great number of bad men of various descriptions," for which reason he wanted the national executive appointed by the State executives.[1]

Apprehension was not confined to generalities. While the Massachusetts Convention of 1788 was considering the Federal Constitution, there appeared in the "Boston Gazette" this letter:

"Bribery and Corruption ! ! !

> "The most diabolical plan is on foot to corrupt the members of the Convention, who oppose the adoption of the new Constitution. Large sums of money have been brought from a neighboring state for that purpose, contributed by the wealthy. If so, is it not probable there may be collections for the same accursed purpose nearer home?
>
> "Centinel"

The printers were requested to appear and give information. Instead they sent a letter which was referred to a committee, but nothing came of it. Doubtless the story was a canard, but the mere fact that it could be entertained shows the atmosphere was murky.

CONGRESSIONAL CORRUPTION

WITH the formation of a Federal Congress, scandal grew apace. Few legislative episodes have been more discreditable than those of the assumption of State debts and the refunding measures of that first Congress. Read some of the entries in the diary of the virulent Maclay:

Jan. 15, 1790. "It appears that a system of speculation for the engrossing certificates has been carrying on for some time. Whispers of this kind come to me from every quarter. Dr. Elmer told me that Mr. Morris must be deep in it, for his partner, Mr. Constable, of this place, had one contract for forty thousand dollars' worth. The Speaker hinted to me that General Heister had brought over a sum of money from Mr. Morris for this business; he said the Boston people were concerned in it. Indeed there is no room to doubt but a connection is spread over the whole Continent on this villainous business. I pray God they may not prosper."

[1] Elliot's Debates, I, 401.

Jan. 18. "Hawkins of North Carolina said as he came up he passed two expresses with very large sums of money on their way to North Carolina for purposes of speculation in certificates. Wadsworth has sent off two small vessels for the Southern States on the errand of buying up certificates. I really fear the members of Congress are deeper in this business than any others."

March 9. "In the Senate chamber this morning Butler said he heard a man say he would give Vining (of Delaware) one thousand guineas for his vote, but added, 'I question whether he would do so in fact.' So do I, too, for he might get it for a tenth part of that sum. I do not know that pecuniary influence has actually been used, but I am certain that every other kind of management has been practiced and every tool at work that could be thought of. Officers of Government, clergy, citizens, Cincinnati, and every person under the influence of the Treasury; Bland and Huger carried to the chamber of Representatives—the one lame, the other sick. Clymer stopped from going away, though he had to leave, and at length they risked the question and carried it, thirty-one votes to twenty-six."

March 10. "What poor, supple things we are, bending down before every dinner and floated away with every flask of liquor!"

July 17. "When I came downstairs, Mr. Clymer came to where I stood with General Irwin. We talked over the general belief that the assumption was forced on us to favor the views of speculation. . . . The whole town almost has been busy at it. Nor have the members [of Congress] kept their hands clean from this dirty work; from Wadsworth, with his boat-load of money, down to the daily six dollars, have they generally been at it. The unexampled success has obliterated every mark of reproach, and from henceforth we may consider speculation as a Congressional employment. Nay, all the abominations of the South Sea bubble are outdone in this vile business. In wrath, I wish the same fate may attend the projectors of both!"

These were, indeed, the railings and revilings of a sour man, warped by suspicion, a bitter partisan looking for evil. Taken alone, they might be greatly discounted, but such beliefs were far from being confined to a solitary Jeremiah, and if widespread acceptance ever proves anything, surely here was a case where the abundance of smoke warrants the conclusion that there

was plenty of fire underneath. So great a man as Thomas
Jefferson, placed where his sources of information would seem
to have been sufficient, had no doubts of the existence of venality. To be sure, he too was biased. His jealousy of Alexander Hamilton probably clouded his judgment, but it is not
likely he was wholly in the wrong. Recording in his "Anas"
under date of February 7, 1793, a conference with President
Washington, he wrote: "My wish was to see both Houses of
Congress cleansed of all persons interested in the bank or public
stocks; and that a pure legislature being given us, I should
always be ready to acquiesce under their determinations even
if contrary to my own opinions, for that I subscribe to the principle that the will of the majority honestly expressed should
give law. I confirmed him in the fact of the great discontents
to the South, that they were grounded on seeing that their
judgments and interests were sacrificed to those of the Eastern
States on every occasion, and their belief that it was the effect
of a corrupt squadron of voters in Congress at the command
of the Treasury, and they see that if the votes of those members
who had an interest distinct from and contrary to the general
interest of their constituents had been withdrawn, as in decency
and honesty they should have been, the laws would have been
the reverse of what they are in all the great questions." [1]

On the 2d of March he wrote to the effect that one half the
House was made up of bank directors, holders of bank stock,
or stock-jobbers, and the next day he recorded a "list of paper-
men" communicated to him by Mr. Beckley, with the summary:
Stockholders in the U.S. Bank, 16 Representatives, 5 Senators;
other paper, 3 Representatives, 2 Senators; suspected, 2
Representatives, 4 Senators. On his list of stockholders
appeared the names of Elbridge Gerry, Fisher Ames, George
Cabot, Roger Sherman, Rufus King, and Robert Morris. [2]

On the 3d of February, 1794, he wrote to Edmund Randolph:
"I indulge myself on one political topic only, that is, in declaring to my countrymen the shameless corruption of a portion of
the Representatives to the 1st and 2d Congresses and their
implicit devotion to the treasury. I think I do good in this,
because it may produce exertions to reform the evil, on the
success of which the form of the government is to depend." [3]

---

[1] *Writings of Thomas Jefferson*, P. L. Ford ed., I, 217.
[2] *Ibid.*, 222, 223.   [3] *Ibid.*, VI, 498.

Of course the partisans accused of such corruption resented the charge. Their temper may be gathered from a few lines in a letter from Fisher Ames to Christopher Gore, written at Philadelphia, January 10, 1795: "Taylor, when he resigned his Senatorship, is said to have assigned, in his letter to the Assembly, as a reason, the extreme corruption of Congress and the President. I wish the crackbrain could be convicted for libelling the government." [1]

Balancing the evidence, it is hard to escape the conclusion that the political standards of the time were distinctly below those now prevailing. That they were lower even than those of the period following the Civil War, so commonly excoriated, was the judgment of George Frisbie Hoar, who in a speech in the House of Representatives, August 9, 1876, came to the defense of his generation. "I believe," he said, "there is absolutely less of corruption and of mal-administration and less of vice and evil in public life than there was in the sixteen years which covered the administration of Washington, the administration of John Adams, and the first term of Jefferson. . . . Why, Mr. Speaker, one of the most famous generals of the Revolutionary War, whose life extended down to the period to which I have alluded, while he was Quartermaster General, was in partnership with a firm for the purpose of selling quartermaster's stores to the Government and making a profit, corresponding with his partner secretly and in cipher. The Attorney General and Secretary of State, Washington's friend, while he was Secretary of State was detected in receiving money from France as a bribe to thwart the foreign policy of the administration of which he was a member. Another cabinet officer of Washington, Hamilton, being charged with a corrupt official relation with a citizen, defended himself by acknowledging to his countrymen, over his own signature, a profligate relation to the wife of the person named."

The reader may have observed that in all this criticism of our early Congressmen and others in public office, there is not much charging of direct bribery. If there was corruption, it did not often take the form of buying and selling votes. At any rate that kind of venality was not countenanced. In December of 1795 three members told the House how one Robert Randall promised to give them land or money for their support of a grant

[1] *Works of Fisher Ames*, I, 161.

of about twenty million acres on the Great Lakes. After several days passed in trying the case, Randall was brought to the bar for reprimand and then committed to the care of the Sergeant-at-Arms, suffering detention of three weeks.

After the first ten or fifteen years, the record of Congress was not greatly besmirched by scandal for a long time. To be sure, Andrew Jackson and his followers tried their hardest to spatter it with mud when John Quincy Adams was elected President by the House. That was when the cry of "bargain and corruption" led great masses of people to implicit faith that two political knaves, Clay and Adams, had cheated an honest soldier out of his rights. John Randolph helped along the slander with a famous speech in which he exhausted the unrivaled resources of his vocabulary in abusing the President and Secretary. Although the word "corruption" was freely used by the Jackson men in characterizing the transaction, it has not come to my notice that anybody supposed money changed hands.

More serious were the imputations in the course of the fight over renewing the charter of the United States Bank. It was charged that in five years through which the contest lasted the Bank lent $1,605,781 to members of Congress, as follows: in 1830, to 52 members, $192,161; in 1831, to 59 members, $322,199; in 1832, to 44 members, $478,069; in 1833, to 58 members, $374,766; in 1834, to 52 members, $238,586. This was more than the total of the salaries of all the members of both Houses during the five-year period.[1] If the charge was true, nearly a quarter of the members were indiscreet, to put it mildly. At the session of 1835–36 attempt was made to investigate the matter, but was abandoned when Adams declared that a like attempt in 1832 had been abandoned because it cut both ways.

The middle of the century passed before any considerable number of men began seriously to think that members of Congress were ever impelled by mercenary motives. The gradual rise of prosperity from financial crisis to financial crisis shows in the period just before each crash a speculative activity that is accompanied by extravagance and by a letting down of all sorts of ethical standards. So it was in the years just before the panic of 1857, and Congress did not escape. The editor of

[1] *Memoirs, Speeches, and Writings of Robert Rantoul, Jr.*, 307.

"Harper's Magazine," in the "Editor's Table" for October, 1856, wrote: "Corruption culminates at Washington. It is a propensity elsewhere, there it is an art. . . . Particulars of individual acts of corruption are not readily ascertained, are not always safe to publish; but the general fact that money is freely and uniformly expended by all successful applicants for Congressional favor, or even Congressional justice, is notorious." This resembles the hyperbolic utterances of a yellow journal of our own day, which we all know to be ridiculously exaggerated, and we suspect that "Harper's Magazine," now sedately venerable, may then have had the irresponsibility of childhood. Yet the records show its allegations were not wholly groundless. For instance, take the case of Colonel Glossbrenner, a former member of the House, who was Sergeant-at-Arms at the time of the two months' contest in the winter of 1855–56 that ended in the election of Banks as Speaker. Ben: Perley Poore says [1] that Glossbrenner obtained a loan of twenty thousand dollars from a bank in Pennsylvania, which enabled him to make advances to impecunious members of both parties, and thus to insure his reëlection. "It then became necessary to divide the spoils, and after an exciting contest Cornelius Wendell, a Democratic nominee, was elected Printer to the House by Republican votes, in consideration of certain percentages of his profits paid to designated parties." [2]

Corrupt lobbying on a large scale was brought out in 1857 in the cases of O. B. Matteson and W. A. Gilbert, Congressmen from New York. The report of a committee of the House, by Henry Winter Davis, chairman, declared Gilbert to have cast his vote on the Iowa land bill for a corrupt consideration, consisting of seven square miles of land and some stock given to him. It also charged him with agreement to procure the passage of a resolution by Congress for purchase of certain books, on condition that he should receive a certain sum out of the appropriation. Matteson was proved to have incited parties interested in the Des Moines land grant to use a large sum of money and interest in railroad stock corruptly, to procure the passage of the grant through the House. After long and acrimonious debate, in the course of which J. W. Simonton, a journalist, was imprisoned for refusing to disclose the names of corruptible members, resolutions to expel both

---

[1] *Reminiscences*, I, 448.   [2] *Ibid.*, 492.

Matteson and Gilbert were reported and would have passed, but both members forestalled the vote by resigning their seats.[1]

Standards of morality change from epoch to epoch. They are largely conventional — matters of agreement. Some are little more than shibboleths. Some are profoundly ethical. Therefore it is with caution that the notions of right and wrong prevalent to-day should be used as a test of what was right or wrong yesterday. Yet I feel warranted in saying at least that the code of legislative conduct in this country in the middle of the nineteenth century was distinctly different from that which is now common. Take for example the case of Stephen A. Douglas. He was looked upon as a great Senator. He was admired and followed by large masses of men. It can hardly be supposed that his conceptions of morality were exceptional, else he would not have retained leadership. That they were tolerated, shows that they were at any rate not grossly repugnant. Parton says there was no artifice to which he would not resort to carry a measure or get a vote. He made not the smallest scruple of selling his own vote, or buying another man's vote, provided the price was of a nature that Congressional morality permitted to be given. In other words, he would vote for a measure of which he was ignorant, in order to induce thereby another member to vote for a measure of which that member disapproved. He thought it quite regular and proper to create false impressions, and, in a pinch, to lie outright. The narrative of some of his exploits of this nature was written and published by an admiring friend, who dedicated the work to "the friends" of the deceased Senator.

"But mark: One day when he was confined to his room after a surgical operation, and was reclining on a sofa, with crutches within easy reach, a man ventured to make a proposal to him which the Congressional standard does *not* recognize as proper. The proposal was in substance this: 'Give *me* a certain document, instead of sending it home to the Secretary of State of Illinois, in whose custody it ought to be. Do this, and I will give you, in exchange, the deed of a tract of land, containing two and a half million acres, and worth twenty millions of dollars.' Such was the proposal. The reply was prompt and clear. 'I jumped for my crutches,' Mr. Douglas used to say;

[1] A. R. Spofford, "Lobby," *Lalor's Cycl. of Pol. Science*, ii, 781.

'he ran from the room, and I gave him a parting blow on the head.'" [1]

Whether there was more corruption, or less, in Washington at that period than at any since is not easy to prove. The writer who contrasts two periods, one of which he has personally observed and the other of which he knows about only by hearsay or the printed record, does not approach both with the same tests. For this reason James Ford Rhodes took some risks when he said in 1895 that "the executive and legislative departments of the national government were undoubtedly as much tainted with corruption between 1850–60 as they are at the present time." To-day the implication that corruption was conspicuous in the Washington of 1895 might be stoutly contested.

For another but kindred reason the writer who contrasts two periods that have each come under his observation, is to be taken with allowances. The earlier, the remoter period is almost sure to be dealt with the more charitably. This is particularly the case where advancing years have brought into play the common instinct of age to think old times the better. That is why we might accept as tolerant the first part of Horace Greeley's judgment, given in 1868 when recalling in his "Recollections of a Busy Life," his brief service in Congress during the winter of 1848–49: "When I was in the House there were ten or twelve members — not more than twelve, I am confident — who were generally presumed to be 'on the make,' as the phrase is; and they were a class by themselves, as clearly as if they were so many black sheep in a large flock of white ones." And we might see less charity in what Mr. Greeley went on to say: "I would gladly believe that this class has not since increased in numbers or in impudence; but the facts do not justify the presumption."

Nevertheless it must be admitted that about this time accusations of Congress began to be so common and severe as to warrant at least the conclusion that the standards of public life had become repugnant to those of private life. For an extreme example of contemporary criticism, take what Sidney G. Fisher wrote in 1862, while war was raging: "The 'lobby' has become an institution — a sort of a sub-Legislature or 'Kitchen Cabinet.' At every session of Congress a committee

---

[1] James Parton, "The 'Strikers' of the Washington Lobby," *Atlantic Monthly*, August, 1869.

is appointed to investigate the frauds of its members and of the Executive departments. Bribery is almost acknowledged as a part of legislation, whilst dishonest jobs and contracts so abound, that they are regarded as things of course. Even in the midst of the patriotic and noble feeling produced by the rebellion, the large expenditure caused by the war has called forth hordes of greedy speculators, who have grown rich on the plunder of the people's money. The habit had been formed; the management of parties had already fallen into the hands of gamblers and traders in votes and offices, who have plied their business, all the more briskly, because the dangers that beset the country multiplied the opportunities for profit. Everything has long been bought and sold, — legislation for the benefit of corporations and cliques of capitalists; grants of public lands; official influence; even the ability to introduce applicants for jobs to those who give jobs."[1]

And read what was said in the same year by whoever wrote for the "North American Review" (October, 1862) a review of Anthony Trollope's "North America": "It is too true, that previously to the present crisis the general government had become corrupt throughout all its functions; that lobbying, which means simple bribery, had become a part of the recognized machinery of legislation; that the whole patronage of the government had been used for political intrigues; and that the grossest frauds had become common in high places. It is further true, that important offices of state were so generally filled by men of mean capacity and questionable honesty, that the very name of politician had become a term of opprobrium and reproach. We cannot deny these facts. Alas! We are paying the penalty of our national sins."

This of course was gross exaggeration, but at any rate it may serve as a warning to those of our own time who incline to swallow avidly nauseous doses of the same type.

The increase of the tax on whiskey in 1864 led to charges of corruption by the "New York Tribune," and the powerful influence of that journal gave them wide credence. It was believed that illegitimate means had been used to defeat the taxation of liquor in stock, and the intimation was that fourteen members changed their votes for money. Rhodes after carefully studying the records reaches this conclusion: "Probably

[1] *The Trial of the Constitution*, 346.

the truth of the matter is that a very small number of Senators and Representatives in the 37th Congress would accept money for their votes and influence in legislation on private bills, and that if there were any change in the succeeding Congress, it was in the way of deterioration." [1] The care and judgment that have given Rhodes a leading place among our historians, warrant acceptance of this conclusion.

That there was deterioration after the War, cannot be disputed. It was another speculative period, leading up to the panic of 1873. Railroad construction was making fortunes. Demands for special privileges were pressed on all the legislative bodies of the land, Congress included, by all the methods that unscrupulous men could command. The scandalmongers reveled. They countenanced Louis J. Jennings in saying that in the annals of Congress might "be found revelations of legislative corruption without a parallel in recent times." [2]

James Parton thought the effect produced upon the country by certain tirades in the Senate showed how general was the feeling that Congress was sliding down toward the bottomless pit of infamy, where aldermen, councilmen, and supervisors of the City of New York were more than content to dwell. Yet, said he, these tirades were plainly untruthful.[3] And he went on to explain that as a rule men disappointed by legislation raise the cry of corruption; often as a means of revenge; often for the purpose of being bought off or "let in"; often in perfect sincerity, since they are truly unable to comprehend how an honest man can oppose a measure so necessary, so wise. "On the very morning in which I am writing these words," said Parton, "I have read a furious communication in a newspaper, denouncing a certain Legislature as corrupt, its members as 'bought and paid for like sheep in the market'; and, a little further on, the writer betrays the fact that the Legislature had just decided against *his* scheme of a railroad — a scheme respecting the wisdom of which the best informed men might honestly differ in opinion, nay, *do* differ, as everyone knows."

A railroad enterprise of this period brought to Congress the most notorious of its scandals, that of the Crédit Mobilier, so called from the name of the construction company organized

[1] *History of the U.S.*, v, 263 *et sqq.*
[2] *Eighty Years of Government in the U.S.*, London, 1867.
[3] "The 'Strikers' of the Washington Lobby," *Atlantic Monthly*, August, 1869.

to build the Union Pacific Railroad. Grossly exaggerated charges made in the heat of the presidential campaign of 1872 led to a committee of investigation, which found that Oakes Ames, a member of Congress and at the head of the railroad enterprise, had sold at least 160 shares of the Crédit Mobilier stock to members of Congress, at par, with interest from the first day of the previous July, the shares at that time being worth at least 200. Some paid the money for their shares; others, unable to pay, had their stock carried for them by Ames. It does not appear that any member was told of any prospective dividend except the first. Some members asked if holding the stock would embarrass them in their legislative responsibility. "No," said Ames, "the Union Pacific has received from Congress all the grants and legislation it wants and shall ask for nothing more." The fact seems to be that Ames and his associates were apprehensive that something might be done in Congress to interfere with their expected profits and what they regarded as their rights. The purpose in distributing the stock was to make friends against a possible time of need. The committee found Ames "guilty of selling to members of Congress" shares in the Crédit Mobilier at prices much below the true value, with the intent "to influence the votes and decisions of such members in matters to be brought before Congress for action"; and it recommended his expulsion. Also it found James Brooks, of New York, guilty of corruption as a member of the House and as a government director of the Union Pacific Railroad, and likewise recommended his expulsion. The House changed the resolution in each case to one of censure. Within three months both men died; their deaths undoubtedly hastened by the mortification and disgrace.

Ames was the product of his time, says Rhodes.[1] In business ethics the man who took a bribe was dishonorable, the man who gave it was not. But Ames did not think he was offering bribes; he had no idea that he was doing an immoral or indelicate act; he thought his transactions with members of Congress were the "same thing as going into a business community and interesting the leading men by giving them shares." "Was there any purpose on your part," asked Poland when Ames was giving his testimony, "of exercising any influence over members of Congress or to corrupt them in any way?" "I

[1] *Hist. of the U.S.*, VII, 11.

never dreamed of it," answered Ames; "I did not know that they required it, because they were all friends of the road and my friends. If you want to bribe a man, you want to bribe one who is opposed to you, not to bribe one who is your friend. . . . I never made a promise to, or got one from, any member of Congress in my life, and I would not dare to attempt it."

It did not develop that those members who took the stock had any expectation that it would have a bearing or influence on their course as members. Those who told a frank, straight story about the transaction never suffered appreciably from it; some of them achieved long careers of distinction in the public service, with no stain on their reputations as a consequence of the Crédit Mobilier. Members who evaded or lied, were pilloried by public opinion, and several of the most distinguished of them never recovered their political standing.

Luke T. Poland, of Vermont, chairman of the investigating committee, voiced the righteous sentiment of the country at the time, and wrote words worth the reflection of the legislator in all times, when he said in his report:

"This country is fast becoming filled with gigantic corporations wielding and controlling immense aggregations of money and thereby commanding great influence and power. It is notorious in many State Legislatures that these influences are often controlling, so that in effect they become the ruling power of the State. Within a few years Congress has to some extent been brought within similar influences, and the knowledge of the public on that subject has brought great discredit upon the body, far more, we believe, than there were facts to justify. But such is the tendency of the time, and the belief is far too general that all men can be ruled with money, and that the use of such means to carry public measures is legitimate and proper. No member of Congress ought to place himself in circumstances of suspicion, so that any discredit of the body shall arise on his account. It is of the highest importance that the national legislature should be free of all taint of corruption, and it is of almost equal necessity that the people should feel confident that it is so. In a free government like ours we cannot expect the people will long respect our laws, if they lose respect for the lawmakers." [1]

[1] *Poland Report*, x.

The chastening given to the country by the hard times following the financial crisis of 1873 seems to have had for one of its effects a purification of conduct. In 1877 James A. Garfield declared it to be demonstrable, as a matter of history, that on the whole the standard of public and private morals was higher than ever before; that men in public and private stations were held to a more rigid accountability; and that the average moral tone of Congress was higher than at any previous period in our history.[1] A decade later Bryce thought that though bribery existed in Congress, it was confined to a few members, say five per cent of the whole number.[2] Speaking to the Massachusetts Constitutional Convention of 1917 Charles G. Washburn, who had served in Congress, said it would be absolutely impossible to reproduce in the House of Representatives at Washington such legislative scandals as existed there within three or four years of the close of the Civil War. He asserted that legislative integrity and commercial honesty were never at a higher point.

As to present conditions there could hardly be testimony resulting from better opportunity to observe and know than that which Frederick H. Gillett has had as Speaker of the House. Commenting on strictures by J. Ramsay MacDonald, the British labor leader, who had been quoted as averring that there is more corruption in the House of Representatives than in the House of Commons, Mr. Gillett said, in November, 1923, that in his four years in the chair he did not remember an instance where he suspected or had reason to suspect any man in the House of being influenced by corrupt motives. This tallies exactly with my own experience through the same period. I have not observed a single vote nor listened to a single speech that I had the slightest reason to suspect was influenced by a venal consideration. I have not been approached, nor have I known of any member who has been approached, with a suggestion having any venal flavor.

The charge that may be brought against members of Congress is not of influence by bribes, but of influence by interest. In Congress far more than in the State Legislatures do men consider the possible effect of their votes upon their political fortunes. The explanation is simple. Many members are solely

[1] "A Century of Congress," *Atlantic Monthly*, July, 1877.
[2] *American Commonwealth*, chap. LXVII.

dependent on their salaries. For the time membership furnishes livelihood. Reëlection means at least temporary freedom from anxiety. If giving offense is avoided, long service may be won. Furthermore, service in Congress can gratify ambition for distinction and advancement to much larger degree than service in a Legislature. All this brings strong temptation to take the positions that will prove least dangerous when election time comes again. In the eyes of men who think Representatives should be nothing but transmitters, the result will not seem unfortunate, but surely it does not increase the public benefits that spring from independent thought and action.

Attention was forcefully called to the dangers of recent developments by a thoughtful journalist, George Perry Morris, observing Washington public life from outside the official circle.[1] He thought that no extra-constitutional phase of practical political reconstruction is going on now comparable in significance with the planting at the nation's political center of the administrative headquarters of the "interests," whether capitalistic or proletarian, agricultural or industrial, educational or philanthropic, commercial or scientific. Millions of dollars already have been invested in elegant quarters, and more are to follow. The scale of expenditure for officials and staff is generous — indeed it excites the wonder of foreigners. Funds are raised by assessment of multitudes of members, and the money is lavishly expended on the instruments of propaganda. Spokesmen come before committees or present themselves in the offices of Congressmen, not to bribe, not to persuade, but to command. Millions of votes are the means of coercion. So Mr. Morris saw the legislator of to-day tending more and more to become the object of a group competition fiercer than he is trained to resist.

The menace is real. Group organization is one of the perils of the times. Yet he who has faith in the common sense of the people will not be unduly alarmed. He will find that the zealots who misrepresent their organizations can rarely make good their threats. Courage, sincerity, integrity will still be respected. Under the new conditions the perils of politics may not after all prove to be seriously greater than they always have been where popular approval has been the instrument of Fate.

[1] *Am. Review of Reviews*, July, 1920.

Venality in the Legislatures

The record of the State Legislatures is no less free from stain than that of Congress, but shameful though some of it has been, yet the proof seems overwhelming that great advance has been made and that the standards of public honor were never so high as they are to-day.   Certainly there has been no single instance of corruption in our own time matching that which disgraced Georgia before she had been in the Union a decade. It was in January of 1795 that the Georgia Legislature sold to four land companies the greater part of what is now Alabama and Mississippi, a tract of the richest farm land in the country, found afterward to contain thirty-five million acres, for about one and a half cents an acre.   The news of the sale produced great excitement and indignation throughout the State.   Every member of the Legislature but one had been bribed.   The method used was the allotment of a certain number of acres to the legislator at a stipulated price which he was excused from paying until the market had risen forty or fifty-fold, when he received the difference.   Righteous men led a campaign that put into the next Legislature a majority pledged to wipe out the blot.   They promptly revoked the sale as a violation of the State Constitution, directed the repayment of the purchase money, and ordered the obnoxious act to be publicly burned. Two days later the sentence was carried out with due solemnity. The two Houses attended in a body in front of the State House. The Committee handed the act to the President of the Senate, he to the Speaker of the House, he to the Clerk, he to the Door-keeper, who threw it into the flames that had been lighted, tradition says, by "fire from Heaven" drawn down by a sun-glass.   All evidence of the passage of the act was expunged from the records.[1]

The Yazoo Frauds brought from the United States Supreme Court one of the opinions that have become landmarks in our constitutional history, that in the case of Fletcher v. Peck, to be found in the 4th of Wheaton.   Here but one phase of it may be noticed — John Marshall's handling of the contention that there had been a breach of a covenant upon a deed because some of the members of the Legislature were induced to vote in favor

[1] C. H. Haskins, *The Yazoo Land Companies*, 26; Alexander Johnston, "Yazoo Frauds," *Lalor's Cycl. of Pol. Science*, III, 28.

of the law which constituted the contract, by being promised an interest in it, and that therefore the act was a mere nullity. "This solemn question," said Marshall, "cannot be brought thus collaterally and incidentally before the Court. It would be indecent in the extreme, upon a private contract between two individuals, to enter into an inquiry respecting the corruption of the sovereign power of a State. If the title be plainly deduced from a legislative act, which the Legislature might constitutionally pass, if the act be clothed with all the requisite forms of law, a court, sitting as a court of law, cannot sustain a suit brought by one individual against another, founded on the allegation that the act is a nullity in consequence of impure motives which influenced certain members of the Legislature which passed the law."

To rehearse all the known episodes of corruption in the Legislatures would be a tedious task and serve no good purpose. Let it suffice to give the salient features of the record in a few of the States where scandal has been most prevalent, to prove first that it is nothing new, and secondly, to see if there is warrant for believing that our times are more virtuous than those that went before.

New York is the most important State for us to examine with care, because it has produced the largest volume of criticism and has done more than any other to give Legislatures a bad name. In its great city are published the periodicals and journals of the country that, taken as a group, do most to shape reputation and form opinion. Their contributors and editors are naturally as a rule more familiar with what goes on in Albany than in any other State capital. It has been a grievous misfortune for most of the Legislatures of the land that they have been assumed to be but replicas of the New York Assembly. If it should appear that even the New York Assembly is not to-day quite so black as it is painted and that it is better than it has been at many periods in its history, perhaps other legislative bodies may now get reflected credit just as they have in the past been so liberally bespattered with reflected damnation.

Bank charters gave birth to corruption in New York. When the Merchants Bank secured its charter in 1805, it was proved that several members had been tampered with, and in the Council of Revision Judge Spencer zealously protested against the bill, partly on the ground that its passage through one if not both branches had been secured by bribery and corruption. He pointed out that in the Senate, where the vote stood 14 to 12, Ebenezer Purdy, who had been bribed, was one of the fourteen, and that if Purdy had voted in the negative the bill would have been rejected. The protest was in vain and the bill became law, but Judge Purdy, who had introduced it, was forced to resign his seat to avoid expulsion for bribery.

One outcome was the enactment of a law exposing both the giver and taker of a bribe to the penalty of a fine not exceeding $1000, or two years of imprisonment. This law brought to grief John Martin, a preacher, as the result of another charter scandal, that of the Bank of America, incorporated in 1812. Martin was convicted of attempt to bribe members and was sentenced to confinement in the State Prison. Several affidavits to be found in the Journals of the Assembly disclose shameless attempts to corrupt in connection with this charter. The odium resulting discouraged bribery for a time, but a dozen years later fresh proofs of human weakness appeared in the circumstances connected with the chartering of the Chemical Bank. An investigation took place. Hammond's language about it ought to satisfy the most censorious. Says he: "The evidence given before the committee affords a most disgusting picture of the depravity of the members of the Legislature, and indeed, I might say, of the degradation of human nature itself." [1]

Episodes like this furnished some of the material that helped Andrew Jackson to rivet his hold on the masses. The Democrats were quick to turn the scandals to account. The country rang with questions like those that Samuel J. Tilden asked of a county convention at Hudson, New York, in 1833. "Can we be insensible to the rapid and fearful strides which a heartless, soulless moneyed power is making in our country? Are not monopolies and corporations springing up like hydras in every part of the nation? Are they not obtaining an alarming ascendancy over our legislative bodies, and over the people themselves?" [2]

These were the queries of a youth of nineteen, and not to be taken as intimating the views of a mature mind, but they reflected an opinion then rife, and indeed in its implication of the

[1] *Hist. of Political Parties in the State of New York*, II, 178.
[2] John Bigelow, *Life of Samuel J. Tilden*, I, 39.

relations between legislation and a heartless, soulless moneyed power, an opinion still familiar.

At the other end of his long public life Mr. Tilden delivered himself of a judgment indicating that either things grew better after the period of his youth, or else that the passage of many years mellowed backward vision. It was in 1874 that he told the Young Men's Democratic Club of New York: "I can remember perfectly well when you might stand in the legislative halls of this State — it is not more than eight and twenty years ago — and no man would suspect any member of being under any influence, consideration, or motive that was not perfectly legitimate." Calculation will show that the immaculate period thus described was about 1846.

He who will may attempt to synchronize this with the timetable of another admirer of the good old days, equally famous in the politics of New York, that astute politician Thurlow Weed. It was in 1866 that recalling the Legislature from 1814 to 1839 he said: "During all this period legislative action was marked, with exceptions few and far between, by honesty and integrity. The principles and habits of the earlier and better days of the government had not yet been weakened by influences which subsequently obtained." [1]

Weed is alleged to have used his political control of the New York Legislature in 1860 to secure the granting of several franchises for street railways in New York City, to a gang of lobbyists, and to have spent the four to six hundred thousand dollars of "campaign contributions" obtained in this manner to back the candidacy of Seward for the presidential nomination at the Chicago convention of the Republican party.[2] The fact that such an allegation could be made, indicates of itself the ground for attaching weight to Weed's conclusions in 1866: "Legislation and legislators have within thirty years become sadly demoralized. There is not in these times that high sense of official responsibility and legislative integrity that pervaded earlier legislation. Formerly the *suspicion* of corruption in a member would have put him 'into Coventry,' while knowledge of such an offense would have secured the expulsion of the offender. Now 'bribery and corruption' prevail to a greater extent than existed in the worst days of the Parliament of England, where,

[1] *Autobiography of Thurlow Weed*, 404.
[2] R. C. Brooks, *Corruption in American Politics and Life*, 71.

happily for England, the practice has been reformed, as it must be here, or corruption will undermine the government. No measure, however meritorious, escapes the attention of 'strikers.' Venal members openly solicit appointment on paying committees. In the better days of legislation, when no unlawful motive existed, it was considered *indelicate* to indicate to the Speaker any preference about committees." [1]

On comparing dates, it may be concluded that in New York State, as we have seen was the case at Washington, the decade of downfall was that just before the Civil War. The degree of deterioration by 1856 may be judged from the "Editor's Table" of "Harper's Magazine" for October of that year, where by indirection it was alleged that the balance of power in the Assembly had been held for two years by men who were ready to sell every vote; "that they did sell, last session, every vote for which they could find a purchaser; that more than one member committed offenses during the session for which they might have been sent to the State's prison, were accused of the same publicly, and dared not deny."

Things went from bad to worse. Jennings cites a letter to the "New York Tribune" dated at Albany March 18, 1867, in which it was asserted that not forty members could have been found for ten years past, willing to vote without a bribe. The New York Central Railroad Company had paid since 1853 half a million dollars in corrupting the members. In a letter in the "Tribune" of March 29, 1867, the same writer asserted a bill was passed through the Senate at a cost of $40,000. In the Assembly "between forty and fifty votes were paid for, at prices varying from $300 to $1500 each." And in a third letter published in the "Tribune," April 3, 1867, the writer said: "During all the many years that I have been accustomed to observe the character of legislators and the proceedings of the body, I have never seen anything to compare with the present assemblage of Representatives in point of shamelessness, rapacity, and recklessness of consequences. Their predecessors have often been noted for venality and greediness, but these people sell their votes openly, haggle about the price without pretense of concealment, and then boast of what they have been paid." The "New York Times" of April 8, 1867, confirmed these statements: "We venture to say that, as a general

[1] *Autobiography of Thurlow Weed*, 409.

rule, for the last ten years, one fifth of the members of each House have been in the habit of taking bribes for their votes — the fact is open, notorious to everyone who has had any personal connection with Albany legislation." And again: "We speak what hundreds of men know from personal experience, that no bill whose passage will confer pecuniary advantage upon any man or any corporation can be passed in Albany except by bribery — except by paying members to pass it. No man can get his rights, or prevent serious damage to his private interests, or avert ruin from himself and his family, except by bribery."

A memorial by the Citizens' Association of New York, September 13, 1867, and signed by Peter Cooper, is quoted as saying: "It is well known to every intelligent man conversant with public affairs, that corruption has become organized throughout our State, and has assumed such alarming proportions that capital, labor, and the industrial and commercial classes are oppressed to a degree unknown even in countries where the most absolute and tyrannical form of government prevails. The demoralizing influences of corruption are rapidly penetrating social life, and tampering with the Press, the Pulpit, and with the Judge upon the bench, poisoning justice at the fountain-head, sapping morals, religion, and education."

All this, had it no further support, might be questioned on the score of bias, and rejected. Jennings was a prejudiced scold. Newspaper correspondents are sometimes irresponsible and often rash of statement. Citizens' Associations are credulous. In this instance, however, some measure of official corroboration is at hand. So insistent were the charges that investigation took place. The usual difficulty in getting at the facts was found, for bribery is one of the hardest things to prove, but we may be sure that the need for action was demonstrated, for the special committee of the Convention of 1867 that made inquiry and took testimony, reported that official corruption was "a crime of deep turpitude, growing prevalence, and dangerous tendency."

It is probable that here as in Washington the low-water mark was reached in the period between the War and the Crisis of 1873. Then gain began. Theodore Roosevelt, reviewing in 1885 his personal experiences and observations during three terms in the Assembly, declared the standard of legislative morals certainly higher than it had been fifteen or twenty-five years before. That there was much viciousness and dishonesty, much moral cowardice, and a good deal of actual bribe-giving in Albany, no one with any practical experience of legislation could doubt; but at the same time he thought the good members always outnumbered the bad, and that there was never any doubt as to the result when a naked question of right and wrong could be placed before the Legislature clearly and in its true light.

Mr. Roosevelt and some of his colleagues interested in getting through certain measures they deemed for the public good, had occasion to "size up" their fellow legislators. "As a result," he said, "and after very careful study, conducted purely with the object of learning the truth, so that we might work more effectually, we came to the conclusion that about a third of the members were open to corrupt influences in some form or other; in certain sessions the proportion was greater, and in some less. . . . We felt absolutely confident that there was hardly a case in which our judgment as to the honesty of any given member was not correct." [1]

It is with great hesitation that one questions such a conclusion by Mr. Roosevelt, yet it is to be remembered that he was then a young man, but a few years out of college, without the wonderful knowledge of human nature which was to be his fortune in later years, and that his temperament inclined him to emphasis. If it was a fact that one third of the New York legislators of that day were open to corruption, the percentage was surely very much larger than has been the rule in American lawmaking bodies.

When he reprinted his article a dozen years later, in "American Ideals," he added in a note: "At present, I should say that there was rather less personal corruption in the Legislature; but also less independence and a greater subservience to the machine, which is even less responsive to honest and enlightened public opinion." He had in 1885 thought it likely that the standard of legislative morals would continue to improve slowly and by fits and starts, "keeping pace exactly with the gradual awakening of the popular mind to the necessity of having honest and intelligent men in the State Legislatures." That is just what has taken place. The nobler impulses that

[1] "Phases of State Legislation," *Century Magazine*, April, 1885.

came with the opening of the twentieth century, to stirring which Mr. Roosevelt himself as President so greatly contributed, showed themselves in New York as everywhere else. In 1907, when Hughes was Governor, "The Outlook" was able to say: "Not in many years has a Legislature of the State been so free from suspicion of corrupt influences; not in many years has a Legislature of the State passed such an array of good measures, or killed so many that were palpably vicious." [1] Three years later the Senate by 40 to 9 voted that charges against Jonathan P. Allds, Senator from Chenango, had been sustained. Allds was accused of soliciting and receiving bribes to stave off legislation adverse to certain bridge corporations. To avoid expulsion he resigned. "The Nation" said (March 31, 1910) that this was the first time the Legislature or one of its Houses had found a member guilty of a criminal act.

Nobody would risk saying that the Legislature of New York is yet stainlessly pure, but that it is vastly more virtuous than its predecessors of half a century ago, cannot be questioned.

Turning to Pennsylvania, we find much the same story as in New York — early instances of corruption, downfall about the middle of the century, attempt at reform after the period of venality following the Civil War, slow and irregular advance since then. Jeremiah S. Black, able and eminent, delivering in the Convention of 1873 a scathing denunciation of the Legislature, traced the corruption to corporate influences, beginning with the charter of the Bank of the United States in 1836, "pushed through the Legislature partly by direct bribery and partly by a base combination of private interests." [2] The early lapses of integrity may have taught men with mercenary instincts how to proceed, but it seems probable that their rascalities did not become customary until the decade from 1850 to 1860. Support of this view may be found in the testimony of Thaddeus Stevens, who was a member of the Legislature much of the time from 1833 to 1841. In a letter in the "Washington Morning Chronicle" of January 7, 1867, he is declared by Jennings to have said: "It cannot be denied, and therefore need not be concealed, that for the last ten or fifteen years the Legislature of Pennsylvania has had a most unenviable reputation." From this it is a fair inference that at any rate the situation was not notorious before 1850. Then it became so bad

---

[1] *The Outlook*, July 6, 1907, p. 484.   [2] *Debates*, II, 487.

that Stevens was able to say: "Corruption, bribery, and fraud have been freely charged, and, I fear, too often proved to have controlled their actions. No matter how honest when chosen, the atmosphere of Harrisburg seems to have pierced many of them with a demoralizing taint. A seat in the Legislature became an object of ambition, not for the per diem, but for the chance of levying contributions from rich corporations, and other large jobs. Corruption finally became so respectable as to seduce candidates for office boldly and to bid for them, and to pay the cash for the delivery of the ballot. The very office of Senator is known to have once been bought with gold, and to have been trafficked for on other memorable occasions in exchange for precious metals. Indeed it has become proverbial that the longest purse is sure to win."

Much dirty linen was washed in the Convention of 1873. Although in the spirited debate aroused by the onslaught of Judge Black, defense was not lacking, yet the volume of denunciation would warrant the belief that for many years the Legislature had in fact been the scene of much venality. Even here, however, it is probable that the volume of depravity was exaggerated. Otherwise John S. Mann would hardly have had the courage to say he believed for three sessions when he was in the Legislature he could write the name of every member who had ever been influenced by improper motives in the passage of bills, and that in no one of these sessions did that number exceed fifteen.

The moral decay that made representative government the despair of thoughtful men during this epoch cannot be said to have been due in any degree whatever to the ravages of time. In some of the older States it did not appear at all; in others it was unimportant; and it appeared in several of the newer communities. Indeed its uneven distribution prevents attempts to generalize. For example, in 1873 Governor E. S. Straw of New Hampshire wrote to a delegate in the Pennsylvania Convention: "There has never been any corruption charged in our House of Representatives." Governor Jewell of Connecticut wrote: "I am proud to say there has never been any corruption of the Legislature." [1]

On the other hand so clean a State as Massachusetts found itself driven in 1869 to investigate a railroad scandal, due to the

[1] *Debates of the Penn. Const. Conv. of 1873*, ii, 281.

Hoosac Tunnel. No such corruption was exposed as had disgraced some other States, but there was ground for carrying one specific case of bribery to the courts. Grants to the Hartford & Erie railroad next roused the better instincts of the State. Largely by the efforts of the "Springfield Republican" public opinion was stirred to such a pitch that Governor Claflin had its backing when in a veto message he wrote: "Great as are the advantages, they are not to be counted for a moment, if the State is to be disgraced by silent acquiescence in the course of deception, peculation, and fraud, practiced by the managers of the company." These episodes contributed to the establishment of the Massachusetts Railroad Commission, the pioneer of such bodies in this country, which, with a general railroad law, led to a great diminution of special legislation and its attendant corruption in public life.[1]

Of scandalous episodes in the newer communities one instance may suffice. A majority of the Wisconsin Legislature of 1856 is believed to have been bought to vote for a valuable land grant to the La Crosse and Milwaukee Railroad Company; $175,000 of stocks and bonds were distributed among thirteen Senators, and $335,000 of stocks and bonds were distributed among members of the Assembly. The bonds were worth forty-eight cents on the dollar, the stock sold in New York at from sixty to seventy-five cents.[2]

Let me spare you other proofs of weakness of some of our predecessors, and particularly let me escape the wretched story of the Southern Legislatures of the reconstruction period. It would only show what everybody knows — that untrained men do poor work and that men without moral standards are usually vicious, whether their skins are black or white. These Legislatures were in the hands of negroes recently freed from slavery, and the worst white element, for the most part adventurers or knaves or both. Their doings were abnormal and the abnormal has little of instruction or edification. It distorts the vision. It gives false values to human nature. It encourages groundless pessimism. It does not help.

---

[1] G. S. Merriam, *Life and Times of Samuel Bowles*, ii, 102 *et sqq.*
[2] *Report of the Joint Select Committee of the Wisconsin Legislature*, 1858.

SAFEGUARDS

PROTECTION against bribery of legislators was for a long time left to the common law and to statutes. There were some constitutional references to bribery, but it was tampering with voters that was in mind. With the alarming growth of the evil after the Civil War came the belief that there should be resort to the more solemn prohibitions of the organic law. In 1867 the special committee of the New York Convention investigating the matter reached the conclusion that the subject should no longer be left to the discretion of the Legislature, and it recommended an article defining bribery of public officers, providing for its punishment by imprisonment of not less than three years, and forbidding pardon or commutation of sentence except on satisfactory proof of innocence.[1]

New York did not act until later, but in that same year Maryland took the lead by directing the General Assembly at its very next session to provide punishment for bribing or attempting to bribe a public officer, as well as for demanding or receiving a bribe. Members and officers of the Assembly were specifically included. As part of the penalty the guilty man was to be forever disfranchised and to be disqualified from holding any office of trust or profit in the State. Next came Virginia, copying this in 1872. Pennsylvania followed, in 1873, by saying much the same thing, in somewhat different language. Since then more than a dozen other States have in one form or another put the subject into their Constitutions.

The New York Convention Committee of 1867 pointed out one serious difficulty in the way of enforcing the laws against bribery. It thought experience had proved the absolute necessity of exempting from punishment one of the parties if we would convict either, and so it recommended that the briber should not be punishable if the bribe was accepted. A committee of the Legislature investigating the scandals of the following year in connection with the Great Erie Railroad War, adverted to the same difficulty, saying the result under the existing law was either a refusal to testify, or remarkable forgetfulness, or something worse. Maryland in 1867 tried to meet the situation by providing that any person compelled to testify against another in bribery proceedings should himself be exempt from

[1] C. Z. Lincoln, *Const. Hist. of New York*, II, 379.

trial and punishment, and West Virginia said likewise. Pennsylvania, in 1873, declared that any person might be compelled to testify and that he should not be permitted to withhold his testimony on the ground that it might criminate him or expose him to public infamy, but that his testimony should not be used against him in any judicial proceeding, except for perjury. When New York acted, in 1874, it provided that if upon the prosecution of a person for receiving a bribe, the briber testified that he had offered it, then the briber should go scot free. All told, ten of the States have now seen fit to permit by their Constitutions, and others by statutes, this, to which the lively American imagination has given the name of "the immunity bath."

Of the various devices for the artificial regulation of the individual conscience, all more or less futile, oaths are among the least efficacious. In ancient times, when the fear of the Gods powerfully influenced human action, solemn obligations were not useless. In as intelligent and civilized a community as that of Athens, we are told [1] that the oath sworn by the dikasts was the occasion of frequent appeals by the orators, who contrasted the dikasts with the unsworn citizens attending the ecclesia, or public assembly. In the course of the centuries, though the old traditions and forms persisted, they gradually lost their vitality. Even in our early colonial days, while theology was yet a dominating influence, men had come to realize that solemn adjurations were likely to be vain. In April, 1649, a petition of the Maryland Assembly to the Lord Proprietor read: "We do further humbly request your Lordship that thereafter such things as your Lordship may desire of us may be done with as little swearing as conveniently may be, experience teaching us that a great occasion is given to much perjury when swearing becometh common. . . . Oaths little prevail against men of little conscience."

Nevertheless, the men who began the giving of written Constitutions to the world, were not ready to abandon the old ceremonies altogether, and so they required public servants to subscribe to professions for the most part abstract and elastic that may have proved of some general value in dignifying the entrance upon public service. It is, however, much to be doubted if any good whatever has been accomplished by apply-

[1] George Grote, *Hist. of Greece*, pt. 2, chap. 46.

ing the principle to specific obligations. A few of the States
have invited criticism on this score. When Illinois revised
her Constitution in 1870, a new form of oath was contrived
for members of the General Assembly, reading in part: "I
have not accepted, nor will I accept or receive, directly or indirectly, any money or other valuable thing from any corporation, company or person for any vote or influence I may give
or withhold on any bill, resolution or appropriation, or for any
other official act." Any member who refused to take this oath
was to forfeit his seat. The idea pleased the fancy of West
Virginia statesmen and they copied it, in 1872.

The next year saw that most fruitful of the more recent Conventions, the body that labored for many months over the Constitution of Pennsylvania. For an illuminating and exhaustive
discussion of oaths for legislators, the student may look with
profit in the second volume of its "Debates" (p. 481 *et sqq.*). It
fought long over a proposal to require from legislators upon
leaving office an oath that they had supported the Constitution; had not "knowingly listened to corrupt private solicitation from interested parties or their agents"; had not received
gifts or promises from such parties or their agents; had not
voted or spoken on any matter on which they had or expected
to have a private interest; had not done any act involving guilt
of bribery; and had observed the order and forms of legislation as prescribed by the Constitution. In the end this was
defeated by but one vote. Jeremiah S. Black had warmly
argued for it, and it received the support of such thoughtful
men as Wayne MacVeagh, Charles R. Buckalew, and Judge
Woodward. On the other hand, strong arguments brought
out the probability that the corrupt man will not hesitate to
swear falsely, making oaths of little or no avail. Nevertheless
the Convention, although unwilling to try to make the parting
legislator disclose his iniquity, thought the coming legislator
might well have his conscience propped by formal declaration,
and so required him to declare that he would not knowingly receive, directly or indirectly, any money or other valuable thing
for the performance or nonperformance of any act or duty pertaining to his office, other than the compensation allowed by
law. Nebraska imitated this in 1875 and half a dozen other
States have since then put it in their organic law.

Fraud and corruption in the processes of lawmaking may

vitiate the product in the esteem of the public, but will not affect its validity. Although the courts have sometimes been urged to inquire into motives, they have never consented.[1] Yet they have gone a long distance in trying to protect the sources of law from contamination. For instance, as far back as 1826 Chief Justice Skinner of Vermont, in Pingry *v.* Washburn, 1 Aiken 264, held that an agreement on the part of a corporation to grant to individuals certain privileges, in consideration that they would withdraw their opposition to the passage of a legislative act touching the interests of the corporation, is against sound policy, prejudicial to correct and just legislation, and void.

[1] Cooley, *Const. Limitations*, 187.

CHAPTER XIX

IMPROPRIETIES OR WORSE

THE appointment of members of Parliament to office became a great evil. The Stuarts brought into full flower the system of influence by means of favors. From the time of James I the King and his Ministers sought to control votes by lavishly granting offices, sinecures, or pensions. The Parliament of 1678 gained the name of "the Pensioned," because so many of its members were provided for out of the public treasury. William of Orange accepted the situation as he found it and if anything made it worse. Hallam tells us no check was put on the number or quality of placemen in the lower House. New offices were continually created, and at unreasonable salaries. The abuse became such a menace that in the Act of Settlement, passed in 1700 to regulate the succession to the Crown, it was provided: "That no person who has an office or place of profit under the King, or receives a pension from the Crown, shall be capable of serving as a member of Parliament."

This was quickly found to be too rigorous. Had it been maintained, among its effects would have been the exclusion of Ministers from the Commons, thus preventing the development of the Cabinet system of responsible government. To get rid of the evident embarrassments, the Commons, in 1706, sought to introduce into the Act of Security, as it was called, a list of officials who might be members. The Lords wanted to abolish the whole prohibition. After a long controversy both sides receded and a compromise was reached by way of enactment that no man enjoying during pleasure a pension from the Crown should sit in Parliament; that no man holding an office created after October 25, 1705, could be elected or reelected; that in case any member accepted from the Crown an office created before October 25, 1705, except a high commission in the army, his seat should thereby be vacated, though he would still be capable of reëlection, the object being to submit the acceptance of office by a representative to the approval of his constituents.

Since then such has been the law in spite of all attempts at modification. At first, however, though the law may have hampered the Crown in the exercise of improper influence, the snake was only scotched, not killed. Under the Georges the evil flourished alarmingly. Out of 550 members of the first Parliament of George I, no less than 271 held offices, sinecures, or pensions, and in the first Parliament of George II there were 257 thus exposed to the charge of being under the royal whip. Walpole dominated Parliament by the corruption of which this was a part. After his fall, it was one of the first of the evils struck at by the reformers of the time. In 1743 they passed a Place Bill excluding a great number of minor officials from the House of Commons. It did not suffice. The evil due to civil offices and pensions continued well into the reign of George III, playing a prominent part in the turbulent and disastrous years before and during the war with the American colonies. In the year when peace was negotiated, 1782, Lord Rockingham's administration came into office pledged to economic reform. The Civil List Act to which his name was given, abolished many useless offices and cut down the pension list. After that the ground for complaint became unimportant.

In the colonies the royal Governors frequently used the patronage as a mode of influencing the Legislature, freely appointing members to profitable positions. Observe, for example, what took place in Massachusetts Bay. In 1707 and 1708 were published three pamphlets on the "Deplorable State of New England," the first a bitter attack on Governor Dudley, the second a defense, and the third a renewal of the savage criticism. The Mathers are supposed to have had a hand in the abuse and their standing was such that at least some ground for their charges may be assumed to have existed, although the evident animosity makes it wise to take them with a grain of salt. "We have already intimated," says the third pamphlet, "how the Governor comes to have so many Friends in the House: that are so set on doing him justice, Right or Wrong. Besides the caresses of the Table, which are enough to Dazzle an Honest Countryman, who Thinks every Body Means what he Speaks; The influence which Preferments and Commissions have upon little Men, is inexpressible. It must needs be a Mortal Sin, to Disoblige a Governour, that has Inabled a Man to Command *a whole Country Town*, and to Strut among his

Neighbours, with the Illustrious Titles of, *Our Major*, and, *The Captain*, or, *His Worship*. Such magnificent Grandeurs, make many to Stagger Egregiously." The writer goes on to tell how Colonel Dudley rewarded a member from Ipswich, sarcastically called a "Sow-Gelder," by making him a Justice of the Peace. "Whether the *Cattle* are in less Danger, or the *People* in more, since this promotion, we who are Strangers to the Man, except by hearsay, know not; we suppose there never was a *Sow-Gelder* made a Justice except in *New England*, and that not till *Dudley* was their Governour." [1]

The lower House of Maryland resolved in 1722 that thereafter any Delegate accepting an office or pension from or under the Government, should be incapable of sitting longer as a member. A dozen years later, by a vote of 37 to 4, it expelled four men for accepting office. Thereupon the Governor, calling the Delegates before him in the upper House, scolded them, declaring that the members in question had not been disqualified by any law, inasmuch as one House could not give its own resolution a force equaling that of the whole Assembly. In punishment he proceeded to dissolve the Assembly. When in 1750 two members were expelled for the same reason, dissolution did not follow, but the lower House seems not to have been sure of its ground, for repeatedly it sent up a bill covering the point, until in 1774 the upper House passed the measure, but with amendments, one of which would require that the members of both Houses should serve without pay. Thus amended the bill was not heard from again.

In Virginia the Governors sometimes got objectionable men out of the House by appointing them sheriffs. Acts of Assembly in 1730 and 1762 absolutely disqualifying sheriffs, provided that Burgesses accepting offices of profit should resign their seats, but followed English example by permitting them to be reëlected. In 1685 Robert Beverly forfeited his seat by being chosen Clerk of the Burgesses. Failure to live up to the principle brought the unfortunate episode of John Robertson's downfall, described in the previous chapter. After 1691 the Treasurer of the province was appointed by the House, and from 1696 whoever might be Speaker served in that capacity. This helped the House in its control of the Governors through the financial powers that went with the office of Treas-

---

[1] *Mass. Hist. Soc. Colls.*, 5th Series, VI, 118.

urer. Upon the discovery after Robinson's death that his estate was seriously involved by reason of his loans of public money to personal and political friends, the House of its own accord and not forced by the home government, decided to separate the offices.

Profiting by their knowledge of Parliamentary diseases in the mother country, by their own experience with insidious Governors, and by such cases as that of Robinson in Virginia, the authors of the Constitutions for the new States took precaution. South Carolina led the way by declaring that if a member of the General Assembly or Legislative Council accepted any place of emolument, or any commission save in the militia, he should vacate his seat. Other of the original States so phrased their prohibitions as to strike with one blow at both the election of office-holders to the Legislature, and the appointment of legislators to office without forfeiting their seats. None of them, however, went to the extent of keeping the Governor from appointing to office members of the legislative branch. The remedy was aimed chiefly at what was thought the bad practice of letting a man exercise legislative power at the same time that he was enjoying the perquisites of other office.

When the Revolutionary War ended, apparently the evil had not got beyond such a remedy on either side of the water. Hatsell, publishing in England his first edition of "Precedents" the year before the close of the war, seems to have had no more in mind. After citing the details of thirty-three cases where members of Parliament had been replaced upon acceptance of office, and describing half a dozen laws on the subject passed in the course of the century beginning with the reign of William III, he went on to say (p. 46): "These laws, which are all passed since the Revolution, show how anxious Parliament has been, at several periods, to diminish, as much as possible, the effect of that influence of the Crown, which, from the disposal of so considerable a number of lucrative offices and employments, might have an improper bias on the votes and proceedings of the House of Commons." The bias he had in mind was that of the member who votes while he holds office. It may be inferred that as yet there was no occasion to prevent the bias that comes from the prospect of office, whether at the hands of the Executive or of the lawmaking body itself. This is also the inference from the fact that Lord Buckingham's

Civil List Act of 1782 says nothing about appointment to offices created during the term of the member.

In the course of the next five years something happened to broaden the field of American apprehension, but what it may have been, has not been recorded, so far as I have learned. The first indication of it that comes to my notice is an instruction given by Massachusetts in May of 1785 to her delegates, directing them to try to get from Congress a resolution that no member should, during the term for which he was elected, be appointed to any office in the gift of Congress. "It requires no very great sagacity to foresee," said the Massachusetts lawmakers, "that some persons forsaking the true interests of their country, will take corrupt measures to become members of Congress, with a view to possess themselves of lucrative employments, whereby offices in themselves unnecessary may be created and multiplied." Congress, however, by unanimous vote buried the proposal.

It came to life in the Federal Convention of 1787, made its mark on the Federal Constitution, and thence went into the fundamental law of many of the States.

Edmund Randolph of Virginia opened the debates in the Convention with a comprehensive address, in which he embodied a series of resolutions covering what he thought should be done. One of these, relating to the National Legislature, provided that its members should be ineligible to any office established during their term of service and for the space of [blank] after its expiration. Charles Pinckney of South Carolina followed with a like outline of a frame of government, his provision in this particular differing in that members of the House should not be eligible to any office under the Union during their term, and that members of the Senate should not be eligible during their term nor for one year thereafter, no reference being made to offices created in the course of the term. When in due time voting began, the Convention rejected, by ten States to one, a proposition to make members ineligible for three years after ceasing to be members; then, by eight to two, approved ineligibility for one year; and, with only Connecticut disagreeing, decided that in this respect the members of the two branches should be on the same footing.

Ten days later Nathaniel Gorham, of Massachusetts, moved to strike out the provision for ineligibility of members of the first branch. He considered it unnecessary and injurious. It was true, abuses had been displayed in Great Britain, but no one could say how far they might have contributed to preserve the due influence of the Government, nor what might have ensued in case the contrary theory had been tried.

Pierce Butler of South Carolina opposed the motion. This precaution against intrigue was necessary. He appealed to the example of Great Britain, where men get into Parliament that they might get offices for themselves or their friends. This was the course of the corruption that ruined their government.

Rufus King of Massachusetts thought this was refining too much. Such a restriction on the members would discourage merit. It would also give a pretext to the Executive for bad appointments, as he might always plead this as a bar to the choice he wished to have made.

James Wilson was against fettering elections, and discouraging merit. He suggested, also, the fatal consequence in time of war, of rendering, perhaps, the best commanders ineligible; and appealed to our situation during the late war, indirectly leading to a recollection of the appointment of the Commander-in-Chief out of Congress.

George Mason of Virginia was for shutting the door at all events against corruption. He enlarged on the venality and abuses, in this particular, in Great Britain; and alluded to the multiplicity of foreign embassies by Congress. The disqualification he regarded as a cornerstone in the fabric.

Alexander Hamilton saw the inconveniences on both sides. We must take man as we find him; and if we expect him to serve the public, must interest his passions in doing so. A reliance on pure patriotism had been the source of many of our errors. He thought the remark of Mr. Gorham a just one. It was impossible to say what would be the effect in Great Britain of such a reform as had been urged. It was known that one of the ablest politicians (Mr. Hume) had pronounced all that influence on the side of the Crown which went under the name of *corruption*, an essential part of the weight which maintained the equilibrium of the Constitution.

Gorham's motion was lost by four States to four, with three divided.

The next day James Madison, of Virginia, renewed his motion, made and waived the day before, to render the members of the first branch ineligible during their term of service, and for one year after, to such offices only, as should be established, or the emoluments augmented, by the Legislature of the United States, during the time of their being members. He supposed that the unnecessary creation of offices, and increase of salaries, were the evils most experienced, and that if the door was shut against them, it might properly be left open for the appointment of members to other offices as an encouragement to the legislative service.

John Rutledge, of South Carolina, was for preserving the Legislature as pure as possible, by shutting the door against appointments of its own members to office, which was one source of its corruption.

Mason came to the front again. He appealed to his colleague as a witness of the shameful partiality of the Legislature of Virginia to its own members. He could not suppose that a sufficient number of citizens could not be found who would be ready, without the inducement of eligibility to offices, to undertake legislative service. Genius and virtue, it may be said, ought to be encouraged. Genius, for aught he knew, might ; but that virtue should be encouraged by such a species of venality, was an idea that had at least the merit of being new.

King repeated the view that they were refining too much, and held that the idea of preventing intrigue and solicitation of offices was chimerical.

Wilson supported Madison. He animadverted on the impropriety of stigmatizing with the name or venality the laudable ambition of rising into the honorable offices of the Government — an ambition most likely to be felt in the early and most incorrupt period of life, and which all wise and free governments had deemed it sound policy to cherish, not to check. The members of the Legislature have, perhaps, the hardest and least profitable task of any who engage in the service of the State. Ought this merit to be made a disqualification?

Sherman and Gerry thought Madison's motion did not go far enough.

Madison further defended his motion, but it was lost, two to eight, with Massachusetts divided.

The main question then coming, it was separated. The part creating ineligibility during the term of service for which members had been elected prevailed by a vote of eight to two, with Massachusetts divided; and the part prescribing it for a year afterward was defeated, four to six, with Pennsylvania divided.

When in the following week the same problem came up in the matter of Senators, it was unanimously voted that they should be ineligible for a year after their terms had expired.

Nearly two months passed before the discussion was resumed. Then Charles Pinckney attacked the proviso as it stood. He argued that the making of members ineligible to offices was *degrading* to them, and the more improper as their election into the Legislature implied that they had the confidence of the people; that it was *inconvenient*, because the Senate might be supposed to contain the fittest men. He hoped to see that body become a school of public ministers, a nursery of statesmen. That it was *impolitic*, because the Legislature would cease to be a magnet to the first talents and abilities.

Colonel Mason thereupon ironically proposed to strike out the whole section, as a more effectual expedient for encouraging that exotic corruption which might not otherwise thrive so well in the American soil; for completing that aristocracy which was probably in the contemplation of some amongst us; and for inviting into the legislative service those generous and benevolent characters, who will do justice to each other's merit, by carving out for it offices and rewards.

Elbridge Gerry read a resolution of the Legislature of Massachusetts, in which her deputies were instructed not to agree in any case to give to the members of Congress a capacity to hold office under the government. This resolution had been repealed in consequence of the act of Congress calling the Convention, but was still the sense of the State.

Much more debate followed, and then the matter was postponed, presumably in that spirit of trying to conciliate and convince which accomplished so much of the work of the Convention.

On the 3d of September Mr. Pinckney tried to get the acceptance of this substitute wording: "The members of each House shall be incapable of holding any office under the United States for which they, or any other for their benefit, receive any salary, fees, or emoluments of any kind; and the acceptance of such office shall vacate their seats respectively."

This won the vote of only two States. Then Hugh Williamson secured by a vote of five to four, with Georgia divided, the insertion of the words "created, or the emoluments whereof shall have been increased," and the contest ended. The paragraph in the Constitution reads: "No senator or representative shall, during the time for which he was elected, be appointed to any civil office under the authority of the United States, which shall have been created, or the emoluments whereof shall have been encreased, during such time; and no person holding any office under the United States shall be a member of either house during his continuance in office."

The ratifying Convention in Maryland refused to ask for an amendment "that no member of Congress shall be eligible to any office of profit under Congress, during the term for which he shall be appointed." [1] The words "under Congress" would seem to indicate that the offices in mind were those over which Congress had control. The broader proposal, that no member should be eligible to any appointment during his term, met with the favor of the Conventions of New York, Virginia, and North Carolina, but nothing came of it. Proposals to amend, brought into the 1st and 11th Congresses, were equally fruitless. Yet on the second occasion a House Committee reported in favor and the vote lacked only three of the two thirds necessary to refer the matter to the States.

The question would not down. Some of the great among the early statesmen of the nation saw real danger in the practice of appointing members of Congress to office. When on one occasion George Washington was driven to it, he felt that the honor of his administration required him to show justification. No less than four persons, among them Patrick Henry, having declined the honor of appointment as Secretary of State to succeed Edmund Randolph, the President saw no other more suitable person outside the Senate and so he offered the place to Rufus King of that body, who, by the way, also declined. In a letter to Hamilton, October 29, 1795, the President spoke of his objections to the practice as being well-known to Hamilton. Monroe looked at it from the same point of view, at any rate, in the matter of diplomats. John Quincy Adams, then Secretary of State, records in his Diary, April 4, 1818, that Monroe told him "he did not approve the principle of appointing members of Congress to foreign missions, but, as it had

[1] *Elliot's Debates,* ii, 553.

been established in practice from the first organization of the present Government, and as members of Congress would not be satisfied with the opposite principle, he did not think proper to make it a rule for himself." [1]

Two years later, in recording that Strother had told him of a publication in the "Georgetown Messenger" severely censuring the President for appointing members of Congress to executive offices, and that Cobb of Georgia had proposed an amendment forbidding such appointment during the term or for a year afterward, Adams commented: "There are strong arguments both for and against such a provision." [2]   Cobb persisted, and in the session of 1825–26 got from a select committee of the Senate a favorable report, which went to the length not only of prohibiting appointment in the course of the term for which a member was elected, but also of directing that a member serving in the first half of the term of the President, should not be eligible for appointment until after the end of the President's term.

Thomas H. Benton was the Chairman of that committee. Writing in his "Thirty Years' View" (chap. 30) a quarter of a century later, he still deplored the practice and declared its abuse was ripening into a chronic disease of the body politic. Yet his next sentences show the disease had long been virulent, for he says: "When I first came to the Senate thirty years ago, aged members were accustomed to tell me that there were always members in the market, waiting to render votes, and to receive office; and that in any closely contested, or nearly balanced question, in which the administration took an interest, they could turn the decision which way they pleased by the help of these marketable votes.   It was a humiliating revelation to a young Senator — but true; and I have seen too much of it in my time — seen members whose every vote was at the service of government — to whom a seat in Congress was but the stepping-stone to executive appointment — for whom federal office was the pabulum for which their stomachs yearned — and who to obtain it, were ready to forget that they had either constituents or country."

It would not be surprising if it was Benton who inspired Andrew Jackson to take up the subject in his first message, in which he said the security of the Government would doubtless

<hr>

[1] *Memoirs of J. Q. Adams*, IV, 72.   [2] *Ibid.*, V, 62.

be promoted by the exclusion of members of Congress from all appointments in the gift of the President, "in whose election they may have been officially concerned." Presumably this was a dig at Henry Clay, whose appointment as Secretary of State after he had thrown his support to Adams in 1825 led to that famous and most unjust charge of "bargain and corruption." Jackson, however, thought that perhaps judges and also diplomats of the highest rank ought to be excepted from the exclusion.

The policy of a President of very different type brought the question to the front again many years afterward. It was William McKinley who, according to Senator Hoar,[1] "made what was before but an individual and extraordinary instance, a practice." Undoubtedly it had been a "practice" in the early years of the Republic, so that from the Senator's use of the word, we are to infer that meanwhile it had ceased to be such. Mr. Hoar characterized as a serious mistake "the appointment of members of the Senate to distinguished and lucrative places in the public service, in which they are to receive and obey the command of the Executive, and then come back to their seats to carry out as Senators a policy which they have adopted at the command of another power, without any opportunity of consultation with their associates, or of learning their associates' opinions."

"I think," said Mr. Hoar, "that sooner or later some emphatic action will be taken, probably in the form of a declaratory resolution, which will put an end to this abuse. But there will always be found men in either branch who desire such honorable employment. They will be men of great influence. There are also frequently men of personal worth who always support whatever the President of the United States thinks fit to do, and trot or amble along in the procession which follows the Executive chariot. So, if any President shall hereafter repeat this attempt it will require a good deal of firmness to defeat it."

Had the patriotic Senator from Massachusetts lived until the end of the Great War, would he have joined the rest of his party in criticizing Mr. Wilson for not naming any Senator as one of the Commissioners to arrange the terms of peace?

In a class by itself has been the question of giving military

[1] *Autobiography*, II, 45–48.

commissions to Congressmen.   The importance our fathers attached to preventing this may be gathered from the strictness with which they interpreted the constitutional provision almost at the start.   It was in the 7th Congress (1803) that they went to an extent well-nigh absurd in the case of John Van Ness, a member from New York.   He had married Marcia, the only child of David Burns, one of the original proprietors of the land on which the Federal City was located.   The Van Ness mansion on the bank of the Potomac adorned what was long the most elegant estate in the city.   In those days every able-bodied man between 18 and 45 (with few exceptions) had to perform military duty, and the District Volunteers, organizing themselves in a battalion, complimented Mr. Van Ness by electing him Major.   The President commissioned him, whereupon the House declared he had forfeited his seat.   As Ben: Perley Poore phrased it, "for the empty honor of wearing a militia uniform three or four times a year, and paying a large share of the music assessments, Major Van Ness lost his seat in Congress." [1]

The question next rose at the time of the Mexican War. Archibald Yell, the only member from Arkansas, accepted a commission as Colonel of volunteers, went to the front, and was killed in the battle of Buena Vista.   Five months after he took the commission, but before his death, Arkansas elected Thomas W. Newton.   Although a committee reported that Newton was entitled to the seat, the House refused to act on the report. Also it refused to act on a report to the effect that Colonel Edward B. Baker had forfeited his membership.   After several months of absence in the service, Baker resumed his seat at Washington, but resigned when controversy rose over his right so to do.   He was more fortunate than Yell in Mexico, but destiny had in store for him death at the unfortunate affair of Ball's Bluff.

In the Civil War and again in the Spanish War the issue was raised in various cases, but although the committee reports adhered to the doctrine of incompatibility, the House found ways to avoid unseating members who went into the military service from the motive of patriotic zeal.

Five sixths of the States have put provision on the general subject into their Constitutions.   About three fifths have

[1] *Reminiscences*, I, 157.

followed the Federal example in making legislators ineligible to offices created during their terms. More than a third have gone to the extreme of entirely forbidding the appointment of legislators to office. In this Georgia led the way, in 1796, by prohibiting the election or appointment of any Senator or Representative to any office having emoluments or compensation.

New York in 1821 said that no member should receive any civil appointment from the Governor and Senate, or from the Legislature, adding in 1874, "or from any city government." Changes of this sort in the organic law, evidently the fruit of experience, are always instructive. Of themselves they attest motives strongly impelling. Occasionally we can find description of what led up to them. For example take Governor Ford's account of the Illinois Legislature in its first dozen years (1818–30). "Offices and jobs were created," he says,[1] "and special laws of all kinds for individual, not general benefit, were passed, and these good things were divided out by bargains, intrigues, and log-rolling combinations, and were mostly obtained by fraud, deceit, and tact. It is related of Mr. Samuel Crozier, a former Senator from Randolph County, who was a remarkable example of the most pure, kind, and single-hearted honesty, that after serving two sessions in the Senate, at the close of the second, and after he had been bought and sold a hundred times without knowing it, he said he 'really did believe that some intrigue had been going on.' Thus it was that a corrupt, cunning, and busy activity blinded the eyes of the people and their representatives, governed in the name of the people, and divided among those who practiced it, nearly all the benefits and advantages of government." Is it any wonder that in revolt against this sort of thing Illinois when remodeling her Constitution in 1848 stopped altogether the appointment of legislators to office?

At least three other States after experience with the narrower form have found it wise to make the prohibition sweeping — Pennsylvania, which applied the Federal limitation from 1790 to 1873, Virginia, doing likewise from 1830 to 1902, and Nebraska, after shorter test, from 1866 to 1885. A committee of the Pennsylvania Commission on Constitutional Amendment and Revision advised in 1919 return to the rule of 1790, but the Commission rejected the advice.

[1] *History of Illinois*, 90.

Indiana began (1816) by excluding only from "any office, the appointment of which is vested in the General Assembly." This of course did not check at all the exercise of improper influence by the Governor, and so, in 1848, was added the familiar provision about offices created or with emoluments increased, during the term. Mississippi at the start (1817) extended the period of ineligibility to one year after the term, but in 1868 dropped the extension. Half a dozen other States still prevent a lawmaker from getting a newly created office for a year after his term expires.

Massachusetts sought to achieve the purpose of the Federal provision by statute, in 1857. This sufficed for more than half a century, and then in two or three cases special provisions were put into office-creating statutes so that members who had shared in passing the bills might be eligible to appointment. Although the men named were exceptionally fitted for the positions, the danger of abuse led in 1918 to placing the prohibition in the Constitution. It received strangely little notice in the Convention, chancing to be tied up with another matter in the same amendment, that of recess committees, on which all the debate was focused. The Vermont Commission of 1908 recommended putting it into the Constitution, but the proposal was not adopted. Whether popular instinct was reflected in the rejection, would be hard to tell, but there may be such an instinct, if we are warranted in drawing any inference from the refusal of the voters of Arizona in 1922, by a vote of 6899 to 25,095, to put the usual prohibition in their Constitution.

Probably, however, such a decision was due to ignorance of the history and nature of the problem. An electorate could hardly be expected to know how and why it has vexed wherever representative institutions have been adopted. For example, under Louis Philippe the French Government obtained its majorities in no small part by dispensing office to Deputies. Nearly half the members of the Assembly were at the same time officeholders. Guizot, himself scrupulously honest, controlled by distributing places, promotions, increases of salaries, contracts, and franchises. His ministry year after year refused assent for the passage of a law forbidding Deputies to hold office, and this was one of the causes contributing to the downfall of Louis Philippe, by reason of the discontent with the corruption that the measure would have ended. The Organic Law of November 30, 1875, declared that every Deputy accepting appointment or promotion to a salaried public position should automatically cease to be a member of the Chamber; but he may be reëlected "if the office which he occupies is compatible with the mandate of a Deputy." Certain incompatibilities are set forth in the case of French Senators. Belgium vacates the seats of members of either branch on appointment to any other salaried public office except that of Minister, but reëlection is permitted. In Chile no Deputy is to be appointed to office until six months after the expiration of his term.

Some of the newer Constitutions show the influences of such experiences as those of England and France. Thus in Poland a Senator or Deputy is to lose his seat on appointment to a paid office other than that of Minister, Under Secretary of State, or Professor in an academic school; and Czecho-Slovakia goes farther by declaring that a member of Parliament cannot enter the civil service until a year after he has ceased to be a member, but this provision does not apply to Ministers nor does the time limit affect members who had been in the civil service when elected, provided they return to the same department.

Nevertheless the sweeping exclusion of lawmakers from eligibility to other offices during their terms is a matter of doubtful expediency. The sapient observations of Judge Story in his "Commentaries" (Sec. 868) are well worth pondering. His reflections were not those of the closet philosopher, but of one who after serving in the General Court of Massachusetts, went to Congress, and then returning to the Legislature, became Speaker of the House, rounding out his close observation of men in lawmaking capacities by service in the Constitutional Convention of 1820. It was after this and while a Justice of the Supreme Court that with other sane comments on the subject he said: "It is not easy, by any constitutional or legislative enactments, to shut out all, or even many of the avenues of undue or corrupt influence upon the human mind. The great securities for society — those on which it must ever rest in a free government — are responsibility to the people through elections, and personal character, and purity of principle. Where these are wanting, there can never be any solid confidence, or any deep sense of duty. Where these exist, they become a sufficient guaranty against all sinister influences, as well as gross offences."

Perhaps, however, this contrast of two possible conditions in public life errs in not recognizing a third condition, that which in fact is the most common, with virtue and weakness intermingled just as in all the other relations of life. We ever need to be protected against ourselves, and it may be wise to thwart temptation by such barriers as this. Each case depends on whether the barrier does more harm than good. This particular barrier was probably more useful a century ago than it is to-day. The range of public activity was narrower, zest for office may have been keener, perhaps fitness was less considered, certainly effort has become far more specialized, thus emphasizing special qualifications. A notable change has come about in the manner of selecting many public officials, and particularly judges. In the days when it was much more common than it is now for judges to be chosen by the Legislature, there was especial reason for making members ineligible, as otherwise there would have been grave danger of the choice of comparatively inefficient men by reason of personal popularity.

It is the personal element that is uppermost in complete exclusion, but exclusion from newly created offices concerns measures more than men. The prime purpose is to prevent the enactment of unwise laws as a result of selfish ambitions. Upon this Judge Story comments: "The chances of receiving an appointment to a new office are not so many, or so enticing, as to bewilder many minds; and if they are, the aberrations from duty are so easily traced, that they rarely, or never escape the public reproaches. . . . The history of our State governments (to go no farther) will scarcely be thought by any ingenuous mind to afford any proofs, that the absence of such a disqualification has rendered State legislation less pure, or less intelligent; or, that the existence of such a disqualification would have retarded one rash measure, or introduced one salutary scruple into the elements of popular or party strife." So broad a generalization is hardly consistent with the course of so many Constitution-makers in providing against the dangers involved. Their apprehensions cannot be supposed to have been wholly imaginary. Yet it is altogether probable that there has been far less ground for their fears than critics would have us think, and that their prohibitions have been of slight practical usefulness.

National and State provisions in these matters have given

the courts repeated occasion to define "office" and "officer." That no clear-cut, unquestionable distinction is possible may be inferred from what followed the appointment by President McKinley, in 1898, of two Senators and a Representative as members of a commission to recommend legislation concerning the Hawaiian Islands. Their eligibility being questioned, the House and Senate, with Speaker Henderson and Senator Hoar as champions, took opposite sides, with learned and forceful arguments that would seem to have exhausted the question. The House contention, that a member of a commission created by law to investigate and report, but having no legislative, judicial, or executive powers, is not an officer within the meaning of the constitutional inhibition, may be presumed now to have become established by the refusal of Congress in 1922 to invalidate the appointment of Senator Smoot and Representative Burton as members of the commission to negotiate an adjustment of the debt of England to the United States arising from the World War. Yet it is to be noted that this conclusion was contrary to the views of a majority of the Senate Committee on the Judiciary (set forth learnedly, together with those of the minority, in Senate Report 563, 67th Cong., 2d Session), and it should not be forgotten that Senator Hoar's colleagues agreed with him in thinking the practice of making such appointments to be on the whole unwise, and that most of them believed it unconstitutional.

The one thing agreed upon by all the judges and text-writers is that an "officer" must be empowered to exercise some part of the sovereign power. As far as this may be legislative or judicial power, little difficulty arises. It is the executive power that makes the trouble. Here to discriminate between an "office" and a mere "employment" or "contractual agency," several tests are applied. Inquiry is made as to tenure, payment, the giving of a bond, the taking of an oath, and as to whether the duty is owed to the government, that is, the people as a whole, rather than the source of the appointment or election. These considerations vary in weight, but taken together have furnished a basis usually adequate for satisfactory conclusion.

Though not connected with dual office-holding, it may not be inappropriate here to say a word as to the legal aspect of the status of a lawmaker. It was held in New Hampshire as early as 1820 (Morrill *v.* Haines, 2 N.H. 246, 251), that a Representative was a "State officer." To the contrary in North Carolina in 1869 it was declared (Worthy *v.* Barrett, 63 N.C. 199): "Members of the Legislature are not *officers.* Theirs are places of trust and profit, but not *offices* of trust and profit." In 1908 it was held in Minnesota (State *ex rel.* Olson *v.* Scott, 105 Minn. 513) that "an office under the State" refers to other than the legislative offices of Senator and Representative. Yet in the Maryland constitutional amendment of 1922 for quadrennial elections is the phrase — "Members of the House of Delegates and all other State and county officers."

In 1912 it was held in Idaho (State *v.* Gifford, 22 Ida. 613, 632) that "the office of Congressman is clearly not a State office; it is provided for by the Federal Constitution, and the only thing left to the State to do is to hold the election." Is it a national office? The question came up in the first case of impeachment, that of William Blount, Senator from Tennessee. He alleged that a Senator was not an officer within the meaning of the Constitution, and hence was not liable to impeachment. The proposition was elaborately argued and the Senate decided it had no jurisdiction. There is no longer contention that a Senator or Representative may be impeached. Various decisions have made it clear that under Article 2, Section 2, of the Constitution there are legally no officers of the United States except those appointed by the President, the courts of law, or the heads of departments. The Supreme Court, however, has held that the same word may have different meanings, according to the context, and it has in some cases given to "officer" its popular meaning. This prevented the escape of Lamar, who was convicted upon an indictment charging him with having "falsely pretended to be an officer of the Government of the United States, to wit, a Member of the House of Representatives; that is to say, A. Mitchell Palmer, a Member of Congress, with intent to defraud J. P. Morgan & Co. and the United States Steel Corporation." The Court held that Congressmen came within the scope of the word "officer" as used in the Criminal Code.

THE LAWYER'S DUTY

THE canons of conduct for a lawyer who is also a member of a lawmaking body have not always been so clear as they are to-day. It is doubtful if now there is a legislature in any part of the world where it would be thought proper for an attorney member to take a fee for any work connected with legislation. That the contrary opinion was once entertained, is shown by the prohibitions found necessary. Evidently there was a time when lawyer members of the House of Commons added to their incomes by helping to get measures through the other branch, for the Commons ordered, November 6, 1666, "That such members of this house as are of the long robe shall not be of counsel on either side, in any bill depending in the Lords' House, before such bill shall come down from the Lords' House to this house."

In the Colonies, while the legislative and judicial functions were still confused and no small part of the important litigation either started in the General Court or Assembly, or was appealed to that body, instincts of propriety kept the people from electing lawyers to be Representatives, or even, as in Massachusetts, they were formally excluded. When in the eighteenth century they began to be admitted, some must have carried the fee habit with them, for we find the Connecticut statute prohibiting members from acting as attorneys, referring back to 1731.

Many years were to pass before the evil would be suppressed. It was still much alive in New Hampshire in 1790. William Plumer, Jr., tells us it was then the practice for members to appear as counsel and argue cases before committees or even before the House in which as members they were themselves bound to act and decide. "Besides the undue advantage which this gave their clients," the younger Plumer admirably observes, "the practice was fatal to their own impartiality of judgment and independence of action." The senior Plumer refused to put himself in the position of an advocate where he was bound to be a judge, and tried to procure the passage of an order prohibiting the practice. The refusal of the Legislature to pass such an order sheds light on the legislative standards of that day. More delicate was the sense of propriety in the Convention of the following year, which at Plumer's instigation put into the Constitution it framed: "No member of the general court shall take fees, be of counsel, or act as advocate in any cause before either branch of the Legislature; and upon due proof thereof such member shall forfeit his seat in the Legislature." [1]

In 1793 Vermont said substantially the same thing, omitting, however, the penalty of forfeiture of seat. Rhode Island put a clause of the same purport into her first Constitution, that of 1842, probably because there the exercise of judicial powers by the Legislature was still not uncommon. Why Mississippi should have had occasion to say essentially the same thing for the first time as late as 1890, has not come to my knowledge.

An allied question, yet with a distinct difference, is that of whether a lawyer may without danger to the public welfare serve as counsel in cases against the government for which he is making laws. John Quincy Adams records in his Diary, December 20, 1845, an offer of $5000 for an argument before the Supreme Court respecting the division of the legislative and judicial powers under the government of the United States. To this offer he replied that he had long ceased to practice law in any of the judicial courts of the United States, but as a member of the House would give an opinion to his visitor without any fee or charge whatever. He goes on to say: "It occurs to me that this double capacity of a counsellor in courts of law and a member of a legislative body affords opportunity and temptation for contingent fees of very questionable moral purity. Of one such transaction I had knowledge last winter, which in my mind was tainted with the vilest corruption; and I have heard of others, which I shall not specify, because they are familiarly spoken of as in no wise exceptionable, but for which the only palliation of which I deem them susceptible is that alleged by Lord Chancellor Bacon in his defence upon his trial before the English House of Peers — that there are 'vitia temporum' as well as 'vitia hominum.' It is a sad contemplation of human nature to observe how the action of the members of legislative bodies may be bought and sold, and how some of the brightest stars in that firmament may pass in occultation without losing their lustre." [2]

It had long been the common practice for members of Congress to prosecute claims against the Government, for fees or rewards, and our most distinguished public men were in the habit of doing it without censure or criticism; but a finer sense of propriety was developing, and in 1853 Congress by enactment made such conduct a misdemeanor.

Another phase of the matter came up in 1862 when Senator James F. Simmons of Rhode Island was threatened with expulsion because he had exercised his official influence over certain heads of departments to procure an order authorizing a certain person to manufacture rifles for the army and navy. The allegation was that the compensation of Simmons was to be $50,000, of which he had received $10,000 in promissory notes. Congress adjourned three days after the committee report, without action thereon by the Senate, and before the next session Simmons resigned. By an act approved March 3, 1863, the law of ten years earlier making it a penal offense for a member of Congress to accept a bribe, was extended to cover such transactions as this. It is now unlawful for a member or for anybody acting in behalf of either House or a committee thereof to receive money with the intent of having his decision or action influenced in any matter that may be brought before him in his official capacity or in his place of trust or profit.

The States seem for the most part not to have found need for regulation in this particular. From 1838 to 1865 the Constitution of Florida contained the provision: "No governor, member of Congress, or of the general assembly of this State, shall receive a fee, be engaged as counsel, agent, or attorney, in any civil case or claim against this State, or to which this State shall be a party, during the time he shall remain in office." Presumably some exceptional abuse led to this prohibition, and also presumably it was found needlessly drastic. Oregon put a provision of the same sort into the Constitution of 1857 with which she came into the Union, but its absence in other States warrants the inference that it is generally believed undesirable.

Another aspect of the relations between lawyer and client is distinctly iniquitous when perverted by corporations in their dealings with the Legislature. In the Pennsylvania Convention of 1873 John R. Reed said: "We all know that it is one of the most approved ways of bribing a member of the Legislature, to retain him as counsel for a particular interest upon which he is asked to legislate." Retaining fees to lawyer members, given with no particular measure designated, but for the purpose of biasing and vitiating judgment on any measure that may affect the corporation responsible for the blanket bribe, have not been confined to Pennsylvania. They are a menace that the legal profession itself should be the first to resent and disown. They are a disgrace to all concerned.

Log-Rolling

"Log-rolling" is the name that has been given to the exchange of votes, or in the vernacular the swapping of votes. The allusion is to neighbors who help each other roll away the logs from their clearings. Undoubtedly the practice goes back to the very beginning of lawmaking assemblies, but I chance not to have seen reference to it in other countries, nor in our own before the early years of the Federal Congress. Senator William Maclay says in his Journal under date of March 26, 1790, apropos of the fight over the assumption of State debts: "How true is the observation made by Henry, of Maryland: 'All great governments resolve themselves into cabals.' Ours is a mere system of jockeying opinions. Vote this way for me, and I will vote that way for you." The credit of inventing the system has been added to Thomas Jefferson's responsibilities, but it is altogether improbable that if he advised its use, he therein conceived anything novel. Perhaps he helped make it somewhat more habitual.

Naturally the evil would develop in the United States more than elsewhere, for we have been conspicuous in emphasizing the theory that the Representative represents his particular district first, the State or Nation secondly. This brings every member to the hall of assembly with local and special interests to be advanced, and as his reëlection may depend on his success with them, he is inevitably tempted to bargain with other members for support.

This is akin to bribery, and very likely most of the constitutional definitions of that offense would permit log-rolling to be punished, though so far as I am aware they have never been invoked for such a purpose. The men who drew the Constitution for the new State of Colorado, in 1876, thought more specific injunction desirable, and so they devoted an exhaustive section to providing that any member offering or promising to give, or giving his vote, in consideration of a vote by another, should be deemed guilty of solicitation and bribery in the one case, of bribery in the other; should be expelled without possibility of reëlection to the same Assembly; and on conviction in the civil courts, be liable to such further penalty as might be prescribed by law. Montana, North Dakota, and Wyoming copied this in 1889. Utah has by statute made log-rolling a felony, and possibly other States have done the same. Louisiana is more sensible in recognizing the uselessness of extreme penalties, its constitutional provision going no farther than to prescribe forfeiture of office for the offense.

A Mississippi legislator, by the Constitution of 1890, must take oath — "I will not vote for any measure or person because of a promise of any other member of the Legislature to vote for any measure or person, or as a means of influencing him or them so to do. So help me God."

Three of the newer States, North Dakota, South Dakota, and Wyoming, have carried to a singular and almost ridiculous degree precaution against that form of log-rolling which involves the swapping of legislative votes for executive favors. All three were admitted in 1889 with Constitutions providing that any Governor "who gives or offers, or promises his official influence in consideration that any member of the Legislature shall give his official vote or influence on any particular side of any question or matter upon which he is required to act in his official capacity, or who menaces any member by the threatened use of his veto power, or who offers or promises any member that he, the Governor, will appoint any particular person or persons to any office created or thereafter to be created, in consideration that any member shall give his official vote or influence on any matter pending or thereafter to be introduced into either House of said Legislature; or who threatens any member that he, the Governor, will remove any person or persons from office or position with intent in any manner to influence the action of said member, shall be punished in the manner now or that may hereafter be provided by law, and upon conviction thereof shall forfeit all right to hold or exercise any office of trust or honor in this State."

North Dakota supplemented this by a statute making it a felony for a member to promise the Governor to give his vote

or influence for or against a bill in consideration of the approval
or veto of any measure by the Governor, or his making of an
appointment or his removing an office-holder. Utah has
enacted to the same effect. Whether this has the more significance in connection with log-rolling or with the separation of
powers, the reader may determine. It is a case of killing two
birds with one stone, or rather of throwing the stone, for the
probability is great that neither bird has been so much as
wounded.

ODD ABUSES

HERE and there may be found odd instances of interference
with legislation, from motives sometimes honest but mistaken,
sometimes malicious, sometimes corrupt. That lively gossip,
Pepys, recorded in his Diary, May 13, 1664: "There was also
in the Commons' House a great quarrel about Mr. Prin, and it
was believed that he should have been sent to the Tower for
adding something to a bill (after it was ordered to be engrossed)
of his own head — a bill for measures of wine and other things
of that sort, and a bill of his owne bringing in; but it appeared
that he could not mean any hurt in it. But, however, the King
was fain to write in his behalf, and all was passed over." Prynne
urged in excuse "that he did not do it out of any evil intent,
but to rectify some matters mistaken in it, and make the bill
accord with the sense of the House." On calling him in after
debating his case, the Speaker acquainted him — "That the
House was very sensible of this great mistake in so ancient and
knowing a member as he was, to break so material and essential an order of the House as this to alter," etc., but were content to remit the offense.[1]

More comprehensive was the method of amendment that
commended itself to the bitter Elijah Lawrence and to Mott
of Monmouth, in the fifth New Jersey Assembly, under Colonel
Inglesby, in 1709. They were of the anti-proprietary majority
on a committee that the House had ordered to prepare a bill
settling the rights of the proprietors. In due time Lawrence
reported they had blotted out the entire bill save the title,
thinking this the best amendment that could be made. The
chairman, however, explained that contrary to his assent as
chairman, Lawrence "did blot out the bill," and Mott forcibly

[1] *Cobbett's Parliamentary History*, IV, col. 293.

detained the chairman in the room while Lawrence so did. The House voted them both in contempt, and ordered them to be brought to the bar of the House to ask forgiveness and to acknowledge the favor of the House in not expelling them. This they did and were then reinstated.[1]

More serious and with less excuse was an episode in the New Hampshire session of 1791, when William Plumer gave great offense to some of the Exeter men by a bill he introduced to tax State notes, in which they were greatly interested. "Your influence," said one of them, "may carry the bill through an ignorant House, as you can carry anything else there, but it will be rejected by the Senate." "We shall see," was the quiet reply. The bill accordingly passed the House, and was sent to the Senate, which, a few days after, sent a message to the House, informing it that the bill had been taken from the files, and could not be found. The House immediately passed it a second time, and sent it to the Senate, by whom it was enacted and became a law. "It is a curious illustration of the kind of men sometimes found in public life," comments Plumer's biographer, "that a member of the House (not from Exeter) afterwards boasted that he had pocketed the first bill, and came near getting the second. It will readily be believed that he was a holder of State notes." [2]

Doubtless some episode of this sort was responsible for the interesting rule of the Maryland House stipulating that "the combination of the safe lock shall not be made known to any other person than the Speaker and the Chief Clerk of the House, and said combination shall be changed during the first week of each session of the General Assembly." Let no reader unfamiliar with our Legislatures infer that such precautions have widespread occasion. Nowhere else have I found the like. Yet instances of tampering with bills are not uncommon. For example, take the case of a bill relating to police pensions in New York that in 1885 passed both Houses and after adjournment was signed by the Governor. It was then found that after it had left the Legislature a new clause had been inserted which retired the superintendent of police, one inspector, five captains, and more than one hundred other members of the force.[3]

---

[1] E. P. Tanner, *The Province of New Jersey*, Col. Univ. Studies, xxx, 368.
[2] William Plumer, Jr., *Life of William Plumer*, 111.
[3] "Sham Legislation," *New Princeton Review*, November, 1886.

In but one State do I note that such possibilities have been thought important enough to deserve constitutional attention. It is one of the youngest and most immature of States, New Mexico, which deems it necessary to provide that a person materially changing, altering, or making away with a bill pending or passed is to be deemed guilty of a felony, and upon conviction is to be punished by imprisonment for not less than one or more than five years.

Possibly some instances of alteration may have led to the unique law enacted by Connecticut in 1917, which requires that within a day after the reference of any bill to a committee, it shall be transmitted to the State Librarian, who is to cause it to be photographed, then delivering it to the committee within another day. A file of the photographs is to be kept by the Librarian, who may sell copies of any bill to the public at a reasonable charge and may on request give not more than three copies free to any member.

CORRUPTION IN GENERAL

CORRUPTION in one form or another having been a feature common to all governments in all lands and all ages, it is of interest and importance to know whether in this particular our time is better or worse, and whether democratic institutions as we have developed them show gain or loss. To encourage fair judgment, let me follow the foregoing record of turpitude with proofs of probity. For once, with whatever permanence this book may give, let the defense be set down. It has none of the morbid attraction that attaches to the abnormal. Is there nothing instructive in the fact that virtue is so commonplace that those avid for sensation think virtue tedious?

First to testify let me summon George S. Boutwell, legislator, Governor, Senator, Cabinet officer. "From 1842 to 1861," says Mr. Boutwell, "I was connected with the public affairs of Massachusetts with the interruption, perhaps, of three years only. In that period of time I heard of one instance of corruption on the part of members of the General Court which seemed, but without legal investigation, to have been well supported. With that exception there was no incident that came to my knowledge that seemed worthy of special condemnation. I should say in addition that in the last forty years I have not been made acquainted with any fact which would justify an adverse conclusion as to the character of legislation in Massachusetts." [1]

Couple with this the emphatic statement of Thomas Wentworth Higginson, author and reformer: "It is my firm conviction that there never was an honester body of men, on the whole, than the two Massachusetts Legislatures with which I served in 1880 and 1881." [2]

In the same State, R. L. Bridgman, oldest State House reporter in point of service, wrote in 1905 after watching Legislatures for a generation: "It is not likely that the purchaseable element of the 240 members of the House ever reaches higher than twenty or thirty, and probably not to that number often. Most of the members are honest and above suspicion." [3]

New Hampshire was one of the States that suffered sadly in reputation as a result of the muckraking period with which the present century opened. That brilliant novelist, Winston Churchill, helped to carry far the knowledge of the shortcomings in its politics. He and other young reformers did a useful service in raising there the standards of political honor. Yet I doubt if those standards had ever fallen as low as the pessimists believed. Speaker Rufus N. Elwell of the New Hampshire House said in 1905 that his experience with the Legislature then covered fourteen years, either as a member or as "one seeking favors." He testified: "I have been interested in bills for charters and would have been likely to know of it had the members been mercenary. In all those years I have never known of more than five or six men who seemed to me desirous of selling their votes. In each of those cases I found the other members ready and anxious to make the support for every meritorious measure so strong that there was no necessity of spending one cent for any man's vote, and I have never been placed in a position where I had to decide whether or not I would purchase votes. In case a man appears whose vote is for sale, he is invariably disliked and blacklisted by nearly every member of the New Hampshire Legislature." [4]

Rhode Island is the New England State with the longest and

---

[1] *Boston Sunday Globe*, April 27, 1902.
[2] "On the Outskirts of Public Life," *Atlantic Monthly*, February, 1898.
[3] "Legislative Efficiency and Morals," *New England Mag.*, May, 1905.
[4] *Boston Globe*, January 8, 1905.

cloudiest reputation for venality. The record of corrupting the very fountain of its laws, the electorate itself, goes back into colonial days. In our own times its Legislature has been reputed to be more under the domination of a boss than almost any other in the land, with rumors of the use of money that have gained wide credence. Yet Alfred S. Kenyon said in 1905: "During the forty odd years I was in the Legislature I was never offered a dollar of any man's money or given or promised any reward for voting for or against any bill. All this talk about graft and of members of the Legislature being thieves and robbers comes from people who do not know what they are talking about." [1]

Said Governor Mann of Virginia to the Governors' Conference of 1913: "I was in the Senate of Virginia for ten years, and I stand here to bear my testimony and would give it under oath, if necessary, that during those ten years of legislative life, I was connected with as high and as pure a set of men as our Commonwealth has ever produced. They made mistakes. Men always make mistakes. The only man who does not make mistakes, is a dead man; but live men make mistakes." [2]

Samuel W. McCall, not yet a Governor, but with twenty years of service in Congress and before that a personal knowledge of the Massachusetts Legislature, should have been qualified to speak by the card when in 1911 he said: "Undoubtedly you will sometimes find a corrupt legislator or a corrupt ring of legislators. But unfortunately you will sometimes find a corrupt voter and even a community of corrupt voters. Notwithstanding this latter circumstance the ballots of the great mass of the American people are pure and without taint, and at the same time I believe that the great mass of the legislators both at the State capitols and at Washington are honest men. It is a singular reflection which these self-anointed champions of the people make upon their purity when they assert that the people generally or often choose corrupt men to represent them." [3]

Lastly, let me take the stand myself. Personal observation

---

[1] *Boston Globe*, January 8, 1905.   [2] *Proceedings*, 317.
[3] "Representative as against Direct Government," Address before Ohio State Bar Association, July 12, 1911, printed as Senate Doc. 273, 62d Congress, 2d Session.

of more than a thousand men with whom I served in the course of nine Legislatures, did not disclose to me ten members whom with any warrant I could accuse of venality. Rumor did not endanger the good names of fifty, that is, five per cent of the whole. With but two cases of bribery did I come in contact. In one of them we expelled a member for guilt we thought to be proved. The other has not before this been brought to public knowledge. One day an acquaintance from another State, whose duty it was to protect the alum baking powder interests from attacks by other baking powder interests in all the Legislatures of the land, came to me with a detailed story of offers of support from certain members if they should be well paid, and threats of defeat if they were not bought off. I gave him the names of half a dozen strong men in the House to whom the story might be usefully told. The result was that the dangerous bill was thrown out, with never an inkling getting abroad as to what killed it.

Much the same measure was handled differently in Missouri. There a decoy "Public Health Society" succeeded in smuggling it through the Legislature of 1899 under the guise of protecting the public against food adulteration. A bill to repeal it passed the lower House in 1901 by a large majority, but was held up in the Senate. At the next session a repeal bill again passed the lower House, but was defeated in the Senate by the casting vote of the Lieutenant-Governor. He confessed that several attempts had been made to bribe him, and that he kept for ten days or so a check for one thousand dollars sent to him after the defeat of the bill, until, as the "St. Louis Post-Dispatch" put it, he saw that exposure was imminent. It was in probing this affair that Circuit Attorney Folk made a reputation. Several Senators confessed to their share in the bribery. One admitted having "boodled" for a long time and having made, as nearly as he could figure it, about fifteen thousand dollars out of his legislative experience. "Money," he said, "was offered on pretty nearly everything of importance." [1]

Painful and depressing as were exposures of this sort, it may have been that they were wiser than our Massachusetts action in preventing scandal. At the time I thought otherwise, for I knew that with us the episode was altogether abnormal, and it seemed imprudent to shake confidence in our General Court

[1] *The Outlook*, April 25 and May 23, 1903.

by furnishing food to the sensation-monger. Looking back over what has followed the exposures of that period, I am not certain that their beneficial results may not have overbalanced their harm. To be sure, while bringing some criminals to book, they wrought tremendous injustice by aspersing thousands of upright, conscientious, honorable servants of the public. For a time the occupation of a seat in a Legislature was in the public mind almost prima facie evidence of turpitude. Great damage was done by impairing the respect for our processes of government. Yet the work of Mr. Folk in Missouri, the remarkable achievements of Mr. Hughes in connection with the New York Life Insurance scandal, the preachments of Mr. Roosevelt, the indignation of a thousand prophets of righteousness, stirred the conscience of the people into establishing new canons of conduct, with the result that the standards of public morality were never so high in any large country as they are in the United States of to-day.

While recognizing the gains that have accrued, those of us who passed through the deluge of mud may be forgiven if we ask that the final record shall in point of accuracy approach the facts. If I might infer from the percentage of criticism of the Massachusetts Legislature I know to have been unwarranted, that a like percentage of criticism of other Legislatures has been unwarranted, a fair conclusion would be that all of them have been far from as black as they have been painted. In a few of them, however, it is altogether probable that conditions have been seriously discreditable. What may be justly emphasized, is that such conditions have been confined to a few of the forty-eight States — at the most not more than eight or ten, say a fifth of the whole number. So great were the cash profits of scandal during the muckraking period that we may be sure the other four fifths of the Legislatures would not have got off so lightly as was their fortune, if pretext for vilification could have been discovered. The grievous thing is that because corruption was shown to be rampant in a few lawmaking bodies, the people jumped at the conclusion that it was the rule in all lawmaking bodies.

As to Congress, Samuel J. Barrows pertinently asked if any pessimist would maintain that there was any such proportion of black sheep in the national folds at Washington as there was among the Twelve Apostles, one of whom was a liar and another a traitorous thief.[1] He well observed that the odor of a single unsavory reputation in a public body frequently creates the impression of general corruption and moral decay. What a pity it is that the spotless records of so many of our statesmen cannot offset the harm done by a few knaves! Barrows pointed out that there is no position in which a man could have better opportunity to grow rich at the public expense through bribery and jobbery than that of holding the strings of the public purse as Chairman of the Committees on Appropriations in House and Senate. Yet the men — William Boyd Allison and Joseph G. Cannon — who for years had administered this trust had remained comparatively poor, while in administering private interests the same intelligence and knowledge they had brought to bear upon public affairs would have made them both immensely rich.

Let him who would sweepingly impugn the honor of those who have served our country in its legislative halls, ponder the closing lines of the inscription that Senator Hoar wrote for a tablet to be placed in the Vice-President's room in the Capitol, where Henry Wilson died:

HE DEALT WITH AND CONTROLLED VAST
PUBLIC EXPENDITURES DURING A GREAT CIVIL WAR,
YET LIVED AND DIED POOR, AND LEFT TO HIS GRATEFUL
COUNTRYMEN THE MEMORY OF AN HONORABLE PUBLIC
SERVICE, AND A GOOD NAME FAR BETTER THAN RICHES.

So it has been with the great majority of our Senators and Representatives at Washington. Venality has been the marked exception; probity the rule. And some have lived on levels of virtue as lofty as any that history records. Let me cite just one instance, that of a man who served in the House for nearly thirty years, reached the office of Speaker, was a great Democrat — Samuel J. Randall. A year before his death, he decided that by reason of expense he must stay in Washington during the summer in a small house owned by his wife. Friends learning of this found for him a comfortable house a dozen miles out of the city. Says Colonel A. K. McClure in his "Recollections of Half a Century" (p. 448): "When Randall came on I met him at the depot and there presented him the lease with the

[1] " Is Our National Congress Representative? " *No. Am. Review*, November, 1903.

receipt for the rental. He hesitated for a few moments when he saw that the rent had been paid, and said with emphasis: 'I cannot accept this unless you agree that I shall refund it when able to do so.' I answered that we would discuss that question when he was in a more comfortable condition."

Two months later Randall handed to McClure the money for the rent. "It was evident that he had denied himself and his family many of the ordinary comforts of life in order to save $500 out of his monthly payments. I told him that it could not be accepted; that there were others besides Mr. Childs and myself who had joined in it, and that none would permit the money to be returned. He answered with emphasis: 'No public man can afford to accept gratuity from any.' I saw that he was very positive and that it was needless to discuss the question with him. I then asked that Mrs. Randall be called, and when she entered the room I handed the package to her and said: 'This money your husband insists shall be returned to those who rented this property for him, and it will not be accepted. You must take it and devote it to the comfort of your suffering husband and your family.' Mrs. Randall hesitated for a moment and finally said she would receive it."

Only a short time before Randall's death, Mr. Childs raised a fund, doubtless made up by Mr. Drexel and himself, that would give Randall and his family an income of nearly two thousand dollars a year, but Randall promptly and peremptorily refused it. Colonel McClure went to Washington to try to persuade him. Randall met the Colonel's first suggestion about the money with a positive refusal to accept. "He insisted that no man in public office could afford to receive aid from any one except as a loan that was certainly to be paid. I then told him that the fund would be presented to Mrs. Randall, and that he must, for the sake of his family, permit that to be done. After much painful hesitation he finally acceded to it, or, rather, said that perhaps he ought not to interpose to prevent it."

We too have had our Catos.

CALUMNY AND ITS EFFECTS

IT is easy to see why publishers of sensational periodicals and newspapers calumniated the servants of the public during the muckraking period. There was money in scandal, and the more gross, the more profitable. What mystified, was the credulity of scholars. Surely it was singular that men whose lives are supposed to be devoted to the search for truth, and in whose training scientific accuracy is nowadays the foremost consideration, should declare, as Professor James H. Hyslop declared,[1] that if honest men secured office, "neither their judgment nor their votes would count for anything in the system of blackmail and tyranny that make up the average legislator's work." To be sure, not many of the scholars went to quite that extreme, but it is within bounds to say that the greater part of them who have written about American public life in the course of the last score of years, have assumed the widespread prevalence of immorality in our lawmaking bodies, have argued from the premise that the tone of our public life is lower than ever before, and have treated those who serve the public as a degenerate caste, markedly inferior to mankind as a whole. It is refreshing to turn from their vague vagaries to the conclusions of one who sought facts, Professor Robert C. Brooks, of the University of Cincinnati, whose book on "Corruption in American Politics and Life" might be studied with profit by those who indulge in extravaganza whenever they approach the subject. Temperate discussion of the theme is so rare that it deserves especial commendation. Professor Brooks reaches these among other conclusions:

"(1) The prevalence of charges of corruption and of actual corruption in American politics is not of itself proof of our inferiority in political morality to the other great nations of the world.

"(2) Considering opportunities and temptations, our current political morality is at least not yet proven to be inferior to our business and social morality in general.

"(3) Unsupported charges of corruption are too frequently indulged in by practical politicians, reformers, and conservatives, the results being a popular moral callousness and a loss of social confidence which renders all constructive work more difficult."

To the injury shown in that third conclusion, I would add another — the disheartening effect upon the courage and enthusiasm of the individual lawmaker. What sort of work can

[1] *Democracy*, 128.

you expect from a man who is conscious that whatever he does, however lofty his aspirations, however noble his ideals, however pure his conduct, he will be reprobated by no small part of his fellow citizens? And how do you appraise the attractions of a career where the chances are only a little more than even that honesty will get public recognition and reward? After his three terms in the New York Assembly, Theodore Roosevelt concluded that in the long run, and on the average, the public will usually do justice to its representatives. "But," he said, "it is a very rough, uneven, and long-delayed justice. That is, judging from what I have myself seen of the way in which members were treated by their constituents, I should say that the chances of an honest man being retained in public life were about ten per cent better than if he were dishonest, other things being equal." [1]

Occasionally, but not often, the chance comes to a man to do something that will stamp on the public imagination the impression that he is conspicuously honest. Without this chance he may serve for years and get none other than a negative reputation — "We never heard anything said against him." Likewise some knaves get exposed and thereby ruined. But most of the honest men may expect no reward save the greatest — the contentment of their own consciences; and most knaves suffer no punishment save the worst — the remorse that conscience brings.

This, however, should be modified by the admission that within the walls of the legislative chamber there is prompt recognition of uprightness, for an American Legislature "sizes up" its distinctly honorable members with remarkable celerity and accuracy. Of course it is illogical not to advance also the converse of the proposition, for to discriminate those who are honest, would naturally involve discrimination of the rest as dishonest. Yet logical or not, the fact is that in the Legislatures with which I have been familiar, it was much easier to tell who were honest than to tell who were dishonest. In this my experience differed from that of Mr. Roosevelt, who averred that "the character of a legislator, if bad, soon becomes a matter of common notoriety, and no dishonest legislator can long keep his reputation good with honest men." [2]

[1] "Phases of State Legislation," *Century Mag.*, April, 1885.
[2] *Ibid.*, April, 1885.

Very likely he was right regarding New York, where venal men were numerous enough to embolden each other, and brazen defiance of morality brought little if any disgrace. In Massachusetts and three quarters of the rest of the States bribery is ordinarily so rare that the few guilty men are shamed into hiding their offenses. Bribery is one of the hardest things to prove, and in this particular most legislators are likely to depart from the habit of mankind in general and to remember that a man is innocent until he is proved guilty. For such exceptional charity there is exceptional reason. Men are rarely elected to public office unless they have some amiable qualities, and many succeed chiefly because they are gifted with the elements of popularity. It follows that a Legislature is peculiarly addicted to good-fellowship. Even the rogues are likeable rogues. Furthermore, their votes count just as much as any other votes, and nobody, however upright, cares to invite hostility to the measures he has at heart by alienating good-will unless that is clearly demanded. Also it has to be admitted that however praiseworthy in theory may be the informer and the accuser, in the actual relations of life human nature does not warm toward them. To pretend otherwise, is hypocrisy.

All this discourages censoriousness. It makes legislators reluctant to attribute guilt to each other, makes them slow to pass sentence, makes even the most righteous of them hesitate to crucify an associate. So it is not, in my judgment, quite the case, as Mr. Roosevelt thought it, that constituents can easily find out the character of a member by inquiring from his fellows. In the doubtful instances a legislator is likely to give the benefit of the doubt to his fellow-member, and not impugn his motives if inquiry is made.

CHAPTER XX

PRIVILEGE

PARLIAMENTARY "privileges" were intentionally left indefinite. Speaker Thorpe's case, in the reign of Henry VI, became famous by bringing out the reason for this. Thorpe, who was Speaker of the House of Commons, was sued by Richard, Duke of York, in the recess of Parliament. The plaintiff obtained a judgment and execution, upon which Thorpe was arrested and committed to the Fleet prison. After the recess the whole House of Commons presented a petition to the Lords, for the "enlargement" of their Speaker. The Lords thereupon propounded a question to the judges, and Sir John Fortescue, replying in the name of his brethren, declared that "they ought not to make answer to that question: for it hath not been used aforetime that the justices should in any wise determine the privileges of the high court of Parliament. For it is so high and mighty in its nature, that it may make law: and that which is law, it may make no law: and the determination and knowledge of that privilege belongs to the Lords of Parliament, and not to the justices."

Blackstone after citing this goes on to say that privilege of Parliament was principally established in order to protect its members, not only from being molested by their fellow-subjects, but also more especially from being oppressed by the power of the Crown. "If therefore all the privileges of Parliament were once to be set down and ascertained, and no privilege to be allowed but what was so defined and determined, it were easy for the executive power to devise some new case, not within the line of privilege, and under pretence thereof, to harass any refractory member and violate the freedom of Parliament. The dignity and independence of the two Houses are therefore in great measure preserved by keeping their privilege indefinite." [1]

In a sense it may still be true that privilege is whatever Parliament or any other legislature may choose to make it, yet

[1] *Commentaries*, I, 164.

Constitutions, statutes, and precedents so restrict the power that at least the customary lines of its exercise are fairly well established. For a classification of these, let us follow Hatsell, who found the principal view that the House of Commons seem always to have had in the several declarations of their Privileges, was to secure to themselves, (1) their right of attendance in Parliament, unmolested by threats or insults of private persons; (2) their thoughts and attention undisturbed by any concern for their goods or estate; (3) their personal presence in the House, not to be withdrawn, either by the summons of inferior courts, by the arrest of their bodies in civil causes, or, what was of more importance, by commitment by orders from the Crown, for any supposed offenses.[1]

Hatsell cites various English cases of arrest for affronting members. For example, take this entry: "On the 12th of February, 1620, Mr. Lovell complains, that one Dayrell had threatened his person: He is ordered to be sent for by the Serjeant; the same day he is brought to the Bar, but denying that he spake the words charged upon him, he is ordered to attend again the next day with his witnesses; he accordingly attends on the 13th, but one of his witnesses being a woman, Mr. Crewe and Sir Edward Coke oppose her being called in, very gravely objecting, on the authority of St. Bernard, 'That a woman ought not to speak in the congregation.' A Committee is therefore appointed to go out, and examine her at the door; and Sir Edward Gyles reports the examination, and Dayrell is ordered to be committed to the Serjeant, and then to come and acknowledge his fault, which if he does not do, then to be committed to the Tower." [2]

Typical of the American cases is that of A. P. Field, who in 1865 assaulted Representative William D. Kelley, of Pennsylvania, with a knife at a hotel in Washington. The House agreed to a resolution reported by a committee, to the effect that Field had been convicted of a breach of privilege "in the attempt, by language of intimidation and bullying, to deter [Kelley] from the free and fearless exercise of his rights, and in following up the attempt with assault." Thereupon Field was reprimanded at the bar by the Speaker.

The theory that a member of Congress has in such matters rights beyond those of any other citizen, was contested by a

[1] *Precedents*, I, 205. [2] *Ibid.*, I, 194.

minority of the House Judiciary Committee in 1870, when Patrick Woods assaulted Representative Charles H. Porter, in Richmond, Virginia, while he was returning to Washington. The minority argued among other things that Congress derived no power whatever from English parliamentary law; that members were exempt only as provided in the Constitution; that they have the same protection as all other citizens for their rights of person and property, no more and no less. These arguments did not prevail, for Woods was sentenced to imprisonment for three months. It is to be noticed that one consideration advanced by the majority of the Judiciary Committee in this case was that assault on members might interfere with the presence of a quorum, and that "assaulting and maiming members might become an inconvenient but sure method of changing a majority in the House in high party times, especially where that majority was not large." The inconvenience of this, particularly to the members maimed, would seem to be beyond cavil.

CRITICISM, SLANDER, LIBEL

WITHIN the right of attendance unmolested by threat or insult, comes the question of criticism. One of the dearest privileges of the citizen is that of scolding public servants. They have not always endured it as meekly as is now their wont. Time was when they resented it and used their power to punish. On the 15th of April, 1559, one Trower, a servant to the Master of Rolls, was ordered to attend, to answer for certain evil words spoken by him against the House. "He attends on the 17th, and is charged with saying, against the state of the House, 'That if a Bill were brought in for women's wyers in their pastes, they would dispute it and go to the question'; for which offence, though he denied the words, he is committed to the Serjeant's keeping." [1] "Paste" is defined by the Standard Dictionary as: (1) A bridal wreath; (2) Lace, trimming, gimp. Apparently ours has not been the only age when lawmakers have been charged with contentious trifling.

In 1586 Bland, a currier, was brought to the bar for using what were adjudged contumelious expressions against the House for something it had done in a matter of little moment. He was discharged by reason of his poverty, on making sub-

[1] Hatsell, *Precedents*, i, 190.

mission and paying a fine of twenty shillings, thus getting off more lightly than Doctor Harris, parson of Blechingley, who toward the end of the reign of James I got into trouble by taking a hand in trying to elect Henry Lovell to Parliament. When the parson appeared before the Committee of Elections and Privileges, his testimony brought him a reprimand, whereupon he preached a sermon criticising the committee and charging the opposing witnesses with falsehood. On the ground, among other things, of "scandalizing the proceedings and justice of the said committee," he was obliged to confess his fault on his knees in the House, to be sharply admonished, and again to witness his fault on beginning his next sermon, "desiring the love of his neighbors and promising reformation." [1]

Hatsell gives us a specimen of the epithets that cut to the quick: "On the 21st of February, 1628, one Burgess, who had called some of the Parliament men, 'Hell-hounds and Puritans,' is ordered to be presently sent for by the Serjeant; and a Warrant likewise for the parties that are witnesses against him." [2]

Even the good name of previous Parliaments was protected. When, in 1614, Mr. Martin, counsel for the Virginia Company, in a speech at the bar of the House had offended it by "taxing" the last Parliament, he was brought to the bar and reprimanded by the Speaker, whereupon was made "a very humble submission." [3]

These were all resentments of slander upon individual members or a committee or the House as a whole. Perhaps it was not until 1714 that anybody suffered for criticizing measures. Then Sir Richard Steele, the author, was expelled for writing articles in the "Crisis" and the "Englishman," "maliciously insinuating that the Protestant succession in the house of Hanover was in danger under Her Majesty's administration," the proceeding being, according to Lord Mahon, "a most fierce and unwarrantable stretch of party violence." For a considerable time, and especially during the reign of Anne, the House of Commons assumed a regular censorship over the press. Asgill was expelled on the pretext of an absurd book, "On the Possibility of Avoiding Death." Defoe was prosecuted by the House of Commons for his "Shortest Way with Dissenters." Tutchin,

---

[1] John Glanville, *Reports of Certain Cases, etc.*, 45.
[2] *Precedents*, i, 204. [3] *Ibid.*, i, 191.

by order of the House, was whipped by the hangman. Well-wood, the editor of the "Mercurius Rusticus," Dyer, the editor of the well-known "News Letter," and Fogg, the proprietor of "Mist's Journal," were compelled in the presence of the House to express on their knees their contrition. Whitehead's poem called "Manners" was voted a libel. Occasionally, as in the case of Hoadly, the House passed resolutions of approval.[1]

The folly of having a lawmaking body deal out punishment for such things, ended with the Wilkes episode, famous chiefly for firmly establishing the freedom of the press to criticize public servants, but also deserving no small credit for leading Parliament to refrain from further usurping the functions of the courts in applying the standards of morality. One of the three reasons for the expulsion of John Wilkes from the House of Commons in 1769 was his share in the preparation and printing of certain poems that unquestionably were in a high degree blasphemous and obscene. Only thirteen copies of the little volume containing them were printed and only the most private circulation was in mind, but the Government, ignoring all scruples in its mad desire to suppress Wilkes, bribed his workmen and got hold of a set of proof sheets. The House of Lords declared the poems "a scandalous, obscene, and impious libel," and addressed to the King a demand for the prosecution of Wilkes for blasphemy. Thereupon, though absent from the country, he was tried and outlawed. When four years later he returned to England and gave himself up, more than half of his punishment of fine and imprisonment was for this publication, and in the following year it was put forward as one of the reasons for expulsion from the House.

Another of the reasons has received much more attention, and deservedly, because it unshackled the newspapers of England. In 1763 Wilkes savagely attacked Bute and the Government in No. 45 of his periodical, the "North Briton." Grenville, who succeeded Bute, made Wilkes a political martyr by having him thrown in prison. Chief Justice Pratt held that Wilkes was exempted from arrest by reason of his privilege as a member of Parliament. His release was hailed with rejoicing in all parts of England, but his troubles had only begun, for the issue was transferred to the House, which voted by a large majority that the famous No. 45 of his paper was a seditious

[1] Lecky, *England in the Eighteenth Century*, I, 474.

libel and ordered it burned by the common hangman. Wilkes fled to France and the House punished him with his first expulsion. After he came back from France and was elected to Parliament from the county of Middlesex, the House expelled him for the second time, whereupon he was returned without opposition, only to have the House declare him incapable of sitting. Twice this was repeated, and then after another display of stubborn persistence by a majority of the electors of Middlesex, the House gave the seat to a minority candidate, Colonel Luttrell, though he had received but three hundred votes. This produced intense indignation throughout the country, for the fight between Wilkes and the Government had come to engross public attention. He had been made a hero of the people. Although in. prison, presents of jewelry, furniture, wines, and plate were showered on him, and £20,000 was raised to pay off his debts. When at last he was released, the City of London made him an Alderman.

In 1774 he was again elected to Parliament and this time was permitted to take his seat. The House got rid of the quarrel with him by deciding that his alleged incapacity to serve had ended with the previous Parliament, but it could not shake off his demand for vindication. In eight successive years he brought forward his motion to clear his record, and then in 1782 he made his victory complete by getting all the declarations, orders, and resolutions regarding the Middlesex election expunged from the Journals, as being subversive of the rights of the whole body of electors.

This memorable contest brought a great boon to the cause of freedom of speech, but it did not establish that liberty could safely sink into license. This was shown when, in 1810, the Commons having committed to Newgate the publisher 'of an offensive placard announcing for discussion in a debating society the conduct of two members of the House, Sir Francis Burdett in his place in Parliament denied the authority of the Commons and enforced his denial in a published address to his constituents. He was himself adjudged by the House to be guilty of contempt, and committed to the Tower by the warrant of the Speaker, but not until the aid of the military had been called in to overcome his forcible resistance. He then brought action for redress against the Speaker and the Sergeant-at-Arms, but the Court of King's Bench, and, on appeal, the Exchequer

Chamber and the House of Lords, successively upheld the authority of the House.[1]

In England the courts have held that though the public career of any member of Parliament or of any candidate for Parliament is of course a matter of public interest in the constituency, not so his private life and history. "However large the privilege of electors may be," said Lord Denman, C.J.,[2] "it is extravagant to suppose that it can justify the publication to all the world of facts injurious to a person who happens to stand in the position of a candidate." Electors, however, are entitled to investigate all matters in the past private life of a candidate which if as alleged would prove him morally or intellectually unfit to represent them in Parliament; but not to state as facts what they only know as rumors.[3]

Slander made trouble early in the American colonies. A Virginian, Francis Willis, in 1640 condemned the laws of the preceding General Assembly as repugnant to justice; and he also spoke in harsh terms of the Gloucester bench. The General Court, taking cognizance of his words, considered to be the more inexcusable because he was the clerk of that county and also a practicing attorney, sentenced him to stand at the door of the court house with a placard attached to his head announcing his offense; deprived him of his clerkship and attorney's license; and required him to pay a fine of twenty-eight pounds sterling, and to suffer imprisonment during the pleasure of the Governor.

P. A. Bruce, in his valuable "Institutional History of Virginia," tells us (II, 448, 449) the Burgess was invested with so much sacredness that it was considered to be as serious an offense to speak of him disrespectfully or scandalously as of the Governor or the members of the Council. "You are one of our Burgesses with a pox," Thomas Fowlkes remarked angrily and sneeringly to Hugh Yeo, a representative from Accomac County in 1666, then adding: "You go to Jamestown, and sett there, and sayes nothing, and comes back like a foole." These words were deemed to be highly derogatory to the general reputation of Yeo as a member of the House, and Fowlkes had to suffer in consequence. An insult offered to the Assembly as a whole was resented with even greater bitterness. For such an offense

---

[1] T. P. Taswell-Langmead, *English Const. Hist.*, 685, 686.
[2] Duncombe *v.* Daniell, 8 C. & P. 22.
[3] *Odgers on Libel and Slander*, 5th ed., 208 and cases cited.

Edward Prescott in 1660 was summarily committed to prison. When Giles Bland, in his rage over Philip Ludwell's failure to keep an appointment to fight a duel with him, nailed his glove, by way of defiance, to the door of the Assembly's hall, Ludwell being a Burgess at the time, the Assembly thought his conduct such an outrage on its dignity that it fined him a hundred pounds sterling and in addition required him to make his submission in its presence, which, we are told, he did with a proud and haughty air. In 1693 Thomas Rooke, for speaking abusively of the same body, and even more opprobriously of Mr. Kemp, one of its members, was sentenced to acknowledge the heinousness of his offense on his knees in the Assembly chamber, and in that humiliating attitude to beg the pardon of the Assembly as well as that of Mr. Kemp; and at the conclusion of the performance he was delivered into the custody of the messenger, who received orders to detain him until the House saw fit to release him.

The lawmakers of Massachusetts Bay found it necessary to protect the colony by general legislation against falsehood and slander. In 1644 the House directed a committee "to drawe upp an order for ye preventinge of falce rumors which are to frequently spread within this jurisdiction."[1] Presumably it was as a result of this that the next year the General Court passed an order that appears in the codification of 1660 as follows:

"Whereas Trueth in Words, as well as in actions, is required of all men, Especially of Christians, who are the professed servants of the God of Trueth; And whereas all Lying is contrary to truth, and some sort of lyes are not only sinfull (as all lyes are) but also pernicious to the Publick weal, and injurious to particular persons; It is therefore ordered by this Court and Authority thereof, That every person of the age of discretion (which is accounted fourteen yeares) who shall wittingly and willingly make, or publish any lye, which may be pernicious to the publick weal, or tending to the damage or injury of any particular person, or with intent to deceive and abuse the people, with false news and reports," shall be fined ten shillings for the first offense, or if unable to pay, set in the stocks; for the second; twenty shillings, or whipped with not more than ten stripes; for the third; forty shillings, or not more than fifteen stripes;

[1] *Records of the Colony of the Mass. Bay in N.E.*, III, 7.

and so on. If he appealed and the appeal was found causeless, the fine was to be doubled.

The first newspaper in America was called "Publick Occurrences" and it appeared in Boston, September 25, 1690. It appeared but once. Then it died, unwillingly. It had touched on local and military matters, innocently enough, we should now think, but the lawmakers thought otherwise. They said it came out "contrary to law" and contained "reflections of a very high nature." So they strictly forbade "anything in print, without license first obtained from those appointed by the government to grant the same."

Fourteen years later, either because the dignitaries had reconciled themselves to the idea of a newspaper or because John Campbell, Postmaster of Boston, had influence enough to get permission, the "News-Letter" was issued by Campbell with better success. That and the "Gazette," which followed in 1719, kept out of trouble with the government, but such was not the fortune of another journal, the "Courant," started by James Franklin in 1721. Its career has been made familiar by the "Autobiography" of Benjamin Franklin, brother of James. Benjamin, a boy of sixteen, was working for his brother when, according to the "Autobiography," one of the pieces in the newspaper on some political point gave offense to the Assembly. James, the account goes on to say, "was taken up, censured, and imprisoned for a month, by the Speaker's warrant, I suppose, because he would not discover his author. I, too, was taken up and examined before the Council; but, tho' I did not give them any satisfaction, they contented themselves with admonishing me, and dismissed me, perhaps, as an apprentice, who was bound to keep his master's secrets. During my brother's confinement, which I resented a good deal, notwithstanding our private differences, I had the management of the paper, and I made bold to give our rulers some rubs in it, which my brother took very kindly, while others began to consider me in an unfavorable light, as a young genius that had a turn for libeling and satire. My brother's discharge was accompanied with an order of the House (a very odd one) that 'James Franklin should no longer print the paper called the "New England Courant" '." After consultation among his friends, it was decided that the paper should be continued under Benjamin's name, and that went on for several months, until

Benjamin quarreled afresh with his brother and went to Philadelphia.

James was imprisoned a second time, in June of 1722, because the "Courant" charged the authorities with tardiness in the matter of a pirate who appeared off Block Island. The Council resolved that "said paragraph is a high affront to this government" and sent James to jail. After a week he said in a petition that he was truly sensible and heartily sorry for the offense he had given, acknowledged his inadvertency and folly, as well as his indiscretion and indecency when before the court, and on the score of ill health was permitted the liberty of the prison house and yard. The next month the Council voted that his paper should not be published "without the same be first perused and allowed by the Secretary, as has been usual"; and put him under bonds to be of good behavior.[1]

William Penn's Frame of Government of 1682 had this provision: "All scandalous and malicious reporters, backbiters, defamers, and spreaders of false news, whether against Magistrates, or private persons, shall be accordingly severely punished, as enemies to the peace and concord of this province." The authorities of Pennsylvania remembered this when the first newspaper there, the "Mercury," which was started in 1719, printed in 1721 this paragraph: "Our General Assembly are now sitting, and we have great expectations from them, at this juncture, that they will find some effectual remedy to revive the dying credit of this Province, and restore us to our former happy circumstances."

For this apparently harmless expression the publisher was summoned before the Council. Upon his averring that it was written and inserted by a journeyman without his knowledge, and his regretting the publication, he was discharged with a reprimand, and a warning never to publish anything more relative to the affairs of any of the colonies. Later, for an equally harmless paragraph that Benjamin Franklin had written, the publisher was arrested, committed to prison, and bound over to the court, but this time he showed some pluck and the matter ended.[2]

When in 1704 the Assembly of Carolina voted that every person thereafter chosen a member should receive the sacrament of the Lord's Supper according to the rites and usages of

[1] Frederic Hudson, *Journalism in the United States*, 51–71.   [2] *Ibid.*, 60.

the Church of England, the Rev. Mr. Marston declared that many of the members of the Commons House passing the act were constant absentees from church and that eleven of them were never known to have received the sacrament. From his pulpit he violently assailed the act and all who supported it. Ordered by the House to lay the minutes of his sermons before its bar, he refused, whereupon he himself was summoned to the bar, was censured, and ultimately was deprived of his living. At the same session Landgrave Thomas Smith was committed to the custody of the Messenger because he had reflected very sharply on the conduct of the House, in private letters that fell into the hands of the Governor. Smith was chosen Speaker of the next House and had the satisfaction of seeing the tables turned, for one of his persecutors, Colonel Risbee, the author of the bill against dissenters, was brought to the bar on a charge of vilifying the Assembly while over a bottle of wine at his tavern.[1] In 1722 when twenty-eight of the merchants of Charleston, among the leading men in the province, presented a petition and memorial against a new issue of paper money, they called attention to the bad faith of the Assembly in repealing several of the sinking fund acts before these could be put in operation. Thereupon the House retorted by declaring the memorial "false and scandalous" and ordered the signers to be taken into custody, where they remained until five or six days later they acknowledged their fault and were discharged after paying heavy fees to the Clerk and Messenger.

Faultfinders much excited the lawmakers of New Jersey. We are told that the overthrow of Coxe and his party in 1716 caused especially bitter feelings in the province, and rendered the members of the loyal party in the Assembly extremely unpopular in certain districts. The supporters of Coxe added fuel to the fire by circulating various writings attacking their opponents. Thus stung to action, the reorganized 7th Assembly named a committee on libels, with power to send for persons and papers, and numerous complaints of insult were brought before the House. William Lawrence reported that he had been insulted by one Benjamin Johnstone, of Monmouth, who declared in slanderous terms that Lawrence had been false to his trust in the Assembly. The House voted the words false and scandalous, and ordered the Sergeant to arrest Johnstone, but he, having

[1] Edward McCrady, *Hist. of So. Carolina*, I, 408 *et sqq.*

notice, escaped. A more serious charge was soon after made against Major Sandford and Thomas Van Buskirk, of Bergen, for scandalizing Philip Schuyler, the representative of the same county. Sandford and Van Buskirk were brought in by the Sergeant and charged with reporting that Schuyler "drank a health to the damnation of the Governor and the justices of the peace." Sandford acknowledged this utterance, and presented an affidavit of John Wright, coroner of Bergen, to prove its truth. Schuyler denied the statement of the affidavit, but admitted a quarrel and that he had kicked John Wright. In the end the House voted that Schuyler was not guilty and he took his seat.[1]

In New York John Peter Zenger, who started the "Weekly Journal" in 1733, got into trouble a year later. After repeated attacks on the government he was arrested on the first charge of newspaper libel in America. The arrest produced great excitement and his trial created intense interest. In the opinion of Gouverneur Morris, Zenger's acquittal was "the dawn of that liberty which afterward revolutionized America." His counsel was the celebrated Andrew Hamilton of Philadelphia. The Common Council of New York presented to Hamilton the freedom of the city for the remarkable service done by him to the city and colony "by his learned and generous defence of the rights of mankind, and the liberty of the Press."

In another episode of provincial New York the reader may find less of inspiration and more of amusement. The Journal of the Assembly for 1738, for the last day but one of the session, after a formal preamble reciting, "whereas on the complaint of Colonel Chambers that one Samuel Bevier had calumniated him by saying that he was a rogue and a liar, and likewise a fool and no fit person to be an Assemblyman, and that he was always drunk, and that the other Assemblymen could always make him do as they had a mind," and whereas Bevier could not be arrested before the dissolution, records that thereupon "the House unanimously certified that the said Colonel Chambers has duly attended the service of the House in a sober and discreet manner, and that he (as far as is known to the other members) always acted as a free representative for the public services of this country." [2]

---

[1] E. P. Tanner, "The Province of New Jersey," *Col. Univ. Studies*, xxx, 365–66.   [2] Ellis H. Roberts, *New York*, i, 283.

In Virginia the struggle to protect members of the Assembly against slander continued in the eighteenth century. As in the century before, the records seem to make little distinction between the privilege of the member and the privilege of the House, for as a rule a slander of even a single member was looked upon as a breach of privilege of the House as well as of that member. Mr. Fife, a clergyman of Norfolk, preached a sermon which reflected on two Burgesses, and the committee on privileges was ordered to investigate to ascertain whether there had been a breach of privilege. In 1735, John Doncastle was declared guilty of a breach of the privilege of the House and ordered into custody because he had used abusive language toward a member. Doncastle made excuse that he was irritable because of ill health and asked pardon for the offense. An assault on or abuse of a member of the family of a Burgess, or an assault upon his servant, was regarded as a breach of privilege and the guilty party was brought before the House, reprimanded and made to pay the costs. From many cases it is clear that the House took much care not only to defend its members, but to protect its own good name. Evidently it believed that to allow an innocent member to be slandered without protest, would have invited wholesale abuse and a consequent discrediting of the House itself.[1]

When the revolutionary crisis expanded the conception of democratic liberty, Pennsylvania led in declaring as to this particular matter: "The printing presses shall be free to every person who undertakes to examine the proceedings of the Legislature or any part of government." The devotees of freedom, however, were not yet quite ready to practice what they preached. For example, in April of 1778 the General Court of Massachusetts dismissed its chaplain, Rev. Dr. Gordon, for some free remarks written by him, and published in the newspapers, in which the Court was charged with "intrigue" in its conduct respecting the newly proposed Constitution. Yet on paper Massachusetts was ready to surpass Pennsylvania in emphasis, and it said in 1780: "The liberty of the press is essential to the security of freedom in a State; it ought not, therefore, to be restrained in this Commonwealth." A dozen years later Delaware modified slightly the Pennsylvania declaration, and added a proviso emasculating it: "The press shall be

[1] E. I. Miller, *The Legislature of the Province of Virginia*, 89–91.

free to every citizen who undertakes to examine the official conduct of men acting in a public capacity; and any citizen may print on any subject, being responsible for the abuse of that liberty."

It was what they deemed the abuse of the liberty that led the Federalists in 1798 to enactment on the subject in the notorious Alien and Sedition laws which proved fatal to their party. They were goaded to it by the venomous attacks of the Republican press. One section of the Sedition Law subjected to a fine of as much as two thousand dollars or imprisonment not exceeding two years, any man who printed or published false, scandalous, and malicious writings against the government of the United States, or either House of Congress, or the President, with intent to defame them, or to bring them into contempt or disrepute, or to excite against them the hatred of the good people of the United States, or to stir up sedition, or to incite resistance to law, or to abet hostile designs of a foreign nation. Prof. Frank M. Anderson made a thorough search to learn of all the arrests that followed. There appear to have been about twenty-five persons arrested. Only ten or eleven came to trial; in ten cases the accused were found guilty, and possibly in one other case there may have been an acquittal. At least eight newspapers were attacked.[1]

The democratic spirit that was assailed by the Sedition Law had already led Tennessee, framing her first Constitution in 1796, to say: "The printing-presses shall be free to every person who undertakes to examine the proceedings of the Legislature, or of any branch or officer of government; and no law shall ever be made to restrain the right thereof." Ohio in 1802 copied the Tennessee language with unessential modifications, and Louisiana (1812) said much the same thing.

Meanwhile the constitution-makers were attacking from another direction restraint of speech. The common-law theory that the truth might not be urged in defense against the charge of libel, was beginning to fall into disrepute. With respect to criticism of men in public life, its harm was especially conspicuous, and there was the weak point for the first inroad. Pennsylvania in 1790 put into her Declaration of Rights: "In prosecutions for the publication of papers investigating the official

---

[1] "The Enforcement of the Alien and Sedition Laws," *Am. Hist. Assn. Ann. Report for 1912*, 120.

conduct of officers or men in a public capacity, or where the matter published is proper for public information, the truth thereof may be given in evidence; and in all indictments for libels the jury shall have a right to determine the law and the facts, under the direction of the court, as in other cases." This was copied, literally or in substance, by Kentucky and Delaware in 1792, Tennessee in 1796, and later, with sundry variations, by other States, until now less than a dozen lack constitutional provision on the subject and rely on statutes. Some have inserted the proviso that the publication shall have been with good motives and for justifiable ends; others phrase it the other way about, to the effect that the publication shall not have been malicious.

Pennsylvania again took the lead, in 1873, by dropping the reference to truth, and saying instead that no conviction shall be had "where the fact that such publication was not maliciously or negligently made shall be established to the satisfaction of the jury," thus making good faith the criterion in the criticism of public officials. In 1809 the Legislature of that State had gone far beyond the Constitution as it then stood, in declaring by statute that no person should be indictable for a publication on the official conduct of men holding a public trust, and the decision of the New York Court of Errors in Thorn v. Blanchard (5 Johns. 508) went just as far, for it appeared to be the doctrine of a majority of the Court that where a person petitioned the Council of Appointment to remove a public officer for corruption in office, public policy would not permit the officer libeled to have any redress by private action, whether the charge was true or false, or the motive of the petitioner innocent or malicious. However, the opinion in Root v. King and Verplanck (7 Cowen 613–1827) frowned on the idea that a false charge should be permitted because its object was somebody seeking or holding office. A newspaper known as the "New York American" had described the Lieutenant-Governor of New York as presiding in the Senate and making a speech while in a state of gross intoxication, an object of loathing and disgust. The libel suit that followed, bringing a verdict for the Lieutenant-Governor, was carried to the full bench, which held that although the criticism was of a public officer, the defendant was bound to show the truth of the charge in order to justify. Chief Justice Savage said of the editors: "Their right to publish the truth is not questioned; but it is denied that, in the capacity of editors of a newspaper, they have any other rights than such as are common to all. The liberty of the press will not be invaded by requiring the conductors of our presses to stand responsible for the truth of what they publish."

In the New Hampshire case of State *v.* Burnham (9 N.H. 34) in 1837 it was decided that if the end to be attained by a publication is justifiable, as, if the object be to prevent the election of an unsuitable person to office, the occasion is lawful. Where, however, there is merely a color of lawful occasion, and the party, instead of acting in good faith, assumes to act for some justifiable end merely as a pretense to publish and circulate defamatory matter, he is liable in the same manner as if no such pretense existed. "If in such case," said the Court, "the defendant justifies by showing the truth, his motives are not in question. If upon a lawful occasion for making a publication, he has published the truth, and no more, there is no sound principle which can make him liable, even if he was actuated by express malice."

By statute in New York the Assembly has the power to imprison for "the publication of a false and malicious report of its proceedings, or of the conduct of a member in his legislative capacity."

Of late years our lawmakers have almost wholly abandoned the unequal contest with editors. The newspaper has the great advantages of the sympathy of the public and of the last word. However flagrant or false may be the charge, however conscious the lawmaker may be of rectitude and probity, he would better grit his teeth and keep still. If he retorts, he is sure to lose. Let him be consoled by the philosophy of the astute politician who cares not what the newspapers say of him, so long as they say something.

Occasionally a legislative body stung beyond endurance, will seek to punish its assailants. Several times to this end newspaper reporters have been excluded from Congress. In March of 1846 the House expelled the reporters and letter-writers of the "New York Tribune," because of a letter that roused the ire of Representative Sawyer, purporting to be a description of some of his personal habits "and otherwise of a very scurrilous and abusive character." Later in the month the Senate exerted the same power by expelling and excluding from the press gallery the editor, publisher, and reporters of the "Washington Times," by reason of charges of corruption it had made. In 1847 James A. Houston, reporter for the "Union," was excluded because of "false and scandalous reports of the proceedings" of the House.

In 1887 one Canfield, a reporter for the "San Antonio Express," published what the plea of the defendant in Canfield v. Gresham (82 Tex. 10) said was "a series of sensational, false, defamatory, and slanderous letters, relating not to any matter affecting the public welfare or concerning the official proceedings of said [Texas] House of Representatives, but to the personal appearance, manners, and habits of certain individual members of that House." Thereupon the House denied him the privileges of the floor. He tried to enter and the Sergeant-at-Arms went far enough toward excluding him to give a basis for the charge of assault, upon which the Speaker was arrested. On the ground that this was an obstruction to its proceedings, the House ordered the imprisonment of Canfield for forty-eight hours. Canfield sued fifty-six members of the House and the Sergeant-at-Arms, but the Supreme Court held they were within their rights.

One of the sorry effects of the fear in which some lawmakers stand of the press, is to be seen in the puerile attempts to forestall criticism by liberalities at the public expense. It is quite legitimate to furnish reporters with suitable accommodations and every reasonable facility for the proper performance of their work, but gratuities are as injurious to the public welfare as they are distasteful to the self-respecting newspaper man. The publishers of Iowa ought to have been more indignant than anybody else when it came out in 1908 that it was the custom for press representatives to allow supplies voted to them with improper generosity, to accumulate till the end of the session, and then take the equivalent in cash. When lawmakers themselves indulge in petty graft of this variety, they cannot expect reporters to have more squeamish consciences, but the employers of the reporters ought to be ashamed of permitting that sort of thing.

Goods and Estate

Hatsell gave it as the second purpose of Parliament in asserting privilege, that they might secure to themselves "their thoughts and attention undisturbed by any concern for their goods or estate." The first instance of privilege that Hatsell found would come under this heading, was cited by Sir Edward Coke, in the "Fourth Institute," p. 24, being the case of the Master of the Temple in the 18th year of Edward I, "whereby it appeareth," says Coke, "that a Member of Parliament shall have Privilege of Parliament, not only for his servants, as is aforesaid, but for his horses, &c. or other goods distrainable." Another instance was this: "On the 14th of June, 1610, Dr. Steward's servant is taken up for getting a woman with child; the Warrant was signed by four Justices, before the Parliament, but executed now; it is referred to the Committee of Privileges, who report on the 16th, and it is determined he should have Privilege." [1] In commenting on this case, Hatsell (I, 154) recalls that the law about bastards required the father to make provision for the child, and that in default of the weekly payment he was to go to jail. "It does not appear from the Journal," says Hatsell, "on what ground this commitment was made, whether only as being an offence *contra bonos mores*, or, upon the Act of Parliament, on his refusal to pay the money; it was however in neither case clearly a 'matter of the peace,' and therefore the House, consistently with that doctrine, determined he should have Privilege."

In 1621, the House was informed that Johnson, Sir James Whitlock's man, had been arrested. "The parties are immediately called to the Bar, and heard, on their knees, in their defence; and after a variety of propositions made for several degrees of punishment, it is ordered upon the question, 'That they shall both ride upon one horse bare backed, back to back, from Westminster to the Exchange, with papers on their breasts with this inscription, "For arresting a servant to a Member of the Commons House of Parliament;" and this to be done presently, sedente Curia.' And this their judgment was pronounced by Mr. Speaker to them, at the Bar, accordingly." This new and extraordinary punishment was awarded notwithstanding it appears from the Journal, and the Parliamentary proceedings, that both these parties had acknowledged their fault and craved forgiveness of the House, and of Sir James Whitlock.[2]

As a matter of practice the protection of servants from arrest

[1] *Precedents*, I, 133.   [2] *Ibid.*, I, 165.

came to an end in England in the reign of George III, but the claim of the privilege in behalf of the Commons was not omitted from the speech at the beginning of each Parliament until Speaker Peel dropped it in 1892. As the Lords do not claim their privileges after the fashion of the Commons, whether they have abandoned protection in regard to their servants is not clear.[1] In this country the privilege prevailed at least in colonial Virginia and Massachusetts Bay. No trace of it since the Revolution has come to my notice.

Freedom from Arrest

FREEDOM from arrest was for hundreds of years a parliamentary privilege of even more importance to lawmakers than freedom of speech. It came into view much earlier than any of the other privileges, dating indeed from the first gatherings of Englishmen for a share in government. The persons of those who were on their way to the King's Court and Council had a sort of sanctity such as is recognized in an ambassador. By the law of Ethelbert, "if the King call his 'leod' to him, and any one there do them evil," the offender must make double satisfaction to the injured person and pay a fine to the King. Canute willed, in a law which must have had a still wider application, "that every man be entitled to grith to the gemot and from the gemot except he be a notorious thief." The laws ascribed to Edward the Confessor recognize a particular immunity for persons going to and from the synods.[2]

With the instituting of Parliaments the importance of the doctrine grew. Manifestly the King could not afford to let anybody interfere with the agents of the shires and boroughs whom he summoned to treat with him about supplying money for his needs. So he made supreme the necessity of attending the business of his highest court and took the members under his protection. Under Edward I and II it was established that it was unbecoming for a member to be distrained while at the session, and a statute of 1432 required the punishment of anybody who molested a member in coming, double damages being imposed as in Ethelbert's time.

At first the House of Commons did not try by virtue of its

---

[1] Adrian Wontner. *The Lords, Their History and Powers*, 21–22.
[2] Stubbs, *Const. Hist.*, III, 494.

own authority to deliver out of custody a member who had been imprisoned, but proceeded by an Act of Parliament to enable the Chancellor to issue his writ for the member's release. Probably the first case where the House went ahead directly was that of George Ferrers, member for Plymouth, who in 1543 was arrested for debt and committed to prison, under the orders of the Judges of the King's Bench. The House, on receiving information of the fact, sent the Sergeant to demand the member. In the execution of his orders he met with resistance, his mace was broken, and his assistant knocked down. In consequence, the Sheriff of London and those who were concerned in the arrests were brought before the House, when some of them were committed to the Tower, others to Newgate, where they remained until they were discharged on the petition of the Lord Mayor.

The proceeding was not repeated till 1575, when they sent the Sergeant to deliver Smallet, a member's servant. Upon discovery that the man had fraudulently procured his own arrest to get rid of a debt, he was committed for a month and ordered to pay the plaintiff a hundred pounds, which was possibly the amount of what he owed.

Before the end of Elizabeth's reign it had become the established rule of privilege that no subpœna or summons for the attendance of a member in any other court ought to be served without leave obtained or information given to the House; and that the persons who procured or served such process were guilty of a breach of privilege, and were punishable by commitment or otherwise, on the order of the House.

In Potter's "Dwarris on Statutes," p. 601, reference is made to expressions of Lord Mansfield, advocating in 1770 the passage of a bill that ultimately became a law, the provisions of which greatly facilitated the prosecution of civil actions against members of Parliament, and restrained only arrests of their persons in such actions. The remarks of Lord Mansfield, made so shortly before the Revolution, and undoubtedly referring to the decision in the Wilkes case (2 Wils. 151), are of special significance. Among other things he said:

"It may not be popular to take away any of the privileges of Parliament, for I very well remember, and many of your Lordships may remember, that not long ago the popular cry was for an extension of privileges, and so far did they carry it at that time that it was said that privilege protected members from criminal actions, and such was the power of popular prejudice over weak minds that the very decisions of some of the courts were tinctured with that doctrine. . . . The laws of this country allow no place or employment as a sanctuary for crime, and where I have the honor to sit as judge neither royal favor nor popular applause shall ever protect the guilty. . . . Members of both Houses should be free in their persons in cases of civil suits, for there may come a time when the safety and welfare of this whole empire may depend upon their attendance in Parliament. God forbid that I should advise any measure that would in future endanger the state. But this bill has no such tendency. It expressly secures the persons of members from arrest in all civil suits." [1]

The privilege was repeatedly abused. In 1558 the House, by 112 to 107, allowed it to a member who had defrauded merchants of London of wares to the value of £300, meaning to defraud them thereof under color of privilege. In another instance a member was held entitled to his privilege although it was notorious that he had bought his seat to escape the payment of his debts, which amounted to £23,000. Lord Beaconsfield described one of the characters in his earliest novel as "so involved that the only way to keep him out of the House of Correction was to get him into the House of Commons." The sneer was justified by the facts. A few years before he wrote "Vivian Grey," a debtor, a prisoner in the Fleet, had been elected for Beverley, whereupon, instead of repairing to his parliamentary duties, he departed from the country. The privilege that had been a necessity in one age had become a scandal in another. Theoretically the scandal that occurred in the election of a debtor for Beverley might recur to-day, but virtually its recurrence is impossible from the course which legislation has assumed. Members of the House of Commons are still free from arrest during the session of Parliament and for a reasonable time before its beginning and after its termination. But no inconvenience has of late years resulted, nor is it likely to result, from the perpetuation of this privilege. [2]

Hatsell did not find a single instance of a member's claiming the privilege in order to withdraw himself from the criminal

---

[1] Quoted by White, J., in Williamson *v.* U.S., 207 U.S. 427 (1908).
[2] Spencer Walpole, *The Electorate and the Legislature*, 99.

law of the land. For offenses against the public peace the members always thought themselves amenable to the laws of their country. They were contented with being substantially secured against any violence from the Crown, or its Ministers; but readily submitted themselves to the judicature of the King's Bench, the legal court of criminal jurisdiction, well knowing that "Privilege," which is allowed in case of "public service for the Commonwealth, must not be used for the danger of the Commonwealth." [1]

On the Continent persecution of legislators by the executive branch or by partisan opponents has made general the prohibition of arrest unless the offender is caught in the act of a criminal offense; and even then prosecution and imprisonment must as a rule be deferred till the end of the session, in some countries unless specifically permitted by the House concerned, in others upon its demand. Germany allows arrest also on the day following the commission of a crime. In Austria and Poland the arrest may be canceled. In Jugoslavia the right of immunity begins on the day of election. In Czecho-Slovakia consent must be given for even a civil prosecution. In Poland proceedings begun before election may be suspended until the end of the term of the Deputy. The Italian Senate is declared to be alone competent to judge of the imputed misdemeanors of Senators. Doubtless it was European experience that led the South American Republics to be equally careful in protecting the immunities of members. It need be noted of them only that Chile shields members from the day of election, Brazil from the day they get their credentials until the next election; and that Argentina calls for a two-thirds vote of Senate or House in order to suspend and to surrender for trial a member against whom charges in writing have been filed before the ordinary tribunals.

Privilege in the matter of arrest was early provided in Virginia, not so much for protection against the Executive as against bothersome creditors. Number 11 of the "Laws and Orders concluded on by the General Assembly [of Virginia], March the 5th, 1623," reads: "That no Burgesses of the General Assembly shall be arrested during the time of the Assembly, a week before and a week after, under pain of the creditor's forfeiture of his debt and such punishment upon the officer as the court shall award." The privilege was extended to servants

[1] *Precedents*, I, 206.

in 1658. Amplification of the law was made in 1705, to the effect that members should be "in their persons, servants, and estates, both real and personal, free, exempted, and privileged from all arrest, attachments, executions, and all other processes whatsoever (save only for treason, felony, or breach of the peace) during his or their attendance upon the General Assembly, by the space of ten days before the beginning, and ten days after the conclusion of every session of the Assembly." [1]

Massachusetts Bay ordered in 1692: "No member of the General Assembly, or his servant, during the time of their sessions, or going to and from thence shall be arrested, sued, imprisoned, or any ways molested or troubled, or compelled to make answer to any suit, bill, plaint or declaration, or otherwise, cases of high treason and felony excepted."

In 1705 William Biles, a Quaker minister, old, self-willed, irascible, lost his head in the Pennsylvania Assembly and assailed the Executive, declaring: "He is but a boy and not fit to be Governor. We'll kick him out." The Governor haled him into court, where his plea of privilege as a member was overruled and he was fined three hundred pounds. The Assembly refused to expel Biles, but instead passed a resolution condemning the sheriff and judges for violating the privileges of the House, whereupon the Governor called the members before him and after addressing them in a most abusive speech, adjourned them. Public opinion was with Biles. The Quaker ladies of the town did not conceal their pride in looking out for the wants of their minister in jail, and after a while he was released.

The Articles of Confederation in 1778 provided: "The members of Congress shall be protected in their persons from arrests and imprisonments during the time of their going to and from, and attendance on, Congress, except for treason, felony, or breach of the peace." This was slightly modified for the Federal Constitution, as follows: "The Senators and Representatives . . . shall in all cases, except treason, felony and breach of the peace, be privileged from arrest during their attendance at the session of their respective houses, and in going to and returning from the same."

All the States but five now recognize in their Constitutions in some way the privilege of freedom from arrest. North

[1] Hening, *Virginia Statutes at Large*, VII, 526–27.

Carolina and Vermont seem never to have mentioned it; Maryland dropped it in 1864, Florida in 1868; New York in her first Constitution said the Assembly should enjoy the same privileges as in the colony. It may be conjectured that in these five States the privilege would be allowed under the common law. Thirty-eight of the States give complete freedom from arrest save in case of treason, felony, or breach of the peace, barring Kansas, which omitted treason (doubtless because of the peculiar conditions in that State when it was organized), and also with the exception of five States that include violation of oath of office, Georgia which includes larceny, and Mississippi which includes theft.

Massachusetts confines the privilege to freedom from arrest or being held to bail on mesne process, and seems to restrict it to the House of Representatives, though as the next section says "the Senate shall have the same powers in like cases," the situation is not clear. There is also some doubt about New Hampshire, for though its Constitution clearly says "no member of the House of Representatives or Senate shall be arrested or held to bail on mesne process," the next section gives authority to imprison "every person guilty of a breach of its privileges in making arrests for debt," as if these were the only arrests in mind. Rhode Island is usually classed among the States that confine the privilege to matters of civil process, but the provision reads: "The person of every member of the General Assembly shall be exempt from arrest, and his estate from attachment in any civil action." It might be argued with force that the comma restricts "any civil action" to "attachment." In Connecticut the wording clearly makes it a privilege in all cases of civil process, and the restriction is equally clear in Nevada. Eleven States besides the general exemption from arrest, say that members shall not be subject to civil process.

A Kentucky statute, strengthening the usual constitutional provision, reads: "The members of the General Assembly shall, in nowise, be disturbed or embarrassed in the great and important business of legislation. They shall not, directly or indirectly, by any ways or means, be arrested, menaced or otherwise disturbed during the existence of their constitutional privilege, except on legal process for treason, felony, breach of the peace or misdemeanor."

In the matter of duration of privilege there is much difference of provision. Blackstone said it covered forty days before and forty after the session. Bradley, C. J., in an exhaustive examination of the subject in Hoppin v. Jenckes, 8 R.I. 453 (1867), concluded the weight of authority overbalanced Blackstone and that by the law of England "it was for a reasonable or convenient time, and not for a period of forty days and more." Such the court held to be the test that should be applied in the case of a member. of Congress. Rhode Island itself allows privilege only during the session and two days before and after. More than half the States with constitutional provisions on the subject allow privilege only during the session. A dozen also allow fifteen days before and after, with some variations, and a few have exceptional provisions of no significance, unless it be in the case of five States that seem to shield the legislator throughout his term of office. The Wisconsin Constitution says: "Members of the Legislature shall in all cases, except treason, felony, and breach of the peace, be privileged from arrest." California, Washington, and Arizona use the same words. Michigan says: "Senators and Representatives shall in all cases, except treason, felony, and breach of the peace, be privileged from arrest." Inasmuch as technically membership continues from the time of taking the oath until the next Legislature convenes (there being always the chance of a special session), in these States members would appear to be immune whether the Legislature is sitting or not.

Although in olden times Parliament enjoyed the invention of humiliating forms of punishment for those who hurt its pride or interfered with its members, nothing but imprisonment, save an occasional fine, has of late years been inflicted by lawmaking bodies. Question has arisen over the length of time of imprisonment. The English conclusion, generally accepted here, has been that the offender may not be kept in confinement beyond the term of the House sentencing him. The reason for this, as given in the case of Anderson v. Dunn (6 Wheaton, 204), is that "the existence of the power that imprisons is indispensable to its continuance." In the next breath the Court said that "the legislative power continues perpetual," and most laymen would suppose this met the condition the Court had just imposed, but it went on to identify "the legislative body" with "the legislative power," by saying: "The legislative body ceases to exist on the moment of its adjournment or periodical dissolution. It follows that imprisonment must terminate with the adjournment." The three months to which Patrick Woods was sentenced by the national House was a specific sentence unusual. In that case the time of sentence expired before the term of the Congress imposing it.

The privilege of exemption from arrest is to-day of far less practical consequence than of old, as arrest or seizure of the person is now rarely authorized except for crime, and all crimes of a serious nature are included within the description of treason, felony, or breach of the peace. Yet occasionally it becomes of importance, as for example in the case of Justice Platt Porter of the New York Supreme Court who in 1870 was summoned to the bar of the Assembly to answer for an alleged breach of privilege in causing an attachment to be issued against Henry Ray, a member, and requiring him to appear before the grand jury. Mr. Ray had been subpœnaed to attend as a witness before the grand jury, but had not obeyed, whereupon the attachment was issued, and he was compelled to attend the grand jury, and give evidence in a pending criminal proceeding. This was deemed by the Assembly a breach of the privilege of its members. The Judge appeared and presented his defense, protesting, however, against the power of the Assembly to inquire into his judicial acts, and saying he came as an individual, not as a judge to defend his judicial action.

He characterized the act of the Assembly as an "aggressive assumption of power," and said that if one department of this government possesses the power to command obedience of another of co-extensive and equal power — if the legislative can usurp the authority to hold in awe or punish the judicial — then indeed have we a despotism, and not a government of freedom. "If for an official act, if for a judicial act of a judge, this House possesses the power to punish, even for a mistaken judgment, where is the boasted protection to an independent judiciary?" He denied that Mr. Ray had been arrested on civil process, averring it was criminal process, issued on behalf of the people to enforce the criminal law.

In the end the Assembly resolved that he was mistaken as to the privileges of the House, and that he did commit a breach of privilege; "but this House do not believe that any intention or desire to interfere with the independence or dignity of the House actuated him in the performance of that which he deemed his official duty." This closed the incident as far as he was concerned. What doubt there may have been as to the privilege was removed by a statute of 1892, reading: "A member of the Legislature shall be privileged from arrest in a civil action or proceeding other than for a forfeiture or breach of trust in public office or employment, while attending upon its session, or for fourteen days before and after each session, or while absent for not more than fourteen days during the session, with the leave of the House of which he is a member. An officer of either House shall be privileged from arrest in such a civil action or proceeding while in actual attendance upon the House. Either House shall have the power to discharge from arrest any of its members or officers arrested in violation of his privilege from arrest." [1]

A more recent case was that of Williamson, a member of Congress, who in 1905 was found guilty of conspiring to commit the crime of subornation of perjury in proceedings for the purchase of public land. He protested against sentence on the ground that he would thereby be deprived of his constitutional right to go to, attend at, and return from the ensuing session of Congress. Having been sentenced to pay a fine and to imprisonment for ten months, he took the matter to the Supreme Court of the United States, where Justice White, for the Court, held that the words "treason, felony, and breach of the peace" should be construed in the same sense as those words were commonly used and understood in England as applied to parliamentary privilege, and as excluding from the privilege all arrests and prosecutions for criminal offenses, and confining the privilege to arrests in civil cases. On other grounds the decision of the lower court was reversed.[2]

It is to be borne in mind that the privilege of freedom from arrest is not primarily for the benefit of the member, but is grounded on considerations of public interest. As Jefferson said in his Manual, "when a Representative is withdrawn from his seat by summons, the 40,000 people whom he represents lose their voice in debate and vote, as they do on his voluntary absence; when a Senator is withdrawn by summons, his State loses half its voice in debate and vote, as it does on his voluntary absence. The enormous disparity of evil admits of no

[1] C. Z. Lincoln, *Const. Hist. of New York*, iv, 607, 612.
[2] Williamson v. United States, 207 U.S. 425 (1908).

comparison." Now that the constituency of a Representative in Congress is five or six times as large as when Jefferson wrote, the loss he described has become so much the more serious, if numbers determine, but of course the principle is the same whatever the size of the constituency. It was for like reason of public interest that in 1787 the Massachusetts General Court resolved "that the right of granting writs of protection to persons who have business pending at the General Court, and whose attendance there, on examination by Committee or otherwise, appears to be necessary, is a right incident to either House," and that either House had the right to order its Clerk to issue such writ, "in the same way as heretofore has been the usual custom." Such a custom has long since passed into desuetude, but doubtless could be revived should occasion arise. Indeed it is safe to say that lawmaking bodies would be sustained in any reasonable assertion of privilege evidently necessary to the proper performance of their duties.

The privilege extends to officers of Congress. In 1800 a spectator, one James Lane, who in the gallery applauded by clapping his hands, was by order of the Speaker taken into custody by the Sergeant-at-Arms and detained for two hours. Lane got a warrant for the arrest of the Sergeant-at-Arms, whereupon it was resolved that the arrest and confinement of an officer of the House of Representatives for an act performed by him in its service and in obedience to its orders must be deemed a high breach of privilege.

CHAPTER XXI

CONTEMPT

THERE would be advantage if "contempt" and "privilege" could be discriminated sharply. It would be well to confine "privilege" to the rights of individual members and to use "contempt" for an invasion of the collective rights of a legislative body. However, the words have been so often used by investigating committees and in findings as if they had something in common, and they have been so confounded in Constitutions and statutes, that perhaps scientific precision is now impracticable. This may be my excuse for having as a matter of convenience treated together individual criticism and collective criticism. Yet it may in general be well to consider contempt from the collective point of view, as willful disobedience of the orders of a legislative body, or disorderly or contumacious behavior in its presence.

Whether the power to punish for contempt inheres in every legislative body, has been the subject of much discussion. There is no question whatever that Parliament has the power. In Burdett v. Abbott, 51 Geo. III, 1811 (14 East, 1), and in Sheriff's of Middlesex Case, 3 Vict., 1840 (11 Ad. & Ell., 273 ; 39 Eng. C.L.), it was held that either House may commit for contempt, and in the latter case that no court will inquire into the grounds of such commitment. Sir Erskine May says that since 1547 the power of commitment by the House of Commons has been exercised more than a thousand times. But is it clear that other legislative bodies may commit without specific authorization by Constitution or statute?

In the leading English case of Kielly v. Carson (4 Moore P.C. 63), decided in 1841, the question rose by reason of the fact that the offense had been committed against a provincial legislature. Kielly was said to have used reproaches, in gross and threatening language, toward John Kent, one of the members of the House of Assembly of Newfoundland. He was brought before the House, where he added to his offense by boisterous and violent language, and was finally committed to jail. The Privy Council held that a local legislature had not what it erroneously supposed itself to possess — the same exclusive privileges which the ancient law of England has annexed to the House of Parliament. "The reason why the House of Commons has this power is not because it is a representative body with legislative functions, but by virtue of ancient usage and prescription; the *lex et consuetudo parliamenti*, which forms a part of the common law of the land." The opinion also discussed at length the necessity of this power in a legislative body for its protection, and to enable it to discharge its lawmaking functions, and decided against the proposition. "The power of punishing any one for past misconduct as a contempt of its authority, and adjudicating upon the fact of such contempt, and the measure of punishment as a judicial body, irresponsible to the party accused, whatever the real facts may be, is by no means essentially necessary for the exercise of its functions by a local legislature, whether representative or not. All these functions may be well performed without this extraordinary power, and with the aid of the ordinary tribunals to investigate and punish contemptuous insults and interruptions." Very likely it was because of this opinion that the framers of the Constitution for the Irish Free State felt it necessary to specify that each House shall have power "to protect itself and its members against any person or persons interfering with, molesting, or attempting to corrupt the members in the exercise of their duties."

The principle involved had in this country been discussed when the editor of the "Aurora" was committed for having inserted in his paper of February 19, 1800, some paragraphs defamatory of the United States Senate. Jefferson in his "Manual" (Sec. III) says it was insisted in support of the legality of this order, "that every man, by the law of nature, and every body of men, possesses the right of self-defense; that all public functionaries are essentially invested with the powers of self-preservation; that they have an inherent right to do all acts necessary to keep themselves in a condition to discharge the trusts confided to them; that whenever authorities are given, the means of carrying them into execution are given by necessary implication; that thus we see the British Parliament exercise the right of punishing contempts; all the State Legislatures exercise the same power, and every court does the same; that, if we have it not, we sit at the mercy of every intruder who may enter our doors or gallery, and, by noise and tumult, render proceeding in business impracticable; that if our tranquillity is to be perpetually disturbed by newspaper defamation, it will not be possible to exercise our functions with the requisite coolness and deliberation; and that we must, therefore, have a power to punish these disturbers of our peace and proceedings."

To this it was answered, that the Parliament and courts of England have cognizance of contempts by the express provisions of their law; that the State Legislatures have equal authority because their powers are plenary; that they represent their constituents completely, and possess all their powers, except such as their Constitutions have expressly denied them; that Congress have no such natural or necessary power, nor any powers but such as are given them by the Constitution; that, moreover, by that article of the Constitution which authorizes them "to make all laws necessary and proper for carrying into execution the powers vested by the Constitution in them," they may provide by law for an undisturbed exercise of their functions, for example, for the punishment of contempts, of affrays or tumult in their presence, etc.; but, till the law be made, it does not exist; that in the meantime, however, they are not unprotected, the ordinary magistrates and courts of law being open and competent to punish all unjustifiable disturbances or defamations. "Which of these doctrines is to prevail," said Jefferson, "time will decide."

It was not many years before time brought the decision, in the case of Anderson v. Dunn (6 Wh. 204–1821). This followed the disclosure that Colonel John Anderson had written a letter to Lewis Williams, of North Carolina, a Representative in Congress, requesting him to accept $500 as "part pay for extra trouble" in furthering certain claims. Upon Anderson's arrest by order of the House, extended debate arose. It was objected that neither the Constitution nor the law gave any authority to the House to punish, and that the great and oppressive powers assumed in this respect by the British Parliament were no precedent here. The House might protect itself from indecorum and insult, but might not punish individuals for acts done elsewhere.

On the other hand it was said that there must be in the House the power to resist the advances of bribery and corruption, since the Constitution, in giving being to the House, must have given it every attribute necessary to its security and purity. The House of Commons acted as a House in its punishments for contempt; therefore the difference in the functions of Parliament as compared with those of Congress did not prevent the precedents of the Commons from being valuable.

The outcome was that Anderson was found guilty, and reprimanded at the bar of the House, then being discharged from custody. He brought suit against the Sergeant-at-Arms for assault and battery, and false imprisonment. It reached the Supreme Court, which decided that the House had the power to punish for contempt, and that it was an implied power, and of vital importance to the safety, character, and dignity of the House. The necessity of its existence and exercise was founded on the principle of self-preservation.

That case, however, if not overruled, was in its findings greatly narrowed in 1880 by Kilbourn v. Thompson (103 U.S. 168). Kilbourn had refused as a witness to answer certain questions put to him by the House, whereupon he had been imprisoned forty-five days. He sued the Sergeant-at-Arms and four members of the House. The court held that neither House of Congress is constituted a part of any court of general jurisdiction, nor has it any history to which the exercise of such power can be traced. Its power must be sought alone in some express grant in the Constitution, or be found necessary to carry into effect such powers as are there granted. The court, without affirming that such a power can arise in any case other than those specified, decided that it can exist in no case where the House attempting to exercise it, invokes its aid in a matter to which its authority does not extend, such as an inquiry into the private affairs of the citizen. Being a legislature of limited powers, Congress cannot measure its powers by those exercised by the English Parliament.

The matter was further clarified in the Chapman case in 1897 (166 U.S. 661), where Chief Justice Fuller gave the opinion, to the effect that Congress possesses the constitutional power to enact a statute to enforce the attendance of witnesses, and to compel them to make disclosure of evidence to enable the respective bodies to discharge their legislative functions. The Senate had created a special committee to investigate charges of corruption in the matter of the tariff bill in 1894. Chapman, a member of a firm of stockbrokers in New York, refused to say whether his firm had bought or sold sugar stocks for any Senator. He defended on the ground that to answer might tend to expose him to criminal prosecution. The court differentiated the case from Kilbourn *v.* Thompson, where it was held that there existed no general power in Congress to inquire into the private affairs of a citizen. The case at bar was wholly different. Specific charges against Senators were to be investigated. The questions were not intrusions into the affairs of the citizens.

What may prove to be the last word on the broad aspect of the subject, at least as far as American lawmaking bodies are concerned, was spoken by Chief Justice White in an opinion handed down April 23, 1917, in the case of Marshall *v.* Gordon (243 U.S. 521). H. Snowdon Marshall, a United States Attorney, conducted a grand jury investigation in New York that led to the indictment of a member of Congress. Acting on charges against Marshall, the House directed its Judiciary Committee to make inquiry and report concerning his liability to impeachment. While the inquiry was in progress, Marshall wrote to the subcommittee chairman and gave to the press an ill-tempered letter charging the chairman with trying to probe into and frustrate the action of the grand jury. This letter was couched in terms calculated to arouse the indignation of the members of the committee and of the House generally. Upon Marshall's arrest because of it, he applied for *habeas corpus.* In the opinion Justice White accepted as indubitable the theory that the power to punish for contempt rested upon an assumed blending of legislative and judicial authority possessed by Parliament when the Lords and Commons were one, an authority that continued after the division of the Parliament, either because it was thought to continue to reside in the Commons or by the force of routine. In view of the separation of powers by our early State Constitutions, he thought the object of the provisions relating to contempt could only have been to recognize the right of the legislative power to deal with the particular acts without reference to their violation of the criminal law. No power of this sort being specifically granted by the Constitution to Congress, its authority could only be one implied from such powers as were granted. The only power to be implied is the power to deal with contempt only so far as necessary to carry out the legislative authority given. "It is a means to an end and not the end itself." It rests only upon the right of self-preservation, that is, the right to prevent acts which in and of themselves inherently obstruct or prevent the discharge of legislative duty or the refusal to do that which there is an inherent legislative power to compel in order that legislative functions may be performed. The act complained of in this case was held to be extrinsic to the discharge of legislative duties and related only to the presumed operation that the letter might have upon the public mind, and the indignation naturally felt by members of the committee. So the lower court was held to have erred in refusing the writ of *habeas corpus*, and the discharge of Marshall was ordered.

Various decisions in the State courts would warrant the inference that the authority of the State Legislatures to punish for contempt is much broader than that of Congress. It has been commonly though not universally held that possessing all powers not expressly or impliedly refused them, they have a general inquisitorial power and a corresponding general authority to punish a refusal to testify or to produce papers.

Such was the attitude of the Supreme Court of Massachusetts in Whitcomb's Case, 120 Mass. 118 (1876). Chief Justice Gray, after citing the Newfoundland case, said that the power doubtless existed in State Legislatures, "which are supreme within their sphere, and not, like the colonial assemblies of Great Britain, created by and subordinate to the national legislature." He went on, however, to hold that a city council is not a legislature, and to say: "The Legislature cannot delegate to or confer upon municipal boards or officers, that are not courts of justice, and whose proceedings are not an exercise of judicial power, the authority to imprison and punish, without right of appeal or trial by jury."

The Massachusetts courts have in other instances had occasion to consider the power of the Legislature over witnesses. In Burnham *v.* Morrissey, 14 Gray 226 (1859), Justice Hoar said: "The House of Representatives has many duties to perform, which necessarily require it to receive evidence, and examine witnesses. . . . It has often occasion to acquire a certain knowledge of facts, in order to the proper performance of legislative duties. We therefore think it clear that it has the constitutional right to take evidence, to summon witnesses, and to compel them to attend and to testify. This power to summon and examine witnesses it may exercise by means of committees. If a witness, duly notified or summoned, by the authority of the House, to attend before a committee, or before the House, refuses to attend, or, when present, and required to testify, or to do any other act which a witness may be lawfully required to do, refuses to obey the lawful commands of the House in that behalf, it is a contempt of the authority of the House; and, upon such refusal to attend, or if such refusal to testify occur before a committee, the House may compel his obedience by arresting him by the proper officer of the House, and bringing him before the House. If, when before the House, he is contumacious and refuses to obey, without lawful excuse, such conduct renders him 'guilty of disrespect to the House by contemptuous behavior in its presence,' within the meaning of the tenth article of chapter 1, §3, of the Constitution, and he may be lawfully imprisoned for such contemptuous behavior, for a term not exceeding thirty days."

In the same case it was brought out that the legislative power in such matters is not above control. "The House of Representatives," said the court, "is not the final judge of its own powers and privileges in cases where the rights and liberties of the subject are concerned; but the legality of its action may be examined and determined by this court. That House is not the Legislature, but only a part of it, and is therefore subject in its action to the laws, in common with all other bodies, officers, and tribunals within the Commonwealth."

In April, 1871, Henry Emery declined to answer certain questions put to him by a committee of the Massachusetts Legislature, on the ground that the answers would criminate himself and tend to furnish evidence against himself. The Senate ordered him committed to jail. Before the Supreme Court, Emery sought to shield himself behind the provision in the Massachusetts Declaration of Rights: "No subject shall be held to answer for any crimes or offense, until the same is fully and plainly, substantially and formally, described to him; or be compelled to accuse, or furnish evidence against himself." The Attorney General, for the Senate, represented that when the Constitution was adopted, a witness in court was excused from giving answers criminating himself, by the rules of common law ; but a witness before Parliament, or a committee of Parliament, had no such protection. The rules of common law and of parliamentary law were directly opposed to each other. He thought the provision of the Declaration of Rights was designed simply to embody the common law rule, and not to affect the parliamentary law. In this the court did not agree with him. Justice Wells submitted the matter to his associates and they unanimously concluded that the Constitution is above, not only the common law, but the Legislature also, and that this safeguard of individual rights cannot be suspended or invaded, either by general laws, or the special order of the legislative body, or of any of its branches. No one can be required to forego an appeal to its protection, unless first secured from future liability, and exposure to be prejudiced, in any criminal proceeding against him.[1]

The problem has been the subject of elaborate discussion by New York courts. The case of People *ex rel.* McDonald *v.* Keeler brought out two long opinions. The Supreme Court (32 Hun. 563) held in 1884 that the Assembly in investigating the Department of Public Works of New York City was not engaged in a judicial function, and that "except when engaged in the judicial functions authorized by the Constitution, neither branch of the Legislature has any power to punish as for contempt for a refusal to answer a question." When in the following year the case reached the Court of Appeal (99 N.Y. 463), a new turn was given to it, for while it was held that the Legislature or one of its committees may punish for contempt witnesses only who refuse to answer questions put with the desire of obtaining information for future legislative action, at the same time it was admitted the court cannot impugn the expressed motives of the Legislature, so that all the Legislature has to do in order to bring itself under the rule stated in this case is to declare in the resolution appointing the committee that it wishes such information.

This case was quoted approvingly in 1889 by Justice Mayham in People *v.* Webb (5 N.Y. Supp. 855). A committee had been appointed to investigate the doings of a committee of a preceding Legislature in the matter of certain repairs in the State capitol. The court found that such knowledge as the investigating committee might get could not be used for purposes of

[1] Emery's Case, 107 Mass., 172.

legislation, and said: "It seems well settled that the Legislature of the State cannot, nor can any committee appointed by it, constitute itself into a court of general jurisdiction, or a grand inquest, for the purpose of inquiring into the conduct of a citizen not a member of its body, nor can it compel the answer of a witness on an inquiry or investigation before it, except for legislative purposes, or in acquiring information upon which to predicate remedial legislation." Nevertheless the Massachusetts General Court of 1921 undertook to investigate the conduct of all the members of the General Court of 1918 in the matter of rumored transactions in the stock of street railway companies while or after certain important street railway legislation was before the Legislature. Inquiry was even directed to whether stock was bought or sold after the adjournment of the session. Authority for this seems to have been sought in the averment of the Supreme Court in Burnham *v.* Morrissey (cited above), that the House "is the grand inquest of the Commonwealth," but examination of the case will disclose that the court coupled with this averment the clause — "and as such has power to inquire into the official conduct of all officers of the Commonwealth, in order to impeachment." No such purpose can be found in an inquiry into the conduct of former legislators, and it seems to me very doubtful if the procedure could be justified by the remote possibility of remedial legislation.

In People *v.* Webb it was also held that since the power of the New York Legislature to punish for contempt, not specifically given by the Constitution, is regulated by a statute, the question must be determined under the provisions of that statute, thus excluding any common law rights.

Herein the New York attitude has been distinctly contrary to the general supposition in the States that the power to punish for contempt is inherent, whether specified in the Constitution or not. It would seem as if few things could be clearer than that this power is essential for the proper performance of the lawmaking function. A Legislature ought not only to be able to command respect, but also be able to secure the information necessary for its guidance. That in this particular it should be restricted by the view of some preceding Legislature as embodied in a statute, is not easy to reconcile with the principle that only Constitutions control Legislatures.

Whether in this matter a Legislature has any extra-constitutional power, springing out of its nature, is of course another question. That confronted the Supreme Court of Texas in 1911. When the Legislature had been called in special session for certain specified purposes and such others as the Governor might present, he declined the request to lay before it anything relating to a recent vote on the prohibition question. Thereupon the House proceeded by itself to create an investigating committee. J. F. Wolters, chairman of the anti-State-wide executive committee, refused to answer questions that would disclose who had contributed to its funds. The court held [1] that as the topic was foreign to the purposes for which the session was called and the Governor had refused to present it, no legislation could result from the action of the committee, and therefore it was powerless to summon witnesses and compel them to testify.

A novel problem in this field confronted the House in the 67th Congress. Representative Oscar E. Keller refused to respect a subpœna issued under power given to the Committee on Judiciary, summoning him to appear and give it certain information relating to impeachment charges he had made against the Attorney General. Did Keller's privilege as a member protect him? A majority of the committee thought not and so told the House,[2] but the matter was not carried to the point of trying to coerce the recalcitrant member.

Massachusetts gave each branch of the General Court power to punish by imprisonment any person who should assault, or arrest, any witnesses, or any other person, ordered to attend the House, in his way going or returning. New Hampshire gave the same power in modified language. Kentucky, silent on the subject of disorder and disrespect, put into her Constitution of 1890 power to "punish for contempt any person who refuses to attend as a witness, or to bring any paper proper to be used as evidence," or "to testify concerning any matter which may be a proper subject of inquiry," imprisonment not to extend beyond the session. In 1912 Ohio added to the powers of each House — "and shall have all powers necessary to provide for its safety and the undisturbed transaction of its business, and to obtain through committees or otherwise, information affecting legislative action under consideration or in contemplation, or with

[1] *Ex. parte* J. F. Wolters, 64 Tex. Cr. Rep. 238.
[2] H. R. 1372, 67th Congress, 4th Session.

reference to any alleged breach of its privileges, or misconduct of its members, and to that end to enforce the attendance and testimony of witnesses, and the production of books and papers." Florida, Mississippi, and Oklahoma have provisions looking to the same result. In four States (Alabama, Arkansas, Colorado, and Pennsylvania) the Constitution says each House may enforce obedience to its processes, which would of course secure the attendance of witnesses, and in Maryland detailed power of investigation is given to the lower House.

The German Constitution of 1919 says that "the members of the National Assembly and the State Assemblies are entitled to refuse to give evidence concerning persons who have given them information in their official capacity, or to whom they have given information in the performance of their official duties, or concerning the information itself." Happily the dangerous possibilities that this anticipates are beyond the range of American contemplation.

Assaults and Contumacy

That class of contempt which consists of disorderly or contumacious behavior, might fill a long chapter with illustrations. There are few legislative bodies whose annals are free from record of altercations and blows. Hot tempers are found in every large assembly, partisanship now and then overthrows judgment, and in too many epochs of parliamentary history strong drink has proved the curse of fine intellects. Any extensive enumeration of all the quarrels of lawmakers would chiefly result in revealing the worse side of human nature. A few instances will suffice the more useful purpose of refuting the notion that we live in a degenerate age, that manners are deteriorating, that self-control is a rarer quality than it was among our ancestors, that legislatures are more disgraceful than ever. Begin with an entry from that famous diary of Pepys, under date of December 19, 1666: "Thence I up to the Lords' House to enquire for my Lord Bellassis; and there hear how at a conference this morning between the two Houses about the business of the Canary Company, my Lord Buckingham leaning rudely over my Lord Marquis Dorchester, my Lord Dorchester removed his elbow. Duke of Buckingham asked him if he was uneasy; Dorchester replied, yes, and that he durst not do this were he anywhere else. Buckingham replied, yes he would, and that he was a better man than himself; Dorchester said that he lyed. With this Buckingham struck off his hat, and took him by his periwig, and pulled it aside, and held him. My Lord Chamberlain and others interposed, and, upon coming into the House, the Lords did order them both into the Tower, whither they are to go this afternoon. This day's work will bring the Lieutenant of the Tower £350."

And farther on in the record of the same day he reports that Sir W. Batten and Sir R. Ford told him "how Sir Allen Brodericke and Sir Allen Apsley did come drunk the other day into the House, and did both speak for half an hour together, and could not be either laughed, or pulled, or bid to sit down and hold their peace, to the great contempt of the King's servants and cause; which I am grieved at with all my heart."

Next turn to colonial history and read the last act of the Rhode Island session of June, 1655: "That in case any man shall strike another person in ye Court, he shall either be fined ten pounds, or be whipt, accordinge as ye Court shall see meete."

Or look into the Journal of the 5th Assembly of New Jersey (1709) and see how "Captain Duncan drew his sword on Mr. Sharp, another Representative, and tried to kill him, 'etc.,' For this offense Duncan was made to acknowledge his fault before being allowed to take his seat."

Those were rude days, you say, and the country was raw. Surely men were wiser and gentler when we had risen to the dignity of a nation and pure patriotism reached a height from which we have sadly fallen. Perhaps so, and yet it is hard to reconcile that view with the story of the attack by Matthew Lyon, of Vermont, on Roger Griswold, of Connecticut, in the House, January 30, 1798, already told in connection with the subject of expulsion.

Of all assaults in the Capitol at Washington the most momentous was that of Preston S. Brooks, of South Carolina, a member of the House, upon Senator Charles Sumner, of Massachusetts. In what Sumner had promised should be "the most thorough philippic ever uttered in a legislative body," he had exhausted the resources of invective, hurled at the champions of slavery. Among those he savagely denounced, was Senator Butler, of South Carolina. Brooks, a kinsman of Butler, undertook to revenge him. Going to the Senate Chamber and finding Sumner writing letters, after the close of the session, Brooks dealt him a terrible blow on the head with his cane. Sumner, though a man of powerful build, was taken by surprise, and could not get away from the desk to defend himself. Brooks kept raining blows on him, broke the cane, and kept on beating him with the stump. Sumner, partly stunned and blinded, wrenched the desk from its fastenings as he struggled to his feet, and in vain tried to ward off the blows. When somebody rushed to the spot and seized Brooks to stop the brutal beating that yet continued, Sumner fell to the floor, bleeding profusely and covered with his blood. The blow would have killed most men, but Sumner's iron constitution saved him from death. The injury, however, affected his spine, made him a complete invalid for three or four years, and weakened him for life. The political result was for the anti-slavery cause an access of support not to be measured. The parliamentary result was that a committee of the Senate, without a Republican on it, reported the assault a breach of the privileges of the Senate, but not within its jurisdiction and to be punished only by the House. In that body a committee reported that the privileges of the House had been violated as well as those of the Senate, and recommended the expulsion of Brooks, but as the vote stood 121 to 95, the necessary two thirds was not secured. Brooks, however, immediately resigned and went back to South Carolina, where, at a banquet numerously attended, his constituents gave him a cane on which was inscribed, "Use knock-down arguments."

It should be noticed that the House Committee held the assault to be a violation of the constitutional provision that Senators and Representatives "for any speech or debate in either House shall not be questioned in any other place," and a breach not only of the privileges of the Senator assailed, but also of the privileges of Senate and House, as well as an act of disorderly behavior.

The Senate has been remarkably patient with offending members. Its tolerance has often left very grave personalities unrebuked, going so far indeed as to ignore the outrageous act of Senator Foote in drawing from his pocket a fully loaded revolver that might have made Benton a martyr. Occasionally, however, even Senatorial latitude has been restrained. For instance, in 1863 Willard Saulsbury went too far in declaring

President Lincoln "a weak and imbecile man." For this he was called to order, and required to sit down. When he refused to stop talking, the Vice-President directed the Sergeant-at-Arms to take him in charge for disorderly conduct.

Far different was the attitude of the Senate toward the next President, Andrew Johnson, for it refused to reverse the judgment of the Chair that Charles Sumner was not out of order when he said: "We have never before had a President of the United States who was an enemy of his country." When L. Q. C. Lamar, March 1, 1879, confessed "surprise and regret that the Senator from Massachusetts should have wantonly, without provocation, flung this insult," he was ruled out of order by the Chair, Mr. Edmunds, who was not sustained on appeal, the vote being 15 to 16. Zachariah Chandler, May 9, 1879, said of twelve Senators, "By fraud and violence you occupy your seats." It was held, however, that no necessary imputation of fraud and violence attached to the Senators themselves. On the other hand Robert M. La Follette was declared to have used disorderly language when he said, June 11, 1909: "The Senator from Rhode Island . . . cannot by any legislative trick in amendments that have been voted upon, plant in the mind of any Senator here who has been exercising some independence, any timidity or error."

An affray in August, 1856, is worth recalling because the House took note of it though it occurred elsewhere. Two members in an omnibus on their way to the House became engaged in a controversy over the prospective failure of the army appropriation bill, and an assault brought some injury to one of them. The majority of the committee investigating the matter deemed there had been invasion of the right to come to the House in safety, but by reason of mitigating circumstances no action was taken.

Another phase of contempt is found in the case where a clerk of a committee was attacked, within the walls of the Capitol, in 1866. The assailant was dealt with by a resolution directing the Sergeant-at-Arms to deliver him to the civil authorities of the District and prosecute him in the criminal courts. One stenographer assaulting another in the presence of the House, in 1836, the assailant, acknowledging his offense, was let off with exclusion.

Among the cases in which one branch or the other of Congress has punished, have been: Attempt to bribe; the sending of a challenge to a member; defamatory publication; contumacy on the part of witnesses; an assault on the private Secretary of the President within the Capitol immediately after he had delivered a message; publishing a treaty pending in executive session. C. F. Gettemy found that from 1789 to 1870 there were 76 attempts to discipline members of Congress; 26 of these were cases of abusive language or disorderly behavior on the floor of the House, and 25 were for treason. The actual censures for all causes in both Houses during that time were 10 and the expulsions 18.

About half the States by constitutional provision give their Legislatures power to punish for disorderly or contemptuous behavior in the presence of the House. Louisiana describes the offense as "disrespect, or disorderly or contemptuous behavior," and does not confine it to the presence of the House, nor does Wisconsin so confine it in speaking of "contempt and disorderly behavior," nor Rhode Island with its comprehensive phrase, "punish for contempts." West Virginia says — "disrespectful behavior in its presence." Four States (Maine, New Hampshire, West Virginia, and Mississippi) extend the power to obstructing proceedings, two (Maryland and West Virginia) to obstructing an officer in the execution of his duties, and New Hampshire elaborates this into "assaulting or disturbing any one of its officers in the execution of any order or procedure of the House."

FREEDOM OF SPEECH

FREEDOM of speech within the walls of a legislative assembly is one of the most important of privileges, and its abuse is one of the most serious of contempts, yet for our purposes as a matter of convenience it has been chiefly treated in connection with the subject of debate.[1] Here, however, it may be appropriately pointed out that freedom of speech is not a privilege which takes away from a legislative body the power to protect itself against its own members when they descend to scurrility or slander. This was established nearly four centuries ago. The Journal of the House of Commons records, January 21, 1547–48, that John Storie, one of the Burgesses, was ordered to be committed to the custody of the Sergeant of

[1] See *Legislative Procedure*, 319–29.

the House. Articles of accusation were read against him, and
the Commons, of their single authority, committed him to the
Tower. The exact nature of his offense is not stated, but he
is known to have been a zealous opponent of the Reformation,
and would appear to have made use of language disrespectful
alike to the House and to the government of the Protector
Somerset.

Hatsell tells us that on the 18th of February, 1557, Mr. Marsh,
one of the Burgesses of London, complained that Mr. Wylde,
Burgess of Worcester, had slandered him to the drapers of
London. The matter was referred to a committee, for them to
examine and report, but Hatsell does not say what befell Mr.
Wylde.[1] Then came the case of Arthur Hall, expelled, as we
have seen, for having published a book slandering Parliament.

In our own time an American Legislature has asserted its
power in this particular. Representative Comerford, a member of the Illinois House, had delivered a lecture before the
Illinois College of Law, in which he scored the Legislature in
biting terms, saying, among other things, that it was "a great
auction mart for the sale of special privileges." The speech
made a sensation, and a commission was appointed to investigate the matter. The commission ruled that it would consider charges against only the Legislature that had just begun
its session, and as Mr. Comerford had little or no proof of corruption in that session, his charges were held to be slanderous,
and by a vote of 121 to 13 he was expelled. The "Chicago
Inter Ocean" and "Journal" criticized the Legislature severely
for this action, but the other Chicago papers thought Mr.
Comerford brought his fate upon himself by making charges he
could not prove. "The Assembly has the right to demand that
it shall not be prejudged, and that no one of its own members
shall, without proof, scandalize it in the public estimation,"
said the "Chicago Tribune"; and the "Chicago Evening
Post" remarked that "no legislative body could retain its
own self-respect or the confidence of its constituents if it
failed to punish one of its members who called his colleagues
boodlers." [2]

Of the same nature was the resentment shown by the Massachusetts House of 1919 against one of its members who in a
public address had said that of course in such a number of men

[1] *Precedents*, I, 190.   [2] *Literary Digest*, February 25, 1905.

(280) as made up the Legislature you would find "some who are not worth two cents and some who might be considered as very near crooked." This truism, known to everybody, applicable to every legislative body in the world, and recognized by a thousand writers, somehow particularly aggrieved the members of the Massachusetts House, and they proceeded to formal censure, which was wisely expunged from the records in the hour of good-will at the close of the session. Afterward I heard a member of Congress, on the floor of the national House, commit a like offense which might have been measured as twice as grave, for he said there were Congressmen not worth one cent. It behooves me to avoid the charge of contempt that might follow were the estimate to be here characterized as also a truism, but inasmuch as the House took no notice of the appraisal when made in its presence, perhaps there will be no danger in the repetition.

If such things are to be taken seriously — and of course they have a serious side — it is clear that any legislator ought to think twice before he asperses the capacity or impugns the integrity of any of his associates. Even generalities may do harm by adding to the disrepute in which so many of the people hold the servants they select. On the other hand if the people are to be incited to choose better servants, that can be achieved only by statement of the facts. Such statement, calm, judicial, without exaggeration, cannot fairly be called "contempt." It is in reality a public service.

In a class by itself, without precedent, was the episode in the national House in October, 1921, of which Representative Thomas L. Blanton of Texas was the central figure. Following the custom, he had secured permission to "extend" his remarks on a subject specified, which means that he was authorized to insert in the "Congressional Record" matter not spoken or read on the floor. This he did by inserting an affidavit of an employee in the Government Printing Office, describing a controversy with another employee in the course of which sundry obscene epithets were used. These were printed elliptically, that is, with hyphens between the first and last letters, but their significance was for the most part easily understood. When the matter was brought to the attention of the House, that body promptly ordered the affidavit to be expunged from the Record. Then indignation waxed — fanned, it is to be feared, by recollection of the annoyance Mr. Blanton had caused his fellow-members through many months by excessive and seemingly unjustifiable use of the power given to any one member to demand quorum calls and otherwise delay the business of the House. The opportunity to get revenge for the waste of some weeks of their lives, together with a genuine resentment of what was felt to be a scandalous outrage, led many members to approve expulsion as a punishment none too severe. Earnest debate on a high plane, with a full house and crowded galleries, resulted in failure to get the two-thirds vote necessary for the extreme penalty, whereupon by majority vote the Speaker was ordered to censure Mr. Blanton, this proving to be an ordeal more severe than expulsion would have brought. The next day, when the House had calmed down and sober reflection had overcome hasty impulses, many who had voted to expel, expressed satisfaction that their views had not prevailed, and conceded that the wiser course was followed.

The obnoxious words were not those of Mr. Blanton himself. They disclosed a blameworthy state of affairs in a government office. They involved the problem of organized labor in the civil service, a problem sharply dividing the public at large and of a nature certain to prevent unprejudiced judgment. The public would look to what it might assume to be Mr. Blanton's motives and not to his methods. Expulsion would be viewed as martyrdom. Justly or unjustly, the reputation of the House would suffer and the very purpose of punishment would be thwarted.

COMMUNICATING WITH CONSTITUENTS

MAY a legislator enjoy freedom of speech in communicating with his constituents? No less a man than Thomas Jefferson once discussed this vigorously. In May, 1797, at a Circuit Court in Richmond, Virginia, the Grand Jury made this presentment:

"We, of the grand jury of the United States, for the district of Virginia, present as a real evil, the circular letters of several members of the late Congress, and particularly letters with the signature of Samuel J. Cabell, endeavoring, at a time of real public danger, to disseminate unfounded calumnies against the happy government of the United States, and thereby to separate the people therefrom; and to increase or produce a foreign influence, ruinous to the peace, happiness, and independence of these United States."

Jefferson took exception to this and wrote a Petition to the Virginia House of Delegates, to be signed by inhabitants of the four counties in Cabell's district, in which he set forth:

"That by the Constitution of this State, established from its earliest settlement, the people thereof have professed the right of being governed by laws to which they have consented by representatives chosen by themselves, immediately: that in order to give to the will of the people the influence it ought to have, and the information which may enable them to exercise it usefully, it was a part of the common law, adopted as the law of this land, that their representatives, in the discharge of their functions, should be free from the cognizance or coercion of the coördinate branches, Judiciary and Executive; and that their communications with their constituents should of right, as of duty also, be free, full, and unawed by any: that so necessary has this intercourse been deemed in the country from which they derive principally their descent and laws, that the correspondence between the representative and constituent is privileged there to pass free of expense through the channel of the public post, and that the proceedings of the legislature have been known to be arrested and suspended at times until the Representatives could go home to their several counties and confer with their constituents. . . .

"That the grand jury is a part of the judiciary, not permanent indeed, but in office, *pro hac vice* and responsible as other judges are for their actings and doings while in office: that for the Judiciary to interpose in the legislative department between the constituent and his representative, to control them in the exercise of their functions or duties towards each other, to overawe the free correspondence which exists and ought to exist between them, to dictate what communications may pass between them, and to punish all others, to put the representative into jeopardy of criminal prosecution, of vexation, expense, and punishment before the Judiciary, if his communications, public or private, do not exactly square with their ideas of fact or right, or with their designs of wrong, is to put the legislative department under the feet of the Judiciary, is to leave us, indeed, the shadow, but to take away the substance of representation, which requires essentially that the representative be as free as his constituents would be, that the same interchange of sentiment be lawful between him and them as would be lawful among themselves were they in the personal transaction of their own business; is to do away with the influence of the people over the proceedings of their representatives by excluding from their knowledge, by the terror of punishment, all but such information or misinformation as may suit their own views; and is the more vitally dangerous when it is considered that grand jurors are selected by officers nominated and holding their places at the will of the Executive."

Elaborated at length, the petition concluded by invoking from the Assembly "that redress of our violated rights which the freedom and safety of our common country calls for. We denounce to you a great crime, wicked in its purpose, and mortal in its consequences unless prevented, committed by citizens of this Commonwealth against the body of their country. If we have erred in conceiving the redress provided by the law, we commit the subject to the superior wisdom of this House to devise and pursue such proceedings as they shall think best; and we, as in duty bound, shall ever pray," etc.[1]

Nothing appears to have come of it, and probably Jefferson did not expect anything to come of it. Presumably the ends of a political manifesto were all he had in mind.

[1] *Writings of Thomas Jefferson*, P. L. Ford ed., VII, 158.

CHAPTER XXII

SALARIES

PAYMENT of lawmakers probably began in England as compensation, in the literal sense of the word. The King could not easily get shires and boroughs to send agents to him for negotiating about the money he needed, unless the agents were compensated for their expenses. The thrifty monarchs saw no occasion for paying these out of their own pockets, and so they ordered the sheriffs to levy on the land-owners. At least one sheriff got into trouble thereby. We find a presentment by the grand jury for the wapentake of West Derby, in 1320, saying that the sheriff of Lancashire had returned two Knights without the assent of the county, and had levied £20 for their expenses; "whereas the county could, by their own election, have found two good and sufficient men, who would have gone to Parliament for ten marks, or at the most for £10." [1]

Not long after this, the compensation was fixed at four shillings a day for a Knight and two shillings for a citizen or Burgess. Payment was due for the whole time of service, including not only the stay in Parliament, but also the journey to and fro, which would indicate that it was looked on as a matter of compensation rather than reward. On the other hand, the giving of twice as much to a Knight as to a Burgess has the flavor of reward, unless we assume that the social standing of the Knight entailed on him a larger burden in the way of keeping up appearances. It is to be remembered that though two and four shillings a day strike us as ridiculously small, the purchasing power of money was then from four to six times what it is now, so that the payment was really considerable. In fact, it was probably enough above the actual outlay of members to justify the common view of it as a wage. We know at any rate it proved so heavy a burden for poor constituencies that they refused to send a member rather than pay the cost. In the time of Henry VIII the city of Canterbury, overjoyed at having saved the wages of one of its members who stayed away from

---

[1] Quoted by Townsend, *Hist. of the House of Commons*, I, 241.

Westminster on account of the plague, actually rewarded him for so doing.

There has been preserved a curious indenture of agreement between John Strange, member for Dunwich, and his constituents, made in 1463, by which it is witnessed that "John Strange granteth by these presents to be one of the Burgesses for Dunwich, at the Parliament to be holden at Westminster, for which, whether it hold for longer time or short, or whether it fortune to be prorogued, the said John Strange granteth no more to be taken for his wages than a cade full of herrings, and a half-barrel full of herrings, to be delivered on Christmas next coming." [1] Had it been only a matter of expenses, Strange and the electors would hardly have bargained.

Wages were regularly paid to the end of the reign of Henry VIII, but thereafter the practice rapidly waned, because the desire to serve in Parliament grew so much that for the sake of getting elected men gladly undertook to pay their own expenses, and indeed went beyond that and paid for the privilege. We read, for instance, that one Thomas Long, "a very simple man, and unfit to serve," had crept into Queen Elizabeth's Parliament of 1571. When questioned how he came to be elected, he confessed "that he gave the mayor of Westbury and another £4 for his place." The House was greatly shocked, in those primitive days, at the notion of their member paying, instead of being paid, for a seat, and immediately ordered the mayor and town council to disgorge the money, to appear to answer such things as should be objected against them, and to suffer a penalty of £20 for their scandalous attempt. This was a precursor of the payments a thousand times as large that became common two centuries later.

By Pepys' time the practice of payment to members had almost disappeared. His Diary records, March 30, 1668: "At dinner we had a great deal of good discourse about Parliament; their number being uncertain, and always at the will of the King to increase as he saw reason to erect a new borough. But all concluded that the bane of the Parliament hath been the leaving off the old custom of the places allowing wages to those that served them in Parliament, by which they chose men that understood their business and would attend to it, and they could expect an account from; which now they cannot: and so the

[1] Quoted by Townsend, *Hist. of the House of Commons*, I, 242.

Parliament is become a company of men unable to give account for the interest of the place they serve for." Andrew Marvell, the poet, who died in 1678, and who had been a member from the time of the Restoration, has frequently been credited with being the last person who accepted wages for his attendance as a member, but one or two later instances are now said to have been found.

A story is told of Marvell that may point a moral in an argument for the payment of legislators. Charles II, wanting Marvell's powerful support, sent Lord Danby, the Lord Treasurer, with offers of place and money. The royal messenger found Marvell in obscure apartments and evidently in narrow circumstances, but all the courtly blandishments could not move the poet. At parting the Treasurer slipped into Marvell's hands an order on the Treasury for a thousand pounds, and was moving toward his carriage when Marvell stopped him, and taking him again up-stairs called the servant-boy. "Jack, child," he asked, "what had I for dinner yesterday?" "Don't you remember, sir, you had the little shoulder of mutton that you ordered me to bring from the woman in the market." "Very right, child, what have I for dinner to-day?" "Don't you know, sir, that you bade me lay by the blade-bone to broil?" "'Tis so, child; go away. My lord, do you hear that Andrew Marvell's dinner is provided? There's your piece of paper; I want it not. I knew the sort of kindness you intended. I live here to serve my constituents; the ministry may seek men for their purpose; I am not one." [1]

IN THE COLONIES

IT will be observed that when legislative assemblies began meeting in America, the custom of compensating members had not died out in England. Furthermore, the conditions of colonial life, with its privations at the outset and with its lack of wealthy men or a leisure class in most of the colonies for many years, postponed the time when any considerable number of representatives could afford to waive compensation, much less to pay for the privilege of election. So here the custom of wages began naturally and came to be looked on as an inevitable adjunct of election to representative office.

[1] G. H. Jennings, *Anecdotal Hist. of Parlt.*, 85, quoting Cooke's *Hist. of Party*.

The question at the start was not whether payment should be made, but who should make it, colony or town. The General Court of Massachusetts Bay ordered in October of 1636 "that the charges of the deputies of the townes bee borne by the townes which they came from, to ease the publike." [1] In the following March, an entry reads: "The order for each towne to beare their owne deputies charge was reversed; & the former order, for the charge of the deputies to be borne by the country is reëstablished." [2] A year later the opposite view again prevailed, and it was ordered, that "every towne shall beare the charges of their owne magistrates & deputies, & to alow for a magistrate 3s. 6d. a day, & for a deputy 2s. 6d. a day, from the time of their going out to the Court until their returne, for their dyot & lodging." [3]

Plymouth, instituting representation in that year, made the charges of the "committees" also two-and-six a day, and put them on the townships. In Massachusetts Bay in 1639 it was ordered that "the charge of dyot of the magistrates & deputies should, after this Court, be borne by the fines." [4] What fines were meant does not appear, but it may have been fines for absences. The change may not have been satisfactory or the amounts may have proved inadequate. Anyhow there is proof of a movement in 1644 for higher salaries and more of them. It was ordered, May 29, that "it shall & may be lawfull for the deputies of the Court to advise with their elders and freemen, & take into serious consideration whether God do not expect that all the inhabitants of this plantation alowe to their magistrates, & all others that are called to country service, a proportionable alowance, answerable to their places & implements, & all other that are called to country service, & (if so) upon what grounds, & that they send in their determinations & conclusions the next Generall Court." [5]

No record appears of any report on this, but at the General Court May 14, 1645, it was voted: "This Court, being sensible of the many publike imploiments that the magistrates are called to, which dayly increaseth, and which necessarily occasioneth much expence of their time, to the prejudice of their families & estates, knowing also the straitnes of things in the country, & the just care that this Court ought to take to see

---

[1] *Records of the Colony of the Mass. Bay in N.E.*, I, 183.
[2] *Ibid.*, 187.   [3] *Ibid.*, 228.   [4] *Ibid.*, 261.   [5] *Ibid.*, II, 67.

that none ought to be unequally burthened, or discouraged from doing service to the country in such places as they may be called to, do therefore hereby order " that the Assistants should have five hundred pounds of estate free from taxes for three years.[1] Five months later the court returned to the system of having each town bear the charges of its own Deputies, and this was reiterated in 1653 when it was ordered[2] that "such townes as have not more than thirty ffreemen shall henceforth be at libertie for sending, or not sending, deputyes to the Generall Court, & all such townes as shall send deputyes into the Generall Court shall beare the whole charges of their respective deputies." [3] Thus it was recognized in New England as it had been long before in Old England that poor places ought not to be required to carry the burden of representation.

In Rhode Island at first there was no payment. Although its handful of towns were close together, presently it was found hard to get the Deputies to attend, and this led in 1666 to the passage of an act to pay all the members of the Assembly, and of the Courts, three shillings a day, while employed on these duties. The per diem of the Assemblymen was not paid in cash, but their accounts, certified by the Moderator, were to be allowed in offset of taxes levied in their respective towns.[4] Six years later came one of the rare instances of lowering the pay of lawmakers. It was reduced to two shillings a day.[5] Massachusetts, on the other hand, in 1692, began what has become the normal practice of raising salaries, providing that the towns should pay their Representatives, "during their attendance upon the Court, and for the necessary time in their journeying to and from thence, three shillings in money per diem."

In New Hampshire the Councilors received nothing for their services when sitting as a Council of State, but were rewarded when officiating as members of the Legislature, receiving like the Representatives, a per diem allowance while they were engaged on legislative business during the session of the General Assembly. As the amount was not named in the commission and instructions, it had to be determined by a vote of both branches of the Legislature, and, as each Assembly had the right to name the amount to be paid, it could be changed.

---

[1] *Records of the Colony of the Mass. Bay in N.E.*, 101.
[2] *Ibid.*, 140.   [3] *Ibid.*, III, 320.
[4] S. G. Arnold, *Hist. of R.I.*, I, 328.   [5] *Ibid.*, 365.

Generally, however, the Councilors received two shillings more a day than the members of the lower House.[1]   In Pennsylvania likewise the members of the upper branch were made more expensive than those of the lower.   By the Frame of Government of 1696 the wages of members of the Council were put at five shillings a day, those of members of the Assembly at four, with payment to be made by the counties.

Perhaps to anticipate the criticism of taxpayers, not uncommonly the provisions for wages were accompanied by reasons, as we have seen in the almost deprecatory language of the General Court of Massachusetts in 1645.   Of more far-reaching significance was the explanation in "The Concessions and Agreements of the Proprietors, Freeholders and Inhabitants of the Province of West New-Jersey in America," setting the allowance to each member of the Assembly at a shilling a day — "that thereby he may be known to be the servant of the people." Contrast the flavor of high hope therein with the sorry proof of result given by the depressing explanation of the Virginia Assembly: "Whereas the excessive expences of the Burgesses causing diverse misunderstandings between them and the people occasioned an injunction to make an agreement with them before their election which may probably cause interested persons to purchase votes by offering to undertake the place at low rates and by that meanes make the place both mercenary and contemptible, Bee it therefore enacted by this present grand assembly that the allowance for their maintenance be ascertained to one hundred and fifty pounds of tobacco per day besides their charge in goeing and comeing." [2]   That seems to have been thought inadequate, for in the codification of the following year they put after the word "rates" — "by which meanes the candour and ffreedome which should be in the choice of persons credited with soe honorable and greate a trust might be very much prejudiced and that place itself become mercenary and contemptable." [3]

The salaries, however, proved to be by no means "contemptable," at any rate from the point of view of the recipients, for we find that in 1673 the wages and expenses of the two members from Lancaster County were burdening it to the tune of $25

[1] W. H. Fry, " New Hampshire as a Royal Province," *Columbia Univ. Studies,* xxix, 2 : 105 (1908).

[2] Hening, *Statutes at Large,* ii, 23 (1660–61).   [3] *Ibid.,* ii, 106.

a day, as we should now calculate value, and a score of years later the total cost of the three members from Lancaster amounted to what would be about $2500 in modern figures. One of the excuses offered for the high cost was the exorbitant charge made for liquors by the innkeepers of Jamestown. Another explanation appeared when King James II wrote to the Governor in 1685, commending him for having put an end to the session of the House of Burgesses, one of his reasons being — "their sinister intentions to protract the time of their sitting to the great oppression of our good subjects, from whome they receive their wages for their attendance in the assembly." [1]

Sometimes the Burgess was paid by the parish or county he represented, sometimes by the colony as a whole. Sometimes he was paid in money, sometimes "in kind" (tobacco). Whether county or colony should pay depended upon the decision of each particular Assembly. After September, 1756, except in 1760 and possibly 1762, the salary was regularly paid from the public treasury. [2]

In 1726, the date of the first Journal of a North Carolina Assembly that we have, each member of the House received ten shillings a day, in colonial bills, then depreciated to a quarter of their face value in English money. The wage covered each day that attendance on the Assembly kept the member from home. Singularly enough, South Carolina took just the opposite view of the matter. Lieutenant-Governor Bull, writing to the Earl of Hillsborough in 1770, said that the members of the Assembly disdained to take any pay for their services, though the members of the North Carolina and Virginia Assemblies received eight or nine shillings sterling a day. [3] There had been at least one attempt to change this. In 1746, when a bill for the payment of members was introduced, the Assembly first struck out the provision for the payment of Councilors, and then by a vote of 18 to 11 killed what was left of the measure.

In the States

WHEN the States came to frame their Constitutions, the idea of compensation was still uppermost. The Pennsylvania docu-

---

[1] Hening, *Statutes at Large*, III, 40.
[2] E. I. Miller, *The Legislature of the Province of Virginia*, 96.
[3] W. Roy Smith, *South Carolina as a Royal Province*, 115.

ment of 1776 set forth the sentiments of the time: "As every freeman to preserve his independence (if without a sufficient estate), ought to have some profession, calling, trade or farm, whereby he may honestly subsist, there can be no necessity for, nor use in establishing offices of profit, the usual effects of which are dependence and servility unbecoming freemen, in the possessors and expectants; faction, contention, corruption, and disorder among the people. But if any man is called into public service, to the prejudice of his private affairs, he has a right to a reasonable compensation: And whenever an office, through increase of fees or otherwise, becomes so profitable as to occasion many to apply for it, the profits ought to be lessened by the legislature."

Although this meant making good to a man what he lost by engaging in the public service, it leaned toward profit by the intimation that the profit must not be considerable. Two years later Thomas Jefferson went a step farther. As a member of the Virginia Assembly, he prepared, and George Mason introduced, a bill for giving its members an adequate allowance. Although the bill was not adopted, part of the preamble is worth quoting:

"Whereas it is just that members of the General Assembly delegated by the people to transact for them the legislative business, should, while attending that business, have their reasonable sustenance defrayed, dedicating to the public service their time and labors freely and without account; and it is also expedient that the public councils should not be deprived of the aid of good and able men, who might be deterred from entering into them by the insufficiency of their private fortunes to be the extraordinary expences they must necessarily incur:

"And it being inconsistent with the principle of civil liberty, and contrary to the natural rights of the other members of the society, that any body of men therein should have authority to enlarge their own powers, prerogatives, or emoluments without restraint, the said General Assembly cannot at their own will increase the allowance which their members are to draw from the public treasury for their expenses while in assembly; but to enable them so to do an application to the body of the people has become necessary." [1]

Jefferson disliked the Virginia Constitution of 1776, and from

[1] *Writings of Thomas Jefferson*, P. L. Ford ed., II, 165.

the time of its adoption tried to get a Convention held to frame a new one. Finding such a Convention a subject of discussion in 1783, he made a draft of the sort of Constitution he thought desirable. In it he put a provision for wages that was far ahead of his time. The acceptance of the economic principle on which it was based might have saved mankind infinite injury. Not even yet are the mysteries of the purchasing power of money understood, and men still persist in bringing on their own heads the calamities due to a fluctuating standard of value, but some day they will awake to the way of ending the needless sufferings they inflict on themselves. Meantime it is interesting to know that Thomas Jefferson recognized what may be called at least the germ of the real remedy for shifting prices, and that he advanced it in connection with the payment of members of the Assembly. By this plan they were to receive daily wages in gold and silver, equal to the value of two bushels of wheat. This value was to be deemed one dollar by the bushel till the year 1790, in which and in every tenth year thereafter, the general court, at their first sessions in the year, should cause a special jury, "of the most respectable merchants, and farmers," to be summoned, to declare what had been the averaged value of wheat during the last ten years; which averaged value was to be the measure of wages for the ten subsequent years.[1]

The rival of Jefferson for the honor of being America's greatest statesman, John Adams, also believed public servants ought to be rewarded, but as usual he approached the question from a point of view more aristocratic than that of the democratic Virginian. Jefferson wanted the poor man to be able to serve. Adams wanted to dignify the public service. Writing to John Jebb in 1785, he said: "In Mr. Hume's perfect Commonwealth, 'no representative, magistrate, or Senator, as such, has any salary. The protector, secretaries, councils, and ambassadors have salaries.' Your opinion coincides with his, excepting that you think the higher magistrates, as the judges for example, should have salaries. I carry the point so far as to desire that all representatives, magistrates, and Senators, as well as judges and executive officers, should have salaries. Not merely upon the principle of justice, that every man has a right to compensation for his time and labor, but to maintain the responsibility of the person, and to raise and support, both in the minds of

[1] *Writings of Thomas Jefferson*, P. L. Ford ed., III, 324.

the people themselves, and of their representatives, senators, and magistrates, a sense of the dignity and importance of the people." [1]

Adams had put these ideas into the Constitution he wrote for Massachusetts. A sonorous article gave the reasons why its Governor should have "an honorable stated salary," amply sufficient so that he should in all cases act with freedom for the benefit of the public, should not have his attention necessarily diverted from that object to his private concerns, and should maintain the dignity of the Commonwealth in the character of its chief magistrate. The judges, too, were to have "honorable salaries." But he failed to make any specification for the lawmakers, except in the matter of what has come to be known as "mileage," that is, traveling expenses. Indeed, none of the early Constitutions, so far as I have observed, went into specifications about salaries, beyond saying who should pay them. South Carolina appears in 1790 to have begun mentioning figures, with a provision that the compensation of legislators should be "a sum not exceeding seven shillings sterling a day." With the admission of new States came the practice of setting forth definitely what the lawmakers might get. Kentucky began (1792) with a constitutional requirement for a wage of six shillings a day, changed seven years later to a dollar and a half. Tennessee (1796) preferred a maximum limit of $1.75 a day. Ohio in 1802 put the limit at two dollars a day. Ten years later Louisiana was so recklessly extravagant as to come out for a plump four dollars a day. Indiana in 1816 copied Ohio, but said that after 1819 the pay was to be regulated by law.

With 1821 the original States began being definite, in their revised Constitutions, New York in that year providing the rate should not exceed three dollars a day. Tennessee in 1834 raised the rate to four dollars flat for the following session, but thereafter it was to be fixed by law, which was done until 1870, when the four-dollar rate was constitutionally established. Michigan set forth a maximum of three dollars a day when framing her first Constitution in 1835.

The practice of prescribing rates in Constitutions really first got headway in the decade from 1840 to 1850. Nine States used figures, ranging from the pittance of a dollar a day in

[1] *Works*, IX, 543.

Rhode Island to the munificence of sixteen a day (for the first session) in California, where gold was cheap. In that decade appears the first lump sum mentioned by a Constitution. New York, which in 1821 had taken up the subject by providing that compensation should be paid out of the State Treasury, now said the aggregate should not exceed $300, except in case of proceedings for impeachment. However, the custom of specifying a per diem to be paid for not more than a maximum of days, or at a reduced rate after a certain time, devised by New Jersey in 1844, and quickly copied, put into effect in various States what was virtually a lump sum payment, for legislators were not anxious to work overtime at reduced rates or with no pay at all.

Since 1850 no new State has failed to regulate the matter in its Constitution. Other of the older States have come to it. To-day only one quarter of the States give their Legislatures a free hand as to the amount, and some of these forbid a Legislature to apply a salary increase to its own session.

Illinois is the most liberal. The record is instructive. The State began in 1818 with no constitutional provision; in 1848 stipulated $2 a day for forty-two days and $1 a day thereafter; in 1870 left the matter to the Legislature, which agreed on $5 a day; in 1895 by statute allowed $1000 for each regular session, with $5 a day for special sessions; in 1907 doubled this, by provision for $1000 a year; in 1909 the total of $2000 was made payable in the first session; and in 1915 the figure was jumped to $3500.

Pennsylvania ranks next. After repeated vetoes of salary-increase bills, at last, in 1919, the cost-of-living argument carried the day and Governor Sproul signed a bill raising the pay from $1500 to $2500. In New York $1000 was recommended by the New York Constitutional Commission of 1872–73, but the Legislature changed it to $1500 and the people approved the change in 1874.

Five States (California, Colorado, Iowa, Minnesota, and Ohio) pay a thousand dollars; Michigan and Nebraska, $800; Nevada pays $600; Mississippi, New Jersey, and Wisconsin pay $500; Virginia pays $480; Maine, $400; Connecticut, $300; New Hampshire and South Carolina pay $200. The rest pay from $3 to $6 a day, save that Arizona gives $7, Wyoming $8, and Louisiana, Kentucky, and Montana give $10.

The Massachusetts record also illustrates changing views and conditions. There the legislators first provided themselves a salary by the year in 1858, putting it at $300. In 1871 this was jumped to $750; in 1876 reduced to $650; in 1879 again reduced, to $500; in 1884 raised to $650 over the Governor's veto; in 1892, to $750. In 1911 it was made $1000, over the Governor's veto. The bill was not to take effect until the following year, but the Governor saw fit to object, on the ground that the sessions were too long, and that by adopting his proposal for a finance board, each Legislature would be able to act promptly upon a mass of financial legislation for which the data had already been prepared. Measures enacted to that end, however, had no perceptible effect in quickening the work of the Legislatures or shortening sessions. Evidently the lawmakers concluded that no relief was possible in this direction, and when the rising price-scale led to readjustments all along the line, they decided, in 1919, to vote themselves $1500, and passed their bill over the Governor's veto. This led to much scolding by the newspapers, and one at least published at frequent intervals up to the next election the names of salary-grabbers. However, this time the public was indifferent and few members suffered any punishment at the polls.

A third of the States make constitutional provision about payment for special sessions. As a rule, the per diem is to be the same as at a regular session, but Arkansas pays only half as much and Wisconsin pays no wage at all for service at special sessions. Two States limit the pay then to fifteen days, two to twenty days, and four to thirty days. Four States paying a lump sum for regular sessions, prescribe a per diem for special sessions.

It took a long time to get rid of the notion that a representative should be paid by his constituency. While that survived, it was a serious obstacle in the way of inducing men to understand that the first duty of a representative in the Legislature is to the State, and not to his district — a theory not yet universally accepted, but now making more headway than in the first century of the republic. When a representative was held here to be what he was at first in England, an agent, naturally it was thought proper for his principals to bear his cost. Only Pennsylvania of the original States, as far as I observe, placed in her Constitution the contrary view, now universal. New

Hampshire and Delaware found wisdom in this respect in 1792, New York in 1821, Virginia in 1830. Perhaps, though, these and other States put themselves in the right path by statute earlier.

It is hard to find just when, why, and how some of these changes took place. For example, my own researches, aided by those of competent investigators, have as yet failed to disclose the whole story for Massachusetts. What has been gleaned, however, is not without interest from various points of view. It would seem that when the State was organized, the colonial idea of payment by the towns was still vigorous. The first draft of a Constitution, rejected in 1778, provided for this. The Constitution as adopted in 1780 required the State to pay traveling expenses, but was silent as to who should pay salaries. At the first session of the General Court thereafter, it was voted (November, 1780) that the Senators be paid thirteen shillings and sixpence a day "for each day they shall attend," and members of the House twelve a day, and that it be charged to the several towns, "agreeable to the Constitution." The last clause was unwarranted, for this was not in fact "agreeable to the Constitution," and in a like order of the following January this clause was dropped.

The Constitution said that each town "may" send Representatives, and although it further said the House should have power to fine towns neglecting to send, apparently for some time they followed their fancy in the matter. Boston, for instance, chose seven each year until 1805, when it voted — "That the town will exercise its Constitutional privilege in the choice of Representatives"; and at the next election it chose twenty-six.

Everything indicates that decision on this point was in Boston and elsewhere a matter either of economy or of politics. With the growth of Democratic sentiment, the rich Federalist towns like Boston abandoned their parsimony in order to get more votes in the House. A singular episode in Gloucester illustrates the part politics played. Fourteen Federalists announced their belief that the Democrats meant to send the extreme number of Representatives the Constitution would allow them, "for the purpose of distracting, disorganizing, and paralising our State Legislature." So these Federalists, "conscious that our fellow citizens of this town have been incalculable sufferers," promised that if the Federal Republican ticket of six should prevail, the expense to the town should not exceed that of the two Representatives the town had been wont to send. The six were elected, whereupon the House unseated them because the giving of a bond guaranteeing the promise was "in the highest degree dangerous to the safety of the State, and tending inevitably to subvert the freedom of elections." [1]

The Democrats, controlling the General Court in 1812, passed a law that the State Treasury should bear the burden. This was repealed in 1813, and although there was further legislation in 1814, the practice of making the towns pay seems to have continued. The thrift of the towns had an odd effect. Ezekiel Whitman, of Portland, told the Maine Convention of 1819 what took place in the State from which Maine was departing. "These seven hundred members have not assembled for the purpose of legislation — they have assembled to try the strength of political parties — and for this purpose only. This done, and they have dispersed. This huge body has vanished, and left, perhaps, a quorum behind. In a very few days after this assemblage had met and organized the government, we have found the Speaker scarcely able to muster a quorum of sixty." So deplorable a state of affairs led the Massachusetts Convention of 1820 to provide for payment out of the State Treasury. "Such mode of payment," it said in its Address to the People, "has been repeatedly voted in the House, and on one occasion it obtained the concurrence of the Senate." The provision for the change was incorporated in the amendment creating a new basis of apportionment, which was doubtless the reason for its defeat, by a vote of 9904 for to 20,729 against.

In the course of the following decade the change was in fact made, but singularly enough no statute can be found authorizing it. The evidence indicates that the State had all along paid the bills and then reimbursed itself, save in 1812, by levying on the towns in the State tax. How this reimbursement was stopped, is a mystery. The only light shed on it is by a committee report in 1839 which said the practice of paying out of the State Treasury without providing for reimbursement by towns had begun twelve or fifteen years before.

Nearly all the recent Constitutions take it for granted that the State Treasury will pay salaries.

[1] *Mass. Reports on Election Cases*, I, 97.

The New Jersey provision of 1844, reducing the pay of members after a specified number of days of service, was copied by Iowa in 1846, and Illinois in 1849, but all three of these States have since dispensed with that practice. Missouri took up with it in 1849, dropped it from 1865 to 1875, and then resorted to it again. Texas applied it in 1876, Oklahoma in 1907. Arkansas used it from 1912 to 1914.

The New York Convention of 1846 was impressed by the New Jersey idea of abbreviating sessions through the efficacy of the pay-roll, but preferred going the whole distance, and so it provided that beginning with 1848 no legislator could collect more than $300, at the rate of $3 a day, a system that continued until 1874, when an annual salary was substituted. Michigan in 1850 followed the New York example, permitting payment for the first sixty days of the session of 1851, but only the first forty days of subsequent sessions, and the restriction stood for a decade. The rejected Massachusetts amendments of 1853 would have limited payment to a hundred days. Oregon in 1857 said legislators should not get more than $120 at the rate of not more than $3 a day. Kansas in 1859 made the possible aggregate $150 at $3 a day. Maryland in 1864 with a wage of $5 a day, put the maximum at $400, but three years later, definitely limiting sessions to ninety days, made no mention of the maximum. Since then a dozen or more of other States have specified either the number of days for which payment may be made or the maximum payable at a specified rate per diem. In practice it makes little difference how a Constitution accomplishes the result, whether by setting a maximum of dollars to be paid, or of days for which payment may be made, or of the length of term permissible, for human nature rarely lets Legislatures sit beyond the limit to which their per diem payment extends.

When the wage of legislators is at the mercy of a popular vote, they are unlikely to find generosity paramount. In no other matter are the American people so parsimonious as in that of the payment of their servants. For instance, between 1891 and 1908 five amendments to the California Constitution relating to the pay of members and allied matters, were rejected at the polls, before a majority was secured for payment of $1000. It is hardly to be supposed that all the Legislatures concerned had been unreasonable in their suggestions. In 1913

Connecticut by a vote of 17,812 to 25,293 defeated an increase from $300 to $500. In 1914 Oregon by 41,087 to 146,278 refused to increase the pay from $3 to $5 a day; Texas, by 37,221 to 89,307 refused to change from $5 a day to $1200 a year; Missouri, by 89,629 to 355,326, refused to change from $5 a day to $1000 a year; Arkansas, by 43,919 to 49,101, refused to change from $6 a day to $750 a year; Wisconsin, by 65,193 to 153,166, refused the trivial increase from $500 to $600; and North Carolina defeated an amendment increasing pay. This took place in spite of the universal knowledge of the increased cost of living, which had cut down the purchasing power of the dollar by perhaps, on the average, a third from what it was when the existing wage had been fixed.

The hardship to legislators was recognized by the New York Constitutional Convention of 1915. In its Address to the People it said: "The salary of members of the Legislature was fixed at $1500 per annum in 1875. In view of the changes in the value of money and the largely increased cost of living during the forty years since that date, we have increased that compensation to $2500 a year, besides the actual railroad fare of the members paid in going to and returning from their homes not oftener than once a week during the session of the Legislature. An additional reason for this increase was furnished by the argument, earnestly pressed upon us, that many competent and desirable citizens cannot afford to become members of the Legislature at the present rate of compensation. We have also increased the salary of the Governor, after January 1, 1917, to $20,000 a year, as more suitable to the dignity and responsibility of the office of Chief Executive of the State." [1]

Inasmuch as the New York Constitution was submitted to the voters as a whole, its rejection leaves us no information as to what the people thought of this particular proposal, but before the vote men familiar with political conditions reported that the salary increases would lead to hostility by some part of the voters, and it is altogether probable this factor contributed to the unfortunate result.

At least three times since then, if I have kept the count correctly, the New York electorate has refused to be generous. The temper of the people may be judged from the vote in 1921 — 542,094 Yes to 1,003,938 No. Everywhere the further rise

[1] N.Y. Conv. Doc. no. 54, p. 6.

in prices brought by the World War had made the voters yet
more unreasonable. Suffering from the burdens due to the
working of economic principles they either could not or would
not understand, they jumped at the chance to retaliate by refusing to their servants even a penny extra, though each and
all demanding of their neighbors more dollars for their own
services. Of the fifteen popular votes on the question that
came to my notice from 1919 to 1922, only one was fair enough
to recognize the facts of the situation, that of West Virginia in
1920, which gave the legislators a salary of $500 a year. Else-
where old limits were maintained.

Of Congressmen

THE United States came near starting with an unpaid Congress.
Opposing opinions in the Federal Convention nearly balanced.
Debate was long. Randolph's resolution provided that members of each branch were "to receive liberal stipends, by which
they may be compensated for the devotion of their time to the
public service." By Pinckney's draft they were to be paid by
the States they represented. Madison moved to insert in
Randolph's provision the words "and fixed." He observed
that it would be improper to leave the members of the National
Legislature to be provided for by the State Legislatures, because it would create an improper dependence; and to leave
them to regulate their own wages was an indecent thing, and
might in time prove a dangerous one. He revived Jefferson's
suggestion of taking for a standard of value wheat, or some
other article of which the average price, throughout a reasonable period preceding, might be settled in some convenient mode.
Colonel Mason supported Madison. He thought it would be
improper to leave the wages to be regulated by the States —
first because the different States would make different provision for their representatives, and an inequality would be felt
among them, whereas he thought they ought to be in all respects equal; and secondly, the parsimony of the States might
reduce the provision so low, that, as had already happened in
choosing delegates to Congress, the question would be, not who
were most fit to be chosen, but who were most willing to serve.
By a vote of eight States to three the words "and fixed" were
inserted.

Then on Franklin's motion, the word "liberal" was stricken out. "He would prefer the word 'moderate,' if it was necessary to substitute any other. He remarked the tendency of abuses, in every case, to grow of themselves when once begun; and related very pleasantly the progression in ecclesiastical benefices, from the first departure from the gratuitous provision for the apostles, to the establishment of the papal system." Nobody objected to Franklin's view.

It was voted, also by eight States to three, that payment should be out of the National Treasury, but that was not to end the discussion, for ten days later (June 22) Ellsworth moved to substitute payment by the States, observing that the manners of different States were very different in the style of living, and in the profits accruing from the exercise of like talents. What would be deemed, therefore, a reasonable compensation in some States, in others would be very unpopular, and might impede the system of which it made a part.

Gorham, on the contrary, wished not to refer the matter to the State Legislatures, who were always paring down salaries in such a manner as to keep out of office men most capable of exercising the functions of them. He thought, also, it would be wrong to fix the compensation by the Constitution, because "we could not venture to make it as liberal as it ought to be, without exciting an enmity against the whole plan. Let the National Legislatures provide for their own wages from time to time, as the State Legislatures do." He had not seen this part of their power abused, nor did he apprehend an abuse of it.

Randolph said he feared they were going too far in consulting popular prejudices. Whatever respect might be due them in lesser matters, or in cases where they formed the permanent character of the people, he thought it neither incumbent on, nor honorable for, the Convention, to sacrifice right and justice to that consideration. If the States were to pay the members of the National Legislature, a dependence would be created that would vitiate the whole system. The whole nation has an interest in the attendance and services of the members. The National Treasury, therefore, was the proper fund for supporting them.

King also urged the danger of creating a dependence on the States by leaving to them the payment of the members of the National Legislature. He supposed it would be best to be explicit as to the compensation to be allowed. A reserve on that point, or a reference to the National Legislature of the quantum, would excite greater opposition than any sum that would be actually necessary or proper. Madison approved of fixing the compensation by the Constitution. He thought members would be too much interested. It would be indecent for them to put their hands into the public purse for the sake of their own pockets.

Ellsworth appeared to have carried the day, for on the question — "Shall the salaries of the first branch be ascertained by the National Legislature?" — only two States voted for, with seven against, New York and Georgia dividing. Then on striking out "National Treasury" four were for, with five against, New York and Georgia again dividing. Massachusetts voted for, not because its delegates thought the State Treasury ought to be substituted, but because they thought nothing should be said on the subject, in which case it would silently devolve on the National Treasury to support the National Legislature. Nobody objected to substituting "adequate compensation" for "fixed stipends."

The next day (the matter having been postponed), on the question "for allowing an adequate compensation, to be paid out of the *Treasury of the United States*," the vote was a tie, New York having united on the affirmative, but on a tie of course the motion was lost.

On the 26th came discussion about Senators. General Pinckney proposed that no salary be allowed them. As the Senatorial branch was meant to represent the wealth of the country, it ought to be composed of persons of wealth; and if no allowance was to be made, the wealthy alone would undertake the service. Franklin took the same view. There were in the Convention a number of young men who would probably be of the Senate. "If lucrative appointments should be recommended, we might be chargeable with having carved out places for ourselves." The motion was lost by the narrowest of margins, five States voting for and six against. Then Ellsworth renewed the views he had presented as to the House, now applied to the Senate, that States should pay. He was opposed by Madison and Dayton who considered the payment of the Senate by the States as fatal to the independence of the Senators. The amendment was lost, five for to six against. Then the question was taken whether the words "to be paid out of the National Treasury" should stand, and this too was lost, five to six, North Carolina having changed, leaving the thing in the air.

Gouverneur Morris, who had left the Convention a few days after it began business, on returning in July referred to the subject, saying he was against paying the Senators. "They will pay themselves, if they can. If they cannot, they will be rich, and can do without it. Of such the second branch ought to consist; and none but such can compose it, if they are not to be paid."

As the Resolutions went to the Committee on Detail, they provided for members of the first branch (the House of Representatives) "to be paid out of the public treasury; to receive an adequate compensation for their services." Senators were "to receive a compensation for the devotion of their time to the public service" — with no reference as to who should pay them. As the provision came back from that Committee it read: "Sec. 10. The members of each House shall receive a compensation for their services, to be ascertained and paid by the State in which they shall be chosen." When debate was resumed on the subject, Ellsworth said that upon reflection he had become satisfied too much dependence on the States would be produced by this mode of payment. Most of the debate was a repetition of previous arguments.

Colonel Mason called attention to the fact that the clause as it now stood made the House of Representatives also dependent on the State Legislatures; so that both Houses would be made the instruments of the politics of the States, whatever they might be. Sherman feared, not that the members would make their own wages too high, but too low; so that men ever so fit could not serve unless they were at the same time rich. He thought the best plan would be to make a moderate allowance to be paid out of the National Treasury, and let the States make such addition as they might judge fit. He moved that five dollars a day be the sum, any further emoluments to be added by the States. Carroll proposed that an act should be passed every twelve years by the National Legislature settling the quantum of their wages. Ellsworth's change of view threw the balance strongly toward payment out of the National Treasury, and only Massachusetts and North Carolina voted in the negative. The proposal to fix the pay at five dollars a day had but two States in its favor.

Dickinson proposed that the wages of both Houses should be required to be the same, and Broome seconded him. Gorham thought this would be unreasonable. The Senate will be detained longer from home, will be obliged to remove their families, and in time of war perhaps to sit constantly. Their allowance should certainly be higher. The members of the Senates in the States are allowed more than those of the other House. The argument led Dickinson to withdraw his motion. Then it was moved and agreed to amend the section by adding, "to be ascertained by law." The section as amended was then agreed to, *nem. con.*

Elbridge Gerry was one of the three members of the Convention who refused to sign the Constitution. Early in the session he had seemed to approve salaries. He had then said of Massachusetts, whence he came: "One principal evil arises from the want of due provision for those employed in the administration of government. It would seem to be a maxim of democracy to starve the public servants." He mentioned the popular clamor in Massachusetts for the reduction of salaries. He had, he said, been too republican heretofore; he was still, however, republican, but had been taught by experience the danger of the leveling spirit. Nevertheless he appears to have thought it most dangerous for Congressmen to fix their own salaries, as he gave that as one of his reasons for refusing to sign. His apprehensions were shared by several of the State Conventions called to ratify the new Constitution. Virginia, New York, and North Carolina proposed that no alteration of the existing rate of compensation should take effect before the following election of Representatives. Madison suggested an amendment to that effect, in the first Congress, and it was one of the twelve amendments submitted, but it failed of ratification, five States rejecting it, with no record of action by three others.

When the matter of compensation first came up in the Senate, William Maclay of Pennsylvania, the original Democrat, moved it be five dollars a day. In his Journal he tells what happened: "Morris [of Pa.], Izard [of S.C.], and Butler [of S.C.], were in a violent chaff. Mr. Morris moved that the pay of Senators should be eight dollars a day. Up now rose Izard;

said that the members of the Senate went to boarding-houses, lodged in holes and corners, associated with improper company, and conversed improperly, so as to lower their dignity and character; that the delegates from South Carolina used to have £600 per year, and could live like gentlemen, etc. Butler rose; said a great deal of stuff of the same kind; that a member of the Senate should not only have a handsome income, but should spend it all. He was happy enough to look down on these things; he could despise them, but it was scandalous for a member of Congress to take any of his wages home; he should rather give it to the poor, etc. Mr. Morris likewise paid himself some compliments on his manner and conduct in life, his disregard of money, and the little respect he paid to the common opinions of people. Mr. King got up, said the matter seemed of a delicate nature, and moved for a committee. This obtained." [1]

Three days later the matter came up again. The Senators wanted to get six dollars a day, giving Representatives five. Maclay moved to make it five for the Senators as well. "Such a storm of abuse," he says, "never, perhaps, fell on any member. 'It was nonsense, stupidity.' 'It was a misfortune to have men void of understanding in the House.' Izard, King, and Mr. Morris said every rude thing they could. I did not retort their abuse, but still explained the consistency of my motion. I stood the rage and insult of the bulk of the House, for what appeared to me an hour and a half, but it was not half so much perhaps. Izard was most vehement that no such motion should be admitted. It was foolish; it was nonsense; it was against all rule, etc. And all this, although there never was a fairer or plainer motion before the House. . . . When abuse and insult would not do, then followed entreaty. [The Senators did not want to go on record.] We adhered to the motion, and had the Yeas and Nays." [2]

The outcome was a compromise, as illogical as most compromises, under which the Senators and Representatives were to be treated alike, at the higher figure, six dollars a day, until 1795, and then the Senators should get seven dollars a day. This preferment, however, lasted for but a year, an act of 1796 making the pay six dollars for each branch. No distinction has since been drawn between the two Houses.

[1] *Journal of William Maclay*, August 25, 1789.   [2] *Ibid.*, August 28, 1789.

Salary-Grabbing

AFTER 1796 the six-dollar rate stood for a score of years. Then came a famous episode. It was in March of 1816 that Mentor Johnson asked for a committee to consider the matter of salaries. Randolph supported the motion. The present manner of payment is disgraceful, said he. Is it wonderful that we are considered by the people at large as no better than day laborers when we are willing to come here and work for something less than a dollar an hour, which is something more than you pay a man for sawing wood? There should, too, be another change made. A member should be paid whether he attends or not. Is it to be presumed that because he is out of his seat he is idle? Is the only diligent member the one who comes each day, writes and franks so many letters, reads so many newspapers, stitches together as many documents as he chances to find on his table, and adjourns when the clock strikes four?

A bill was reported changing the pay to $1500 a year for each member, with twice that for the Speaker and Vice-President. As McMaster tells the story, Randolph heartily approved of the bill, but did not believe the new plan would shorten the session a day. Members would still have to be roused from slumber to hear the question and to vote on bills concerning the merits of which they knew nothing; the House would still at times be prevented from adjourning because such men had not finished their letters or sent off the last newspaper; debates would still be swelled to great length by the inattention of members who would never be attentive, while the House continued to be a bookbinder's shop. Calhoun declared that he would like to see the sum made twenty-five hundred. The sole check on an undue executive power was an able, intelligent, and experienced House. But such a House could not be had unless the pay was enough to draw men of ability into its seats and keep them there.

The House passed the bill within forty-eight hours after its introduction, and, though the Senate was less hasty, it met with small opposition and in two weeks was a law. That some grumbling and complaint would be called forth was fully expected. But that every man who voted for it would be denounced from one end of the country to the other was not expected. The excitement was out of all proportion to the interests concerned. Grand juries presented the conduct of the supporters of the law as deserving universal detestation, and called on the voters to return no man to Congress who was not hostile to the measure. Effigies meant to represent its supporters were burned. Mass meetings demanded that members who had voted for it should instantly resign. "Wherever I went," said Henry Clay to the House some months later, "I do not recollect to have met with one solitary individual who was not opposed to the act; who did not, on some ground or other, think it an improper and unjust law." In the elections next following, from Ohio, Delaware, and Vermont not one member was returned. Georgia sent back but one of the old members, South Carolina but three out of nine, Maryland but four out of nine, and Pennsylvania thirteen out of twenty-three. "The punishment was unreasonable, and, as is so often the case in great outbursts of popular anger, was harmful, for, of all the Congresses which up to that time had assembled under the Constitution, the ablest and most useful was that so ruthlessly swept away." [1]

In the course of the excitement the Legislatures of Massachusetts and Tennessee had resolved in favor of the amendment that had been rejected when proposed by the First Congress, but nothing came of their action.

Clay had not voted at all on the question; but he was Speaker when the bill passed, and was, therefore, held responsible for its passage. Opposed for reëlection by one-armed John Pope — one of the ablest men then living in Kentucky, but who labored under the serious disadvantage of having been a Federalist — Mr. Clay had all he could do, by popular addresses and personal appeals, to stem the tide of discontent. Even his barber — a naturalized Irishman, who had hitherto been one of his most enthusiastic, efficient supporters — maintained an ominous silence on the subject, until Mr. Clay himself canvassed him, saying: "I trust I may count on *your* hearty support, as usual?" He replied "Faith, Mr. Clay, I think I shall vote *this* time for the man who can get but one hand into the Treasury." [2]

Every member of Congress from Kentucky who had voted for the Compensation Bill, except Colonel Johnson and Clay, was defeated, and these two were spared only upon their prom-

---

[1] J. B. McMaster, *Hist. of the People of the U.S.*, iv, 358–62.
[2] Horace Greeley, *Recollections of a Busy Life*, 218.

ises to vote for the repeal of the obnoxious measure. On the first day of the next session Colonel Johnson obtained leave to bring in a bill to repeal the act, and in February it passed with little or no discussion.

Nevertheless Congressmen felt they were not fairly treated, and the next year they raised their wages to eight dollars a day, this time without arousing much indignation. The per diem stood at that figure until 1856, when a bill not retroactive was introduced, substituting payment by the year, the rate being $2500. It was amended to make the amount $3000, was made retroactive, and was passed. Although embodying the same dubious principle that had roused such a storm in 1816, it met with hardly a murmur. Conditions were very different. In 1816, just after the war with England, funds in the Treasury were low and times were hard. In 1856 money was plenty and times were good. In 1816, with "the era of good feeling" at hand, partisan issues were scarce and the country was hungry for political excitement. In 1856 the controversy over the slavery issue was engrossing attention.

William Stickney, in the "Autobiography of Amos Kendall" (p. 178) suggests another factor. "It is not to be disguised," he says, "that the disposition of the manufacturing and other interests of the country, which profit by the mode in which the public revenue was raised, was to deplete an overflowing treasury by extravagant and reckless expenditures, thus introducing abuses and corruptions into the public service, and blunting the susceptibilities of the people, who, scarcely knowing that they were taxed at all, became indifferent as to the manner in which the public moneys were expended." Some weight may be attached to the suggestion, but not much. It is an example of criticism altogether too frequent, based on the curious assumption that it is possible for "the interests" to combine in order secretly to affect the general course of legislation. This is a favorite chimera of the demagogue. Its absurdity is known to every man who ever served in a legislative body. The truth, of course, is that the community alternates between moods of extravagance and parsimony. When money spending is the thought uppermost among the people, salaries can be raised without remonstrance. When the era of money saving comes, it is rash to raise salaries.

The Civil War was followed by an epoch of prosperity, at

any rate for the North, and furthermore an inflated currency had raised all prices excessively. So it was possible for Congressmen to escape severe censure when they put up their salaries to $5000, even though the measure was retroactive, reaching back more than a year, was said to be fraudulently coupled with another measure, and was alleged to have been hurried through. Only one member refused to accept the increase, and he was defeated for reëlection. Just the opposite happened the next time salaries were raised. That was in 1873, when business conditions were in bad shape. The increase to $7500 brought a repetition of the wrath of 1816. From one end of the land to the other the "salary grab" was denounced. Early in the next session it was repealed.

In the course of the excitement Ohio ratified the constitutional amendment that had failed of adoption just after the Union was formed. The theory that an amendment once proposed by Congress is always open to ratification, makes it possible that this one may yet prevail. If the people get roused again as they were in 1873, such an outcome is not out of the question, but happily occasion for it is not likely to arise, if we may judge by the procedure of Congress when the attempt to get more pay next succeeded. The increase of one half, to $7500, in 1907, was hardly noticed, doubtless in part because business was reasonably good, the purchasing power of money had fallen much in the decade preceding, and the country had become accustomed to higher scales of remuneration in nearly all fields of business and professional activity — but mainly because the increase was not retroactive. As the first Congressional increase in our history not applying to the Congress that made it, the course pursued should be recognized as indicating a higher standard of political honor than the nation had yet seen, and as at least one proof that our public life is not degenerating.

Of course the motive for provisions in the State Constitutions about pay was not to secure payment for legislators, but to prevent them from getting too much. In the older States, with the matter left to the Legislatures, it was quickly found that the lawmakers had not such fine sense of propriety as would keep them from raising their own salaries. So when South Carolina set a maximum, in 1790, she also deemed it prudent to declare that no alteration in the pay should take effect in the term of the Legislature making the change. Two years later Delaware saw the wisdom of that. Louisiana, Indiana, Mississippi, Maine, and Missouri all included a like provision in their Constitutions. New York put it into her second Constitution. Virginia in 1830 went farther still by providing that no law increasing compensation of members should take effect until the end of the next session, the evident purpose being that self-interest should not affect even those members who counted on reëlection. In the Constitution of 1850 this was changed so as to limit the restriction to the term of the Legislature altering the rate, but though we may infer that the experience of Virginia showed they had gone too far with their barriers, Illinois theorists put the same idea into the proposed Constitution that was rejected in 1922.

The Republic of Texas began in 1836 with the singular injunction that no diminution of salary should take effect in the session when made. It was not deemed necessary to continue the precaution against self-sacrifice when the Republic became a State.

The Constitutions of eighteen States now head off salary-grabbers. Elsewhere the fear of public opinion ordinarily suffices. There can be no question that Governor Robinson of Massachusetts voiced the common belief when in vetoing a salary increase in 1884 he said: "I maintain that no safer principle can be established than that they shall not appropriate to their own use, except for the most urgent reasons, any money to apply on account of services already rendered, upon terms well understood by themselves and by the people." This but responds to the general conviction that it is not wise for servants to fix their own pay.

In Other Countries

Our example in paying wages to lawmakers has now been generally followed throughout the world. England returned late to the practice, and only after long agitation. The Chartist movement that followed by some years the Reform Bill of 1832, had payment of members as one of the planks of its platform, but that went by the board with all the other proposals, in the storm of middle-class opposition. In 1870 Peter Taylor moved for leave to introduce a bill "to restore the ancient constitutional practice of payment of members," but the motion was rejected by 211 to 24. Gradually, however, the idea made headway. Gladstone in 1891, when conversing with Morley, suggested that from the Inland Revenue books it should be found what incomes of members fell below the limit of exemption, and that a check say for £300 should be sent to such members. He thought it desirable that poor men should have access to the House of Commons and should stand there on the same footing as anybody else.[1]

It was the entrance of labor representatives into Parliament that brought home sharply the need of support for the man who gave up a wage in order to serve a constituency. At first the Labor Party furnished the money to pay its representatives, but in 1909 the House of Lords, in the Osborne judgment, said the payment of members as such from the dues of labor organizations was contrary to law. Naturally this brought the matter to a head. It was decided in 1911 not formally to reverse the ruling of the Lords, but instead to vote salaries to all members not already in receipt of income as officers of the House, such as Ministers, or as officers of Her Majesty's household. The amount was put at £400 a year. At the end, opposition was not serious. Criticism from the outside, however, has not been lacking. For example, J. A. R. Marriott, writing in the "Nineteenth Century" for January, 1914, speaks of "the corrupt and cynical conduct of the present House of Commons in voting to the existing members a salary out of the public purse." He says Goldwin Smith, whose radicalism was above suspicion, told him that "the gratuitous service of Members of Parliament was the last great barrier which averted from the House of Commons the fate which had overtaken the majority of elected Chambers."

In all the Parliaments of the British Dominions some payment is made. In Canada the salary of the members of the Federal Parliament, now become $4000, is liberal compared with that of our Congressmen, considering the comparative volume of work. The Provinces, too, with salaries running from $500 in New Brunswick to $1500 in Manitoba and Saskatchewan, are more liberal than our States of corresponding size. In Australia the lead in providing payment was taken by Victoria, which gave it to members of the lower House in 1870. Salaries in the Australasian States run from $1500 to $1800 a

[1] John Morley, *Life of W. E. Gladstone*, iii, 479.

year. It is said that there money scandals have been absent since payment began. The Constitution of the Irish Free State says that Parliament shall make provision for payment.

On the Continent of Europe, Belgium was first to act, providing a small payment for members of the lower House by the Constitution of 1831, as reimbursement rather than salary, for Brussels members could not take it, since they were under no unusual expense. In 1921 the payment became sizable, being raised from 4000 to 12,000 francs. As only men of means can be Senators, it has not been thought necessary to pay them, but they get an allowance of 4000 francs for expenses. The Constitution adopted in 1848 by the French Republic contained an article providing that every representative of the people should receive a remuneration which he was not at liberty to renounce. Three years later the Constitution framed by Louis Napoleon prohibited any payment, either to Senators or Deputies. Immediately after the fall of the Second Empire, salary was restored, and in 1875 Senators and Deputies were placed upon the same footing. The amount was raised from 9000 to 15,000 francs a year in 1906.

Writing of Germany Lowell said in 1896: "Universal suffrage was looked upon as an experiment of a somewhat hazardous character, and Bismarck insisted on the non-payment of the members of the Reichstag, as a safeguard. This has been a bone of contention with the Liberals ever since — the Reichstag having repeatedly passed bills for the payment of the members, which the Bundesrath has invariably rejected. The absence of remuneration has not been without effect, for it has deterred university professors and other men of small means, usually of liberal views, from accepting an office which entails the expense of a long residence in Berlin, but it has not fulfilled the predictions that were made either by its foes or its friends, for it has not caused a dearth of candidates, or discouraged the presence of men who make politics their occupation. The provision has, however, a meaning one would hardly suspect. In 1885, when the Socialist representatives were paid a salary by their own party, Bismarck, claiming that such a proceeding was illegal, caused the treasury to sue them for the sums of money they had received in this way, and, strange to say, the Imperial Court of Appeal sustained the suits. The object of withholding pay from the members is, of course, to prevent the power of the working classes from becoming too great; but a much more effectual means to the same end is the habit of holding elections on working days, instead of holding them on Sundays, as is done in France and most of the other Catholic countries." [1]

In 1906 Liberal views of the matter at last prevailed and a salary of 3000 marks was provided. The Constitution of 1919 established that the members of the Reichstag should have the right to compensation by law. That of Prussia says refusal of it shall not be permitted.

Italy in 1912 decided to pay a salary of 6000 lire. In Spain neither Senators nor Deputies have been paid. Of the newer Constitutions those of Poland and Czecho-Slovakia direct that the amount shall be fixed by statute or standing order. Finland sets a figure of 1400 marks. Esthonia, leaving the figure to be fixed by law, says it can be altered only for subsequent Assemblies. As far as I have observed only Brazil previously had a like safeguard against salary-grabbing, in its provision that each Congress at its close shall fix the salaries to be paid to the members of the next one.

Japan introduced payment of members by the Constitution of 1889. It is said the result was not satisfactory, "for at the first general election of the Japanese Parliament the creditors of honorable members who had run into debt were ready to move heaven and earth to secure the return of their debtors, as the only means of securing their money." [2]

How Much Should be Paid

THE variation in the payments to legislators reflects the variation in belief on the subject. Wise men differ widely in their conclusions. In this country no voice is now raised in favor of prohibiting any payment whatsoever, but here and there somebody thinks payment should be confined to reimbursement. For instance, so stanch a Democrat as Simeon E. Baldwin, Governor of Connecticut after being one of her Judges, has said: "To one whose station puts it in his power, without abandoning his ordinary means of livelihood, to share and direct in such a work, no reward ought to be needed that ambition does not supply. No doubt there are enough who seek a seat

[1] *Governments and Parties in Continental Europe*, I, 253, 254.
[2] *Westminster Review*, January, 1898.

in the Legislature from motives very different, and make the want of a salary an excuse for selling their vote or petty pilfering from the public treasury. . . . There are, on the other hand, many of our best citizens who have no time that they can afford to give to the public, and are thus shut out of our Legislatures, to make room for richer and weaker men. . . . But this is a difficulty inherent in the practical administration of republican government in a country without the traditions of a court. . . . The rule of confining salaries to an indemnity for the expenses ordinarily incurred rests, therefore, upon solid foundations. . . . The absence of remuneration is the least objectionable form of a property qualification for office." [1]

The minds of two Massachusetts Governors have run in much the same channel, though probably each would have gone farther in liberality than Judge Baldwin. Both gave their views in vetoing bills for salary increases. Said John A. Andrew in 1864: "I do not for a moment weigh the intrinsic value to the Commonwealth of the services rendered by its legislators, against the price proposed for their compensation. I do not understand that ever they are paid, or ever were expected to be rewarded, in the form of any pecuniary wages, for the experience, good judgment, and intelligent patriotism which the Commonwealth expects to be employed in their annual work of legislation. She claims the right to draw hither, each year, by the votes of the people, a sufficient number of sound heads and true hearts to perform certain of the gravest and most responsible functions intrusted by organized civil society to its members." Twenty years later Governor George D. Robinson observed: "No one will undertake the argument that even the increased allowance granted in the proposed bill constitutes adequate pay, viewed in the light of wages, for the performance of the duties imposed on the members of the Legislature. In the legislative branch of the government, as is the rule in municipal affairs and in the management of great concerns by boards of trustees and commissioners, it has been the practice from the foundation of the State to intrust important interests, for a limited period, to men selected for their fitness and disinterestedness, who regard it somewhat a duty to undertake the public work for the general good; and when but a portion of their time is required, and they have the unquestioned right to determine the days and the

[1] *Modern Political Institutions*, 338–40.

hours of their session, to avoid interruption and disturbance of private interests, too great a sacrifice does not seem to be demanded."

Other Governors, however, equally public-spirited and conscientious, can be quoted to the opposite effect. For example, Governor Hoffman of New York said in his message urging a Constitutional Commission, in 1872: "There is no true economy in withholding from public servants a just compensation for their labor." Governor Dix of the same State elaborated this in his message of the following year. "It is neither just nor creditable to the State," he said, "that its legislators should be kept at a distance from their homes, to labor for the welfare of the people, and to protect the interest of their constituents, and be compelled to have recourse to their private means to meet their personal expenses. All who give their time and talents to the State should receive a compensation for their services proportionate to the importance of their duties, and to the expenditures which they must necessarily incur in performing them." Some more recent Governors have used even stronger language. Governor Dunne of Illinois declared to the Governors' Conference of 1913: "It is shocking and indecent to ask people to represent a State in the Legislature and pass upon laws and help in the passage of laws of tremendous and far-reaching effect upon the people, and pay them the nigardly salaries that are paid in some of the States of the United States." [1] Governor O'Neal of Alabama was just as emphatic. "The present salary in almost every Legislature is utterly inadequate," he protested. "It would be better for the State to invite free service from her citizens than the miserable pittance she now offers. It is too often the case that the leading candidates are young men just commencing their careers, or professional politicians who hope to find in legislative halls an avenue to political preferment. The reorganization of our Legislatures should be accompanied with the payment of salaries sufficient to command the services of the ablest men in the State." [2]

Here, it will be seen, is a distinct adhesion to the doctrine that the pay must be big enough to command the best services. That eminent authority on constitutional law, Judge T. M. Cooley, has usefully commented on such doctrine. Although

[1] *Proceedings*, 270.
[2] "Distrust of State Legislatures," *No. Am. Review*, May, 1914.

he had especially in mind the salaries of judges and other State officers, his views were in at least some measure applicable to the payment of legislators. "The opinion is often and very strongly expressed," he observed, "that to secure the best talent in the service of the State, the compensation must be equal to what the best talent secures in the various branches of private business. There is some degree of truth in this opinion; at the same time it is probably true that no citizen of Michigan ever declined one of its leading offices for the reason solely that the salary fixed by the Constitution was inferior to what he might reasonably look for in private life. And it is also probably true that the low compensation for public services has had a powerful tendency to keep alive ideas of economy and frugality in official circles and in all branches of State expenditure, and even among the people at large; and that we may justly attribute to it some influence in securing the remarkable exemption from official peculations and legislative scandals and corruption which the State for the most part has enjoyed." [1]

Yet the very cause to which Judge Cooley ascribed in part the purity of Michigan Legislatures was the cause to which Thurlow Weed ascribed in part precisely the opposite effect in New York. Weed, recalling in 1866 his intimate knowledge of the New York Legislature from 1814 to 1839, said that legislation and Legislatures had within thirty years become sadly demoralized. "Insufficient compensation," he went on to aver, "is one cause of legislative dishonesty. A member who receives from the State for his services less than is absolutely necessary to pay his expenses, is wronged, and therefore subject to temptation." [2]

Perhaps, though, these conclusions are not so contradictory as they seem at first blush. Weed was criticizing salaries below the living point. Cooley may have favored having those of legislators above that point, although as Michigan up to the time he wrote had been paying three dollars a day, not many men would see therein much of a margin above the subsistence level. Right there is the insolvable problem. Who can tell what it ought to cost another to live? Family, illness, environment, habit, tastes — these and dozens of other factors complicate. Of course nothing but an average can be attempted, and even that is wholly unsatisfactory. Suppose you were to

---

[1] *Michigan*, 302–03.   [2] *Autobiography of Thurlow Weed*, 410.

say the members of a Legislature ought to get what on the average would equal daily earnings in their usual occupations. That would not compensate professional men for the loss of clients or business men for the interference with their affairs.

The same difficulty rises if you pay attention only to the circumstances of that group of legislators who would not ordinarily be called prosperous. We hold that a Legislature should contain representatives of all walks in life and all grades in the social scale. This implies that some will be without independent resources. Such men were in the mind of the majority of the New York Convention Committee on Legislative Organization when it reported in 1915: "At the present rate of compensation it has become practically impossible for a poor man to accept the office and properly attend to its duties, and particularly is it impossible for the laboring man whose absence not only prevents him from otherwise earning support for his family, but frequently results in his being compelled, after his period of service, to seek a new position." As the proposal was to raise the salary from $1500 to $2500, it may be presumed that the majority of the committee thought $1500 for such part of the year as a New York Assembly sits, to be below the minimum of the earning capacity of a poor man in New York, plus what should be allowed for possible loss of position, which will surprise men accustomed to the standards of other States.

The minority of the committee presented a different view of the case. "We believe," it said, "that the best service to the State in the Legislature is not rendered by the man devoting his whole time to political life and who is lured by the salary, but rather by those who, busy in their own affairs, are yet willing to sacrifice of their time in serving the public in places of honor, and who find much of their compensation for such service in the confidence and regard of the constituency electing them and in the satisfaction that comes from the consciousness of duty well performed. It must be borne in mind that the active duties of a member of the Legislature are not continuous, do not usually engage more than a third of the year, and that they are so distributed as to leave reasonable time for a man diligent in business to care somewhat for his private affairs, while still serving well the public." [1]

This brings us nearer what seems to me the heart of the prob-

[1] N.Y. Conv. Doc. no. 20, p. 4.

lem. The minority said that we want representatives who are willing to make sacrifice. Against this set such a view as that of Professor Jones: "We must rely for the most part on men who cannot afford to sacrifice their own interests to those of the public, or at least cannot afford to do so for a succession of years, as is necessary if the State is to reap the advantage of their previous legislative experience. The salary of the legislator should therefore be a reasonable return for the sacrifice which an ordinary citizen would be called upon to make."[1] Individual decision between these two contentions will depend so much upon the mental habit and the material environment of the judge, that after all it will have little value. As a matter of fact the statutory result will depend on the relative strength of these contentions in the community concerned.

Professor Jones concludes that poor payment of legislators is the poorest investment the State can make. "The salaries we pay are high enough for the small politician who is not too careful of the subsidiary income which may come his way, but they are not high enough to secure the continued service of our solid citizenship. No better way could be devised to work to the advantage of the lobbyist than to keep the salary of the legislator low." Professor Holcombe argues to like effect, saying that "unless legislators are to supplement their official wages by prostituting their public position to purposes of private gain, the only men who can afford to go to most Legislatures are those so poor that they have nothing to lose or so rich that they need not care how much they lose."[2]

After weighing these considerations and opinions, and adding the result of personal observation, I hazard these beliefs:

The pay of a State legislator ought not to be large enough to make it a material factor in candidacies for the position.

It ought not to be so small as to impose real hardship on a man without resources.

It ought to contemplate an element of money sacrifice.

As a matter of fact the money sacrifice will usually be offset by advantages in the way of gratification of ambition, satisfaction in exercising power and playing an honorable part in public affairs, and the more tangible benefits that come through increase of acquaintance, through greater prestige, and through additions to knowledge of men and matters.

[1] C. L. Jones, *Statute Lawmaking*, 8.   [2] *State Government in the U.S.*, 236.

With Congressmen it is a different matter. We properly expect a member of Congress to abandon his profession or business, and to devote himself wholly to public affairs. Also we ask him to live away from his usual home half to three quarters of the time, or even more, under domestic conditions commonly much more expensive than those to which he has been accustomed. Occasionally the reputation and prestige he gets will accrue to his advantage on leaving Congress; occasionally he secures appointment to office at a salary larger than he could elsewhere earn; but in the great majority of cases he suffers net loss in the end by disappearance of his clientage, by disruption of his business, by the inability to pick up the threads and resume his vocation. Furthermore, it is of real importance that strong men shall be able to continue in the service of the nation and that statesmanship can be a career in the United States as it is elsewhere in the world. It may not be unwise in the State Legislatures to base the rate of pay on the standards of the least prosperous members. Sessions are for the most part brief, terms of service are for the most part few, and the requirement of some degree of sacrifice does no great harm, but on the other hand does some good. In Congress the salaries ought to be based on the situation of the most capable men. The country can well afford to pay excessively for the less capable, that it may keep in its service those who are competent to decide great questions of war and peace, of commerce and finance, the questions that affect the welfare and the safety of a hundred million human beings.

Robert Lincoln O'Brien, an experienced newspaper man who was long in Washington, writing on "The Troubles of a New Congressman" in "The Outlook" of December 2, 1905, observed that the small salary was driving out of Congress an increasing number of useful men who, in the prime of life and with growing families, could not afford to stay. He quoted Congressman Knox, of Massachusetts, as saying, after he had received visits one morning from a number of constituents, nearly all of whom needed pecuniary assistance: "The Congress of the United States is the proper place for either of two classes of men — those who are so rich that they can respond cheerfully to the requests of every charitable organization, political club, Grand Army post, or church improvement enterprise in the district without feeling the drain in the least; and, second, those who are so poor that the meanest beggar would not waste time trying to extort anything from them.   For a man who belongs to neither of these classes, who, like myself, is in between the two — Congress is no place."

The increase in the salary soon afterward, from $5000 to $7500, proved but a brief palliative, for it no more than offset the drop in the purchasing power of money between 1896 and 1910. With the drop of another third from the 1896 level, brought about chiefly by the currency inflation connected with the World War, the salary became totally inadequate to the needs of members having no other income.   At the same time the opportunity to earn other income was greatly reduced, for the exigencies of the war period compelled extra sessions and made the work of a Congressman almost continuous.   Up to this period he could count on having about half of every twenty-four months available for private affairs.   Whether with the vastly expanded scope of governmental activities, in other words the huge growth in public business, long intervals between sessions will ever again be possible, remains to be seen.   One Senator, Edward J. Gay, of Louisiana, convinced that the new conditions would be permanent, announced early in 1920 that he would not be a candidate for reëlection, for he was unwilling to accept an office to which he could not continue to give his undivided attention.

Although the members of Congress of course appreciated the bearing of the situation upon their individual welfare, and some of them knew its menace to the public welfare, although it was clear that the salary had become grossly inadequate in comparison with the real value of the salary of a generation before, yet they hesitated to act.   Nearly all the citizens of the country belonging to the professional class were in much the same plight; the suffering due to the maladjustments of swiftly rising prices was widespread; and there was natural reluctance to make any addition to the burdens of taxation.   So Congressmen were among the last to begin talking about the need of more pay.

As things stand now, I should hesitate to advise any man having a family and without independent resources, to be a candidate for Congress.   He cannot hope to dress and to dwell and generally to live as his constituents would expect and his self-respect demand, with decent regard to the dignity of his position, and yet escape constant anxiety.   He will be unable to lay aside anything against sickness or the needs of old age. He will be lucky if he keeps out of debt. If he hopes to stay in office long enough to win standing and influence, he will face the certainty that upon the failure of reëlection which sooner or later ends almost every public career in America, with practice or clientage or business prestige gone, with the earning habit broken, perhaps with bodily and mental powers impaired, his remaining days will lack many a comfort enjoyed by his compeers who have not sought the chance to be of service to their fellow-citizens. It happens that I can say this without personal bias. My only motive is to disclose the situation to any reader who may chance to aspire to a seat in Congress, as well as to awaken all my readers to the folly of under-paying the men whom they intrust with the affairs of the nation.

INCIDENTAL OUTLAY

THE critic who finds fault with the salaries of lawmakers usually forgets or ignores the outlays that are incidental to public service. They are a serious matter to the man without independent income. Election costs alone make no small inroad on earnings. Theoretically, these are quite unjustifiable, and the time will doubtless come when they will be taken away from individuals, the public assuming all the costs of selecting its servants. At present, however, not only must the candidates as a practical matter usually go to material expense, but also that expense is in effect made legitimate by corrupt practices acts. For instance, Massachusetts says any candidate may spend $150, may not expend more than $5000, and within these limits may expend $25 for each thousand voters in his district. Thus that which a candidate is virtually invited to spend, takes a not insignificant part of the salary he gets if successful.

This is only the beginning of drains on his purse, if he is elected. As long as he is in office, he is the target for every sort of solicitation. He is expected to be a generous contributor to all the organizations of his party, to charities and philanthropies, and a host of devices for the rapid circulation of money. Such a burden has this become that in at least one State the statute book has been invoked as a shield. The Massachusetts law against corrupt practices was amended in 1911 so as to make it an offense to solicit either from a candidate for, or from any person occupying, an elective public office, any payment or gift for advertising, gratuities, donations, tickets, programmes, or any other purpose whatever; and also an offense for a candidate or a person holding elective public office to make such payment or gift; the solicitation or making in good faith of gifts for charitable or religious purposes excepted. Of course no prosecutions ever take place under such a law, but it has its uses as a protection to the pocketbook of the man who wants to cite it, though its efficacy was much lessened by permitting the solicitation for charitable or religious purposes.

With courage and tact it is possible safely to deny the greater part of the unfair demands, though never without anxiety over the possible effect on political fortunes. There are other outlays, though, that the man in public life feels he must make beyond the degree probable were he not in office. He is expected to dress well. He is expected to be more than ordinarily generous in hospitality. He should not be over thrifty when traveling. If he has to use hotels, it must be the higher priced hotels. In a dozen other ways his scale of living is usually higher than that to which he has been accustomed. The result is that even when the salary is liberal, very few men save anything. Furthermore, when they return to private life, often it is to find clientage gone or business impaired. To many, the acceptance of public office under the uncertain conditions of American politics spells ruin. To others it spells sacrifice to an amount never appreciated by the public. Political honor is dearly bought.

Very rarely an over-conscientious man raises the question of whether he ought to accept any payment at all for serving the public. If he can easily afford it, his scruples, or some other cause, may lead him to refuse to draw his salary, or having drawn it, to give it to some charity. Unfortunately there is occasional ground for fear that his course is due to some other cause than pure scruple. From early times men have sought to ingratiate themselves with electorates by the pretense of generosity. As long ago as 1678 the House of Commons had occasion to make a standing order declaring it bribery if a candidate for the House should give or promise any gift or reward to the county, town, or borough from which he sought to be returned to Parliament, after writs of election had been issued; and the order punished the person so offending by expulsion and a limited disqualification. In our country this kind of bribery has here and there taken the form of an offer to forego all or part of the salary attached to the desired office.

Such a course has been severely condemned. An early case was that of William Cole and Cole Diggs, charged in 1715 with having made preëlection promises that they would not draw any salary if elected to the Virginia House of Burgesses. Finding that the charges were true, the House declared Cole and Diggs not to have been duly elected, and asked Governor Spotswood to issue writs for a new election. The offenders were among Spotswood's few supporters in the House, which may have had something to do with his indignation over their treatment, but another election was held and the same men being returned, were this time admitted. The Burgesses based their contention on the law disabling anybody who made or promised a gift of money or anything else to any "person or persons in Particular" or to any "county, Town, or corporation, in general." As each county then paid the salary of its two Burgesses, the offer of service without salary was held to be a promise of reward to the county.

When in 1873 J. E. Newell offered the voters of Vernon County, Wisconsin, to serve as county judge for $700 a year, $1000 being the salary, and later reduced his offer to $600, the court held (State v. Purdy, 36 Wis. 213) that votes given by reason of such an offer were void. The voice of justice spoke still more emphatically as a result of what took place in Calloway County, Missouri, in 1878. About a thousand citizens held a mass meeting and passed resolutions in which they said the salaries of their county officers were larger than they could afford to pay, and that there were plenty of good men, competent and honest, who were willing to perform the services at lower rates set forth in the resolutions. It was voted to support no man who would not agree to serve for an amount specified. One Collier was elected Judge of Probate under such an agreement. The matter was carried to the Supreme Court, which held against him.[1] The ground for the decision was that such a promise tends to swerve the voter from his duty as a citizen; to blind his perceptions to the sole question he should consider — the qualifications of the candidate; and to fix them upon

[1] State v. Collier, 72 Mo. 13 (1880).

considerations altogether foreign to the proper exercise of the
highest right known to free men, the right of suffrage.   However
laudable the promise in its object, it is demoralizing in its tendencies, and utterly contrary to the plainest dictates of public
policy.

CHAPTER XXIII

EXPENSES

It was early established in the colonies that a man ought not to be out of pocket for serving the public. He ought to be reimbursed at least for his living expenses while away from home. So we find the Massachusetts General Court ordering, March 4, 1634 /5, "that the charges of dyett for the Governor, Deputy Governor, Assistants, and Deputyes of severall townes, dureing the time of every Court, as also the dyet for the commissioners of martial discipline, att the tymes of their meeteings, shalbe paid out of the tresury." [1] When the Body of Liberties came to be framed (1641), the matter was deemed of importance enough to be treated in the fundamental law. Paragraph 63 reads: "No Governor, Deputy Governor, Assistant, Associate, or grand Jury man at any Court, nor any Deputie for the Generall Court shall at any time beare his owne chardges at any Court, but their necessary expences shall be defrayed either by the Towne or Shire on whose service they are, or by the Country in generall."

It would seem that the towns tried to evade the duty thus prescribed, for it was found necessary in 1645 to enact: "The Court, considering of the difficulties that such meete with that make provisions for the Court, at his motion who now maketh provision for the same, for some such proportionable pay to be made him out of the next country rate as may enable him comfortably to go through with that which he is called to, & may be expected from him, do order, that whatsoever charge for dyet shalbe expended for the time to come by the present session of the Courts it shalbe satisfied by the severall townes, according to their equal proportions, in cattle, wheate, mault, or barly, within three months from the date hereof." [2]

Three years later there was occasion for further ordering, to this effect: "For the avoydinge of all unnecessary charges by the expences of the deputies in theire comings to, continuance at, or returnes from, the General Court, its ordered, that

[1] *Records of the Colony of the Mass. Bay in N.E.*, I, 142.　[2] *Ibid.*, II, 101.

560

henceforth, from time to time, the first day of the session of this howse after the Speaker is chosen, that there shalbe two of their members chosen for stewards for that session of Court, who shall order & regulate the dyet of the howse, & to take care that there be no further charges put on the country account, but the just & necessary expences of the members only, except of such persons as shalbe invited by the Speaker or stewards, or at least brought in by their consents." [1]

Read between the lines of this and you may see our venerable ancestors fussing over the menu, ordering delicacies at the public expense, asking a friend to get a free meal, entertaining constituents, imposing on the people, just as some of us do to-day. They ate together, not a bad idea for tempering the acerbities of legislation, as the Deputies showed they believed when they voted in 1654: "Whereas it is judged most comly, convenient, and conduceable to the dispatch of publicke service, that the Deputies of ye Generall Court should dyett together, especially at dynner, it is therefore ordred, that the Deputyes of the Generall Court, the next ensuing yeare, viz. 1655, shall all be provided for at the Shipp Taverne, at Boston, in respect of dynner, and that they shall all accordingly dyne together."

The order went on to direct that from time to time before the dissolving of each session, some like course should be taken, so that the Deputies of the next Court might not have to make arrangements.

Lieutenant Phillips, the keeper of the tavern, agreed that at the next Court the Deputies should sit in the new court chamber, and "be dyeted with breakfast, dynner, and supper, with wine, and beere between meales, with fire and beds, at the rate of three shillings per day," but he stipulated that only such as had all their "dyet" there should have beer between meals, and it was set forth that "by wine is intended a cupp each man at dynner & supper, and no more." [2]

In Virginia as early as 1636 the inhabitants of each county were strictly enjoined by statute to defray all the charges incurred by their lawmakers. The burden was by no means trifling. The figures of one county in 1659 show expense payments for the two Burgesses amounting to about ten thousand pounds of tobacco, which meant at least one thousand dollars in buying value. The bill of particulars presented by the Bur-

---

[1] *Records of the Colony of the Mass. Bay in N.E.*, III, 122.   [2] *Ibid.*, 352, 353.

gesses of Lower Norfolk in 1641 suggests almost a feudal retinue, there being charges for four hogs, twenty pounds of butter, two bushels of peas, a hogshead of beer, and a case of strong spirits. Also there was a claim for the wages of the cook who had dressed the food. It seems not to have been uncommon for the costs of servants to be paid out of the public treasury — an illustration of the aristocratic ways of the Southern colonies. A delightful Virginia privilege was that of getting credit for drinks at the Williamstown ordinaries during sessions. Prudently enough, this was not permitted when the Assembly was not in session.[1]

Only one colonial instance has come to my notice where the costs of travel were independently recognized. The General Court of Massachusetts, in its laws about ferries, enacted from 1641 to 1647, "ordered, that all Magistrates, and such as are, or from time to time shall be chosen Deputies of the General Court, with their necessary attendance, viz. a Man and a Horse at all times, during the time of their being Magistrates or Deputies (but not their Families) shall be Passage-free over all Ferries, that pay no Rent to the Country."

It is altogether probable that traveling expenses were generally cared for out of the public treasury. Their payment had been the origin of wages for members of Parliament, a practice not yet abandoned when the first American colonies were founded. The Massachusetts vote of 1648 spoke of the expenses of the Deputies "in theire comings to, continuance at, or returnes from, the General Court."

With the gathering of the Continental Congress the matter became of importance. To reach Philadelphia from the remoter settlements, was a journey of weeks. Each State paid its own delegates and the rates varied. Jefferson wrote to M. de Meusnier in 1786 : "Some are on fixed allowances, from 4 to 8 dollars a day. Others have their expenses paid & surplus for their time. This surplus is two, three, or four dollars a day." [2] The Southern States were the more liberal. Jefferson estimated that the Virginia allowance averaged seven thousand dollars a year in gold. Fortunes were fewer in the North, habits were simpler, and the allowances much less. Thrifty States econo-

[1] E. I. Miller, *The Legislature of the Province of Virginia*, 89, 96. P. A. Bruce, *Institutional Hist. of Virginia*, II, 435–38.
[2] *Writings of Thomas Jefferson*, P. L. Ford ed., IV, 155.

mized. Connecticut was in the habit of electing six delegates and providing that only three should be in attendance at any one time at the public expense, though others might go if they paid their own way.

When the first Federal Congress put the pay of members at six dollars for every day's attendance, it granted an equal amount for every twenty miles of travel going to and returning from the "seat of Congress." It was believed that every member should net the same amount for his services, whether he lived in New Hampshire or Georgia or near by. When in 1818 the compensation of each Senator and Representative was fixed at eight dollars for every day's attendance, eight dollars was allowed "for every twenty miles of estimated distance, by the most usual road from his place of residence to the seat of Congress, at the commencement and end of every such session and meeting." In 1866, mileage at the rate of twenty cents a mile to and from each regular session, was to be "estimated by the nearest route usually travelled." What was known as the salary-grab law of 1873 gave actual individual traveling expenses to and from each session "by the most direct route of usual travel." The repeal of 1874 put mileage at the rate of twenty cents a mile to and from each regular session. There has been no general law allowing mileage for attendance upon special or extraordinary sessions. When authorized, it has been by special act applicable to the particular session.

The earliest of State Constitutions paid no attention to the expenses of lawmakers. Massachusetts, however, making no constitutional provision for wages, oddly enough gave thought to travel costs, saying that "the expenses of traveling to the general assembly, and returning home, once in every session, and no more, shall be paid by the government, out of the public treasury." In those days all but a small part of the members stayed in Boston until they went home for good. Long after railroads made it possible for members to go home every night, the old provision remained; not until 1893 was it annulled and the matter left to statute. Nearly half the States now specify in their Constitutions the number of cents to be paid for each mile of one journey each way; five others specify a maximum. Ten cents a mile is the favorite figure; South Carolina and Louisiana allow only five cents a mile.

When Connecticut, in 1876, made constitutional provision for payment of members, with the pitiful maximum of three hundred dollars a year, it was so inconsistently extravagant as to set the mileage at twenty-five cents a mile. Such an outrage on Yankee notions of thrift was endured for forty years, and then economy got at least the chance of a hearing, for in 1916 the Constitution was so amended that the General Assembly should "provide by law for the transportation of each member by public conveyance by the most convenient route between his home station and the place of meeting." Even the lavishness of Connecticut was miserly compared with the bounty of California in the flush times when that State framed her Constitution, for it gave sixteen dollars for every twenty miles going and coming, but now the California lawmaker is not to get more than ten cents a mile. No mileage figure specified in a Constitution to-day exceeds twenty-five cents a mile.

Those who defend the putting of such things in Constitutions can buttress their argument by citing the Massachusetts Legislature of 1919, which, not content with two dollars and a half a mile (figured on the one-way distance), changed the statute to make it read three dollars. Or they can point to Illinois, where the Legislature, in addition to the constitutional allowance of ten cents a mile, tried to get two cents a mile for each of twenty-one round trips between the capital and home — a scheme balked by the Supreme Court, which said it violated the provision expressly limiting allowances to members for incidental expenses.[1] The same plan seems not to have met constitutional obstacles in Ohio, where every member gets mileage at the rate of two cents a mile each way by the most traveled route once a week through the session.

Maine in 1819 for some singular reason restricted the payment of traveling expenses to members of the lower House. Perhaps it was thought Senators would be wealthy men who could pay their own bills without sacrifice.

Mileage looked like so much clear gain to many lawmakers while the evil of free railroad passes flourished. That era has now passed into history, but for the sake of the record the evil should be here set down as having reached a demoralizing pitch after the Civil War, and having required a generation for its mastery by public opinion. The Pennsylvania Convention

[1] Fergus v. Russel, 270, III, 626 (1915).

of 1873 took the lead with the declaration : "No railroad, railway or other transportation company shall grant free passes, or
passes at a discount, to any person except officers or employes
of the company." First and last, fifteen States have followed
the example with varying constitutional provisions aimed at
this insidious form of bribery, and others have met the situation with statutes. Now that there has been federal prohibition of the practice, we are not likely to see it ever revive.

New Hampshire has met the situation singularly. Its general
law prohibiting free transportation, enacted in 1878, was not
properly obeyed. When in 1881 an attempt was made to put
teeth into the law by making it a crime not only for railroad
officials to give, but also for any person to receive, one legislator rose and frankly stated his dilemma. He had a pass and
wanted to use it going home. Enough others were in the same
box or aroused sympathy enough to get the proposition defeated
by a vote of nearly three to one. In March of 1897 there was
extraordinary legislation. The exceptions in the law of 1878
were extended by adding after "persons poor and in misfortune,
who are unable to pay said fare," the words "and others," so
that the concluding exception read — "and others to whom
passes have been granted." A member frankly said on the
floor that this was designed to make legal the issuance of passes
to members of the Legislature, and the bill was passed. Men
with a sense of propriety outraged by this, were unable to get
the Convention of 1902 to recommend a constitutional amendment, but the Convention voted, 221 to 101, to recommend
that "the Legislature consider the subject and enact such legislation, if any, as in their opinion the public good may require."
When in accordance therewith in 1907 the railroads were forbidden to give passes, the Governor was authorized to contract
for the transportation of members, officers, and employees of
the General Court. They were to get no mileage unless their
homes were more than two miles from a railroad station, in
which case members and officers were to get every week twenty
cents for each mile to and from home to station. In 1915 it
was found necessary by statute to threaten with a fine as high
as a hundred dollars any member or employee who might let
anybody else use his legislative ticket.

An Oklahoma legislator has to take oath that he will not
receive, use, or travel upon any free pass or free transportation

during his term of office. In Canada, by statute, members of both Houses of Parliament are entitled to free transportation at all times upon railways under the jurisdiction of Parliament. The Constitution of the Irish Free State says that Parliament may provide its members "with free traveling facilities in any part of Ireland." It is common in the countries of Continental Europe to give legislators their transportation free or at greatly reduced rates. In Italy and Germany it is free; French Deputies get a large discount. Railroads on the Continent, however, are for the most part owned by the government, which might be argued as altering the situation somewhat.

With the great lessening in the cost of transportation, American legislators seem to have come to make money out of their mileage. Railroad fares at three cents a mile appear to leave a handsome profit, even taking into account the incidentals of travel, provided the member goes to and fro but once or twice in a session. This of course accrues most to the advantage of members living at a distance from the capital. The Congressman from the Pacific Coast is supposed to be lucky. In the course of the session of any Legislature some newspaper is reasonably sure to call attention to the plum falling into the lap of the legislator who comes from the most remote corner of the State. Naturally this encourages criticism of the system and adds to the absurd but prevalent notion that all lawmakers are petty grafters. As a result reduction or abolition of mileage is a favorite resort of those demagogues whose hypocritical demands for economy are designed to get them into office, as well as of some sincere patriots whose information does not match their motives.

Is it to be conceived that the system would have withstood the innumerable assaults upon it if to honorable legislators acquainted with the facts of the situation, the system had not seemed to accomplish, however roughly and crudely, a justifiable purpose?

Misunderstanding has come from uncertainty as to just what "mileage" does or should mean. Critics too hastily assume that it means nothing but transportation costs. Even if that were so, there remain the questions of whether it includes those for a member's family, and whether but one journey to and fro should be taken into account. In origin and early development, however, we have seen that the payment, whatever its name, was meant to cover what we call traveling expenses. Why should it not now go at least that far? Indeed would there be injustice in having it approximate the additional living costs entailed by service in a legislative body? No general rule could be devised that would measure these fairly and accurately for every member, so diverse are the conditions. Probably distance furnishes as good a criterion as can be found. Speaking broadly, the farther a member lives from the seat of government, the more it costs him, directly and indirectly, to share in making laws. With that in mind, the criticisms of mileage become narrow, unreasonable, unjust.

PERQUISITES

NEW JERSEY in 1844 summarily freed itself from all perplexing problems of mileage or other legislative perquisites by declaring that besides the salary of five hundred dollars, members should receive no other allowance or emolument, directly or indirectly, for any purpose whatever. Nebraska and South Dakota have forbidden any pay or perquisites other than per diem and mileage. Arkansas and Colorado have forbidden any compensation, perquisite, or allowance except as provided in their Constitutions. Pennsylvania prohibits any extra compensation, whether for service upon committee or otherwise, a restriction that would bring gloom to lawmakers in various States where recess committees flourish. When Ohio prohibits extra compensation, it discloses the particular evil there aimed at by specifying postage.

That it has been deemed necessary to give to such provisions the solemn weight of constitutional declaration, precludes denial of the existence among legislators of traits of human nature that are to be found in other bodies of men. In any considerable group of human beings you are sure to find some individuals who are greedy or thriftless, some who lack a fine sense of honor, many who are indifferent. The result in most of our Legislatures has been a luxuriant growth of petty graft, of no very great consequence in its aggregate burden on the taxpayers, but extremely annoying to men with scruples, and having various demoralizing effects calling for remedy. It has not always been easy to draw the line between expenditures reasonably to be incurred for the proper performance of duty and those that savor of individual benefit. Furthermore, while some perquisites of office are harmful, others are harmless and may be accepted safely by the most conscientious. These things, too, are often matters of convention, with standards changing from generation to generation or from place to place. Time was when the item for flip or punch was a normal entry in the expenses of ordaining a New England clergyman. Yet even before the prohibition amendment came, the legislative committee that put in a bill for champagne or even beer, was rash indeed. Opinion, however, did not seriously frown on a charge for cigars.

Our ancestors were not above perquisites, as you may see by an entry of the Massachusetts General Court, October 27, 1648: "It is ordered, by the full Courte, that the bookes of lawes, now at the presse, may be sould in quires, at three shillings the booke; provided that every member of this Courte shall have one without price." [1] Doubtless they salved their consciences by arguing that there was special need for lawmakers to have "the bookes of lawes." More than two centuries later the temptation to get books at the public expense survived still in Massachusetts, for we find that when in 1858 the Legislature fixed by law the compensation of its members at three hundred dollars a year, it felt moved to put in the statute: "No periodicals, publications or books, other than those printed for the use of the Legislature, shall hereafter be ordered for members at the charge of the Commonwealth."

Since 1850 the Michigan Constitution has declared that a member "shall not receive, at the expense of the State, books, newspapers, or other perquisites of office not expressly authorized by this Constitution." Maryland in 1851 ordained: "No book or other printed matter not appertaining to the business of the session shall be purchased or subscribed for, for the use of the members, or be distributed among them at the public expense." About that time the book agent must have been abroad in the land. Horace Greeley, who served in Congress for the short session of the winter of 1848–49, tells us in his "Recollections of a Busy Life," of his vote against paying for the books that for years it had been the custom to buy for each new member, consisting of "American Archives," "Debates in Congress," etc., at that time swelled (by enormous charges) to a

---

[1] *Records of the Colony of the Mass. Bay in N.E.*, II, 262.

cost of about one thousand dollars a man. He says it was well known that many to whom the books were voted never took nor saw them — merely drawing an order for them, and selling it to the book-suppliers for so much cash in hand, less than half what the books cost the Treasury. In one case, a member well-known to Greeley was reputed to have sold his order and gambled away the proceeds before going to his lodging the night after the appropriation was voted.

Nowadays the only advantage the lawmaker has in the matter of books is that he has his pick of the government publications. Not many of these have permanent worth enough to warrant filling up library shelves with them, but now and then some publication *de luxe* comes along, or something of real historical value. The chief complaint the public may make on the score of books is the wastefulness of the system of government publication. In the seventeen years after the Act of 1895 the excess accumulation of documents in Washington that neither Congress nor the Departments had been able to distribute, amounted to more than ten million publications. Senator Smoot estimated that the actual loss in that time due to defective methods of distribution had been not less than $25,000,000. On a smaller scale the same sort of thing is to be found in every State capitol. An efficiency engineer backed up by intelligent legislation could save the people of the country vast sums in the aggregate, while placing a huge amount of reading matter now wasted where it would have at least the chance to be of service. The burden put on the lawmakers themselves by the duty of trying to help distribute this matter properly, is no small item. Congressmen have the advantage of the franking system. Is it not penny-wise pound-foolish for the States not to pay at least the cost of distributing the documents they print?

About the first thing the members of the very first Congress did was to provide themselves with newspapers, to be paid for out of the public treasury. The committee reporting on the matter said just as would be said to-day: "Public economy requires that the expenses of government be retrenched." Then it went on sapiently: "But as your committee consider the publication of newspapers to be highly beneficial in disseminating useful knowledge throughout the United States and deserving of public encouragement, they recommend that each member of Congress be supplied, at the public expense, with one paper, leaving the choice of the same to each member."

Beginning with the first legislative Assembly of the Territory of Iowa and extending down to 1872 it was customary for the members to vote themselves from five to thirty daily newspapers apiece, or their equivalent in weeklies. The papers so received were then mailed to constituents, all at the public expense. Other postage was paid for members, but in 1868 by statute the amount was restricted to three dollars a week. Of late no allowance has been made.

Stationery has furnished the biggest field for petty profit at the public charge. It would be but fruitless repetition to rehearse the sins of all the States in this respect. Let a few figures from one suffice, with the knowledge that the same sort of waste can be found in nearly every Legislature in the land, though not always to such marked degree. Minnesota is taken for illustration, not because there is any reason to suppose its Legislature has been the most careless, but because the figures in detail chance to be available through their publication in the little book of Lynn Haines, on "The Minnesota Legislature of 1911." They show 708 pocketknives to have been bought for that body of 63 Senators and 120 Representatives. The average price was about $1.75, which would indicate that the Minnesota lawmakers needed better knives than most of us can afford to carry and lose. In the matter of fountain pens they were not quite so luxurious, for the price paid averaged only $3.13. One of the Representatives inquired in his capacity as a druggist, the wholesale price of pens corresponding in quality to nearly 400 that had been sold to the State at $3 apiece. The dealer was so rash as to quote him a price of $1.80 if he would buy two dozen at a time, and offered to throw in "a handsome oak, plate-glass display case." The Legislature enjoyed the blessings of just one less than 500 fountain pens, all told. The supplies mostly went home with the lawmakers, or somewhere else. Of 180 ink-wells costing $1.26, 32 survived the session, according to the checking of the custodian. Carpet-sweepers held out better, three of the six enduring, but only one of twelve turkey dusters remained to serve another term.

Nevada may have been the first State to dignify this matter by constitutional provision. In 1864 it directed that an appropriation might be made for postage, express charges, newspapers, and stationery, not to exceed sixty dollars for each member. Illinois in 1870 set fifty dollars as the allowance for such incidentals. Half a dozen other States have deemed it necessary by constitutional requirement to take the same sort of precaution. Trivial specifications about incidentals are quite foreign to the purpose of a Constitution. Furthermore, any allowance at all often fails of its purpose when the account can be taken in cash. In such case it may become nothing but an enlargement of salary and would be better covered therein. More than this, the presence of such provisions in Constitutions may have unforeseen results that harmfully interfere with the proper performance of public duty. For instance, nobody nowadays would question the propriety of adequate telephone service. Yet in 1915 the Supreme Court of Illinois felt compelled to declare unconstitutional an appropriation of twenty-five hundred dollars for telephone tolls for members of the General Assembly, as a violation of the limit for incidental expenses. [1]

Time was when the stationery allowance to Congressmen permitted to many of them a commutation that helped a little toward eking out their salaries, but in these days few pocket much from this source. So great has been the growth of correspondence, other perfectly legitimate use of the mails, and office work, that the allowance now more often proves inadequate than excessive.

A quite different aspect of the matter of stationery and printing is presented by the constitutional provisions looking to the prevention of petty grafting in connection with purchases and contracts. Many a scandalous episode has developed in connection with the State printing. The profit therein is often sought by the publishers of some newspaper that gives important political support to the party or faction in power. To scan over-closely a contract made under such conditions, would be ungrateful. The resultant reciprocity in favors has cost the public much money. For example, in Iowa it was alleged that five hundred dollars each had been paid for two blankbooks that could be reproduced at a profit for fifteen dollars. Somebody wanted the passage of a resolution that should lead to inscribing over one of them, in part: "The Twenty-Eighth General Assembly, believing this to be the most valuable book

[1] Fergus v. Russel, 270, ill, 304, 332.

of its kind ever owned or ever to be owned by the State, ordered its deposit in this case in the historical building, that it might ever be preserved as a fitting climax of the printer's art, at the close of the nineteenth century." [1]

In view of such episodes it is not surprising that we find various drastic provisions in the Constitutions. It would be of little use to enumerate their variations. A typical illustration of their nature will suffice, and a section from the Louisiana Constitution of 1875 will do as well as any. It reads: "All stationery, printing, paper, and fuel used in the legislative and other departments of governments, shall be furnished, and the printing, binding, and distributing of the laws, journals and department reports, and all other printing and binding, and the repairing and furnishing the halls and rooms used for the meetings of the General Assembly and its committees, shall be done under contract, to be given to the lowest responsible bidder below such maximum price, and under such regulations as shall be prescribed by law; provided, that such contracts shall be awarded only to citizens of the State. No member or officer of any of the departments of the government shall be in any way interested in such contracts, and all such contracts shall be subject to the approval of the Governor, the President of the Senate, and Speaker of the House of Representatives, or any two of them." A third of the States provide to much the same effect in their Constitutions and probably most if not all of the rest provide in the same way by statute.

It was an odd provision that the Know-Nothing Legislature of Massachusetts made about stationery in 1855. That Legislature was the product of the agitation against men and things foreign. So it carried its principles to a logical conclusion by prescribing that the lawmakers should use no stationery save that of American manufacture.

Another kind of undue profit at the cost of the taxpayer has been so frequent that an identifying name has been given to it in the word "junket." From the earliest times, in this country at any rate, it has been found necessary on occasion to send legislative committees on errands of investigation or for other quite legitimate purposes. No question can be raised of the propriety of paying the proper expenses of such committees. Unfortunately, payment has given a chance for weak human

[1] *Statute Lawmaking in Iowa*, 673.

nature to yield to temptation in the way of indulging appetite or gratifying extravagant tastes. For example, in 1915, the New York Assembly Committee on Privileges and Elections spent in two election cases $9,075.98 for hotel expenses alone.[1]

Despite such instances of dereliction, if all the facts could be gathered, it is probable they would show that higher conceptions of duty are gradually coming to prevail, stimulated by reasonable statutes and rules. In Massachusetts, committee junketing, at least of the old type, has almost disappeared. Wives and friends do not now go along at the public expense. Requests for leave to travel are most carefully scrutinized, and unless such requests are formally granted, legislators travel at their own cost. Monthly reports of committee expenses are published in detail in a public document. A majority of the committee must approve every bill before it is paid. The sooner like standards become common throughout the land, the better.

Occasionally Legislatures have gone on junkets in a body, with their officers and friends. The General Assembly of Iowa, for example, thus was wont to visit various State institutions at public expense. Of little value as such visits were, of even less value and of probable injury were junkets at the expense of corporations. It was charged that an excursion of the Iowa legislators to Chicago in 1892 was contrived by the Pullman Palace Car Company in order to affect the action of the Legislature on several bills adverse to Pullman interests. The General Assembly of Iowa has indulged in no such junket since 1904.

Whether there is real value in having visits of inspection made by groups as large as a whole legislative standing committee, may well be considered. The Louisiana House requires such visits to be made by subcommittees of not more than three. Why is not that enough for all practical purposes?

FRANKING

POSTAGE wastes have been insignificant in the State Legislatures, but the topic has some interest, historical and otherwise, in connection with Congress, by reason of the abuse of the franking privilege. Franking, by which is meant the privilege of

[1] H. W. Dodds, *Procedure in State Legislatures*, 21.

sending and receiving letters post-free, is of English origin. It appears to have been first mentioned at the time of the Commonwealth, in 1658. When a Post Office bill was under consideration in 1660, it was proposed to recognize the privilege. Sir Heneage Finch said it was "a poor mendicant proviso, and below the honour of the House." The question being called for, the Speaker, Sir Harbottle Grimstone, was unwilling to put it, saying he was ashamed of it. Nevertheless the proviso was carried, but it was rejected by the Lords. At a subsequent period, however, both Houses did not feel it below their honor to secure for themselves this exemption from postage. They justified it on the ground of the desirability of frequent communication between members and their constituents. "Supposing it is true," said Sir William Yonge, in opposing in 1745 a motion in the House of Commons for annual Parliaments, "that some members never see their constituents from the time they are chosen until they return to solicit their votes at a new election, which I believe is very rarely the case, is there not, or may there not be, a constant intercourse by letter? Are not all letters from or to members of Parliament made free of postage for this very purpose?" [1]

Complaint of abuse of the privilege appears early in the eighteenth century. It was declared that His Majesty's revenue was lessened, that scandalous and seditious libels were transmitted, and that these evils were due to a reckless use of the privilege, which extended even to the franking of enormous numbers of letters, without the slightest examination, and the sending of franks by post to be used by persons not members, and valid for any length of time. It was, therefore, directed that for the future the franks must be in the member's own handwriting. Even then the most remarkable abuses were perpetrated. Hampers of game, baskets of fish, parcels of all sorts — even in some cases girls and able-bodied men — were carried at His Majesty's expense by the magic of a member's signature.

In 1760 the privilege was limited to franking parcels not exceeding two ounces in weight. Later, in the course of the American war, Lord North proposed to relieve the strain on the revenue by suppressing the exemption altogether, but his statement was received with such a general howl of disapprobation that the idea was dropped at once for fear of alienating

[1] *Parl. Hist.*, XIII, 1077.

votes. Mr. Pitt succeeded, however, in placing some limits on the abuse. He proposed that all franks should be dated with the time and place. This measure, which practically limited the right to the personal use of members — for which it was originally intended — was carried unanimously. From this time the privilege was watched with considerable jealousy; and though innumerable frauds must have been perpetrated — especially on the eve of an election — yet they were no longer committed openly and unblushingly in the light of day. The privilege was not finally given up till the establishment of the penny post, in 1840.[1]

Abuses of the same sort have been plenty in the exercise of the privilege in this country. The postmaster at Washington declared that in the course of three weeks in 1841 the number of letters franked by members of Congress was 20,392, and the number franked by the Post Office Department 22,038, and the number of franked documents and packages more than 392,000. Not only did Congressmen frank their own letters, but they franked for their friends. A man in the West would write to a friend in Boston and enclose the note in a letter to the Congressman from his district with the request to forward it to Boston. This made a double letter and called for fifty cents postage, but it was addressed to a member of Congress and went free. The member would inclose it to the person to whom it was addressed, thus making another double letter, which likewise went free.[2]

Reduction in postal rates has ended this particular kind of abuse, but in other ways the privilege continues to be perverted. It appears impossible to devise regulations that will prevent the evils and yet not hamper the legitimate use of the practice, for it is really of public consequence that legislators shall not be restrained in proper communication with their constituents and that publications of the government shall have wide circulation.

Misunderstanding of the facts of the case, or deliberate misrepresentation, has brought to Congress as a body unmerited reproach and has caused excusable annoyance to those members, the large majority, who have not been guilty of questionable procedure. Exaggerating critics have given the public to under-

[1] B. C. Skottowe, *Short History of Parliament*, 199–200.
[2] McMaster, *Hist. of the People of the U.S.*, VII, 111.

stand that all Representatives and Senators, without any cost
to themselves but wholly at the expense of the taxpayer, crowd
into the mails enormous masses of printed matter, chiefly
for the purpose of advancing prestige and securing reëlection.
As far as the attack is aimed at the circulation of speeches, the
critics refrain from disclosing that the Congressman pays for
the paper and press-work out of his own pocket, and ten per
cent more, for the law puts him in this respect on the same footing with any other citizen. Anybody can get at the Government
Printing Office as many copies as he wants of an official publication by paying cost plus ten per cent. The Congressman
also pays for envelopes if beyond his stationery allowance, as
is usually the case. The addressing is often done in his own
office. He may have the speeches inserted in the envelopes
without cost, by the clerks in the Folding Room. The only
really important thing he gets free is the use of the mails.

Such documents as are printed in accordance with specifications in the statutes or by order of Congress, are for the most
part limited to small editions, which are apportioned to the
members so that generally they get less than half a dozen copies
each, though where it is expected that a volume will be in great
demand, the allowance may be much larger. Waste enters
because the system pays no attention to the greatly varying
needs and wishes of the members. The startling figures printed
from time to time about the accumulation of out-of-date volumes
that must go to the paper-mill, really prove only that many
members have not distributed their allotments. In other words,
they have used the mails too little rather than too much. In
point of fact it is hard to tell where to send a good deal of the
matter with any likelihood that it will be acceptable. On the
other hand, requests frequently come for documents that ought
to be available, and of which the supply has been exhausted.
It is just as hard for the Government as for any other publisher
to tell in advance what quantity will exactly meet the demand.
Therefore rarely may it be said with fairness that the statute
or resolution is injudicious in respect to the quantity specified.

Still more difficult is the problem presented by publications
of the various Departments, printed upon their own responsibility under blanket appropriations. Congressmen can without
cost to themselves get copies of these, but in numbers far more
restricted than is commonly supposed. No doubt sometimes

a Department is grossly extravagant in its publishing and sometimes a Congressman presses a Department for copies beyond all reason. Abuses might be checked by requiring that sizable requests shall be approved by some legislative or administrative committee or official, but for the most part the necessities of the case will compel reliance upon the personal sense of honor and fair dealing.

Deceptive and virulent attacks upon the franking privilege have poisoned the public mind to such an extent that not a few credulous citizens have come to view the frank as savoring of discredit even when used on official correspondence. The misconception has occasionally been fostered by men of large means who have thought to win favor as purists by putting stamps on all their letters. Such a practice is just as blameworthy as that of the wealthy candidate for office who handicaps his less prosperous rival by promising to forego the salary or give it to some charity — a promise held by the courts to be against public policy as in the nature of bribery. The theory of the frank is perfectly legitimate. It contemplates that public service shall not entail money loss upon a public servant. The expense of the public business should be borne by the public. For this reason there is ample warrant in declaring that a Congressman ought not to be asked to pay postage on any letter or document he would not have mailed but for his official position.

An odd illustration of changed conditions is given by a provision that remained in the Michigan Constitution from 1850 to 1908: "The Legislature may provide by law for the payment of postage on mailable matter received by its members and officers during the sessions of the Legislature, but not on any sent or mailed by them."

Franking has also developed evils in connection with the use of the telegraph and telephone. New York in 1894 found it advisable to include prohibition of the practice when forbidding persons elected or appointed to public office to ask or receive for their own use or benefit, or that of another, a free pass or free transportation. Louisiana in 1898 made like provision. Of course there is no legitimate ground for permitting legislators or other servants of the public, to receive individual favors from telegraph, telephone, or any other corporations likely to be especially interested in legislation.

All Italian deputies receive two thousand lire a year to cover the expenses of correspondence.

PATRONAGE

WASTE of public funds by the employment of superfluous assistance is no product of modern decadence. When the salary of committee clerks in Virginia, which in 1656 had been fixed by statute at fifteen hundred pounds of tobacco, twenty years later reached four thousand pounds, there was grave discontent, not only because of its size, but also because not infrequently, it was alleged, a clerk did not have so much as twenty lines to write in the course of a session. The mischief, however, did not become widespread and conspicuous until the spoils system inflicted on the American people by Jacksonian Democrats had deadened the consciences of lawmakers. Since then patronage has brought disgrace to many a Legislature, and it still works its baneful influence here and there.

The demoralization of the Civil War and the coincident growth of corporations brought the evil to its height. The rapid growth of legislative extravagance permitted for party purposes in the period when Legislatures were beginning to pursue the downward path, was shown by William Lilly in the Pennsylvania Convention of 1873. He said that when he was a member twenty-two years before, the Legislature had but nine employees and it was well served. Now there had come to be between fifty and sixty. "Each man of the dominant party who has influence will get some friend appointed. The friend's name is then placed on the roll, and he goes home, and does not present himself again, except, perhaps, once a week, until the end of the session, when he draws his salary." [1]

A bulletin of the Legislative Voters' League of Illinois in 1903 disclosed a yet more scandalous situation. "The Legislative pay-roll," it said, "is created on the first day of the session, and in the confusion and, to the new members, novelty of the situation, resolution after resolution is put through, creating a needless and extravagant pay-roll. At the same time a bill to provide $100,000 for this pay-roll is started on its way to the Senate. Of this sum $75,000 used during the last session was clear waste, to pay for positions not provided by statute

[1] *Debates of Penn. Convention of 1873*, II, 631.

and not necessary to the work of the session. Ninety-three janitors and seventy policemen formed a portion of the 261 sinecure jobs paid for out of this fund, and the only service required was to appear at the auditor's window and draw pay. The pay-roll, by judicious distribution, was used to further the ends of the organization."

Take the figures from another State. Hichborn in his "Story of the California Legislature of 1909" says (pp. 23–24): "At the session of 1901 the Assembly patronage ran about $580 a day, the Senate patronage about $610. This was only $80 a day more in the Assembly, and $110 more in the Senate, than the limit now fixed by the Constitution. In 1903 the patronage in the Senate totaled $6312.50 a week, more than $900 a day. In the Senate it was $5612.50, or $800 a day. The increase continued in 1905. In that year Assembly patronage totaled $7956.50 a week, or $1135 a day, while the Senate patronage was $6002.50 a week, or $857 a day. The climax came in 1907, when the Assembly patronage went to $9660.50 a week, or $1350 a day, and the Senate patronage to $6893.50 a week, or $985 a day."

In 1907 a sarcastic amendment offered in Iowa to a resolution for the retaining of certain superfluous employees would have instructed the chief clerk "to place on the pay-roll any others desiring employment."

Governor Stubbs of Kansas said to the Governors' Conference of 1911: "We had only a few years ago, only eight years ago, 432 men and women on the pay-roll of the Legislature. I was just new in the business then; I had never been in politics. I wanted to know what these fellows were doing and I made an investigation, went to the pay-roll, and found that over a hundred of them were carried on the pay-roll as assistant superintendents of ventilation — three hundred dollars a day for regulating a thousand windows in the State House. We cleaned them out!"[1]

The Nebraska Legislature of 1913 declared in a resolution (House Journal, 1348) that "in Nebraska as in many other States the number and kind of employees is largely determined not by the amount and kind of work to be done, but by the importunity of persons desiring to be placed on the legislative pay-roll." According to figures gathered by the Nebraska

[1] *Proceedings*, 248.

Legislative Reference Bureau, there had been more employees than members in the preceding Legislatures of California, Maryland, Missouri, Montana, Nebraska, New Jersey, New York, and Oregon. The worst showing in ratios was that of Missouri, where there were 315 employees for 177 members, with Oregon next, having 157 employees for 90 members. New York and New Jersey each had about three employees for every two members. New Hampshire, with its large membership, easily made the best showing, one employee to fourteen members. Mississippi and Connecticut came next, with one to eight, then Alabama and Maine, with one to six.

Oregon has a statute requiring that all expert stenographers for House and Senate must present a certificate from the Secretary of State as to their proficiency and ability before they can be employed in either branch or by committees. Yet Elbert Bede, in the "National Municipal Review" for September, 1923, writing of the recent session declares: "The inefficiency of many of the minor clerks and of many of the stenographers was something of a scandal." Of the clerk situation as a whole he says: "The inefficient ones got their positions because of acquaintance with some committee chairman, because of pleas that they needed the money, because of most any plea except that of ability to serve. Attempts to hire all clerks upon an efficiency basis have been made at several sessions, but have proved unsuccessful. Probably fifty thousand dollars was wasted at the recent session because of this kind of deadwood on the pay-roll."

Indiana follows the happy plan of making appointments for half the session, employing a new corps for the last thirty days.[1]

For a diverting illustration of system and efficiency in politics, examine some of the schemes of apportionment of patronage — for example, the scheme that may be found in the Journal of the Maryland House of Delegates for January 13, 1916. No crew of pirates ever more fairly divided the loot. However, the Legislature of that year decreased its running expenses by eighty thousand dollars. It stopped the extra compensation or gratuities it had been the custom to give to some of the members, a great number of employees, newspaper reporters, and others.

Pests breed their own cure, and the spoils system bred civil

[1] H. W. Dodds, *Procedure in State Legislatures*, 23.

service reform, which now for twoscore years has been slowly bringing back the standards of public duty to the proper level. In this particular matter encouraging signs are to be found in sundry constitutional provisions, in statutes, and in legislative rules.

The favorite precaution has taken the form of constitutional provisions requiring laws specifying the number and pay of employees. These provisions were expected to prevent the off-hand creation of places under political or personal pressure, by securing at least the formality and deliberation of a statute. Thus Pennsylvania in 1873 said: "The General Assembly shall prescribe by law the number, duties and compensation of the officers and employees of each House, and no payment shall be made from the State Treasury, or be in any way authorized, to any person, except to an acting officer or employee elected or appointed in pursuance of law." Alabama in 1875 copied this, and was followed to like effect by Colorado, Montana, and Wyoming. Texas put into her Constitution of 1876 a general provision that the Legislature should employ no one in the name of the State unless authorized by preëxisting law. Virginia in 1902 directed that the General Assembly should by general law prescribe the number of employees and fix their compensation at a per diem for the time actually employed in the discharge of their duties.

Other States have tried to check the evils of patronage by specifying the employees the Legislature may have, or limiting the total expenditure, or combining the two modes of restraint. Georgia in 1868 directed that the officers of the two Houses, besides President and Speaker, should be a Secretary of the Senate and Clerk of the House, and an assistant for each; a journalizing clerk, and two engrossing and two enrolling clerks for each House. The number was not to be increased save by vote of the House — a precaution that would seem hardly adequate. In 1877 this was changed so that the Secretary and Clerk might appoint such assistants as they saw fit, but the total of the clerical expenses of the Senate was not to exceed sixty, nor of the House seventy, dollars a day. Louisiana in 1879 provided the same maximum for the expenses for clerks and employees. Evidently this was found too small, for in 1898 the figures were changed to one hundred dollars for the Senate and one hundred and twenty dollars for the House, with the article strengthened by "including the Sergeant-at-Arms, of each House, together with all clerks of committees and all other employees of whatever kind."

Kentucky in 1890 enumerated the employees allowed, ten for the Senate and twelve for the House, their salaries to be fixed by law. New Mexico likewise enumerated in 1910 thirteen employees for the Senate and fifteen for the House, specifying their salaries, and gave authority for the employment of other assistants at a cost not to exceed twenty dollars a day for the Senate and thirty for the House. In 1908 California by amendment limited the total expenditure for officers, employees, and attachés of the Legislature to five hundred dollars a day for either House at regular sessions; two hundred dollars a day at special sessions. In 1914 the people by a vote of 87,315 to 494,272 defeated an increase to six hundred dollars a day. New Mexico (1910) not only itemized in its Constitution the officers and more important employees each branch might have, but also set their salaries, and limited the additional expenditure for subordinate employees to twenty dollars a day for the Senate and thirty dollars a day for the House.

Statutes looking in the same direction have in part failed of their purpose. Relying on the principle that a Legislature cannot bind its successor, in various States appointments have been made with little or no regard to the law. Thus in Indiana, where an act of 1905 strictly limited the number and pay of legislative employees, allowances in disregard thereof increased, until in 1913 the amount spent for help exceeded all previous records. Several members and officers of both Houses were indicted and tried for making out fraudulent warrants to pay men employed contrary to law. The court rejected the contention that the act of 1895 was binding on the two Houses until repealed. It held that the power of each House to fix the number of its employees inhered in its nature, and therefore was a power that the General Assembly acting as a lawmaking body could not curtail or limit.[1]

The opposite view has been taken by some of the Supreme Courts. In general their position is that the Legislature, although the lawmaking power, is itself regulated and controlled by law. If employees are desired in addition to those authorized by statute, they must be provided by amending the statute,

[1] H. W. Dodds, *Procedure in State Legislatures*, 15 et sqq.

which of course would prevent either House from determining the matter itself.[1]

New York in 1915 thought it best to bring the law into conformity with the practice, and amended the statute so that either House could at will increase the number of its employees. In August of that year Elihu Root, President of the Constitutional Convention, said to one of its committees: "We all know that the halls of this capitol swarm with men during the session of the Legislature on pay day. A great number, seldom here, rendering no service, are put on the pay-rolls as a matter of patronage, not of service, but of party patronage. Both parties are alike; all parties are alike." [2]

In New Jersey the passage of an act defining the number and compensation of employees has greatly lessened the abuse, but has not been entirely successful. In Vermont the law has failed of observance only in unimportant details.

In Wisconsin the application of the civil service law to legislative positions began in 1907. In the Senate Manual of 1913 Chief Clerk F. M. Wylie said the law displaced the spoils system, "under which clerks not qualified were likely to be appointed, and most of the clerks did not expect and were not expected to render services commensurate with their compensation." Mr. Wylie further said: "The idea of clerical efficiency is a comparatively new one in legislative bodies, and even the civil service law could not bring about a revolution in Wisconsin in this respect. The idea has grown through the several sessions since 1907, however, and by reason of the better qualifications of the men, the changing idea of the nature of the service, greater requirements, and better organization, the clerical force of the Senate of 1913 very nearly reaches the percentage of efficiency that is obtained in permanent business establishments, under conditions which the nature of the employment makes much more adverse than would be met in such establishments."

Proof that legislative self-respect is growing may be found in some other States. For instance, among the reforms of the Nebraska Legislature in 1915 was the reduction of the number of Senate employees from seventy-one to fifty, of those of the

[1] State v. Holliday, 61 Mo. 229 (1875) ; State v. Wallichs, 14 Neb. 439 (1883) ; People v. Spruance, 8 Colo. 307 (1885) ; Walker v. Coulter, 113 Ky. 814 (1902).
[2] N.Y. Conv. Doc. no. 50, p. 16.

House from seventy-one to thirty-three, with a total wage saving of $26,316.76. The Illinois Assembly of 1917, under competent presiding officers and with conscientious chairmen of committees on contingent expenses, did away with unnecessary employees and the sources of other unnecessary expenses to such a degree that the total cost of the session was less than half that of the regular sessions of the two preceding Assemblies, in spite of the fact that in one of them the House had won praise for economy.

Do not imagine that the occasion for such reform has been universal. In Massachusetts the abuse is not to be found; it has been unknown in our time, and I do not recollect ever hearing of its existence. Undoubtedly there are other States that have had the same good fortune.

Clerk hire in the Legislatures straddles the line between personal perquisites and public functions, but in Congress there is no longer any question of its nature, for within the last score of years it has become a common and absolute necessity for the proper performance of what is now accepted as public duty. Once what was slightingly called the errand-boy work of a Congressman consisted largely of visiting the Departments in connection with seeking offices for constituents, preventing their discharge, or pushing favor in some other direction. This has largely disappeared, and in its place has come a huge volume of business consequent upon the great expansion of governmental activities. The office of the Congressman is now the medium through which hundreds of the people deal with their government. They might, of course, approach it directly and in many cases just as effectively, if they knew how, but even the best informed of them are sometimes at a loss to know which way to turn, and for the multitude official Washington is a city of mystery. This has made each Congressman the agent of two hundred thousand and more of his fellow citizens in the matter of their grievances, their perplexities, their desires, connected with a governmental machine that by its very size produces countless individual problems.

The growth in volume of this work compelled about a score of years ago erection of two large office buildings, one for Senators and the other for Representatives. Also it compelled the hiring of assistance in the way of clerks and stenographers. Instead of extravagance in this direction, public parsimony was the rule. Afraid of criticism, Congressmen chose to meet much of the additional cost of clerical help out of their own pockets. In 1919, however, this had become so burdensome to many members that it was agreed, though with reluctance, to allow to each Representative $3200 for clerk hire. As a matter of fact, the pay-roll in not a few offices exceeds this amount. Some members are more fortunate than others. Representatives having many constituents employed in manufacturing industries are the most burdened. Suburban constituencies are not excessive in their demands. Agricultural districts are the least arduous to serve. Senators carry a big load. Some of them sometimes receive between one and two thousand pieces of mail in a day. It is not uncommon for them to need six or eight employees in their offices.

The need of a secretary for each member of a State Legislature is open to grave question. Yet in Oregon, by rule, each member of the House can appoint an expert stenographer at five dollars a day or one "common clerk" at three dollars a day. To a man having had experience with only a New England Legislature, this seems a straightout levy on the public treasury under false pretenses, but perhaps conditions elsewhere are different.

In the Iowa Senate there are fifty committee clerks, one for each Senator. They must be competent stenographers and, it is pleasant to learn from the rules of the Senate, must be of good moral character. The number of committee clerks for the House is determined at each session, of late being forty or more. In some cases one clerk is assigned to several committees. Since 1906 the minority has been allowed a certain number of committee clerks. When not on committee duty, clerks are subject to other assignments of work by the Speaker or Chief Clerk; and any Representative may request a committee clerk to do work for him. The majority of the clerks are women. As early as 1873 the Senate decided that the "employment of ladies" as clerks was "no longer an experiment" and recommended the practice to future Assemblies. It is matter of congratulation that since then we have in all occupations stopped employing "ladies" while widely adding to the opportunities for "women" to be of service, thus dignifying their share in the world's work.

Each Kansas Senator is by rule entitled to a clerk, who is

the clerk of any committee of which the Senator is Chairman, and also is subject to the order of the President or the Committee on Employees, when not needed by the Senator employing him. The Maryland House has a stenographer for the Speaker, one for the minority members, and ten for the majority, parcelled out by regions. The Constitution of New Mexico includes among the employees authorized, six stenographers for the Senate and eight for the House.

Every legislator nowadays must engage in much correspondence. Whether or not it directly relates to his work as a legislator, it takes his time, and so interferes with proper attention to his legislative duties. It would be good policy to face this fact. With the modern applications of the phonograph, it would be an easy matter to arrange a typewriting department. The members could dictate their letters on cylinders, the letters to be transcribed as in many large business offices, then carried to the authors for signing, and then duly mailed. This would be much more economical than the system of individual stenography, would treat everybody alike, would be a great convenience to members, and would benefit lawmaking far more than enough to offset its cost.

Governor Clarke of Iowa in his message of 1915 condemned the practice of hiring extra legislative help, characterizing it as "pure unadulterated graft." He said of the employment of clerks: "Every man of legislative experience knows that many more committee clerks and other clerks are employed than are needed. Every Senator and Representative knows of clerks sitting around these chambers in luxurious ease from one end of the session to the other, doing practically nothing at all, and every Senator and Representative knows that such a thing should fall under his condemnation." A warm controversy followed between the Governor and the outraged Senate, with the result that the virtuous Senators declared the expression, "pure unadulterated graft," to be "an unhappy choice of words to express the thought which the Governor's reply to your committee shows he had in his mind, and that it was unwarranted by the facts as they have been disclosed to this committee." At this distance the Governor's phrase would seem accurate.

Congress still endures the spoils system. There are on the pay-roll something more than two hundred persons attached to committees, appointed by the chairmen, and likely for the

most part to be displaced when the seniority rule or a change
in party control brings a new man into that position. Then
there are about five hundred employees in miscellaneous positions who constitute what is known as "the patronage." This
means that their places are looked upon as perquisites of the
majority members, to each of whom is allotted the designation
of his proportional share of appointment as nearly as this can be
accomplished. When the Republicans regained control of the
House in 1919, the system gave to each Republican Representative not having the benefit of the positions at the disposal of
a committee chairman, patronage to the extent of nearly two
thousand dollars a year. In most cases this was covered by two
designations for appointment. Not in our day had the system
been of less consequence. The drop in the purchasing power
of money, due to the inflation of the currency, and the opportunity to get employment at high wages anywhere in the country, had made the salaries of these positions unattractive. Few
men cared to come from homes at any considerable distance,
to face the cost of living in Washington with no more income
than that of an elevator man or messenger. So the places were
for the most part filled by resident applicants, and without
bearing on political fortunes.

Nevertheless the result was about the same as usual — inefficiency and waste. Men who owe their places to personal
favor and do not work under the eyes of their patrons, rarely
work well. Discipline is next to impossible. If a superior
blames or complains, the personal appointee knows he can turn
to his patron for support almost sure to be given. There is
no fear of discharge, no incentive for diligence and care. So
in a multitude of little things the Congressman accustomed,
say, to the atmosphere of a successful industry, finds himself
in the Capitol or the office buildings annoyed by indifferent
service and wasteful practice.

The most scandalous features of the system have in the past
developed in connection with committee employees. Clerks
have been known never to come to the committee rooms, indeed in some cases not even to come to Washington. It is
said that occasionally chairmen have drawn the salaries of
dummy clerks, pocketing the money without apparent scruple.
Nepotism has been far from uncommon, and though near rela-
tives of Congressmen have often well earned their pay, it is to

be feared that in other cases no real service has been performed. Many of the committees do little or no work, perhaps not meeting once in the course of a session, and the provision for clerks for them has given rise to no little occasion for criticism, much of it in the past well founded.

All this has greatly changed of late.   The growth in the volume of work has destroyed the sinecures.   The chairman whose committees is without work as such, occupies its nominal employees with tasks for which he otherwise might have to pay in part out of his own funds.   A fellow-member who as a youth twenty years ago saw Congressional life in Washington at close range, tells me that the busiest Senator of those days had less of routine business on his hands than now confronts the most inconspicuous member of the House.

To-day, therefore, the reformer would find little ground for valid criticism of Congressional expenditure for personal services.   The method of employment for office purposes could not be materially improved.   Such services have a confidential element that precludes the application of the merit system. It ought, however, to be applied in the choice of the working force of each House as a whole.   "The patronage" could well be abolished, not only to the gain of the public treasury, but also, by way of better service, to the benefit of Congressmen themselves.

In Canada appointments in the legislative service are made by the Government without confirmation or ratification by any other authority, just as in all other branches of the Canadian public service.   In practice clerical assistance is largely detailed from the regular civil service.   It is against the rules for any member of a legislative assembly there to propose any expenditure whatever unless first recommended by the administration.   So what money the lawmaking body grants for the public service in any field, creates patronage in which it does not share.   Hence its natural tendency is to keep down such appropriations just as it is the natural tendency of an American Legislature to expand them.   In 1908 such contrasts as these appeared north and south of the line, in amounts paid to legislative employees: Manitoba, $6623.85, as against $69,477 in Minnesota and $31,861 in North Dakota; British Columbia, $2590, as against $30,756 in the State of Washington.[1]

[1] Henry Jones Ford, "American and Canadian Political Methods," *No. Am. Review*, November, 1911.

GRATUITIES

A WASTEFUL source of lavish generosity at the expense of the tax-payer has been the practice of giving gratuities, allowances, bonuses, or some like form of benefaction. It is hard to refuse such gifts to persons with whom friendly acquaintance has been established, particularly if they are in position to do favors of the personal and intimate variety. Public employees are quick to take advantage of this. As an illustration of how it has been worked, read one of Horace Greeley's "Recollections of a Busy Life," telling (p. 229) of an experience in his brief service as a Congressman (1848–49).

"An abuse had crept in, a few years before, at the close of a long, exhausting session," he says, "when some liberal soul proposed that each of the sub-officers and attachés of Congress (whose name is Legion) be paid $250 extra because of such protracted labor. Thenceforth, this gratuity was repeated at the close of each session — the money being taken by the generous members, not from their own pockets, but Uncle Sam's, and the vote being now that, 'The *usual* extra compensation,' etc. As our session was a light as well as a short one, some of us determined to stop this Treasury leak; and we did it once or twice, to the chagrin of the movers. At length came the last night of the session, and with it a magnificent 'spread,' free to all members, in one of the Committee-rooms, paid for by a levy of five dollars per head from the regiment of underlings who hoped thus to secure their 'usual' gratuity; giving each a net profit on the investment of $245. After the House had been duly mellowed and warmed, a resolve to pay the 'usual extra compensation' was sprung, but failed — two thirds in the affirmative being necessary to secure the requisite suspension of the rules. Nothing daunted, the operators drew off to repair damages; and soon there was moved a resolve to pay the chaplain of the House his stipend from the Contingent Fund, and to suspend the rules to accord this resolve an immediate consideration.

"'I object, Mr. Speaker,' I at once interposed; 'we all know that the chaplain's salary has not been left unprovided for to this time. This is a *ruse*, — I call for the Yeas and Nays on suspending the rules.'

"'Shame! Shame!' rose and reverberated on every side;

'don't keep the chaplain out of his hard-earned money! Refuse the Yeas and Nays!'

"They were accordingly refused; the rules were indignantly suspended, and the resolution received.

"'And now, Mr. Speaker,' said the member who had been cast for this part, 'I move to amend the resolve before us by adding the usual compensation to the sub-clerks, door-keepers, and other *employees* of the House.'

"No sooner said than done; debate was cut off, and the amendment prevailed. The resolve, as amended, was rushed through; and our employees pocketed their $250 each, less the five dollars so recently and judiciously invested as aforesaid."

Episodes of this sort became so frequent in the State Legislatures that it was deemed necessary to dignify them by constitutional attack. Nevada appears to have been the first to resort thereto. When it became a State, in 1864, it forbade payment to any officer or employee of the Legislature except under law passed prior to his election; and also forbade increasing or diminishing compensation during the session. Missouri said in 1875: "No allowance or emolument, for any purpose whatever, shall ever be paid to any officer, agent, servant, or employee of either House of the General Assembly, or of any committee thereof, except such per diem as may be provided for by law, not to exceed five dollars." California declared in 1879: "The pay of no attaché shall be increased after he is elected or appointed." In the same year Texas provided: "No donation of any unexpended balances shall be made as extra compensation or for any other purpose." Oklahoma provided in 1907: "The Legislature shall not increase the number or emolument of its employees, or the employees of either House, except by general law, which shall not take effect during the term at which such increase was made."

It is not clear that constitutional prohibition of gratuities is necessary. In the New York case of People *ex rel.* Kene *v.* Olcott, 11 Hun., 610 (1877), it was held that the Legislature cannot authorize the payment of extra compensation to its clerks and employees, nor compensation for a period prior to their appointment. "Where one is compensated by the day, this compensation is measured by the number of days during which he is in the employ for which he is paid. Anything beyond is a gratuity." Nevertheless, since what is everybody's business is nobody's business, impositions of this sort are seldom likely to be taken into court and so it may be well to provide against them.

All honor to Iowa for having positively forbidden, since 1909, the giving of extra compensation to House employees in the form of "tips"; for an employee there to accept a tip, is cause for his removal. More than anybody else public servants should be kept from the debasing influences of the tip system.

Illinois, Mississippi, and Nebraska try by publicity to secure some check on expenditure, the requirement being that the Auditor shall within sixty days after adjournment publish a detailed statement of all money expended.

EXPENDITURE TOTALS

WITH that singular lack of sense of proportion which so often shows itself in republics, the people at times resent the cost of their legislatures, particularly when matters of salary are brought to general attention. Yet the cost of making the laws is an insignificant proportion of the whole cost of government. The legislative department of the United States is debited with an annual charge of between thirteen and fourteen million dollars. Between five and six millions of this, however, is for public printing and binding, much of which is not really part of the expense of legislation, and the Congressional Library, with functions far beyond those of helping to make laws, costs six or seven hundred thousand. It is probably fair to say that the cost of Congress itself is less than ten cents per capita, or forty-five cents a family, and is only about one per cent of the total disbursement of the national government for routine expenses.

The Census Bulletin on Financial Statistics of States for 1915 gives the total expenditure for the legislative branch of State governments as $6,344,341; the Bulletin for 1916 makes it $8,832,240. Adding these and dividing by two, to compensate for the biennial factor, and then dividing by the estimated population of 1915, gives an average per capita cost of 7.7 cents, just under two per cent of the total disbursements for running expenses. That makes the cost for the average family less than thirty-five cents a year for State lawmaking. Even in an annual session State like Massachusetts the cost is less than fourteen cents per capita or sixty-five cents for each family.

Critics are wont in a matter like this to look at the total of dollars spent rather than at average costs per capita. This leads them to forget growth in population, particularly if as historians their minds have been accustomed to the days of small things. Millions terrify them and they produce all sorts of strange generalizations. For example, note the conclusion of so sane a writer as Professor Dealey: "No one for a moment supposes that the States get their money's worth in return for this enormous expenditure. Unquestionably better results might be secured at half the cost under a more efficient system." [1] I am one of those rash enough to think that taken by and large the average American family does get the worth of thirty-five cents a year from the lawmaking of the State in which it dwells, and forty-five cents a year from that of Congress. Is it really true that these are excessive prices to pay for the redress of grievances and for the adaptation of law to the ever-changing needs of a diversified and developing society? On the contrary, might it not be said with reason that so restricted an expenditure is niggardly economy, penny-wise and pound-foolish?

I quite agree with Professor Dealey that better results might be secured under a more efficient system, particularly if he has in mind a system whereunder the making of administrative law would be chiefly performed by administrative agencies, but that the cost would be wisely cut in two is altogether improbable. On the other hand, would it not be better economy in the long run to spend twice the money, that the laws may be properly framed after adequate research — the most pressing need of the moment? Professor Dealey does well in calling attention to "the burden of needless litigation necessitated by defective laws." It is not alone the litigation that costs, but also the needless hardships imposed on citizens, the uncertainties injected into commerce and industry, the interferences with the normal currents of trade and enterprise. We need better lawmaking more than we need less lawmaking. To get it we shall have to spend more money rather than less, and it will be worth far more than the cost.

[1] J. Q. Dealey, *Growth of Am. State Constitutions*, 279.

CHAPTER XXIV

CUSTOMS AND HABITS

SOMETHING should be said about the personal, the human side of lawmaking, not so much here for any entertainment it may furnish, as for the light it may throw on the development of the most important of human institutions. That which men achieve is the achievement of men, of human beings, compounded of wisdom and folly, smiles and tears, of habits, am- bitions, passions — the myriad motives of human action. Were lawmakers mere logic machines, then the measuring devices of science might suffice our need, but as they are men the sketch- brush must be used, even if to get no more than an impression of legislative life and some of the material conditions that shape its course.

We are told that we are creatures of environment. Without carrying that theory to extreme application, it is not unreason- able to say that men do well to make their laws in surroundings dignified, even ornate. It is not for the sake of vain display that public buildings are among the most imposing and sump- tuous edifices man can erect. Their beauty, their solidity, their magnificence give a perpetual lesson in public self-respect. They encourage honorable pride. They instill the sense of power. They inspire reverence for the authority of law. They are the symbols of what government means.

Likewise it is fitting and useful that the halls of legislation and their adornment shall be the best a people can afford, not for the comfort and gratification of those who frequent them, but to keep the makers of law ever mindful of the supreme importance of their labors. These are the reasons why the finest buildings of the modern world, taken as a class, are its capitols, and its finest chambers, again as a class, are those designed for legislators.

Of the same nature are the reasons why the processes of law- making have always been conducted with some degree of pomp and parade, etiquette and ceremonial. In a democratic coun- try like ours, with small patience for what we scornfully speak of as fuss and feathers, these things are little encouraged, yet enough of them survive to call for recognition of their significance. The fact that they are only survivals, is of itself instructive, for it tells us that we have been growing more and more democratic, with less and less regard for pretentious forms. As far as they conduce to reasonable dignity and decorum, we tolerate them, but everything savoring of class distinction has been discarded. Here is at least one aspect of our social relations that may help to dissipate the fears of those who imagine wealth to be reviving class and caste. If they suppose invidious discrimination something new in America, just for a single illustration to the contrary, let them be informed that a century or so ago the Massachusetts House of Representatives had what was called the Boston seat, reserved exclusively for the Boston members, who sat together, on cushions, while other members were left to such accommodations as they could find on bare benches.[1]

Matters of costume throw side-lights on the changes that have taken place. In 1805 the President of the South Carolina Senate wore a blue satin gown trimmed with white ermine, and by resolution of December 19 of that year the Speaker of the House was directed to wear one of the same sort.[2] A Philadelphia newspaper of 1791 said the Senators of the United States appeared every morning full-powdered and dressed in the richest material.[3] Going back to the first Legislature in the country, that of Virginia, we find sitting in the choir of the church where the first Assembly met, the Governor and Council, their coats trimmed with gold lace. By the statute of 1621, no one was allowed to wear gold lace except these high officials and the commanders of the hundreds.[4]

Do not infer that our forefathers sent to represent them none but those who could afford to dress elegantly. Sometimes friends of improvident statesmen looked out for their needs. Such was the good fortune of Sam Adams when he went to Congress in 1774. Adams, then in his fifty-third year, had never left his native town of Boston except for places a few miles distant, his biographer tells us.[5] The expenses of the

---

[1] Charles Sumner, *Debates in Mass. Conv. of 1853*, II, 597.
[2] *Am. Hist. Assn. Rep. for 1896*, I, 864, 866.
[3] J. W. Moore, *The American Congress*, 143.
[4] John Fiske, *Old Virginia and Her Neighbours*, I, 231.
[5] J. K. Hosmer, *Samuel Adams*, 307, 308.

journey and the sojourn in Philadelphia were arranged for by the legislative appropriation. But the critical society of a populous town, and the picked men of the thirteen colonies were to be encountered. A certain sumptuousness in living and apparel would be not only fitting, but necessary in the deputies, that the great Province which they represented might suffer no dishonor. Samuel Adams himself probably would have been quite satisfied to appear in the old red coat of 1770, in which Copley had painted him, and which no doubt his wife's careful darning still held together; but his townsmen arranged it differently. John Andrews, in a letter to William Barrell, told how they did it. "Some persons (their name unknown) sent and asked his permission to build him a new barn, the old one being decayed, which was executed in a few days. A second sent to ask leave to repair his house, which was thoroughly effected soon. A third sent to beg the favor of him to call at a tailor's shop, and be measured for a suit of clothes, and choose his cloth, which were finished and sent home for his acceptance. A fourth presented him with a new wig, a fifth with a new hat, a sixth with six pair of the best silk hose, a seventh with six pair of fine thread ditto, an eighth with six pair of shoes, and a ninth modestly inquired of him whether his finances were not rather low than otherwise. He replied it was true that was the case, but he was very indifferent about these matters, so that his *poor* abilities were of any service to the public; upon which the gentleman obliged him to accept of a purse containing about fifteen or twenty Johannes."

Another story of kind-hearted neighbors is told by Governor Thomas Ford in his "History of Illinois" (p. 284), about John Grammar, who was elected to the territorial Legislature of Illinois from Union County about the year 1816, and was continued in the Legislature most of the time for twenty years. It is said that when first elected, lacking the apparel necessary for a member, he and his sons gathered a large quantity of hazelnuts, which were taken to the Ohio Saline and sold for cloth to make a coat and pantaloons. The cloth was the blue strouding used by the Indians for breech-cloths. When it was brought home the neighboring women were assembled to make up the garments of the new member. The cloth was measured every way, cross, lengthwise, and from corner to corner, but still the puzzling truth appeared that the pattern was scant. The women concluded to make of it a very short bob-tailed coat, and a long pair of leggings, which being finished, and Mr. Grammar arrayed in them, he started for Kaskaskia, the seat of government. Here he continued to wear his leggings over an old tattered garment until the poetry bill (a partial appropriation) passed, when he provided himself with a pair of breeches.

Lawmakers no longer think it necessary to "dress up" and wear their "Sunday best." Nowadays they wear what would be worn by the business or professional man about his ordinary work. He who dresses in the height of fashion may become the butt of ridicule. He who wears what he would wear at a wedding or funeral is liable to the loss of influence with his fellow members, for they will suspect him of snobbery or stupidity.

In England the advance in common sense has been even more remarkable than in America, for the Englishman had farther to travel. A generation ago no London business man, not to speak of a professional man or member of Parliament, ever thought of appearing at shop or office without silk hat and black coat. It was but a little more than half a century ago that no member of the House of Commons who respected himself and his constituency sat in the presence of the Speaker without wearing gloves. Henry W. Lucy recalls how one named Monk, who sat for Gloucester session after session, created a sensation, on the whole painful, by presenting himself on sultry days in a dove-colored suit. It is true his late father had been a Bishop, but it was felt that he was rather imposing on the distinction.

"I distinctly remember," Lucy goes on, "another shock suffered by the House when Lord Randolph Churchill entered wearing a pair of tan shoes. The Fourth Party was then at the height of its impudence, the plenitude of its power. Its young leader had, for months, alternately bullied the Prime Minister and tweaked the nose of the Leader of the Opposition. These things had been suffered, not gladly, it is true, but in recognition of impotence to withstand them. This tan shoes atrocity was, on both sides of the House, felt to be going literally a step too far. At this date it is curious to reflect upon these dead-and-gone emotions. On sultry afternoons the benches of the twentieth-century House of Commons present an appearance suggestive of Henley on Regatta day. The cylindrical silk hat, which, within the memory of the present Speaker, was regarded in the light of one of the pillars that sustain the British Constitution, is rarely seen. Straw hats, Homburg hats, and the common bowler have rudely shunted its solemnity. A working-man Member, returned for the first time to the present Parliament, has beaten the record by presenting himself in a soft brown wide-awake, the rim of which is in size and proportions planned on the scale of the sloping roof of a Swiss chalet. As for clothes, anything will do, the lighter in color, the less conventional in cut, the better. It was by the last Parliament elected in the reign of Queen Victoria — the first King Edward VII opened in person — that this revolution was completed." [1]

Nevertheless, Sydney Brooks thought Parliament "the best-dressed assembly in the world." [2]

With us unconventionality rarely gets conspicuous save in hot weather. Of late years men have sought comfort on torrid days at any cost. Presiding officers, however, occasionally draw the line. When a Congressman took off his coat and flaunted his shirt-sleeves before the nation, Speaker Reed promptly dispatched a page to order the coat restored to its proper domain.

Thomas Jefferson is said to have attributed the signing of the Declaration of Independence in part to a matter of clothes. A livery stable nearby the hall where the Congress met, bred such a swarm of flies that the delegates, wearing the short breeches and silk stockings then the fashion, kept their handkerchiefs very busy in switching the pestiferous nuisances from their legs. The annoyance was so great that it hastened if it did not aid the appending of the ever-memorable signatures.

THE SYMBOLICAL HAT

THE article of costume that has played the biggest part in the history of lawmaking bodies is the hat. To remain covered by cap or hat has for centuries been the evidence and emblem of liberty and independence. Thereby the commoners of England showed that no King could interfere with their freedom. By the same token they showed their joint superiority to any one of their number who sought from them the favor of a hear-

---

[1] Henry W. Lucy ("Toby, M. P."), "Reminiscences of the House of Commons," *Putnam's Monthly*, January, February, 1907.

[2] *Harper's Weekly*, March 5, 1904.

ing.   Uncovered he must address the House.   This came to be a help to procedure.   Sir Thomas Smith tells us of Parliament in Queen Elizabeth's time : "In the disputing is a marvellous good order used in the lower House.   He that standeth up bare headed is understood that he will speak to the bill."   The rule yet survives.   It has, however, one exception, for if a member wishes to address the chair on a point of order in the course of the two minutes after debate has finished and while the division bells are ringing, he must retain his place and wear his hat. Once Gladstone forgot and rose to his feet without his hat, for he never brought a hat into the House.   On the cry of "Order," he sat down until he could lay hands on the hat of one of his lieutenants.   As Gladstone's head was of abnormal size, the makeshift was much too small, and perched on the great head of the statesman, delighted the House exceedingly.   Absentminded members every once in a while amuse the House by sitting down on their hats after speeches.   On one such occasion an Irish representative rose and gravely said : "Mr. Speaker, permit me to congratulate the honorable member that when he sat on his hat his head was not in it."

The chamber in which the House of Commons meets is much too small for the full membership, no member save a Minister or Privy Councillor has a right to any particular seat, and good seats are scarce.   This has given rise to a custom of much importance to the member who wishes to hear a debate comfortably or take part therein.   If he attends prayers, he is entitled to keep during the whole evening the seat he then secures — a reward for piety.   He may record his right of possession by slipping a card reading, "At prayers," in a receptacle at the back of the seat, or by putting his hat on the seat.   The hat must be the only hat he has on the premises, for he forfeits his right if he brings two hats, leaves one on the seat, and wears off the other.   In 1892 an Irish member brought a dozen soft hats with him and secured places for a dozen members who showed up later, but the Speaker repeated the rule laid down in 1880 and insisted on restricting the privilege to a solitary hat.   Augustine Birrell says these seemingly trivial matters are deemed by the House to be of the utmost importance, and the solemn tones of the Speaker are not infrequently heard expounding to a gravely attentive House the law of Parliament on the great hat question.

In France the hat serves yet another purpose. There it is needed as a last resort to quell the disorder to which the excitable French nature makes the Deputies peculiarly susceptible. When they become wholly unmanageable, the President puts on his hat, and unless quiet is immediately restored, the House stands adjourned for an hour, to give the members time to cool off.

The wearing of the hat by representatives of the people is a custom that Englishmen have taken with them to all parts of the world, but when transplanted, though sometimes surviving, as in the case of the Canadian House at Ottawa, often it has been abandoned, as in the case of all the lawmaking bodies of the United States. Yet more than two centuries passed before it here disappeared. Massachusetts began with it and was one of the last to give it up. The records of the General Court show that May 30, 1644, it was ordered "that henceforward noe member of this howse shall sitt or stand with his hatt on whiles ye Speaker is propounding any vote." The marginal note says — "Repeald." [1] Just what were the variations of the custom, it is now impossible to say. That it was not invariable would appear from an entry in the Journal of the Second Provincial Congress of Massachusetts, February 7, 1775, in the middle of its most serious proceedings: "In consideration of the coldness of the season, and that the Congress sit in a house without fire, Resolved, That all those members who incline thereto may sit with their hats on while in Congress." When George S. Boutwell began his public service, in the Massachusetts House of 1842, he says there were four wood fires — one in each corner of the great hall. Members sat in their overcoats and hats, and in one of the rules it was declared that when "a member rises to speak, he shall take off his hat and address the speaker." [2]

Senator William Plumer, of New Hampshire, wrote from Washington to his son William, February 22, 1803: "The members of the House sit with their hats on, but take them off when they speak. It has rather an odd appearance to see the House covered, and the Senate, and Heads of Departments, who frequently go in to hear the debates, with their hats in their hands." [3] The Senator was familiar with the New Hamp-

[1] *Records of the Colony of the Mass. Bay in N.E.*, III, 2.
[2] *Sixty Years in Public Affairs*, I, 71.
[3] William Plumer, Jr., *Life of William Plumer*, 256.

shire Legislature, so it may be inferred the wearing of the hat had long ceased to be the practice there. John Fiske, in describing the first American Legislature, that of Virginia, says all the members sat with their hats on,[1] but I have seen it stated somewhere that the House of Burgesses, though studiously observant of all the forms of the House of Commons, never adopted the practice of wearing hats during the session. Possibly Fiske presumed the English custom was followed, or it may have been abandoned very early.

Edward Hooker tells us in his Diary that in 1805 the members of the South Carolina House sat with their hats on, taking them off only when they rose to speak.[2] The rule of the South Carolina House still says "the members may keep on their hats while actually sitting in their respective seats, but at all other times they shall be uncovered (except such as shall be conscientiously restrained from uncovering their heads)." A Senate rule says no Senator shall with his head covered pass the President when the President is in the chair. Quakers are permitted to wear their hats by rule of the North Carolina House.

By the first Constitution of Georgia (1777), the members of a committee of the Council, sent to the Assembly with any proposed amendments to a bill, were to deliver their reasons "sitting and covered"; the whole House, except the Speaker, was to be uncovered. The superior dignity of the Council was recognized in this fashion until 1789.

In the Congress of the Confederation and afterward for a long time in the Federal House, the English custom was followed. The Speaker wore his hat with the rest, though he would generally doff it when he rose to call the attention of the House to any matter. Apparently the notion that the House of Representatives was peculiarly the popular body was not reflected in difference of practice from that of the Senate in this particular, for we find Edward Livingstone, of Louisiana, saying in the Senate in January, 1820: "Sir, the privilege of being covered during the debates of this House is one which of all others I hold to be most worthless; it is one of which I do not frequently avail myself, and which, if it were not sanctioned by such high authority, I should think somewhat indecorous." [3] A few

---

[1] *Old Virginia and Her Neighbours*, I, 244.
[2] *Am. Hist. Assn. Rep. for 1896*, I, 865.
[3] C. H. Hunt, *Life of Edward Livingstone*, 301

years earlier the Congressmen had begun agitating the desirability of abandoning the practice. Several times change was refused. One of the objectors to the custom was James K. Polk, afterward President, but when in 1833 he suggested its abolition, objection was made successfully that members would have no place in which to put their hats if they did not wear them, and also that the custom of wearing hats was the sign of the independence of the Commons of England, and therefore a good usage to preserve in the American House. About that time cloak rooms were established, the members gradually stopped wearing hats during the session, and in 1837 the practice was forbidden.

MOURNING

To wear any badge of mourning for a dead member or illustrious statesman not a member, is no longer customary. Once the matter led to sharp controversy in the United States Senate. John Quincy Adams, the instigator of the trouble, tells about it in his diary, under date of October 31, 1803: "Mr. Breckenridge introduced a resolution to wear crape a month for the three illustrious patriots, Samuel Adams, Edmund Pendleton, and Stevens Thompson Mason. I asked for the constitutional authority of the Senate to enjoin upon its members this act; and he referred to the manual, that such a regulation was merely conventional and not binding upon the members. I then objected against it as improper in itself, tending to unsuitable discussions of character, and to an employment of the Senate's time in debates altogether foreign to the subjects which properly belong to them. This led to a debate of three hours, in the course of which the resolution was divided into two — one for Mr. Mason, as a matter of form and of course, to a member of the Senate holding the office at the time of his decease; the other for the two other illustrious patriots. The first was unanimously agreed to; the last by a majority of twenty-one to ten."

Congress continued the custom until 1884. As a further token of grief the desk of a dead member was draped. Such melancholy symbolism is in a legislative body usually quite perfunctory. It savors too much of barbarous ostentation. Perhaps something is to be said for the emblems of sorrow displayed by those who have been very near to the dead, for such emblems may ward off levity and mutely explain the sad demeanor inevitably accompanying bitter loss. But on the part of those who are little more than chance acquaintances, thrown together for a brief time by the accidents of life, to continue the pretense of a mourning that has quickly faded serves no useful purpose whatever. It is even doubtful whether we do well in keeping up the practice of adjournment out of respect to those who die. It was long the custom in Congress for the death of a member to be formally announced at the opening of a session and for the House then to adjourn. Gradually, by necessity of the pressure of business, scruples gave way, until announcement was delayed till the close of the session, though the pretense of adjourning out of respect remained. State Legislatures pursue the same course. When an unexpected death comes as a great shock, it may be that the news of it will for the moment unfit for work those who were most closely associated with the member who has died, or his prominence may have been such that it would be manifestly improper to forego exceptional formality. In most cases, however, the best procedure would be an announcement of the death, with some simple and dignified expression of sorrow not so exaggerated as to intimate insincerity.

Prayers and Sermons

To invoke the blessing of the Deity on work about to be done by an assembly is one of the oldest of customs. In Athens priests offered a sacrifice. A large circle was traced by pouring lustral water upon the ground, and within this sacred circle the citizens gathered. The auspices were consulted, and if any unfavorable sign appeared in the heavens, the assembly broke up at once. Before any orator began to speak, a prayer was offered, with the people silent. The hall where the Senate met contained an altar and a sacred fire. Every Senator on entering approached the altar and pronounced a prayer. While the session lasted, every Senator wore a crown on his head, as in religious ceremonies. The Romans proceeded likewise. The augurs were required to declare that the gods were propitious. The assembly began with a prayer, which the augur pronounced, the consul repeating it after him. The Senate met always in a temple. If a session had been elsewhere than in a sacred place, its acts would have been null and void; for the gods would not have been present. At the altar each Senator on entering offered a libation and invoked the gods. Before every deliberation the president offered a sacrifice and pronounced a prayer.[1]

Prayers in Parliament appear to have come after Protestantism prevailed. The Journals show that in Elizabeth's time, immediately after the Speaker of the House of 1571 had been chosen, a resolution directed that "the litany shall be read every day as in the last Parliament, and also a prayer said by Mr. Speaker as he shall think fittest for the time." Some of the prayers preserved in the Journals were of a high order of merit. However, this did not long remain a function of the Speaker. In the first of the Parliaments under Cromwell a Chaplain appears, and after the Restoration he becomes recognized as an officer of the House. Now Mr. Speaker's Chaplain, as he is known, besides money payment, usually receives some advancement in the church.

With the Chaplain survives a relic of ancient ceremonial in the manner of his departure after he has performed his office. He must walk out backward. As attendance is good because of the advantage of being present in order to reserve seats for the day, the result is a performance that Justin McCarthy says has always seemed to him particularly ridiculous, for every member of the House rushes out the moment prayers are said and he has secured his seat — there is a short interval before actual business begins — and there you see a stream of men all rushing out in the ordinary manner, looking the way they are running, and in the midst of the stream one mild gentleman in clerical garb, who is trying to walk backward down the floor in the same direction, with the chance of collision against some fugitive who is just struggling to the front.

The Canadian Parliament now follows the English custom of having prayers read by the presiding officers. When there are two sittings on the same day, prayers must be read at the opening of each.

The official report of the first representative Assembly in America, at James City in Virginia, July 30, 1619, reads: "Prayer being ended, to the intente that as we had begun at God Almighty, so we might proceed with awful and due respect

[1] Fustel de Coulanges, *The Ancient City*, Willard Small, trans., 216, 217.

towards his Lieutenant, our most gratious and dreade Soveraigne, all the Burgesses were intreatted to retyer themselves into the body of the Churche, which being done, before they were duly admitted, they were called in order and by name, and so every man (none staggering at it) tooke the oathe of Supremacy and then entred the Assembly." Virginia pastors who read prayers for the Assembly were compensated by fees. The source of the remuneration, the revenue from the tax on liquors, seems not to have disturbed the Reverend Cope Doyley and the Reverend Samuel Eborne, who were each allowed five pounds sterling in 1695.

The "Records of the Colony of the Massachusetts Bay in New England," virtually the Journals of the General Court from 1631 to 1686, do not contain entries such as are found in legislative Journals now, recording that sessions were opened with prayer. That the custom had been established, one entry, of September 11, 1666, shows not to be improbable: "Itt is ordered, that some of the reverend elders that are or may be in toune be desired to be present with the Generall Court on the morrow morning, and to beginn the Court, & spend the forenoone in prayer." [1]

The early records do not show the election of a Chaplain at the beginning of each Massachusetts session, but surely it was the practice by the time of the Revolution, for we know that William Gordon lost the place. Gordon, a clergyman of Roxbury, wrote widely and well on the politics of the time. When the Legislature drew up the Constitution of 1778, he directed against it four moderate but weighty articles, printed in four issues of the "Independent Chronicle" in April of that year. The first of these treated somewhat incisively the conduct of the General Court, and led to his summary removal from the office of Chaplain.

It is probable that an opening prayer was the custom in all colonial assemblies. Yet that it did not continue universal custom may be inferred from a memorable episode in the Federal Convention of 1787. Things were looking very dark for the friends of a closer union. It seemed as if opposing views could not be reconciled and that the Convention might break up in failure. In this dire crisis the venerable philosopher, Benjamin Franklin, rose to move that the sessions be opened

[1] *Records*, IV, pt. 2, p. 314.

every morning with prayer. "The small progress we have made after four or five weeks close attendance, and continual reasonings with each other," he sadly observed, "our different sentiments on almost every question, several of the last producing as many *noes* as *ayes*, is, methinks, a melancholy proof of the imperfection of the human understanding. . . . In this situation of this assembly, groping, as it were, in the dark, to find political truth, and scarce able to distinguish it when presented to us, how has it happened, sir, that we have not hitherto once thought of humbly applying to the Father of Lights to illuminate our understandings? In the beginning of the contest with Britain, when we were sensible of danger, we had daily prayers in this room for the Divine protection. Our prayers, sir, were heard — and they were graciously answered. . . . I have lived, sir, a long time, and the longer I live the more convincing proofs I see of this truth, *that* GOD *governs the affairs of men.* And if a sparrow cannot fall to the ground without his notice, is it probable that an empire can rise without his aid?"

To the original draft of this speech there is the following note appended in the handwriting of Dr. Franklin: "The Convention, except three or four persons, thought prayer unnecessary." His motion was referred to a committee, which did not report. "The time that had elapsed without prayers," the editor thinks, "sufficiently explains the failure of Franklin's motion." [1]

The new Congress was more observant of ancient custom. The committee to prepare a system of rules reported that each House should have a Chaplain, that the two should be of different denominations, and that they should interchange weekly. When Edward Hooker visited Washington in December of 1808, he recorded in his diary how sessions of the House were opened. About eleven o'clock "the Speaker rapped on the table and Mr. Brown, a Baptist clergyman, the Chaplain of the House, went into the Clerk's place fronting the Speaker's chair and addressed the throne of grace in a modest, appropriate, *republican* prayer of about eight or ten minutes, about half the members being in and observing great decorum and apparent seriousness." [2]

The Republicans, as the Democrats of to-day were then

[1] *Works of Benjamin Franklin,* John Bigelow ed., IX, 428–31.
[2] *Am. Hist. Assn. Rep. for 1896,* 923.

known, controlled the House, but whether Hooker used the term to imply that the prayer had a partisan flavor, modest but appropriate, the reader may imagine for himself. However that may have been, prayerful partisanship half a century later put an end to the custom of having two clergymen of different denominations serve Senate and House in turn. During the prolonged Speakership contest of 1855 the House employed various local ministers. Their prayers, it seemed, too often evinced something of the partisan spirit that characterized the pending controversy, and in the following Congress (1857) certain members who asserted that the employment of chaplains conflicted with the spirit of the Constitution and tended to promote a union of Church and State, made a determined effort to discontinue their use. This aroused the churches of the country, and at the end of an acrimonious debate the House, by an overwhelming majority, adopted the following resolution: "Whereas the people of the United States, from their earliest history to the present time, have been led by the hand of a kind Providence and are indebted for the countless blessings of the past and the present and dependent for continued prosperity in the future upon Almighty God; and whereas the great vital and conservative element in our system is the belief of our people in the pure doctrines and divine truths of the Gospel of Jesus Christ, it eminently becomes the representatives of a people so highly favored to acknowledge in the most public manner their reverence for God: Therefore, be it resolved, that the daily sessions of this body be opened with prayer, and that the ministers of the Gospel in this city are hereby requested to attend and alternately perform this solemn duty." The adoption of this creed ended objection to the presence of a Chaplain.[1]

Many a parson has dangerously yielded to the temptation to mix advice and warning on secular matters with his petitions to the Almighty. Resentment of allusion to pending legislation has not been uncommon, but perhaps there was no precedent for the revolt of the Colorado House of 1923 when the Chaplain emulated Jeremiah in a burst of pessimism covering the sins of society in general and in particular. After heated debate, first in public and then for several hours in executive session, the House adopted a resolution of censure.

[1] De A. S. Alexander, *Hist. and Procedure of the House of Representatives*, 98.

A novelty of different nature was the question raised in Congress in February of 1921 when a member of the House from Oklahoma who had started on a campaign for securing attendance by demanding quorum calls, carried his zeal to the point of doubting the presence of a quorum before the prayer. The Speaker at first thought this was within the right of the member from Oklahoma, but reflection led to the conclusion that there was force in the counter-argument presented by Mr. Watson of Pennsylvania and so the Speaker in the end held that prayer by the Chaplain "is not a matter of business, but that it is a matter of ceremony, of devotion, and that its appeal is not to the duty of members to hear it, but to their sense of reverence." Inasmuch as the rule calls for the appearance of a quorum before the reading of the Journal, which is the first business after prayer by the Chaplain, the Speaker thought it was indicated by indirection that the prayer did not require the presence of a quorum, and in this he was overwhelmingly sustained upon appeal.

As far as I am aware, the sittings of the State Legislatures are all opened with prayer. Sometimes, as in Iowa, it is the custom to invite clergymen of all creeds and denominations from all parts of the State. Sometimes, as in Massachusetts, the same clergymen serve throughout the session and receive a salary. Michigan and Oregon by their Constitutions forbid the payment of money for religious services in either House. In the early years of the nineteenth century it was customary for the South Carolina Legislature to appoint a Chaplain to perform divine services on Sundays. Edward Hooker, chancing to be present when the appointment was made in 1805, tells us in his Diary that the House by a large majority voted the appointee a salary of a hundred dollars, although "one plain-looking old fellow with flap hat and each hand in a pocket, got up hastily, and in rather an ill-humored tone said, 'Let them that go to hear him put their hands in their pockets and pay him themselves.'"[1]

Too often the election of the Chaplain has been accompanied by unseemly campaigning, repugnant to all men who find in a scramble for office something incompatible with the solemnity of the clerical function. When a struggle for the place threatened the Massachusetts House of 1923 as a result of the resig-

[1] *Am. Hist. Assn. Ann. Report for 1896*, I, 864.

nation of the incumbent, who had himself been chosen out of many candidates the year before, the danger was avoided by a unanimous vote empowering the Speaker to appoint a Chaplain for the remainder of the session. That might wisely be made the practice everywhere.

Views vary as to the wisdom of having prayer in lawmaking bodies. James Parton, for instance, criticized the practice severely. "Never was there a religious service that seemed more ill-timed or more ill-placed than that which opens the daily sessions of the House of Representatives," he declared. "There is a time for all things; but members evidently think that the time to pray is *not* then nor there. The prayer can have no effect in calming members' minds, opening them to conviction, or preparing them for the duties of the occasion, because members' minds are absorbed, at the time, in hurrying the work of their committee-rooms to a conclusion. . . . In fixing times and places for devotional acts, we are now advanced far enough, I trust, to use our sense of the becoming and the suitable, and to obey its dictates. Members should certainly come in and 'behave,' or else abolish the chaplain." [1]

The complaint of non-attendance is amply justified, not only by the conduct of Congress, but also by that of the Legislatures. In Parliament the doors of the press and public galleries are not opened until after prayers have been read, and the same is the usage at Ottawa. If it should be copied in the States, the public would lose an opportunity to see and deplore the indifference of Congressmen and legislators to the ministrations of the Chaplain. Yet in spite of the force in criticisms like those of Mr. Parton, there are many of us who would grieve to see the ancient custom abandoned. Apart from religious considerations that need not be here advanced, it is well for the serious function of lawmaking to be dignified by some measure of solemn ceremony. No man who attends can fail to profit by having his thoughts for a brief space lifted above the turmoil and contention of the day. We may not be able to measure the subtle influence of prayer more than that of music or anything else that appeals to the finer instincts of our being, but the universal experience of mankind has taught us that there is value and help in whatever tends to ennoble and purify human conduct.

[1] "The Pressure upon Congress," *Atlantic Monthly*, February, 1870.

The didactic phase of religious observance is another matter. Few will regret that it is no longer the custom for lawmakers at the beginning of the session to submit themselves to the admonitions and instructions of the clergy. However beneficial it may be for any man to profit at frequent intervals by the homilies of those earnest men who devote their lives to the culture of the soul, it has not been shown that there is pertinence or advantage in their addressing themselves particularly to the obligations and tasks of lawmakers. Clergymen have too often found it impossible to resist the temptation to use the opportunity for advancing partisan views that have embittered rather than conciliated. For an instance of the embarrassments of this, read Lecky's story of what happened in Parliament in 1772. Dean Nowell was appointed to preach the customary sermon before the House on the anniversary of the Restoration. Only three or four Members were present, and they are said to have been asleep during the sermon, but the House, as usual, passed, unanimously, a vote of thanks to the preacher, and in terms of high eulogy ordered the sermon to be printed. When it appeared it was found that the preacher, being an extreme Tory, had availed himself of the occasion to denounce in the strongest language the Puritans and their principles, to extol the royal martyr in terms of which it can be only said that they were a faithful echo of the Church service for the day, and to urge that the qualities of Charles I were very accurately reproduced in the reigning sovereign. The House of Commons, which was at this time strongly Whig, was both exasperated and perplexed. It was felt that it would be scarcely becoming to condemn to the flames a sermon which had been printed by its express order and honored by its thanks, and it accordingly contented itself with ordering, without a division, that its vote of thanks should be expunged.[1]

A colonial incident of kindred nature had taken place in Maryland a century before. Charles Nichollet preached to the Delegates a sermon in which he advanced doctrines dangerous to the peace of the colony. He told them "they were chosen both by God and man, and had a power put into their hands"; that they "should read the proceedings of the Commons of England, to see what brave things they had done"; and, above all, that they should "beware of the sin of permission" — mean-

[1] *England in the Eighteenth Century,* i, 475.

ing they ought to let things alone which it was in their power to disquiet. Nichollet was rather a brawler than a fanatic, for, on being called to account by the Upper House, he humbly acknowledged his fault, and asked pardon on his knees, and so came off with a fine of forty shillings.[1]

The "election sermon" annually preached to the General Court of Massachusetts made trouble from the earliest days. It appears to have been often the subject of sharp controversy, and not unfrequently to have been the precursor, if not the cause, of the precise event which it aimed at averting. When in 1634 John Cotton preached against rotation in office, Winthrop was immediately left out of the chief magistracy; and in 1643, when Ezekiel Rogers declaimed with vehemence against choosing the same man twice in succession, Winthrop was forthwith reëlected.[2]

Yet as long as the clergy controlled in Massachusetts, the election sermon was an important episode of each year. A century ago it was still a fashionable function. A writer in the "Columbian Centinel" of May 28, 1814, tells of going to the Old South Meeting House, "where a very appropriate and learned Discourse was delivered by the Rev. President of Bowdoin College." We are informed that "the audience was crowded and highly respectable, and the satisfaction unanimous and complete." Such was not always the verdict. The election sermon preached in 1810 was deemed so disrespectful to those newly installed in office that the House by a large majority voted a censure instead of the customary resolution of thanks. It is told that not many years afterward when a Democratic majority proposed refusing to print a sermon that had been obnoxious, Josiah Quincy, then President of the Senate, though it may have been somebody else, suggested that in case of such action the resolution should instruct the preacher of the next election sermon to take for his text the verse of the Psalm which says, "I will keep my mouth with a bridle, while the wicked is before me."

Toward the end of the Convention that framed the Constitution of Maine in 1819, Judge Cony of Augusta expressed the thought that it would be proper to observe the usual practices and religious observances at the day of election, and therefore

[1] W. H. Browne, *Maryland*, 120.
[2] R. C. Winthrop, *Life and Letters of John Winthrop*, II, 305.

he would move that an hour be assigned to elect a clergyman to preach the election sermon in May next. General Wingate asked if they were to have all the parade and pageantry of the government of Massachusetts. He hoped they would be more republican. The practice had been much abused. Judge Thacher said he did not know that preaching a sermon was anti-republican. Other States had always practiced it, and it was a good and wholesome custom. After a little conversation the matter subsided and no vote was taken on the subject.

The custom of a sermon to the General Court survived in Massachusetts until 1880, when its consequence had so dwindled that with very little discussion it was abandoned.

This does not mean that the attitude of men in public life toward religious matters has changed more for the worse than that of the community at large. On the contrary, I am inclined to think that our public men have clung somewhat more loyally to old institutions and ways of thought than the greater part of their constituents. It might be supposed that their wider experience with the worse phases of human nature and that in general the circumstances of their lives would turn them into cynics and materialists, with small regard for the higher emotions and for the deeper springs of human conduct. This, however, is more than offset by the consideration that their work is essentially altruistic and that they are constantly faced with serious problems concerning man and his destiny. Whatever the cause, it is the fact that an unexpectedly large number of lawmakers will be found to be righteous, God-fearing men, who mean to meet their religious obligations and to perform the duties imposed upon them by the Church.

Sometimes perplexity results. For example, what should be the course of a representative who believes in the strict observance of the Lord's Day? I have seen colleagues refuse to attend a committee meeting on Sunday, yet ask to be recorded on the important vote to be taken. Were they consistent? They recall the quandary of John Fairfield, member of Congress from Maine in 1836, when at midnight of a Saturday the House was still in session. Writing to his wife he told of his embarrass-ment: "I hesitated about my course but finally concluded I would stick to my post, a post assigned to me by the people. But then, being satisfied that more injury would result to the public morals by the example set, than political good from con-

tinuing this session into the Sabbath, I felt inclined to adjourn.
But my political friends were opposed to adjournment. What,
then, should I do? I finally concluded to stand by but take
no part except under imperious circumstances. Accordingly
there were three lists of yeas & nays when my name will not
be found." [1] A somewhat casuistical decision!

By the way, Fairfield's "Letters" elsewhere (p. 110) show
how times have changed in this matter of Sabbath observance. When he was in Congress, there were still those in
New England who held that the Sabbath began at sundown
of Saturday. He went to a party of a Saturday evening, and
in telling his wife of it, felt obliged to apologize. "It is strange,"
he said, "how soon we become accustomed to the habits and
manners of those with whom we happen to be placed and how
readily we slide into their views and modes of thinking and feeling." Then in a religious vein he went on to explain himself.

HOURS OF WORK

IN days when candles furnished the only artificial light for
assembly rooms, men did as much of their work as they could
in the daytime. Nothing better than the hours of sitting of
Parliament illustrates the changes wrought by gas and electricity. Up into the fourteenth century the House of Commons
met at sunrise. In 1642 the hour was seven in the morning.
Then it was resolved to meet at eight, and a year later the hour
was changed to nine. In Queen Elizabeth's time, according
to Sir Thomas Smith, "at the afternoon they keep no Parliament." It was usual for the House to rise at twelve o'clock.
Now that body also rises at or about twelve o'clock, but it is
twelve midnight and not twelve noon. Debate on opposed matters stops ordinarily at eleven, but the work may go on an hour
or two longer. The House meets at a quarter of three. It was
in the early part of the eighteenth century that the hour had
been delayed till noon and Bishop Burnett complained that
the sitting began too late in the day. Then evening sittings
were comparatively rare. The motion to bring in candles that
debate might be continued into the evening was likely to rouse
angry objection, for it was equivalent to the application of
closure. Even Mr. Gladstone could remember when the

[1] *Letters of John Fairfield*, 117.

House was wont to rise at six or seven o'clock in the evening. Long before his parliamentary career was ended, this had so changed that in hotly controversial times the sittings frequently lasted till four o'clock in the morning, sometimes an hour or two later. Mr. Dillon told the Select Committee on Procedure in 1914 that it killed a good many members. He had no doubt it killed Mr. W. H. Smith.

Sittings of most of the lawmaking bodies on the Continent usually last from five to seven hours. In Belgium, however, three hours has been the normal time, and in Denmark three to four hours.

When lawmaking began in this country, men used the daylight. The first Virginia Assemblies came together at the third beat of the drum, an hour after sunrise. The Plymouth General Court met at 7 A.M. in summer, 8 A.M. in winter, with dinner at eleven. The men of Rhode Island were yet earlier risers, meeting usually at six o'clock or half an hour, sometimes an hour, after sunrise. Even as late as Revolutionary times these early hours continued. The committees of the Virginia Convention of 1776 met at seven, the Convention itself at nine.

Ten o'clock is the most common meeting hour for Legislatures nowadays. Four States grouped in the heart of the country, Missouri, Arkansas, Iowa, and Nebraska, show an admirable virtue by convening their Legislatures at nine o'clock. The Nebraska House allots to committee meetings the time between three and six in the afternoon.

The Houses of Congress ordinarily now meet at noon. Through most of the session the day's work is finished in the course of from five to six hours, with no intermissions. Experiments in the way of recesses have not been satisfactory. John Fairfield's report of one in 1836 shows how the habits of society have changed in less than a century. He wrote to his wife that he feared he would no longer have any evenings to himself, for the House had voted to take a recess each day from half past two to four, thereby giving time to go home to dinner. "I understand," he said, "Congress has always been afraid to have a session after dinner, on the ground that the members would be rather too winy and of course too talkative." Nowadays once in a while when haste seems imperative there are evening sittings, beginning at eight o'clock and lasting till perhaps ten thirty, but it is hard to get a quorum, and for various

reasons they are disliked. In the last month evening sittings
are more frequent, and the last two days may witness a continuous sitting.

The Canadian Parliament meets at 3 P.M., except that on
Wednesdays the House of Commons meets at 2. If the House
is in session at six the Speaker leaves the chair and the sitting
is automatically adjourned till eight; but on Wednesdays at
six the Speaker adjourns the House, without question put.
Unless otherwise ordered there is adjournment from Friday to
Monday, but toward the close of the session there are frequent
sittings on Saturday, and meetings are at an earlier hour.

The British House of Commons does not sit on Saturday.
The holiday is said to have owed its origin to Sir Robert Walpole's wish to devote the day to hunting. Parliament finds
very inconvenient on Fridays the practice whereby the Speaker
and other members must stay till four o'clock before the House
can be counted out — a relic of old custom the House seems
unable to abandon. Members waiting to vote against a bill if
it comes up must wait till four lest a quorum may present itself.

In France, Belgium, and Holland sittings are regularly held
on only four days in the week. In France the Assembly also
sits sometimes on Wednesday, rarely on Saturday; in Holland,
occasionally Monday afternoon or Saturday. In Italy sittings
are held every week day and sometimes on Sunday. In Sweden
Wednesday and Saturday are regular days for meeting.

Congress works six days in the week. If it is to keep on sitting much the greater part of the year, it might wisely husband
the vitality of its members by imitating the British Parliament
with a Saturday holiday. Under present conditions Sunday
is the only day when members can regularly shake off their
cares and without compunction enjoy the open. As things have
been going of late, Congressmen have not had enough opportunity for the rest, recreation, and change necessary to keep mind
and body in the best condition.

PUNCTUALITY

HISTORY does not disclose any era when lawmaking bodies
were not bothered by tardiness. In 1562 it was ordered by the
House of Commons "that every man of this House, that cometh
after the prayer, which shall begin at eight of the clock, shall

pay fourpence to the poor man's box." In the early Assemblies of Virginia those not present at prayers were fined a shilling; in 1659 those who failed to attend at the beginning of the session were to be fined three hundred pounds of tobacco; in 1663 this was made a hogshead of tobacco, and the rules adopted in that year also provided "that every member of this House for each time of his absence upon call of the clerk shall forfeit twenty pounds of tobacco, lawful impediments excepted." In Plymouth sixpence was the penalty "for any default." The Massachusetts Deputies in 1646 resolved that those who were present at the hour to which the House stood adjourned, might fine the rest, "though they be ye major parte that be absent." It was voted in 1650 that a Deputy who did not answer at the second call should pay threepence, and for every hour's absence afterward sixpence.

In the early days of 1777, a resolution was passed by the Continental Congress requiring the Secretary to note upon the Journal what States were represented in Congress later than ten o'clock, the regular meeting time. This was ordered with a view to transmitting the information to the State Legislatures, on account of the tardiness in attendance of the delegates to Congress.[1] If since that time there have been any attempts to make tardiness costly for legislators anywhere in the country, they have been few and insignificant. In a dozen Legislatures the rules require that the presiding officer shall take the chair at "precisely" the hour to which Senate or House may stand adjourned. Curiously enough, sometimes this is required only of the Speaker, sometimes only of the President of the Senate. In but four of the dozen is the admonition found in the rules of both branches. The clerk of the Delaware House is to call the roll every day before the House proceeds to other business.

Once a Member has arrived, it is commonly assumed that he will stay through the sitting, or at any rate it seems to be thought useless to try to control him. Two odd exceptions, however, come to my notice. A rule of the Colorado House requires that no member shall absent himself for more than twenty consecutive minutes without leave previously obtained, and in New Jersey the House is even more stringent, limiting the time to quarter of an hour.

[1] Herbert Friedenwald, "Journals and Papers of the Continental Congress," *Am. Hist. Assn. Rep. for 1896*, I, 116.

Each House of Congress invariably begins the day without a quorum. So often does this result in ringing the roll-call bells, that the aggregate waste of time in the course of a session is really a serious matter. The suggestion of a drastic remedy, for example, the timeclock system now found in nearly all large industrial and commercial establishments, would be indignantly resented as an outrage upon Congressional dignity. However, the present situation outrages patience, and of the two this strikes me as the greater evil. Who steals my time, shortens my life.

ABSENCE

Loss of wages has long been a common punishment for non-attendance. History shows no time when what we now clumsily call absenteeism has not, at any rate in English-speaking bodies, been a troublesome evil. As far back as Edward III we find the Knights for the counties of Gloucester and Oxford refused their wages, for the simple reason bluntly stated, "because they neglected their work." A statute enacted in the reign of Henry VIII declared the law and custom of Parliament to be, "that no members have writs to levy their expenses but those who staid to the end of the session, such only excepted who had licence to depart, who should have their expenses down to the time of departure, provided they returned to the performance of their duties. This loss was accounted a great disparagement, yea punishment, in former times, making them contemptible in the counties and cities for which they served." The Burgesses, however, appear to have had, and to have exercised, a more free license in the matter, their presence or absence not being deemed a matter that required much consideration. Hallam thinks it highly probable that a great part of those elected for the boroughs did not trouble themselves with attending in Parliament.[1]

In the twenty-third year of Elizabeth's reign, a list of the names of those who had not attended was handed to the clerk of the Crown, with instructions to issue no writs for their wages, but to deliver in their names on the first day of the ensuing session, when each Knight who had persisted in absenting himself was fined £20, and each Burgess £10 — a very heavy fine, when we take into account the comparative poverty

[1] W. C. Townsend, *History of the House of Commons*, ii, 362.

of the time, and the diminution since then of four fifths in the standard of value. Omissions being thus sharply visited, the attendance of members became so general under James, that fresh seats were required for their use.[1] Clarendon says that in debates of the highest consequence in the course of the reign of Charles I, there were not usually present in the House of Commons the fifth part of their just members, and very often not above a dozen or thirteen in the House of Peers.

Pepys has an entry in his Diary under date of December 8, 1666, which shows that two hundred and fifty years ago members of Parliament had to be gathered in on the occasion of important votes much as they are to-day, though it is to be hoped the search has not now to be made in the same places, for Pepys says: "The great Proviso passed the House of Parliament yesterday; which makes the King and Court mad, the King having given order to my Lord Chamberlain to send to the playhouses and brothels, to bid all the Parliamentmen that were there to go to the Parliament presently. This is true, it seems; but it was carried against the Court by thirty or forty voices." In 1668 an order was passed that absent members be sent for by the Sergeant-at-Arms, be fined £40, and be committed to the Tower until the fine should be paid. A plea of sickness was allowed, but leave of absence was required even for purposes of business. When, for instance, Sir John Maynard, the celebrated lawyer, ventured to go on the Western Circuit without having first obtained permission, his conduct was brought to the notice of the House, and his son was allowed to write to him to order him to return on pain of being sent for by the Sergeant-at-Arms. If leave was granted, the member having it was expected to use it. On one occasion Sir Richard Temple was permitted to visit his sick wife; but, rising to speak when he was supposed to be away, an objection was raised to his being heard. Sir Richard, perhaps because his wife was better, good-humoredly parried it by calling it a "merry motion, a Christmas motion," and the subject was quietly dropped.[2]

In the eighteenth century, members of Parliament appear, with schoolboy glee, to have caught at any pretext for playing

---

[1] W. C. Townsend, *History of the House of Commons*, II, 363.
[2] C. B. Roylance Kent, "The Parliamentary Machine," *Longman's Mag.*, *Living Age*, October 11, 1902.

truant. No House could be formed to discuss the rival claims of the old and new East India Company, the members having dispersed to see a tiger baited by dogs. The performance of Othello at some private theatricals by the fashionable Mr. Delaval, lured away the House on another important night. Burke remonstrated in vain against their adjourning for a *fête champêtre* to be given by Lady Stanley. A general toleration of Wednesday dinners, a counting out of the House on Derby day, an abstinence from divisions, and adjournment over Saturday, marked the mezzo-termino of George the Second's reign. Horace Walpole, in his amusing letters, furnishes us several instances, for example March 7, 1751: "The seventh was appointed for the Naturalization Bill, but the House adjourned to attend at Drury Lane." [1]

When Hatsell wrote, he declared that "notwithstanding the great anxiety, trouble, and expence, which many persons put themselves to, to obtain a seat in the House of Commons, it is inconceivable how many of these very persons neglect their duty, by not attending and taking a part in the business that is depending, and with what difficulty they are prevailed upon to give up their amusements, and other less important avocations, for this, which, whilst they continue Members, ought to be their first and principal object." [2]

The habits of lawmakers abroad have not changed. Bryce thought American Congressmen more assiduous in their attendance than the members of most European legislatures. The House of Commons finds difficulty, through many private members' days and on government days from 8 to 10 P.M., in making up its modest quorum of forty. Herbert Sidebotham says a House of fifty or sixty is not noticeably thin.[3] T. P. O'Connor has caustically described what takes place. "If it should happen," he says, "that the business under discussion is of vast importance, and yet presents no hope of picturesqueness or general interest, the House again empties. For instance, the Navy estimates, the Army estimates, dealing as they do with the defense of the country — one of its supreme interests, and involving expenditure by tens of millions — are always debated in a House that is practically empty. I have seen millions of money voted by a House consisting at most of ten or

[1] W. C. Townsend, *History of the House of Commons*, 377.
[2] *Precedents*, II, 71 (1781).   [3] *Political Profiles*, 17 (1921).

fifteen members. Indeed, one might almost venture on the paradox, with regard to the House of Commons, that its attendance and its interest are in inverse proportion to the importance of the subjects which it is debating. A small personal squabble between two members will often bring to the House a crowded, excited, and interested audience, while the interests of the Empire will leave the House cold and empty." [1] Mr. O'Connor said he had seen a member addressing the House when there were but two other members present, and indeed had seen a member speak when his only audience was the Speaker. Mr. Asquith told the Select Committee of 1914 that he could remember sitting on the Treasury Bench with Mr. Gladstone and Sir William Harcourt when the Home Rule bill of 1893 was up, and not a soul was near them. On the Opposition side of the House were about six men, one of whom was talking on the supremacy of Parliament or something of the sort. Said Mr. Asquith: "We sat for about half an hour like that very happily."

Up to 1902 the House used to suspend business informally for half an hour, that the Speaker might take what was called his "chop," but now business goes on continuously, though with a ridiculously small attendance during the dinner period, ten or a dozen members being present, sometimes less. Often three quarters of the members are absent until ten or half-past.

Non-attendance through most of the debates is encouraged by a device unfamiliar in American assemblies, but that would appeal to at least some members of Congress. In all the smoking and reading rooms there is an indicator that shows who may be speaking. Herbert Sidebotham seems to find in this the reason why three fourths of the members who vote in the average division have not heard a word of the debate. [2] In excuse he says that "in many cases the arguments used are only hotted up from the committee room, and everything that can be said for or against is familiar."

The House of Lords, where the quorum is but three, usually has less than thirty peers present. Absenteeism has become such a scandal that Lord Phillimore, urging omission of the Writ of Summons unless a peer petitions for it, advises that the

---

[1] "Some Absurdities of the House of Commons," *No. Am. Review*, August, 1900.

[2] *Political Profiles*, 17.

petition present an undertaking to attend and take part in business for a period of say three or five years.

The Canadian Parliament is to deduct from the salary fifteen dollars a day for each day beyond fifteen days on which a member does not attend a sitting of the House. Exception is made for days of illness when a member is at or within ten miles of the capital and unable to attend; for days of absence by a military man when on duty with his corps; and for days on which the House is not sitting.

In Switzerland a member loses his per diem if he does not answer the roll-call at the opening of the day's session, unless he appears later and gives the secretary a sufficient excuse for his dilatoriness. If subsequently, in the course of that day's session, there is a vote by roll-call (*appel nominal*), or if there is a count of the House to ascertain the presence of a quorum, the compensation of the members whose absence is disclosed is forfeited for that day. This law is not a "dead letter," but is strictly enforced, and with a frugal-minded people tends to keep the members in their seats.[1] Before the World War members of the German Reichstag were to be docked twenty marks a day for absence; the rule may continue. The only provision about the matter I find in a European Constitution is in that of Finland, where absentees may be condemned to a loss of fifteen marks out of salary for each day of absence and in addition a fine not to exceed fifteen marks.

Some years ago (1910 or 1911) an attempt was made in the French Chamber to organize a system of attendance sheets signed by each member entering the Chamber, but the measure was repealed after two years.

Our colonial ancestors were not a whit more faithful to the performance of their duties than are their descendants, if we may judge from the laws found necessary almost at the outset. The Plymouth revision of 1636 commands "that all such as depart any his Majesties Courts before they be dismissed without due leave be amerced in three shillings sterling."[2] At least one entry, that of December 25, 1689, shows the law was no idle threat: "John Cushing, Esq., John Hall, Seth Pope, & Henry Head, for their disorderly departing from this Generall Court, fined each of them 20 shillings."[3]

[1] Boyd Winchester, *The Swiss Republic*, 68 (1891).
[2] *Plymouth Colony Records*, XI, 13.   [3] *Ibid.*, VI, 225.

Not by reason of direct bearing on the making of laws, but as showing the spirit of the times, observe this curious anticipation of the compulsory voting reform, a statute of June 10, 1660: "Whereas the Court hath taken notice that divers of the freemen of this Corporation doe neither appeer att Courts of election nor send theirs voates by proxey for the Choise of majestrates &c. It is enacted by the Court and the Authoritie thereof; that whosoever of the freemen of this Corporation; that shall not appeer att the Court of election att Plymouth in June annually nor send theire voate by proxey according to order of the Court for the choise of Governor Assistants Comissioners and Treasurer shall bee fined to the Collonies use the sume of ten shillinges for every such default; unlesse some unavoidable impediment hinder such in theire appeerance." [1] Later in the year (October 2) appears this cryptic entry: "The Court have ordered that the law conserning not coming to our meetings that the fines shall not be levied untill the Court shalbee in a capasitie to order otherwise." [2]

Massachusetts Bay, much the larger colony, naturally gives us more instances of early practice in these matters. It appears by the "Records" (I, 230) that June 8, 1638, four gentlemen (Magistrates and Deputies) were fined five shillings each for absence when the Court was called. In 1643 (as appears by the revision of 1660) came a law commanding every freeman to attend the annual Court of Elections in person or by proxy, and imposing a severe fine on absent Magistrates or Deputies: "From which General Court, no Magistrate or Deputie shall depart or be discharged, without the consent of the Major part both of Magistrates and Deputies, during the first foure daies of the first session, under the penaltie of one hundred pounds, nor afterwards, under such penaltie, as the Court shall impose." The House of Deputies May 30, 1644, ordered (III, 2) that "henceforward noe member of this howse, (uppon pretence of businesse with any man,) shall absent himselfe from ye occasions thereof without leave first granted him from ye howse."

The next year, June 16th, it was resolved (III, 19), "uppon ye quaestion, by vote, that no member of this howse shall have liberty henceforward to enter his contradicent to any vote that shall passe this howse in ye absence of such members, when such absence is occacioned by their oune private occa-

---

[1] *Plymouth Colony Records*, XI, 127. [2] *Ibid.*, XI, 129.

cions." In 1654 it was provided that all persons chosen as Deputies and accepting the office, absent from the House during the time of the sitting without just grounds so judged by the House, should pay twenty shillings a day, "for every such defect." In 1655 it was provided (III, 373) that as the presence of the Magistrates was more necessary than that of any Deputies, a Magistrate absent without consent should forfeit forty shillings a day, against twenty shillings for an absent Deputy. Perhaps the fining fell into disuse, for we find (IV, pt. 2, 333) that May 15, 1667, a fresh order was passed: "Henceforth it shall not be lawful for any member of the Generall Court to absent himself from the Court without license of both houses first had & obteyned, on peonalty of twenty shillings a day, and for the first fower dayes of the Court of Elections, the poenalty to be as in the printed law; and that there may be due observance hereof, the secretary & clarke of the deputies shall, in their respective places, enter in their daybooks all defaults made by any members of either house, & before the rising of the Court present the same to the whole Court."

A generation later it seems to have been necessary to provide in still greater detail, for in October, 1692, it was enacted: "Every person chosen to serve for, and represent any town in the general assembly, and accepting thereof, shall give his constant attendance during their sessions, on pain of forfeiting five shillings per diem for his neglect, without just excuse made and allowed of by the House of Representatives, to be paid unto the clerk of said House, and is to be disposed of and employed as the House may direct, and in default of payment to be levied by distress upon such delinquent's goods, by warrant from the said clerk, by order of the House, directed to the sheriff of the county, his under-sheriff or deputy, or constable of the town where such representative dwells; and no representative shall depart or absent himself from the general assembly, until the same be fully finished, adjourned or prorogued, without the license of the speaker and representatives assembled, to be entered upon record in the clerk's book, on pain to every one so departing or absenting himself in any other manner to lose his wages. And the inhabitants of such town for which he serves shall be clearly discharged of the said wages against such person and his executors for ever."

Other colonies had the same difficulties and tried to meet

them in the same way. The Fundamental Orders of Connecticut, 1638–39, declared: "The said deputyes shall haue power to fyne any that shall be disorderly at their meetings, or for not coming in due tyme or place according to appoyntment." In the Fundamental Order for the government of the New Haven Colony, agreed to at a General Court October 27, 1643, appears: "If any of the said magistrates or Deputyes shall either be absent att the first sitting of the said Generall Court, (unless some providence of God hinder, which the said Court shall judge of,) or depart, or absent themselves disorderly before the Court be finished he or they shall each of them pay twenty shillings fine, with due considerations of further aggravations if there shall be cause." In Rhode Island in 1672 the fine for absence from the Assembly was made twenty shillings, or if a quorum was not present, double that amount.[1]

At the first meeting of the first legislative body in New Jersey, 1668, among the provisions made in the four days' session, was one to the effect that for the absence of any Deputy, he should be liable to pay a fine of forty shillings, as a fine to the county, unless the Assembly should see cause to remit the same.[2]

It was particularly important that there should be as many present as possible on the first day of a session, for work could not proceed until a quorum presented itself, and the more who took part in electing the Speaker, the less likelihood of friction afterward. So in Virginia it was enacted in 1659–60 that the Burgess who failed to present himself on the day appointed should be fined 300 pounds of tobacco for every absence of twenty-four hours, unless offering acceptable excuse. It was customary for the letters of explanation to be read and approved or rejected. Sometimes the explanation given was regarded as aggravating the offense.[3] Like precaution appears in North Carolina, the revision of the laws made in 1715 directing that if a Representative-elect did not make his appearance by a time specified in the summons, he should be fined twenty shillings for each day he delayed.

After he had once presented himself, the Virginia Burgess, by the Orders adopted at the opening of the session of 1658–59, was forbidden absence "without leave first obtained (unless prevented by sickness) when any matter shall be debated of."

[1] S. G. Arnold, *Hist. of R.I.*, I, 365.   [2] Mulford, *Hist. of N.J.*, 147.
[3] P. A. Bruce, *Institutional Hist. of Va.*, II, 464.

Notice that this seems to have condoned absence when debate was not in progress, but although the language is ambiguous, presumably voting also was provided for by another rule — "Any member of this House, for any time of his absence upon call of the clerk, shall forfeit twenty pounds of tobacco, to be disposed of by the major part of this House, upon every Saturday in the afternoon, lawful impediments excepted." A generation afterward the penalty for absence Mondays was made a hogshead of tobacco, to discourage members from leaving town over Sunday.

The original States put nothing in their Constitutions about the matter. Kentucky was the first to use in the fundamental law phraseology that might be construed as contemplating deduction for absence. It said members should get "six shillings a day during their attendance on, going to and returning from the legislature," but one might safely conjecture that the word "during" was not construed too harshly. Kentucky still says "during," but Ohio, copying it in 1802, dropped it from the Constitution in 1851 when compensation was directed to be fixed by law. Ohio did not undertake to pay the legislator for the days spent in coming and going, but Louisiana did and kept it up until 1879, when the phrase was cut down to "during their attendance." Now in Ohio by statute if on a call of either House the members present refuse to excuse an absentee, he shall not be entitled to compensation during his absence.

Alabama put into her Constitution of 1819 and has kept there this provision: "It shall be the duty of the General Assembly [now Legislature] to regulate, by law, the cases in which deductions shall be made from the salaries of public officers, for neglect of duty in their official capacities, and the amount of such deduction." Wisconsin appears to have been the pioneer in definitely restricting payment to the time actually given, saying in its first Constitution (1848) that members should receive pay "for each day's attendance during the session," and such was the provision until in 1881 a salary was substituted. Michigan liked the idea and copied it in 1850, with the addition of compensation "when absent on account of sickness," maintaining the practice until a salary was substituted. Kansas in 1859 took the Wisconsin wording. Maryland in 1864 preferred the Michigan modification with changed phraseology, and added in

1867 — "or by leave of the House of which he is a member." Nebraska in 1866 said the payment should be "for each day's attendance," and that has since been said by South Dakota, Washington, and New Mexico. Nebraska, however, in 1886 changed it to "during the sitting." Tennessee in 1870 forbade payment to a member for any day when absent from his seat in the Legislature, unless physically unable to attend. Rhode Island said in 1900 payment should be "for each day of actual attendance."

Massachusetts at the first General Court after the adoption of her Constitution, directed that members be paid "for each day they shall attend." Later statutes changed this to payment "for each and every day's attendance," and such was the stipulation until in 1858 payment by the session was substituted for the per diem practice. Then it was directed that three dollars a day be deducted for each day of absence, a provision repealed in 1865. It is to be doubted if the law was ever efficacious. At any rate Boutwell says of the General Court of 1842: "The attendance of members was never enforced, and it was quite irregular. A full House consisted of about 350 members, but 60 was a quorum. It was common for merchants and lawyers to call at the House, look at the orders of the day, and then go to business. In an exigency they were sent for and brought in to vote." [1]

A unique provision was that of Massachusetts enacted in 1826 and standing as long as members were paid by the day, to the effect that the per diem of any member taken sick while going to, returning from, or attending the General Court, and who could not be removed to his home, should continue during his disability, though not beyond the first session of the next General Court — a provision that we may surmise was due to sympathy for some one unlucky member. Georgia provides by statute that an absent member shall get no pay unless the absence is due to sickness of himself or in his family, or unless he has express leave of the House. Possibly other States have statutory provisions on the subject.

A few eccentricities appear. Indiana in 1851 decided that if either House failed to organize itself within five days after a quorum presented itself, its members should get no pay until organization should be effected. Oregon copied this, and so

[1] *Sixty Years in Public Affairs*, i, 71.

did Idaho, making the time four instead of five days. From 1860 until a salary was provided, Michigan allowed members from the Upper Peninsula three dollars a day more than the rest. California does not pay members for a recess of more than three days, but now that it pays a lump sum for regular sessions, this would presumably affect only special sessions.

The Continental Congress had the rule: "No member shall leave Congress without permission of Congress or his constituents." Palpably there was difficulty in determining when a member had the permission of his constituents, unless they were supposed to be the Legislatures. More sensible was the form the rule took in the first Federal Congress, "that no member absent himself from the service of the House, unless he have leave or be sick and unable to attend." A simpler form now prevails: "Every member shall be present within the hall of the House during its sittings, unless excused or necessarily prevented." For the upper branch Jefferson's Manual prescribed: "No member shall absent himself from the service of the Senate without leave of the Senate first obtained." Such is still the Senate rule, save for the omission of the last five words.

When the Federal Congress first came together, a remarkable spasm of virtue overcame the impulses of human nature. Fisher Ames wrote to George Richards Minot, July 8, 1789: "There is a most punctual attendance of the members at the hour of meeting. Three or four have had leave of absence, but every other member actually attends daily, till the hour of adjourning." [1] Nothing indicates that such a phenomenal state of affairs lasted after the novelty wore off. Half a century later John Fairfield could write to his wife: "To-day, at one time, we were without a quorum, many of the members having gone off to the race-course, where a purse of $20,000 was to be run for. At three o'clock we adjourned on account of the absence of members." This he thought "disgraceful to the last degree," and he declared it "a foul stain upon the character of an American Congress." [2] But he did not object to the sport itself, for three days later he wrote that after the House had adjourned, he too "joined in the dissipation."

Benton recalled that in the Journals of the two Houses, for the first thirty years of the Government, there was in the index a regular head for "absent without leave," but that it had disap-

[1] *Works of Fisher Ames*, I, 62.   [2] *Letters of John Fairfield*, 226.

peared. He recollected "no instance of leave asked since the last of the early members — the Macons, Randolphs, Rufus Kings, Samuel Smiths, and John Taylors of Caroline — disappeared from the halls of Congress." [1] At the time of the 47th Congress the rule requiring a Senator to ask leave of absence had so long been disregarded that when a Senator asked for such leave a question was raised as to the necessity of his so doing, and the Vice-President stated that, though the rule was perfectly explicit, it had not been the practice of the Senate to enforce it.

In the House, some members still go through what is usually the idle form of asking leave of absence for themselves or others. Customarily it is granted without opposition, but there have been instances of denial. In 1816 John Sargeant was refused leave, his intention being to depart for Europe. It was urged in the debate that a member's absence was a question between him and his constituents, but on the other hand it was replied that the House should not by vote sanction a relinquishment of public duties.

Publicity is one of the methods used for inciting attendance. In 1864 the Senate, by a vote of 20 to 13, directed the Reporter in making up the proceedings for the "Congressional Globe" to insert a separate list of the names of the absentees in each call for the Ayes and Noes. Eight and ten years later attempts to rescind this were without avail. The House non-voters also get their names published. Furthermore, when a Committee of the Whole finds itself without a quorum it rises and reports to the House the names of the absentees, which are to be entered on the Journal.

The colonial practice or pretense — we cannot now in most cases tell which it was — of deducting from a member's salary for absence, naturally suggested itself to Congress for imitation. The Senate first tried it in 1816, discarded it in 1817, and tried it again in 1818, but the exceptions, including sickness, providential causes, and necessary business, were loopholes as wide as a barn-door, and the rule was useless. About Van Buren's time, some attempts seem to have been made to enforce it. Their evident futility may have led to the belief that only a statute could meet the difficulty. To that end Section 40 of the Act of August 18, 1856, authorized the Sergeant-at-Arms to deduct a day's salary for each day of unexcused absence.

[1] *Thirty Years' View*, I, 178.

This official had no desire to risk his popularity by the enforcement of any such law, and it had been almost forgotten when in 1894 it was brought to the aid of Speaker Crisp for the purpose of maintaining a quorum. The Sergeant-at-Arms prepared a form of certificate the Speaker approved, by which the members were to certify the number of days they had been absent in the course of the month. Discussion followed as to whether the law was really in force. On a question of privilege the Speaker ruled it was alive and the Sergeant-at-Arms had simply done his duty. The law exempted the member who assigned as the reason for his absence the sickness of himself or some member of his family. Many conscientious members suffered deduction, but a remarkable amount of sickness prevailed in the families of others. In the next Congress a paragraph to return the sums deducted was stricken from an appropriation bill. Again in 1914 the old law was remembered, late in August when a hot summer had kept the attendance very slim. Animated was the debate. Of course the virtuous attendants denounced unmercifully the guilty absentees. One member said the average daily absence for three months had been 205, and that the truants had drawn from the public treasury at least $442,800 for services not rendered. By a vote of 212 to 27 deductions were ordered. Again at the next session the question of reimbursement came up, and this time it was provided for, without discussion and without a dissenting vote.

Senator George F. Hoar, writing with long experience as a legislator, spoke strongly on the subject of absentees. "We ought," he said, "to have laws upon the statute book, both national and State, punishing by sufficient penalties every Senator and Representative who absents himself from the body to which he belongs, and declaring that such absences shall operate as a resignation of the seat." [1] Such a Spartan course might be in theory admirable, but even to attempt its practice would be quite futile. Laws of such a sort simply would not be generally enforced. Always the motive behind the attempts to enforce would be suspected. Partisanship or animosity or jealousy or ambition or ulterior purpose would be attributed to the complainant, and whether rightly or not, this would create sympathy and breed excuse for the culprit. No, the remedy would better be left to conscience and public opinion.

[1] "Has the Senate Degenerated?" *Forum*, April, 1897.

As a matter of fact, there are legitimate occasions for absence, particularly in the case of Congressmen. Many members must occasionally go home for a few days, to give reasonable attention to domestic or business affairs. Such visits are indeed not without distinct benefit to the public. Washington is the worst place in the country for knowledge of what the people are really thinking. Every Senator and Representative may well at no infrequent intervals mix with his constituents and benefit by the reaction. Also the giving of information on public questions and the stimulating of opinion, by way of addresses and speeches, form an eminently desirable element of Congressional service.

A word, too, may be said for occasional absence that has nothing in view but rest and recreation. Most Congressmen are well along in years. Their work is often arduous. They toil six days in the week without even Saturday afternoon off or adjourning over all the holidays. The capital has during several months of the year as detestable a climate as there is in the country, for the site, though almost at sea level, is too far from the ocean to benefit by sea breezes, and on the other hand the mountains are many miles away. From June to October the air is humid, lifeless, enervating; exercise is almost out of the question; sleep eludes. A city that in autumn has many delights, in winter is comfortable, and in spring is unsurpassed in charms, becomes almost intolerable after the arrival of hot weather. Yet of late years Congress has worked nearly or quite through almost every summer. Is it unforgivable for a member to run away once in a while in the hope that a little relief may bring him strength enough to do better work on his return?

Taking into account these causes of absence, and others equally reasonable, such as illness of members themselves or in their families, it is not especially reprehensible that at any given time about a quarter of the membership is likely to be found away from Capitol Hill. A hundred roll-calls in the 66th Congress (1919–21) examined at random showed an average of 286 members voting. Adding the paired members present and those sitting in committees with due authorization, makes it probable that well over 300 are ordinarily in the Capitol or the office buildings. The largest number recorded on any one of these votes was 361, the total membership (with no vacancies) being 435.

Much of the absence from the sessions of the House, without actual absence from town, is equally defensible, but on quite different grounds. A great deal of the work of Congress is of no general interest or concern, either to the members or to the public. Take, for example, the annual discussion of Indian affairs. Few of the Senators or Representatives from the eastern half of the country know or care anything about them. As a rule it is better to leave their consideration to men who have some acquaintance with the subject. Or take the government of the District of Columbia, which is supposed to get from the House two days in each month. It is the work of a City Council. Why demand the attendance of four hundred and more Representatives? Or take the details of the appropriation bills, which at any rate in the House may consume more time than everything else together. Conclusion on these will almost invariably be just as wisely reached by forty men as by four hundred. Sir H. S. Maine, writing in 1885, recalled that Jeremy Bentham used to denounce the non-attendance of members of Parliament at all sittings as a grave abuse; but, said Maine, "it now appears that the scanty attendance of members, and the still scantier participation of most of them in debate, were essential to the conduct of business by the House of Commons, which was then, and still is, the most numerous deliberative assembly in the world." Although the House of Representatives at Washington is much smaller, yet the presence of the full membership is the last thing to be desired for the efficient transaction of most of the business. On the contrary, ordinarily the smaller the attendance, the better the work.

In view of such considerations members feel it is no dereliction of duty to pass in their offices or the lobbies a considerable part of the hours when the House is in session. If anybody thinks attendance has fallen below the safety-point, he can by doubting the presence of a quorum, bring in enough absentees to better the situation, at least for a while, for the members will stay until in their judgment no harm is likely to result from departure. On the whole, the practice of ignoring the absence of a quorum works out satisfactorily, and there is no real ground for the criticisms either of the stranger in the gallery who chafes because he thinks his Congress is not attending to business, or of the demagogical member who abuses the confidence of his constituents by boasting to them that he is one of the few members always at the post of duty.

CHAPTER XXV

DECORUM

Decorum in lawmaking bodies is to be looked at from two points of view. The customary conduct of such bodies may be orderly or disorderly; their abnormal periods may be few or many, mild or violent.

It is probable or at any rate not improbable that in customary conduct there has been steady improvement with the gain in the manners of mankind and with the perfecting of rules of order for assemblies. Lacking much definite evidence on the subject, it is permissible to draw from rules made in early times the inference that there was decided occasion for them. Thus when we find Parliament ordering in 1640, "those who go out of the House in a confused manner before the Speaker to forfeit 10s.," we are warranted in imagining a considerable degree of indecorous conduct. So when we find the Pennsylvania Assembly in 1703 making a rule of like tenor, "that no Member presume to go in or out of the House before the Speaker, he being present, nor depart the House without his Leave," and another, "that the Members forbear talking to each other, and keep Silence, unless they have Occasion to speak in order as aforesaid," again we suspect an impolite and unruly body; and our suspicions are strengthened when we see it was at the same time provided "that any Member indecently carrying himself towards the Speaker, or any of the Members, by Reflections, or other uncomely Behavior, in the House, or shall transgress this or any other of the following Rules, shall for the first Offence be reproved, for the second and after fin'd, as the House thinks fit, not exceeding *Ten Shillings*."

The Massachusetts General Court found it necessary to provide in 1640 that "if any bee speaking about private business, whilst the business of the Court is in hand, hee shall forfect 12d."[1] The Rhode Island Assembly of May, 1648, was more concise, and in the matter of the penalty more lenient, ordering "that they that whisper or disturb ye Court, or useth nipping terms, shall forfeitt sixpence for every fault." The

[1] *Records of the Colony of the Mass. Bay in N.E.*, I, 304.

enforcement of such a fine nowadays would permit the lowering of the tax-rate by the income from whispers, but nipping terms are not now so plenty that at sixpence apiece they would largely profit the Treasury.

More delicate and diffuse was the injunction among the Orders adopted at the opening of the Virginia Assembly of 1658–59: "Every member shall keep order, and give due attention to the reading or debating of whatsoever shall be proposed or presented for the consideration of the House; and every burgesse shall, with due respect, address himself to Mr. Speaker in a decent manner, and not entertain any private discourse, while the public affairs are treated of."

It is to be presumed that restless members by moving about have always bothered the others. At any rate, among the Notes of Rules for the Continental Congress prepared by Jefferson in July, 1776, were: "No person to walk while question putting. Every person to sit while not speaking." Nowadays American legislative bodies endure commotion with little protest. Members perambulate as the whim takes them, and the constant flitting of pages and messengers is accepted as a matter of course. Very different is the custom in the House of Commons. There no attendant nor messenger dare pass beyond what is called the bar. A messenger stands at the bar with letters or telegrams until some member comes and takes them from him and passes them on to their rightful owners. In the House of Lords, however, messengers and attendants are allowed to pass up and down the chamber delivering notes and telegrams very much as in the Capitol at Washington.

Sydney Brooks noticed in Congress perpetual violations of the rule that forbids a man to pass between the Speaker and the member who is addressing the House. He says the House of Commons is punctilious to what some think an absurd degree in the observance of such points of order. If a member moves about the House with his hat on or puts even a toe beyond the line on the floor which no man may cross while speaking, cries of "Order! Order!" are heard on every side. Brooks thinks this very wholesome. "It may seem trivial in a given solitary instance, but it is only by ceaseless stringency in the small points of decorum that the intimacies of daily strife in a contentious and excitable body can be kept on a high plane."[1]

[1] "Congress and Parliament: A Contrast," *No. Am. Review*, January, 1900.

A famous English observer of earlier date, Charles Dickens, tells us of an episode he saw when he visited Washington in 1841. "A member who was speaking," he records, "being interrupted by a laugh, mimicked it, as one child would in quarreling with another, and added, 'that he would make the honorable gentlemen opposite, sing out a little more on the other side of their mouths presently.' But interruptions are rare; the speaker being usually heard in silence. There are more quarrels than with us, and more threatenings than gentlemen are accustomed to exchange in any civilized society of which we have record; but farm-yard imitations have not as yet been imported from the Parliament of the United Kingdom." [1]

Dickens was not wholly ungenerous in his observations. He paid a high compliment to the Massachusetts Legislature of that day, saying: "Such proceedings as I saw here, were conducted with perfect gravity and decorum; and were certainly calculated to inspire attention and respect." [2]

Probably when in Boston he did not chance to observe one difference between American and English canons of parliamentary conduct that brings criticism from many foreign visitors. The habit of reading the news of the day during routine proceedings or while dull speakers have the floor must have begun early with us, for the precise Jefferson jotted down in 1776 the need of a rule — "No person to read printed papers." [3] In the Massachusetts Convention of 1820 Mr. Dana, of Groton, moved that the Secretary be ordered to furnish each of the members daily with two newspapers such as each member should choose. He observed that it was usual for members of deliberative bodies to be furnished with newspapers. In the present instance it would tend not only to their own instruction and gratification, but would enable them to furnish their constituents at a distance with a full account of their proceedings, by transmitting the journals of the day which contained a regular report of their doings. James T. Austin hoped if the resolution was adopted, there would be an addition requiring that the newspapers should be read out of the House and not by members in their seats. Mr. Dana, however, believed a sense of decorum would be a sufficient restraint. Mr. Saltonstall, of Salem, thought the members had better be attending to what was

---

[1] *American Notes*, ed. of 1910, 144.   [2] *Ibid.*, 30.
[3] *Writings of Thomas Jefferson*, P. L. Ford ed., II, 60.

going on before them in the House. It was an unpleasant sight in the Legislature to observe legislators reading advertisements and the news of the day to the neglect of the duties they were chosen to perform. Daniel Webster said it was a standing rule of all the legislative bodies he had any acquaintance with, that no member should be employed in reading in his place either newspapers or any printed paper except the printed Journal of the House or some other paper printed by order of the House, and he should consider it the duty of any one who saw this rule infringed, to call to order the member who violated it. The question was then decided in the affirmative by a large majority, and the members got their newspapers.[1]

Webster had already served two terms in Congress and of course he spoke with authority about the rule, but if up to that time it had been enforced, certainly it fell into disuse not long afterward. It is related of James K. Polk, who was Speaker from 1835 to 1839, that one morning there was some important news in the papers, and all the members were eagerly reading when he called the House to order. After the Journal had been read, Mr. Polk announced that the House was ready for business. No one paid the slightest attention to the announcement, and thereupon Mr. Polk took a newspaper, turned his back to the House, and began reading himself. Ten, fifteen, twenty minutes passed away; the members had finished their papers and wondered what the matter was. The Speaker sat absorbed in reading. "Mr. Speaker! Mr. Speaker!" shouted one member after another. Finally a member rose and thus addressed the Clerk of the House: "There does not seem to be any Speaker present, and I move, Mr. Clerk, that we proceed to a choice of Speaker *pro tem.*" Instantly Mr. Polk turned in his chair and said: "The Speaker is present, and begs to say to the honorable House that, in accordance with established custom, he notified the House that it was ready for business, but found it was not ready, and trusts it is now ready to proceed." The House burst into laughter, and it was agreed by all that the Speaker had given a good lesson in politeness.[2]

So far as I am aware, no member of an American legislative body is now disturbed in his perusal of the news. Yet according to the rules, no member of the Wisconsin Assembly is to

[1] *Mass. Convention of 1820*, pp. 33–35.
[2] J. W. Moore, *The American Congress*, 311.

read a newspaper within the bar of the House. No Senator of Louisiana, Nebraska, or Wyoming is to enjoy the news of the day or profit by editorial advice while the Journal or public papers are being read, or any member is speaking in debate. The Iowa House, with less regard for the feelings of dreary orators, confines its prohibition to the time while the Journal is being read.

In Parliament, it is a conspicuous breach of order for a member to read a newspaper in the House. He may quote an extract from one in the course of a speech, but if he attempted to peruse it as he sat in his place his ears would soon be assailed by a stern and reproving cry of "Order! Order!" from the Chair. [1] Members, however, often slip a newspaper or periodical into the "Orders of the Day," and read it while the Speaker imagines they are industriously studying the clauses of a bill or its amendments. It is equally reprehensible to read a book.

Writing was once as obnoxious as reading in the House of Commons. No man was to write a letter in the debating chamber itself, nor even to jot down a line, except for actual purpose of the debate, in which case he might make a note of something said in a speech to which he intended to reply. As far back as the days of the Stuarts note-taking was looked upon as blameworthy. On one occasion Sir Edward Alvord was required to give up his notes to the Speaker. For a while the severity of the prohibition seems to have been relaxed. We read that Sir Henry Vane told his neighbor, D'Ewes, who records it, that he could remember when no man was allowed to make notes, and wished it to be now forbidden. D'Ewes commented: "If you will not permit us to write, we must go to sleep, as some among us do, or go to plays, as others have done."

Apparently the rule is no longer in force, if indeed it is still supposed to exist. Lord Robert Cecil told the Select Committee on Procedure in 1914 that he knew nothing out of order in the writing of letters in the House. He said that Mr. Gladstone used to write his letters to the Queen while he was on the bench. This was in response to a question by Sir David Brynmor Jones as to whether the witness would favor allowing members to read or write their letters in the House if there were a con-

[1] Michael MacDonough, "The Quaint Side of Parliament," *Nineteenth Century*, February, 1898.

venient table or ledge at hand.   Lord Robert replied that he saw no reason at all why they should not so write their letters.

Had he served in an American lawmaking body, perhaps he would not have been so confident.   One of the advantages sought in removing the desks from the chamber of the lower House at Washington was the preventing of this very thing. It was expected that if members had no place to write, they would listen.   Yet there may be more gain in having an inattentive member where his mind can be on occasion diverted from his avocations to the discussion in progress, than in having him in the writing-room or an office where he can be reached only with the help of the roll-call bells.   Certainly, too, desks are greatly useful for the storing of calendars and other current documents, as well as material for the needs of debate.   In other directions, however, the gains from the absence of desks are so decisive that they are not likely to be returned to the national House, and they might well be removed from the chamber of any legislative body with large membership.

By the way, that same hearing before the English Select Committee brought to light a singular rule probably unknown to almost everybody.   At any rate Lord Robert Cecil did not know it was out of order for a private member to lift both feet from the floor.   Sir David Brynmor Jones called it to his attention that this was one of the many things permissible to a Minister, but not to a private member.   The observant Herbert Sidebotham tells us that when the legs of Ministers are short, they have to get their shoulders well down to reach the table, giving the impression of men trying to stand on their heads.[1] We Americans had supposed we had a monopoly in the way of easing our legs by disposing both feet comfortably at any elevation preferred.   Not everywhere in the United States has the practice been approved.   The story goes that one afternoon a member of Congress decorated the desk in front of him with two feet inside of low shoes and white socks.   Speaker Reed thereupon sent him the message, "The Czar commands you to haul down those flags of truce!"   It sufficed.

[1] *Political Profiles*, 20.

Smoking and Drinking

TOBACCO has brought pleasure and trouble to many generations of lawmakers. Evidently it did not take the settlers of Massachusetts Bay long to establish commerce enough with Virginia to secure for themselves the new solace, for we read of the House of Deputies, November 4, 1646: "It is ordered, that if any person shall take any tobacco within the roome where the Courte is sitting he shall forfeite, for every pipe so taken, 6d.; and if they shall offend againe in contemning this wholesome order, he shall be called to ye barr for his delinquency, & pay double his fyne." [1] Even in Virginia itself the use of the staple that made the fortunes of the colony had to be regulated. Number 8 of the Orders of the House of Burgesses of 1663 declared "that every member that shall pipe it after the House is begun to be called over, until adjournment or publick license by consent of the major part of the House, in the vacancy from any business, shall be fined twenty pounds of tobacco." [2] Parliament had to meet the same situation in the interest of those whom tobacco offended. About the middle of that century the Standing Orders of the House of Commons contained this: "Ordered, that no member of the House do presume to smoke tobacco in the gallery, or at the table of the House, sitting as Committee." Nevertheless, at any rate on this side of the water, smoking long continued in legislative halls. It was not stopped in Congress until 1871, and even after that time violations of the rule were not unknown. One of the merits accredited to Speaker Reed was that he would not permit smoking on the floor of the House. In various Western Legislatures no such asceticism has prevailed. When women lawmakers began to appear, it was wondered whether their presence would expel the cigar.

Formal prohibition of the practice is now to be found in the rules of nearly all the Legislatures. The rule of the California House makes the generous exception that at evening sessions it may be suspended by majority vote without notice or reference to a committee. The Michigan Senate says the prohibition shall not extend to the Committee of the Whole. Probably there are few rooms of standing committees where smoking is forbidden. Yet a decent regard for the rights of others should

[1] *Records of the Colony of the Mass. Bay in N.E.*, III, 83.
[2] Hening, *Statutes at Large*, II, 207.

preclude it if women are in attendance. This truism would be both superfluous and smug were it not for the astonishing fact that some men with brains enough to be preferred for public office by their fellows, do fail to use them in this particular. When none but men are in the room, question of propriety is not so fairly raised, for most men who take part in public affairs are quite accustomed to tobacco smoke, and it is expected that the unlucky exceptions to the rule will submit in silence rather than interfere with the satisfactions of their neighbors.

Snuff-taking, no longer customary with the mass of mankind, was once as familiar a habit with "the well-born" as with those of lowlier origin. A century ago it was the custom in both Houses of Congress to have great silver urns, filled with the choicest and most fragrant "Maccaboy" and "Old Scotch" snuff, placed where the members could help themselves freely to the nose-titillating pulverized tobacco. It was no unusual thing to see a speaker, while pouring out words of eloquence on the floor of the House or Senate, stop suddenly, walk over to the snuff-urn, fill his nose, sneeze two or three times, flourish a bandanna handkerchief, and then walk back to his place and resume his remarks. Some of the old members had considerable reputation as graceful snuff-takers. Mr. Macon, who presided over the Senate, took snuff with such perfection that he was admired by all the Senators; and Mr. Clay, who imitated the French, was not far behind him in grace and polished ease.[1] The snuff-urn of the National House of Representatives was never empty during the session until 1876.[2] In Massachusetts the banishment of snuff from the Speaker's desk was one of the triumphs of the Know-Nothing Legislature of 1855.

The chewing of tobacco is a form of its use that is disappearing among those who care anything for the standards of social intercourse. Time was when its critics dignified it by prohibition. In the Journal of the Virginia House of Burgesses of 1769 there is to be found in the long list of standing orders one to the effect that no member should chew tobacco in the House while the Speaker was in the chair or while the House was in the Committee of the Whole House. Attempts of this sort to suppress the practice were vain, and during many years it was so prevalent that the United States became notorious by reason

[1] J. W. Moore, *The American Congress*, 253.
[2] James A. Garfield, "A Century of Congress," *Atlantic Monthly*, July, 1877.

of its disgusting manifestations. Visitors from abroad rarely failed to make it the target of their scorn. Notable among them was Dickens, who wrote after his visit to Congress: "Both Houses are handsomely carpeted; but the state to which these carpets are reduced by the universal disregard of the spittoon with which every honorable member is accommodated, and the extraordinary improvements on the pattern which are squirted and dabbled upon it in every direction, do not admit of being described. . . . It is strange enough, too, to see an honorable gentleman leaning back in his tilted chair, with his legs on the desk before him, shaping a convenient 'plug' with his penknife, and when it is quite ready for use, shooting the old one from his mouth, as from a popgun, and clapping the new one in its place. I was surprised to observe that even steady old chewers of great experience, are not always good marksmen." [1]

Had Dickens examined the legislative history of his own land, he might have found that the vice of expectoration was neither novel nor peculiar to Americans. He might have read how in the time of Queen Elizabeth, Parliament "meeting to go through the form of choosing a Speaker with all proper solemnity, the comptroller of the household, Sir William Knolls, said, 'I will deliver my opinion unto you who is most fit for this place, being a member of this House, and those good abilities which I know to be in him' (here he made a little pause, *and the House hawked and spat*, and, after silence made, he proceeded)," etc.[2] We may be thankful that this particular method of disapprobation no longer prevails in Parliament or anywhere else.

The part played by intoxicating liquor in lawmaking would make a sorry, saddening tale. The only good that could come from it would be to show us that men are gaining on the enemies of their happiness. Manifold as are yet the injuries wrought by strong drink on legislators, never since representative assemblies began have those injuries been so rare as now. Surely it is not the least of present-day virtues that excessive indulgence in liquor has become disgraceful, and that total abstinence arouses no scorn. Measure the change in conditions by

---

[1] *American Notes*, ed. of 1910. 140 *et sqq.*

[2] Sir Symonds d'Ewes, quoted in Townsend's *History of the House of Commons*, I, 15.

learning that when, in 1701, the Connecticut Legislature was to meet for the first time in New Haven, the town meeting voted authority to five more men to "Sell Rum only while the Court sits." Or if that seems too remote a period for comparison, read about the favorite beverage of Congressmen a century ago, "switchel," compounded of molasses, ginger, and water from the celebrated Capitol spring, and "flavored" with the finest Jamaica rum. Many gallons of it were consumed daily, and whenever there was an exciting debate the supply had to be renewed time and again.[1]

Come still nearer our own day and note in the letters of John Fairfield to his wife the report of case after case of gross intoxication, and of deaths of members from *mania a potu*. Or find in George W. Julian's reminiscences the proof of conditions now almost unbelievable that prevailed in Washington as late as the middle of the nineteenth century. The vice of intemperance, Julian says, was not, as now, restricted to a few exceptional cases, but was fearfully prevalent. A glass of wine could sometimes be seen on the desk of a Senator while engaged in debate, and the free use of intoxicating drinks by Senators was too common to provoke remark. It was still more common in the House; and the scenes of drunkenness and disorder in that body on the last night of the session beggared description. Much of the most important legislation of the session, involving the expenditure of many millions, remained to be disposed of at that sitting; and, as a preparation for the work, a large supply of whiskey had been deposited in a room immediately connected with the Hall of Representatives, which was thronged by members at all hours of the night. The chairman of the Ways and Means Committee became so exhilarated that he had to be retired from his post; and some of his brethren, who had been calling him to order in a most disorderly manner, were quite as incapable of business as himself, while order had sought her worshipers elsewhere. The exhibition was most humiliating.[2]

Many State legislators were no more self-respecting, at an even later period. Senator Isaac Stephenson served two terms in the Wisconsin Legislature just after the Civil War. In his "Recollections of a Long Life" he says (p. 194): "These

[1] J. W. Moore, *The American Congress*, 253.
[2] *Political Recollections*, 105, 106.

were tumultuous days in Madison. Lobbyists in profusion, especially those in the employ of the railroads, hovered in the shadow of the capitol; whiskey flowed freely, and many legislative plans were laid over steaming bowls of 'hot Scotch.' Not infrequently men remained all night drinking at the bar." He tells of harmonizing a committee by taking a recess of fifteen minutes in order to visit the largest saloon in the capital. Also he describes the effect on Horace Greeley of an orgy in a hotel room next that in which Greeley chanced to be staying. "The famous editor observed afterwards that he had been in the worst places in New York City, but none so bad as Madison appeared to be."

Palpable though the evils of strong drink must always have been, attempts to combat them before our own day were as rare as they were ineffective. Almost an oasis of common sense in the desert of folly is one of the Orders adopted by the Virginia Assembly at the opening of the session of 1658–59 : "The first time any member of this House shall, by the major part of the House, be adjudged to be disguised with overmuch drink, he shall forfeit one hundred pounds of tobacco ; and for the second time he shall be so disguised, he shall forfeit 300 of tobacco ; and for the third offence 1000 lb. tobacco."

Not until within a few years has the nation itself realized the stupidity of permitting within the very walls of its Capitol the sale of poison to befuddle the brains of its lawmakers. Liquor was there dispensed without restriction until 1837, when under the influence of the Washingtonian movement, it was prohibited. The rule proved imperfect and the sale went on, under severe restrictions, until 1867, when it was again prohibited, only to be renewed under other conditions until 1903, when by reason of the growing temperance sentiment of the country the thing was stopped for good by a vote taken without debate or division.

In Georgia the messenger and doorkeeper of the House are "especially charged with the rigid enforcement" of the rule that no member shall be permitted to enter or remain when in an intoxicated condition. The probability is strong that such a rule is no longer of consequence. It is now exceedingly rare to see any member of our lawmaking bodies under the influence of liquor while in attendance. Many months passed after I entered Congress before a single instance came under my observation, and that remained unique for a long time.

Former Speaker Champ Clark came to the defense of Congress in this matter in his "Quarter Century of American Politics" (I, 197). "Another railing accusation, also false," said he, "is that Representatives and Senators spend much time in guzzling, gambling, and in other manner of riotous living, when as a matter of fact they do little of that sort of thing. The truth is that a vast majority of them are sober, serious, industrious, intelligent, capable, and patriotic men, most of them discharging their religious duties more completely in Washington than at home." Mr. Clark died just before the close of the 66th Congress, and his body was awaiting burial when the members assembled for the last evening sitting, an occasion previously always marked by disorder. He had not been reëlected, and the tragic coincidence of his death just at the end of his long and brilliant Congressional career combined with the universal affection for him to prevent any hilarity or breach of decorum. Perhaps a bad custom thus once broken will not be easily resumed.

Strong Language

In the heat of debate, men usually moderate and considerate sometimes say things likely to provoke bad temper or even altercations. It was early found that these could not prudently be allowed to go unrebuked. Sir Thomas Smith, describing the Parliament of Queen Elizabeth's time, says: "No reviling or nipping words must be used; for then all the House will cry 'it is against the order.'" Nevertheless reviling and nipping words became almost the fashion. It is doubtful if the intemperance of speech in both Houses of Parliament during the American war and at some periods of the administration of the younger Pitt has ever been equalled in Congress or any other of our lawmaking bodies. For example, the "Debates" shows that February 7, 1775, "Lord Mansfield rose in great passion, — he charged the last noble lord (Earl of Shelburne) with uttering gross falsehood." And: "The Earl of Shelburne returned the charge of falsehood to Lord Mansfield in direct terms."

The lie direct and the *tu quoque* have been heard in other lawmaking bodies, but in none where it would be so unexpected as in the British House of Lords. There a single instance might be set down to the infirmities of human nature and rejected as an insufficient basis for general criticism, but to find that coarse and angry epithets were frequent if not habitual gives cause for gratitude that manners have improved.

So eminent a man as Canning complained of "the practice in the House of Commons, of calumniating public men on either side of the House, by imputing to them motives of action, the insinuation of which would not be tolerated in the intercourse of private life." This gentleman allowed himself, on the floor, to stigmatize Mr. Lambton, one of the most distinguished orators of the opposition, as "a dolt and an ideot." In February, 1817, Mr. Bennett exclaimed, in his place, against "such Ministers as the noble Lord, Castlereagh, who had already imbrued their hands in the blood of their country, and been guilty of the most criminal cruelties." Lord Castlereagh replied by giving the lie direct to his accuser. Upon another occasion in the same year, when vilified by Mr. Brougham, the noble Lord described the speech of the honorable and learned gentleman as "a strain of black, malignant, and libellous insinuation." [1]

Let it not be supposed that our colonial forefathers were without offense in this regard. They were, however, often rude, unlettered yeomen, with no pretension to the culture of an English lord, nor with anything like the opportunity for polish that was at any rate open to every member of the English gentry. There is no occasion for surprise that even Virginia, more aristocratic than any other colony, found it wise to insert in the rules of order adopted at the opening of the session of 1658–59, "that no irreverent or indigne forme of speech be uttered in the House by any person against another member of this House, upon the penalty of five hundred pounds of tobacco; the House to be judge therein."

Singularly enough the public men of Virginia and the neighboring colonies, where wealth first created classes in America and groups of men first came to think themselves better than other groups, were long the most conspicuous in the halls of Congress for violations of taste and even of decency in the use of language. Indeed, the most flagrant offender of all was a Virginian, John Randolph. That strange genius reached the height of his extravagance when John C. Calhoun became Vice-President, and in presiding over the Senate made the surprising discovery that he had no authority to call Senators to order for

[1] *Walsh's Appeal*, 300, 301.

words spoken in debate. It is believed he was led to this by the wish to let Randolph say what he might. The bitter partisanship aroused by the circumstances of the election of John Quincy Adams as President was tainting the work of both House and Senate. Virulence marked many a speech, and the most virulent of all the speakers was John Randolph. His powerful intellect was broken. His best friends excused him on the ground that he was partly insane; his enemies declared his insanity due only to drink. His biographer, Henry Adams, says perhaps a charitable explanation will agree with his own belief that all Randolph's peculiarities had their source in an ungovernable temper, which he had indulged until it led him to the verge of madness. He would take the floor, and, leaning or lolling against the railing that in the old Senate Chamber surrounded the outer row of desks, he would talk two or three hours at a time, while Calhoun sat like a statue in the Vice-President's chair, until the Senators one by one retired, leaving the Senate to adjourn without a quorum, a thing until then unknown to its courteous habits; and the gallery looked down with titters or open laughter at this exhibition of a half-insane, half-intoxicated man, talking a dreary monologue, broken at long intervals by passages beautiful in their construction, direct in their purpose, and not the less amusing from their occasional virulence.[1]

These long speeches, if speeches they could be called, were never reported. The reporters broke down in trying to cope with the rapid utterance, the discursiveness and interminable length of such harangues. One sentence, however, made history. "I was defeated," he said, "horse, foot, and dragoons — cut up and clean broke down by the coalition of Blifil and Black George — by the combination, unheard of till then, of the Puritan with the blackleg." This characterization of Adams and Clay made them furious. The President contented himself with applying the words of Ovid, which the biographer translates —

> His face is livid; gaunt his whole body;
> His breast is green with gall; his tongue drips poison.

Clay resorted to the reply of the time — a challenge to a duel, which affair you may find graphically described in the

[1] Henry Adams, *John Randolph*, 297.

pages of Benton.[1] It was, he says, "about the last high-toned duel that I have witnessed, and among the highest-toned that I have ever witnessed, and so happily conducted to a fortunate issue — a result due to the noble character of the seconds as well as to the generous and heroic spirit of the principals."

The President indignantly charged that Calhoun permitted Randolph "in speeches of ten hours long to drink himself drunk with bottled porter and in raving balderdash of the meridian of Wapping to revile the absent and the present, the living and the dead." Certain it is that Calhoun put no check whatever on Randolph's maunderings. His course, however, was not permitted to escape Senatorial attention. In 1828 the rules were modified after a debate in which it appeared that Senators thought the change gave their presiding officer power to enforce order without being called on so to do by one of their number. Yet for more than twenty years it continued to be the practice for the presiding officer not to interfere unless a question of order was raised. Then, in April, 1850, Vice-President Millard Fillmore faced the question, and in a careful discussion of the subject, told the Senate he intended to take the responsibility.[2] "I know," he said, "how difficult it is to determine what is and what is not in order — to restrain improper language, and yet not abridge the freedom of debate. But all must see how important it is that the first departure from the strict rule of parliamentary decorum should be checked, as a slight attack, or even insinuation, of a personal character often provokes a more severe retort, which brings out a more disorderly reply — each Senator feeling a justification in the previous aggression."

Fillmore regretted that the rule was not so explicit as that of the House in making the duty imperative. It now so reads: "If any Senator in speaking or otherwise transgress the rules of the Senate, the Presiding Officer shall, or any Senator may, call him to order."

The story of Roscoe Conkling furnishes an instructive illustration of the danger in allowing personal reflections to be made in a legislative assembly. When the Army Bill was before the House in April, 1866, Conkling, in a speech supporting his motion to strike out the appropriation for the provost-marshal-general, assailed the office and the officer in a manner calculated

---

[1] *Thirty Years' View*, I, 70 *et sqq.*   [2] *Gilfry's Precedents*, 567.

to kindle resentment. James G. Blaine in reply read from his seat in the House a letter from General Fry, the incumbent of the office, to himself, containing charges of improper conduct on the part of Conkling. A committee was asked, and it exonerated Conkling. Its report criticized the practice of reading in the House letters that reflected upon the House, or upon the acts or speeches of any member. This started the controversy that ended only with Conkling's death, and which in one way or another so seriously affected the politics of a score of years.[1]

Lawmakers have usually contented themselves with trying to prevent language arousing the animosity of individuals. The United States Senate goes farther by saying that no Senator shall refer offensively to any State of the Union. No longer ago than May 14, 1920, Vice-President Marshall, presiding, had occasion to remind Senator Sheppard of this, when the Senator said that New Jersey in the matter of the prohibition amendment had put itself "on the side of revolution and anarchy." Accordingly the Senator formally withdrew the remark from the Record. Arizona carried the Senate precaution to a unique extreme with a rule reading: "No Senator shall refer offensively to any county in the State."

For novelty, at any rate, that can be matched by a rule of the Georgia Senate: "In nominating candidates for any office no laudatory remarks shall be allowed nor shall other candidates be disparaged."

TUMULTUOUS DISORDER

THE spirit of disorder that occasionally sweeps a whole assembly off its feet furnishes an interesting study in psychology. It is a manifestation of the mob spirit. Men in the mass give way to passion, throw reason to the winds, for the time become irresponsible beings, from causes that operating upon the same men isolated would leave most of them unmoved and sane. Tumultuous episodes may therefore be expected now and then in every legislative body.

Lowell has suggested that "familiarity with legislative bodies seems to breed contempt, for the last half century has been marked by an increase of disorderly scenes in the legislatures

[1] George S. Boutwell, *Sixty Years in Public Affairs*, II, 260 *et sqq.*

of many countries." [1] It may be that such an increase has been more apparent than real. Perhaps the newspapers now acquaint us with them more generally. Perhaps they attract more attention than in days when society itself was more tumultuous. Certainly they are not novel, even in their abundance. The history of Parliament discloses many of them in every century of which we have copious information. Intimations of them are to be found scattered through the records of our colonial assemblies.

Congress became acquainted with them early. For example, read Jefferson's description of one. "Yesterday witnessed a scandalous scene in the H. of R.," he wrote. "It was the day for taking up the report of their committee against the Alien & Sedition laws, &c. They held a Caucus and determined that not a word should be spoken on their side, in answer to anything which should be said on the other. Gallatin took up the Alien, & Nicholas the Sedition law ; but after a little while of common silence, they began to enter into loud conversations, laugh, cough, &c., so that for the last hour of these gentlemen's speaking, they must have had the lungs of a vendue master to have been heard. Livingston, however, attempted to speak. But after a few sentences the Speaker called him to order, and told him what he was saying was not to the question. It was impossible to proceed. The question was taken & carried in favor of the report, 52 to 48." [2] Here you may see the mob spirit, which always seeks to vent itself in noise, turning instinctively to a course directly the opposite of that which had been agreed upon to secure the desired end.

Horace Binney recalled that when he was in Congress in 1834 and "Tom Benton brought in his bill to debase the gold coin," after a small house had listened attentively to a speech by Binney in opposition, when a gentleman took the floor to speak on the same side, the house suddenly filled as if by magic. Every member was soon in his seat, and then they began such coughing and scraping of feet that the member could not go on. Next they called for a vote and passed the measure without a pause. "Here," says Binney, "was an organized conspiracy to carry through this party measure without reference to argu-

[1] *The Government of England*, i, 261.
[2] Thomas Jefferson to James Madison, February 26, 1799, *Writings of Thomas Jefferson*, P. L. Ford ed., vii, 371.

ment or the honor of the country. It made an impression on me at that time, and showed how thorough party training had even then become." [1]

For an instance of the same sort of thing in Parliament, before the half-century of which President Lowell spoke, take Macaulay's account in his diary, June 11, 1840: "I have never seen such unseemly demeanour or heard such scurrilous language in Parliament. Lord Norreys was making all sorts of noises. Lord Maidstone was so ill-mannered that I hope he was drunk. At last, after much grossly indecent conduct, a furious outbreak took place. O'Connell was so rudely interrupted that he used the expression 'beastly bellowings.' Then rose such an uproar as no mob at Covent Garden Theatre — no crowd of Chartists in front of a hustings — ever equalled. Men on both sides stood up, shook their fists, and bawled at the top of their voices. O'Connell raged like a mad bull. . . . At last the tumult ended from a physical weakness. It was past one and the steady bellowers had been howling since six o'clock."

In our own time even so eminent a man as Gladstone was not spared humiliation by Parliament become a mob. He complained pathetically of the intolerant treatment given to him upon his introduction of the first Home Rule Bill in 1885. He declared "it struck a fatal blow at the liberties of debate and at the dignity of Parliament." Upon objection to having the Colonial Secretary answer questions on Chinese labor addressed directly to the Premier, the Opposition prevented his speech by yelling continuously for an hour.

Justin McCarthy goes so far as to say that the House of Commons is almost the noisiest and rudest legislative assembly with which he has any manner of personal acquaintance. For this he gives a sound reason. "The House of Commons," he says, "is too large in numbers and too contracted in space to be orderly when any exciting question is under debate. I do not know how any assembly could in very exciting times be decorous and orderly when men are crammed together within hearing of every interruption and indeed of every word. The recent riot — for it was nothing short of a riot during the short time it lasted — in the House of Commons was mainly caused by the fact that men were pent up so closely together that the movement of one man from his place suggested to another man

[1] C. C. Binney, *Life of Horace Binney*, 124.

that he who first sought to push his way through must have had it in his mind to assault somebody." [1]

The apprehension that the same kind of result might follow was one of the reasons for the delay in removing the desks from the chamber of the House of Representatives at Washington, an improvement postponed long after its desirability for various reasons became evident.

Riots made up chiefly of noise will doubtless continue to develop from time to time in both Parliament and Congress, and of course are to be deprecated, but their actual harm to anything save the sense of public dignity, is not often serious. Fortunately we seem to have outgrown the manners that put bodily injury among their possible results. No longer may it ever be said as James H. Hammond, of South Carolina, said in the bitter Speakership contest of 1859: "I believe every man is armed with a revolver — some with two and a bowie knife." Former Speaker Grow, telling De A. S. Alexander of his experience in the fifties, remembered a revolver slipping from the hip pocket of a member and falling noisily to the floor in front of the Speaker's desk. In answer to the Chair, its owner explained that he had carried it the night before as a protection against vicious dogs and forgot to remove it from his pocket. This explanation raised a roar of derisive laughter, but the matter received no further notice. "It is doubtful," added Grow, "if a revolver has been carried in the House for forty years." [2]

Of course legislative tumults are quite inconsistent with good lawmaking. Nothing calls more for calm, cool, sane judgment than the deciding upon a statute. What could be more foreign to the proper conduct of such a process than the circumstances of the passage by the Illinois Legislature of what was believed to be the first general legislative act in the United States providing for the municipal ownership of street railways? Edwin Burritt Smith described the episode in the "Atlantic Monthly" for January, 1904. Evidently he was a strong partisan in a bitter fight, so that his description is to be taken with allowances, but the essential facts were doubtless accurately given. When the Senate Bill for public ownership came to the House, its opponents decided to favor instead the Lindley Bill, with cer-

[1] "Parliamentary Manners," *No. Am. Review*, December, 1893.
[2] *Hist. and Procedure of the House of Reps.*, 265.

tain amendments. As soon as Mr. Lindley offered the first of these, the opposition leader moved to lay it on the table. His followers, to the number of ninety-six, rose in their seats and shouted, "Roll-call! Roll-call!" By the Constitution, a roll-call should have been granted on request of five. But the Speaker, an "organization" man, refused to hear the shout, and declared the amendment adopted by *viva voce* vote. "You lie!" shouted Representative Allen.

Then amid the utmost confusion and excitement, with the majority members standing on their desks and shouting, "Roll-call! Roll-call!" Mr. Lindley hastily offered his six other amendments. The Speaker, without the formality of reading or a vote, declared them all adopted. Without motion, he also declared the bill passed to its third reading, beyond the reach of further amendments. Representative Burke made a rush for him, but was intercepted and thrown roughly to the floor.

A riot might have followed had not the Speaker precipitately fled to his room, declaring that the House had taken a recess until afternoon. At once Representative Murray, of Springfield, standing on his seat near the Speaker's desk, solemnly called the House to order and said: "It appears that the House is without a presiding officer; I move that Mr. Allen, of Vermilion, be chosen Speaker *pro tem.*" The motion carried, Mr. Allen took the deserted chair, and the confusion quickly subsided. Thereupon the Lindley Bill was recalled from its third reading and the Senate Bill substituted. The ninety-six members who did this next signed a resolution that they would not vote on any question until the House records should show this reconsideration, and the House should during the rest of the session be assured of the continuous observance of the constitutional right of a roll-call. This brought the Speaker to terms and he permitted the roll-call. His excuse was that he had been approached with intimations that he could make money by allowing a roll-call, and was fully convinced that "there was something wrong with this effort on the part of outside parties to push this bill."

The wisest and strongest of presiding officers have a hard task in such emergencies. Often they are quite helpless for the time inasmuch as the wit of man has not been equal to providing adequate remedy. Sometimes the Speaker can restore order with the help of the Sergeant-at-Arms, whose mace by its symbolism of authority brings offenders to their senses. Sometimes for equally mysterious reasons efficacy will be found in the use of the parliamentary device known as naming a member. The House of Commons, on the 23d of January, 1693, resolved, "to the end that all debates should be grave and orderly, as becomes so great an assembly, and that all interruptions should be prevented, that no member of this House do presume to make any noise or disturbance while any member shall be orderly debating, or whilst any bill, order, or other matter shall be in reading or opening; and, in case of such noise or disturbance, that Mr. Speaker do call upon the member by name making such disturbance, and that every such person shall thereby incur the displeasure and censure of the House."

W. C. Townsend, in his "History of the House of Commons" (II, 92), tells the story of Speaker Onslow, who, in his anxiety to tighten the lax bands of discipline, used to fulminate in deepest baritone the threat of naming the disorderly member, "Order, sir; I will name you presently; order, order; I will name you." He was one day asked by an inquisitive rebel to his authority, using the privilege of a very young member, what would actually be the consequence if the Speaker should name him. The Speaker, after a grave pause, replied solemnly, "The Lord in heaven only knows!" But, says Townsend, the answer must have been made in a spirit of pompous waggery, or a resolution not to relieve the mysterious terrors of ignorance; for he well knew the penalty, that the member thus called upon by name would have to withdraw, and, even if the most lenient view of his case be taken, have to be committed to the custody of the Sergeant.

When once in a great while an American legislator gets named, his case is usually turned over to a committee, which persuades him to make an apology. Until he yields, he is precluded from any share in the business of the House. It happened to me to be the innocent cause of about the only episode of the sort in Massachusetts in our time. Some remarks of mine led to their characterization by a domineering fellow-member as "nonsense, buncombe, and rot." He might not have suffered had he not been engaged for some time in provoking the Speaker. At last his effrontery had brought patience to its limit, and this seemed an opportunity to teach him a lesson. Great was the bewilderment when he was named. At first nobody knew what to do about it. Then misty recollection suggested a committee which gravely approved of the ruling that "rot" was an unparliamentary term, and the next day the penitent offender duly apologized.

The Massachusetts Legislature has an institution that in theory is presumed to have for one of its purposes the maintenance of discipline. It is of ancient origin. This entry in the Journal of the House of Deputies, May 31, 1644, follows an order that no member should speak a second time if another wished to speak: "It is ordered, that Capta: Cooke & Mr. Tory are chosen comptrolers of ye howse for this Courte, & particulerly to see to ye exact keepeing of ye foregoeinge order." [1]

The "comptrolers" of old are now known as "monitors." They may illustrate how easy it is for a stranger to draw from printed rules an inference not in fact warranted by the actual practice. L. G. McConachie, in "Congressional Committees" (p. 367), says of them: "The House of Representatives divides itself into four sections, for each of which the Speaker appoints two lieutenants or monitors, who take the number of votes, or of members present, for the Chair, and assist him in preserving order. If their authority is defied, they report to the House, which may see fit to deprive an unruly member of his right to vote or to speak."

As a matter of fact, the share of the monitors in preserving order is negligible. I never saw one exercise any authority, or even take any interest in so doing or manifest an inclination so to do. Almost their only function is to count rising votes and report the totals to the Speaker, by divisions, which are formed by the aisles running from the entrances down to the Speaker's desk. Incorrect reports by them, sometimes suspected not to have been unintentional, occasionally add a little gayety to the proceedings, but are never seriously harmful, for errors are usually noted by some interested member, who will ask that the count be verified by repetition, which, with the chance for the Yeas and Nays, in the end gets accuracy.

Those who take to heart the scenes of disorder now and then witnessed in our legislative halls, may at least find cause for encouragement in the fact that to-day the bad behavior of lawmakers is at any rate kept within doors. Our fathers were

[1] *Records of the Colony of the Mass. Bay in N.E.*, III, 4.

sometimes less considerate. Edward Hooker tells us in his diary that as the session of the South Carolina Assembly for 1805 was nearing its end, on Sunday, December 15, a riotous scene took place which made considerable disturbance. "The Speaker of the House of Representatives is said to have been a principal actor in it. He and several members of both Houses together with some others went through the streets in high glee with a drum and fiddle; to *set the town to rights* as they term it. They went to the lodgings of a number of the members, and in case of their failing to rise and admit them voluntarily, broke down the doors of their rooms." [1] Surely we have made some gain in self-respect since then.

Governor Thomas Ford in his "History of Illinois" (p. 81) tells a delightful story of public life in pioneer days. It seems that in 1827 there was in the Legislature a very exciting election for a State Treasurer, in which the former incumbent of the office was defeated. After the election was over the Assembly immediately adjourned; but before the members got out of the House the unsuccessful candidate walked into their chamber and administered personal chastisement upon four of the largest and strongest of those who had voted against him. The members broke one way or another out of the house and fled like sheep from a fold invaded by a wolf. No steps were ever taken to bring the offender to punishment, but the same session he was appointed clerk of the circuit court, and recorder for Jo Daviess county.

Admission to the Floor

In the Federal House the first rule regulating admission to the floor was adopted in January of 1802, and restricted the privilege to "Senators, officers of the General and State Governments, and such persons as Members might introduce." In 1805 officers of State governments were excluded; in 1809, judicial officers and ex-Members of Congress admitted. In 1833 a change was made to admit "such persons as the Speaker or a Member might introduce," and this lasted fifty years, the House rescinding it almost unanimously December 10, 1883.

John Randolph, on one occasion, deliberately insulted James Lloyd, one of "the solid men of Boston," then a Senator

[1] *Am. Hist. Assn. Rep. for 1896*, i, 880.

from Massachusetts, who had, in accordance with the custom, introduced upon the floor of the Senate one of his constituents, Major Benjamin Russell, the editor of the "Columbian Sentinel." The sight of a Federalist editor aroused Mr. Randolph's anger, and he at once insolently demanded that the floor of the Senate be cleared, forcing Major Russell to retire. Mr. Lloyd took the first opportunity to express his opinion of this gratuitous insult and declared in very forcible language that, as he had introduced Major Russell on the floor, he was responsible therefor. Mr. Randolph indulged in a little gasconade, in which he announced that his carriage was waiting at the door to convey him to Baltimore, and at the conclusion of his remarks he left the Senate Chamber and the city. Mr. Calhoun, who had not attempted to check Mr. Randolph, lamented from the chair that anything should have happened to mar the harmony of the Senate, and again declared that he had no power to call a Senator to order, nor would he for ten thousand worlds look like an usurper.[1]

The State Legislatures have been very lax in this matter. Of late years many of them have seen the danger of allowing lobbyists to circulate among the members, and have stopped the practice. There is not yet, however, that strict exclusion of strangers from the floor which is desirable for the proper conduct of business. The situation in at least one of the States, which it is to be feared is not exceptional, may be learned from what Victor J. West writes of the California Legislature, in the "National Municipal Review" for July, 1923. "In both Houses," he says, "almost any visitor is permitted to enter the chamber, move freely up and down the aisles, and confer with members even during the formal transaction of legislative business. Indeed, it is no uncommon thing, in the Assembly especially, for the seats of members to be occupied by persons who have no right to be in the chamber at all." Mr. West further avers that in the past fifteen years there have been many instances of fights directed from the floor by lobbyists, who, seated at the desks of members and acting through committee chairmen, "commanded the opposing forces as effectively as generals on the field of battle."

Even the presence of disinterested spectators is unfortunate. Manifestly a member will not give his attention so well to the

[1] Ben: Perley Poore, *Reminiscences*, I, 70.

question before the House if he must entertain the visitor at
his side, and the conversation adds to the noise that is always
a disturbing factor. The matter seemed of such importance
to the framers of the Alabama Constitution of 1901, that
they made it the subject of a constitutional provision: "No
person shall be admitted to the floor of either House while the
same is in session, except members of the Legislature, officers
and employees of the two Houses, the Governor and his secretaries, representatives of the press and other persons to whom
either House, by unanimous vote, may extend the privileges of
its floor." The insertion of such a provision in the fundamental
law ought not to be necessary. A legislative rule strictly enforced should suffice.

The admission of women visitors to the floor, still common
in sundry Legislatures, may bring embarrassments of another
kind, springing from the deference that men pay to the opposite
sex. They are nothing new. In 1675 Lord Shaftesbury complained of "the drove of ladies" that attended Parliament,
and added that it was quite the custom for men to hire or borrow
of their friends "handsome sisters or daughters to deliver their
petitions." From Horace Walpole and Lady Mary Wortley
Montagu we get the amusing story of the struggle of the peeresses for admission to the galleries of the House of Lords nearly
two centuries ago, and of their triumph over every obstacle.
The peeresses' galleries are set apart for the unmarried daughters
of peers. They had been admitted, but made such a noise
that orders were issued that their presence could no longer be
tolerated.

Yet they came again. Lady Montagu, writing to Lady
Pomfret (1738), gives lively details of what followed: "The
ladies have shown their zeal and appetite for knowledge in a
most glorious manner. . . . I look upon them to be the boldest
assertors and most resigned sufferers for liberty I ever heard of.
. . . Sir William Saunderson respectfully informed them that
the Chancellor had made an order against their admittance.
The Duchess of Queensbury, as head of the squadron, pished
at the ill-breeding of a mere lawyer, and desired him to let
them up the stairs privately. After some modest refusals, he
swore by G—— he would not let them in. Her grace, with a
noble warmth, answered by G—— they would come in, in spite
of the Chancellor and whole House. This being reported, the

peers resolved to starve them out; an order was given that the doors should not be opened till they had raised their siege. These amazons now showed themselves qualified for the duty even of foot-soldiers; they stood there till five in the afternoon, without either sustenance or intermission, every now and then playing volleys of thumps, kicks, and raps against the door, with so much violence that the speakers in the House were scarce heard." Though this stopped the debate, it failed to open the doors. Then silence was called for half an hour, when the peers, confident that the enemy must be gone, and thirsting for fresh air, ordered the doors to be opened, and in rushed the victorious band. Lady Mary ends her account by saying: "You must own this action to be very well worthy of record and I think it not to be paralleled in any history, ancient or modern."

Toward the middle of that century, attendance upon the debates of both Houses of Parliament had become a fashionable amusement. Lord Royston wrote to Lord Hardwicke in 1761: "The House was hot and crowded — as full of ladies as the House of Lords when the King goes to make a speech." In 1779, in the course of an interesting debate, a great crowd of ladies assembled. Since many were unable to obtain seats, the Speaker declared that the House should be cleared of all the male strangers. This was followed by such an irruption of ladies that all the seats below the bar and both galleries were filled. A member, irritated by the expulsion of some male friend, insisted on the removal of all the strangers, and a ridiculous scene ensued. The ladies refused to go at all, expostulated and resisted violently, so that it took the officers nearly two hours to turn them out, during which time there was such a rustling of dresses and clatter of voices, and altogether such an extraordinary turmoil and confusion, that ladies were rigorously excluded henceforth until after the Reform Bill. They were still allowed to appear in the House of Lords, but the place allotted to them was behind the curtains on each side of the throne. After their exclusion from the Commons, they resorted to disguise in order to obtain admission. The Duchess of Gordon went to the Strangers' Gallery disguised as a man, and the beautiful Mrs. Sheridan imitated this example in order that she might listen to her husband's oratory.[1]

[1] B. C. Skottowe, *Short History of Parliament*, 195.

The keen interest taken in the work of Parliament by English women of social standing has continued to the present time and must be reckoned with as one of the influences powerfully affecting English public life. Nothing like it has ever been common in America. Women who visit our lawmaking bodies come from personal curiosity or because of interest in individual members rather than by reason of any sympathetic concern in the issues debated, save of course in matters directly affecting their sex. They have rarely attended in numbers except on ceremonial occasions or when exceptional oratory was promised. McMaster says that when Washington resigned his commission before Congress, December 23, 1783, the gallery and floor of the hall of Congress, then sitting at Annapolis, were filled with ladies, with high functionaries of the State, and with many officers of the army and navy. Seaton's biography gives a lively sketch of the scene at the Missouri debates in 1820. The ladies crowded into the Senate chamber, not less than a hundred of them being on the floor, whenever Pinkney was expected to speak, encompassing the Senators to the exclusion of the Representatives and foreign ministers. The gallant Vice-President, as it appears, invited a small party of ladies to take the floor; and as soon as the company in the gallery saw them comfortably seated on the sofas, with warm footstools and other luxuries, they left their seats above and came flocking in, to the annoyance of many of the Senators, Tompkins himself appearing disconcerted. The next day a note was affixed to the door, excluding all ladies not introduced by some Senator; but this rule still permitted the sex to be largely represented.

When Harriet Martineau visited Washington, in 1835, she was not pleased with the bearing of those of her sex she saw in the Capitol. "I wished every day," she wrote, "that the ladies would conduct themselves in a more dignified manner than they did in the Senate. They came in with waving plumes, and glittering in all the colors of the rainbow, causing no little bustle in the place, no little annoyance to the gentlemen spectators, and rarely sat still for any length of time. I know that these ladies are no fair specimens of the women who would attend parliamentary proceedings in any other metropolis. I know that they were the wives, daughters, and sisters of legislators, women thronging to Washington for purposes of convenience or pleasure, leaving their usual employments behind them, and seeking to pass away the time. I knew this, and made allowance accordingly; but I still wished that they could understand the gravity of such an assembly, and show so much respect to it as to repay the privilege of admission by striving to excite as little attention as possible, and by having the patience to sit still when they happened not to be amused, till some interruption gave them the opportunity to depart quietly. If they had done this, Judge Porter would not have moved that they should be appointed seats in the gallery instead of below; and they would have been guiltless of furnishing a plea for the exclusion of women, who would probably make a better use of the privilege, from the galleries of other Houses of Parliament." [1]

For a long time the rule against the admission of ladies to the floor was often suspended.

Miss Martineau had another complaint to make. "When I was at Washington," she said, "albums were the fashion and the plague of the day. I scarcely ever came home but I found an album on my table or requests for autographs; but some ladies went much farther than petitioning a foreigner who might be supposed to have leisure. I have actually seen them stand at the door of the Senate Chamber, and send the doorkeeper with an album, and a request to write in it, to Mr. Webster and other eminent members. I have seen them do worse; stand at the door of the Supreme Court, and send in their albums to Chief-Justice Marshall while he was on the bench hearing pleadings. The poor President [Jackson] was terribly persecuted; and to him it was a real nuisance, as he had no poetical resource but Watts's hymns. I have seen verses and stanzas of a most ominous purport from Watts, in the President's very conspicuous handwriting, standing in the midst of the crowquill compliments and translucent charades which are the staple of albums. Nothing was done to repress this atrocious impertinence of the ladies. I always declined writing more than name and date; but Senators, judges, and statesmen submitted to write gallant nonsense at the request of any woman who would stoop to desire it." [2]

The New York Senate, as far as I have observed, is the only branch of a State Legislature that directly provides in its rules for the admission of ladies to the floor. The rules of the Kansas

---

[1] *Retrospect of Western Travel*, i, 180.   [2] *Ibid.*, i, 154.

House, but not the Senate, specify "the wives and families of members.' The Missouri Senate by rule provides seats in the rear and at the side of the chamber for wives and families. Doubtless in various other assemblies they are admitted by custom. It is not a wise practice from any point of view.

THE END

INDEX

Chiltern Hundreds, and resignation from Parliament, 273.

Chittenden, L. E., tells of lobbying in Vt., 368.

Christie, Robert, reëlected after expulsion, 288.

Churchill, Captain, escapes expulsion from Parliament, 292.

Churchill, Lord Randolph, and tan shoes, 596.

Churchill, Winston, and shortcomings of N.H., 462.

Cicero, on the qualifications of Senators, 361.

Cilley, Jonathan, killed in duel, 261, 285.

Cities, councils of, not Legislatures, 37; representation of, 339.

Citizenship qualification, 215.

Civil service reform, 392.

Claflin, William, on an episode of corruption in Mass., 431.

Claiborne, William C. C., admitted to Senate though below age limit, 211.

Clarendon, Earl of, on attendance, 617.

Clark, Champ, defends Congress, 642.

Clarke, George, consents to frequent elections in N.Y., 107.

Clarke, George W., on patronage in Iowa, 586.

Clay, Henry, opposes Jackson as to adjournment, 140; admitted to Senate though below age limit, 211; fights duel with Randolph, 260; on criticism of public men, 301; accused of corruption, 412, 446, 644; and salary-grabbing, 542; as a snuff-taker, 638.

Cleisthenes, modifies the Athenian Senate, 44.

Clergymen, in Parliament, 3; eligibility of, 248. *See also* Chaplain, Prayers, Religious tests.

Clerke, Sir Phillips Jennings, urges exclusion of contractors, 254.

Clerks, 580, 584, 587.

Cleveland, Grover, never sought office, 325.

Clifford, Lord, a briber, 401

Clinton, De Witt, and dual office-holding, 269.

Clinton, George, prorogues twice before assemblage, 188; letter of Hamilton to, quoted, 304.

Clymer, George, and assumption of debts, 409.

Cobb, William C., as to appointment of members to office, 445.

Cockran, W. Bourke, urges longer term for Representatives, 115.

Coke, Sir Edward, on minors in the Commons, 208; and exclusion of lawyers, 251; complains of monopolies, 257; threatened with exclusion when made a sheriff, 266; and the aversion to lawyers, 331; objects to woman as witness, 472; on privilege, 488.

Cole, William, excluded because of pre-election promises, 558.

Colepepper, Lord, and two chambers in Va., 18.

Colepepper, Lord John, speaks against monopolists, 257.

Collier, ——, excluded because of pre-election promise, 558.

Colorado, continuity of Senate in, 63; session limits in, 139, 143; pressure in closing days of session in, 158; age requirement in, 210; attorneys in, 252, 330; disqualifies duelists, 263; solicitation by employees in, 389; provision against log-rolling in, 457; witnesses in, 509; salaries in, 529; perquisites in, 567; patronage in, 581; a chaplain censured in, 606; attendance in, 615.

Colquitt, Oscar Branch, favors large legislative bodies, 90.

Comerford, Frank D., expelled for slander, 514.

Committees, between sessions, 168.

Commons, John Rogers, as to character of representation, 320.

Communicating with constituents, 516.

Competency, 206.

Confucius, quoted, 309.

Congress, Washington's illustration as to framework of, 36; under the Confederation an elastic body, 91; and special sessions, 137; time schedule of, 148; length of sessions of, 153; pressure in closing days of, 160; unfinished business in, 164, 166; convening, 174, 178; and adjournment, 189; and contested elections, 200, 201; and residence qualification, 223; proposal to exclude contractors from, 255; duelists in, 260; and dual office-holding, 269; and resignation, 274; and expulsion, 284; criticized, 299 *et sqq.*; defended, 310, 313; lawyers

criminal action, 490; uses strong language, 642.

Marriott, J. A. R., condemns salaries, 546.

Marsh, Mr., complains of slander, 514.

Marshall, A. J., and lobbying contracts, 379.

Marshall, H. Snowdon, and contempt, 503.

Marshall, John, quoted, 117; elected though a non-resident, 222; on inquiry as to corruption, 422; besought for autographs, 658.

Marshall, Samuel S., contest over election of, 269.

Marshall, Thomas R., and offensive reference to a State, 646.

Marshfield, and Webster's residence qualification, 224.

Marston, Gilman, defends large House, 88.

Marston, Rev. Mr., punished for criticizing Assembly, 481.

Martin, John, convicted of bribery, 424.

Martin, Josiah, criticizes N.C. legislators, 307.

Martin, Recorder, on youth in the Commons, 207.

Martin, Secretary, and corruption, 404.

Martineau, Harriet, on criticism of public men, 301; on disastrous effects of rotation, 353; on conduct of the ladies in Washington, 657; and on albums, 658.

Marvell, Andrew, attempt to bribe, 521.

Mary Queen of Scots, and May marriages, 138.

Maryland, two chambers in, 17, 24; new method of choice of Senators in, 22; Charles Pinckney on Senate of, 30; continuity of Senate in, 62; indirect election in, 65; size of Houses in, 86, 87; requires frequent elections, 109; changes to biennials, 113; terms of Senators in, 119; frequency of sessions in, 124; limits sessions, 139; adjournment in, 187; contested elections in, 198; qualification in, 206; age requirement in, 209; property qualification in, 234; Catholics in, 238; religious tests in, 240, 245; clergymen in, 249, 251; excludes contractors, 255; disqualifies violators of election law, 259; and duelists, 263; and sheriffs, 266; and other officeholders, 267; compulsory service in,

273; expulsion in, 283; attorneys in, 332; farmers in colonial, 338; rotation in, 346, 348; and appointment of members to office, 438, 444; and the meaning of "office," 453; odd rule about the safe in, 460; arrest in, 494; contempt in, 513; salaries in, 533; resents salary grab, 542; perquisites in, 568; patronage in, 580, 586; an obnoxious sermon in, 609; absence in, 624.

Mason, George, draft of Virginia Constitution by, 21; on age qualification, 209; on citizenship qualification, 215; on property qualification, 232; in connection with quality of Virginia legislators, 306; urges rotation, 352; on appointment of members to office, 441; introduces bill for wages, 526; on salaries, 535, 538.

Mason, Stevens T., and the wearing of crape, 601.

Massachusetts, the negative voice in, 4, 25; names of legislative bodies in, 22, 23; Shays's Rebellion in, 31; bosses in, 38; the upper branch in, 47, 57; large House in, 89; terms in, 103, 132; requires regular elections, 110; adopts biennials, 113; frequency of sessions in, 123, 132; limiting sessions in, 140, 143; length of sessions, 146; the split session in, 149, 151; little pressure in closing days of session in, 158; location of capital in, 170, 173; time of convening in, 175; adjournment in, 183, 186, 188; contested elections in, 195, 201, 205; average age of legislators in, 211; and the citizenship qualification, 217; and the residence qualification, 219, 224; property qualification in, 234; religious tests in, 237, 241, 242, 244; clergymen in, 249, 250, 251; lawyers in, 251; declares against monopolies, 257; dual office-holding in, 268; compulsory service in, 272; vacancies in, 279, 294; legislators of criticized by Gerry, 306; quality of present-day legislators in, 310, 314; college-bred men in, 328, 329; lawyers in, 329, 330; farmers in, 337; city and rural representation in, 339; Masons in, 341; rotation in, 345, 348, 350, 351, 363; lobbying in, 368, 371, 384, 387, 388; contributions in, 389; bribery charge in, 408; corruption in, 430, 461, 463,